WORLD WAR II from
an American Perspective

This bibliography was conceived and compiled from the periodicals database of the American Bibliographical Center by editors at ABC-Clio Information Services, Inc.

Robert de V. Brunkow, Assistant Editor
Lance Klass, Assistant Editor
David J. Valiulis, Assistant Editor

Pamela Byrne, Associate Editor
Gail Schlachter, Vice President, Publications

WORLD WAR II from an American Perspective

an annotated bibliography

ABC-Clio, Inc.
Santa Barbara, California
Oxford, England

Copyright © 1983 by ABC-Clio, Inc.

All rights reserved. No part of this publication may be reproduced, stored in a retrieval system, or transmitted, in any form or by any means, electronic, mechanical, photocopying, recording, or otherwise, except for the inclusion of brief quotations in a review, without prior permission in writing from the publishers.

US ISBN 0-87436-035-8

ABC-Clio, Inc.
2040 Alameda Padre Serra, Box 4397
Santa Barbara, California 93103

Clio Press Ltd.
Woodside House, Hinksey Hill
Oxford, OX1 5BE, England

Manufactured in the United States of America

American Bibliographical Center
ABC-Clio, Inc.

CONTENTS

INTRODUCTION v

LIST OF ABBREVIATIONS vi

ABSTRACTS 1

SUBJECT INDEX 213

INTRODUCTION

The responses of the United States and Canada to World War II and its antecedents have been exhaustively recorded and analyzed in a vast array of journal articles over the years — and more articles continue to issue forth. Because of this proliferation of scholarship on World War II, there is a critical need for a convenient, annotated bibliography on the subject covering a wide range of periodical literature — a bibliography useful to the undergraduate as well as the advanced student and research scholar.

World War II from an American Perspective was created to meet this need. It provides bibliographic control for a full decade (1971-1981) of scholarly writing in historical journals and journals of the related social sciences and humanities. All 1,107 citations in this volume are drawn from the American Bibliographical Center's data base, the largest history data base in the world, an immense storehouse of article abstracts selected from more than 2,000 journals published in 42 languages. All non-English article titles are translated into English, and all abstracts are written in English, thereby providing even the beginning student with access to scholarship from all over the world.

This bibliography covers all aspects of World War II as it relates to North America. Researchers will find, for example, not only citations to articles on traditional diplomatic, political, and military topics but also to articles on social history (including published primary sources like letters, diaries, and government communiqués), for much that is being written on World War II concerns the effects of the war on society. Other topics represented in these pages are the debate on American culpability for the Japanese attack on Pearl Harbor, the controversy over the World War II origins of the Cold War, America's efforts to remain neutral during the 1930's, military campaigns, and political leadership. Historians of science and technology will find information on technological innovations induced by the war. Entries on wartime society range over such topics as women in the workplace, films, the effects of rationing, and the internment of Japanese Americans.

The bibliographic entries are arranged alphabetically by author and provide sentence or paragraph annotations. Prepared by a worldwide staff, the annotations summarize the contents of the articles. The abstracts are expertly indexed by editor/indexers, using the American Bibliographical Center's Subject Profile Index System (ABC-SPIndex). The subjects of each entry are indexed as a set of terms (an index string) that provides a complete profile of the subject matter of the cited article — in effect giving the user an abstract of the abstract. By spending a few minutes perusing the index profiles, the researcher should be able to reduce considerably the time that must be spent finding relevant articles. See the explanatory note at the beginning of the index for more information about ABC-SPIndex.

LIST OF ABBREVIATIONS

A	Author-prepared Abstract	*Illus*	Illustrated, Illustration
Acad	Academy, Académie, Academia	*Inst*	Institute, Institut-.
Agric	Agriculture, Agricultural	*Int*	International, Internacional, Internationaux, Internazionale
AIA	Abstracts in Anthropology		
Akad	Akademie	*J*	Journal, Journal-prepared Abstract
Am	America, American	*Lib*	Library, Libraries
Ann	Annals, Annales, Annual	*Mag*	Magazine
Anthrop	Anthropology, Anthropological	*Mus*	Museum, Musée, Museo
Arch	Archives	*Nac*	Nacional
Archaeol	Archaeology, Archaeological	*Natl*	National, Nationale
Art	Article	*Naz*	Nazionale
Assoc	Association, Associate	*Phil*	Philosophy, Philosophical
Biblio	Bibliography, Bibliographical	*Photo*	Photograph
Biog	Biography, Biographical	*Pol*	Politics, Political, Politique
Bol	Boletim, Boletín	*Pr*	Press
Bull	Bulletin	*Pres*	President
c	century (in index)	*Pro*	Proceedings
ca	circa	*Publ*	Publishing, Publication
Can	Canada, Canadian, Canadien	*Q*	Quarterly
Cent	Century	*Rev*	Review, Revue, Revista, Revised
Coll	College	*Riv*	Rivista
Com	Committee	*Res*	Research
Comm	Commission	*RSA*	Romanian Scientific Abstracts
Comp	Compiler	*S*	Staff-prepared Abstract
DAI	Dissertation Abstracts International	*Sci*	Science, Scientific
Dept	Department	*Secy*	Secretary
Dir	Director, Direktor	*Soc*	Society, Société, Sociedad, Società
Econ	Economy, Econom-.	*Sociol*	Sociology, Sociological
Ed	Editor, Edition	*Tr*	Transactions
Educ	Education, Educational	*Transl*	Translator, Translation
Geneal	Genealogy, Genealogical, Généalogique	*U*	University, Universi-.
Grad	Graduate	*US*	United States
Hist	History, Hist-.	*Vol*	Volume
IHE	Indice Histórico Español	*Y*	Yearbook

Abbreviations also apply to feminine and plural forms.
Abbreviations not noted above are based on *Webster's Third New International Dictionary*
and the *United States Government Printing Office Style Manual*.

WORLD WAR II FROM AN AMERICAN PERSPECTIVE

1. Abbott, Carl. THE AMERICAN SUNBELT: IDEA AND REGION. *J. of the West 1979 18(3): 4-18.* The American South and West is a new urban region whose growing economic and political strength began during World War II with military expansion. The prosperity of the war years continued as manufacturing interests were attracted by low costs, and tourists and retirees were attracted by the mild climate. The shifts of population and production to the Sunbelt have made it a new American region. Based on published sources; 2 maps, 10 photos, 3 tables, 27 notes.   B. S. Porter

2. Abella, Irving and Troper, Harold. "THE LINE MUST BE DRAWN SOMEWHERE": CANADA AND JEWISH REFUGEES, 1933-9. *Can. Hist. Rev. [Canada] 1979 60(2): 178-209.* Canada's immigration policy had always been ethnically selective and economically self-serving. During the 1930's, it became even more restrictive, barring nonagricultural immigrants of non-Anglo-American extraction. Frederick Charles Blair was put in charge of the immigration service. He feared that Canada would be overrun by Jewish refugees and intractably refused their admission even when pressured by Canadian pro-Jewish and humanitarian groups. Even at the onset of World War II, he would not relent: German Jews would be denied admission because as nationals of a hostile power they were enemy aliens expressly excluded by law. Based on manuscripts from the Archives of Canada and secondary sources; 117 notes.   S

3. Ackoff, Russell L. A REVOLUTION IN ORGANIZATIONAL CONCEPTS. *Naval War Coll. R. 1972 24(5): 4-14.* Analyzes traditional patterns of thought and conceptualization to argue that modern approaches to solving problems differ in philosophic terms from past practice. All major organizational questions today relate to either system design or the relationship of the organization with its human and natural environments. For a century preceding World War II, the physical sciences provided the organizing concepts of matter and force, creating a mechanical image of the world. World War II initiated a new era of thought in which systems became the new mode of thought, based on synthesis rather than analysis. This revolution in conceptualization has created three problems: planning-system design, humanization of organizations, and environmentalization of organizations. American leaders must understand the issues involved in this revolution and the nature of change in our society, to find the means by which these issues can be constructively directed. Undocumented.
R. M. Rudoff

4. Addington, Larry H. THE U.S. COAST ARTILLERY AND THE PROBLEM OF ARTILLERY ORGANIZATION, 1907-1954. *Military Affairs 1976 40(1): 1-6.* In 1907 Congress enacted legislation which separated the artillery into Field and Coast Artillery, creating problems for the coastal artillery in their mission and relationship with the Army Chief of Staff. Coast Artillery became responsible for the fixed and movable defenses of land and coast fortifications. Yet, the status of coastal artillery within the War Department was a constance

source of study and argument during its 43-year history. Based on primary and secondary sources; 36 notes.   A. M. Osur

5. Adler, Selig. THE UNITED STATES AND THE HOLOCAUST. *Am. Jewish Hist. Q. 1974 64(1): 14-23.* The US government did less to mitigate the catastrophe that befell European Jews than it could have because 1) Washington initially made incorrect assumptions concerning the extent and possible alleviation of the holocaust, 2) measures taken lacked a sense of urgency because of low priority on the war timetable and the end of war political maneuvers, and 3) measures taken came too late to save any considerable number of Jews. Proofs for these points constitute a new approach to the entire question. 23 notes.
F. Rosenthal

6. Aga Rossi, Elena. LA POLITICA DEL VATICANO DURANTE LA SECONDA GUERRA MONDIALE: INDICAZIONI DI RICERCA E DOCUMENTI INEDITI SULLA MISSIONE DI MYRON TAYLOR [The policy of the Vatican during World War II: directions of research and unedited documents on the mission of Myron Taylor]. *Storia Contemporanea [Italy] 1975 6(4): 881-928.* Publishes documents relating to the three visits of Myron Taylor, President Roosevelt's special representative, to the Vatican in February 1940, September 1941, and September 1942. Taylor, at one time President of the US Steel Corporation, was an Episcopalian but a personal friend of Pope Pius XII. His third mission, from which stem the most documents, was to convince the Vatican that the Allies would keep fighting until Hitler and Nazi-Fascism were destroyed; there could be no compromise. In the postwar era, too, Taylor continued to be an important voice in the United States on Italian affairs. The documents contain information on the massacres of Jews by the Nazis. 80 notes.
J. C. Billigmeier

7. Ainsworth, Catherine Harris. AMERICAN FOLKTALES FROM THE RECENT WARS. *New York Folklore Q. 1973 29(1): 38-49.*

8. Albers, Lawrence C. PERRY WOLFF AND *AIR POWER*: A FILM MAKER'S CONTRIBUTION TO HISTORICAL UNDERSTANDING. *Southern Q. 1976 14(3): 231-235.* An analysis of Perry Wolff's role as writer-producer of the 1950's television series *Air Power*. The contention is that Wolff was a good researcher and included new or little known historical facts in his productions, thus adding to the knowledge of air warfare during World War II and its aftermath. Reference is made to the second bombing of Poland by Germany in 1939 and the Berlin airlift of 1948. Concludes that filmmakers can use this medium to assist in a more complete understanding of historical events. 13 notes.
R. W. Dubay

9. Alberts, Robert C. PROFILE OF A SOLDIER: MATTHEW B. RIDGWAY. *Am. Heritage 1976 27(2): 4-7, 73-82.* Following graduation from West Point in 1917, Matthew B. Ridgway (b. 1895) embarked on a long military career. In 1943, he led the 82nd Airborne Division in the European war. In August 1945, Ridgway went to the Far East to assume command of all airborne operations in that theater when the war ended. After an assignment in the Caribbean, and one at Fort Myers, Ridgway became involved in the Korean War. Sent to Korea in 1950, he replaced MacArthur in April 1951. In 1952, he assumed command of

NATO forces in Europe, and in 1953, he became Army Chief of Staff, where an unpleasant relationship developed with Defense Secretary Wilson. He retired from the Army in 1955. Based on conversations and published works; 9 illus.

J. F. Paul

10. Alden, John D. ANDREW IRWIN MCKEE: NAVAL CONSTRUCTOR. *US Naval Inst. Pro. 1979 105(6): 49-57.* Rear Admiral Andrew Irwin McKee (1896-1976) had a great deal to do with developing and constructing the US Navy's submarine force. He was an all-around naval constructor and was considered to be a "designer's designer." He made his mark as a member of the Navy's Construction Corps before and during World War II. He retired from the Navy in July 1947 and joined the Electric Boat Company as design director; he later became that company's vice-president of engineering and director of research and design. During 1947-61, he was responsible for 14 new submarine designs that went into production, several conversions of World War II fleet submarines to new configurations, and for many experimental efforts. Primary and secondary sources; 10 photos, 9 notes. A. N. Garland

11. Aleksin, A. SSHA I CHILI V GODY VTOROI MIROVOI VOINY [The US and Chile during the Second World War]. *Novaia i Noveishaia Istoriia [USSR] 1970 (6): 78-91.* In 1939 a Popular Front government was elected in Chile. The United States, however, managed to frustrate attempts to take over control of American business interests by attaching conditions to the US credits which the Chilean government needed. World War II enabled the Americans to take an even stronger position in the Chilean economy. They gradually took charge of Chilean copper output and sales, and they insisted on the freezing of the assets of rival Axis corporations. They eventually persuaded Chile to sever diplomatic relations with the Axis powers, although she did not declare war on Germany until 1945. Based heavily on *Foreign Relations of the United States* (Diplomatic Papers 1939-43), and secondary sources; 78 notes.

C. I. P. Ferdinand

12. Allen, Louis. THE HISTORIAN AS LITTLE PETERKIN. *Durham U. J. [Great Britain] 1979 2(1): 89-98.* Reviews Peter Lowe's *Great Britain and the Origins of the Pacific War. A Study of British Policy in East Asia 1937-1941* (Oxford: Clarendon Pr., 1977), which discusses the breakdown of Anglo-Japanese relations up to 1940. The focus on British sources results in an imbalance in interpretation. The author considers British and US policy in Asia and the Pacific in relation to Raymond Callahan's *Burma 1942-45* (Davis-Poynter, 1978) and William Roger Louis's *Imperialism at Bay: The United States and the Decolonization of the British Empire, 1941-1945* (Oxford: Clarendon Pr., 1977). S

13. Almaráz, Felix Díaz, Jr. THE LITTLE THEATRE IN THE ATOMIC AGE: AMATEUR DRAMATICS IN LOS ALAMOS, NEW MEXICO 1943-1946. *J. of the West 1978 17(2): 72-82.* The development of the little theatre in Los Alamos was a response to the social and cultural needs of the public employees assigned to this isolated community. A company of amateur performers organized the Little Theatre Group on 8 November 1943. Some initial difficulties were encountered in scheduling rehearsal space and performance dates, but audience response was enthusiastic and the group's treasury reflected its success. Under the guidance of dedicated leaders, the amateur actors experimented with

a variety of drama projects. Minutes of the Board of Directors of the Los Alamos Little Theatre and secondary sources; illus., 4 photos, 29 notes.

B. S. Porter

14. Altherr, Marco. LES ORIGINES DE LA GUERRE FROIDE: UN ESSAI D'HISTORIOGRAPHIE [The origins of the Cold War: a historiographical essay]. *Relations Int. [France] 1977 (9): 69-81.* Notes the extent and the passion of the debate among historians about the origins of the Cold War. Divides opinions into traditional, realist, revisionist, and postrevisionist schools, the revisionists in turn being classified as "hard" and "soft." Reviews leading points of controversy, including eastern Europe, the role of Harry Truman, the atomic bomb, and economic determinism. A conflict of generations with different historical experiences helps explain the historiographical disagreements.

R. Stromberg

15. Alvarez, David J. THE UNITED STATES, THE VATICAN, AND WORLD WAR II. *Res. Studies 1972 40(4): 239-250.* The object of American diplomacy with the Vatican during 1937-45 was to keep the Vatican from collaborating with the Axis and to obtain Vatican cooperation for Allied war policies and interests.

16. Anderson, Carroll R. MCGUIRE'S LAST MISSION. *Air Force Mag. 1975 58(1): 59-64.* An acount of the last mnission of Major Thomas McGuire on 7 January 1945, while leading a fighter sweep over the Philippines.

17. Anderson, Elaine. CONSUMER RATIONING IN LUCAS COUNTY DURING WORLD WAR II. *Northwest Ohio Q. 1975 47(3): 79-99.* Examines rationing and price controls into 1943.

18. Anderson, Henry H., Jr. THE 920TH FIELD ARTILLERY BATTALION IN ACTION AT METZ, NOVEMBER, 1944. *Military Collector and Hist. 1978 30(4): 148-157.* Discusses the US 3d Army's 920th Field Artillery Battalion.

19. Anderson, Herbert L. EARLY DAYS OF THE CHAIN REACTION. *Sci. and Public Affairs 1973 29(4): 8-12.* Reminisces about the first controlled nuclear chain reaction, in a laboratory at the University of Chicago in 1942 where the first nuclear pile was built.

20. Anderson, Herbert L. [FERMI, SZILARD, AND ATOMIC ENERGY].
THE LEGACY OF FERMI AND SZILARD. *Bull. of the Atomic Scientists 1974 30(7): 56-62.* Discusses Leo Szilard's and Enrico Fermi's research on nuclear fission during 1933-39, particularly at Columbia University.
FERMI, SZILARD AND TRINITY. *Bull. of the Atomic Scientists 1974 30(8): 40-47.* Reminiscences on working with Fermi and Szilard at Columbia, at the University of Chicago collaborating on the first controlled chain reaction, and at Los Alamos, New Mexico, 1940-45.

21. Anderson, Irvine H. LEND-LEASE FOR SAUDI ARABIA: A COMMENT ON ALTERNATIVE CONCEPTUALIZATIONS. *Diplomatic Hist. 1979 3(4): 413-423.* Examines the role of Standard Oil of California and the Texas Company (Texaco) in influencing the US government to provide Lend-Lease aid for Saudi Arabia. Fearing that Ibn Saud would turn to the British for financial

aid and consequently favor British oil interests over US interests, the two oil companies lobbied for financial aid for Saudi Arabia. Their influence was not crucial, for the government was moved by strategic concerns. The US military was aware of the decline in US oil reserves and wanted to have access to Arabian oil sources. The government concurred and provided aid to the Saudis. Based on archival and published primary sources; 44 notes.   S

22. Anderson, Irvine H., Jr. THE 1941 *DE FACTO* EMBARGO ON OIL TO JAPAN: A BUREAUCRATIC REFLEX. *Pacific Hist. R. 1975 44(2): 201-231.* Heretofore unused documents reveal that President Franklin D. Roosevelt did not intend to terminate Japan's oil supply when he froze funds in July 1941. He correctly anticipated that Japan would attack the Netherlands East Indies if oil was cut off, but Roosevelt allowed the order to be written as all-inclusive so that policy could be changed day-to-day without issuing further orders. Neither the public nor the British, Dutch, or Japanese were given a clear idea of the American policy. This ambiguity allowed a bureaucracy biased against Japan, specifically the Foreign Funds Control Interdepartmental Committee, to establish a de facto oil embargo which Roosevelt and Cordell Hull supported by mid-September out of fear that a relaxation would be interpreted as a sign of weakness. Based on government documents at the Federal Records Center, Suitland, Maryland and the National Archives, private papers at Hoover Institution and Yale University, and other primary and secondary sources; 107 notes.
W. K. Hobson

23. Anderson, Richard M. and Baker, Arthur D., III. CV-2 LEX AND CV-3 SARA. *Warship Int. 1977 14(4): 291-336.* Examines the specifications, plans, and construction of US aircraft carriers *Lexington* and *Saratoga*, 1922-30; summarizes both ships' record during World War II.

24. Anderson, Richard M. THE *MIDWAY* CLASS CARRIERS. *Warship Internat. 1975 12(2): 166-175.* Provides photographs and general descriptions of the aircraft carriers first developed in 1941.   S

25. Andrade, Ernest. THE BATTLE CRUISER IN THE UNITED STATES NAVY. *Military Affairs 1980 44(1): 18-23.* Survey of the historical arguments for and against battle cruisers in the United States and the US plans for their use. World War I seemed to prove their worth, but the Washington Conference and Five Power Treaty of the early 1920's restricted the building of battle cruisers; thus the heavy cruiser became the dominant type of surface warship to be constructed during the interwar period. Two US battle cruiser-type vessels were built during World War II, but it is not clear whether that was a good investment. Based on US Navy sources; 30 notes.   A. M. Osur

26. Andrews, John A. C. THE FORTY, THE SPIT, AND THE JUG. *Aerospace Hist. 1979 26(4): 202-207.* The author recalls his flying experiences during World War II as he flew the Curtiss P-40, the Spitfire, and the P-47. Discusses the pilot procedures and the handling characteristics of each aircraft. 4 photos.   C. W. Ohrvall

27. Andrews, Paul M. SEVENTEEN BITS AND PIECES: BOEING'S B-17 FS AND GS ASSIGNED TO THE 8TH U.S. ARMY AIR FORCE, AUGUST 1942-MAY 1945. *Am. Aviation Hist. Soc. J. 1979 24(3): 202-213, (4): 303-312.*

Part I. Broken down by bombardment squadrons, lists the Boeing B-17 Gs and B-17 Fs used by pilots in the First Air Division of the Eighth Army Air Force. Part II. Broken down by squadron, lists all of Boeing's model B-17 Gs and B-17 Fs employed in the Third Air Division of the Eighth Army Air Force, 1942-45.

28. Ano, Masaharu. LOYAL LINGUISTS: NISEI OF WORLD WAR II LEARNED JAPANESE IN MINNESOTA. *Minnesota Hist. 1977 45(7): 273-287.* During and after World War II, the Military Intelligence Service Language School at Camp Savage and later at Fort Snelling, Minnesota, gave 5,500 Nisei men and women an opportunity to train for the war against Japan and the resultant American occupation. The school was commanded by, and owed its existence largely to, Kai E. Rasmussen. Captain (later Colonel) Rasmussen had had prewar experience with the US Army in Japan, and he had genuine empathy for the often-abused Nisei under his command. The students were intensely and extensively trained in Japanese language and culture, enabling them to decipher Japanese plans and military documents in combat situations. The graduates used their knowledge in combat situations in the Aleutians and later in the South Pacific and Okinawa. Off-duty contacts between the Nisei and native Minnesotans were generally free of tension. Based on primary sources. N. Lederer

29. Arcidiacono, Bruno. LA GRANDE-BRETAGNE ET LES ÉTATS-UNIS FACE AU PROBLÈME DE L'ARMISTICE AVEC L'ITALIE ET DU CONTRÔLE DU TERRITOIRE ITALIEN LIBÉRÉ [Great Britain and the United States and the problem of the armistice with Italy and the control of liberated Italian territory]. *Relations Int. [France] 1977 (10): 143-161.* As the first Axis country to be liberated, Italy provided a significant example of the debate between Great Britain and the United States on the administration of liberated territory. Following their disagreement on whether or not to invade Italy at all, the two allies disagreed over whether to govern directly or indirectly via an Italian central government, then argued whether there should be a one- or two-stage armistice. The disagreement delayed Italian surrender and gave the Germans time to occupy much of Italy. The author views it as an example of differing US-British military and strategic conceptions of the war and world politics.
R. Stromberg

30. Arden, Stuart. THE GOOD SOLDIER SCHWEIK AND HIS AMERICAN CARTOON COUNTERPARTS. *J. of Popular Culture 1975 9(1): 26-30.* Compares the character in Jaroslav Hasek's satirical, antiwar novel *The Good Soldier Schweik* with his counterparts in American cartoons. Characters such as Dave Breger's G.I. Joe, George Baker's Sad Sack, Dick Wingert's Hubert, Bill Mauldin's Willie and Joe, and Beetle Bailey are caricatures of losers whereas Schweik is physically sturdy. The American versions deal only with military life and usually in an inoffensive manner, but Hasek lampooned religion and the entire military establishment. The American cartoons do not satirize or genuinely oppose war and militarism, they merely make fun of them. 12 notes.
J. D. Falk

31. Armstrong, David M. BATTLE OF SEALARK CHANNEL. *Am. Hist. Illus. 1973 8(6): 4-9, 44-48.* Author's reminiscence of the Battle of Guadalcanal. S

32. Armstrong, David M. PEARL HARBOR! AN EYEWITNESS ACCOUNT. *Am. Hist. Illus. 1974 9(5): 4-11, 41-48.* The author, an ensign on the *USS Zane,* gives a personal account of the Japanese attack on Pearl Harbor, 1942.

33. Armstrong, William J. AIRCRAFT GO TO SEA: A BRIEF HISTORY OF AVIATION IN THE US NAVY. *Aerospace Hist. 1978 25(2): 79-91.* From its inception in 1911 the main goal of naval aviation has not been to build an air force but to increase the operational effectiveness of the Navy. Thus the stress has been on the need for sea-going aircraft rather than those tied to land bases. Gives a brief history of the Navy's efforts to achieve this goal. Based on official sources, 7 references to letters in official archives, 22 photos. C. W. Ohrvall

34. Arnold, Joseph C. OMENS AND ORACLES. *US Naval Inst. Pro. 1980 106(8): 47-53.* Since 1945, it has become increasingly apparent that the military's use of information provided by various sources must improve. The Battle of the Bulge, the Chinese Communist entry into the Korean War, and the Soviet introduction of missiles into Cuba in the early 1960's are but three of the most recent failures of US military intelligence agencies to evaluate information properly. Once gathered, intelligence has been neither properly nor promptly interpreted. The United States must devise a way of ascertaining an enemy's capabilities, and should discard its policy of trying to determine enemy intentions. Secondary sources; 4 photos, 3 notes.

35. Artal Delgado, José A. DE LOS BARCOS [About ships]. *Rev. General de Marina [Spain] 1978 194(2): 151-169.* Describes the histories of the first five destroyers transferred from the United States to the Spanish navy under the 1953 convention. The USS *Capps* and *David W. Taylor* were ceded in 1957, the *Converse* in 1959, and the *Jarvis* and *McGowan* in 1960. All were of the *Fletcher* class, the first such transferred to a foreign navy. All were named after 19th-century American naval officers and had been active in World War II. In the Spanish Navy they were named respectively: *Lepanto, Almirante Ferrándiz, Almirande Valdés, Alcalá Galiano* and *Jorge Juan.* 5 illus. W. C. Frank

36. Ashkenazy, Irvin. AS THE GUAYULE BALL BOUNCES. *Westways 1977 69(9): 56-60.* Discusses the importance to the rubber industry of a process involving a native California rubber-producing shrub called guayule, developed in 1942 by the Agriculture Department's Emergency Rubber Project (ERP) and Dr. Shimpe Nishimura.

37. Avery, Norman L. NORTH AMERICAN'S B-25 TRANSPORTS. *Am. Aviation Hist. Soc. J. 1977 22(2): 136-141.* Discusses North American Aviation's B-25 transports, used as personnel transports by the American armed forces in World War II; focuses on modifications, 1942-49.

38. Bache, William B. THE HERO SYNDROME. *Dalhousie R. [Canada] 1975 55(1): 93-102.* A whimsical account of an incident near the end of World War II in Germany when the author drove a jeep for General Anthony McAuliffe to the city of Ludwigshafen under rather dangerous conditions. C. Held

39. Bagnasco, Erminio. CORREGIDOR: STORIA DI UN' ISOLA-FORTEZZA [Corregidor: history of an island fortress]. *Riv. Marittima [Italy] 1979 112(11): 43-54.* History of Corregidor, an island at the entrance of Manila Bay,

from 1795; focuses on battles during World War II which made the island famous.

40. Bainbridge, Kenneth T. A FOUL AND AWESOME DISPLAY. *Bull. of the Atomic Scientists 1975 31(5): 40-46.* Recounts participation in the Manhattan Project construction of the first nuclear bomb at Los Alamos, New Mexico, and his impressions of its detonation in 1945.

41. Baines, John M. U.S. MILITARY ASSISTANCE TO LATIN AMERICA: AN ASSESSMENT. *J. of Inter-Am. Studies and World Affairs 1972 14(4): 469-486.* In the early years of the 20th century, U.S. interest in Latin America centered on preserving security in the Western Hemisphere. With the advent of the Good Neighbor Policy in 1932, the United States tried to pull out of the internal affairs of Latin America. But by 1938, arms were being shipped into the area from the north, to compete with military assistance from Germany, France, and Italy. During World War II, the United States became the primary supplier of arms from Latin America; soon, extensive military assistance grants of equipment and military missions were flowing from Washington. The U.S. Military Assistance Program has come under fire because it is charged that it brings the Defense Department into diplomacy. The program also has been castigated for aiding the takeover of governments by military establishments. These accusations have not been proven, but even a hint of such activity tends to bring suspicion on the Military Assistance Program. Based on U.S. Government documents and on secondary sources; 6 tables, biblio. J. R. Thomas

42. Baker, Arthur Davidson, III. THE 1945 ANTI-AIRCRAFT ARMAMENT AUGMENTATION OF U.S. NAVY DESTROYERS: *PORTER* THROUGH *SIMS* CLASSES. *Warship Int. 1978 15(1): 51-61.* Presents 12 photographs of antiaircraft armament on Navy destroyers, 1945.

43. Balashov, P. GOD TIAZHELYKH ISPYTANII [The year of heavy ordeals]. *Voenno-Istoricheskii Zhurnal [USSR] 1976 (3): 116-121.* Reviews the fifth volume of the Soviet *History of the Second World War* which covers 1942.

44. Baldwin, Paul H. THE ENDING OF WORLD WAR II. *Aerospace Hist. 1976 23(3): 136-139.* The author graduated in physics from Carnegie Institute of Technology in 1937 and applied to the Mellon Institute of Industrial Research for work as an atomic physicist. He felt that Hitler would be the one to use the atomic bomb in World War II. During the war the author was a Radar Observer with the 547th Night Fighter Squadron in the Philippines. Describes the training and utilization of night fighter squadrons to intercept enemy fighters. The night fighter operation and the A-bomb would have helped end the war sooner. President Truman made the correct decision in using the bomb. 3 photos.
C. W. Ohrvall

45. Balfour, Michael. THE ORIGIN OF THE FORMULA: "UNCONDITIONAL SURRENDER" IN WORLD WAR II. *Armed Forces and Soc. 1979 5(2): 281-301.* There is some uncertainty whether the formula "unconditional surrender" had been given serious study before being enunciated by President Franklin D. Roosevelt at his Casablanca press conference. A careful consideration of all pro and con factors affecting its advisability as a basis for achieving early surrender and the best possible foundation for postwar settlements would

suggest, given the personalities and circumstances involved, that an adequate change in the character of the peace to be achieved was not an available option. Primary sources; 37 notes. R. V. Ritter

46. Balkoski, Joseph. PATTON'S 3RD ARMY: THE LORRAINE CAMPAIGN, 8 NOV.-1 DEC. '44. *Strategy and Tactics 1980 (78): 4-15.* Story of Lieutenant General George S. Patton's US Third Army in the Lorraine campaign and the battle of Metz in France between 8 November and 1 December 1944.

47. Baram, Philip. UNDERMINING THE BRITISH: DEPARTMENT OF STATE POLICIES IN EGYPT AND THE SUEZ CANAL BEFORE AND DURING WORLD WAR II. *Historian 1978 40(4): 631-649.* In Egypt, friendly competition existed between Britain and the United States in the political, military, economic, and public relations areas as British strength gained or diminished. Overall, however, US wartime relations with Egypt as conducted by the State Department's Division of Near Eastern Affairs and by the Foreign Service were limited and secondary. Even the State Department's postwar planning for Egypt was deliberately passive. No question of competition existed over the Suez Canal, however. The State Department's view was that the Canal was totally a British military responsibility, essentially separate from Anglo-American relations in the rest of Egypt. M. S. Legan

48. Barclay, G. St. J. AUSTRALIA LOOKS TO AMERICA: THE WARTIME RELATIONSHIP, 1939-1942. *Pacific Hist. Rev. 1977 46(2): 251-271.* Australian policy makers developed the erroneous impression during 1939-42 that the United States was committed to a Pacific first policy. Hence, Australian leaders came to look to the United States rather than to Great Britain for assistance against the Japanese threat. When US actions failed to meet Australian expectations, Australian leaders, especially Prime Minister John Curtin, became embittered. Based on manuscript collections in Australian Commonwealth Archives Office, National Library of Australia, National Archives of New Zealand, British Public Record Office, and Washington Navy Yard Archives, and primary sources; 63 notes. W. K. Hobson

49. Barclay, Glen St. John. SINGAPORE STRATEGY: THE ROLE OF THE UNITED STATES IN IMPERIAL DEFENSE. *Military Affairs 1975 39(2): 54-59.* Before and during the early years of World War II, Great Britain faced the dilemma of defending the security of the United Kingdom as well as its naval base at Singapore. As the British did not have the resources to do this, they had to enlist the aid of the United States. Australia and New Zealand were particularly concerned about the lack of any solid military force in the Pacific. The United States would not base its main force beyond Hawaii, and Winston Churchill's promises for extended protection were never fulfilled. By the end of 1941, there was no credible deterrent in the western Pacific to stop Japanese aggression. Based on primary and secondary sources; 62 notes. A. M. Osur

50. Barham, Wayne. GUAM: D-DAY PLUS 30 YEARS. *Guam Recorder 1975 5(2): 3-10.* Recalls the American invasion of Guam, 21-27 July 1944.

51. Barr, William. NEWFOUNDLAND SHIP MADE SOVIET ARCTIC HISTORY. *Can. Geographic [Canada] 1979 99(2): 30-35.* Traces the cargo-running career of the Newfoundland steel steamer, the *Beothic,* from the ship's

launching in 1908 to 1915, and describes its involvement as the Soviet vessel *Georgi Sedov* in World War I and World War II, particularly its epic 812-day crossing of the Arctic basin in 1940. Follows its career until 1967 when the name was removed from Soviet shipping lists.

52. Barral, Pierre and Tavernier, Yves. MOUVEMENTS PAYSANS VISANT À ADAPTER L'AGRICULTURE À L'ECONOMIE [Peasant movements concerning the adaptation of agriculture to the market economy]. *Cahiers Int. d'Hist. Écon. et Sociale [Italy] 1976 6: 36-51.* Synthesizes reports at the International Colloquium (Naples, 1969) on peasant movements in the industrialized societies of Europe and North America in the late 19th and 20th centuries. The evolution of "capitalistic agriculture" added to the old peasant struggle for land, new problems created by salaried employees, technical equipment, and transport. World War II brought the peasant into direct encounter with the technical revolution of the 19th century and thereby altered the history of peasants. Peasant movements developed from pressure groups to political parties, and peasant voters forced all political groups to formulate policies for agricultural problems.
F. X. Hartigan

53. Barrett, Allen M. I FOUGHT AT IWO—TWICE! *Marine Corps Gazette 1979 63(2): 43-52.* The author describes his experiences as a Marine at Iwo Jima in 1945.

54. Barry, P. S. THE PROLIFIC PIPELINE: FINDING OIL FOR CANOL. *Dalhousie Rev. [Canada] 1977 57(2): 205-223.* Canol, coined from "Canada" and "oil," was conceived by the US War Department in the spring of 1942 as a 600-mile pipeline from Norman Wells on the Mackenzie River to Whitehorse, Yukon. Its "hydra-headed monster" nature was commented on by Colonel S. W. Dzuiban, an American historian, and Canada's Major General W. W. Foster attempted to control it in 1943. Before the project ended in 1945 it included roadbuilding, river freighting, airfields, wildcat oil drilling, and other minor projects unrelated to the original authorization. During World War II there were several full-blown investigations of Canol by the United States and Canadian Governments. The wildcatting by Imperial Oil is noted. 44 notes.
C. H. Held

55. Barry, P. S. THE PROLIFIC PIPELINE: GETTING CANOL UNDER WAY. *Dalhousie Rev. [Canada] 1976 56(2): 252-267.* The Canol project of World War II was called prolific because its originally projected 600-mile length from Norman Wells to Whitehorse grew to 1600 miles with branches to Skagway and Fairbanks, Alaska. There is much to be learned by studying the history of Canol's construction in the early 1940's in the Mackenzie River basin by the planners and builders of the current Mackenzie Valley project. The Berger Commission, established to look into the impact of this current project, would also be greatly instructed by the resurrection of Canol's history. Costs mounted from an original estimate of $30 million to $300 million, and manpower from 8,000 to 25,000. Roads were an important but useful proliferation. Illus., map, 31 notes.
C. Held

56. Barry, P. S. "PUNCH" DICKINS AND THE ORIGIN OF CANOL'S MACKENZIE AIR FIELDS. *Arctic [Canada] 1979 32(4): 366-373.* Examines the letters between Canadian flyer C. H. "Punch" Dickins and the Canadian government in Ottawa in 1942 indicating that the US government was building a secret "unauthorized" Mackenzie Air Route to the Norman Wells, an oil field to be tapped for defense purposes, that the Canadian government knew about but that Canada's Cabinet War Committee did not.

57. Bartlett, C. J. INTER-ALLIED RELATIONS IN THE SECOND WORLD WAR. *History [Great Britain] 1978 63(209): 390-395.* A review article prompted by four works on the diplomatic relations among Great Britain, the United States, and the USSR during and after World War II. Despite wartime disagreement between US and British policymakers over the status of the British colonial empire, a growing concern over Soviet military intentions after the war led the United States to see benefits for itself in the global network of British military bases. In the early years of the Cold War, then, the convergence of Anglo-American military interests was far more significant than were any outstanding differences. 12 notes. R. P. Sindermann, Jr.

58. Battillo, Anthony. THUNDER IN THE PO VALLEY. *Am. Hist. Illus. 1976 10(10): 22-30.* The Po Valley campaign, the last in Italy (14 April-2 May 1945), is recounted by a participant. The speed of attack of Lieutenant General Willis D. Crittenberger's IV Corps, the rapid crossing of the Po River, and the vast Po Valley which permitted long, wide, sweeping attacks by tanks and infantry, were responsible for the surrender of Italian Marshal Rodolfo Graziani's Army of Liguria in less than 18 days from the start of the campaign. Primary and secondary sources. 9 illus., map. D. B. Dodd

59. Bauer, Yehuda. "ONKEL SALY": DIE VERHANDLUNGEN DES SALY MAYER ZUR RETTUNG DER JUDEN 1944/45 ["Uncle Saly": the negotiations of Saly Mayer to save Jews, 1944-45]. *Vierteljahrshefte für Zeitgeschichte [West Germany] 1977 25(2): 188-219.* Describes the negotiations of Saly Mayer (1882-1950), Swiss industrialist and chairman of the Union of Jewish Communities in Switzerland, with representatives of SS Chief Heinrich Himmler. The American Jewish Joint Distribution Committee and the US government authorized negotiations in order to gain time, but did not authorize the offer of dollars and goods desired by the Nazis. With very limited means Mayer was able to delay and finally to prevent the deaths of many thousands of Jews. Based on records at the Roosevelt Library and in British, Israeli, and US archives, published documents, memoirs, and secondary sources; 64 notes. D. Prowe

60. Bayne, Walter J. WEIRD, WONDERFUL WARPLANES. *Air Force Mag. 1975 58(6): 64-68.* Discusses the development of fighter aircraft in the US Army Air Force from 1940 to 1945.

61. Beardsley, E. H. DOCTORS TO THE BARRICADES! AMERICAN PHYSICIANS AND THE BATTLE OF BRITAIN. *Bull. of the Hist. of Medicine 1977 51(2): 278-292.* In 1940, when the Battle of Britain began, a number of American physicians sought to volunteer for service in Britain. One organization, the American Hospital in Great Britain, Ltd., wanted to send an organized and equipped surgical unit. When the British began to recruit Ameri-

can volunteers, they let the American Hospital In Britain screen applicants. Few Americans served, however, and of those who did volunteer, many were not professionally licensed. The British attitude did not help the cause, as American doctors had to pay their own transportation costs, received the same pay as British physicians, and paid the same high taxes. Moreover, the US Army, Navy, and Public Health Service were recruiting doctors and refused to defer to British needs. The British hesitated to employ German American or Italian American physicians, and refused to accept Negro applicants. After a vigorous campaign of recruitment, only 53 physicians left for Britain, far less than the 1000 sought. 53 notes. M. Kaufman

62. Beardsley, E. H. NO HELP WANTED: MEDICAL RESEARCH EXCHANGE BETWEEN RUSSIA AND THE WEST DURING THE SECOND WORLD WAR. *Medical Hist. [Great Britain] 1978 22(4): 365-377.* Describes the Anglo-American attempts to establish a medical research exchange with the USSR during World War II. Although both sides would have benefited, the Western powers' efforts were rebuffed. Cooperation and information sharing certainly could have saved lives in the Russian typhus epidemic, but Soviet recalcitrance was based on the fear of the establishment of a permanent mission. The attempts at medical exchange also caused ill feeling between the United States and Great Britain. Primary sources; 55 notes. S. Patterson

63. Beardsley, E. H. SECRETS BETWEEN FRIENDS: APPLIED SCIENCE EXCHANGE BETWEEN THE WESTERN ALLIES AND THE SOVIET UNION DURING WORLD WAR II. *Social Studies of Sci. [Great Britain] 1977 7(4): 447-474.* Describes the inability of the United States and Great Britain to agree on scientific information exchange with the Soviet Union during World War II; first the US feared an exchange of secrets with the enemy, and then Britain feared strengthening the Soviet hand after the war.

64. Beaumont, Roger A. A MYTH OF CHIVALRY: VARIATIONS ON A THEME BY GABRIEL AND SAVAGE. *Military Rev. 1980 60(5): 64-75.* Examines the hypothesis of Richard A. Gabriel and Paul L. Savage's *Crisis in Command* (New York: Hill and Wang, 1978) that the organization man mentality in World War II eclipsed traditional soldierly values in the officer corps. The experience of the American military in the 20th century seems to validate this. Efforts to demilitarize the Army, to remove special status from various elements of it, and suppression of most innovations all indicate that Gabriel and Savage are probably right. 3 photos, 3 notes. D. H. Cline

65. Becton, Wendell R. and Maunder, Elwood R. MILITARY FORESTRY IN FRANCE AFTER 1944. *Forest Hist. 1972 16(3): 38-43.* The author was one of 15 foresters in the German theater of operations during WWII, supervising the production of lumber from eastern France for the allied invasion forces. The Germans did not destroy lumber on their retreat, thereby making it possible for the allied armies to use locally-produced lumber. Due to the intelligence information accumulated by the Oxford School of Forestry, the Allies knew exactly how much timber they could get out of France and Germany, the locations of the mills, and what specific kind of wood supply was needed. Based on interview; illus., 2 photos. D. R. Verardo

66. Beecher, Lloyd, Jr. THE SECOND WORLD WAR AND U.S. POLITICO-ECONOMIC EXPANSION: THE CASE OF LIBERIA, 1938-45. *Diplomatic Hist. 1979 3(4): 391-412.* Before World War II, US relations with Liberia were primarily sentimental. As war approached, the US military understood Liberia's strategic value and promoted that country's development for military reasons. As the security of the region improved, the military's interest in the country declined, but the State Department became more active, promoting economic development to benefit the United States and planning reform measures. Based on archival and published primary sources; 53 notes.   S

67. Bell, Charles. SHOOTOUT AT SAVO. *Am. Hist. Illus. 1975 9(9): 28-38.* A report on the World War II naval battle at Savo Island, off the coast of Guadalcanal. The Allied fleet protecting the invasion beachhead was large and well-armed. The small Japanese fleet took advantage of Allied blunders to enter the bay without alerting the guard ships. The battle was a one-sided Japanese victory. The defeat caused Allied commanders to remain alert thereafter, and never again did they underestimate the enemy. 2 maps, 14 photos.
V. L. Human

68. Bell, Roger. AUSTRALIAN-AMERICAN RELATIONS AND RECIPROCAL WARTIME ECONOMIC ASSISTANCE, 1941-6: AN AMBIVALENT ASSOCIATION. *Australian Econ. Hist. Rev. [Australia] 1976 16(1): 23-49.* Both the United States and Australia made sufficient contributions and concessions to ultimate victory over Japan, during World War II, but neither country was prepared seriously to compromise its immediate or long-term economic interests to further this end. Each attempted to exploit the wartime economic arrangements for national economic and trade benefits after the war. Based on archival materials in the United States and Australia; 103 notes.
R. B. Orr

69. Bell, Roger. AUSTRALIAN-AMERICAN DISCORD: NEGOTIATIONS FOR POST-WAR BASES AND SECURITY ARRANGEMENTS IN THE PACIFIC 1944-1946. *Australian Outlook [Australia] 1973 27(1): 12-33.* By early 1944 Australia was no longer looking primarily to America. It was prepared to foster American involvement in the South Pacific by negotiating reciprocal base rights, a tripartite defence scheme, or a regional security arrangement, but was opposed to US proposals for the unilateral use of Manus Island, and US expansion in the Southwest Pacific. Failure to negotiate a compromise was a result of US policy revision in early 1946. Based on State Department documents of 1941-45 and declassified British and Australian war records; 89 notes.
E. Plumridge

70. Bell, Roger. AUSTRALIAN-AMERICAN DISAGREEMENT OVER THE PEACE SETTLEMENT WITH JAPAN, 1944-46. *Australian Outlook [Australia] 1976 30(2): 238-262.* Analyzes the disagreement over the peace settlement which was a continuation of friction over Allied strategic priorities precipitated by rapid Japanese advances in 1942. Australia opposed the Anglo-American policy of defeating Germany first; and, after 1943, Australian criticism of America became more pronounced. The reluctance of the USSR to sustain the temporary wartime alliance after 1945 and growing American suspicions of Soviet intentions in occupied Germany and Eastern Europe increased American deter-

mination to dominate the Far Eastern counteroffensive and monopolize control of defeated Japan. Australia's resistance to American policy was largely unsuccessful although it did obtain some powers of advisory consultation and led the British Commonwealth Occupation Force and the Allied Control Council in Japan. Primary and secondary sources; 88 notes. R. G. Neville

71. Bellingacci, Isabella. NOTE SULL'ORGANIZZAZIONE DEL TRATTATO DELL'ATLANTICO DEL NORD [Notes on the organization of NATO]. *La seconda guerra mondiale nella prospettiva storica a trent'anni dall'epilogo* (Como: Casa Editrice Pietro Carioli, 1977): 485-491. Follows the evolution of US intervention in world affairs, particularly its participation in World War II and its role in international organizations such as the UN and NATO. NATO can be considered, in retrospect, the means by which direct confrontation with Eastern European countries was avoided. The subsequent creation of the Warsaw Pact established an equilibrium that led to the crystallization of events and subsequently to peace. Biblio. M. T. Wilson

72. Belz, Herman. CHANGING CONCEPTIONS OF CONSTITUTIONALISM IN THE ERA OF WORLD WAR II AND THE COLD WAR. *J. of Am. Hist. 1972 59(3): 640-669.* A broad analysis of political theory and ideas concerning constitutionalism reveals a reaction against the "realist" concept of the Constitution as a "parchment barrier against social reform and a defense of the laissez-faire status quo," and of law as a static justification of economic self-interest. The rise of Nazi and Communist totalitarian movements led many earlier realists such as Charles Beard and Carl Becker to reassess the constitution more positively as a valuable restraint on the power of government. Even radical movements of the 1960's, while proclaiming the need for more opportunities for political action on the part of citizens, worked within the structure of constitutionalism as a normative mode of conducting public affairs. 117 notes.
K. B. West

73. Bennett, Geoffrey. THE DEVELOPMENT OF THE PROXIMITY FUZE. *J. of the Royal United Services Inst. for Defence Studies [Great Britain] 1976 121(1): 57-62.* Describes the little-known development, by US scientists, of the proximity fuse for antiaircraft gunnery. Dangers to Allied naval vessels from air attack from the beginning of World War II necessitated research on an "influence fuse," the main work on which was passed to the United States in 1940. By the beginning of 1942 US electronics firms had produced a viable model. During the next two years the proximity fuse proved significant in reducing losses to air attack in both the US and Royal Navies. In Britain the device proved invaluable in dealing with German V-1 flying bomb attacks. 10 notes.
D. H. Murdoch

74. Ben-Zvi, Abraham. AMERICAN PRECONCEPTIONS AND POLICIES TOWARD JAPAN, 1940-1941: A CASE STUDY IN MISPERCEPTION. *Internat. Studies Q. 1975 19(2): 228-248.* An attempt to develop a new typology of American policymakers involved in US-Japanese relations during 1940 and 1941. The typology consists of three major categories: 1) the globalist-realists, Henry Stimson, Henry Morgenthau, and Stanley Hornbeck, 2) the globalist-idealists like Cordell Hull, and 3) the nationalist-pragmatists, Franklin D. Roosevelt and Joseph Grew. 5 notes. G. J. Boughton

75. Ben-Zvi, Abraham. THE OUTBREAK AND TERMINATION OF THE PACIFIC WAR: A JUXTAPOSITION OF AMERICAN PRECONCEPTIONS. *J. of Peace Res. [Norway] 1978 15(1): 33-49.* The article juxtaposes the predominant preconceptions and beliefs pertaining to Japanese military capabilities and predisposition to take risks, held by a number of U.S. decision makers on the eve of the Pacific War, with those adhered to during the last phases of that conflagration. The analysis indicates that misperceived notions contributed both to the outbreak of the War and to the manner in which it was terminated. The central lesson emerging from this study is misperception can be formulated as the need to evaluate tactical field information on its own, and to avoid interpreting such data solely in the light of a *priori* strategic assumptions which inevitably reflect the decision maker's images of an opponent. As the article demonstrates U.S. policy makers on both occasions analyzed tended to discount the flow of tactical indicators which contradicted their assessments of the opponent's capabilities and propensity to take risks. Thus, as a means for improving the decision-making process, particularly during periods of acute crisis or war (when policy makers are especially susceptible to the influence of preconceived images), the article suggests that increased weight should be given to tactical indicators when these are at variance with strategic assumptions. J

76. Ben-Zvi, Abraham. PERCEPTION, ACTION AND REACTION: A COMPARATIVE ANALYSIS OF DECISION-MAKING PROCESSES IN BILATERAL CONFLICTS. *J. of Pol. Sci. 1980 7(2): 95-111.* Decisionmakers in foreign policy act in accordance with their perceptions of reality, not in response to reality itself. Breaking away too sharply from misperceptions can prove as harmful as clinging to the original notions. Based on studies of the Arab-Israeli conflict, 1967-73, and the United States and Japan, 1941-45. 58 notes. T. P. Richardson

77. Ben-Zvi, Abraham. THE STUDY OF SURPRISE ATTACKS. *British J. of Int. Studies [Great Britain] 1979 5(2): 129-149.* Examination of surprise attacks (Pearl Harbor, the Korean War, and the October War) indicates that neither the analytic-revisionist nor the cognitive-cybernetic school of research has successfully explained the element of surprise.

78. Bérard, Armand. LA FIN DE ROOSEVELT ET LA DOUBLE CAPITULATION [The death of Roosevelt and the double capitulation]. *Nouvelle Rev. des Deux Mondes [France] 1978 (2): 280-289.* Discusses US-European diplomacy, February-August 1945.

79. Berkin, Carol Ruth. NOT SEPARATE, NOT EQUAL. Berkin, Carol Ruth and Norton, Mary Beth, ed. *Women of America: A History* (Boston: Houghton Mifflin Co., 1979): 273-288. Examines the apparent disintegration of the women's liberation movement after the passage of the 19th Amendment. The media held up the flapper as an indication that women were liberated in the 1920's. Real jobs were difficult to obtain, however, and feminist leaders could not decide which issues to attack after the amendment had passed. The Depression brought with it the idea that "one unemployed woman meant one more working man." World War II brought many women back into the work force. Many resisted leaving their jobs when men returned from the war, but they were still reduced from 25% to 7.5% of the labor force. In the 1960's, a new feminist movement emerged based on the reforms of the decade. K. Talley

80. Bernard, Elaine. A UNIVERSITY AT WAR: JAPANESE CANADIANS AT UBC DURING WORLD WAR II. *BC Studies [Canada] 1977 (35): 36-55.* The impact of World War II on the University of British Columbia must be considered in the context of race relations in the province and national policy. The 1940 National Resources Mobilization Act meant compulsory military training on the campus in the Canadian Officers' Training Corps, including the Canadian students of Japanese descent. The Japanese Canadians were abruptly discharged from the service, however, after Pearl Harbor. Eventually some 70 "Japanese" students were forced out of the university and the coastal area. 30 notes, 4 appendixes. D. L. Smith

81. Bernhard, George K., Jr. TEN FEET, MORE OR LESS. *Aerospace Hist. 1979 26(1): 21-24.* An account of the author's experiences as an Aviation Cadet in pilot training with the US Army Air Forces during World War II. The title of the article comes from his flight in a PT-17 trainer. He continually flew the traffic pattern 10 feet over the prescribed 500 feet. His instructor slapped the control column and the student "flew" out of the cockpit and parachuted to the ground. Possibly the extra 10 feet of altitude saved his life, as the parachute apparently opened when he was only inches from the ground. C. W. Ohrvall

82. Bernson, Sarah L. and Eggers, Robert J. BLACK PEOPLE IN SOUTH DAKOTA HISTORY. *South Dakota Hist. 1977 7(3): 241-270.* Lewis and Clark were accompanied by a black slave. Dakota had few blacks, and they were prohibited from voting. After the Civil War, a few were among the advancing settlers and miners. Minor racial incidents occurred near military forts in the 1870's and 80's. There were concentrations of black people in Yankton and rural Sully County. The state had only 832 blacks in 1920. The following decade was marked by Ku Klux Klan activity and the formation of an NAACP chapter. The Great Depression was weathered through the efforts of black churches, the NAACP, and group cooperation. Following a black increase during World War II, especially at cities near military bases, discrimination in housing and services became serious issues. These problems have been legislated away. The recent national civil rights movement and black awareness have helped the black population (1,627 in 1970) establish themselves as full and equal citizens. Secondary sources; 8 photos, 95 notes. A. J. Larson

83. Bernstein, Barton J. HIROSHIMA RECONSIDERED—THIRTY YEARS LATER. *Foreign Service J. 1975 52(8): 8-13, 32-33.* Reviews the decision to use atomic warfare against Japan in 1945. S

84. Bernstein, Barton J. THE PERILS AND POLITICS OF SURRENDER: ENDING THE WAR WITH JAPAN AND AVOIDING THE THIRD ATOMIC BOMB. *Pacific Hist. Rev. 1977 46(1): 1-27.* The ambiguous American response to Japan's 10 August 1945 surrender offer strengthened the militarists in Japan and nearly prolonged the war. President Truman and Secretary of State James F. Byrnes were reluctant to retain the Emperor. Byrnes and Truman were concerned about domestic political effects and feared a popular backlash if the surrender terms were not harsh enough. They were therefore willing to consider using a third atomic bomb or mounting a costly invasion of Japan. Secretary of War Henry L. Stimson and Admiral William Leahy urged accep-

tance of Japan's surrender terms in order to end the war quickly, keep Russia out of the peace settlement, and avoid world-wide horror at the use of a third atomic bomb. Based on documents in numerous manuscript collections; 92 notes.

W. K. Hobson

85. Bernstein, Barton J. THE QUEST FOR SECURITY: AMERICAN FOREIGN POLICY AND INTERNATIONAL CONTROL OF ATOMIC ENERGY, 1942-1946. *J. of Am. Hist. 1974 60(4): 1003-1044.* Overriding the objections of some scientists, the administration of Franklin D. Roosevelt made the decision *not* to share atomic secrets with the USSR. Henry Stimson considered promising such secrets in return for an opening of Soviet society, and had F.D.R. lived he might quite possibly have used "atomic diplomacy" to ease America's postwar role. President Truman later saw the United States as a trustee for the awesome weapon. Although at times he seemed disposed to listen to Stimson and Acheson who suggested a more open and direct approach to the Soviet Union, he was averse to sharing secrets that might end America's nuclear monopoly. The Acheson-Lilienthal report was so amended by Bernard Baruch (with provisions for inspections and giving up veto power in the UN) as to make it obviously unacceptable to the Soviet military chief. The climate of political opinion in 1946 made it difficult for the United States to offer any proposal which might have been acceptable to the Soviet Union. The controversy over atomic energy was both cause and consequence of the Cold War. 81 notes.

K. B. West

86. Bernstein, Barton J. SHATTERER OF WORLDS: HIROSHIMA AND NAGASAKI. *Bull. of the Atomic Scientists 1975 31(10): 12-22.* US policymakers in the Roosevelt and Truman administrations had little doubt about the desirability of using atomic weapons both for ending the war in the Pacific and for intimidating the USSR.

87. Bernstein, Barton J. THE UNEASY ALLIANCE: ROOSEVELT, CHURCHILL, AND THE ATOMIC BOMB, 1940-1945. *Western Pol. Q. 1976 29(2): 202-230.* Reinterprets the wartime Anglo-American relationship on atomic energy, defined primarily by Roosevelt and Churchill. Atomic energy represented, potentially, the cornerstone of a postwar Anglo-American entente in which only these "two policemen" (the United States and Great Britain) would have the atomic bomb. Roosevelt was a shrewd administrator in this important area, as revealed by his wartime foreign policy: his understanding of power, his attitudes toward the Soviet Union, his view of the United Nations, and his expectations about the postwar world. He was not naïve or innocent, but astute, about power in international affairs. He was not a Wilsonian internationalist but a firm believer in big-power politics. Based on the recently declassified American and British archives.

J/S

88. Best, Gary Dean. TOTALITARIANSIM OR PEACE: HERBERT HOOVER AND THE ROAD TO WAR, 1939-1941. *Ann. of Iowa 1979 44(7): 516-529.* Before the Japanese attack on Pearl Harbor, Herbert C. Hoover opposed US involvement in World War II. Hoover's opposition stemmed from diverse causes: his Quaker background, his experiences in World War I, his perception of the Communist USSR as a totalitarian government more objectionable than Nazi Germany and Fascist Italy, and his fear that US involvement

in the war would bring about domestic regimentation even greater than the New Deal. The United States could best serve the cause of freedom, said Hoover repeatedly, by remaining aloof from a war between totalitarian nations. Primary and secondary sources; 2 photos, 30 notes. P. L. Petersen

89. Bhana, Surendra. AN ATTEMPT BY THE ROOSEVELT ADMINISTRATION TO "REINFORCE" SELF-GOVERNMENT IN PUERTO RICO: THE ELECTIVE GOVERNOR BILL OF 1943. *Rev. Interamericana [Puerto Rico] 1973 2(4): 559-573.* World War II and internal politics in Puerto Rico influenced the Roosevelt administration to allow Puerto Ricans to elect their own governor. Congress opposed self-government in Puerto Rico and blocked enabling legislation during 1943-44. Primary and secondary works; 74 notes.
J. Lewis

90. Billinger, Robert D., Jr. WITH THE WEHRMACHT IN FLORIDA: THE GERMAN POW FACILITY AT CAMP BLANDING, 1942-1946. *Florida Hist. Q. 1979 58(2): 160-173.* Florida received only a small fraction of the total Wehrmacht prisoners of war in America. The experiences at Camp Blanding were typical: strikes, riots, and public complaints. Camp Blanding demonstrated the need for more local and regional research into the POW camps. Based on records from the Modern Military Archives Division of the National Archives; 56 notes. N. A. Kuntz

91. Binkley, John C. HISTORY OF US ARMY FORCE STRUCTURING. *Military Rev. 1977 57(2): 67-83.* Military force structuring determines how effectively the unit will operate and what can be accomplished on the battlefield. There are four factors that determine how and why US forces are structured and these have operated from the Civil War to the present-day Reorganization Objective Army Divisions. G. E. Snow

92. Birdsall, Steve. TARGET: RABAUL! *Air Force Mag. 1975 58(9): 108-113.* General George Kenney's fifth air force in the South Pacific destroyed Japan's air and naval power on New Britain Island in October 1943.

93. Bittner, D. F. SHOULDER PATCHES: A POLAR BEAR FOR THE MARINES. *Marine Corps Gazette 1980 64(11): 76-82.* Discusses the polar bear shoulder patches worn by some US Marines divisions when they were stationed in Iceland during 1941 and 1942 and accepted an offer by the British to adopt the polar bear motif.

94. Black, Gregory D. *KEYS OF THE KINGDOM:* ENTERTAINMENT AND PROPAGANDA. *South Atlantic Q. 1976 75(4): 434-446.* Uses the history of *The Keys of the Kingdom,* a 1944 20th Century-Fox movie about early 20th-century missionary life in China, to show the Office of War Information's (OWI) involvement in American wartime film industry. Only with the greatest persuasion could the filmmakers conceive of Chinese society in terms other than the mysterious East, but the stereotyping forced on them by the government agency was equally unrealistic. The OWI was promoting Franklin D. Roosevelt's concept of China as a fourth world power and obviously used this movie to improve relations between Washington and Chungking. Primary and secondary sources; 19 notes. W. L. Olbrich

95. Black, Gregory D. and Koppes, Clayton R. OWI GOES TO THE MOVIES. *Foreign Service J. 1974 51(8): 18-23, 29-30.* Discussses how during World War II (1942-43) the Office of War Information analyzed Hollywood films for the US propaganda effort. S

96. Black, Gregory D. and Koppes, Clayton R. OWI GOES TO THE MOVIES: THE BUREAU OF INTELLIGENCE'S CRITICISM OF HOLLYWOOD, 1942-43. *Prologue 1974 6(1): 44-59.* A commentary on the Bureau of Intelligence's criticism of Hollywood's motion pictures produced during 1942-43 when Elmer Davis was appointed head of the Office of War Information by President Roosevelt on 13 June 1942. "As the central coordinating agency between the government and mass media, Davis' organization was to inform the public of the 'progress of the war effort and of war policies, activities, and aims of the government and mass media.' " In the spring of 1943, intelligence operations were cut back, and analyses of motion pictures were suspended. "Through its desire to press artistic expression into government-sanctioned molds, the bureau courted the danger of undermining the ideals for which it fought." Illus., 2 photos, 40 notes. D. D. Cameron

97. Blair, Leon B. AMATEURS IN DIPLOMACY: THE AMERICAN VICE CONSULS IN NORTH AFRICA 1941-1943. *Historian 1973 35(4): 607-620.* Early in 1941 the United States and Vichy France concluded an agreement which allowed for the posting of 12 vice consuls in North Africa ostensibly for the purpose of distributing consumer goods purchased in America with frozen French assets. The men appointed to these positions had business experience but neither diplomatic nor political abilities. This proved unfortunate because their functions included gathering military intelligence and generating broad political support for the Allied landings scheduled for 1942. Their work proved seriously defective when they began to align the United States on the side of repressive pro-German French groups and continued by setting a 20 year pattern of uncritical support for French rule in North Africa. Based on primary sources found in the National Archives, Washington; 44 notes. N. W. Moen

98. Bland, Larry I. AVERELL HARRIMAN, THE RUSSIANS AND THE ORIGINS OF THE COLD WAR IN EUROPE, 1943-45. *Australian J. of Pol. and Hist. [Australia] 1977 23(3): 403-416.* Portrays W. Averell Harriman, Roosevelt's lend-lease expediter in London, and later ambassador in Moscow, as representative of "the best in the American diplomatic tradition." The rich, well travelled son of a railroad magnate broke with his class in 1932 and became a New Dealer. He took a "Wilsonian liberalism" into diplomatic affairs, but by 1943 urged hard reciprocal bargaining with the Russians. His optimism about Soviet postwar intentions was shaken in 1945 by the fate of Poland and the prisoners of war issue, and he became a pioneer "cold warrior." By the 1960's he was wanting to "de-escalate the rhetoric." Concludes that the irony of Harriman's ambassadorship is that some of his sound advice of 1943-44 was ignored, while his rather shrill rhetoric of 1945 was accepted as expert advice. Private papers, official archives, memoirs, and monographs. W. D. McIntrye

99. Blasier, Cole. THE UNITED STATES, GERMANY, AND THE BOLIVIAN REVOLUTIONARIES (1941-1946). *Hispanic Am. Hist. R. 1972 52(1): 26-54.* Examines the US campaign against Nazi Fascism in Bolivia involv-

ing three interrelated episodes: the "Nazi Putsch" of 1941, the initial refusal of the US to recognize the Villarroel government in 1944, and the 1946 publication of the Blue Book against Juan Perón. The US anti-Nazi campaign hampered rather than promoted US purposes. Notes the lack of authenticity of the Belmonte-Wendler letter, though it served the purposes of the US and Britain. Based on captured German documents, US State Department archives, recently published memoirs, and interviews with leading participants; 77 notes.
R. V. Ritter

100. Blayney, Michael S. HERBERT PELL, WAR CRIMES, AND THE JEWS. *Am. Jewish Hist. Q. 1976 65(4): 335-352.* Herbert Claiborne Pell, a Harvard classmate of Franklin D. Roosevelt, was one of Roosevelt's political appointees in various foreign service posts. Pell was an early and vigorous denouncer of Nazi policies; his letters to the President stand in marked contrast to the restrained style and attitude of the State Department. His 1943 appointment to the UN War Crimes Commission led almost from the beginning to increased conflict with the State Department, which did not agree with his definition of war crimes and atrocities. The question whether crimes against Jews, regardless of location and nationality, came within the jurisdiction of the commission was another issue that divided Pell and the Department. All of this led to his abrupt dismissal in 1945. 45 notes.
F. Rosenthal

101. Bloom, Lynn Z. THE DIARY AS POPULAR CULTURE. *J. of Popular Culture 1976 9(4): 794-807.* Diaries have been popular since the Renaissance. They are the raw materials of history, full of repetitive minutia written to record, interpret, gain perspective, or, in the case of prison diaries, to maintain sanity. Bloom edited the 5,000-page World War II diary of Natalie Stark Crouter, prisoner of the Japanese in the Philippines, during 1941-45. Details the food, recreation, organization, and hierarchy of the 500 alien civilian prisoners and their relations with their guards. A communal democracy emerged among the prisoners which maintained order, discipline, and hope, despite malnutrition, regimentation, and lack of privacy. Quotes from the diary.
D. L. Grant

102. Blum, Albert A. ROOSEVELT, THE M-DAY PLANS, AND THE MILITARY-INDUSTRIAL COMPLEX. *Military Affairs 1972 36(2): 44-46.* The industrial mobilization plans developed in the 1920's and 1930's resulted from close cooperation between military and business leaders. They were also drawn in isolation from the growing labor union movement and from the ideologies reflected in the New Deal. The proposals were therefore politically unrealistic in calling for a mobilization office staffed with businessmen and a strong director of mobilization. With the May 1940 establishment of the Advisory Commission to the Council of National Defense, President Franklin Delano Roosevelt ensured that the control of mobilization rested in the White House. Based on the author's "Birth and Death of the M-Day Plan," in Harold Stein, ed., *American Civil-Military Decisions* (Montgomery: U. of Alabama Press, 1963); 2 notes.
K. J. Bauer

103. Bocca, Geoffrey. "WHEN DOES THIS PLACE GET TO NEW YORK?" *Am. Heritage 1979 30(4): 80-91.* Built between 1930 and 1936, the *Queen Mary* served during the golden age of ocean travel and then as a transporter of American G.I.s to war in Europe. Returned to passenger service in 1947,

Mary fell victim to improved air service. Her last voyage was completed in 1957, and later *Mary* was sold to the City of Long Beach, California. 25 illus.

J. F. Paul

104. Boghosian, S. Samuel. "THE ONE-MAN PURSUIT FORCE." *Air Force Mag. 1973 56(9): 94-98.* Describes the career of air ace Lieutenant Boyd D. "Buzz" Wagner, one of a handful of pilots in the Philippines after Pearl Harbor, 1941-42.

105. Bonder, Seth. SYSTEMS ANALYSIS: A PURELY INTELLECTUAL ACTIVITY. *Military R. 1971 51(2): 14-23.* Operations research activities in World War II were primarily directed at analysis of existing military systems to improve their operating efficiency. Much of systems analysis today is not scientific, but rather "natural philosophy." It is an intellectual art used in making necessary and useful predicitions in problem areas where experiment and verification are difficult or impossible. Cites specific examples where failure to recognize this change has resulted in gross misuse of systems analysis by the defense community. Suggests four methods to change systems analysis activity. 4 charts.

G. E. Snow

106. Booth, Larry. WARTIME SAN DIEGO: 1943. *J. of San Diego Hist. 1978 24(2): 197-220.* Reprints and comments on 25 photographs.

107. Boothe, Leon E. THE BRUSSELS CONFERENCE AND CONFLICT WITH JAPAN. *World Affairs 1972 135(3): 240-259.* Failure to align with Britain, France, and the USSR at the Brussels Conference following Japanese aggression in China in 1937, indicated to Japan and Germany that the United States was unwilling to unite with antifascist powers against the former's imperialistic endeavors and figured decisively in the string of events leading to World War II.

108. Borisiuk, V. I. OT ZAKONA VAGNERA K ZAKONU TAFTA-KHARTLI: POVOROT K REAKTSII V TRUDOVOM ZAKONODA-TEL'STVE SSHA (1935-1947 GG.) [From the Wagner Act to the Taft-Hartley Act: the shift to reactionary labor legislation in the United States, 1935-47]. *Vestnik Moskovskogo U., Seriia 9: Istoriia [USSR] 1971 26(5): 15-31.* The Wagner Act (US, 1935), considered the most radical piece of labor legislation of the New Deal, generated sharp opposition from the right, manufacturers, and capital, and from their representatives in Congress. At first they sought to prove it unconstitutional; failing this they tried to amend it. They called the power of unions "un-American." During World War II there was a reactionary shift under the guise of protecting the war effort. After the war, with controls lifted, the number of strikes increased sharply. This set the stage for the victory of the right, the Taft-Hartley Act (US, 1947), which strictly regulated union activities. Based on published sources; 67 notes.

G. E. Munro

109. Bothwell, Robert and English, John. CANADIAN TRADE POLICY IN THE AGE OF AMERICAN DOMINANCE AND BRITISH DECLINE, 1943-1947. *Can. Rev. of Am. Studies [Canada] 1977 8(1): 52-65.* Traces the development of Canadian tariff, monetary, and other fundamental economic policies between 1943 and 1947. Canada alternately followed policies designed to preserve its preferential trading position in the British Empire, bilateral trade

policies characterized by special agreements between Canada and its "trading partners," and finally multilateral trade policies that the United States favored and Canada accepted as a means of curing its post-World War II economic ills. Canada made its postwar economic choices largely out of fear of returning to the poverty experienced during the 1930's. Based on Canadian archival sources and secondary works; 52 notes. H. T. Lovin

110. Bowen, John E. DECEMBER 7, 1941: THE DAY THE HONOLULU FIRE DEPARTMENT WENT TO WAR. *Hawaiian J. of Hist. 1979 13: 126-135.* On 7 December 1941, the 12 men of the Honolulu Fire Department Engine Companies 4 and 6 found that they were the entire firefighting force available. The fire department fought fire and enemy bombing at Hickam Field near Pearl Harbor. The Honolulu Fire Department is the only civilian fire department in the United States to fight fires caused by enemy action under combat conditions. Notes. M. J. Wentworth

111. Bowers, Ray L. AFTER THIRTY YEARS: CONVERSATIONS ON THE AIR WAR. *Aerospace Hist. 1974 21(2): 65-69.* US and German airmen discuss their experiences in Europe during World War II, 1942.

112. Bowers, Thomas A. THE BANKHEAD BILL: HOW A THREATENED PRESS SUBSIDY WAS DEFEATED. *Journalism Q. 1976 53(1): 21-27.* The bill introduced by John H. Bankhead in the Senate in 1943 would have required the federal government to purchase War Bond advertising to subsidize smaller newspapers. It raised controversy among journalists, legislators, and advertising professionals. In the House of Representatives, the Bankhead Bill (1943) and two others similar to it were tabled. The bills lacked media guidelines and advertising objectives, and were opposed by the Treasury Department. Based on primary sources; 47 notes. K. J. Puffer

113. Bowles, Dorothy. NEWSPAPER SUPPORT FOR FREE EXPRESSION IN TIMES OF ALARM, 1920 AND 1940. *Journalism Q. 1977 54(2): 271-279.* Editorials in large-city newspapers were generally supportive of freedom of expression during two periods of alarm in the United States; such support was not dependent on whether the threat directly affected the press, nor do the data indicate that newspaper support differed significantly across geographical areas.

114. Bowman, Marvin S. WORLD WAR II: STOPPING OVER AT IVAN'S AIRDROME. *Air Force Mag. 1972 55(4): 51-55.* A US Air Force veteran recalls the bombing missions from Great Britain to Russia in June 1944 when some crews put in at Mirgorod and escaped the Poltava tragedy.

115. Boyd, Carl. ATTACKING THE *INDIANAPOLIS:* A REEXAMINATION. *Warship Int. 1976 13(1): 15-25.* Examines the sinking of the *USS Indianapolis* by the Japanese submarine *I-58;* includes histories of both vessels and analyses of why the 1945 attack took place, including the possibility of the use of kaitens, the submarine equivalent of kamikaze planes.

116. Bozhinov, B. POLITIKATA NA SASHT SPRIAMO BULGARIIA PREZ 1944 G [The policy of the United States toward Bulgaria in 1944]. *Istoricheski Pregled [Bulgaria] 1966 22(6): 67-82.* Throughout World War II the United States wished to remove Bulgaria from the war so that American military,

political, and economic power could have a free hand. The Americans had worked out a plan of capitulation for Bulgaria, and feared an agreement between Bulgaria and the USSR. Moreover, the United States wished to gain control of the Bulgarian Army, and use it in Thrace as a policing force. The USA also decided not to support Bulgaria's claim to Macedonia. The Greek government eagerly pursued a policy of territorial expansion, and Turkey wished to play an active role in the Balkans. The timely arrival of Soviet liberating forces averted a potential catastrophe. Based on *Foreign Relations of the United States, Diplomatic Papers, 1944,* Vol. III (Washington, 1965); 58 notes. A. J. Evans

117. Bradley, Mark E. THE P-51 OVER BERLIN. *Aerospace Hist. 1974 21(3): 125-128.* Discusses the development and role of this plane in World War II. S

118. Bradley, Omar Nelson. POVESTEA UNUI SOLDAT [A Soldier's Story]. *Magazin Istoric [Rumania] 1975 9(5): 33-36, 40.* Prints excerpts from Bradley's book. 5 notes. J. M. McCarthy

119. Bradshaw, Russell. TO RUSSIA: ONE WAY. *Aerospace Hist. 1978 25(4): 198-205.* The author discusses his participation as an Air Force Intelligence Officer in the first USAF combat missions to fly from Russian airfields in World War II. Aircraft from the 2nd, 97th, and 99th Bomb Groups stationed in Italy were flown to airbases in the Ukraine on 2 June 1944. From there they operated against German Army targets for 10 days before returning to Italy. 6 photos. C. W. Ohrvall

120. Brady, E. C. WHITE ENSIGN FOUR STACKERS. *Can. Forces Sentinel [Canada] 1972 8(8): 31-36.* After World War I, the United States was left with surplus numbers of fleet destroyers, the famous "Four Stackers." By 1940, the British, facing German invasion and the submarine blockade, appealed to the United States. Franklin D. Roosevelt responded by turning over 50 Four Stackers amid great controversy. Six of these were given to Canada. Despite the fact that they were not designed for their job and their age created immense maintenance problems, the Four Stackers performed heroically and helped turn the tide of battle against the U-boats. The saga of the *St. Croix* is representative; taking part in many major battles, sinking two U-boats, and helping in several other kills before she was lost. By 1945, the Four Stackers were out of active service but their heroism has been perpetuated in the names of newer ships.
W. E. Pittman, Jr.

121. Brady, Lawrence K. MARSHALL'S STRATEGY. *Army Q. and Defence J. [Great Britain] 1972 103(1): 52-62.* A general study of the strategic thinking of Chief of Staff General George C. Marshall 1939-50. Traces the development of his planning through 1941 to its culmination in the "basic strategy of a global war before [the United States] was involved in it," and the decision to aim for total military defeat of Germany. His strategic thinking at this stage indicated basically traditional attitudes toward international politics. Marshall underestimated the dynamic element in Fascism, and more importantly, in Soviet Communism. This underestimation affected his strategic outlook to the point where "there appears to be an abandonment of the idea that realistic policy objectives can be the only true basis for strategy." In 1947, as Secretary of State,

he immediately was faced with conflict with the Soviet Union in Europe. Marshall's solution, the European Recovery Program, ultimately showed that he "had analysed the problem in Europe accurately and had devised a most effective strategy to meet the threat." D. H. Murdoch

122. Brandon, Donald. THE LAST TIME WE HAD A MULTIPOLAR WORLD THINGS DIDN'T WORK OUT VERY WELL. *Worldview 1974 17(3): 5-9.* Compares foreign relations among the seven Great Powers in the 1930's with those of the two superpowers in the 1970's, recommending a balance of power policy to the US rather than the multipolar politics that led to World War II.

123. Bravo Nuche, Ramón. SERVICIOS DE INTELIGENCIA [Intelligence services]. *Rev. General de Marina [Spain] 1977 193(8-9): 185-197.* The development of US intelligence services demonstrates the complexity of the interrelationships among the various armed services and agencies of government. During World War II, intelligence services were highly decentralized among the various services and only coordinated at the joint chiefs of staff level. This was clearly inadequate and led to the establishment of the Central Intelligence Agency in 1947. Intelligence functions then became too heavily centralized, leading to a partial decentralization after 1961 with the establishment of the Defense Intelligence Agency. The resulting balance between centralization and decentralization serves as a basis for the author's model intelligence organization, in which the armed services and governmental agencies individually provide intelligence requirements to a centralized evaluative department which compiles data from various sources and provides intelligence estimations to a central director of intelligence who oversees the entire process. 3 fig., biblio. W. C. Frank

124. Brax, Ralph S. WHEN STUDENTS FIRST ORGANIZED AGAINST WAR. *New-York Hist. Soc. Q. 1979 63(3): 228-255.* College student unrest was not new in the 20th century. However, before the 1930's it usually was directed against campus problems. During the Great Depression unrest increased, not, as one might have expected, against the economic system, but concentrating by the mid-1930's on an opposition to war. Sparked at first by socialist and communist groups, three nationwide student strikes were held, the last in 1936 supposedly including half a million students, but probably no more than 350,000. The majority of the million college students took little or no active part. Yet, some success was attained even though the movement collapsed when the nation found itself in World War II. Primary sources; 4 illus., 56 notes. C. L. Grant

125. Britsch, R. Lanier. THE CLOSING OF THE EARLY JAPAN MISSION. *Brigham Young U. Studies 1975 15(2): 171-190.* On 7 August 1924, after 23 years of effort and sacrifice by missionaries and church members, the Mormon Church ended its first mission in Japan. The missionary effort of the Mormons, begun in 1901, was not notably successful. Analyzes the conditions in Japan that caused the leaders of the Church to abandon missionary activity there. 2 tables, 49 notes. M. S. Legan

126. Brockel, Harry C. WORLD WAR II SECRETS OF LAKE MICHIGAN. *Inland Seas 1978 34(2): 103-112.* Several wartime activities on Lake Michigan are little known. These include the training of 14,000 naval aviators on

the side-wheel aircraft carriers *Sable* and *Wolverine;* the storage of 4,000 tons of Philippine hemp at Milwaukee; the rental of the Milwaukee Harbor Commission's 20-ton crane by the Navy for use in the submarine building program at Manitowoc Shipbuilding Company; the training of as many as 50,000 men at a time at the Great Lakes Naval Training Station; use of the Chesapeake and Ohio Railroad's car ferries to train merchant seamen; and the service of the Coast Guard cutter *Mackinaw* as a training vessel for Russian engineers preparing to take over a group of American-built icebreakers. Illus. K. J. Bauer

127. Brooks, Jim. THE DAY THE 31ST FIGHTER GROUP WON ITS UNIT CITATION. *Air Force Mag. 1972 55(10): 73-75.* A former P-51 pilot recounts 21 April 1944, when fighter aircraft escorted B-24's and B-17's in the massive raids on the Rumanian oil fields.

128. Brotherton, Bruce. BATFISH BEATS THE BONEYARD. *Warship Internat. 1973 10(4): 400-408.* Discusses the World War II fighting record of the antisubmarine vessel *USS Batfish*. S

129. Brown, Reginald J. THE MEANING OF PROFESSIONALISM: PURPOSES AND EXPECTATIONS IN A DEMOCRATIC SOCIETY. *Am. Behavioral Scientist 1976 19(5): 511-522.* Discusses the definition of military professionalism in contemporary American society, distinguishing between traditional conceptions of professionalism and the current concept of professional conduct, and giving a historical perspective from World War II through the Vietnam era.

130. Brown, Richard G. TARAWA: LEST WE FORGET. *Marine Corps Gazette 1980 64(11): 46-50.* The controversial assault by US Marines on the island of Betio, Tarawa Atoll, in the Gilbert Islands, 20 November 1943 resulted in 3,300 casualties before American troops took the island in 72 hours.

131. Brune, Lester H. CONSIDERATIONS OF FORCE IN CORDELL HULL'S DIPLOMACY, JULY 26 TO NOVEMBER 26, 1941. *Diplomatic Hist. 1978 2(4): 389-405.* The Japanese occupation of much of Indochina in mid-1941 resulted in Secretary of State Cordell Hull's disillusionment with the prospects for successful negotiations, but resulted also in a decision—to defend the Philippines when hostilities commenced—which laid upon him the task of continuing negotiations solely for the military purpose of buying time. Hull, who never seemed to appreciate the practical connections between diplomatic and military considerations, was not the man for this job, and he bungled it rather badly. On 26 November Hull and Roosevelt, reversing a war council decision of the previous day, scrapped plans to offer the Japanese a few token concessions, and thus abandoned the effort to extend negotiations until American preparations were complete in February or March 1942. Published primary and secondary sources; 48 notes. L. W. Van Wyk

132. Bryson, Thomas A. ROOSEVELT'S QUARANTINE SPEECH, THE GEORGIA PRESS AND THE BORG THESIS: A NOTE. *Australian J. of Pol. and Hist. 1975 21(2): 95-98.* Franklin D. Roosevelt delivered the quarantine speech in Chicago on 5 October 1937 as a response to Japanese military operations in China, and German and Italian involvement in Spain and Ethiopia respectively. Dorothy Borg maintained that the speech, contrary to popular

interpretation, did not represent a sharp change in policy, or anticipate the use of economic sanctions, but was an attempt to avoid war. Roosevelt was not attempting to establish a form of Wilsonian collective security but probably envisaged collective neutrality. He dropped plans to "quarantine" aggressors because of the intense opposition of leading isolationists. This thesis is tested by sampling 65 Georgian newspapers. The editors misrepresented the speech and read more into it than was intended, but the evidence suggests that it was primarily public opinion, rather than a few isolationists, which caused Roosevelt to forego plans to curb belligerent acts by the Axis powers. Primary and secondary sources; 22 notes. R. G. Neville

133. Buckley, Gary J. AMERICAN PUBLIC OPINION AND THE ORIGINS OF THE COLD WAR: A SPECULATIVE ASSESSMENT. *Mid-America 1978 60(1): 35-42.* A case study of American public opinion regarding the USSR during and shortly after World War II. At no time was American public opinion more favorable than a 55% positive attitude in February 1945 and 54% in August 1945. The negative and undecided opinions of Americans toward the USSR generally outweighed the positive responses. Several answers have been suggested for the opinions given by Americans, and more research is suggested to delineate possible reasons for anti-Soviet opinions during wartime cooperation. Secondary material; table, 15 notes. J. M. Lee

134. Buell, T. B. BATTLE OF THE PHILIPPINE SEA. *US Naval Inst. Pro. 1974 100(7): 64-79.* This excerpt from the author's recently published biography of Admiral Raymond A. Spruance, *The Quiet Warrior* (Boston: Little, Brown, 1974), deals exclusively with Spruance's decisions during the June 1943 battle of the Philippine Sea and their aftermath. There is still considerable discussion among naval writers, officers, and historians about Spruance's decision to protect the amphibious operations at Saipan rather than to attack the Japanese aircraft carriers; "their judgments vary widely, reflecting the complexity of the problems that Spruance had to solve in the pressure of war." It appears that "Spruance's failure to meet the enemy fleet in decisive action would forever haunt him," but "to his death, Spruance clung to his belief that Turner's transports were needed off the Saipan beaches." 9 photos. A. N. Garland

135. Buell, Thomas B. GUADALCANAL: NEITHER SIDE WOULD QUIT. *US Naval Inst. Pro. 1980 106(4): 60-65.* In the spring and summer of 1942, Admiral Ernest J. King, the US Chief of Naval Operations, fought hard in meetings of the US Joint Chiefs of Staff for a limited offensive in the Pacific. He was opposed by General George C. Marshall, the Army's Chief of Staff, who believed strongly in a Germany-first policy and who did not want to divert any army or air force resources to support a Pacific offensive. Eventually, King threatened to go ahead on his own, using as his authority several ambiguous memoranda that had been approved earlier by the President. Thus, on 7 August 1942, the US invasion of Guadalcanal took place, and this soon became a battle of attrition in which neither side would quit. Marshall never gave his full support to the operation, but it continued and the US forces were finally successful. Extracted from the author's book, *Master of Sea Power* (Little, Brown and Co., Inc., 1980). A. N. Garland

136. Buhite, Russell D. SOVIET-AMERICAN RELATIONS AND REPATRIATION OF PRISONERS OF WAR, 1945. *Historian 1973 35(3): 384-397.* Thousands of Americans taken prisoner during World War II fell into Soviet hands as Russian armies advanced into Manchuria, eastern Europe, and Germany. Negotiations for their return to the United States demonstrated the inhumanity of the Stalinist system which regarded Russian P.O.W.'s as traitors, and which attempted to repatriate American soldiers in exchange for US recognition of the communist government newly established in Poland. Based on the Yalta Papers and other published State Department documents. 35 notes.
N. W. Moen

137. Buller, H. L. "Duffy." THE C-46 AND C-47 IN CBI OPERATIONS. *Aerospace Historian 1975 22(2): 80-83.* Describes the C-46 and C-47 aircraft from a pilot's point of view. The author, who has flown both aircraft, discusses and compares the flying characteristics of both. Concludes that the superior aircraft was the one being flown at any given time. The article is a revision of one previously published in the *Hump Pilot's Newsletter.* 4 photos.
C. W. Ohrvall

138. Bundy, William P. DICTATORSHIPS AND AMERICAN FOREIGN POLICY. *Foreign Affairs 1975 54(1): 51-60.* Examines the balance maintained between the three basic US foreign policy objectives of 1) security against attack, 2) the maintenance of an international community, and 3) the encouragement of representative government. World War II made opposition to totalitarian dictatorship a cornerstone of US policy, but Richard M. Nixon's administration changed American policy toward democracies and dictatorships with serious consequences at home. American policy toward dictatorships has been uneven and contradictory as exemplified in Greece, the Philippines, and Chile. From a paper read to the American Philosophical Society in 1975.
C. W. Olson

139. Burkholder, Robert C. NEW THOUGHTS ON THE OLD MUSTANG. *Aerospace Hist. 1972 19(2): 66-68.* A retrospective look at the P-51 Mustang airplane. Until the winter of 1943, US bombers had no protection on their deep penetrations into Western Europe. The entrance of the P-51 afforded protection and fighter superiority for the Americans until the introduction of the German Me262 jet fighter in early 1945. The P-51 allowed the B-17s and B-24s to reach their full offensive potential while breaking the back of the Luftwaffe fighter defenses. Secondary sources; 5 photos.
C. W. Ohrvall

140. Bush, Edward F. SIR LYMAN DUFF AND THE HONG KONG INQUIRY. *Dalhousie Review [Canada] 1972 52(2): 203-211.* Examines the controversy that arose over William Lyon Mackenzie King's decision to send two battalions (Royal Rifles of Canada and the Winnipeg Grenadiers) to reinforce the garrison at Hong Kong just prior to the Japanese attack in 1941. Describes Sir Lyman Duff's career and his role in the Royal Commission established to investigate the whole affair. George Drew's attacks on King's government forced inquiry and when Duff's conclusions generally exonerated the government Drew turned his ire on the distinguished jurist. Concludes that Duff's report was a sound one and that Drew's waspishness was politically motivated, serving only to put a blot on an otherwise brilliant career. 26 notes.
C. H. Held

141. Butera, J. L. RESCUE CONCEPTS, BEFORE AND AFTER. *Aerospace Hist. 1974 21(1): 8-11.* "Evaluates the impact and validity of US military rescue concepts before, during, and after World War II, Korea, and Vietnam."
                                                                                                                            S

142. Butler, Joseph T., Jr. PRISONER OF WAR LABOR IN THE SUGAR CANE FIELDS OF LAFOURCHE PARISH, LOUISIANA, 1943-44. *Louisiana Hist. 1973 14(3): 283-296.* Discusses the use of German prisoners of war to farm sugar cane fields in 1943-44.

143. Butow, R. J. C. BACKDOOR DIPLOMACY IN THE PACIFIC: THE PROPOSAL FOR A KONOYE-ROOSEVELT MEETING, 1941. *J. of Am. Hist. 1972 59(1): 48-72.* Many historians have been quite critical of Franklin Delano Roosevelt and Cordell Hull for not responding to the Japanese proposal for a summit meeting in the summer of 1941. A careful analysis, however, shows that the idea of holding such a conference originated not with the Japanese Government but with a well-meaning but disruptive group of "John Doe Associates" led by James M. Drought of the Catholic Foreign Mission Society of America. The Japanese believed erroneously that the proposal originated with the U.S. Government, rejected it in May 1941, and resurrected it with hope of success in July. The U.S. Government considered the offer then as a desperation move, and were fearful of appearing to "appease" Japan. Regardless of Washington's justifiable apprehension, the meeting was a last opportunity to break out of a stalemated situation, and in fact the U.S. and Japanese positions were sufficiently flexible to have promised at least some chance of success. 82 notes.
                                                                                                                     K. B. West

144. Byrd, Martha. THE WAR'S FIRST HERO. *Am. Hist. Illus. 1978 13(8): 10-14.* The need for optimism and an air of success caused US government sources to claim that Captain Colin P. Kelly, Jr., dove his crippled B-17 into a Japanese ship, whereas he actually crashed near Mount Arayat, Philippines, 10 December 1941.

145. Byrd, Martha H. BATTLE OF THE PHILIPPINE SEA. *Am. Hist. Illus. 1977 12(4): 20-35.* Chronicles the Battle of the Philippine Sea, a naval and air battle of World War II between US forces and Japan, June 1944.

146. Byrd, Martha H. IWO JIMA. *Am. Hist. Illus. 1976 10(9): 4-13, 48-49.* Iwo Jima, an eight-square-mile pear-shaped island of volcanic ash in the Bonins midway between B-29's based in Saipan and their Tokyo target, was strategically significant as a base for fighters flying escort for the B-29's and as an emergency field for crippled B-29's. Thus General Tadamichi Kuribayashi and 22,000 of his 23,000 troops defended it to the death with a network of caves, tunnels, and pillboxes so secure that two months of softening up by naval and air bombardment had barely touched the emplacements. From 19 February to 16 March 1945, marines under General Holland M. Smith suffered 25,851 casualties (5,931 dead) in taking the island. Primary and secondary sources; 15 illus., map.
                                                                                                                     D. B. Dodd

147. Byrd, Martha H. SIX MINUTES TO VICTORY: THE BATTLE OF MIDWAY. *Am. Hist. Illus. 1975 10(2): 33-43.* Discusses the battle between US and Japanese naval forces near the Pacific island of Midway in 1942.

148. Byrnes, Robert F. UNITED STATES POLICY TOWARD EASTERN EUROPE: BEFORE AND AFTER HELSINKI. *R. of Pol. 1975 37(4): 435-463.* The Allies failed to counter Soviet land aggression during World War II because FDR placed politics and military strategy in different spheres. However, containment policy against Communist aggression after World War II has worked remarkably well. Many feel that the Helsinki agreement may have weakened the West defensively. In reality, by providing the United States and its allies with greater access to Eastern Europe, and by an aggressive policy of demonstrating the cultural, economic, and technical strengths of the West, the West may be able to use politics and culture to gradually end the "Soviet Empire over Europe."
L. E. Ziewacz

149. Cable, John N. VANDENBERG: THE POLISH QUESTION AND POLISH AMERICANS, 1944-1948. *Michigan Hist. 1973 57(4): 296-310.* Michigan's Republican Senator Arthur H. Vandenberg, best remembered for his strong bipartisanship as World War II ended and the Cold War began, was only moderately bipartisan on the Polish issue. Responding sympathetically to his staunchly anti-Communist, heavily Polish American constituency, Vandenberg articulated and championed the Polish cause at the national level. While critical of alleged diplomatic errors committed during the war and after, he realistically understood the impossibility of repudiating the East European agreements made at the Yalta Conference. Based largely upon primary sources; 2 photos, 43 notes.
D. W. Johnson

150. Caldwell, Hamlin A., Jr. AIR FORCE MARITIME MISSIONS. *US Naval Inst. Pro. 1978 104(10): 28-36.* Today, as much as it was needed and desired during World War II, US Air Force participation in its collateral maritime missions—aerial mining, ocean surveillance and reconnaissance, interdiction, and the like—is desirable and probably inevitable. Cooperation between the appropriate naval and air elements is essential and can certainly be arranged, despite the competition for scarce resources, the differing personalities and interservice rivalries, and the doctrinal differences concerning aircraft employment. Arranging this cooperation can be made easier if the two services will carefully and honestly examine the World War II precedents, during which the Air Force performed a number of significant maritime missions. Secondary sources; 8 photos, 20 notes.
A. N. Garland

151. Campbell, John P. THE SKIES OVER DIEPPE, AUGUST 19, 1942. *Canada 1975 3(1): 3-19.* Discusses the Royal Canadian Air Force's participation in the air battle of Dieppe during World War II in 1942, emphasizing the military strategy of British Air Vice-Marshal Trafford Leigh-Mallory.

152. Campbell, Thomas M. NATIONALISM IN AMERICA'S U.N. POLICY, 1944-1945. *Internat. Organization 1973 27(1): 25-44.* Presents an interpretation of the conflicts between universalism and nationalism as they affected United States policy toward the creation of the United Nations. Drawing on heretofore unavailable sources, the author stresses the rising influence of nationalism in the evolution of decisions on the veto power, trusteeships, and regionalism. His focus is on the decision-making process during Roosevelt's last year and the initial months of the Truman administration. He contends that Cordell Hull's universalist UN blueprint, which Roosevelt supported, was inexorably eroded by

critics within the American government, especially military spokesmen. These leaders took advantage of the apprehension about the Soviet Union's future policy to further their own ambitions for a strong post-war military posture. Truman was sympathetic to the voices of nationalism, and when he became president the shift away from a strong UN became more pronounced. J

153. Campion, Martin C. WAR GAME: WORLD WAR II IN THE WEST. *Hist. Teacher 1977 10(4): 575-585.* Discusses war games, especially those involving the Western European Theater in World War II. Games on war are competitive enough to keep the students' interest, and do not require too much reading preparation. Their chief advantage is that they clearly illustrate the confusion of life and the complexity of the decisionmaking process. Discusses and evaluates several war games. Lists games. P. W. Kennedy

154. Cannistraro, Philip V. GLI ITALO-AMERICANI DI FRONTE ALL-'INGRESSO DELL'ITALIA NELLA SECONDA GUERRA MONDIALE [Italian Americans and the entry of Italy into World War II]. *Storia Contemporanea [Italy] 1976 7(4): 855-864.* During the 1920's and 1930's, most Italian Americans had a favorable attitude toward Fascist Italy. The strong nationalism and alleged (by massive propaganda directed by Rome) accomplishments of Mussolini's regime attracted Italian Americans to whom Italy was an important psychological support in the often hostile American environment. Italy's entry into World War II on the Axis side—the famous "stab in the back"—caused an abrupt change in Italian American opinion, so that by the time Italy declared war on the United States in the wake of Pearl Harbor, the vast majority of Italian Americans were firmly in the anti-Fascist camp. Includes as an appendix a memorandum of 5 July 1940 on Italian American public opinion by A. Colonna of the Italian Embassy in Washington. 27 notes, appendix.
J. C. Billigmeier

155. Carano, Paul. LIBERATION DAY, PRELUDE TO FREEDOM. *Guam Recorder 1973 3(3): 3-9.* Discusses World War II on Guam, February-August 1944, from Japanese control to liberation by US forces which turned Guam into an outpost of democracy in three months.

156. Careless, J. M. S. SUBMARINES, PRINCES AND HOLLYWOOD COMMANDOS, OR AT SEA IN B.C. *BC Studies [Canada] 1980 (45): 3-16.* Recounts "certain lighter aspects" of the naval history of British Columbia. In World War I, as the German navy began to pose a threat in the Pacific, the provincial premier purchased two submarines built in Seattle, Washington, to assuage public anxiety over the otherwise defenseless west coast. In World War II, the *Prince Robert, Prince David,* and *Prince Henry,* armed merchant cruisers of the Royal Canadian Navy, afforded similar protection against the Japanese. The *Prince David* appeared in a Hollywood production, *The Commandos Strike at Dawn,* filmed off Vancouver Island in 1942. 29 notes. D. L. Smith

157. Carlisle, Rodney. THE FOREIGN POLICY VIEWS OF AN ISOLATIONIST PRESS LORD: W. R. HEARST & THE INTERNATIONAL CRISIS, 1936-41. *J. of Contemporary Hist. [Great Britain] 1974 9(3): 217-227.* William Randolph Hearst's press represented 12-14 percent of the total readership of daily newspapers in the United States during the mid-1930's. His isolation-

ist opinion had the largest, single editorial influence of the time. Hearst believed the United States should establish a deterrent armed force, not threaten Germany, nor make moves on the European continent in support of the Versailles Treaty or the League of Nations, give no encouragement to Britain or France, and should watch Japan and the Soviet Union very carefully. He was at once a militant nationalist, anti-communist, and suspicious of the British, French, Japanese, and Russians. Primary sources; 24 notes. — M. P. Trauth

158. Carter, Carolle J. IRELAND: AMERICA'S NEUTRAL ALLY, 1939-1941. *Éire-Ireland 1977 12(2): 5-14.* During World War II, Ireland, although technically neutral, favored the United States. Americans, however, accused the Irish during and after the war of harboring German spies, refueling submarines, and providing information about US troops. Ireland did not contradict these claims, because the government's support rested on its anti-British stance, even though secretly the government was actively cooperating with the British. Based on German Foreign Office records received by the US Department of State and on secondary sources; 23 notes. — S

159. Caruso, Samuel T. AFTER PEARL HARBOR: ARIZONA'S RESPONSE TO THE GILA RIVER RELOCATION CENTER. *J. of Arizona Hist. 1973 14(4): 335-346.* Sixteen thousand Japanese Americans were imprisoned 1942-45 at Sacaton, a barbed-wire city better known as the Gila River Relocation Center, in south central Arizona. Whites reacted to them as they had to their Apache predecessors—open hostility drowning out sympathetic understanding and concern. Whatever the racial slurs, the restrictive legislation, and other degradations they suffered, the Japanese produced millions of tons of vegetables and performed much labor on state roads. 2 illus., 46 notes. — D. L. Smith

160. Cary, Otis. THE SPARING OF KYOTO: MR. STIMSON'S "PET CITY." *Japan Q. [Japan] 1975 22(4): 337-347.* There have been a number of stories told about why the city of Kyoto was not heavily bombed by the US air forces during World War II or why the city was spared from nuclear attack even though its name had appeared high on the list of target cities prepared by various US air commanders. One story credits Florence Denton, a long-time teacher at Dōshisha Women's College, as the person responsible for having Kyoto removed from the target lists. Another credits Langdon Warner, from Harvard's Fogg Museum. A third gives credit to Professor Edwin O. Reischauer, also of Harvard University. It was really Henry L. Stimson, US Secretary of War in 1945, who caused Kyoto to be removed from the US target lists, and he did so with President Truman's knowledge and approval. 20 notes. — A. N. Garland

161. Cawthon, Charles. PURSUIT: NORMANDY, 1944: AN INFANTRYMAN REMEMBERS HOW IT WAS. *Am. Heritage 1978 29(2): 80-91.* A personal recollection of Normandy by a battalion major and executive officer. Joining the battle on 28 July, his account covers events through 9 August 1944. 10 illus. — J. F. Paul

162. Cawthon, Charles R. JULY, 1944: ST. LÔ. *Am. Heritage 1974 25(4): 4-11, 82-88.* Discusses World War II battle in the city of St. Lô, France, during the Normandy invasion. — S

163. Cawthon, John Ardis. A SCHOOL TEACHER GETS DRAFTED. *North Louisiana Hist. Assoc. J. 1974 5(4): 130-134.* On March 1942 the author was inducted into the US Army and sent to Camp Beauregard, Louisiana. Recalls events of his first days in the Army. Photo, 12 notes. A. N. Garland

164. Chan, K. C. THE ABROGATION OF BRITISH EXTRATERRITORIALITY IN CHINA 1942-43: A STUDY OF ANGLO-AMERICAN-CHINESE RELATIONS. *Modern Asian Studies [Great Britain] 1977 11(2): 257-291.* In 1929 the Nationalist government announced its intention of terminating extraterritoriality in China. Sino-British negotiations on the subject ended with the Japanese invasion in 1937, but recommenced in 1942 on the joint initiative of Britain and America, now allies of the Chinese. The United States succeeded in protecting its immigration policies. Britain, however, failed to secure guarantees for the freedom of British commerce in China. The treaty ending extraterritoriality was signed on 11 January 1943. Based on British archival materials released in 1972; 136 notes. L. W. Van Wyk

165. Chandler, David. THE BRIDGE AT REMAGEN, MARCH 7TH, 1945. *Hist. Today [Great Britain] 1979 29(3): 194-197.* Recounts the American capture of the bridge across the Rhine River at Remagen, Germany, during World War II.

166. Chandler, Harriette L. ANOTHER VIEW OF OPERATION CROSSWORD: A REVISION OF KOLKO. *Military Affairs 1978 42(2): 68-74.* Operation Crossword was the preliminary effort to secure a surrender on the northern Italian front in the spring of 1945. The operation fits into the Cold War struggle because of the Anglo-American decision to deny Soviet participation in the negotiations. This prompted historian Gabriel Kolko to suggest that the move was politically motivated. However, recently declassified material confirms that the decision was based solely on military considerations related to the need to save lives. 52 notes. A. M. Osur

167. Chandler, Harriette L. THE TRANSITION TO COLD WARRIOR: THE EVOLUTION OF W. AVERELL HARRIMAN'S ASSESSMENT OF THE U.S.S.R.'S POLISH POLICY, OCTOBER 1943-WARSAW UPRISING. *East European Q. 1976 10(2): 229-245.* Although W. Averell Harriman helped develop the philosophical foundations of the Containment Policy he approached his job as Ambassador to the USSR with considerable understanding and acceptance of the goals of Soviet foreign policy. His position was generally conciliatory toward the Soviet Union until her stern refusal to aid the beleaguered Poles in the Warsaw Uprising convinced him that the "Soviet will could be bent, if at all, only by hard bargaining, a readiness to apply pressure by withholding favors, and a willingness to do without Soviet assistance in some other areas." Based on recently declassified documents; 40 notes. C. R. Lovin

168. Child, John. LATIN AMERICA: MILITARY-STRATEGIC CONCEPTS. *Air U. Rev. 1976 27(6): 27-42.* Identifies and analyzes eight US military-strategic approaches to Latin America between 1850 and 1976. In chronological order, the approaches are: the American Lake policy (1850-1933), benign neglect (1933-39), quarter-sphere defense (1939-42), hemisphere defense (1939-present), special bilateral relationships between the United States and Mex-

169. Christian, Calvin L. and Showalter, Dennis E. DOCTORAL DISSERTATIONS IN MILITARY AFFAIRS, SUPPLEMENT VII. *Military Affairs 1979 43(1): 35-41.* Compilation of military affairs dissertations as a supplement to *Doctoral Dissertations in Military Affairs: A Bibliography* (1972). The dissertations are listed by subject: Structures in World Military History, Military Affairs of the United States, and Studies of War and the Military.
A. M. Osur

170. Christie Wasberg, Gunnar. DEN GLEMTE FLÅTE: BRITENE I STILLEHAVSOMRÅDET 1941-1945 [The forgotten fleet: the British in the Pacific area, 1941-45]. *Norsk Militaert Tidsskrift [Norway] 1972 142(6): 249-252.* Reviews John Winton's *The Forgotten Fleet* (London: Michael Joseph, 1969), which considers Great Britain's involvement in the Pacific after the Japanese conquest of Singapore on 15 February 1942, and examines the achievements of both the Americans and the English in this area, 1941-45.

171. Christman, Calvin L. and Showalter, Dennis E. DOCTORAL DISSERTATIONS IN MILITARY AFFAIRS: SUPPLEMENT VIII. *Military Affairs 1980 44(1): 35-41.* Compilation of military affairs dissertations as a supplement to *Doctoral Dissertations in Military Affairs: A Bibliography* (1972), classified by subject.
A. M. Osur

172. Christman, Calvin L. DONALD NELSON AND THE ARMY: PERSONALITY AS A FACTOR IN CIVIL-MILITARY RELATIONS DURING WORLD WAR II. *Military Affairs 1973 37(3): 81-83.* The struggle between the War Production Board and the armed services over the division of national production during World War II involved many factors. Often overlooked was the personality clash between Donald M. Nelson (Chairman of the WPB) and various key Army officers, notably General Brehon Somervell. Nelson's tendency toward indecisiveness brought him into sharp conflict with the driving and quick-minded Somervell. Their struggle became the focus of the civilian-military struggle for direction of the wartime economy. Based upon interviews and WPB records; 29 notes.
K. J. Bauer

173. Cigliana, Carlo. LA FINE DELLA GUERRA IN ESTREMO ORIENTE, 1945 [The end of the war in the Far East, 1945]. *Riv. Militare [Italy] 1972 28(1): 46-59.* Discusses military strategy employed in the Far East, 1944-45, which ended the war against Japan.

174. Clagett, John. ADMIRAL H. KENT HEWITT, U.S. NAVY. PART I—PREPARING FOR HIGH COMMAND. *Naval War Coll. R. 1975 28(1): 72-86.* Although his impressive list of accomplishments ranks Adm. H. Kent Hewitt among the most successful of World War II naval commanders, he also remains one of the least well known. Here, Hewitt's early

exploits are recounted—exploits that range from a role in the Great White Fleet's round-the-world cruise, the almost Kiplingesque adventures in revolutionary Cuba, to the command of the cruiser *Indianapolis*—all of which molded him into the man who would successfully command amphibious forces greater than those found at the Normandy landing, deployed over greater distance.

PART II—HIGH COMMAND. *Naval War Coll. R. 1975 28(2): 60-86.* In December 1939, H. Kent Hewitt reached a milestone for which he had prepared most of his adult life, selection for promotion to the rank of rear admiral. His role in the round-the-world cruise of the Great White Fleet, his adventures in revolutionary Cuba, his much enjoyed days in command of the *Indianapolis* were all behind him. Ahead lay the challenges of the greatest naval war in history. This, the second of a two-part series, reviews Hewitt's final preparations for his role in the conflict and describes his unqualified success in one of the first major counteroffensives made by the Allies in World War II—the amphibious attack on French Morocco. J

175. Clendenin, John. "CRAZY" YEARS AS A GLIDER PILOT. *Aerospace Hist. 1976 23(3): 121-123.* Describes the flying of gliders during World War II, based on an interview with Major Jack Riddle, USAF (retired). 5 photos.
C. W. Ohrvall

176. Clifford, John G. GRENVILLE CLARK AND THE ORIGINS OF SELECTIVE SERVICE. *R. of Pol. 1973 35(1): 17-40.* The Selective Service originated in 1940-41 out of proposals from Grenville Clark and the Plattsburg Movement, a group of civic-minded New Yorkers who originally met during World War I. S

177. Clifford, John Garry. THE ODYSSEY OF "CITY OF FLINT." *Am. Neptune 1972 32(2): 100-116.* Describes the diplomatic and political ramifications of the German capture of a U.S. merchant ship, the *City of Flint,* in 1939. The United States was a neutral, but the ship's cargo was defined as contraband under German national law. A German party commandeered the ship and sailed it to Murmansk, Soviet Union. International law required the release of the ship, but the Soviet Union, basking in the security of its recent nonaggression pact with Germany, sought means by which the prize could be sent to Germany. The pretext was found and the ship set sail before American diplomatic circles were notified. The resulting furor helped dispel isolationist sentiment in the United States, but exerted only minor influence on President Franklin Delano Roosevelt's efforts to increase aid to Great Britain. Based on secondary sources; 2 photos, 84 notes.
V. L. Human

178. Cline, Ray S. US FOREIGN INTELLIGENCE, 1939-41. *Foreign Service J. 1976 53(11): 17-20.* Describes steps in the formation of US intelligence units such as the Foreign Broadcast Information Service (1941), which were indispensable to the Foreign Service, but only experimental at the outbreak of World War II.

179. Clive, Alan. THE MICHIGAN FARMER IN WORLD WAR II. *Michigan Hist. 1976 60(4): 291-314.* Michigan farmers' contribution to the World War II effort, obscured by the preeminent position of the automobile

industry, has been largely ignored and forgotten. Although total land under production and acres harvested increased only modestly during the war, agricultural production during 1942 broke all records; and it remained substantial thereafter. The war's impact seemed to augur well for the future of the family farm in Michigan, but proved, in the end, to be nothing more than a momentary postponement of agriculture's gradual decline. Primary sources; 10 photos, 99 notes. D. W. Johnson

180. Clive, Alan. WOMEN WORKERS IN WORLD WAR II: MICHIGAN AS A TEST CASE. *Labor Hist. 1979 20(1): 44-72.* Examines women and World War II in Michigan to test national-level generalizations, tracing changes in the work force, attitudes of industry, labor organizations, and government, and the experience of women. Details resistance to working mothers and provision for day-care for children, which largely failed. The war created no revolution in attitudes, just a series of expedient measures as the traditional concept of womanhood was reaffirmed. Census data, state and federal documents, and newspapers; 61 notes. L. L. Athey

181. Clodfelter, Mark A. CULMINATION DRESDEN: 1945. *Aerospace Hist. 1979 26(3): 134-147.* Examines the controversy over the military and moral implications of the bombing of Dresden by the Royal Air Force, 13-14 February 1945, and the US 8th Air Force, 14 February. Dresden was not a singular sort of terror raid but a logical culmination of the doctrine of total war. Discusses strategic bombing from World War I through World War II. Based on official documents in the Air Force Archives and the National Archives; 9 photos, 85 notes. C. W. Ohrvall

182. Coffman, Edward M. and Herrly, P. F. THE AMERICAN REGULAR ARMY OFFICER CORPS BETWEEN THE WORLD WARS. *Armed Forces and Soc. 1977 4(1): 55-73.* Statistical analysis of the Official Army Register 1919-41 reveals that American Army officers were usually middle-aged (nearly 40), veterans of World War I, educated (West Point or civilian college), and born either in the South or the Midwest. Within the officer corps, southerners predominated in the higher ranks, especially the combat arms. Prior to World War II the vagaries of peacetime influenced officer expectations. Officers who attended in-service schools were better prepared for leadership roles in World War II. Based on official records, congressional testimony, archival sources, and secondary literature; 10 tables, 27 notes. J. P. Harahan

183. Cohen, Michael J. AMERICAN INFLUENCE ON BRITISH POLICY IN THE MIDDLE EAST DURING WORLD WAR TWO: FIRST ATTEMPTS AT COORDINATING ALLIED POLICY ON PALESTINE. *Am. Jewish Hist. Q. 1977 67(1): 50-70.* US entry into Middle Eastern politics during World War II inevitably led to friction with Great Britain. The British feared a US challenge to their political, military, and economic hegemony. The United States suspected British imperialism would exploit American resources. The author examines problems blocking an Anglo-American consensus on the Palestine question, such as attitudes toward Zionism, immigration quotas, and the formation of a Jewish Army. Franklin D. Roosevelt's attempts to placate the British on these issues highlight the dilemma American policymakers faced. 63 notes. F. Rosenthal

184. Cohen, Susan. WORLD WAR II UGLY DUCKLING COMES HOME. *Hist. Preservation 1980 32(2): 18-23.* The *Jeremiah O'Brien,* one of the 60 Liberty Ships, emergency freighters mass-produced during World War II, survived the war. Never adapted for peacetime use, the old-fashioned steamer attracted the attention of Captain Thomas J. Patterson in 1962. Resolved to save it from the scrap yard and aided by the National Trust's Maritime Preservation Office, by 1977 Patterson had organized a group of preservation enthusiasts within the maritime industry. Grants from various sources now committed to the *Jeremiah O'Brien's* restoration will provide for its future upkeep, as well as a museum, the Liberty Ship Memorial. 8 photos. P. M. Cohen

185. Cole, David L. PERCEPTIONS OF WAR AND PARTICIPANTS IN WARFARE: A TEN-YEAR REPLICATION. *J. of Peace Res. [Norway] 1973 10(1-2): 115-118.* Ten years ago, college students were asked to ascribe adjectives to one or both sides of a military battle in US history. The "United States was perceived as the rational, intelligent, self-possessed participant in the battle, and the enemy perceived in terms of his brutality [and] irresponsibility...." In the recent repeat test, the preponderance of "ego" adjectives was markedly lower, especially in the case of Pearl Harbor and the Alamo. Between 1961 and 1971 perceptions of the US Cavalry at the Little Big Horn have changed dramatically. There is less willingness to stereotype than formerly. "War clearly carries little glory in the eyes of these students.... Some students are willing to see the enemies of the United States forces as heroes.... Negative images of the Mexicans at the Alamo have lessened, as have negative images of the Japanese at Pearl Harbor." 2 tables. E. P. Stickney

186. Conrad, Margaret. APPLE BLOSSOM TIME IN THE ANNAPOLIS VALLEY 1880-1957. *Acadiensis [Canada] 1980 9(2): 14-39.* By the 1880's, improvements in steamship service and lowered freight rates helped create a ready market for Nova Scotia apples in Great Britain. By 1914, the expanding apple industry had transformed agriculture in the Annapolis Valley. By the 1930's, Nova Scotia produced more than 40% of Canada's apples and was a major supplier to Britain. Shippers dominated much of the industry, however, and were more concerned about volume than quality. World War II closed the British market, and the Canadian government failed to find new markets afterwards, while allowing extensive imports from the United States. By the 1950's, apples represented less than 4% of Nova Scotia's agricultural output, and the largest landowners in the Valley included multinational processing corporations. 3 tables, 100 notes. D. F. Chard

187. Conway, John S. A GERMAN NATIONAL REICH CHURCH AND AMERICAN WAR PROPAGANDA. *Catholic Hist. Rev. 1976 62(3): 464-472.* In 1941 American sources obtained a secretly circulated pamphlet from Germany outlining a plan to abolish Christianity and substitute a National Reich Church complete with Nazi symbols, liturgies and ideology. Franklin D. Roosevelt used this for his propaganda campaign, designed to attack Nazi Germany and to denounce the persecution of the Churches. He assumed that this plan was an official Nazi proposal and used it to win over opponents, particularly American Roman Catholics. In fact, Gestapo reports showed that the proposal stemmed from a pro-Nazi fanatic. But, the anticlerical and anti-Christian aspects of the program closely resembled the Gestapo's own plans.

188. Conway, John S. MYRON C. TAYLOR'S MISSION TO THE VATICAN 1940-50. *Church Hist. 1975 44(1): 85-99.* The mission of Myron C. Taylor, personal representative of Roosevelt and Truman to Pope Pius XII remains an anomaly in US foreign relations. Since the United States maintained no formal mission to the Vatican, Taylor was the main link between the papacy and Washington in the trying days preceding World War II. By remaining aloof from the religious controversies concerning his mission, Taylor maintained cordial relations between Roosevelt and Pius XII in their mutual quest for peace. With the entry of the United States into the conflict, Taylor continued to deal with the Vatican on controversial subjects such as the overthrow of Mussolini and the American bombing of Rome. Present US-Vatican relations have been influenced by Taylor's tenure (1940-1950) as personal envoy. His mission is also significant because Congress later refused to establish a permanent mission to the Vatican. 54 notes. M. D. Dibert

189. Cook, Charles O., Jr. THE PACIFIC COMMAND DIVIDED: THE "MOST UNEXPLAINABLE" DECISION. *US Naval Inst. Pro. 1978 104(9): 55-61.* There has never been a satisfactory explanation as to why the command in the Pacific during World War II was not united under one commander. Two military theaters of operation were established —the Southwest Pacific headed by General Douglas MacArthur and the Pacific Ocean Areas commanded by Admiral Chester W. Nimitz. From the available evidence, it seems clear that President Franklin D. Roosevelt had lost faith in General MacArthur as a result of the latter's actions during the battle for the Philippines, 1941-42, and did not think that MacArthur could be trusted with the increased authority of an undivided Pacific command. The decision to divide the Pacific appears to have been the President's, and the Joint Chiefs of Staff because they knew how he felt, gave him the plan that was put into effect in March 1942. Primary and secondary sources; 5 photos, 14 notes. A. N. Garland

190. Cook, Charles O., Jr. THE STRANGE CASE OF RAINBOW 5. *US Naval Inst. Pro. 1978 104(8): 67-73.* Rainbow-5 was a joint Army-Navy plan that described the military strategy US forces would follow in the event the US entered World War II. Although the plan did not state it specifically, the US military leaders assumed that the Philippines could not be held. Rainbow-5 was the plan when the war broke out for the United States in December 1941. Its provisions governed US actions during the first few months of World War II. General Douglas MacArthur's call for a change in the direction of the war effort created some embarrassment—an action for which he should have been relieved —but there was really nothing the United States could do to save the islands. Unfortunately, several high-ranking military people had their reputations besmirched because no one in Washington would admit that the Philippines could not be saved, and because the Hawaiian debacle was used as an excuse to cover up what was intended to be all along. Primary and secondary sources; 14 notes, 6 photos. A. N. Garland

191. Cornelius, Wanda and Short, Thayne R. "WHEN TIGERS FLEW IN CHINA." *Am. Hist. Illus. 1979 14(1): 40-42.* Discusses shoulder patches designed for the American Volunteer Group and the 23rd Fighter Group depicting Flying Tigers, a popular image derived from their air defense in China against the invading Japanese, 1930's-45.

192. Corrigan, Robert A. LITERATURE AND POLITICS: THE CASE OF EZRA POUND RECONSIDERED. Hague, John A., ed. *American Character and Culture in a Changing World: Some Twentieth-Century Perspectives* (Westport, Conn.: Greenwood Pr., 1979): 81-98. Analyzes the educational, psychological, political, public, and personal travails and travels of Ezra Pound. Controversial even in 1909, when he first arrived in Europe, Pound's increasingly extreme economic and social theories and later adulation of Mussolini, and shrill anti-Semitism and anti-American war propaganda—which despite their blatant irrationality were considered persuasive by ethically and ideologically principled thinkers—raised questions about moral responsibility and guilt.In 1945 Pound was incarcerated for treason. Illustrious friends then and subsequently ignored the law, supporting and honoring the mentally ill poet. Based on unpublished correspondence, Pound's friends' and associates' recollections, newspapers, and secondary sources; 65 notes. S

193. Couture, Paul M. THE VICHY-FREE FRENCH PROPAGANDA WAR IN QUEBEC, 1940 TO 1942. *Hist. Papers [Canada] 1978: 200-216.* The legality of the government established at Vichy by Marshall Petain in June 1940 was contested by a rival group under General de Gaulle with headquarters in England. The struggle of these two factions had strong repercussions in Canada. The discussions were ideological, social, and diplomatic. The people of Quebec took sides, Petain having a stronger following with emphasis on restoration of the Third Republic and of clericalism. The propaganda programs from France are given prominence. "The propaganda from the pro-de Gaulle people became associated with the 'total war' campaign. . . . The Vichy propaganda and Petain sympathisers in Quebec became closely identified with the anti-conscription efforts." In 1942 the Allied invasion of North Africa, Canada's termination of diplomatic relations with France, and the German occupation of Vichy's territory resolved the most contentious issues and were thus fortunate for Canada. 81 notes.   E. P. Stickney

194. Creighton, Alice S. THE EDWARD J. STREICHEN COLLECTION, U.S. NAVAL ACADEMY, ANNAPOLIS, MARYLAND. *Aerospace Hist. 1977 24(1): 27-29.* Discusses the photographic collection at the US Naval Academy, named for Edward J. Streichen, who was in charge of all Naval combat photography during World War II. The collection is mainly of naval combat photographs, but includes various aspects of the American scene as recorded by many famous photographers. 3 photos.   C. W. Ohrvall

195. Cripps, Thomas and Culbert, David. *THE NEGRO SOLDIER* (1944): FILM PROPAGANDA IN BLACK AND WHITE. *Am. Q. 1979 31(5): 616-640.* Discusses the symbiotic relationship among the army, blacks, social scientists, and the Hollywood film community that made the World War II army orientation film *The Negro Soldier* in 1944. Frank Capra chose Stuart Heisler to direct it. The result was a 43-minute documentary of high technical quality that portrayed blacks with middle class values and stressed black history. Both black and white troops were enthusiastic, as were most civilian audiences. The impact of *The Negro Soldier* with its well-executed theme of racial integration extended into three areas: promotion, in that black pressure groups learned that film could be a tool for social change; production of "message films"; and the demise of "race movies." 6 photos, 74 notes. S

196. Critchlow, Donald T. COMMUNIST UNIONS AND RACISM. *Labor Hist. 1976 17(2): 230-244.* Studies the responses of the United Electrical Radio and Machine Workers and the National Maritime Union to the "Black Question" during World War II. The U.E. ignored Negroes while the N.M.U. prided itself on its black members. This ambiguity of policy casts doubt on the assumption that "Communist-dominated" unions were essentially identical in interests. Based on proceedings of the U.E. and the N.M.U.; 38 notes.
L. L. Athey

197. Crouter, Natalie. FORBIDDEN DIARY. *Am. Heritage 1979 30(3): 78-95.* Natalie Crouter, husband Jerry, and their two children, ages 12 and 10, were captured in the Philippines by the Japanese shortly after Pearl Harbor. Natalie's diary, which had to be kept hidden from her captors, survived to recount some of the family's experiences during more than three years of internment. Excerpted from *The Internment of Natalie Crouter,* forthcoming. 13 illus.
J. F. Paul

198. Crumb, Charles V. YOU CAN'T LEAD IF YOU DON'T KNOW HOW TO FOLLOW. *Marine Corps Gazette 1979 63(8): 26-36.* The author, a retired Marine 1st Lieutenant, recounts principles of leadership displayed by 11 Marines during his Marine career, 1936-67, which included 20 years' active service.

199. Culbert, David. EDUCATION UNIT IN WORLD WAR II: AN INTERVIEW WITH ERIK BARNOUW. *J. Popular Culture 1978 12(2): 275-284.* Erik Barnouw, head of programming for the Armed Forces Radio Service, relates his experiences in originating educational broadcasting during World War II; 1942-45.

200. Culbert, David H. "THIS IS LONDON": EDWARD R. MURROW, RADIO NEWS AND AMERICAN AID TO BRITAIN. *J. of Popular Culture 1976 10(1): 28-37.* Suggests that Murrow's personal commitment and mastery of the arts of effective radio news broadcasting helped pre-World War II America identify with the British war effort and helped pave the road toward America's inevitable involvement. 45 notes.
D. G. Nielson

201. Culver, John A. A TIME FOR VICTORIES. *US Naval Inst. Pro. 1977 103(2): 50-57.* Victory ships significantly contributed to the US effort in World War II, and many of them gave outstanding service after the war. Some of the 414 cargo and 117 transport type ships built during 1944-46 are still operating with either the Military Sealift Command or with private companies. About 130 of them were taken out of the National Defense Reserve Fleet (NDRF) to support the Vietnam War effort. These old ships can be replaced by building 200 breakbulk Victory ships to rescue the Merchant Marine from its present sadly depleted state. The Victory has a good simple design, is a good ship, and could save us again. 11 photos.
A. N. Garland

202. Cuneo, Carl J. STATE, CLASS, AND RESERVE LABOUR: THE CASE OF THE 1941 CANADIAN UNEMPLOYMENT INSURANCE ACT. *Can. Rev. of Sociol. and Anthrop. [Canada] 1979 16(2): 147-170.* Uses the Canadian Unemployment Insurance Act (1941) as a case study comparing the validity of the Marxist instrumental and structural theories of the capitalist state.

Examines the interests of capital accumulation, social control of labor, and labor's wage subsistence on this legislation. Shows that the federal state introduced unemployment insurance to control unrest among the unemployed and to assist its own accumulation of capital in the context of World War II. The capitalist class consistently opposed state unemployment insurance during 1920-41, although its opposition weakened somewhat during the Depression of the 1930's. Labor organizations have consistently supported unemployment insurance since 1919. The radicalism of some of their proposals reached a high point during the Depression. Concludes that because the federal state introduced unemployment insurance largely over the objections of Canadian business, Marxist structural theory, in which the state displays a relative autonomy from business and thereby accommodates some working-class demands, is the most valid theory for this case. J/S

203. Dahlie, Jorgan. THE JAPANESE CHALLENGE TO PUBLIC SCHOOLS IN SOCIETY IN BRITISH COLUMBIA. *J. of Ethnic Studies 1974 2(1): 10-23.* Reviews the history of the Japanese communities of British Columbia from 1900 until sweeping evacuation orders in 1942 shipped thousands into camps in the province's interior. Ever since the beginning of the century prejudice and discrimination were overt and thinly disguised, based on "economic, political, and social rationalizations." The constant theme was that of non-assimilability, and by the interwar years the "Oriental Menace" was a threat to a white British Columbia. The maintenance of separate Japanese-language schools and Buddhist religious centers added to the discriminatory feeling, and by the 1940's their dual nationality automatically meant fifth column activities. Paradoxically most of the Issei and Nisei coped extremely well with the restrictions and persecutions, both official and unofficial, which they experienced. The only bright spot was the work of various Christian missionary groups among the Japanese children and in the relocation camps. Since World War II conditions for minorities have improved markedly in British Columbia with the establishment of a policy of multi-culturalism. Based on contemporary sources; 58 notes.
G. J. Bobango

204. Dainelli, Luca. ROBERT MURPHY [Robert Murphy (1894-1978)]. *Riv. di Studi Pol. Int. [Italy] 1978 45(1): 118-123.* A biographical tribute to Robert Murphy focusing on his role as an American diplomat in Europe during World War II.

205. Dallek, Robert. LIMITED INFLUENCE: AMERICAN OPINION LEADERS AND EAST ASIA. *Rev. in Am. Hist. 1979 7(3): 401-405.* Review article on Warren I. Cohen's *The Chinese Connection: Roger S. Greene, Thomas W. Lamont, George E. Sokolosky, and American-East Asian Relations* (New York: Columbia U. Pr., 1978) emphasizes the import of international affairs and public opinion in forming American foreign policy toward China and Japan, 1900's-40's, and the relative lack of influence among apparent opinion leaders Greene, Lamont, and Sokolosky.

206. Daniels, Roger. AMERICAN HISTORIANS AND EAST ASIAN IMMIGRANTS. *Pacific Hist. R. 1974 43(4): 449-472.* After a summary description and tabulation of five periods of Asian immigration during 1849-1974, concentrates on an analysis of the historiography and attitudes of American

historians. Divides the study by national origins, discussing writings about the Chinese and Japanese, with concentration on the Japanese relocation camps of World War II. Little has been published about Filipinos, East Indians, Koreans, and other Asian ethnic groups. There has been some acceleration in Asian American studies as a result of the heightened emphasis on minority rights and the rise of a number of Asian American study centers. 73 notes. R. V. Ritter

207. Danilov, A. I. and Sharifzhanov, I. I. ISTORIIA SSSR NA STRANITSAKH SHKOL'NYKH UCHEBNIKOV CSHA [The history of the USSR in the pages of US school textbooks]. *Prepodavanie Istorii v Shkole [USSR] 1979 (5): 71-78.* Sees bias, distortions, omissions, and overall hostility to the USSR in US school textbooks, especially in coverage of the Civil War, collectivization, and the Nazi invasion.

208. Danovitch, Sylvia E. THE PAST RECAPTURED? THE PHOTOGRAPHIC RECORD OF THE INTERNMENT OF JAPANESE AMERICANS. *Prologue 1980 12(2): 91-103.* Discusses the value of photographs as historical documents while focusing on an analysis of the 12,500 photographs in the National Archives that the War Relocation Authority made in connection with the forced evacuation and internment of Japanese Americans after the bombing of Pearl Harbor. This study concentrates on preevacuation photographs, evacuation photographs, Manzanar and Tule Lake Camps photographs, and relocation or resettlement photographs. The purpose of the photographing of the War Relocation Authority Program set forth in Administrative Instruction no. 74 dated 2 January 1943 was to document the program as fully as possible. Based on National Archives photographs of the War Relocation Authority; 41 notes.
M. A. Kascus

209. Daugherty, Fred A. and Woods, Pendleton. OKLAHOMA'S MILITARY TRADITION. *Chronicles of Oklahoma 1979-80 57(4): 427-445.* Surveys Oklahoma's military contributions since 1890, when the Oklahoma Territorial Militia was created. The Oklahoma National Guard served in the Spanish American War and on Mexican border duty in 1916, and participated in suppression of the Crazy Snake Rebellion of 1909 and of various domestic problems of the 1920's. During World War I, the Oklahoma Guard joined units from Texas to form the 36th Infantry Division and fought with distinction in France. During World War II, Oklahomans joined with troops from neighboring states to form the 45th Infantry Division and won praise for meritorious service in Sicily, Italy, France, and Germany. The 45th Infantry Division fought again in the Korean War and was disbanded in 1968. 12 photos. M. L. Tate

210. Davis, Frank. OPERATION OLYMPIC: THE INVASION OF JAPAN: NOVEMBER 1, 1945. *Strategy & Tactics 1974 (45): 4-20.*

211. Davis, Gerald H. PRISONERS OF WAR IN TWENTIETH-CENTURY WAR ECONOMIES. *J. of Contemporary Hist. [Great Britain] 1977 12(4): 623-634.* The experience of both sides during World War I and World War II demonstrated little economic advantage in keeping war prisoners, who were costly to maintain and inefficient, poorly-motivated workers ill-suited to their tasks. Erich von Ludendorff provided a rare exception when, after World War I, he extolled the great value of Russian POW's to the German economy. Based

on US National Archives reports on POW camp inspection in Russia, 1914-17, as well as published primary and secondary sources; 51 notes. M. P. Trauth

212. Davis, W. L. and Sweet, John J. T., ed. THE BRIDGES ON THE RIVER KWAI. *Aerospace Hist. 1973 20(1): 7-9.* W. L. Davis, a British prisoner of war, was forced to work on railway bridges over the Kwae Mae Khlong River and witnessed the destruction of these bridges by US B-24 Liberator bombers.

213. De Angelis, Mark J. AO-24 U.S.S. *PLATTE. Warship Internat. 1973 10(3): 299-310.*

214. DeBenedetti, Charles. THE AMERICAN PEACE MOVEMENT AND THE NATIONAL SECURITY STATE, 1941-1971. *World Affairs 1978 141(2): 118-129.* Describes the movement in the United States, after the attack on Pearl Harbor, toward global military preparedness, and the reactions of American pacifists, both liberal and radical.

215. Debus, Allen G. A TRIBUTE TO MORRIS FISHBEIN. *Bull. of the Hist. of Medicine 1977 51(1): 153-154.* Morris Fishbein was not only a historian, he was history. "It will be impossible in future years to write the history of 20th century medicine without referring to him as a central figure." His *Doctors at War* remains the basic study of the medical profession during World War II, and his massive history of the American Medical Association is a monument to his industry.
M. Kaufman

216. de la Sierra Fernández, Luis. PEARL HARBOR [Pearl Harbor]. *Rev. General de Marina [Spain] 1977 192(6): 645-651; 193 (8-9): 169-184; 193(12): 629-635; 1978 194(2): 137-150; 194(4): 403-424.* Part I. For thousands of years before the Spanish discovery of the Pacific, Micronesian, Melanesian, and especially Polynesian sailors had conquered that vast ocean. These sailors had learned accurate celestial navigation and were used to sailing thousands of miles. Their heroic exploits form a fitting perspective on the equally heroic naval struggle between the United States and Japan which began with the attack on Pearl Harbor in 1941. Part II. The rise of Japan as a Pacific Asian power, the clash of US and Japanese interests in China and the Pacific, and racial antagonism led to each considering the other as a potential enemy by 1909. The acquisition of mandated islands after World War I greatly expanded Japan's power into the Pacific, and thus readied the area for a future conflict. Japan built a modern fleet up to treaty limits. A US building program led Japan to withdraw from naval limitation in 1936 and begin construction of the *Yamato* super-battleships. The United States then entered a naval race with Japan. Part III. Discusses Roosevelt's concentration of the US fleet at Pearl Harbor in 1940, impositions of serious trade restrictions on Japan, and increased pressure on Japan to abandon imperial ambitions in Asia. The United States deliberately intensified tensions and rejected Japanese offers of compromise, yet never foresaw a Japanese attack on Pearl Harbor. Part IV. Admiral Isoroku Yamamoto's war Plan Z entailed use of carrier aircraft to destroy the US Pacific Fleet, after which the United States would sue for a compromise peace. The naval staff accepted the plan in October 1941. Yamamoto always hoped that a diplomatic breakthrough might allow a cancellation, but it never came. The overconfident US Admiral Husband E. Kimmel took

inadequate precautions, but unfortunately for Japan, the US aircraft carriers were at sea. The Japanese naval staff decided that the moored battleships were sufficient targets. Part V. Despite US detection of Japanese aircraft and submarines, the surprise on 7 December 1941 was complete. The US vessels were either sunk or severely damaged, and only the US carriers remained at large. Fearing counter attack, Admiral Nagumo turned for home. Japan's tactical and strategic victory allowed Japanese consolidation of its position in China and the Pacific. The Japanese selection of the US battleships as the primary targets and the decision to withdraw were correct. Washington was responsible for the unpreparedness at Pearl Harbor. 8 notes. W. C. Frank

217. Delmas, Claude. LES SECRETS DES ARCHIVES AMÉRICAINES [Secrets of the American archives]. *Nouvelle Rev. des Deux Mondes [France] 1980 (1): 98-103.* A review of Nerin E. Gun's *Pétain-Laval-De Gaulle* (Paris, Editions Albin Michel, 1979), a book which, although dealing with an already well-known subject, reveals new and valuable information based on American archival documents, previously secret, covering 1939-45.

218. De Luna, Giovanni. LA RICERCA DELLA DOCUMENTAZIONE SULLA RESISTENZA EUROPEA NELLE FONTI CHE SI TROVANO NEGLI STATI UNITI [Research on the documentation of the European resistance as found in American sources]. *La Seconda Guerra Mondiale nella Prospettiva Storica a Trent'Anni dall'Epilogo* (Como: Casa Editrice Pietro Cairoli, 1977): 441-446. The recent release of official government documents by the US National Archives have proved an innovative source for the study of the European resistance. These documents allow not only a closer look at particular decisions made at political and military levels but also provide insights into the decisionmaking process itself. Reviews the most important works to date concerning the European resistance. M. T. Wilson

219. DeNovo, John A. THE CULBERTSON ECONOMIC MISSION AND ANGLO-AMERICAN TENSIONS IN THE MIDDLE EAST, 1944-1945. *J. of Am. Hist. 1976 63(4): 913-936.* William S. Culbertson's special economic mission to the Middle East in 1944 to survey postwar business prospects illustrated a deep-rooted American emphasis on free enterprise as a stabilizing political force. Culbertson's prescription for expanded official American participation in the Middle East favored the economic primacy of the United States. The British, struggling to retain their international position, found Americans brash and insensitive to vital British interests. Culbertson's report documented Anglo-American differences arising during World War II. It integrated a hard-headed commercial self-interest with a messianic idealism and an urge to national power. Primary and secondary sources; 76 notes. W. R. Hively

220. Desai, Tripta. AMERICAN ROLE IN THE INDIAN FREEDOM MOVEMENT. *Indian Pol. Sci. Rev. [India] 1977 11(1): 1-32.* The American government chose not to give overt support to the Indian national movement up to 1945, lest the joint Anglo-American war effort be affected adversely. After the war the United States encouraged the British to end the political conflict in India but took no active part in the negotiations among the various groups.
J. C. English

221. DeSantis, Hugh. CONFLICTING IMAGES OF THE USSR: AMERICAN CAREER DIPLOMATS AND THE BALKANS, 1944-1946. *Pol. Sci. Q. 1979 94(3): 475-494.* US career diplomats serving in the Balkans underwent drastic changes in their attitudes toward the USSR. The period 1944-46 was a watershed during which American foreign service officers began to overcome earlier negative views of the USSR based on perceptions of the Russian Revolution, the Moscow purge trials of the 1930's, and the Nazi-Soviet Nonaggression Pact of 1939. The heroic Soviet war effort gained the admiration of American officials in 1944-45, but the brutalizing effects of Soviet behavior in the Balkans at the end of World War II once again engendered hostility against the Kremlin. 84 notes. S

222. de Vries, John A. THE GREAT AIR CORPS MUTINY. *Aerospace Historian 1975 22(2): 92-95.* Recounts an incident at Maxwell Field, Montgomery, Alabama, at Christmas-time, 1943. Maxwell Field was a pilot pre-flight school for the Army Air Corps during World War II. Potential pilots received academic instruction there before being sent to flying schools throughout the southeastern United States. By late 1943 the Air Corps realized that its need for aircrew members was beginning to diminish, which resulted in a slow-down of the training program. Rumors began to fly at Maxwell as the pre-flight program was extended and soon the cadets began to rebel, demanding furloughs. After a week of incidents headquarters issued the order for two-week furloughs so that cadets could be home for Christmas. Photo. C. W. Ohrvall

223. Dick, Everett N. THE ADVENTIST MEDICAL CADET CORPS AS SEEN BY ITS FOUNDER. *Adventist Heritage 1974 1(2): 18-27.* The Adventist Medical Cadet Corps was founded in 1934 by the author to train Adventist boys to serve in the Army medical department, if conscripted, in order to avoid the moral difficulties encountered with arms bearing and Sabbath observance in the service; covers World War II and Korean War service.

224. Dick, Everett N. THE MILITARY CHAPLAINCY AND SEVENTH-DAY ADVENTISTS: THE EVOLUTION OF AN ATTITUDE. *Adventist Heritage 1976 3(1): 33-45.* The Seventh-Day Adventist General Conference officers in 1944 attempted to guide Adventist ministers away from military chaplaincy, but by 1955 supplied financial aid and special training for that field.

225. Dickson, W. David. NAVAL TACTICS: AN INTRODUCTION. *Warship Int. 1976 13(3): 168-176.* Discusses naval tactics in terms of maneuvering, gunnery formation, torpedo use, and naval communications pertaining to the US, British, and Japanese navies, during World War II, 1943-45.

226. Diubaldo, Richard J. THE CANOL PROJECT IN CANADIAN-AMERICAN RELATIONS. *Can. Hist. Assoc. Hist. Papers [Canada] 1977: 178-195.* The Canol Project was a part of the Northwest Defense Projects conceived following Pearl Harbor. An examination of the motivations for and the principal steps in the implementation of the 577-mile oil pipeline from Norman Wells to Whitehorse reveals a case of US Army willfulness and bungling which became a cause for alarm as it threatened Canadian sovereignty in its own Northwest. Revelations from Senator Harry S. Truman's Special Committee Investigating the National Defense Program left the War Department defense-

less. Canada finally realized what was happening and took a firm stand thereby forming a safer basis for future defense coordination with the United States. 94 notes.
R. V. Ritter

227. Divine, Robert A. OLD WINE IN A NEW BOTTLE. *Rev. in Am. Hist. 1977 5(2): 286-291.* Review article prompted by Joseph P. Lash's *Roosevelt and Churchill, 1939-1941: The Partnership That Saved the West* (New York: W. W. Norton, 1976).

228. Dobbs, Charles M. AMERICAN MARINES IN NORTH CHINA, 1945-1946. *South Atlantic Q. 1977 76(3): 318-331.* To stall a communist takeover in north China in October 1945, 50,000 US soldiers of the Marine Amphibious Corps were sent in to accept the surrender of the 500,000 Japanese soldiers there. Quickly occupying ports, railroads, and the cities of Peking, Tsinan, and Tientsin, the marines settled into garrison duty. Both the Nationalists and the Communists soon began harrying the marines: the Communists by guerilla attacks, the Nationalists by demands for control of American-held areas. The Japanese troops were actually pressed into active service while they awaited repatriation, which was accomplished by mid-1946. Embarassed now by Soviet heckling, bewildered by the byzantine situation of the Chinese civil war, and confronted by the demands of US Senators Allen Ellender and Hugh Butler for their removal, the marines were slowly withdrawn by early 1947. 30 notes.
W. L. Olbrich

229. Dobney, Fredrick J. THE EVOLUTION OF RECONVERSION POLICY: WORLD WAR II AND SURPLUS WAR PROPERTY DISPOSAL. *Historian 1974 36(3): 498-519.* Discusses methods regarding the best way to dispose of government-owned surplus property at the close of World War II, and the procedures actually developed as implemented by the Surplus Property Act of 1944 as administered by Will Clayton, Surplus War Property Administrator, and later by a three-man board. There was a basic disagreement in philosophy between Clayton and the Senate in its desire to achieve social and economic objectives. The latter proved to be impossible to realize simultaneously with its rapid disposal policy. 88 notes.
R. V. Ritter

230. Doenecke, Justin D. HARRY ELMER BARNES. *Wisconsin Mag. of Hist. 1973 56(4): 311-323.* Revisionist Harry Elmer Barnes (d. 1968) belonged to the intellectual elite, and his articles, reviews, and books were topics of conversation in and out of academe, until his adamant opposition to U.S. involvement in World War II and to the Allied response to Germany in Europe made him an intellectual pariah and closed the doors of publishers and universities to him. As he began to support scholars who were developing revisionist themes on World War II he became increasingly popular with ultrarightists. Although they agreed with his criticisms of Churchill and Roosevelt, they did not support his sympathetic defense of Stalin and the USSR. In this stand, as in others, Barnes was outside the mainstream of the intellectual establishment. 4 photos, 38 notes.
N. C. Burckel

231. Doenecke, Justis D. THE STRANGE CAREER OF AMERICAN ISOLATIONISM, 1944-1954. *Peace and Change 1975 3(2/3): 79-83.* Describes the ups and downs of the isolationist movement, notably during World War II and the Cold War, from 1944-54.

232. Doenecke, Justus D. BEYOND POLEMICS: AN HISTORIOGRAPHICAL RE-APPRAISAL OF AMERICAN ENTRY INTO WORLD WAR II. *Hist. Teacher 1979 12(2): 217-251.* Revisionism is a continual process, particularly in this controversial subject area. The earliest works were by historians and writers such as Beard, Barnes, and Tansil who opposed Roosevelt's interventionism. Internationalist historians who followed defended the basic Roosevelt diplomacy. The key work in this school was by Langer and Gleason. Recently economic factors, particularly in regard to Japan, have received much attention, but the study of religious, ethnic, psychological and emotional factors have continued to be neglected. 156 notes.
L. C. Smith

233. Doenecke, Justus D. THE ISOLATIONIST AS COLLECTIVIST: LAWRENCE DENNIS AND THE COMING OF WORLD WAR II. *J. of Libertarian Studies 1979 3(2): 191-207.* Columnist Lawrence Dennis earned popular disdain and disfavor (and eventually a sedition trial), 1940-45, for his strongly collectivist attitudes and his unmitigated belief in Germany's ability to defeat Allied forces in World War II, but more modern critics applaud him for his apparent foresight in predicting the problems of a warfare/welfare state and in cutting through the conventional rhetoric of his time.

234. Doenecke, Justus D. THE ISOLATIONISTS AND A USABLE PAST. *Peace and Change 1978 5(1): 67-73.* Review article prompted by James T. Patterson's *Mr. Republican: A Biography of Robert A. Taft* (Boston: Houghton Mifflin, 1972), Wayne S. Cole's *Charles A. Lindbergh and the Battle Against American Intervention in World War II* (New York: Harcourt Brace Jovanovich, 1974), Ronald Radosh's *Prophets on the Right: Profiles of Conservative Criticism of American Globalism* (New York: Simon and Schuster, 1975), Michele Flynn Stenehjem's *An American First: John T. Flynn and the America First Committee* (New Rochelle, New York: Arlington House, 1976), and Joan Hoff Wilson's *Herbert Hoover: Forgotten Progressive* (Boston: Little, Brown, 1975).

235. Doenecke, Justus D. ISOLATIONISTS OF THE 1930'S AND 1940'S: AN HISTORIOGRAPHICAL ESSAY. *West Georgia Coll. Studies in the Social Sci. 1974 13: 5-39.*

236. Doenecke, Justus D. NON-INTERVENTION OF THE LEFT: THE KEEP AMERICA OUT OF THE WAR CONGRESS, 1938-41. *J. of Contemporary Hist. [Great Britain] 1977 12(2): 221-236.* After Norman Thomas visited Europe in 1937, he was ordered by the Socialist Party to form an antiwar coalition. Accordingly, the Keep America Out of War Congress was officially founded in New York on 6 March 1938, under the veteran pacifist reformer, Oswald Garrison Villard. The KAOWC was a makeshift coalition of left-wing pacifist groups. Its ideological tenets were also a potpourri: jobs at home rather than abroad, anti-Asian involvement, neutrality, food not guns, etc. With the proximity of war, the movement dwindled. It died after Pearl Harbor. Based on materials in the Papers of the Socialist Party, Duke University; 51 notes.
M. P. Trauth

237. Doenecke, Justus D. PROTEST OVER MALMÉDY: A CASE OF CLEMENCY? *Peace and Change 1976 4(2): 28-33.* Frederick J. Libby of the National Council for the Prevention of War campaigned for justice for the German soldiers responsible for the Malmédy massacre of 1944, maintaining that the United States should apply the same rules to the Axis powers it did to itself.

238. Doenecke, Justus D. VERNE MARSHALL'S LEADERSHIP OF THE NO FOREIGN WAR COMMITTEE, 1940. *Ann. of Iowa 1973 41(7): 1153-1172.* Cedar Rapids Gazette editor Verne Marshall played a major role in forming and leading the No Foreign War Committee directly prior to American involvement in World War II. S

239. Domínguez, Jorge I. A SKEPTICAL VIEW OF WORLD WAR II. *Worldview 1975 18(3): 56-59.* Speculates on the reasons for US entry into World War II, in a review article prompted by Bruce M. Russett's *No Clear and Present Danger: A Skeptical View of the U.S. Entry Into World War II* (New York: Harper & Row, 1972).

240. Dominique, Pierre. LA GRANDE ÉCLIPSE FRANCO-AMÉRICAINE [The great Franco-American mistake]. *Écrits de Paris [France] 1973 (321): 29-35.* At the beginning of World War II, America was persuaded that France had not been beaten but betrayed by Marshal Pétain and his followers.

241. Doolittle, James H. and Lay, Beirne, Jr. IMPACT: DAYLIGHT PRECISION BOMBING. *Am. Hist. Illus. 1980 14(10): 8-12, 42-47.* Discusses the advantages of daylight bombing over night bombing by the US Air Force during World War II in Europe and the Pacific based on the authors' experiences during 1941-44.

242. Dougherty, James J. LEND-LEASE AND THE OPENING OF FRENCH NORTH AND WEST AFRICA TO PRIVATE TRADE. *Cahiers d'Études Africaines [France] 1975 15(3): 481-500.* With French possessions in West and North Africa separated from France by World War II, new mechanisms for supplying consumer goods to those regions had to be developed. At first the American administration favored government-to-government assistance (Lend-Lease) rather than private trade, but toward the end of the war American private companies pressed the government for a resumption of private trade. This the French resisted until 1946, in the hope of reestablishing their own merchants' dominance. Based on materials in the US National Archives, the private papers of American war leaders, and on printed sources; 64 notes. B. S. Fetter

243. Douglas, W. and Brereton, Greenhous. L'HISTORIOGRAPHIE CANADIENNE ET LA SECONDE GUERRE MONDIALE [Canadian historiography and the Second World War]. *Rev. d'Hist. de la Deuxième Guerre Mondiale [France] 1976 26(104): 67-87.* Analyzes historical writing concerning Canada during World War II, referring to approximately 50 works. 28 notes.
G. H. Davis

244. Downey, Fairfax. THE LAST CHARGE. *By Valor and Arms 1976 2(4): 41-43.* Discusses the Army's use of the Philippine Scouts cavalry regiment to hold off Japanese forces in the battle of Luzon and enable General Douglas

MacArthur to withdraw his forces to Bataan, Philippines, during World War II.

245. Doyle, Michael K. THE U.S. NAVY AND WAR PLAN ORANGE, 1933-1940: MAKING NECESSITY A VIRTUE. *Naval War Coll. Rev. 1980 33(3): 49-63.* War Plan ORANGE assumed that America alone would face Japan in a Pacific war after Germany had been defeated, that there would be no threat in the Atlantic and Caribbean areas. As late as October 1940 it remained the only well developed plan—even after Europe was overrun and England was bracing for invasion. Little wonder that critics of that time and since have faulted the plan and the Navy's unmoving support of it. Another view can be taken, however; a wider view that considers naval officers' analysis of strategy and diplomatic questions regarding the pre-1941 Pacific. J

246. Dreifort, John E. INDOCHINA IN ALLIED WARTIME DIPLOMACY: THE FRENCH PERSPECTIVE. *Res. Studies 1980 48(1): 25-39.* From a French perspective, particularly that of Charles de Gaulle, discusses the delicate matters of foreign policy between France and the United States and Great Britain with respect to France's claims in Indochina during World War II.

247. Drier, John A. KENTON COUNTY, KENTUCKY: RE-EVALUATING THE ETHNIC ORIGINS OF ISOLATIONISM. *Filson Club Hist. Q. 1977 51(3): 262-275.* Kenton County, Kentucky, a suburban area south of Cincinnati, was not a stronghold of isolationist sentiment in 1940 despite the presence of a large German population. A strong attachment to the Democratic Party may have been a significant cause for the absence of isolationist feeling. Statistical data are presented. Based on Cincinnati newspapers and federal census reports; 8 tables, 41 notes. G. B. McKinney

248. Droker, Howard A. SEATTLE RACE RELATIONS DURING THE SECOND WORLD WAR. *Pacific Northwest Q. 1976 67(4): 163-174.* Seattle's relatively small black population doubled during World War II as thousands of people came for jobs in defense industries. Jim Crowism became more prevalent and racial tension increased. To combat the possibility of race riots, Mayor William Devin created the Civic Unity Committee in February 1944. This multiracial group, dominated by conservatives, avoided conflict as it worked to defuse potential problems. Its quiet, behind-the-scenes efforts achieved limited success for black employment opportunities, but it never solved the discriminatory housing practices. The committee's efforts in behalf of displaced Japanese Americans in 1945 insured its credibility as a broad-based race relations organization which could effectively accomplish its goals. Primary and secondary sources; 6 photos, 51 notes. M. L. Tate

249. Druks, Herbert. U.S. FOREIGN POLICY BEFORE WORLD WAR II. *East Europe 1972 21(10): 17-21.* In the 1930's the United States issued neutrality laws with the goal of insulating itself from world affairs. "Only after Germany took over the rest of Czechoslovakia did Franklin D. Roosevelt openly support efforts to revise the Neutrality Laws that aided only the aggressors.... Because of their inaction and mutual distrust, the World War I victors were greatly responsible for the success of the aggressors." US isolationism of the 1920's and 1930's encouraged aggression and helped bring on World War II.
E. P. Stickney

250. Dunaeva, N.   LEND-LIZ: FAKTY I VYMYSLY   [The Lend-Lease: facts and fiction]. *Voenno-Istoricheskii Zhurnal [USSR] 1977 (3): 102-106.* Accuses bourgeois historians of exaggerating the importance of Lend-Lease to the USSR during World War II, presenting figures to prove that Allied aid was in fact minimal; 1941-45.

251. Dunn, William R.   THE ACE.   *Air Force Mag. 1976 59(9): 76-82.* The author, the first American fighter ace of World War II, recounts his 27 August 1941 mission with the Royal Air Force.

252. Dunn, William R.   THE IMMORTAL SPITFIRE.   *Air Force Mag. 1975 58(4): 55-60.* The author, a pilot with the Royal Air Force's No. 71 Eagle Squadron, and the first American ace of World War II, describes his experiences flying a Spitfire in 1941.

253. Dunn, William R.   P-47: THE BEAUTIFUL BEAST.   *Air Force Mag. 1975 58(9): 91-98.* Discusses the role of the Republic P-47 Thunderbolt in the US Army Air Force in World War II.

254. Duroselle, Jean-Baptiste.   FRANCE-ÉTATS UNIS: DU MYTHE LA FAYETTE À L'INCOMPREHENSION MUTUELLE   [France-United States: from the Lafayette myth to mutual lack of understanding]. *Rev. des Travaux de l'Acad. des Sci. Morales et Pol. et Comptes Rendus de ses Séances [France] 1976 129(2): 529-551.* Explodes the myth of uniformly cordial Franco-American relations since the time of Lafayette. Though Frenchmen have shown more interest in America than Americans have shown in France, both peoples have allowed ignorance of each other to produce periods of hostility as well as periods of friendship. Mutual lack of understanding, typified by the Roosevelt-de Gaulle feud during World War II, stems from the small number of Americans of French origin, differences in religious and moral values, conflicting views of the state, and contrasting experiences with the availability of land.   J. R. Vignery

255. Eaker, Ira C.   THE FLYING FORTRESS AND THE LIBERATOR. *Aerospace Hist. 1979 26(2): 66-68.* The commanding general of the US Eighth Air Force in Europe during World War II discusses in general terms which aircraft was considered the best, the B-17 *Flying Fortress* or the B-24 *Liberator.* Both had their good points. Concludes that the combat crews considered the aircraft in which they trained and fought as the better of the two. 3 photos.
C. W. Ohrvall

256. Eaker, Ira C.   SOME MEMORIES OF WINSTON CHURCHILL. *Aerospace Hist. 1972 19(3): 120-124.* Ira C. Eaker met with Prime Minister Winston Churchill several times during and after World War II; discusses in particular, his successful efforts to persuade Churchill to continue to use the American Air Force for daylight bombing raids.

257. Eastman, James N., Jr.   LOCATION AND GROWTH OF TINKER AIR FORCE BASE AND OKLAHOMA CITY AIR MATERIEL AREA. *Chronicles of Oklahoma 1972 50(3): 326-346.*

258. Eaton, E. L. EUGENE BUTLER COATES, O. B. E.: SKIPPER UNUSUAL. *Nova Scotia Hist. Q. [Canada] 1979 9(3): 257-267.* Eugene Butler Coates (1891-1978) began his career at sea at the age of 15 and progressed from cabin boy to cook, able seaman, mate, and finally to Captain. He earned a certificate as Master in Sail in 1914 and another for passenger steamships in the coastal trade three years later; both from Yarmouth Navigation School. He won honors for his participation in World War II, and was employed by the Department of Transport of Canada (1950-1958) on various lightships.

H. M. Evans

259. Eckardt, Alice L. THE HOLOCAUST: CHRISTIAN AND JEWISH RESPONSES. *J. of the Am. Acad. of Religion 1974 42(3): 453-469.* Surveys, with some analysis and evaluation, the writings of leading Jewish and Christian scholars who have offered responses to the slaughter of six million Jews by Hitler. While most agree that no solution can be considered adequate, some explanation must be attempted. Stresses the nature of this theological problem for Jews and Christians. 68 notes.

E. R. Lester

260. Eckes, Alfred E., Jr. OPEN DOOR EXPANSIONISM RECONSIDERED: THE WORLD WAR II EXPERIENCE. *J. of Am. Hist. 1973 59(4): 909-924.* An analysis of U.S. economic policy during World War II throws doubt on the radical historians' contention that that policy was designed to expand U.S. exports and to further the Cold War. First, most business people and politicians did not believe that exports represented the best way to avoid depression, but rather stressed planning for domestic markets. Second, there was a genuine belief that liberalizing trade benefited all parties. Third, Henry Morgenthau, Jr. (1891-1967), and Harry Dexter White *welcomed* Soviet cooperation in postwar economic planning. Fourth, the alternatives to liberalized trade were inefficient mini-economics and nationalistic autarchy. Based largely on the Morgenthau diaries; 30 notes.

K. B. West

261. Edgar, John D. THE TEXAS PINBALL MACHINE. *Air Force Mag. 1976 59(8): 57-61.* Discusses combat training devices used by the US Army Air Forces during World War II.

262. Edgerton, Ronald K. GENERAL DOUGLAS MAC ARTHUR AND THE AMERICAN MILITARY IMPACT IN THE PHILIPPINES. *Philippine Studies [Philippines] 1977 25(4): 420-440.* Although the US government had postwar plans for the Philippines, US actions there in 1945-46 were actually shaped by Gen. Douglas MacArthur. His personal acquaintance with the island, his strong personality, and his decision to place military priorities before postwar developments were the significant factors in shaping Philippine policies. He was not consistent in such matters as handling collaborators; he commented on situations and made his feelings known on the basis of how such decisions would affect the war effort, not on whether or not certain Filipinos were indeed collaborators. Based primarily on US military and civilian correspondence, as well as government reports. 64 notes.

D. Chaput

263. Edwards, P. G. R. G. MENZIES'S APPEAL TO THE UNITED STATES, MAY-JUNE 1940. *Australian Outlook [Australia] 1974 28(1): 64-70.* Australian prime minister Robert Gordon Menzies's appeal to the United States

in May and June 1940 for material aid for the British war effort indicated the growing realization that Australian security depended more on the United States than on Great Britain. Based on Menzies's correspondence May-June 1940, now in the Commonwealth Archives Office; 27 notes. D. L. Robinson

264. Egan, Robert S. and Roberts, Stephen S. USS NEW ENGLAND AD-32. *Warship Int. 1977 14(3): 229-243.* Examines US Navy tenders and their design changes during 1937-44, focusing on the USS *New England,* a 1944 ship which incorporated all design changes ordered by the Navy for the AD 32 model.

265. Eggleston, Noel C. ROLE PLAYING: THE ATOMIC BOMB AND THE END OF WORLD WAR II. *Teaching Hist. A J. of Methods 1978 3(2): 52-58.* Describes in detail the development of an historical role playing exercise for classroom use revolving around the question, "Should the United States drop an atomic bomb on Japan?" Discusses setting in 1945, character participants, discussion questions, and the historical works used as well as the specific goals, results, and benefits of this exercise. Examines the value of role playing technique for history instructors. 8 notes.

266. Einhorn, Marion. GRUNDZÜGE UND ERGEBNISSE DER BRITISCHEN UND AMERIKANISCHEN SPANIENPOLITIK WÄHREND DES ZWEITEN WELTKRIEGES [The fundamentals and results of Anglo-American Spanish policy during World War II]. *Jahrbuch für Geschichte [East Germany] 1975 13: 243-291.* Though sympathetic to Nazi Germany and Fascist Italy, the Franco regime in Spain remained neutral during World War II. It did, however, send the Blue Division to fight for the Wehrmacht against the USSR. During 1939-43, the Western powers attempted to keep Spain out of the war by both friendly approaches and pressure, such as an oil embargo. In 1943-45, the American and British governments showed increasing reluctance to work actively for Francisco Franco's downfall. They feared that the resulting instability would threaten their nationals' investments in Spain, as well as undermine the Western position in the Mediterranean. 206 notes. J. C. Billigmeier

267. Ekebjär, Göran. PROBLEM RÖRANDE ATOMBOMBINSATSEN MOT JAPAN 1945 [The problem concerning the atomic bombing of Japan in 1945]. *Kungliga Krigsvetenskaps Akademiens Handlinger och Tidskrift [Sweden] 1965 169: 469-486.* Describes the events leading up to the atomic bombing of Hiroshima and Nagasaki in 1945. The bombs were dropped in the belief that they would prevent a longer war and thus save many lives. The Americans, however, did not consider alternative military strategies; and Japan, weakened by years of war and a shortage of raw materials, would have capitulated within five months at the most. Secondary sources; biblio. U. G. Jeyes/S

268. Elliott, Mark. THE UNITED STATES AND FORCED REPATRIATION OF SOVIET CITIZENS, 1944-47. *Pol. Sci. Q. 1973 88(2): 253-275.* Discusses the West's acquiescence in the question of repatriation of Soviet citizens after World War II. As a result of World War II, "Europe not only 'solved' many of its longstanding minority problems, but avoided a new one owing to Russian insistence and Western compliance with a policy requiring the forced repatriation of Soviet citizens." 93 notes. E. P. Stickney

269. Elliott, Peter. THE LEND-LEASE 'CAPTAINS'. *Warship Int. 1972 9(3): 255-269.* Discusses the transfer of 78 destroyer-escorts to Great Britain during 1943-45 under the Lend-Lease Plan. S

270. Ellwood, David W. and De Luna, Giovanni. *L'INTRODUCTORY GUIDE TO AMERICAN DOCUMENTATION OF THE EUROPEAN RESISTANCE MOVEMENT IN WORLD WAR II* ET LA PHASE ACTUELLE DE LA RECHERCHE DOCUMENTAIRE AUX ÉTATS-UNIS [The *Introductory Guide to American Documentation of the European Resistance Movement in World War II* and the present phase of documentary research in the United States]. *Résistance Européenne [Italy] 1976 (1): 50-58.* Discusses the changes in interpretation and emphasis that resulted from the declassification of national security information by the US government in 1972 and describes the recently published *Introductory Guide* by David Ellwood and James E. Miller.

271. Ellwood, David W. NUOVE FONTI AMERICANE SULL'ITALIA NELLA SECONDA GUERRA MONDIALE [New American sources on Italy in World War II]. *Rassegna degli Archivi di Stato [Italy] 1976 36(1): 115-130.* David W. Ellwood and James F. Miller are the authors of the *General Guide to the American Documentation of European Resistance Movements in World War II,* recently published by the Institut Universitaire d'Etudes Européennes in Turin. Surveys the sources concerning Italy that can be traced back to three different groups of documents: the papers of the Foreign Economic Administration, the Foreign Occupied Areas Reports, and the archive of the Patriots Branch of the Allied Control Commission for Italy. The documentation material is interesting for studies of the military, economic conditions, civilian administration and Allied policy during the occupation of Italy. J

272. Emmerson, John K. CHINA-BURMA-INDIA. *Foreign Service J. 1977 54(10): 8-12; 54(11): 11-14.* Part I. Discusses battalions in the China-Burma-India Theater during World War II, 1941-43. Part II. Discusses his remembrances of fighting in the China-Burma-India Theater, 1944.

273. Emmerson, John K. JAPANESE AND AMERICANS IN PERU, 1942-1943. *Foreign Service J. 1977 54(5): 40-47, 56.* Reminisces about duties in the US embassy in Peru, 1942-43, and of the internment (in the USA) of Japanese Peruvians.

274. Emmerson, John K. TOKYO 1941. *Foreign Service J. 1976 53(4): 10-14, 25.* Describes life in the US embassy in Tokyo and US-Japanese diplomacy during 1941.

275. Emmerson, John K. TOKYO 1941. *Foreign Service J. 1976 53(5): 5-9, 26.* Continued from a previous article (see abstract 15A:1307). Part II. Discusses differing evaluations in the US State Department in Washington, D.C., and in the US embassy in Tokyo over diplomatic negotiations with Japan during 1941.

276. Ethell, Jeff. "LIGHTNING OVER AFRICA": THE STORY OF AMERICA'S VERSATILE AND DURABLE P-38 DURING WW-II ACTION OVER NORTH AFRICA. *Aviation Q. 1979 5(1): 88-104.* Traces the history of the P-38 campaigns over North Africa during World War II and discusses the plane's characteristics.

277. Etzold, Thomas H. THE (F)UTILITY FACTOR: GERMAN INFORMATION GATHERING IN THE UNITED STATES, 1933-1941. *Military Affairs 1975 39(2): 77-82.* German intelligence service operations in the United States 1933-41, in spite of their volume and scope, were not particularly effective, and they contributed little to the formulation and conduct of an operative policy. Internal failings doomed German intelligence work from the outset. Primary and secondary sources; 26 notes. A. M. Osur

278. Evans, Robert L. and Palmer, Fitzhugh L., Jr. CINDERELLA CARRIERS. *US Naval Inst. Pro. 1976 102(8): 52-63.* During World War II small aircraft carriers, converted from cargo and tanker merchant ships, played a major role in the American victory by transporting aircraft from the mainland to an operation theater, performing escort duties for merchant convoys, and supplementing fleet-type carriers during amphibious landing operations. Includes the recollections of a "jeep" carrier pilot. 35 illus. J. K. Ohl

279. Fahrney, Delmar S. THE BIRTH OF GUIDED MISSILES. *US Naval Inst. Pro. 1980 106(12): 54-60.* The Navy Bureau of Aeronautics developed the world's first air-to-surface guided missile (1938, an N2C-2 radio-controlled airplane drone), the first surface-to-surface guided missile (1942, a TG-2 torpedo plane drone), the first surface-to-air guided missile (1950, a Convair Lark missile), and the first air-to-air guided missile (1952, a Douglas Sparrow missile). The author played a prominent role in the development of the first two, starting in 1936. Because of opposition to the program at naval headquarters in the Pacific, the drone program was never given a fair combat test during World War II, although a number of drone missions were permitted, during which the drones performed well. Many of today's guided missiles, such as the cruise missile and the Regulus missile, can be traced back to the Navy's pioneering efforts. 8 photos. A. N. Garland

280. Farley, Ena L. PUERTO RICO: ORDEALS OF AN AMERICAN DEPENDENCY DURING WORLD WAR II. *Rev. Interamericana [Puerto Rico] 1976 6(2): 202-210.* Although World War II often has been viewed as a time of prosperity for Puerto Rico, there was another side to the war years. The island suffered greatly from food shortages in 1942, and, throughout the war, had a very high rural unemployment rate. Primary and secondary sources; 34 notes. J. A. Lewis

281. Fay, Bernard. "UN GRAND AMI DE LA FRANCE: FRANKLIN DELANO ROOSEVELT" ["A great friend of France: Franklin Delano Roosevelt"]. *Écrits de Paris [France] 1974 (339): 46-50.* President Roosevelt championed the cause of France, even before America entered World War II and as early as 1938.

282. Fein, Helen. ATTITUDES IN THE U.S.A., 1933-1945: TOLERATION OF GENOCIDE. *Patterns of Prejudice [Great Britain] 1973 7(5): 22-28.* Alleges toleration of genocide by the Roosevelt administration in its refusal to aid Jewish refugees from Germany by amending US immigration laws, 1933-45.

283. Feingold, Henry L. FAILURE TO RESCUE EUROPEAN JEWRY: WARTIME BRITAIN AND AMERICA. *Ann. of the Am. Acad. of Pol. and Social Sci. 1980 (450): 113-121.* Far more than Washington, London decision-

makers felt threatened by the Nazi ability to "dump" thousands, perhaps millions of Jews. That accounts for the 1939 White Paper and for the consistent failure to act on rescue opportunities. But Bernard Wasserstein has documented how the reluctance of British decisionmakers to save Jewish lives often went beyond wartime priorities and strategic needs. They rejected plans to send food packages to certain camps, blocked the forming of a Jewish army, and thwarted the bombing of the death chambers, despite the approval of Churchill and Eden. Clearly the failure to seriously attempt the rescue of millions of Jewish lives went beyond the exigencies of war. J/S

284. Feingold, Henry L. THE LIMITS OF HYPHENATE POWER: NAZISM IN AMERICA. *Rev. in Am. Hist. 1974 2(4): 563-568.* Review article prompted by Sander A. Diamond's *The Nazi Movement in the United States, 1924-1941* (Ithaca, N. Y.: Cornell U. Pr., 1974), depicting the relation between Nazism, German efforts to form ties with German Americans, and responses in the United States to these efforts.

285. Feingold, Henry L. RESCUE THROUGH MASS RESETTLEMENT: SOME NEW DOCUMENTS, 1938-1943. *Michael: On the Hist. of the Jews in the Diaspora [Israel] 1975 3: 302-335.* Presents 12 documents from the James G. McDonald papers relating primarily to ideas for the resettlement of European Jews under Nazi control. McDonald (1886-1959) headed the President's Advisory Committee on Political Refugees. The documents reflect the unwillingness and inability of the United States and the other major powers to confront the Jewish refugee problem directly, and include plans for diverting the Jews to places like Brazilian rubber plantations (Henry Ford's scheme), Surinam, Angola, the Dominican Republic, the Philippines, British Guiana, and Alaska. Also included is a proto-Zionist scheme by an American Christian woman, and a letter from Valdimir Jabotinsky, leader of the Zionist Revisionists. 28 notes.

T. Sassoon

286. Feingold, Henry L. WHO SHALL BEAR GUILT FOR THE HOLOCAUST: THE HUMAN DILEMMA. *Am. Jewish Hist. 1979 68(3): 261-282.* Analyzes the inability to save Jewish lives during the Holocaust and indicts the Roosevelt administration, the Vatican, the British government, other governments, and American Jewry's leadership. Political and military priorities were compounded by the sheer impossibility for most Americans, including Jews, to absorb what was happening, even as late as December 1944. F. Rosenthal

287. Ferguson, Robert C. AMERICANISM IN LATE AFTERNOON RADIO ADVENTURE SERIALS, 1940-45. *North Dakota Q. 1972 40(4): 20-29.* Americanism, because of World War II, was highly focused and intense in adventure serials on radio, 1940-45.

288. Ferraiolo, Guy. THE ORGANIZATION OF THE U.S. ARMY, EUROPE, 1944-1945. *Strategy and Tactics 1972 (30): 3-17.* Describes the military organization of the US Army in Western Europe during World War II.

289. Finkle, Lee. THE CONSERVATIVE AIMS OF MILITANT RHETORIC: BLACK PROTEST DURING WORLD WAR II. *J. of Am. Hist. 1973 60(3): 692-713.* Black newspapers were often accused of advocating radical action in pressing for an immediate end to segregation and an "overnight revolution"

in race relations. In fact, because of the betrayal of promises after World War I, unemployment, and the continued riots and segregation in the armed forces, many black Americans were disillusioned with democracy at home and were half-hearted about fighting to promote it abroad. As a result, black editors adopted a militant rhetoric and promoted a "double V" program of urging young black soldiers to fight while their fellows at home worked to secure liberties. Black newspapers were patriotic and generally denounced the more militant all-black approach of Asa Philip Randolph. 90 notes. K. B. West

290. Finnie, Richard Sterling. MY FRIEND STEFANSSON. *Alaska J. 1978 8(1): 18-25, 84-85.* In 1931 the author met Vilhjalmur Stefansson (1879-1962), Canadian-born Arctic explorer and researcher. The author worked under him during World War II for the Office of the Coordinator of Information, which later became the OSS and much later the CIA. Having a brilliant intellect, Stefansson finished a four-year arts program at the State University of Iowa in one year, and later developed the very rare skill of speaking one of the Eskimo languages correctly as well as fluently. He made a few enemies, for example Roald Amundsen, who denounced him as a charlatan, but in general he was and is highly respected as an Arctic expert and pioneer. 8 illus., map.
L. W. Van Wyk

291. Fitch, Val L. THE VIEW FROM THE BOTTOM. *Bull. of the Atomic Scientists 1975 31(2): 43-46.* An enlisted soldier present at the first test of the atomic bomb at Los Alamos, New Mexico, 1945, describes the preparations and his impressions of that portentious explosion.

292. Fleury, Antoine. LES ÉTATS-UNIS ET LA SUISSE À L'ISSUE DES DEUX GUERRES MONDIALES: ÉTUDE COMPARÉE DE DIPLOMATIE ÉCONOMIQUE [The United States and Switzerland after two world wars: a comparative study in economic diplomacy]. *Relations Int. [France] 1977 (10): 127-141.* The economic agreements negotiated early in 1919 and the pressures applied to Switzerland in 1944-45 both reflected an American failure to appreciate the Swiss position and traditions of neutrality. R. Stromberg

293. Flick, Alvin S. THE GREAT MARIANAS TURKEY SHOOT. *Aviation Q. 1979 5(3): 214-235.* The Japanese aerial-naval offensive of June 1944 failed to control the Marianas Islands; it was called the most lopsided air battle of World War II.

294. Fornari, Harry D. THE BIG CHANGE: COTTON TO SOYBEANS. *Agric. Hist. 1979 53(1): 245-253.* Soybean cultivation in the United States is comparatively recent, coming ultimately from China where soybean history goes back to 3000 B.C. After World War I they became a major source of feed and oil, the big boom coming during World War II. When the surplus of cotton became a major problem at the beginning of the Great Depression however, there was a push by the Agriculture Department to substitute beans in southern agriculture. Diversified uses for soybean products greatly spurred their replacement of cotton as the major staple crop. Table, 16 notes. R. V. Ritter

295. Fowler, John G., Jr. COMMAND DECISION. *Military Rev. 1979 59(6): 2-6.* General George C. Marshall balanced personal career goals against professional responsibilities. Though he desired the field command of the Allied

invasion of Europe in World War II, Marshall refused to allow personal preferences to influence President Franklin D. Roosevelt's decision. Roosevelt decided that Marshall's global strategic vision and diplomatic ability made him indispensible as US Army chief of staff. The field command was given to Dwight D. Eisenhower. 17 notes. J. Moore

296. Fram, Leon. DETROIT JEWRY'S FINEST HOUR. *Michigan Jewish Hist. 1978 18(2): 14-19.* The author reminisces about his leadership role in Detroit's League for Human Rights during 1930's-40's, boycotting Nazi goods and services, and organizing a campaign of resistance to Nazism.

297. Francis, Michael J. THE UNITED STATES AT RIO, 1942: THE STRAINS OF PAN-AMERICANISM. *J. of Latin Am. Studies [Great Britain] 1974 6(1): 77-95.* Explains why at the Rio Conference (1942) a rupture of diplomatic relations with the Axis powers rather than a joint declaration of war or a unanimous termination of relations with the Axis was recommended. In explaining this outcome, the author focuses on the domestic and foreign policy considerations of representatives from Chile, Argentina, and Brazil. Different analyses of Latin American realities, plus sharp personal rivalry between Under Secretary Sumner Welles and Secretary Cordell Hull, added to the difficulties of the United States in obtaining the unanimous break which Hull thought more desirable. Based on the US National Archives, Department of State, and *Foreign Relations of the United States* and some secondary works; 95 notes. K. M. Bailor

298. Francis, Michael J. THE UNITED STATES AND CHILE DURING THE SECOND WORLD WAR: THE DIPLOMACY OF MISUNDERSTANDING. *J. of Latin Am. Studies [Great Britain] 1977 9(1): 91-113.* The US government felt that all American nations were morally obligated to fight the Axis, but the Chilean government felt that the war was beyond Chile's influence, "and, therefore, beyond its responsibilities." Chile's political parties of the Left were pro-Allied because the Allies were against fascism and the parties of the Right had the closest social and legal ties with US corporations, but both were more concerned with Chile's internal problems than with the rest of the world. Thus, what was almost "an exercise in bookkeeping," i.e., getting the last two Latin American nations (Chile and Argentina) to break relations with the Axis, became a "diplomatic crisis." Published and unpublished State Department documents relating to Chile in the US National Archives; 78 notes.

K. M. Bailor

299. Frank, Benis M. THE STORY OF A FAMOUS PHOTOGRAPH: IWO JIMA FLAG-RAISING. *Am. Hist. Illus. 1968 3(7): 40-42.*

300. Frank, Larry J. THE UNITED STATES NAVY V. THE *CHICAGO TRIBUNE*. *Historian 1980 42(2): 284-303.* On 7 June 1942 an article, authored by Stanley Johnston, appeared in the *Chicago Tribune* relating the Navy's advance knowledge of the Japanese plans for an attack at Midway Island. Fearing that the Japanese would discover that the Navy had broken the Japanese Fleet Operations Code, the US Office of Censorship cited the *Tribune* for violation of the Voluntary Censorship Code. Unfortunately, for the government, a grand jury failed to indict the newspaper. Recently declassified US Navy documents and *Chicago Tribune* Archives provide a new story to this case. The *Tribune* had

gone beyond criticism of the Roosevelt administration to dissemination of a story that was harmful to the war effort. The entire affair produced more censorship regulation and greater threats to the First Amendment and free press which were so passionately defended by the *Tribune* owner-publisher Robert McCormick. Primary sources; 97 notes. R. S. Sliwoski

301. Frazer, Heather T. and O'Sullivan, John. FORGOTTEN WOMEN OF WORLD WAR II: WIVES OF CONSCIENTIOUS OBJECTORS IN CIVILIAN PUBLIC SERVICE. *Peace and Change 1978 5(2-3): 46-51.* Holding philosophies contrary to popular opinion led to social and psychological stress complicated by financial need and insecurity (resulting from federal refusal to provide funds for dependents of conscientious objectors) and served to isolate wives and dependents of participants in Civilian Public Service.

302. Fredeen, Mel. SCRAPPING OUR WORLD WAR II NAVY: A PICTORIAL. *US Naval Inst. Pro. 1979 105(2): 63-73.* More than 1,400 warships were built for the US fleet in US shipyards during World War II. Today, no more than 30 of those ships are still on active service. Most of the rest have been scrapped, although a few are still in the Navy's various mothball fleets and a number have been transformed to friendly foreign navies. 32 photos.
A. N. Garland

303. Freeborn, Dallas W. THE EVOLUTION OF THE MCCLELLAN CAVALRY SADDLE. *Military Collector and Hist. 1979 31(2): 53-65.* In 1857 Captain George Brinton McClellan entered a contest sponsored by the Ordnance Department to find a saddle suitable for US mounted regiments; in 1943 the McClellan saddle was last used by the US cavalry.

304. Freedman, Lawrence. THE STRATEGY OF HIROSHIMA. *J. of Strategic Studies [Great Britain] 1978 1(1): 76-97.* Follows the Roosevelt Administration's decisionmaking on the operational use of the first atomic bombs. Cities were attacked because of the lack of significant military targets and to increase the bomb's shock value over conventional strategic bombing, and not for experimental value or to intimidate the Soviet Union. The bombing of Nagasaki was the logical extension of the decision to use the bomb in the first place. Primary sources; 45 notes. A. M. Osur

305. Freeman, Joshua. DELIVERING THE GOODS: INDUSTRIAL UNIONISM DURING WORLD WAR II. *Labor Hist. 1978 19(4): 570-593.* Discusses historiography on industrial unionism during World War II which argues that militancy and conservatism coexisted in a dynamic relationship. Unions became dependent on decisions by government agencies, notably the WLB, but the activity of industrial unionists often had a spontaneous, even reactionary, quality to it. Widespread support for the war effort helps explain the dichotomy. Based on published works; 46 notes. L. L. Athey

306. Fretz, L. A. SOCIAL WELFARE IN THE UNITED STATES, 1932-64. *Hist. News [New Zealand] 1977 (34): 12-15, (35): 7-11.* Continued from a previous article. Part II. Discusses New Deal federal regulation, planning of public welfare, assistance to organized labor, and the initiation of social security, 1932-39. Part III. Chronicles public welfare during 1939-64, examining limitations of the New Deal, the effects of World War II, the Fair Deal, the Eisenhower

era, the New Frontier, the Great Society, the Cold War, and the civil rights movement.

307. Frisch, Otto R. "SOMEBODY TURNED THE SUN ON WITH A SWITCH." *Sci. and Public Affairs 1974 30(4): 12-18.* The author, a Danish physicist, discusses his career in nuclear physics and the construction of the first atomic bomb at Alamogordo, New Mexico, in 1945.

308. Fry, D. G. MURRAY. *Can. Forces Sentinel [Canada] 1972 8(4): 27.* Discusses the naval career of Rear Admiral Leonard W. Murray during 1913-45. 8 photos.
W. E. Pittman, Jr.

309. Fry, Garry L. "BOISE BEE": THE DUANE BEESON STORY. *Am. Aviation Hist. Soc. J. 1978 23(4): 242-259.* Duane Beeson (1921-47) of Boise, Idaho, joined the Royal Canadian Air Force in June 1941 and in 1942 was transferred with his outfit to the US Army Air Force; in P-47's and P-51's he scored 24 victories, was shot down by antiaircraft fire, and spent 1944-April 1945 as a POW in Germany.

310. Fuller, Daniel J. and Ruddy, T. Michael. MYTH IN PROGRESS: HARRY TRUMAN AND *MEETING AT POTSDAM*. *Am. Studies (Lawrence, KS) 1977 18(2): 99-106.* A review essay about the popular rehabilitation of Harry S. Truman, one of the few remaining American presidents with dramatic potential. Image-makers have enthusiastically seized upon Truman, but the accuracy of their portrayals is questionable. The film skirts the major issues of the Potsdam Conference and focuses on personalities. This raises the broader issue of historical license on the part of authors and film-makers. Primary and secondary sources; 18 notes.
J. A. Andrew

311. Fuller, John F. WEATHER AND WAR. *Aerospace Historian 1976 23(1): 24-27.* After briefly reviewing the effect of weather on armies and navies from the time of Xerxes through World War I, the author details the use of weather in planning and conducting several actions of World War II and Vietnam. Weather is never neutral in war and the US Air Force learned that even in the Vietnam War it fell short of its all-weather operations capability goal. 2 photos.
C. W. Ohrvall

312. Gattei, Giorgio. LA STORIOGRAFIA SULLE ORIGINI DELLA GUERRA FREDDA [Historiography on the origins of the Cold War]. *Studi Storici [Italy] 1976 17(4): 185-210.* Revisionism in historiography always occurs; now it is being applied to the Cold War. Historians in the United States, and elsewhere, are reexamining the sources of the long confrontation between the Western Allies and the USSR and its satellites. The revisionists maintain that Joseph Stalin took only those countries in Eastern Europe that were his rightful "sphere of influence" and were recognized as such by Winston Churchill. Their opinions of American actions in the last stages of World War II and its immediate aftermath are often critical. Surveys the arguments in detail. 102 notes.
J. C. Billigmeier

313. Gavin, James M. THE JUMP INTO SICILY. *Am. Heritage 1978 29(3): 46-61.* Excerpts from Gavin's forthcoming memoirs, *On to Berlin: Battles of an Airborne Commander, 1943-1945,* which tell of the first large-scale invasion of Europe by airborne troops in July 1943. 24 illus.
J. F. Paul

314. Gear, James L. FACTORS INFLUENCING THE DEVELOPMENT OF GOVERNMENT SPONSORED PHYSICAL FITNESS PROGRAMMES IN CANADA FROM 1850 TO 1972. *Can. J. of Hist. of Sport and Physical Educ. 1973 4(2): 1-25.* A few government officials advocated physical training in the mid-1800's, but the U.S. Civil War and the threat of annexation of Canada prompted Parliament to promote military training. A trust fund of $500,000 from Lord Strathcona in 1909 stimulated physical and military training. World Wars I and II stimulated military drill in the schools. The federal government supported Provincial-Recreation Programmes in the 1930's, and a National Physical Fitness Act during World War II. In 1961 the government passed legislation to enhance amateur sport and national prestige. In the 1970's there was a strong move to encourage physical fitness to help keep down the cost of government medical services. The government has used physical fitness to accomplish various societal ends. Based on primary and secondary sources; 80 notes.
R. A. Smith

315. Gelfand, Lawrence E. AMERICAN FOREIGN POLICY AND PUBLIC OPINION: SOME CONCERNS FOR SCHOLARS. *Rev. in Am. Hist. 1977 5(3): 418-425.* Review article prompted by Richard E. Darilek's *A Loyal Opposition in Time of War: The Republican Party and the Politics of Foreign Policy from Pearl Harbor to Yalta* (Westport, Conn.: Greenwood Pr., 1976), Michael Leigh's *Mobilizing Consent: Public Opinion and American Foreign Policy 1937-1947* (Westport, Conn.: Greenwood Pr., 1976), and Ralph B. Levering's *American Opinion and the Russian Alliance 1939-1945* (Chapel Hill: U. of North Carolina Pr., 1976).

316. Genizi, Haim. AMERICAN NON-SECTARIAN REFUGEE RELIEF ORGANIZATIONS (1933-1945). *Yad Vashem Studies on the European Jewish Catastrophe and Resistance [Israel] 1976 11: 164-220.* Examines the activities and role of the American nonsectarian organizations in the general field of aid and relief to refugees from Nazi Germany. The creation of nonsectarian committees comprising Jews and Christians was designed to ensure the greatest possible public support for a task which also involved the fight against the rising wave of anti-Semitism in the United States. The establishment of nonsectarian committees also stemmed from the need to care for professional groups with specific problems. Based on archival and published sources; 185 notes.
J. P. Fox

317. Gerrard-Gough, J. D. TINY TIM: THE NAVY'S UNUSED SUNDAY PUNCH. *Aerospace Hist. 1974 21(3): 160-168.* Describes this Navy rocket and its planned use in 1944.
S

318. Gertsch, W. Darrell. THE STRATEGIC AIR OFFENSE AND THE MUTATION OF AMERICAN VALUES, 1937-1945. *Rocky Mountain Social Sci. J. 1974 11(3): 37-50.* Examines the changes in public opinion toward the air war of World War II, especially attitudes about the bombing of civilians.
S

319. Gingerich, Melvin. EDWARD C. EICHER AND THE SEDITION TRIAL OF 1944. *Palimpsest 1980 61(1): 18-25.* In 1944, Iowa-born New Dealer and federal judge Edward Clayton Eicher presided over the largest sedition trial in American history, a 7 1/2-month trial of 30 assorted anti-Communists, anti-Semites, and fascist sympathizers, who had 22 lawyers; after Eicher's

death at the end of November, a mistrial was declared, and all charges were dismissed in 1947.

320. Glasebrook, Rick. FLYING THE NORTH AMERICAN O-47 AND THE CURTISS-WRIGHT O-52. *Aerospace Hist. 1978 25(1): 5-11.* Describes flying these two observation-type aircraft in Puerto Rico during World War II and gives a brief history of observation aircraft from World War I through World War II. Charts, 4 photos, 4 notes. C. W. Ohrvall

321. Godfrey, Donald. HISTORY HELD AS A MICROPHONE. *Film and Hist. 1973 3(1): 13-16.* The Milo Ryan Phonoarchives at the University of Washington originated with recordings of World War II radio newscasts and set a precedent in cataloging audiovisual materials. S

322. Goldsworthy, Harry E. THE BATTLE OF BORINQUEN. *Aerospace Historian 1975 22(4): 185-187.* The author was a junior officer stationed at Borinquen Field, 10 December 1941. With everyone jittery after the sneak attack on Pearl Harbor, the field was blacked out at night and under constant alert. This battle was the result of misunderstandings and hysteria. It appeared that night that a transport was landing enemy soldiers on the near-by beach. The base B-18's were evacuated and machine gun sites opened fire on anything that moved. The irony of this was that Borinquen was in Puerto Rico. The enemy ship turned out to be an American freighter and the "landing craft" were fishing boats. Fortunately there was only one casualty. 2 photos. C. W. Ohrvall

323. Goldsworthy, Harry E. A TOAST FROM STALIN. *Aerospace Hist. 1979 23(3): 161-165, 170.* An account of the around-the-world flight of an LB-30 transport in the fall of 1941, to ferry the staff of Ambassador W. Averell Harriman's "President's Special War Supply Mission to the USSR," the beginning of Lend-Lease to the USSR. The flight began at Bolling Field, Washington, and traveled via Gander and Prestwick to Moscow. After the conference they returned to Washington via the Middle East, India, Singapore, Australia, Port Moresby, Wake Island, Hawaii, and bases in the United States. Besides the mission of transport, the crew reported on airfields and facilities which provided invaluable information as World War II enveloped the areas. Based on interviews with the participants; 4 photos. C. W. Ohrvall

324. Goncharov, V. M. ZACHAROVANNYE OSTROVA (ISTORIA BOR'BY ZA GALAPAGOSY) [Enchanted islands: history of the struggle for the Galapagos Islands]. *Voprosy Istorii [USSR] 1975 (8): 139-147.* Discusses repeated efforts by the United States and Europe to dominate politically the beautiful and strategically important Galapagos Islands. Discovered in 1535, the islands became the property of Ecuador at its independence in 1830, and since then have become the object of overt and covert negotiations between the United States, major European powers and the government of Ecuador, in which the latter has often been unfairly pressurized to sell or lease at least part of the islands. America gained a foothold during World War II, but US naval forces were eventually forced to depart in June 1946 after public protest against their continued presence. 46 notes. V. Sobeslavsky

325. Gosiorovský, Miloš. AMERICKÍ KRAJANIA A 30. VÝROČIE OSLOBODENIA ČSSR [Czechs and Slovaks in the USA and the 30th anniversary of the liberation of Czechoslovakia]. *Slovanský Přehled [Czechoslovakia] 1975 61(2): 124-131.* Examines the participation of a million Czechs and Slovaks in the United States in 1940 in the liberation of Czechoslovakia and in securing aid to the anti-German coalition during World War II. 36 notes. G. E. Pergl

326. Gottlieb, Moshe. IN THE SHADOW OF WAR: THE AMERICAN ANTI-NAZI BOYCOTT MOVEMENT IN 1939-1941. *Am. Jewish Hist. Q. 1972 62(2): 146-161.* Describes the boycott activities initiated after 1933 under the leadership of the Non-Sectarian Anti-Nazi League to Champion Human Rights and the Joint Boycott Council of the American Jewish Congress and the Jewish Labor Committee. Describes the US Jewish organizational efforts to suppress the smuggling of diamonds—an industry largely in Jewish hands—the question of food packages to occupied Europe, and efforts to counter German inroads in trade with Latin America. Based on primary sources, especially archives of the Joint Boycott Council in the New York Public Library; 33 notes.
S

327. Gowing, Margaret. REFLECTIONS ON ATOMIC ENERGY HISTORY. *Bull. of the Atomic Scientists 1979 35(3): 51-54.* Secrecy surrounding nuclear arms testing and experimentation caused ill feelings between scientific communities in Great Britain and France and those in the United States, since progress was closely guarded even against allies, 1939-45.

328. Grace, Richard J. WHITEHALL AND THE GHOST OF APPEASEMENT: NOVEMBER 1941. *Diplomatic Hist. 1979 3(2): 173-191.* Great Britain refused to support Cordell Hull's peace initiative with the Japanese in 1941. Ultimately the US position was that both the United States and Japan would disavow military action for three months, Japan would reduce its presence in Indochina, the United States would remove the freeze on Japanese assets and would encourage the allies to do the same, and the Americans would encourage Japan and China to negotiate a peace. Britain could have used this period to strengthen its defenses in the Far East. Its refusal to support the US position was due in part to its desire to apply pressure on the Japanese to insure that they would not invade the USSR. Mainly, however, the refusal was due to its experience with appeasement in 1938. Based on archival and published primary sources; 52 notes.
S

329. Graml, Herman. ZWISCHEN JALTA UND POTSDAM: ZUR AMERIKANISCHEN DEUTSCHLANDSPLANUNG IM FRÜHJAHR 1945 [Between Yalta and Potsdam: On American plans for Germany in Spring, 1945]. *Vierteljahrshefte für Zeitgeschichte [West Germany] 1976 24(3): 308-323.* At the Yalta Conference in January, 1945 Allied leaders, Winston Churchill excepted, had talked of dividing Germany, but at the Potsdam Conference in July 1945 they decided on preserving its unity. Franklin D. Roosevelt favored partition, but Edward Stettinius, Secretary of State, dissuaded him. The creation of a part state, *Teilstaat,* was not originally intended, and was merely a later development. As a means of decentralizing Germany's political structure, the American group commander suggested federalism and the division of Prussia to remove the threat of its militarism. Based on the Decentralization Reports of the American Group Commander of 1 and 23 March, 1945; 21 notes. A. Alcock

330. Granatstein, J. L. GETTING ON WITH THE AMERICANS: CHANGING CANADIAN PERCEPTIONS OF THE UNITED STATES, 1939-1945. *Can. R. of Am. Studies 1974 5(1): 3-17.* Geographic, economic, and security considerations produced growing Canadian-American cooperation during World War II. Policies of William Lyon Mackenzie King (1874-1950), designed to effect closer ties to the United States, speeded the achievement of that end. Based on the King and Franklin Roosevelt Papers and other archival sources; 44 notes.
H. T. Lovin

331. Granatstein, J. L. and Cuff, Robert D. THE HYDE PARK DECLARATION 1941: ORIGINS AND SIGNIFICANCE. *Can. Hist. R. 1974 55(1): 59-80.* Examines the intricacies of Canadian-American war finance, 1939-41, as part of a broader Anglo-American-Canadian nexus. Concludes that the Hyde Park Declaration was a result of Canadian negotiating success—and American benevolence. Based on Canadian, British and American governmental and private collections.
A

332. Granatstein, J. L. INDÉPENDANCE ET DÉPENDANCE: LA POLITIQUE ÉTRANGÈRE DU CANADA PENDANT LA SECONDE GUERRE MONDIALE [Independence and dependence in Canadian foreign policy during the Second World War]. *Rev. d'Hist. de la Deuxième Guerre Mondiale [France] 1976 26(104): 49-66.* Despite independence in foreign affairs since 1929, Canada was a minor world power before World War II. Canada acknowledged limited responsibility in the war. Economic problems included dislocation of foreign exchange, high costs of a British-Canadian air training program, suspicion of British financial negligence, and a major dislocation which threatened when the United States offered the United Kingdom armaments which Canada insisted on being paid for. Canada wrote off a donation of $1,000,000,000 as a comradely act toward Great Britain, but received little gratitude for it. Canada struggled to be included in Allied decisionmaking, especially in mixed commissions. Canadian-US relations emerged from the war in a positive condition, partly because Canada feared the Soviet Union. 23 citations from Canadian and British archives.
G. H. Davis

333. Granatstein, J. L. LE QUÉBEC ET LE PLÉBISCITE DE 1942 SUR LA CONSCRIPTION [Quebec and the Plebiscite of 1942 regarding conscription]. *R. d'Hist de l'Amérique Française [Canada] 1973 27(1): 43-62.* Quebec voted against conscription on 27 April 1942, while English-speaking provinces voted in favor of it. The LPDC (Ligue pour la Défense du Canada) actively worked against conscription. Premier William Lyon Mackenzie King, who had initiated the plebiscite, respected Quebec's decision until 1944, when limited conscription was decided upon. 62 notes.
C. Collon

334. Granatstein, J. L. SETTLING THE ACCOUNTS: ANGLO-CANADIAN WAR FINANCE, 1943-1945. *Queen's Q. [Canada] 1976 83(2): 234-249.* Examines the nature of Canada's financial contribution in World War II, especially its impact on relations with Great Britain. The period saw the triumph of Keynesian economics as well as something of a reversal of Canada's traditional financial role vis-à-vis Britain, but Canada's generosity was justified. Table, 46 notes.
J. A. Casada

335. Grant, Philip A., Jr. THE KANSAS CONGRESSIONAL DELEGATION AND THE SELECTIVE SERVICE ACT. *Kansas Hist. 1979 2(3): 196-205.* Studies Kansas congressional reaction to the Burke-Wadsworth or Selective Training and Service Act (US, 1940) and the establishment of peacetime conscription. Democrat John M. Houston (1890-1975) was the only member of the nine-man delegation to support the bill. A review of House and Senate debate shows that many of them either resorted to emotional rhetoric or tended to minimize the Nazi military menace. The delegation reflected the isolationism. There was no senatorial election in 1940; Houston was the only one of the seven representatives to be defeated, an outcome to which the draft debate and vote undoubtedly contributed. Based on the *Congressional Record,* House and Senate Hearings, public opinion polls, and newspaper articles; illus., 40 notes.
W. F. Zornow

336. Gravel, J. Yves. LE CANADA FRANÇAIS ET LA GUERRE 1939-1945 [French Canada and the war, 1939-45]. *Rev. d'Hist. de la Deuxième Guerre Mondiale [France] 1976 26(104): 31-47.* World War II accentuated the differences between the English and French Canadians. In general, the French opposed conscription and participation in overseas warfare. As a compromise, only volunteers went overseas but conscription was instituted for home defense. Anglo Canadians tended to volunteer and readily supported the Commonwealth, but French Canadians tended to wait for conscription. Officers' schools and entrance exams were conducted in English only. French-speaking officers came from a different class (bilinguals or teachers) than the English-speaking officers. Before 1941 the air force ignored French Canadians, but after that some classes were taught in English and French, and courses in mechanics were offered in French. One of 85 squadrons was French Canadian. The navy modeled itself after the British fleet and gave no chance to French-speaking volunteers. 107 notes.
G. H. Davis

337. Gray, Andrew. THE AMERICAN FIELD SERVICE. *Am. Heritage 1974 26(1): 58-63, 88-92.* Piatt Andrew went to France in 1914 to drive an ambulance for the American Hospital in Neuilly-sur-Seine. "Within months he was to organize and direct an ambulance service that would serve virtually the entire French army until after America's entry into World War I." The American Field Service also provided ambulance services in World War II. After 1945 the A.F.S. became a world-wide student exchange program. 9 illus.   B. J. Paul

338. Gray, Robert C. ECONOMIC AND POLITICAL ASPECTS OF THE ORIGINS OF THE COLD WAR. *Polity 1977 9(3): 356-363.* Review article prompted by Lynn Etheridge Davis' *The Cold War Begins: Soviet-American Conflict Over Eastern Europe* (Princeton: Princeton U. Pr., 1974), George C. Herring, Jr.'s *Aid to Russia, 1941-1946: Strategy, Diplomacy, The Origins of the Cold War* (New York: Columbia U. Pr., 1973), Bennett Kovrig's *The Myth of Liberation: East-Central Europe in U.S. Diplomacy and Politics since 1941* (Baltimore: Johns Hopkins U. Pr., 1973), and Thomas G. Paterson's *Soviet-American Confrontation: Postwar Reconstruction and the Origins of the Cold War* (Baltimore: Johns Hopkins U. Pr., 1973). These four volumes discuss the relative significance of economic and political factors in the development of Soviet-American hostility. "In sum, neither American economic goals nor the use of economic weapons can be said to have caused the Cold War." 21 notes.
E. P. Stickney

339. Graybar, Lloyd J. ADMIRAL KING'S TOUGHEST BATTLE. *Naval War Coll. Rev. 1979 32(1): 38-47.* Admiral King was never noted for his smooth press relations but during World War II some two dozen journalists came to know and respect him as few outside the service did—and came to believe that his contributions were too valuabale to be forfeited, as some called for, because of mishandled public relations.

340. Graybar, Lloyd J. AMERICAN PACIFIC STRATEGY AFTER PEARL HARBOR: THE RELIEF OF WAKE ISLAND. *Prologue 1980 12(3): 134-150.* Discusses the circumstances leading up to the decision to terminate US commitment to Wake Island after Pearl Harbor. The American military defenders of Wake Island successfully fought off the first Japanese attack on 11 December, but were forced to surrender on 23 December after repeated attacks. Until then, they awaited and expected the arrival of relief supplies and personnel. Such a relief effort was in fact planned for 24 December, but it was called off before receipt of knowledge of the actual surrender. The manner of withdrawal was not considered to be particularly heroic, but the decision to withdraw was considered strategically sound. Based on CINCPAC Command Summary, Operational Archives, Marine Corps Oral History Collection, Tangier log, military despatches, correspondence; 13 photos, 43 notes. M. A. Kascus

341. Green, James. FIGHTING ON TWO FRONTS: WORKING-CLASS MILITANCY IN THE 1940'S. *Radical Am. 1975 9(4-5): 7-48.* Changes occurred in labor unions with the entrance of women and Negroes into the labor force. S

342. Green, James. WORKING-CLASS HISTORY IN THE 1940'S: A BIBLIOGRAPHICAL ESSAY. *Radical Am. 1975 9(4-5): 206-213.* The dearth of research on the working class is "partially due to the fact that the labor movement seemed to be on the 'offensive' in the Depression and in a 'defensive' position during and after World War II." S

343. Greenhous, B. and Douglas, W. A. B. CANADA AND THE SECOND WORLD WAR: THE STATE OF CLIO'S ART. *Military Affairs 1978 42(1): 24-28.* Reviews the state of the historiography of Canada's participation in World War II. Works document Canada's emergence from a colonial status to true independence. Others show the growth of social reforms, strengthening of the economy, and the role of the military services—the main weakness is in the realm of military aviation. Interest is increasing but more so on the social, political, and economic impact rather than military developments. 10 notes. A. M. Osur

344. Greenhous, Brereton. CANADA AND THE SECOND WORLD WAR: A HISTORIOGRAPHICAL PERSPECTIVE. La seconda guerra mondiale nella prospettiva storica a trent'anni dall'epilogo (Como: Casa Editrice Pietro Cairoli, 1977): 411-417. The extent of Canadian historiographical consideration of World War II is severely limited, despite several excellent works. Canadian preoccupation with federal-provincial relationships and the sociopolitical clash of two cultures pervades World War II historiography. 5 notes.
M. T. Wilson

345. Grefrath, Richard W. WAR INFORMATION CENTERS IN THE UNITED STATES DURING WORLD WAR II. *Lib. Hist. Rev. [India] 1974 1(3): 1-21.* Surveys libraries throughout the United States during World War II which sought to offer information on foreign countries and aims and progress of the war effort, 1941-45.

346. Griffith, Samuel B., Jr. MEMORIES AND IMPRESSIONS: GUADALCANAL AND TULAGI, 1978. *Marine Corps Gazette 1978 62(11): 49-56.* Reminiscences of Tulagi and Guadalcanal, 1942-43 while fighting with the Marines in World War II.

347. Grobman, Alex. THE WARSAW GHETTO UPRISING IN THE AMERICAN JEWISH PRESS. *Wiener Lib. Bull. [Great Britain] 1976 29(37-38): 53-61.* To establish the response of American Jewry to the Warsaw Ghetto revolt (1943), suggests that it is necessary to determine if American Jewry knew what was happening in Poland and in the Warsaw Ghetto prior to the revolt, and their reaction. It is also essential to examine and critically analyze the type of information received about the uprising and investigate the response of the American Jewish community. Finds that there was a steady stream of accurate information about the deteriorating plight of the Jews in the Warsaw Ghetto long before the rebellion. Furthermore, there was little response to the news of the uprising. Based on primary sources; 56 notes. J. P. Fox

348. Grobman, Alex. WHAT DID THEY KNOW? THE AMERICAN JEWISH PRESS AND THE HOLOCAUST, 1 SEPTEMBER 1939-17 DECEMBER 1942. *Am. Jewish Hist. 1979 68(3): 327-352.* Examination of more than 20 periodicals and newspapers for the period in question shows that, while details often were inaccurate or incomplete, a general idea of the Nazi concentration camps was available. By 1942, the full horror story was known and was continuously being published in the general American press and the Yiddish press. American Jews reacted with protest meetings, memorial services, and days of fasting. 142 notes. F. Rosenthal

349. Grube, John. LES HÉROS DE LA PAIX [The heroes of peace]. *Action Natl. [Canada] 1980 69(7): 549-561.* François-Albert Angers was a heroic Quebec pacifist whose writings opposed 1) conscription during World War II, 2) European conflicts and the Cold War, and 3) war itself. His opposition to participation in World War II partially derived from the defensive neutrality of the French Canadian minority who saw conscription as a force for their assimilation into English Canada. He argued that Canada, as a small power, was in a position to preserve civilized values during a brutal era. As an ardent Catholic, he constantly recalled the traditional and contemporary teachings of the Church which stressed the ideal of Christian pacifism. 42 notes. A. W. Novitsky

350. Guggisberg, Hans R. DOKUMENTE ZUR AMERIKANISCHEN AUSSENPOLITIK VON 1940 BIS 1950: DAS QUELLENWERK FOREIGN RELATIONS OF THE UNITED STATES [Documents on American foreign policy from 1940 to 1950: The source collection, "Foreign Relations of the United States"]. *Hist. Zeitschrift [West Germany] 1978 226(3): 622-635.* The official US publication series entitled *Foreign Relations of the United States* is superbly edited and necessary for research in American foreign policy. The faults of the

series involve deletions because of governmental secrecy and because publication is 20 years behind schedule. Includes a list of 89 volumes of the series which refer to the period 1940-50. Several of the most important volumes are described in greater detail. G. H. Davis

351. Guinsburg, Thomas N. THE GEORGE W. NORRIS "CONVERSION" TO INTERNATIONALISM, 1939-1941. *Nebraska Hist. 1972 53(4): 477-490.* Discusses the reasons that Nebraska Senator George Norris, who had opposed entry into World War I, supported internationalism and American entrance into World War II. Norris, who was never an extreme irreconcilable with regard to the Versailles Peace Treaty, supported most of the measures dismantling neutrality that led to American entrance into the war during the 1939-41 period. R. Lowitt

352. Gutiérrez de la Cámara Señán, J. M. LA BATALIA DE LEYTE [The Battle of Leyte]. *R. General de Marina [Spain] 1972 182(4): 437-443.* Describes the decisive battle of Leyte Gulf, 23-26 October 1944. Admiral Soemu Toyoda's plan was a near success. Admiral William Frederick Halsey's Task Force 38 was successfully drawn off, and the pincers attack from both north and south on the American invasion fleet almost broke through to its target. The southern attack sacrificed itself without direct success, but it had kept American warships occupied to the south and made them run short of ammunition. The northern attack surprised and could have broken through American defenses to attack the undefended invasion fleet, but its commander, Admiral Takeo Kurita, grew cautious and withdrew, preventing any hope for a Japanese victory. Japanese losses were so great that the navy never recovered. 3 photos, map.
W. C. Frank

353. Habibuddin, S. M. FRANKLIN D. ROOSEVELT'S ANTICOLONIAL POLICY TOWARDS ASIA: ITS IMPLICATIONS FOR INDIA, INDO-CHINA AND INDONESIA (1941-45). *J. of Indian Hist. [India] 1975 53(3): 497-522.* Examines the anticolonial policies of President Franklin D. Roosevelt with special emphasis on India, Indochina, and Indonesia. Roosevelt's support of Asian aspirations for national independence reflected a commitment to humanitarian ideals. The strategic importance of India after the Japanese capture of the British, French, and Dutch colonies in Asia prompted American officials to urge concessions from the British. Roosevelt wanted the imperialistic powers of Europe to follow the American example in the Philippines and grant independence to subject nationalities. By the end of World War II, however, American anticolonialist policy became passive, particularly after the publication of the William Phillips letter on India in the summer of 1944. War Department and Navy interests were opposed to any trusteeship system which would weaken American control of strategic islands in the Pacific Ocean. Although the Netherlands gave a wartime pledge of greater autonomy to its Asian colonies, neither France nor England indicated any willingness to liquidate overseas empires. Asian nationalists were inspired by the American president's continuing efforts in their behalf. Secondary sources; 105 notes. S. H. Frank

354. Hachey, Thomas. WALTER WHITE AND THE AMERICAN NEGRO SOLDIER IN WORLD WAR II: A DIPLOMATIC DILEMMA FOR BRITAIN. *Phylon 1978 39(3): 241-249.* World War II was in part a crusade

against Nazi-Fascist racism, and it had as a by-product the end of colonial domination of colored peoples by European empires. Yet American black soldiers were still the victims of much racial discrimination. In 1944, Walter F. White, executive secretary of the National Association for the Advancement of Colored People, traveled to Great Britain to investigate race discrimination in the US Army. White's journey deeply concerned the British Foreign Office who kept close watch on his movements. After interviewing black GI's, he wanted to go to India but was dissuaded, being told he would not be able to see interned nationalist leaders, including Gandhi. He did, however, travel widely in Africa. The Foreign Office, though worried by his presence there, told its people in the capitals of Africa to "show him every courtesy." Walter White's sojourn in England was an important contribution to the process which led to President Truman's order to desegregate the Armed Forces in 1948. 23 notes.
J. C. Billigmeier

355. Hachey, Thomas E., ed. AMERICAN PROFILES ON CAPITOL HILL: A CONFIDENTIAL STUDY FOR THE BRITISH FOREIGN OFFICE IN 1943. *Wisconsin Mag. of Hist. 1973/74 57(2): 141-153.* During World War II the British government had a strong interest in the role of the US Congress in determining American foreign policy. On 19 April 1943, Viscount Halifax sent Foreign Secretary Anthony Eden a confidential dispatch on the Senate Foreign Relations Committee and the House Foreign Affairs Committee. Professor Isaiah Berlin was the author of that memorandum, here reprinted, which provided an overview of the nature and functions of the two committees and short biographical paragraphs of each committee member. These thumbnail sketches summarized members' political affiliation, influence, and foreign policy views, especially regarding reciprocal trade treaties, intervention or isolation, and attitude toward England. 4 photos, 11 notes.
N. C. Burckel

356. Hachey, Thomas E. ANGLOPHILE SENTIMENTS IN AMERICAN CATHOLICISM IN 1940: A BRITISH OFFICIAL'S CONFIDENTIAL ASSESSMENT. *Records of the Am. Catholic Hist. Soc. of Philadelphia 1974 85(1/2): 48-58.* Presents the text of a confidential report on the 1940 meeting of the American Catholic hierarchy by Robert Wilberforce of the British Library of Information in New York. 12 notes.
J. M. McCarthy

357. Hachey, Thomas E. THE INFLUENCE OF ROMAN CATHOLICS AND THEIR CHURCH IN AMERICAN POLITICS: A BRITISH ANALYSIS IN 1943. *Am. Benedictine R. 1974 25(1): 123-136.* John R. A. Nicoll, an English-born academic whose specialty was the English theater, served as a consultant to the British Embassy at Washington during World War II. Nicoll's memorandum "The Political Role of Roman Catholics in the United States" (1943), reproduced and analyzed in this article, suggests that Catholic influence would force the Roosevelt administration to become more isolationistic. 14 notes.
J. H. Pragman

358. Hachey, Thomas E. JIM CROW WITH A BRITISH ACCENT: ATTITUDES OF LONDON GOVERNMENT OFFICIALS TOWARD AMERICAN NEGRO SOLDIERS IN ENGLAND DURING WORLD WAR II. *J. of Negro Hist. 1974 59(1): 65-77.* Describes the situation of the black American soldier in Great Britain during World War II, discriminated against by both the

US Army and British officials. Based on recently opened documents in the Public Records Office; 9 notes. N. G. Sapper

359. Hachey, Thomas E. THE WAGES OF WAR: A BRITISH COMMENTARY ON LIFE IN DETROIT IN JULY, 1943. *Michigan Hist. 1975 59(4): 227-238.* Reports on the 1943 Detroit race riot, and on other aspects of wartime life there, transmitted to London by Acting British Consul-General Cyril H. Cane, illustrate the fact that modern legations continue to be indispensable sources for informed opinion. Rejecting the common contemporary claim that the riots were Axis-inspired, Cane discussed psychological, social, and economic factors which he believed had produced the riot. Cane felt that the majority of Detroit's population was apathetic toward the war. The dispatches also revealed Cane's own racism and elitism. Based on primary sources, chiefly Cane's Foreign Office dispatches; 7 notes. D. W. Johnson

360. Hachey, Thomas E. WINNING FRIENDS AND INFLUENCING POLICY: BRITISH STRATEGY TO WOO AMERICA IN 1937. *Wisconsin Mag. of Hist. 1972 55(2): 120-129.* Reprints the entire dispatch (dated 22 March 1937) of British Ambassador Sir Ronald Lindsay, Washington, to British Foreign Secretary Anthony Eden, answering a request for information on how the British Government might retain the goodwill of the U.S. Government and public opinion in the event of a major crisis. Lindsay's dispatch dealt with psychological factors, cordiality of present relations, American isolationism, the importance of the character of American neutrality, a political versus an economic approach, the distinction between Congress and Executive, military information, British policy toward Europe, propaganda, war debts, the New York World Fair, and trade agreement. Under the new ruling on public records, this report and others for 1937 were made available for the first time in 1968. 11 notes.
Edith P. Stickney

361. Haight, David J. and Curtis, George H. ABILENE, KANSAS AND THE HISTORY OF WORLD WAR II: RESOURCES AND RESEARCH OPPORTUNITIES AT THE DWIGHT D. EISENHOWER LIBRARY. *Military Affairs 1977 41(4): 195-200.* The Dwight D. Eisenhower Library has become a major repository for historical materials relating to World War II and has realized the early aims of the Eisenhower Foundation and the people of Abilene. An important collection, nicknamed the "sixteen-fifty-two file," is Eisenhower's Pre-Presidential Papers, 1916-52. The largest, single body of World War II military records is the collection designated "U.S. Army, Unit Record 1940-1950." 5 notes. A. M. Osur

362. Haight, John McVickar, Jr. FDR'S "BIG STICK." *US Naval Inst. Pro. 1980 106(7): 68-73.* From late 1937 to early 1938, President Franklin D. Roosevelt tried to find some way to blunt Japan's aggression in China. As he intimated privately to close associates and publicly in the famous Quarantine Speech in Chicago in early October 1937, he wanted a naval blockade of Japan. He realized, though, that he needed American public opinion behind him before proceeding and that unless he could get Great Britain to commit the British fleet, a blockade of Japan would be unsuccessful and damage US interests in the Far East. Despite the Japanese attack on the USS *Panay* in China in December 1937, Roosevelt failed to rally the American people. When Prime Minister Neville

Chamberlain rebuffed Roosevelt's suggestion about using the British fleet, the blockade idea died. A preliminary version of this article appeared in the *Pacific Historical Review,* May 1971 (see abstract 10:489). 5 photos, 14 notes.

A. N. Garland

363. Haines, Gerald K. THE ROOSEVELT ADMINISTRATION INTERPRETS THE MONROE DOCTRINE. *Australian J. of Pol. and Hist. [Australia] 1978 24(3): 332-345.* Franklin D. Roosevelt and his advisers selectively used the Monroe Doctrine to legitimize and support their objectives. In the 1930's, they converted it into a common hemispheric defense policy, but avoided the term "Monroe Doctrine" in favor of "continental solidarity" or "Pan American unity." By 1938, assurances had been given to Canada. In 1940, British and French colonies west of the International Dateline had been included, and Greenland and West Africa were also considered. By the late 1930's, military officials planned to deny to enemies bases from which they could threaten the United States or the Panama Canal, and business executives supported the administration's desire to counter German or Japanese economic or cultural penetration in Latin America. Based on Department of State archives and on the Roosevelt and Hull Papers; 69 notes.

W. D. McIntyre

364. Haines, Gerald K. UNDER THE EAGLE'S WING: THE FRANKLIN ROOSEVELT ADMINISTRATION FORGES AN AMERICAN HEMISPHERE. *Diplomatic Hist. 1977 1(4): 373-388.* The Franklin D. Roosevelt administration evolved a comprehensive program for minimizing the influence of the Axis Powers in Latin America. Secret police of friendly nations were trained by FBI agents, and Axis aid to local military forces was displaced by American aid. Newspapers, firms, and radio stations thought to be pro-Axis were blacklisted; e.g., American firms were told to restrict their tax deductible Latin American advertising to friendly newspapers and stations. Government censorship was encouraged, while the region was blanketed with pro-American propaganda. Beginning in 1940, the US effort was coordinated by the Office of the Coordinator of Inter-American Affairs headed by Nelson A. Rockefeller. Based on archival and secondary sources; 60 notes.

L. W. Van Wyk

365. Haines, Gerald K. "WHO GIVES A DAMN ABOUT MEDIEVAL WALLS." *Prologue 1976 8(2): 97-106.* The American Commission for the Protection and Salvage of Artistic and Historic Monuments in War Areas had an almost hopeless task in its attempt to fulfill its mission during World War II. Understaffed and outranked, poorly equipped, with a low priority and generally scorned by field commanders and the rank-and-file, the military personnel of the commission endeavored to persuade the Army and Air Force to preserve the artifacts of Western civilization on the field of battle and in rear areas. The little that they accomplished in this regard was far overshadowed by the enormous, often wanton, destruction of artistic and historic monuments and their contents in Allied and enemy areas. Based on files in the National Archives.

N. Lederer

366. Halász, Nicholas and Halász, Robert. LEO SZILÁRD, THE RELUCTANT FATHER OF THE ATOM BOMB. *New Hungarian Q. [Hungary] 1974 15(55): 163-173.* Leo Szilárd (1898-1964), a Hungarian émigré in the United States, was one of three Hungarian American scientists who induced Albert

Einstein to sign the famous letter to President Franklin D. Roosevelt urging establishment of an American atomic weapons program during World War II; later he became a crusader for world peace and disarmament.

367. Haldstead, Charles R. DILIGENT DIPLOMAT: ALEXANDER W. WEDDELL AS AMERICAN AMBASSADOR TO SPAIN, 1939-1942. *Virginia Mag. of Hist. and Biog. 1974 82(1): 3-38.* Weddell (1876-1948) successfully negotiated a dispute over the National Telephone Company, Spain's American-owned (ITT) telephone system. The author describes Weddell's long and sometimes frustrating negotiations on U.S. economic aid and Spanish neutrality in World War II. His last year of tenure was profoundly affected by mutual antipathy toward the Falangist Foreign Minister Ramón Serrano Suñer, but in 1942 he concluded a commercial agreement. Weddell labored well in a difficult environment and gained more than he lost for his government. Based on diplomatic correspondence; illus., 180 notes. E. P. Stickney

368. Haley, J. Frederick. RECONNAISSANCE AT TARAWA ATOLL. *Marine Corps Gazette 1980 64(11): 51-55.* Personal account of a mission to find a native of this Gilbert Islands atoll, a New Zealand Army World War I veteran who could help US Marines in their assault on Tarawa during 21-24 November 1943.

369. Hall, George M. MIDWAY TO TONKIN: A GENERATION OF CARRIERS. *Seapower 1972 15(6): 14-19.* Primarily an account of the June 1942 naval battle with emphasis on the roles of American and Japanese aircraft carriers. The ability of seaborne airpower to move swiftly to danger spots (illustrated by that engagement) is of great importance today. The Vietnam conflict demonstrates how American carriers, impervious to personnel or political problems of ground air bases, should remain in the first line of national defense. These considerations, in turn, should lead Congress to grant permission for the building of a third nuclear-powered carrier. Undocumented, 8 photos.
M. J. Smith, Jr.

370. Hall, Tom G. AGRICULTURAL HISTORY AND THE "ORGANIZATIONAL SYNTHESIS": A REVIEW ESSAY. *Agric. Hist. 1974 48(2): 313-325.* Demonstrates the growth and development of agricultural coops. Reviews Joseph G. Knapp's *The Advance of American Cooperative Enterprise: 1920-45* (Danville, Ill.: Interstate Printers & Publishers, 1973), Robert D. Cuff's *The War Industries Board: Business-Government Relations During World War I* (Baltimore: Johns Hopkins Press, 1973), and Walter W. Wilcox's 1947 *The Farmer in the Second World War* (New York: Da Capo Press, 1973). Examines the relationship of coops and the Department of Agriculture, and the maturation of the coops themselves as they grow in size and acceptance. Based on secondary sources; 24 notes. R. T. Fulton

371. Halle, Louis J. O.K. *Virginia Q. R. 1975 51(2): 213-221.* Describes Louis Halle's inspiring and visionary high school teacher, Dr. Otto Koichwitz. After World War II he discovered Koichwitz was the Nazi propagandist "O.K.," who committed suicide when Allied troops occupied Germany. O. H. Zabel

372. Halstead, Charles R. HISTORIANS IN POLITICS: CARLTON J. H. HAYES AS AN AMERICAN AMBASSADOR TO SPAIN, 1942-45. *J. of Contemporary Hist. [Great Britain] 1975 10(3): 383-405.* Carlton J. H. Hayes was appointed ambassador to Spain in March 1942. The eminent historian was instructed to keep Spain from allying with the Axis powers, to dissuade Spanish authorities from cooperating with the enemy against the Allies, and to try to obtain facilities for the American war effort. Hayes professed to have a *carte blanche* to secure these aims. His belief in his own powers sometimes led him to override his superiors, fraternize with the *franquistas,* and thus arouse the hostility of liberal opinion at home. After his resignation in 1945 Hayes wrote his memoirs, *Wartime Mission to Spain* (New York, 1945), a book not equal to his historical works because he suppressed data detrimental to himself. Based partly on documents in the British Public Record Office; 74 notes. M. P. Trauth

373. Hamerow, Theodore S. WOMEN, PROPAGANDA, AND TOTAL WAR. *Rev. in Am. Hist. 1979 7(1): 122-127.* Review essay of Leila J. Rupp's *Mobilizing Women for War: German and American Propaganda, 1939-1945* (Princeton, N.J.: Princeton U. Pr. 1978) and Allan M. Winkler's *The Politics of Propaganda: The Office of War Information, 1942-1945* (New Haven, Conn.: Yale U. Pr. 1978).

374. Hammersmith, Jack L. FRANKLIN ROOSEVELT, THE POLISH QUESTION, AND THE ELECTION OF 1944. *Mid-Am. 1977 59(1): 5-17.* Examines Democratic Party strategies to retain Polish American voters in 1944. The Republicans made major gains in the 1942 congressional elections and concentrated on winning ethnic minorities, especially Polish Americans, in 1944. Roosevelt and the Democrats took special care to retain and woo the Polish Americans by keeping the Polish-Russian question at arm's length and appealing to the special interests of Poles. Although Roosevelt won by the narrowest margin ever, it was perhaps the Polish-American vote which contributed the most to his victory. Primary and secondary sources; 66 notes. J. M. Lee

375. Hammersmith, Jack L. THE U.S. OFFICE OF WAR INFORMATION (OWI) AND THE POLISH QUESTION, 1943-1945. *Polish R. 1974 19(1): 67-76.* Shows how the Office of War Information's Overseas Branch disseminated propaganda without creating friction between Poland and the USSR.

376. Hammett, Hugh B. AMERICA'S NON-POLICY IN EASTERN EUROPE AND THE ORIGINS OF THE COLD WAR. *Survey [Great Britain] 1973 19(4): 144-162.* "The Roosevelt administration did not know what it was doing in Eastern Europe." One result is that historians have been arguing about the origins of the Cold War ever since. Surveys Cold War historiography and discusses the US wartime attitude toward Eastern Europe. Roosevelt had a puzzling, well-intentioned idealism, but never a policy, and this accounts for his behavior at Teheran and Yalta. Truman never reversed Roosevelt's conciliatory policy; he just made the decisions Roosevelt had been putting off. Based on documents and secondary sources; 56 notes. R. B. Valliant

377. Hammon, Stratton Owen. THE PHOENIX OF STANDIFORD AIRFIELD: A MILITARY INCIDENT OF WORLD WAR II. *Filson Club Hist. Q. 1973 47(2): 161-170.* The author relates his role in the improvement of a

Louisville, Kentucky, airport during World War II. Determined to make the air field useful for civilian traffic after the war, Hammon had to overcome military opposition to construction. Quotes extensively from military orders about the project. G. B. McKinney

378. Hammond, Thomas T. "ATOMIC DIPLOMACY" REVISITED. *Orbis 1976 19(4): 1403-1428.* The theses of Gar Alperovitz in his *Atomic Diplomacy—Hiroshima and Potsdam* (New York: Simon and Schuster, 1965), "are either implausible, exaggerated or unsupported by the evidence" and do not stand up under careful analysis. 86 notes. A. N. Garland

379. Hand, Samuel B., ed. WILLIAM E. BROWN, DEAN OF UVM'S MEDICAL COLLEGE, 1945-52: AN ORAL HISTORY INTERVIEW. *Vermont Hist. 1973 41(3): 158-172.* Recorded accounts of a public health administrator's struggle in Egypt and Greece 1942-45 against dysentery, typhus, measles, and wounds. He secured scarce equipment and supplies in spite of conflicting British and American policies and the civil war in Athens. Recorded by Paul K. French, M.D. T. D. S. Bassett

380. Hansell, Haywood S., Jr. BALAKLAVA REDEEMED. *Air U. R. 1974 25(6): 93-106.* Reviews Edward Jablonski's *Double Strike: The Epic Air Raids on Regensburg-Schweinfurt, August 17, 1943* (Garden City: Doubleday, 1974), which describes the massive air raid conducted by the US Air Force during World War II. Analyzes the major concepts of strategic bombing as well. Concludes that the mission was an example of strategic air warfare at its best and would have been more successful if the Royal Air Force Bomber Command had participated as originally planned. 4 illus. J. W. Thacker, Jr.

381. Hansen, Arthur A. and Hacker, David A. THE MANZANAR RIOT: AN ETHNIC PERSPECTIVE. *Amerasia J. 1974 2(2): 112-157.* Describes a riot at the Manzanar War Relocation Center, California, in 1942 following the arrest of Harry Ueno for assaulting a Nisei. The Project Director's decision to appoint only Nisei to the planned Self-Government Commission led to Kibei rejection. Based on archival and secondary sources; 126 notes.
M. R. Underdown

382. Hansen, Chuck. HAMILTON AIR FORCE BASE, 1931-1950: A PICTORIAL TRIBUTE. *Am. Aviation Hist. Soc. J. 1979 24(4): 269-272.* Provides photographs and briefly discusses Hamilton Air Force Base, located north of San Rafael, California, where departures for the Pacific theater occurred during World War II.

383. Hare, Raymond A. THE GREAT DIVIDE: WORLD WAR II. *Ann. of the Am. Acad. of Pol. and Social Sci. 1972 (401): 23-30.* "From the beginning, the American government had followed a conscious and usually consistent policy in the Middle East confined to protection of its rights and those of its nationals, while avoiding political involvement or responsibility in what was regarded as primarily an area of European interest and maneuver. During World War II we did become significantly involved, but since this activity consisted almost exclusively of logistical support of the British war effort, its importance and significance attracted relatively little attention. Soon after the war, however, we were drawn into the area, not as a matter of fulfilling some national objective,

but in our role as a world power in a situation where the weakened British were no longer able to play their traditional role, but where the Russians were heavy-handedly aggressive. In the current situation in which the Middle East looms as an area of numerous and complex crosscurrents, it can be useful to look back to the little-publicized background of how we initially became involved and, in so doing, be able to assess present problems in better perspective." J

384. Harp, A. Norman. THE GRUMMAN HELLCAT. *Aerospace Hist. 1979 26(4): 215-220.* The author discusses his experiences in flying the F6F, Grumman Hellcat, as a US Navy pilot toward the end of World War II. Describes pilot procedures and the handling characteristics of the aircraft. 3 photos.
C. W. Ohrvall

385. Harrington, Daniel F. A CARELESS HOPE: AMERICAN AIR POWER AND JAPAN, 1941. *Pacific Hist. Rev. 1979 48(2): 217-238.* Hope and rationalization shaped US military strategy in the Pacific during the months before the Japanese attack on Pearl Harbor. Before 1941, American military planners had considered the Philippines indefensible, and the War Department had been uninterested in developing military aviation. In the summer and fall of 1941, US military policy shifted to strategic air power in the Philippines with the intention of halting Japanese expansion without the risk of war. When the Japanese attacked Pearl Harbor, the Far Eastern Air Force in the Philippines was insufficient, unprepared, and quickly destroyed by Japanese air attacks. Based on military archives, records of Congressional hearings, diaries and personal papers of military officers, and secondary sources; 47 notes.
R. N. Lokken

386. Harris, Arthur T. THE THREE VICTORIES OF THE BOMBER OFFENSIVE. *Air Force Mag. 1976 59(12): 36-39.* Presents a new interpretation of the results of the Combined Bomber Offensive during World War II.

387. Harrison, Barbara Grizzuti. RED, WHITE AND GRAVEN: WITNESSES AND THE FLAG (BOOK EXCERPT). *Civil Liberties Rev. 1979 5(4): 36-49.* Excerpt from Barbara Grizzuti Harrison's *Visions of Glory: A History and a Memory of Jehovah's Witnesses* (Simon and Schuster, 1978), which traces the Jehovah's Witnesses' fight against the courts for refusing to participate in World War II and for not saluting the US flag, prior to and during World War II.

388. Harrod, Frederick S. [BLACKS IN THE US NAVY].
JIM CROW IN THE NAVY (1798-1941). *US Naval Inst. Pro. 1979 105(9): 46-53.* The US Navy from its beginnings was hesitant about accepting blacks into its ranks. Blacks did serve, however, usually in the lowest ranks and doing the most menial tasks. During the War of 1812, however, blacks composed almost 20% of the Navy's enlisted force; during the Civil War, blacks made up almost eight percent of the enlisted strength of the US Navy. At all times, blacks served side by side with the white sailors in the same vessels. After the Civil War, though, and into the 20th century, the Navy restricted black enlistments, and segregation aboard ships became more evident. By 1932, there were only 441 blacks in the Navy. By this time, the few blacks that were enlisted could serve only in the messman branch. Adapted from *Manning the New Navy: The Development of a Modern*

Enlisted Force, 1899-1940 (Greenwood Press, 1978). 6 photos, table, 18 notes.

INTEGRATION OF THE NAVY (1941-1978). *US Naval Inst. Pro. 1979 105(10): 40-47.* During and since World War II, the role of blacks in the US Navy has changed. The Navy eventually accepted blacks for general service. In May 1949, Wesley A. Brown, became the first black midshipman to graduate from the US Naval Academy. The 1960's and 1970's saw increasing racial tension in the Navy, and the service created human relations councils and affirmative action programs to address grievances. But many black sailors today still feel they are being discriminated against and that more of the better jobs go to white sailors. Official naval figures tend to support their feelings. 10 photos, 11 notes. A. N. Garland

389. Hart, Eric H. RESEARCH PROJECT NO. 7424: HAWK EIGHTY-ONE. *Am. Aviation Hist. Soc. J. 1980 25(1): 19-25.* Story of the Curtiss-Wright Corporation's Curtiss P-40/Model H-81 pursuit plane between 1938 and 1940, and unsuccessful attempts by the French to buy planes from the United States; instead France cancelled the contracts and gave purchasing rights to Great Britain in the early days of World War II.

390. Hart, Franklin A. YAMASHITA, NUREMBERG AND VIETNAM: COMMAND RESPONSIBILITY REAPPRAISED. *Naval War Coll. R. 1972 25(1): 19-36.* "Domestic political conflict in the United States over the propriety of the conduct of U.S. forces in combat in Vietnam has centered most recently about Professor Telford Taylor's thesis which holds American commanders as senior as General Westmoreland directly responsible for battlefield tragedies such as My Lai. Despite the widespread confusion generated by these contentions, international legal precedents established at Nuremberg do not confirm Professor Taylor's judgment. In fact, both the Nuremberg trials and the Yamashita case itself, when reexamined in the light of new evidence, set forth the relatively unambiguous standard of command responsibility for war crimes which requires evidence proving a commander's personal negligence or participation in criminal behavior before he may be properly convicted." J

391. Hartigan, Richard S. WAR AND ITS NORMATIVE JUSTIFICATION: AN EXAMPLE AND SOME REFLECTIONS. *R. of Pol. 1974 36(4): 492-503.* Uses World War II as an example of the inadequacy of certain moral judgment frames and the need to establish a more universal base on which to make moral judgments. S

392. Hartmann, Susan M. PRESCRIPTIONS FOR PENELOPE: LITERATURE ON WOMEN'S OBLIGATIONS TO RETURNING WORLD WAR II VETERANS. *Women's Studies 1978 5(3): 223-239.* The claim that war produces a positive change in the status of women was challenged by the realities of World War II. War encouraged economic inequality of sexes and generated sex polarization. Demobilization created needs that could not be fulfilled without strengthening traditional sex roles. Business and labor persisted in sex inequality. Government refused to integrate women into the labor force on equal basis. Women leaders failed to organize a unified movement with an effective program leading to positive alteration of women's place in the society. Based on secondary sources: books, articles, professional journals, novels, short stories, and pamphlets. S. P. Forgus

393. Hasdorff, James C. REFLECTIONS ON THE TUSKEGEE EXPERIMENT: AN INTERVIEW WITH BRIG. GEN. NOEL F. PARRISH, USAF (RET.). *Aerospace Hist. 1977 24(3): 173-180.* Based on an oral interview with Brigadier General Noel F. Parrish, discusses the development of his career and his relationship with the black flying program during World War II. As commander of Tuskegee Army Air Field, Parrish became a principal figure in the training of Negroes. His involvement began as an evolutionary process in which he gave some support to a civilian pilot training school for blacks in Chicago which gradually increased its activities during the war years. Includes Parrish's assessment of the Tuskegee program. Primary and secondary sources; 12 notes.
A. M. Osur

394. Hatch, F. J. ALLIES IN THE ALEUTIANS. *Aerospace Hist. 1974 21(2): 70-78.* Discusses the Aleutian campaign during World War II, "the only instance in the conflict in which Canadian squadrons served under American command."
S

395. Hayes, F. Ronald. TWO PRESIDENTS, TWO CULTURES, AND TWO WARS: A PORTRAIT OF DALHOUSIE AS A MICROCOSM OF TWENTIETH-CENTURY CANADA. *Dalhousie R. [Canada] 1974 54(3): 405-417.* Compares the direction taken by Dalhousie University through two presidents' administrations: A. Stanley Mackenzie (1911-31) and Carleton Stanley (1931-45). 9 notes.
C. Held

396. Haygood, William Converse. A GI'S WARTIME LETTERS. *Wisconsin Mag. of Hist. 1975-76 59(2): 101-134.* Presents World War II recollections in an edited series of letters from the author to his wife and parents, beginning in France in January of 1945 and ending by August of that year. Haygood, who was later editor of the *Wisconsin Magazine of History* for nearly 20 years, records his war experiences, especially in the Public Relations Office of the 76th Infantry Division. Instead of letters home, he occasionally sent his news stories, including one on his visit to a prisoner-of-war compound in Luxembourg, and his encounter with German soldiers. He records his reaction to death, the destructiveness of war, foreign allies, and the effect of "liberation" as Allied forces advanced from France through Germany. In early July Haygood was transferred to Supreme Headquarters, Allied Expeditionary Force in Paris where he taught enlisted men how to establish libraries in occupied areas and at redeployment depots. His last letter is a commentary on the atomic bomb. 16 illus., 12 notes.
N. C. Burckel

397. Head, Timothy E. and Daws, Gavan. THE BONINS—ISLES OF CONTENTION. *Am. Heritage 1968 19(2): 58-64, 69-74.* The Bonins are a 40-square-mile cluster of islands about 500 miles southeast of Japan. They were explored by the Japanese in 1675, claimed by the British in 1827, and sporadically inhabited by various groups for almost 25 years. In 1853, Commodore Matthew Perry bought an anchorage, for 50 dollars, on the northern shore of Chichi Jima. Perry believed that the islands had strategic value for creating an American sphere in the western Pacific. The Americans and British discussed possible dual sovereignty, but nothing official was enacted. Fearful of Perry, the Japanese took the Bonins in 1862. However, internal political dissent reversed a policy of systematic colonization. There was no order until the Japanese returned to effect

control in 1882. During the first stages of World War II, Chichi Jima became a supply depot, but when the tide of battle was reversed the island was bombed and bypassed by the Americans. Surrender came in September 1945, and the Japanese-American Treaty of 1952 allowed Japan "residual sovereignty" under American administration. Agreements were reached during President Lyndon Baines Johnson's administration to eventually return the islands to Japan. Illus., maps, photos.
J. D. Born, Jr.

398. Heath, Jim F. AMERICAN WAR MOBILIZATION AND THE USE OF SMALL MANUFACTURERS, 1939-1943. *Business Hist. R. 1972 46(3): 295-319.* Traces the governmental and private attempts at involving smaller manufacturers in the federal industrial mobilization program during World War II. The federal government was not clearly committed to using small businesses in the war effort, but Franklin D. Roosevelt's reluctance to centralize power in the hands of any single person or group did contribute to the preservation of economic democracy among American firms. Based largely on governmental archival materials; 52 notes.
C. J. Pusateri

399. Heath, Jim F. FRUSTRATIONS OF A MISSOURI SMALL BUSINESSMAN: LOU E. HOLLAND IN WARTIME WASHINGTON. *Missouri Hist. R. 1974 68(3): 299-316.* Discusses the problems encountered by Lou E. Holland as head of the Smaller War Plants Division and Corporation (SWPC) during World War II. Begun in 1942, the SWPC was formed to help small business and was a part of the War Production Board (WPB) chaired by Donald M. Nelson. Holland worked to obtain war contracts for small companies. Unfamiliar with federal bureaucracy, he constantly faced problems with the WPB over board appointments, jurisdiction, staffing and cooperation with the military. Greater difficulties ensued when Congress became dissatisfied with the SWPC and Holland's administration of it. Nelson came to his defense and admitted the WPB's lack of support, but these belated actions and support from the War and Navy departments did not keep Holland from losing his job. Based on US government documents, contemporary newspaper reports, primary and secondary sources; 3 illus., 4 photos, 31 notes.
N. J. Street

400. Hechler, Ted, Jr. LIKE SWATTING BEES IN A TELEPHONE BOOTH. *US Naval Inst. Pro. 1980 106(12): 72-74.* The Japanese attack on Pearl Harbor on 7 December 1941 is still remembered in vivid detail by many US Navy personnel who were aboard the Navy's ships in Hawaii on that date. So it is with the author, who as an ensign was serving on the USS *Phoenix* (CL-46), a new light cruiser then moored on the east side of Ford Island. He recalls what he saw of the attack and of what his ship did to defend itself and nearby ships. His ship was lucky that day: it was practically untouched, and it eventually steamed out of Pearl Harbor for the open seas before late afternoon. 2 photos.
A. N. Garland

401. Helmreich, Jonathan A. THE DIPLOMACY OF APOLOGY: U.S. BOMBINGS OF SWITZERLAND DURING WORLD WAR II. *Air U. Rev. 1977 28(4): 19-37.* Discusses the problems caused by the inadvertent bombing of Swiss territory in 1943, 1944, and 1945 by elements of the 8th Air Force. The most serious damage was inflicted in the cities of Schaffhausen, Zurich, and Basel. The causes of these accidents of war can be traced to bad weather, incompetence,

faulty equipment, and excess pilot zeal. US efforts to solve the problem and handle the diplomatic situation are examined in detail. Based on government documents; 4 illus., 60 notes. J. W. Thacker, Jr.

402. Henderson, Alexa B. FEPC AND THE SOUTHERN RAILWAY CASE: AN INVESTIGATION INTO DISCRIMINATORY PRACTICES DURING WORLD WAR II. *J. of Negro Hist. 1976 61(2): 173-187.* For the first time, hearings into discrimination by railroad employers, all members of the Southeastern Carriers Conference, were held by the Fair Employment Practice Committee during World War II. Hundreds of black rail workers cooperated with the field investigators in building the FEPC's case against the railroads and all-white unions. However, the resolve of the FEPC was undermined by presidential vacillation. Based on the records of the FEPC; 45 notes. N. G. Sapper

403. Henderson, William A. ABOUT THAT BRIDGE ON THE RIVER KWAI. *Air Force Mag. 1972 55(2): 42-46.* Historical account of a World War II event popularized in a novel and a subsequent motion picture. Takes issue with the fictional accounts of the bridge's destruction in 1945. Contends that the strategic bridge in Thailand built by prisoners of the Japanese was destroyed by US aerial bombardment, not a ground demolition team, and further that there were two bridges, not one. R. W. Dubay

404. Hennesey, James. AMERICAN JESUIT IN WARTIME ROME: THE DIARY OF VINCENT A. MC CORMICK, S.J., 1942-1945. *Mid-America 1974 56(1): 32-55.* Brooklyn-born Vincent A. McCormick, a Jesuit since 1903, served in Rome from 1934 until after World War II. Among his few personal papers he left several small notebook diaries reflecting his life in Rome during 1942-45. While much of the material involves internal Jesuit matters, many entries refer to contemporary church and political affairs. Some critical remarks are directed toward the Holy See's stance toward the Fascist countries, and secular matters such as the Church's expressed concern at the damage to the San Lorenzo Basilica being more pronounced than its abhorrence of the loss of life from a bombing attack. His own deep loyalty to the Pope and the Church caused him much anguish, some of which is clearly expressed in the diary. Based on the diary and printed secondary sources; 40 notes. T. D. Schoonover

405. Henrikson, Alan K. CALMING THE PACIFIC. *Reviews in Am. Hist. 1975 3(4): 489-493.* R. J. C. Butow's *The John Doe Associates: Backdoor Diplomacy for Peace, 1941* (Stanford, California: Stanford U. Pr., 1974) examines "private efforts for a Japanese-American peace settlement in 1940-41" and Stephen E. Pelz's *Race to Pearl Harbor: The Failure of the Second London Naval Conference and the Onset of World War II* (Cambridge: Harvard U. Pr.) concentrates on the naval arms race in the 1930's; both authors emphasize avoidable mistakes in diplomacy that led to the outbreak of war.

406. Herman, Mark. RAID: COMMANDO OPERATIONS IN THE 20TH CENTURY. *Strategy and Tactics 1977 (64): 4-16.* The creation, history, and deployment of commando units, are traced through specific incidents from World War II and Vietnam through Entebbe; provides charts on current commando forces worldwide.

407. Hess, Gary R. FRANKLIN ROOSEVELT AND INDOCHINA. *J. of Am. Hist. 1972 (59)2: 353-368.* During World War II, President Franklin Delano Roosevelt, determined that the French were finished as imperial masters in Indochina, endorsed a vague trusteeship arrangement for postwar implementation. By the time of the Teheran Conference (November 1943), he obtained support for his policy from the Russians and the Chinese, but without their formal commitment and without explicit details. Moreover, the British, French, and Dutch adamantly opposed trusteeship. In general discussion at the Yalta Conference (February 1945), trusteeships were ruled out except for former League of Nations mandates or conquered enemy territory. French military presence in a British-dominated Southeast Asia command grew as Roosevelt remained opposed to U.S. military assistance to French liberation forces. The French and U.S. positions were irreconcilable, but new President Harry S. Truman declined to push a trusteeship plan. Such a policy nevertheless was realistic and might have been accepted by Ho Chi Minh. It did not, however, receive vigorous and intelligent advocacy. 61 notes. K. B. West

408. Hibel, Franklin. CHENNAULT: MAVERICK TO MARVEL. *Air Force Mag. 1974 57(11): 90-94.* General Claire Lee Chennault (1890-1958), the leader of the Flying Tigers, fought the Japanese in air warfare over China during World War II.

409. Hicken, Victor. *UNDINE* AND THE AIRMAN. *Aerospace Hist. 1979 26(1): 40-44.* The account of the rescue of United States Navy Lt. Willard Parker by the Royal Navy destroyer, *Undine,* in March 1945. Lt. Parker, flying a Corsair fighter against targets near Okinawa, was forced to ditch the aircraft due to engine trouble. He was picked up by the *Undine* which was assigned with other British warships to the Okinawa invasion fleet. Based on the diary which Lt. Parker kept during his time on the *Undine.* 4 photos. C. W. Ohrvall

410. Hicks, Clifford B. TALES FROM THE BLACK CHAMBERS. *Am. Heritage 1973 24(3): 56-61, 95.* Episodes in US foreign policy when cryptography was used to decipher secret codes. S

411. Higham, Robin. THE HISTORIOGRAPHY OF AMERICAN WRITING ON THE SECOND WORLD WAR IN EUROPE, 1945-1975. *La seconda guerra mondie nella prospettiva storica a trent'anni dall'epilogo* (Como: Casa Editrice Pietro Cairoli, 1977): 419-439. Evaluates American historiography of World War II in Europe, including popular novels, magazines, and government and university publications. 171 notes. M. T. Wilson

412. Hill, Ann Corinne. PROTECTION OF WOMEN WORKERS AND THE COURTS: A LEGAL CASE HISTORY. *Feminist Studies 1979 5(2): 247-273.* History of labor law pertaining to women's job protection in the United States, focusing on four periods: from 1876 (when the Massachusetts Supreme Court upheld the first piece of protective legislation for women workers) until 1923; from 1935 to 1948, when unemployment during the Depression and women working at traditionally male-held jobs during World War II raised contradictory questions in the courts about equality in the work force; from 1964 to 1971, when women challenged labor laws; and from 1974 to 1979, characterized by more Supreme Court cases on discrimination against women in the labor force than in

any other period in American labor history. Examines specific court cases and legislation.　　　　　　　　　　　　　　　　　　　　　　　　　　　　　　G. Smith

413. Hill, Thomas Michael. SENATOR ARTHUR H. VANDENBERG, THE POLITICS OF BIPARTISANSHIP, AND THE ORIGINS OF ANTI-SOVIET CONSENSUS, 1941-1946. *World Affairs 1975-76 138(3): 219-241.* Analyzes Arthur Hendrick Vandenberg's policy of bipartisanship, his isolationism followed by interventionism after Pearl Harbor, and the impact of these policies on the anti-Soviet consensus.

414. Hilliker, J. F. THE BRITISH COLUMBIA FRANCHISE AND CANADIAN RELATIONS WITH INDIA IN WARTIME, 1939-1945. *BC Studies [Canada] 1980 (46): 40-60.* British Columbia's efforts to enact exclusion legislation were disallowed by federal authorities, so the province resorted to other discriminatory measures, including denial of the franchise. During World War II, Canada was interested in India because of the Commonwealth connection, concern for the common war effort, and the impact of external events on domestic politics. This in turn was reflected in Canada's effectiveness as a combatant. Deepening racial tensions in British Columbia complicated the situation. 78 notes.　　　　　　　　　　　　　　　　　　　　　　　　　　　　　　D. L. Smith

415. Hilliker, John F. NO BREAD AT THE PEACE TABLE: CANADA AND THE EUROPEAN SETTLEMENT, 1943-47. *Can. Hist. Rev. [Canada] 1980 61(1): 69-86.* Examines Canadian objectives in the European peace negotiations and strategies adopted in the effort to overcome great-power resistance to significant participation by small states. Although Canada's efforts were not successful, the experience was important in its adjustment to the realities of post-war diplomacy.　　　　　　　　　　　　　　　　　　　　　　　　　　A

416. Hilton, Stanley E. BRAZILIAN DIPLOMACY AND THE WASHINGTON-RIO DE JANEIRO "AXIS" DURING THE WORLD WAR II ERA. *Hispanic Am. Hist. Rev. 1979 59(2): 201-231.* The major work in wartime Brazilian-American relations, Frank D. McCann's *The Brazilian-American Alliance, 1937-1945* (Princeton U. Pr., 1973), indicates that the United States was deceitful in dealing with Brazil and aimed its policy toward "economic and political hegemony." On the contrary, Brazil juggled the Axis and the United States to gain the most benefits for Brazil. The US government cultivated Brazil while respecting its sovereignty. Based on documents and letters of Americans and Brazilians of the period, including those of Getúlio Vargas; 114 notes.
　　　　　　　　　　　　　　　　　　　　　　　　　　　　　　B. D. Johnson

417. Hoffer, Peter C. AMERICAN BUSINESSMEN AND THE JAPAN TRADE, 1931-1941: A CASE STUDY OF ATTITUDE FORMATION. *Pacific Hist. R. 1972 41(2): 189-205.* Justification for continued trade with Japan following the Japanese invasion of Manchuria gave the American businessman an opportunity to defend his way of life and his outlook on the world. Until well into 1941, economic leaders and business journals supported U.S. neutrality, arguing that the maintenance of contact with Japanese businessmen was a contribution to future peace as well as profitable and essential to the American economy. With the imminent threat of U.S. involvement in war, American businessmen shifted to their role as leaders in preparedness and national defense.

The Japanese then became a threat to the survival of the American way of life, for which businessmen had assumed the role of creator and defender. 33 notes.

E. C. Hyslop

418. Hofmann, George F. A SELF MADE AUTOMOTIVE ENGINEER FINALLY CONVINCED THE MILITARY THAT AN LVT EXISTED IN THE 1920'S. *Marine Corps Gazette 1977 61(9): 42-50.* Examines tank warfare and its evolution into tracked landing vehicles (used in amphibious warfare) or LVT's through the creative expertise of J. Walter Christie; examines his work in the 1920's and the vehicles' effect during World War II.

419. Hofrichter, Paul. TELEVISION BROUGHT BACK MEMORIES OF WWII GLORY FOR OLD CORSAIR PILOTS. *Marine Corps Gazette 1979 63(5): 79-83.* Describes air warfare in the Pacific Theater between US Marine F4U Corsair pilots and Japanese Zero pilots, 1943-45, memories triggered by the television program, "Baa, Baa, Black Sheep."

420. Holbrook, Francis X. THE ROAD TO DOWN UNDER. *Aerospace Hist. 1974 21(4): 225-231.* Describes the Navy's strategic interest in Pacific islands, 1934-42.

421. Holder, William and Glassmeyer, Clifford. B-24: THE LIBERATOR. *Aviation Q. 1979 5(3): 288-304.* Discusses the development, career, and characteristics of the Consolidated-Vultee B-24, the most produced bomber of World War II, from its introduction in 1942 to the end of the war.

422. Holder, William G. EPITAPH TO THE *LADY*—30 YEARS AFTER. *Air U. R. 1973 24(3): 41-50.* Discusses the causes of the crash (4 April 1943) of the *Lady Be Good,* a B-24, and the evaluation of the wreckage, which was found in the Libyan Desert in 1959. The importance of the study is that most of the airplane's parts were in good working condition after 17 years in the desert. 12 photos.

J. W. Thacker, Jr.

423. Holley, I. B., Jr. THE MANAGEMENT OF TECHNOLOGICAL CHANGE: AIRCRAFT PRODUCTION IN THE UNITED STATES DURING WORLD WAR II. *Aerospace Hist. 1975 22(3): 161-165.* From an article previously published in *Revue d'Historie de la deuxieme guerre mondiale.* The fall of France in 1940 triggered an expansion in the war production effort in the United States. Lack of coordination in specifications between purchasers caused the creation of the Joint Aircraft Committee in the fall of 1940 to coordinate United States services and British purchases. In addition, President Roosevelt created the National Defense Advisory Commission. Because it was only "advisory" in nature it was not too effective. In December, 1940 he created the Office of Production Management. Describes the work of the aircraft industry under the OPM and concludes that the study of the operation of these controlling bodies can help in preparing future agencies to do their jobs better. Based on Senate Committee Hearings and secondary sources; photo., 8 notes.   C. W. Ohrvall

424. Holloway, Bruce K. THE P-40. *Aerospace Hist. 1978 25(3): 136-140.* The author, a retired USAF General, describes the P-40 aircraft and his experiences in flying it in the 14th Air Force, the former American Volunteer Group (Flying Tigers), in China, 1942-43. Provides an informal exchange of correspon-

dence between the editor of the *Aerospace Historian* and General Holloway regarding the aircraft. 2 photos.
C. W. Ohrvall

425. Holmes, Wilfred J. PEARL HARBOR AFTERMATH. *US Naval Inst. Pro. 1978 104(12): 68-75.* Describes service with the Navy's Combat Intelligence Unit at Pearl Harbor after the Japanese attack on 7 December 1941. Concludes with the arrival of Admiral Chester W. Nimitz, the new naval commander, in late December and tells how Nimitz's arrival buoyed the spirits of all of the Navy men at Pearl Harbor. Excerpt from the author's *Double-Edged Secrets,* soon to be published by the US Naval Inst. Pr. 7 photos.
A. N. Garland

426. Homan, Gerlof D. THE UNITED STATES AND THE INDONESIAN QUESTION, DECEMBER 1941-DECEMBER 1946. *Tijdschrift voor Geschiedenis [Netherlands] 1980 93(1): 35-56.* The United States showed no concern about Dutch colonial policy in Asia before World War II. The Roosevelt administration was aware of the colony's economic significance and encouraged the Dutch to resist Japanese encroachments. During the war, various American officials urged the Dutch to make substantial reforms in their colonial administration and to prepare the Netherlands East Indies for independence. After the war the United States showed less concern and hoped that the Dutch, assisted by the British, would make important concessions to the Indonesian nationalists. Still most American officials preferred a strong Dutch presence. Primary materials; 112 notes.
A

427. Hone, Thomas C. THE DESTRUCTION OF THE BATTLE LINE AT PEARL HARBOR. *US Naval Inst. Pro. 1977 103(12): 49-59.* Of the eight US battleships at Pearl Harbor (one was in drydock) on 7 December 1941, five were sunk; all were damaged. The ships that sank were hit by bombs and torpedoes. Of those five, two *(Oklahoma* and *Nevada)* were sunk because of design defects; one *(West Virginia)* was "overwhelmed" by seven torpedo hits; one *(California)* "was sunk because of the performance of her officers and crew;" and one *(Arizona)* remains unknown because the hull has never been examined. None of these were first-line ships; all were unprepared and poorly defended. Although the damage to the ships was great, it was no "greater than what was to be expected under the circumstances." Primary and secondary sources; 2 photos, 8 diagrams, 28 notes.
A. N. Garland

428. Hooper, Paul F. A FOOTNOTE ON THE PACIFIC WAR. *Hawaiian J. of Hist. 1975 9: 121-127.* Describes the efforts of David L. Crawford, then president of the University of Hawaii, to bring about a peace pact between the United States and Japan in 1940-41. Crawford worked through the Institute of Pacific Relations, and the position paper was completed on 5 December 1941.
R. Alvis

429. Horder, Mervyn. IF NO ATOM BOMB? *Blackwood's Mag. [Great Britain] 1975 318(1918): 110-115.* Discusses the military strategy and circumstances of the release of two atom bombs over Japan in 1945.

430. Hosoya, Chihiro. JAPANESE-AMERICAN RELATIONS. *Pacific Hist. 1979 23(4): 9-27.* Japanese Prime Minister Konoe Fumimaro's idea of a summit conference with Franklin D. Roosevelt in October 1941 was intended to

work out a settlement in the Pacific area. Some historians have placed the blame for Pearl Harbor on the State Department's cool reception to Konoe's proposal, but through his 1934 trip to the United States Konoe had so alienated important American businessmen and statesmen that his actions as prime minister were suspect, and this was what prevented Roosevelt from proceeding with the conference with Konoe. H. M. Parker, Jr.

431. Howard, George W. BRIDGES IN THE DESERT: EARLY DAYS OF THE YUMA PROVING GROUND. *J. of Arizona Hist. 1976 17(4): 431-450.* During its early years, 1943-50, and especially during World War II, the Yuma Proving Ground tested floating military bridges, methods of passing vehicles over rice paddy fields, and similar water related military materiel and problems. The facility was situated upstream on the Colorado River from Yuma, Arizona. 4 illus., 49 notes. D. L. Smith

432. Hoyt, Ross G. METAMORPHOSIS OF THE FIGHTER. *Air Force Mag. 1975 58(10): 80-85.* Discusses the development of the fighter in the US Army Air Force and its increasingly important role, 1933-45.

433. Hoyt, Ross G. THE P-26. *Aerospace Hist. 1976 23(2): 62-64.* The Boeing P-26 aircraft was assigned to the United States Army Air Corps (USAAC) in the 1930's. Assigned as commander of a fighter group which flew the P-26, the author discusses the general characteristics of the aircraft. It was a low-winged, open-cockpit monoplane of metal construction with fixed landing gear and swiveling tailwheel. It had a range of 360 miles. Armament consisted of two .30 caliber, fixed machineguns which fired through the propeller. A bomb rack could be installed under the fuselage. Also discusses the aircraft's flying characteristics and combat performance. It was used by several foreign Air Forces at the beginning of World War II. It was the USAAC's last procured fighter plane with fixed landing gear. 2 photos. C. W. Ohrvall

434. Hudson, Gossie Harold. NOT FOR ENTERTAINMENT ONLY. *Negro Hist. Bull. 1977 40(2): 682-683.* Josephine Baker was more than a black entertainer. Her World War II service through the Red Cross, underground intelligence, and the Free French; her postwar experiment of adopting a dozen orphans of various races and nationalities; and her work as a civil rights activist made her the personification of black contributions to the struggle for freedom for all peoples. Based on newspaper accounts and secondary sources; photo, 9 notes. R. E. Noble

435. Hudson, James J. THE P-39 AIRACOBRA IN EUROPE. *Aerospace Hist. 1977 24(3): 129-134.* Personal account of World War II missions in a P-39 Airacobra off France and how to fly and use the fighter. The P-39, along with the P-38 and P-40, carried the early wartime burden of America's fighter effort. But the Airacobra was never popular and suffered from an exaggerated evil reputation about some flying characteristics and psychological misgivings about the location of the engine. In the Mediterranean theater, P-39s were used frequently as fighter-bombers and in convoy-patrol work. Secondary sources.
A. M. Osur

436. Hughes, William. THE PROPAGANDIST'S ART. *Film and Hist. 1974 4(3): 11-15.* Discusses the use of propaganda in films released during World War II. S

437. Hunter, T. Murray. COAST DEFENCE IN BRITISH COLUMBIA, 1939-1941: ATTITUDES AND REALITIES. *BC Studies [Canada] 1975/76 (28): 3-28.* Traces the history of Canada's west-coast defenses since 1862 and examines the attitudes and realities governing military preparations 1939 to December 1941, specifically the coast defense artillery. Based on primary and secondary sources; map, 3 tables, 70 notes. W. L. Marr

438. Hunter, William A. THE REUNION. *Modern Age 1979 23(2): 178-182.* Founded in 1891 and having seen service in both World Wars, the 48th Highlanders of Canada is the only regiment in the Commonwealth which still parades in ceremonial doublets and bonnets. Its strong allegiance to ceremony and tradition have both reflected and nurtured high morale. The author recalls his service with the unit in World War II and laments the influence of "leftist" and liberal elements which he argues have morally and spiritually weakened Canada. C. D'Aniello

439. Hurford, Grace Gibberd. MISSIONARY SERVICE IN CHINA. *J. of the Can. Church Hist. Soc. [Canada] 1977 19(3-4): 177-181.* A personal recollection by a Canadian missionary-educator in China. During her years of service she was a nurse, English instructor, and Christian teacher. Her work offered many rewarding experiences, but from 1937 on she and her fellow workers had to contend with the problems caused by the Japanese invasion. She was injured only once by Japanese bombs, but the danger was omnipresent. Consequently, her work in China was disrupted by the necessity to move on several occasions and by the orders of the Chinese government to close all schools. Her service in China ended with the conclusion of World War II.

J. A. Kicklighter

440. Hurt, R. Douglas. FORT WALLACE, KANSAS, 1865-1882: A FRONTIER POST DURING THE INDIAN WARS. *Red River Valley Hist. R. 1974 1(2): 132-145.* Fort Wallace was deep in Indian territory, depriving the Indians of necessary hunting grounds and providing protection for settlers. S

441. Hurt, R. Douglas. NAVAL AIR STATIONS IN KANSAS DURING WORLD WAR II. *Kansas Hist. Q. 1977 43(3): 351-362.* Both the Olathe and Hutchinson Naval Air Stations began operation in 1942 as primary flight training bases, using Stearman N2S two-seater biplanes. In 1944, combat losses being less than expected, the Navy found itself with a surplus of pilots, and both bases shifted to advanced training in specific areas. Olathe trained transport pilots for the remainder of World War II, using DC3's and DC4's. Hutchinson trained bomber pilots using the PB4Y *Liberator.* The Hutchinson base was closed down in 1946, but Olathe remained in operation until 1969. Based on government documents, contemporary newspaper accounts, and secondary sources; 2 illus., 22 notes. L. W. Van Wyk

442. Iakovev, N. N. F. RUZVEL'T—STORONNIK SOTRUDNICHESTVA S SOVETSKIM SOIUZOM [Franklin D. Roosevelt—a confirmed advocate of cooperation with the Soviet Union]. *Voprosy Istorii [USSR] 1972*

(12): 77-91. Traces the motives that guided Franklin D. Roosevelt in shaping his policy in relation to the USSR between 1933 and 1945. Particular emphasis is laid on the fact that Roosevelt was prompted above all by considerations of political realism, which enabled him to analyze soberly the alignment of forces on the international arena in the period preceding the war, and within the anti-Hitler coalition during the war years. The "balance of forces" principle was the chief doctrine underlying Roosevelt's policy in relation to the USSR. The American President was able to prove to his compatriots that cooperation with the USSR accorded with the national interests of the United States. J

443. Iakovlev, N. N. F. ROOSEVELT: PROPONENT OF COLLABORATION WITH THE SOVIET UNION. *Soviet Studies in Hist. 1974 12(4): 3-29.* President Roosevelt's recognition of the USSR in 1933 and his policy of cooperation with the Soviet Union against fascism were dictated by his astute understanding of *Realpolitik* and his ability to see the true interests of the United States beyond the reactionary prejudices of many segments of American and Western European society during 1933-45.

444. Iiyama, Patty. AMERICAN CONCENTRATION CAMPS: RACISM AND JAPANESE-AMERICANS DURING WORLD WAR II. *Internat. Socialist R. 1973 34(4): 24-33.*

445. Infield, Glenn B. WORLD WAR II: SHUTTLE RAIDERS TO RUSSIA. *Air Force Mag. 1972 55(4): 46-50.* Describes the bombing missions of B-17 aircraft which flew from Great Britain during World War II, attacked factories in Germany, and landed in the USSR, referring to the tragedy of June 1944 when the Luftwaffe caught the Flying Fortresses at the Russian base of Poltava.

446. Iriye, Akira. THE MAKING OF A *REALPOLITIKER*. *Rev. in Am. Hist. 1980 8(1): 109-114.* Review essay of Robert Dallek's *Franklin D. Roosevelt and American Foreign Policy, 1932-1945* (New York: Oxford U. Pr., 1979).

447. Isby, David C. "CA": TACTICAL NAVAL WARFARE IN THE PACIFIC, 1941-43. *Strategy and Tactics 1973 (38): 5-19.* Discusses the development (from the 1920's to 1943) of US and Japanese tactics used in early naval battles in the Pacific during World War II.

448. Isby, David C. DREADNOUGHT: THE BATTLESHIP ERA, 1905-1971. *Strategy and Tactics 1975 (50): 21-35.* A survey of battleships and their activities in naval warfare during 1905-71. S

449. Isby, David C. ISLAND WAR: THE U.S. AMPHIBIOUS OFFENSIVE AGAINST IMPERIAL JAPAN, 1942 TO 1945. *Strategy & Tactics 1975 (52): 21-36.* Describes American amphibious operations against Japanese-occupied Pacific islands during World War II.

450. Iwaasa, David B. THE JAPANESE IN SOUTHERN ALBERTA, 1941-45. *Alberta Hist. [Canada] 1976 24(3): 5-19.* At the outbreak of World War II, many Japanese from British Columbia were removed to southern Alberta, which already had Japanese communities at Raymond and Hardieville. At first limited to working in sugar beet fields, the newly arrived Japanese had severe housing, school, and water problems. In the following years some of the Japanese were

permitted to work in canning factories, sawmills, and other businesses. There was constant controversy in the press about the role and freedom of the local Japanese. Farm production increased markedly, and after the war few of the Japanese took advantage of the repatriation plan. The Japanese in Alberta today are well assimilated, but little of Japanese heritage remains. Based on newspaper accounts and government documents; 6 illus., 76 notes. D. Chaput

451. Jackson, Charles O. THE AMPHETAMINE DEMOCRACY: MEDICINAL ABUSE IN THE POPULAR CULTURE. *South Atlantic Q. 1975 74(3): 308-323.* The invention of amphetamine drugs in the early 1930's brought with it a period of use and abuse which is still very much alive. Amphetamines were widely used during World War II; soldiers returned to civilian life with the propensity ingrained. Truck drivers were the next big users, followed by hippie youth. The drug has succeeded in crossing all class and race borders. The very catholicity of amphetamine use has hampered the strong efforts which have been undertaken to control abuse. 34 notes. V. L. Human

452. Jackson, Frances. BOMBS IN A NATIONAL PARK: MILITARY USE OF HAWAII NATIONAL PARK DURING WORLD WAR II. *Hawaiian J. of Hist. 1976 10: 102-107.* Early in 1938, the Army Air Corps decided that it needed a bombing range in Hawaii and that a location on the Ka'u coast of the Hawaii National Park was the "only suitable site." Details the resistance to this by the Department of the Interior, the passage of the legislation making it possible, and the final return of the land in 1950. That Hawaii was under martial law only complicated the relations between the War Department and the Department of the Interior. R. Alvis

453. Jacob, Ian. THE TURNING POINT: GRAND STRATEGY 1942-43. *Round Table [Great Britain] 1972 (248): 529-535.* Reviews Michael Howard's *History of the Second World War: Grand Strategy*, vol. 4, August 1942-September 1943 (1972). The volume covers the period of the highest level of cooperation in war planning by Great Britain and the US. Differences in planning structure were marked, but there was a common belief in the necessity of a European invasion to ensure the defeat of Germany. The development of a suitable strategy, however, involved further broad differences of opinion, not wholly resolved in the decision to make the North African landings in November 1942. "This history shows that the suspicions that grew up in America and Britain during and since the war about the strategy advocated by the two allies and debated with such intensity for so long were largely unjustified. Each contestant had good military reasons for the policy proposed to the other." D. H. Murdoch

454. Jacobs, William A. TACTICAL AIR DOCTRINE AND AAF CLOSE AIR SUPPORT IN THE EUROPEAN THEATER, 1944-1945. *Aerospace Hist. 1980 27(1): 35-49.* Analyzes tactical air operations in Europe in 1945 in comparison with the ideas of the Army Air Corps Tactical School in the 1930's. Concludes that these tactics did not alter the fundamental priorities established by the School doctrine. This was the result of a remarkable coincidence of circumstances: an appropriate weapons system had been developed in the field, sufficient aircraft were available, technology drawn from other functions made it possible to monitor and control aircraft in the battle area, old prejudices against close air support were softened, and above all, organizations especially designed

for and attuned to the close air support mission were created. Based on lecture notes, texts, and miscellaneous papers in the USAF Archives, Albert F. Simpson Historical Research Center, Maxwell AFB, Alabama; 7 photos, 3 fig. reflecting USAAF command structures, 69 notes. C. W. Ohrvall

455. Jacobson, Harold K. STRUCTURING THE GLOBAL SYSTEM: AMERICAN CONTRIBUTIONS TO INTERNATIONAL ORGANIZATION. *Ann. of the Am. Acad. of Pol. and Social Sci. 1976 428: 77-90.* There are important connections between the ideals embodied in the Declaration of Independence and the Constitution and policies that the United States pursues in the United Nations and other international institutions. The concepts inherent in the American Revolution, the doctrine that government should rest on the consent of the governed, and the doctrine of limited government, could have provided a basis for American involvement in international politics or for American isolation. During the nineteenth century, the latter was followed, except that the United States expanded its commercial relations with other countries as had been implied in the Constitution. By proposing the League of Nations, Woodrow Wilson attempted to establish an institutional framework within which American participation in international politics would be consistent with American ideals. A similar effort was made during World War II. The United States was crucial in structuring the world order that emerged. Achievement of American ideals in this world order has proved to be a complex and demanding task: early euphoria yielded to disillusionment. The U.S. now appears to have a more mature understanding of its shortcomings and the importance of other countries' ideals. It has evidenced a willingness to engage in international institutions to attain American ideals in the same way as within domestic institutions. J

456. Jaunal, Jack W. THIRTY YEARS A U.S. MARINE. *Marine Corps Gazette 1973 57(2): 31-35.* Traces the history of women's service in the US Marines during 1918-22 and since 1943.

457. Jensdóttir Hardarson, Sólrún B. "REPUBLIC OF ICELAND" 1940-44: ANGLO-AMERICAN ATTITUDES AND INFLUENCES. *J. of Contemporary Hist. [Great Britain] 1974 9(4): 27-56.* The Danish-Icelandic Union, which came into force 1 December 1918, allowed either country to sever the union after 25 years. Negotiations for revision of the Act of Union could begin after 1940. Newly opened Foreign Office Archives make it possible to assess British attitude toward a proposed Republic of Iceland. Strategic questions were paramount: German submarine and air bases in Iceland would have serious consequences for North Atlantic traffic. Most Icelanders wanted neutrality; Britain was determined to stop Iceland's trade with Germany but to continue Anglo-Icelandic commerce. Germany invaded Denmark on 9 April 1939. To prevent a like fate, Iceland determined to sever the Union. The British occupied the island on 10 May. The military protection of Iceland was taken over by the United States in July 1941, a step hinting at American participation in the war. Neither Great Britain nor the United States had Danish-Icelandic relations in mind when undertaking to guarantee the absolute independence of Iceland, although the Icelanders adopted that interpretation. A referendum of 20-23 May 1943 resulted in an immediately recognized republic. 111 notes. M. P. Trauth

458. Johnson, Edwin L. BETWEEN WIND AND WATER. *Nautical Res. J. 1977 23(4): 202-206; 1978 24(1): 23-28, (2): 81-84, (3): 147-150.* Continued from a previous article (see abstract 16A:598). Part II. Chronicles the naval career of the third US naval vessel named *Enterprise,* a schooner, against the French, the Barbary States, Great Britain, and pirates in the Caribbean, 1799-1823. Part III. Describes the fourth (1831), fifth (1874), and sixth (1916) US naval vessels named *Enterprise,* 1831-1931. Part IV. Discusses the aircraft carrier *Enterprise* launched in 1936, and its participation in World War II during 1941-44. Part V. The aircraft carrier *Enterprise* served throughout the South Pacific during World War II; unable to accommodate jets, it was scrapped by the Navy in 1956 because modernization would not be efficient. The eighth *Enterprise,* another aircraft carrier, was launched in 1961 and served in the Vietnam War 1965-69, 1971-73, and 1975.
D. J. Engler

459. Johnson,Clyde. CIO OIL WORKERS' ORGANIZING CAMPAIGN IN TEXAS, 1942-1943. Fink, Gary M. and Reed, Merl E., eds. *Essays in Southern Labor History: Selected Papers, Southern Labor History Conference, 1976.* (Westport, Conn.; London, England: Greenwood Pr., 1977): 173-188. A narrative (by an ex-organizer) of strategies and results in the efforts of the Congress of Industrial Organizations to organize oil workers in Texas in the early years of World War II. Covers the campaigns in Port Arthur, the Pan American campaign in Texas City, the Southport campaign, the Ingleside Humble campaign, the Baytown Humble Oil campaign, and the Gulf oil campaign. Notable were the company's exploitation of race issues and its appeals to "patriotism."
R. V. Ritter

460. Johnson, Neil M. and Lagerquist, Philip D. RESOURCES AT THE HARRY S. TRUMAN LIBRARY ON WESTERN ISSUES AND PROGRAMS. *Government Publ. Rev. 1980 7A(2): 159-166.* Identifies holdings of the Harry S. Truman Library on federal policy toward Indians, 1945-66, water power and supply, 1945-52, migratory labor, 1950-51, Japanese American relocation, 1940-45, and oral history of the presidential campaign of 1948.

461. Johnson, Randall A. JAPANESE BALLOONS BOMBED WEST. *Pacific Northwesterner 1976 20(3): 33-43.* During the final year of World War II, Japan sent balloon-carried bombs via wind currents to the United States, many of which landed in the Pacific Northwest.

462. Johnston, Francis J. GROUND CREW. *Aerospace Hist. 1978 25(4): 244-252.* The author served as an armorer on the ground crew of B-29 aircraft in India, China, and Tinian, 1944-45. 9 photos.
C. W. Ohrvall

463. Jones, Alfred Haworth. THE MAKING OF AN INTERVENTIONIST ON THE AIR: ELMER DAVIS AND CBS NEWS, 1939-41. *Pacific Hist. R. 1973 42(1): 74-93.* Using the Milo Ryan Phonoarchive at the University of Washington of the CBS radio news broadcasts 1932-, the author studied the early development of foreign newscasts, especially those of Elmer Davis. His analysis of Davis' daily reports from 1939 to Pearl Harbor reveal the way his viewpoint was shaped by historical events as he changed from a noninterventionist to an advocate of belligerency during World War II. A major source of public information and progaganda during that period, the radio newscast provides an important primary resource for the historian. 48 notes.
E. C. Hyslop

464. Jones, Kenneth Macdonald. THE ENDLESS FRONTIER. *Prologue 1976 8(1): 35-46.* The wartime performance of science convinced most Americans by the closing months of World War II that some sort of program to encourage postwar scientific inquiry sponsored by the federal government was desirable. The debate over the kind of governmental assistance to be made available was furthered through the publication of *Science, The Endless Frontier* by Dr. Vannevar Bush, wartime director of the Office of Scientific Research and Development. He and others felt that government support of science was not incompatible with scientific freedom. After July 1945, the public's rather vague, open-ended image of science gradually narrowed and became more utilitarian as affected by the atomic bomb and the onset of the Cold War. Based on primary and secondary sources. N. Lederer

465. Jones, Philip Dwight. US ANTITANK DOCTRINE IN WORLD WAR II. *Military Rev. 1980 60(3): 57-67.* American antitank doctrine in World War II was imaginative and appeared to utilize the most modern technology, but it failed because it did not reflect battlefield reality. The doctrine relied on the idea of a mass tank attack, and strong reserves against tank attacks. This doctrine failed then, but current doctrine has many of the same attitudes and assumptions, and thus should be reconsidered. Based mainly on Army studies and manuals; 4 photos, 22 notes. D. H. Cline

466. Jörlin, Gösta. SLUTSTRIDEN [The final fight]. *Kungliga Krigsvetenskaps Akademiens Handlingar och Tidskrift [Sweden] 1967 171(2): 64-75.* Describes the Soviet, American, and British policies, 1941-45, concerning the division of a defeated Germany and considers the political and military implications of the capture of Berlin. The Allied failures at the conferences in Tehran (1943) and Yalta (1945) and the different strategies adopted by Bernard Montgomery and Dwight D. Eisenhower explain why the Allies failed to reach Berlin before the Russians. Based on Cornelius Ryan's *Slutstriden. Slaget om Berlin 16 april-2 maj 1945* (Stockholm: Bonniers, 1966); note. U. G. Jeyes/S

467. Juda, Lawrence. UNITED STATES' NONRECOGNITION OF THE SOVIET UNION'S ANNEXATION OF THE BALTIC STATES: POLITICS AND LAW. *J. of Baltic Studies 1975 6(4): 272-290.* Discusses legal, political, and diplomatic aspects, 1940-70's.

468. Kabalin, N. NAD MOREM: STRATEGICHESKIE BOMBARDIROVSHCHIKI [Strategic bombers over the sea]. *Morskoi Sbornik [USSR] 1980 (3): 81-84.* Although British and American experience in World War II suggested that using planes to bomb ships and lay mines was not always effective, since then the United States has developed considerable capacity through adapting the B-52 bomber for operations against ships. Discusses the extent of this capacity in range, speed, and armaments, and mentions the possible use of SR-71, F-111, and B-1 and of tactical aircraft in this role. 2 tables. C. J. Read

469. Kahn, David. WORLD WAR II HISTORY: THE BIGGEST HOLE. *Military Affairs 1975 39(2): 74-76.* Certain areas of intelligence operations during World War II merit further historical research; these include codebreaking, aerial reconnaissance, prisoners of war, press coverage, attachés and diplomats, ground reconnaissance, spies, and the evaluation of intelligence. 21 notes.
A. M. Osur

470. Karamanski, Theodore J. THE CANOL PROJECT: A POORLY PLANNED PIPELINE. *Alaska J. 1979 9(4): 17-21.* During the early days of World War II, the US Army decided that oil in northern Canada was needed for the war effort. The Canol Project pipeline was built by the United States for $138 million during 1942-44 to bring the oil to Whitehorse. Describes the project and its lack of contribution to the war effort. The project was shut down in 1945. 3 photos, map, 21 notes. E. E. Eminhizer

471. Kaufmann, Perry. CITY BOOSTERS, LAS VEGAS STYLE. *J. of the West 1974 13(3): 46-60.* Examines the role of modern city boosters in the development of Las Vegas, Nevada, as a major tourist center. The boosters were public relations men who "carried on a slick publicity and advertising campaign" to promote the city. Major selling points were the lack of moral restrictions and lack of tax encumberments. The early 1940's were pivotal to promotion because the first resort hotels and casinos were built then. World War II was a stimulus to growth because a gunnery school and magnesium plant were established in the vicinity. After the war, promotion was enlarged to a full-scale advertising campaign with funds raised from the community and businesses. This was successful beyond expectation but as Las Vegas increased in size and fame, the community spirit declined. Based on contemporary newspaper reports, articles from advertising and other journals, promotional pamphlets, interviews, and secondary sources; 25 notes. N. J. Street

472. Keating, John S. MISSION TO MECCA: THE CRUISE OF THE *MURPHY*. *US Naval Inst. Pro. 1976 102(1): 54-63.* In February 1945, the US destroyer *Murphy* was ordered to transport King Ibn-Saud of Saudi Arabia from Jidda to the Great Bitter Lake for a conference with President Franklin D. Roosevelt, who was then in the area after attending the Yalta Conference. The article tells of how the officers and crew of the *Murphy* experienced and resolved problems "both diplomatic and pragmatic, which boggled the imagination." The problems were eventually resolved to everyone's satisfaction and on 13 February, the King was delivered safely to the USS *Quincy* for his meeting with the President. 7 photos. A. N. Garland

473. Keegan, John. THE HISTORIAN AND BATTLE. *Int. Security 1978-79 3(3): 138-149.* Discusses the historiography of battles, both arcane and classic, of World War I and World War II; 1914-45.

474. Keeran, Roger R. EVERYTHING FOR VICTORY: COMMUNIST INFLUENCE IN THE AUTO INDUSTRY DURING WORLD WAR II. *Sci. and Soc. 1979 43(1): 1-28.* The decline of Communist influence within the United Automobile Workers of America during World War II can only partially be traced to the group's support for incentive pay and the no-strike clause; both of which were highly popular among many workers. In these matters the Communists were acting in accordance with the "win-the-war" philosophy of the UAW and CIO leadership. The waning of Communist power owed a great deal to the general anti-labor and rightwing political influences that gained strength during the war and to the confusion within Party ranks over Earl Browder's post-Teheran policies. Communists remained influential among black workers and despite the election of Walter Reuther in 1946 were by no means a negligible force in the UAW in the immediate postwar period. Printed primary and secondary sources. N. Lederer

475. Keiderling, Gerhard. ZUR HALTUNG DER WESTMÄCHTE BEI DER VORBEREITUNG DES MILITÄRISCHEN VIER-MÄCHTE-BESATZUNGS- UND KONTROLLSYSTEMS FÜR DEUTSCHLAND (1943-1945) [The attitude of the Western powers toward the preparation of the Four Power system for the military occupation and control of Germany, 1943-45]. *Jahrbuch für Geschichte [East Germany] 1975 13: 293-349.* Traces the negotiations and maneuvers among the four Allies which produced the partition of Germany into US, British, French, and Soviet occupation zones after World War II. President Franklin D. Roosevelt and other US officials wanted larger occupation zones for the Western powers but were forced to agree to smaller zones because of the rapid advance and large size of the Russian armies. 230 notes.

J. C. Billigmeier

476. Keim, Albert N. SERVICE OR RESISTANCE? THE MENNONITE RESPONSE TO CONSCRIPTION IN WORLD WAR II. *Mennonite Q. Rev. 1978 52(2): 141-155.* Mennonites' experiences during World War I caused them to seek an alternative military conscription in the event of another war, an impulse which quickened as World War II approached during the 1930's. Representatives of the Peace Churches approached the federal government with a plan for alternative service in the United States. Neither Congress nor President Roosevelt was enthusiastic about it, but eventually it was adopted. The Mennonites were satisfied with this solution, because they opposed not conscription but war. Some Quakers were more reserved. Ironically, the civilian service units operated under military control, although the individual churches acted as "camp managers." 52 notes.

V. L. Human

477. Kelly, John Joseph. INTELLIGENCE AND COUNTER-INTELLIGENCE IN GERMAN PRISONER OF WAR CAMPS IN CANADA DURING WORLD WAR II. *Dalhousie Rev. [Canada] 1978 58(2): 285-294.* About 40,000 German prisoners of war and civilian internees were held at 25 sites in Canada on behalf of the British government, 1940-47. The decision to establish a Psychological Warfare Committee in Canada in 1943 followed obviously well-organized riots in camps at Ozada (Alberta) and Espanola (Ontario). Gestapo elements within the camps were responsible for many of the problems experienced in Canada. One of the major goals of the Canadian authorities was to reeducate the young, physically fit, thoroughly indoctrinated Nazis before they were returned to Germany following the war. Murder, even mass murder, plotted by the Gestapo, was one of the major worries of Canadian officials. 15 notes.

C. Held

478. Kelly, Vicki L. IN THE SHADOW OF FAME: THE SAN JACINTO ORDNANCE DEPOT, 1939-1964. *Military Hist. of Texas and the Southwest 1976 13(2): 39-46.* Short history of the San Jacinto Ordnance Depot which served as a munitions storage area, 1939-64.

479. Kennan, George F. THE UNITED STATES AND THE SOVIET UNION, 1917-1976. *Foreign Affairs 1976 54(4): 670-690.* US-Soviet relations have moved through several phases during the years 1917-76; from nonrecognition of the Soviets after World War I to cooperation in 1933-45, when Russia was viewed as sharing our noble, antityrannical motives, to the 1945-65 Cold War years when it was considered a military threat, through favorable changes in

1966-68 which led to the Nixon-Kissinger detente in the 1970's. A constant set of impediments have underlain these fluctuations. The United States has objected to the USSR's internal practices of repression, denunciations of the United States, support of anti-US factions in third world countries, and maintenance of armed forces on a large scale, all under a blanket of secrecy. The United States on the other hand has dealt with the USSR subjectively, frequently exploiting the nation's fear of the Russians. There will be no improved relations without greater commitment to the task and a deeper understanding of the reasons behind the constants in Russian behavior. S. Tomlinson-Brown

480. Kerr, Joseph R. MEMORIAL WINDOWS: CAMP LEJEUNE'S STAINED GLASS MASTERPIECES. *Marine Corps Gazette 1980 64(12): 45-48.* Stained glass windows designed and installed by the J. and R. Lamb Studios of Tenafly, New Jersey, in the Main Protestant Chapel at Camp Lejeune, North Carolina, when the chapel was built in 1942-43, portray Marine Corps history from 1775 to World War II.

481. Kimball, Warren F. CHURCHILL AND ROOSEVELT: THE PERSONAL EQUATION. *Prologue 1974 6(3): 169-182.* Reviews the personal correspondence between President Franklin D. Roosevelt and Prime Minister Winston Churchill. Nearly all of the voluminous correspondence has been preserved and presents a remarkable portrait of relations between the two world leaders. These relations were generally amicable, but the few disagreements were of a fundamental nature. Churchill resented playing a secondary role and was very distrustful of Soviet motives. It is doubtful if their friendship could have withstood the rigors of postwar problems. 3 photos, 45 notes. V. L. Human

482. Kimball, Warren F. THE COLD WAR WARMED OVER. *Am. Hist. R. 1974 79(4): 1119-1136.* A review article on: John L. Gaddis, *The United States and the Origins of the Cold War, 1941-1947* (Columbia U. Press, 1972), Joyce and Gabriel Kolko, *The Limits of Power: The World and United States Foreign Policy, 1945-1954* (Harper & Row, 1972), and Robert J. Maddox, *The New Left and the Origins of the Cold War* (Princeton U. Press, 1973). Examines the current state of Cold War historiography. Gaddis typifies a new generation of scholars who eclectically combine many of the findings of orthodox and left-revisionist historians. The Kolkos exemplify determinist historians whose arguments often seem to have been forced into a suitable pattern. Maddox's intemperate and sketchy attack on the left-revisionists lacks both civility and validity. A

483. Kimball, Warren F. THE ROOSEVELT RIDDLE: STILL ANOTHER VIEW. *Rev. in Am. Hist. 1976 4(3): 458-463.* Review article prompted by *The Diaries of Edward R. Stettinius, Jr., 1943-1946* (Thomas M. Campbell and George C. Herring, eds.; New York: New Viewpoints, 1975); discusses American foreign policy under Roosevelt, 1943-45.

484. Kindleberger, Charles P. WORLD WAR II STRATEGY. *Encounter [Great Britain] 1978 51(5): 39-42.* Review article prompted by Solly Zuckerman's autobiographical *From Apes to Warlords* (Hamish Hamilton); criticizes the author's interpretation of strategy used in the 1944 aerial bombing of France by the United States in support of Operation Overlord.

485. King, Michael. EZRA POUND AT PISA: AN INTERVIEW WITH JOHN L. STEELE. *Texas Q. 1978 21(4): 49-61.* For seven months in 1945, Ezra Pound was in custody at the US Army Disciplinary Training Center (DTC) at Pisa, Italy. The commanding officer talked often with Pound about monetary theory and other items of interest to the poet. To protect his sanity the facility made paper and a typewriter available to Pound so that he could continue writing. Pound used the materials and produced verses on the DTC and the commanding officer. While at the DTC Pound impressed his guards with his memory and single-minded approach to whatever problem he addressed himself. 5 notes.
R. H. Tomlinson

486. Kir'ian, M. NEKOTORYE UROKI I VYVODY IZ OPERATSII VOORUZHENNYKH SIL SSHA I ANGLII VO VTOROI MIRIVOI VOINE: MATERIALY DLIA SLUSHATELEI I KURSANTOV VVUZOV [Some lessons and conclusions from the operations of the armed forces of the United States and Great Britain in World War II: materials for students in higher education]. *Voenno-Istoricheskii Zhurnal [USSR] 1979 (7): 70-77.* Discusses the events and tactics of five Allied operations in World War II: El Alamein, the Sicily and Normandy landings, the defensive operations in the Ardennes in 1944, and operations in the Pacific in 1945. Western historians have overstressed the importance of the first two. Allied successes in Western Europe resulted from the heavy German commitment on the Russian Front. All Allied operations had a political motive: the installation in liberated countries of regimes friendly to the Allies. 2 notes.
J. S. S. Charles

487. Kirichenko, V. EKSPANSIONISTSKAIA VOENNAIA POLITICA S.SH.A. V LATINSKOI AMERIKE VO VREMIA VTOROI MIROVOI VOINY [Expansionist military policy of the United States in Latin America during World War II]. *Voenno-Istoricheskii Zhurnal [USSR] 1977 (11): 115-120.* Discusses "two constant aspects" of US defense policy in Latin America: 1) "a part of the global military policy of American imperialism," and 2) an important instrument of US neocolonialism and their Latin American policy in general. Interprets US defense policy in Latin America in 1940-45 as proof of these two assertions.

488. Kistiakowsky, George B. TRINITY—A REMINISCENCE. *Bull. of the Atomic Scientists 1980 36(6): 19-22.* Discusses the Trinity plutonium bomb test in the White Sands military reservation, about 200 miles south of Los Alamos, in 1945.

489. Klaassen, Walter. MENNONITES AND WAR TAXES. *Pennsylvania Mennonite Heritage 1978 1(2): 17-22.* Traces traditional views of government and taxation held by Anabaptists in Switzerland and Germany during the 16th century; examines Anabaptists' refusal to pay taxes connected with war in the United States from the American Revolution to the Vietnam War.

490. Kleiler, Frank M. THE WORLD WAR II BATTLES OF MONTGOMERY WARD. *Chicago Hist. 1976 5(1): 19-27.* Discusses Montgomery Ward's Chairman of the Board, Sewell Avery, and his steadfast refusal to comply with arbitration set down by the War Labor Board in an attempt to settle a strike of Ward workers, which led to Franklin Roosevelt's order for US Army troops to seize the Ward plant, 1941.

491. Kniffin, Ogden. A BASEMENT VIEW OF SIR WINSTON. *Am. Heritage 1972 23(6): 42-43.* A brief account of the visits of Sir Winston Churchill to the White House Map Room during World War II. Written by a night duty officer in the map room. Illus. J. F. Paul

492. Kodachi, Zuigaku; Heikkala, Jan, transl.; and *Cormack, Janet*, ed. PORTLAND ASSEMBLY CENTER: DIARY OF SAKU TOMITA. *Oregon Hist. Q. 1980 81(2): 149-171.* Saku Tomita, who came from Japan to the United States in 1921, was in her 40's when she was evacuated with her family (husband, daughter and son) to the Portland Assembly Center in the early days of World War II. Her diary describes daily occurrences there during May-August 1942 while they were awaiting transfer to a relocation camp. 10 photos, 72 notes.
G. R. Schroeder

493. Koistinen, Paul A. C. MOBILIZING THE WORLD WAR II ECONOMY: LABOR AND THE INDUSTRIAL-MILITARY ALLIANCE. *Pacific Hist. R. 1973 42(4): 443-478.* Examines the junior partnership role of organized labor during World War II through agencies such as the War Production Board and the War Manpower Commission. Challenges the theory that big labor became the equal of the business community or the military establishment. War production set records, but industrial unrest increased as the industrial and military complex successfully maintained the status quo. The Roosevelt administration avoided supporting changes not only because they might interfere with the overseas war effort, but also because the administration was committed to preserving the corporate capitalist system. Labor was no match for its opponents. 66 notes. C. W. Olson

494. Koppes, Clayton R. and Black, Gregory D. WHAT TO SHOW THE WORLD: THE OFFICE OF WAR INFORMATION AND HOLLYWOOD, 1942-1945. *J. of Am. Hist. 1977 64(1): 87-105.* Details the activities of the Office of War Information (OWI), particularly its Bureau of Motion Pictures (BMP). Led by Nelson Poynter, the Bureau analyzed the content of Hollywood films and limited the export of films that did not project a positive image of America and the war effort. Discusses many of the films produced during 1942-44, how Hollywood eventually cooperated with the BMP, and how both Hollywood and the OWI undermined the principles of liberalism by releasing films that did not depict reality. 35 notes. J. B. Reed

495. Kraminov, D. THE END OF THE WAR IN THE WEST. *Int. Affairs [USSR] 1978 (11): 113-122.* After the Anglo-American troops crossed the Rhine in March 1945, they encountered remarkably little resistance on their way to Berlin, and British Field Marshal Montgomery decided on taking the prize of the German capital, but American General Dwight D. Eisenhower thwarted this plan and held the British and American troops on the banks of the Elbe until the Soviet forces entered Berlin. Then the British and Americans swept in to prevent Soviet encirclement of the city, but Eisenhower's actions created friction between the British and Americans.

496. Krammer, Arnold P. GERMAN PRISONERS OF WAR IN THE UNITED STATES. *Military Affairs 1976 40(2): 68-73.* Discusses the problems involved in establishing and administrating camps for German POW's. Two

fundamental principles affected their treatment: the humanitarian intent of the Geneva Convention, and the fact that enemy nations held American soldiers. At the beginning of the war, the government's inefficient division of responsibility led to unpreparedness, but problems were soon worked out and prisoners were working in a variety of tasks. Some complications arose around the ire of American labor unions, the special position of Italy, and political leadership in the camps. The program's success was partly responsible for the healthy postwar reconstruction of American-German relations. Based on primary and secondary sources; 41 notes. A. M. Osur

497. Krammer, Arnold P. WHEN THE *AFRIKA KORPS* CAME TO TEXAS. *Southwestern Hist. Q. 1977 80(3): 247-282.* Almost 79,000 German prisoners of war were held in Texas, 1943-46. They generally liked their lenient treatment but a few tried to escape, and the pro-Nazi element persecuted anti-Nazis inside the camps. Besides sports and education, POW's worked on military bases, farms, and in small businesses. Local communities liked having the extra labor force. Today the old camps are deserted but POW reunions still occur in Germany and Texas. Based on primary and secondary sources; 15 illus., 64 notes.
J. H. Broussard

498. Krasuski, Jerzy. STOSUNKI FRANCJA-USA [Relations between France and the USA]. *Przegląd Zachodni [Poland] 1979 35(5-6): 1-32.* France helped the United States in the American Revolution. America reciprocated by sending US troops to France in World War I. Then came disillusionment. British-American guarantees to France were annulled when the US Senate refused to ratify the Treaty of Versailles. The US demand for repayment of the French war debt cooled relations further. In World War II Roosevelt preferred to deal with the Vichy French, and treated de Gaulle as a British invention. De Gaulle in turn feared the US-Soviet rapprochement as a threat to French independence. After the War the French had colonial obligations to which the United States was inimical. When France lost its colonies de Gaulle hoped for a special French-US relationship. Instead, the British and West Germans received the privilege. Many nuisance acts by the French government followed. French presidents after de Gaulle were forced into the same position, mainly because they also insisted on French status as leader of Western Europe. M. Krzyzaniak

499. Kulish, V. M. SOVETSKO-AMERIKANSKOE SOTRUDNICHESTVO V GODY VTOROI MIROVOI VOINY [Soviet-American collaboration during World War II]. *Novaia i Noveishaia Istoriia [USSR] 1974 (2): 55-76.* During World War II the Soviet Union and America fought together against Nazism, both in governmental and in social spheres. The Communist Party of America was one of the most important progressive forces in the struggle. The two nations were aided by Poland, Czechoslovakia, France, Yugoslavia, and others, with a united single aim of defeating Germany, Japan, and Italy. The other countries recognized the importance of Soviet aid for their own survival, both through the defeat of fascism and in the conclusion of international peace. The collaboration was important as the first significant unification of communist and capitalist governments with a common goal. Primary and secondary sources; 84 notes.
L. Smith

500. Kumamoto, Bob. THE SEARCH FOR SPIES: AMERICAN COUNTERINTELLIGENCE AND THE JAPANESE AMERICAN COMMUNITY 1931-1942. *Amerasia J. 1979 6(2): 45-75.* Counterintelligence activities of the Army and Navy and the Federal Bureau of Investigation (FBI) vis-à-vis Japanese living in the United States, during 1931-42 were marked by excessive paranoia, racism, and stupidity, and fired by the economic jealousy of white Americans. Every Japanese fraternal or business organization was suspected of subversion; old and poor fishermen were irresponsibly accused of having sophisticated espionage equipment aboard. Reliable counterreports have come to light, such as that of Curtis B. Munson of the State Department and FBI Special Agent in Charge N. J. L. Peiper showing no indictable evidence of subversive activities. In spite of this, after Pearl Harbor and US entry into World War II, Japanese citizens of the United States were herded en masse into relocation centers, despoiled of their property and civil rights. 63 notes. H. F. Thomson

501. Kuter, Laurence S. THE GENERAL VS. THE ESTABLISHMENT: GENERAL H. H. ARNOLD AND THE AIR STAFF. *Aerospace Hist. 1974 21(4): 185-189.* Discusses the problems faced by General Henry H. Arnold in the Army Air Force during World War II. S

502. Kuter, Laurence S. GODDAMMIT, GEORGIE! *Air Force Mag. 1973 56(2): 51-56.* George Patton's famous North African campaigns of 1943 were marked by his inability to understand that US tactical air cover should be coordinated with ground operations, rather than subordinated to them.

503. Kuter, Laurence S. HOW HAP ARNOLD BUILT THE AAF. *Air Force Mag. 1973 56(9): 88-93.* Discusses the unorthodox methods, and the outstanding results of the military planning of General Henry H. 'Hap' Arnold in expanding the newly-created Army Air Forces after Pearl Harbor.

504. Kuznetsov, N. G. NEKOTORYE VOPROSY OKEANSKO-MORSKIKH OPERATSII ANGLIISKOGO I AMERIKANSKOGO FLOTOV V GODY VTOROI MIROVOI VOINY [Certain aspects of US and British naval operations in World War II]. *Novaia i Noveishaia Istoriia [USSR] 1975 (4): 95-106.* Describes the struggle for control of the Atlantic, which was a turning point in the naval war. Describes the US strategy against Japan in the Pacific, which ultimately led to the postwar deployment of Polaris submarines. Considers the differing views of the Allies toward the strategic importance of the Pacific theater. 6 notes. E. R. Sicher

505. La Plante, John B. THE EVOLUTION OF PACIFIC POLICY AND STRATEGIC PLANNING: JUNE 1940-JULY 1941. *Naval War Coll. R. 1973 25(5): 57-72.* "Coordinated policy planning and management have long been recognized as being fundamental to the success of any country's foreign policy. Military preparedness and strategic planning should always play an important part in this process, but in periods of acute international tension, as characterized in the 18 months before Pearl Harbor, the integration of the military planning process into national policy circles is mandatory. While U.S. policy and strategic planning were in harmony by late 1941, this foundation upon which the next 4 years' war effort would be based was not the result of close coordination between strategic planners and foreign policy experts as has generally been assumed." J

506. Lademan, J. U., Jr. USS GOLD STAR—FLAGSHIP OF THE GUAM NAVY. *US Naval Inst. Pro. 1973 99(12): 67-79.* A firsthand account of the South Pacific voyages (July 1941-July 1942) of the USS *Gold Star*, a converted ocean tramp which had served for 17 years as Guam's station supply ship before World War II. 4 illus., map.   J. K. Ohl

507. LaFeber, Walter. ROOSEVELT, CHURCHILL, AND INDOCHINA, 1942-1945. *Am. Hist. R. 1975 80(5): 1277-1295.* During 1942-44 Franklin D. Roosevelt hoped to place the French colonies in Southeast Asia under an international trusteeship after the war. He further hoped that China would become the "policeman" in the area, and that the United States could work through China to stabilize and develop Southeast Asia. The president believed that once this precedent was established and China became a great power, the British colonies would also be given their independence and opened to world trade. Roosevelt thought little of the French and strongly disliked the new French leader, General Charles de Gaulle. Fully realizing Roosevelt's plans, Winston Churchill and the British Foreign Office concluded by 1943 that they needed de Gaulle's cooperation if British interests in Asia and Europe were to be protected after the war. As they worked to undercut Roosevelt's policy, they were helped by European specialists in the US Department of State, who also wanted to restore French power, and, most important, by the near-collapse of the Chinese government in 1944. After the summer of 1944 Roosevelt gave up in large measure on Chiang Kai-shek, and as he did so (and as Southeast Asia became less important to American military strategy), he slowly allowed the French to return to Southeast Asia. Above all, Roosevelt wanted an orderly, non-revolutionary Southeast Asia open to Western interests. It was therefore not illogical that when his trusteeship plan failed, he allowed the colonial powers to reenter the area.   A

508. Laidlaw, Lansing S. ALEUTIAN EXPERIENCE OF THE "MAD M." *Oregon Hist. Q. 1979 80(1): 30-49.* Although 47 years old, Lansing Laidlaw enlisted in the Coast Guard during World War II. Assigned to the USS *Arthur Middleton*, or "Mad M", Laidlaw saw action in the Aleutians and the South Pacific The *Arthur Middleton* was odered to the Aleutians and arrived in Constantine Harbor on Amchitka Island 12 January 1943. Soon afterward a storm blew the *Middleton* onto the rocks. The ship was finally refloated three months later and towed to Bremerton, Washington, for repairs. While on the rocks the *Middleton* was attacked frequently by Japanese air forces. However, despite the fact that the ship was aground the air attacks inflicted no serious damage. 8 illus.
D. R. McDonald

509. Lane, James B. A NOTE ON *STEEL SHAVINGS:* FAMILY HISTORIES OF THE CALUMET REGION. *Indiana Mag. of Hist. 1980 76(2): 123-128.* The first five annual issues of *Steel Shavings,* a publication committed to recording local history, as remembered by the people of the Calumet region of Indiana, are devoted to tales of the Great Depression, World War II, and Gary, Indiana. Based on *Steel Shavings;* 2 photos.   A. Erlebacher

510. Langer, John Daniel. THE HARRIMAN-BEAVERBROOK MISSION AND THE DEBATE OVER UNCONDITIONAL AID FOR THE SOVIET UNION, 1941. *J. of Contemporary Hist. [Great Britain] 1979 14(3): 463-482.* US presidential adviser Harry Hopkins, suggested a mission to Moscow to deter-

mine Russian needs after the Nazi invasion. In mid-September 1941 W. Averell Harriman, US lend-lease representative in London, and Lord Beaverbrook, British supply minister, met with Joseph Stalin and offered incredibly generous aid. It was vainly anticipated that the USSR would reciprocate with information. Instead the formal protocol sealing the conference was but a restatement of Allied promises of specific help. The United States treated the protocol as sacred and even after Pearl Harbor gave preference to supplies to Russia before meeting the needs of American forces. Friendship with the Soviet Union, in the interest of peace, was to be won at any price. Based on British and American archival sources; 70 notes. M. P. Trauth

511. Langer, John Daniel. THE "RED GENERAL": PHILIP R. FAYMONVILLE AND THE SOVIET UNION, 1917-52. *Prologue 1976 8(4): 209-221.* Brigadier General Philip R. Faymonville's long absorption in Soviet affairs brought him into a position of influence when the United States granted diplomatic recognition to the USSR in 1933. During his five years as military attaché in Moscow, 1933-38, he gained a reputation as a pro-Soviet observer, in spite of his often unfavorable opinion of Soviet actions. His overall positive stance toward Soviet affairs antagonized many of his military colleagues who assiduously worked, with ultimate success, to undermine his position. During World War II Harry Hopkins used Faymonville as his military representative on the Russian end of the Lend-Lease program. An unfavorable and biased report on Faymonville's loyalty and credibility, coupled with Franklin D. Roosevelt's failure to support him, caused the termination of the General's role in American-Soviet affairs. Based on records in the National Archives. N. Lederer

512. Langer, William L. WASHINGTON BUREAUCRAT AND DIPLOMATIC HISTORIAN. *Soc. for Hist. of Am. Foreign Relations. Newsletter 1978 9(2): 2-15, (3): 15-24.* Part I. Based on the author's memoirs, written in 1975; discusses his World War II and postwar diplomatic service in Great Britain, 1941-46. Part II. The author discusses his career as a diplomatic historian, relating his experience with historiography on Vichy France and US foreign policy, 1946-54; mentions European lecture tours and controversy over his published works.

513. Lansing, Marjorie. POLITICAL CHANGE FOR THE AMERICAN WOMAN. Iglitzin, Lynne B. and Ross, Ruth, eds. *Women in the World* (Santa Barbara, Ca.: Clio Books, 1976): pp. 175-181. The 19th-century feminist movement was begun by women abolitionists who wanted equality with men "in the state, the church and the home." After the passage of the 15th Amendment, which granted the vote to black men but not to women, the feminist movement directed its energies toward securing the vote for women. After the franchise was extended to women in 1920, the feminist movement remained largely inactive until the 1960's. Although there was no organized movement, the status of women changed dramatically during World War II when they entered the work force in large numbers. Concomitant to the rise in employment for women was a rise in the number of female voters. Moreover, the number of women voters increased as they became more educated. In recent years, women politicians have been increasingly accepted by the public. Secondary sources; 13 notes.
J. Holzinger

514. Laqueur, Walter. JEWISH DENIAL AND THE HOLOCAUST. *Commentary 1979 68(6): 44-55.* Describes the dissemination of information about Hitler's Final Solution during the 1940's and Jews' reluctance to believe the extent of Nazi genocide.

515. Laqueur, Walter. REWRITING HISTORY. *Commentary 1973 55(3): 53-63.* Revisionist historiography is found in the writings pertaining to Nazism, World War II, and the origins of the Cold War. S

516. Larsen, Lawrence H. GERALD NYE AND THE ISOLATIONIST ARGUMENT. *North Dakota Hist. 1980 47(1): 25-27.* Text of a speech bitterly critical of President Franklin D. Roosevelt (who was then rumored to be at a secret meeting with Churchill and Stalin) by noninterventionist North Dakota Republican Senator Gerald P. Nye in Chicago, Illinois, on 13 August 1941. "A rare and valuable document [because] few transcripts or tapes of addresses by noninterventionists exist in their entirety." Illus., 3 notes. G. L. Olson

517. Larsen, Lawrence H. WAR BALLOONS OVER THE PRAIRIE: THE JAPANESE INVASION OF SOUTH DAKOTA. *South Dakota Hist. 1979 9(2): 103-115.* In project FUGO, the Japanese launched thousands of armed balloons between late 1944 and August 1945 which were intended to land and explode in the United States. Of the 300 balloon landings, at least nine dropped on South Dakota. Because of military censorship, nothing about the balloons appeared in South Dakota newspapers until after the war. This attack caused an additional expenditure of time and money for American defense measures, but did not affect the outcome of the war, even though it represented the only prolonged threat against the continental United States during World War II. Primary sources; illus., 5 photos, 20 notes. P. L. McLaughlin

518. Larson, Arthur D. THE SECRET SIDE OF WAR: ANGLO-AMERICAN AND GERMAN INTELLIGENCE IN WORLD WAR II. *J. of Pol. & Military Sociol. 1980 8(1): 121-124.* Review article of David Kahn's *Hitler's Spies: German Military Intelligence in World War II* (New York: Macmillan, 1978) and Anthony Cave Brown's *Bodyguard of Lies* (New York: Harper and Row, 1975).

519. Lauderdale, William B. A PROGRESSIVE ERA FOR EDUCATION IN ALABAMA, 1935-1951. *Alabama Hist. Q. 1975 37(1): 38-67.* The progressive education movement reached its peak just before World War II. Alabama became one of the most important states in the progressive movement. The first educational innovations were introduced by Dr. C. B. Smith, Director of the Division of Instruction, who developed a problem-centered approach to education. He was followed by W. Morrison McCall. Peabody College consultants aided curriculum development. The practical application of the new ideas and their effect on the community is illustrated by a case study of the schools at Cold Springs and Fairview. World War II had a negative effect, and in 1951 a conservative was elected State Superintendent. 39 notes. E. E. Eminhizer

520. Laughlin, C. H. FERRY FLIGHT. *Am. Aviation Hist. Soc. J. 1978 23(1): 51-59.* The author discusses his part in ferrying airplanes from Accra, Gold Coast, to Kunming, China, 1942.

521. LaViolette, Forrest E. THE CANADIAN JAPANESE: A NEW LOOK. *Pacific Affairs [Canada] 1977 50(1): 107-111.* Review article prompted by Ken Adachi's *The Enemy That Never Was: A History of the Japanese Canadians.* The first Japanese immigrants came to Canada in 1877. Their acceptance in frontier Canada was restricted, racially biased, and feared. Vigorous measures by the Canadian government during World War II, which included concentration camps, were the most flagrant examples of the unfair and unjust treatment of persons of Japanese ancestry. Primary and secondary sources; 10 notes.
S. H. Frank

522. Lawrence, Derek. THE ENEMY UNSEEN. *Hist. Today [Great Britain] 1974 24(8): 534-541.* Traces the origins and development of submarines from the 17th century through World War II.

523. Lee, Carol F. THE ROAD TO ENFRANCHISEMENT: CHINESE AND JAPANESE IN BRITISH COLUMBIA. *BC Studies [Canada] 1976 (30): 44-76.* Traces the issue of Chinese and Japanese enfranchisement in British Columbia from 1935-49. Considers the events, trends, and concepts which finally eroded the long standing provincial hostility to Orientals. Enfranchisement symbolized a significant change in public attitudes and reflected a change in the prevailing conceptions of the nature of citizenship and political rights in Canada. 64 notes.
D. L. Smith

524. Leiser, Edward L. MEMOIRS OF PILOT ELWYN H. GIBBON, THE MAD IRISHMAN. *Am. Aviation Hist. Soc. J. 1978 23(1): 2-18.* Recounts the flying career of Elwyn H. Gibbon, an American who worked for various American airline companies, saw service in China, 1937-38, and was killed in a crash when flying out of Karachi, 1942.

525. Lemann, Nicholas. FROM WORLD WAR II TO CLAY FELKER: HOW AMERICA BOUGHT ITS WAY TO HAPPINESS. *Washington Monthly 1977 9(1): 5-12.* Reviews John Morton Blum's *V Was for Victory* (New York: Harcourt Brace Jovanovich, 1976), which deals with politics and American culture during World War II, specifically the ways in which the federal government was able to "sell" the war to the American public, 1940-45.

526. Leonard, Thomas M. STANLEY K. HORNBECK: MAJOR DETERRENT TO AMERICA-JAPANESE SUMMITRY, 1941. *Towson State J. of Internat. Affairs 1974 8(2): 113-121.*

527. Leonard, Thomas M. THE UNITED STATES AND WORLD WAR II: CONFLICTING VIEWS OF DIPLOMACY. *Towson State J. of Internat. Affairs 1972 7(1): 25-30.*

528. Leopold, Richard W. THE FOREIGN RELATIONS SERIES REVISITED: ONE HUNDRED PLUS TEN. *J. of Am. Hist. 1973 59(4): 935-957.* Summarizes the contents of 35 volumes of the *Foreign Relations* documents series for the years 1943-46, including the subseries of volumes on the conferences at Washington (1941-42), Casablanca (1943), Washington (1943), and Quebec (1943). The papers cover a broad spectrum of documents from embassy files and overseas posts and constitute a more complete record than those of a decade earlier. The prestige of the series has diminished due to a distrust of political

leaders, the time gap of 20 years, and the lack of serious reviews. Beginning with the 1947 volumes, the series will be systematically reviewed in *The Journal of American History.* 49 notes. K. B. West

529. Leopold, Richard W. HIROSHIMA THIRTY YEARS LATER. *Rev. in Am. Hist. 1976 4(3): 464-470.* Review article prompted by Margaret Gowing's two-volume study, *Independence and Deterrence: Britain and Atomic Energy, 1945-1952* (New York: St. Martin's Pr., 1974) and Martin J. Sherwin's *A World Destroyed: The Atomic Bomb and the Grand Alliance* (New York: Alfred A. Knopf, 1975) which discuss the impact of science on government, warfare, and foreign policymaking, 1938-52.

530. Leopold, Richard W. SARELL EVERETT GLEASON. *Massachusetts Hist. Soc. Pro. 1974 86: 90-94.* Everett Gleason (1905-74) was elected a member of the Massachusetts Historical Society in 1963. Ev Gleason was educated at Harvard, and taught medieval history there and at Amherst before entering a career in government beginning with World War II. He is best known as the coauthor (with William L. Langer) of the still-admired multivolume history entitled *The World Crisis and American Foreign Policy*, the story of US diplomacy in World War II. Gleason also served as editor of *Foreign Relations* from 1963-72. Based on an autobiographical sketch published in 1952, the author's personal friendship dating to 1937, letters from William L. Langer, Charles H. Taylor, Elting E. Morison, and Abbott Gleason, and materials provided by Malcolm Freiberg; index. G. W. R. Ward

531. Leutze, James. THE SECRET OF THE CHURCHILL-ROOSEVELT CORRESPONDENCE SEPTEMBER 1939-MAY 1940. *J. of Contemporary Hist. [Great Britain] 1975 10(3): 465-491.* A careful examination of the Roosevelt-Churchill file does not disclose a plot on the American side to get the USA in the war to help Britain. The revelations of the letters do include the spy case of Tyler Gatewood Kent, a code clerk in the American embassy, who had hundreds of classified documents in his possession when he was arrested and convicted in London in 1940. Kent had felt that Franklin D. Roosevelt was trying to involve the USA in the war while openly saying the opposite to the American people. More importantly, it is now clear that the United States broke neutrality, among other ways, by informing the British of German ship movements in the neutrality zone, of movements of Japanese ships, and of miscellaneous intelligence picked up in Berlin and Tokyo. An appendix lists FDR messages to Winston Churchill and Churchill messages to Roosevelt, 11 September 1939 to 20 May 1940. 89 notes. M. P. Trauth

532. Leutze, James R. TECHNOLOGY AND BARGAINING IN ANGLO-AMERICAN NAVAL RELATIONS: 1938-1946. *US Naval Inst. Pro. 1977 103(6): 50-66.* Between 1938 and 1946, the United States and Great Britain exchanged a great deal of technical information, although there were people on both sides who did not fully accept the arrangements that were worked out and who saw to it that the exchange of information proceeded very slowly, if at all. It was not until early 1941, when President Franklin D. Roosevelt signed the lend-lease act, that there began a more open and extensive exchange of technical and scientific information. Unfortunately, as in the matter of sharing atomic technology, there was much bitterness on the part of the British scientific commu-

nity regarding the outcome of the joint effort. Both sides often proved selfish; both sides were hard bargainers; and agreements were often overturned. Primary and secondary sources; 9 photos, 25 notes. A. N. Garland

533. Lewandowski, Richard B. THE PHANTOM GOVERNMENT: THE UNITED STATES AND THE RECOGNITION OF THE CZECHOSLOVAK REPUBLIC, 1939-1943. *Southern Q. 1973 11(4): 369-388.* Studies Germany's takeover of Czechoslovakia in 1939, mentioning activities of Germans, Americans, and Czechs, such as Eduard Beneš, Franklin D. Roosevelt, Cordell Hull, and Adolf Hitler. The decision by the United States not to recognize the Munich Agreement and the occupation of Czechoslovakia led to the creation of a government-in-exile by the Czechs. The United States steadfastly extended diplomatic recognition to this government throughout World War II. 72 notes.
R. W. Dubay

534. Lewis, Jerry D. A LONG JOURNEY... FIRST PURSUIT GROUP. *Aerospace Hist. 1977 24(1): 34-39.* Chronicles the 1st Pursuit Group in France, 5 May 1918, through its present designation, the First Tactical Fighter Wing, stationed at Langley AFB, Virginia. During World War I the group fought 1,413 aerial combats and destroyed more than 200 enemy aircraft and balloons. Two of its members, 1st Lieutenant Edward V. Rickenbacker and 2d Lieutenant Frank Luke, Jr., were awarded the Medal of Honor for action. After the war the unit was assigned to Selfridge Field, Michigan, as the 1st Pursuit Group. It was the only US pursuit group active during the 1920's. During World War II the First, flying P-38s, was sent to England where it first helped defend England, and then it participated in the North African and Italian campaigns. After the war the First was reactivated at March Field, California. In 1950 it was redesignated a fighter-interceptor unit. In 1955 it was moved to Selfridge AFB, Michigan, in 1970 to Hamilton AFB, California, and then to MacDill AFB, Florida. Since 1975 it has been stationed at Langley AFB, Virginia. Based on official sources. 12 photos, chronological list of aircraft flown by the Wing, and chronological list of duty stations of the Wing. C. W. Ohrvall

535. Libby, Justin H. THE AMERICAN-JAPANESE RELATIONS AND THE COMING WAR IN THE PACIFIC: A CONGRESSIONAL VIEW. *Pacific Hist. 1978 22(4): 379-390.* A study of congressional opinion regarding Japan during the final months of peace preceding the attack on Pearl Harbor. Earlier hesitancy to antagonize Japan was, by autumn, replaced by a climate of opinion favorable to belligerent measures. Four forces had effected the change: Japan's continuing threat to the status quo in Asia, sympathy for China's deteriorating plight, Tokyo's signing the Tripartite Pact, and American pressure groups lobbying for sanctioning legislation for action. An analysis of statements and calls to action by congressional leaders indicated a rapid shrinking of the influence of noninterventionists. Already, before Pearl Harbor, Congress had reversed itself, and was ready for confrontation. 50 notes. R. V. Ritter

536. Libby, Justin H. ANTI-JAPANESE SENTIMENT IN THE PACIFIC NORTHWEST: SENATOR SCHELLENBACH AND CONGRESSMAN COFFEE ATTEMPT TO EMBARGO JAPAN. *Mid-America 1976 58(3): 167-174.* Analyzes the efforts in the 1930's of Senator Lewis B. Schellenbach and Congressman John M. Coffee, Democrats of Washington State, to enact an

American embargo of Japan. Both were concerned with the fishing interests of their state, and this led to their anti-Japanese efforts. Both were noninterventionists and desired to keep the United States out of a war with Japan. A militarily weak Japan was also one of their objectives. Eventually, an anti-Japanese initiative was taken by Franklin D. Roosevelt in 1940, and it achieved what Schwellenbach and Coffee failed to do in Congress with outside support. Based on archival material, news accounts, and speeches; 22 notes. J. M. Lee

537. Libby, Justin H. THE IRRECONCILABLE CONFLICT: KEY PITTMAN AND JAPAN DURING THE INTERWAR YEARS. *Nevada Hist. Soc. Q. 1975 18(3): 128-139.* Analyzes the anti-Japanese views of Key Pittman during the period between the two world wars. Pittman, Chairman of the Senate Committee on Foreign Relations during the 1930's, worked unsuccessfully for stronger American resistance to Japanese aggression in the Far East. Based on primary and secondary sources; photo, 53 notes. H. T. Lovin

538. Libby, Justin H. SENATORS KING AND THOMAS AND THE COMING WAR WITH JAPAN. *Utah Hist. Q. 1974 42(4): 370-380.* Growing enmity toward Japan during the interwar years was mingled with hopes for renewed accord, and Utah's senators reflected these opposing views. Senator William King was fond of China and hostile toward Japan. Senator Elbert Thomas was a student of Japan, but as Japanese aggression intensified in the Orient, he moved gradually to an anti-Japanese position. By 1940 both men were in agreement. 3 photos, 42 notes. V. L. Human

539. Lichtenstein, Nelson. AMBIGUOUS LEGACY: THE UNION SECURITY PROBLEM DURING WORLD WAR II. *Labor Hist. 1977 18(2): 214-238.* Mass industrial unions gained in membership during World War II and solidified their position, but the wartime experience represents a transition from the aggressive period of the 1930's to a quiescent postwar stage. The unions achieved security at the expense of the rank-and-file and union democracy. Based on union records and reports of the National War Labor Board; 45 notes.
L. L. Athey

540. Lichtenstein, Nelson. AUTO WORKER MILITANCY AND THE STRUCTURE OF FACTORY LIFE, 1937-1955. *J. of Am. Hist. 1980 67(2): 335-353.* Analyzes United Automobile Workers of America (UAW) worker militancy concerning production standards and workplace discipline during 1937-55 and stresses the centralization of power in the UAW itself after World War II. Militancy in the 1930's arose from efforts by semiskilled workers to assert some control over the conditions of their labor. Changes in both the workforce and the factory itself spawned additional militancy during World War II at Detroit, Michigan. In attempting to influence production standards and factory discipline, UAW locals found themselves at odds with both industry management and the national union's leadership and goals. Based on personal interviews and other primary sources from the Archives of Labor History, Wayne State University, Detroit; 62 notes. T. P. Linkfield

541. Lichtenstein, Nelson. DEFENDING THE NO-STRIKE PLEDGE: CIO POLITICS DURING WORLD WAR II. *Radical Am. 1975 9(4-5): 49-76.* Discusses the Congress of Industrial Organizations' cooperation with govern-

ment and industry in forcing its members to forego strike activity during the war.

S

542. Liddell Hart, B. H. MARINES AND STRATEGY. *Marine Corps Gazette 1980 64(1): 22-31.* Using historical examples, particularly from World War II, emphasizes the strategic significance of amphibious forces such as those in the US Marine Corps.

543. Lindbergh, Anne Morrow. THE CHANGING CONCEPT OF HEROES. *Minnesota Hist. 1980 46(8): 306-311.* Anne Morrow Lindbergh reflects on the major crusades of Charles A. Lindbergh's life: aviation, antiwar sentiment about World War II, and the quality of life on earth, seeking clues of how they reflected both his roots and the aspirations of his times. A talk before the 1979 annual meeting of the Minnesota Historical Society, including the question and answer session; 2 illus., 10 notes. C. M. Hough

544. Linn, Don. ART AND THE AIRMAN: THE 192ND TACTICAL FIGHTER SQUADRON. *Am. Aviation Hist. Soc. J. 1979 24(2): 154-156.* Provides a brief introduction to, and shows photographs of, the artwork on the F-105 planes by members of the 192d Tactical Fighter Group of the Virginia Air National Guard beginning in 1977, a rediscovery of the nose art common on United States military planes during World War I, World War II, the Korean War, and Vietnam.

545. Littell, Franklin H. UPROOTING ANTISEMITISM: A CALL TO CHRISTIANS. *J. of Church and State 1975 17(1): 15-24.* Christian anti-Semitism, rooted in the theological teaching that Jews are guilty of the crucifixion of Christ, has had social and political implications, exhibited notably in the Holocaust of World War II, as well as in the theology and historiography of such anti-Semitic liberals as Arnold Toynbee.

546. Loebs, Bruce D. NAGASAKI: THE DECISION AND THE MISTAKE. *Rendezvous 1972 7(1): 53-69.* Discusses the background of the atomic bombing of Nagasaki, Japan, in 1945, emphasizing the roles of President Harry S. Truman, General Leslie Groves, Japan's Emperor Hirohito and the Potsdam Conference.

547. Lord, Walter. ORDEAL AT VELLA LAVELLA. *Am. Heritage 1977 28(4): 30-43.* In 1943, American survivors of a naval battle in the Solomon Islands landed on Vella Lavella. After months of avoiding contact with Japanese forces occupying the island, the men were rescued by the US Navy. 12 illus., map.

B. J. Paul

548. Lotchin, Roger W. THE METROPOLITAN-MILITARY COMPLEX IN COMPARATIVE PERSPECTIVE: SAN FRANCISCO, LOS ANGELES, AND SAN DIEGO, 1919-1941. *J. of the West 1979 18(3): 19-30.* During the interwar period, military planners and city boosters joined forces to create the Navy's Pacific Fleet and to build huge shore facilities near major metropolitan areas. Los Angeles and San Diego were the first to benefit by the naval expansion. Several factors delayed large Navy investments in the San Francisco Bay region until the mid-1930's. The civilian-military relationship was mutually beneficial: government money assisted urban commerce while the cities cooperated by pro-

viding harbor improvements and land donations. Study of the relationship of cities and the military offers new understanding of city politics and planning. Based on Congressional documents and on newspapers; 13 photos, 58 notes.

B. S. Porter

549. Louis, Henriette. RÉACTIONS AMÉRICAINES À LA DÉFAITE FRANÇAISE DE 1940: TÉMOIGNAGES ET ENSEIGNEMENT [American reactions to the defeat of France in 1940: eyewitnesses and lessons learned]. *Rev. d'Hist. de la Deuxième Guerre Mondiale [France] 1980 30(119): 1-16.* News and subsequent discussion of the defeat of France in 1940 helped cause a major shift in US policy from isolationism to war preparedness. A main theme of US discourse on the fall of France stressed the need to protect the country against the "fifth column," against subversion, espionage, and sabotage. Based on US preparedness literature; 37 citations.

G. H. Davis

550. Louis, J.-Henriette. XÉNOPHOBIE ET CONCEPTS DE "CINQUIÈME COLONNE" AUX ÉTATS-UNIS: 1939-1941 [Xenophobia and concepts of a Fifth Column in the United States: 1939-41]. *Rev. Française d'Études Américaines [France] 1980 5(9): 89-97.* During 1939-41, Americans came to fear a Fifth Column in their midst, whether Nazi or Communist (or both, since this was the period of the Stalin-Hitler Pact); this fear helped overcome the previously prevalent Anglophobia.

551. Love, Peter. CURTIN, MACARTHUR AND CONSCRIPTION, 1942-43. *Hist. Studies [Australia] 1977 17(69): 505-511.* Disputes the view of Paul Hasluck in *The Government and the People 1942-43* (Canberra, 1970) that Prime Minister John Curtin's appeal to the Australian Labor Party to allow the use of the Citizen Military Forces outside Australia was based on electoral calculations and a shrewd response to the campaign of the opposition. Recently available evidence of journalist F. T. Smith and British Liaison Officer G. Wilkinson suggests that General Douglas MacArthur influenced Curtin, and the move should be seen in the light of Curtin's appeal for greater assistance from the United States at a time when the Southwest Pacific was low on the list of global priorities. Official archival sources, private papers, and war histories.

W. D. McIntyre

552. Lovin, Hugh T. THE CIO AND THAT "DAMNABLE BICKERING" IN THE PACIFIC NORTHWEST 1937-1941. *Pacific Hist. 1979 23(1): 66-79.* In 1937, the Congress of Industrial Organizations (CIO) successfully invaded the AFL-dominated Pacific Northwest. But in spite of the initial success, national CIO officers were increasingly concerned about disputes among the CIO unionists. In 1940, John L. Lewis reprimanded them for their "damnable bickering." Two factions gradually emerged in the CIO ranks: the Opposition (rightists) and the Left. The latter favored America's isolation posture in the late 1930's, and was definitely pro-Soviet in its attitudes. However, after Germany attacked the USSR in 1941, the Left renounced the isolationism it had so fervently advocated. Gradually the Left lost its dominance and the "pork chop" unionists emerged triumphant on the eve of America's entry into World War II, to the relief of the Washington CIO leaders. Based largely on union publications such as the *Timberworker, Voice of the Federation,* and *Tacoma Labor Advocate,* on collections of personal papers as well as union archives, and on secondary sources; photo, 53 notes.

H. M. Parker, Jr.

553. Lowe, Thomas E. and Reinert, Earl. THE LAST LANCER. *Am. Aviation Hist. Soc. J. 1978 23(2): 112-119.* The YP-43 Lancer, built by Seversky Aircraft Corporation, from 1939 saw domestic service and service in China and India during World War II. Lancer was outmoded by aeronautic developments in Europe; its last known specimen was housed at Freemen Field in Seymour, Indiana, until 1959.

554. Lowe, Thomas E. RARE INTERSTATE BOMBER FLYS AGAIN. *Am. Aviation Hist. Soc. J. 1977 22(4): 308-311.* The Interstate Aircraft and Engineering Corporation of DeKalb, Illinois, built the TDR-1 torpedo and bombardment airplane for the Navy in 1943-44; in 1976 the National Air and Space Museum of the Smithsonian Institution donated the last known TDR-1 to the Antique Airplane Association-Airpower Museum of Blakesburg, Iowa, which sold it to Hurley Boehler, who has restored and flown the aircraft.
D. J. Engler

555. Ludlow, Peter W. THE INTERNATIONAL PROTESTANT COMMUNITY IN THE SECOND WORLD WAR. *J. of Ecclesiastical Hist. [Great Britain] 1978 29(3): 311-362.* During 1900-40 the ecumenical movement found expression in four main types of groups: international, inter-confessional bodies; international youth organizations; international confessional groups; and national committees with international links. Notwithstanding high ambitions on the eve of the war, the movement was divided on the main issues. The war revitalized the ecumenical movement, and was decisive in contributing to the emergence of a vigorous international religious community. Focuses on the history of the Scandinavian Lutherans, with particular attention to the Norwegian Church during the German occupation, and the Reformed Protestant churches of Switzerland, France, and Holland. Also discusses the relation of the above to the resistance movements and ecumenical relief organizations. Reviews the historiography of the various aspects of the subject, and draws attention to major archival collections in Europe and the United States. 301 notes.
P. H. Hardacre

556. Lukas, Richard C. THE BIG THREE AND THE WARSAW UPRISING. *Military Affairs 1975 39(3): 129-134.* Discusses the impact of the 1944 Warsaw uprising on the Big Three and analyzes the policies each power pursued during the crisis. It nearly ruptured the Allied alliance and may well have been the starting point of the Cold War. The Warsaw uprising demonstrated the importance for the USSR of a political settlement in Poland on their terms. Primary and secondary sources; 50 notes.
A. M. Osur

557. Lund, W. G. D. THE ROYAL CANADIAN NAVY'S QUEST FOR AUTONOMY IN THE NORTH WEST ATLANTIC: 1941-43. *Naval War Coll. Rev. 1980 33(3): 73-92.* In early 1941 the United States and Great Britain agreed that strategic responsibility for the Western Atlantic would rest with the United States when that nation entered the war. The United States did assume such responsibility. It is little remembered, however, that the US Navy contributed only 2% of the escort forces to the subsequent Battle of the Atlantic while Canada contributed 48%. With this force disparity and with the US Navy's relative inexperience in antisubmarine warfare (and the charge of its unwillingness to learn), little wonder that Canada was dissatisfied and sought to regain control of her own seapower. She finally succeeded and the revised relationships that were then established are reflected in those of today.
J

558. Lundestad, Geir. THE AMERICAN POLICY TOWARDS POLAND, 1943-1946. *Am. Studies in Scandinavia [Sweden] 1972 (8): 5-28.* Surveys the shifts of American policy toward Poland from public support in 1943 to the conviction three years later that Poland was totally under USSR control. Franklin D. Roosevelt's objective of ensuring postwar cooperation between the major powers and Harry S. Truman's interest in winning substantial economic concessions for the United States were both important relative to the recognition of a Polish government and the establishment of postwar Polish boundaries. Based on published government documents and secondary sources; biblio.

J. E. Findling

559. Lunt, J. D. OPERATION MARKET-GARDEN. *Army Q. and Defence J. [Great Britain] 1975 105(1): 22-24.* Review article, prompted by Cornelius Ryan's *A Bridge Too Far* (Hamish Hamilton), on the German defeat of the Allied airborne operation near Arnhem in the Netherlands in 1944.

560. Luttwak, Edward N. CHURCHILL AND US. *Commentary 1977 63(6): 44-49.* From 1933 until the outbreak of World War II, Winston Churchill warned constantly and in detail of the dangers of the German war threat and Hitler's ambitions, while Crown Ministers and "responsible" journals decried his militarism and patronized his lack of understanding the modern spirit of internationalism. Churchill refused to accept the fact that war was obsolete, as do many critics of US foreign policy today. He ignored establishment insistence on Germany's desire for peace and when British papers and the BBC ignored him he broadcast his predictions of war to American audiences. His prediction proved accurate and Britain went to war, a war Churchill was later to call "the unnecessary war" brought on by British and French refusal to take proper measures for military preparedness. The same warnings are reflected today, such as by Senator Henry Jackson, who fears a lack of preparedness due to current US foreign policy.

S. R. Herstein

561. MacCarthy, Esther. CATHOLIC WOMEN AND THE WAR: THE NATIONAL COUNCIL OF CATHOLIC WOMEN, 1919-1946. *Peace and Change 1978 5(1): 23-32.* Examines attitudes toward women and war in the National Catholic Welfare Conference; the National Council of Catholic Women actively participated in the peace movement, 1919-46.

562. MacCreary, Eugene. LA PROPAGANDE CINÉMATOGRAPHIQUE ET L'OPINION AMÉRICAINE: LES FILMS "POURQUOI NOUS COMBATTONS" [Moving picture propaganda and American opinion: The *Why We Fight* films]. *Rev. d'Hist. de la Deuxième Guerre Mondiale [France] 1976 (101): 63-86.* The *Why We Fight* series was produced by the US War Department to indoctrinate some eight million citizen-soldiers during World War II. General George C. Marshall ordered the production, and Frank Capra carried it out. Building upon US public opinion trends in the late 1930's, the series contrasted the "dark" and "evil" world of fascism with the "light" and "good" democracies. The films established credibility by discussing some allied faults and made extensive use of German propaganda films. The impact seems to have been effective during the war and probably affected American attitudes for decades thereafter. 64 notes.

G. H. Davis

563. MacDonald, Charles B.   HORROR IN THE HUERTGEN FOREST. *Am. Hist. Illus. 1972 7(2): 12-22.* The Allies sought to clear the Huertgen Forest of German units to protect their flank in the drive to pierce the Siegfried Line. General Courtney H. Hodges, 1st U.S. Army commander, sent General Norman D. Cota's 28th Infantry Division to do the job. The Germans were ordered by Hitler to stop the allied advance at the Roer River because the Huertgen Forest was considered critical to Hitler's counteroffensive. The battle left 6,184 casualties from the 28th Infantry and a total of 24,000 killed, captured, or wounded. Based on the author's *The Battle of Huertgen Forest* (Philadelphia: Lippincott, 1963); 12 illus.
D. Dodd

564. MacDonald, J. Fred.   GOVERNMENT PROPAGANDA IN COMMERCIAL RADIO: THE CASE OF *TREASURY STAR PARADE*, 1942-1943. *J. of Popular Culture 1978 12(2): 285-304.* The "Treasury Star Parade," a radio program sponsored by the Treasury Department during World War II, used propaganda techniques which appealed to basic American values, made an appeal for domestic unity, intimidated by direct threat, and portrayed the enemy as demonic and the Allies as noble, in order to sell war bonds, 1942-43.

565. MacDowell, Laurel Sefton.   THE FORMATION OF THE CANADIAN INDUSTRIAL RELATIONS SYSTEM DURING WORLD WAR TWO. *Labour [Canada] 1978 3: 175-196.* Union membership more than doubled during World War II, a period marked by labor unrest and antagonistic government-labor relations. Union opposition to wage controls and government's failure to enact collective bargaining legislation or to provide for labor representation on policymaking boards united the Trades and Labour Congress and the Canadian Labour Congress in a common front. The latter organization entered politics through an alliance with the Cooperative Commonwealth Federation. Strikes, political action, and Ontario legislation convinced the government to change its position; in 1944, it enacted an order-in-council to provide protection and legal status for union organizing and collective bargaining. The new policy became a model for postwar legislation. Primary sources; 74 notes.
W. A. Kearns

566. MacLean, Donald.   'QUEEN MARY' MEMORIES. *Blackwood's Mag. [Great Britain] 1974 316(1905): 59-73.* The *Queen Mary* was launched in September 1934 and made her maiden voyage from Southampton to New York in May 1936. Because of her 81,237-ton gross tonnage, the ship had an unpleasant roll that was not corrected until 1958. The ship transported troops during World War II. It has been suggested that the availability of the two Queens to transport troops shortened World War II by a year. In 1967, after 1000 Atlantic crossings, the *Queen Mary* made her final voyage to a permanent berth in Long Beach, California. Personal recollections.
S. R. Herstein

567. MacLean, Elizabeth Kimball.   JOSEPH E. DAVIES AND SOVIET-AMERICAN RELATIONS, 1941-1943. *Diplomatic Hist. 1980 4(1): 73-93.* The personal contacts which Joseph Edward Davies had established with Soviet leaders during his tenure as US ambassador to the USSR (1937-38) enabled him to serve as an unofficial personal liaison between the White House and the Soviet Embassy in Washington in the early years of World War II. Retaining the confidence of both sides, he was able to explain to each the views of the other.

After a last official mission to Soviet Premier Joseph Stalin in 1943, he became less influential, for growing tensions between the two countries made a continuation of his role impossible. 56 notes. T. L. Powers

568. Maddox, Robert Franklin. THE POLITICS OF WORLD WAR II SCIENCE: SENATOR HARLEY M. KILGORE AND THE LEGISLATIVE ORIGINS OF THE NATIONAL SCIENCE FOUNDATION. *West Virginia Hist. 1979 41(1): 20-39.* Discusses the role of West Virginia Democratic Senator Harley M. Kilgore in the creation of the National Science Foundation from 1942, when Kilgore found the wartime administrative machinery for science and technology to be confusing, to 1950, when President Harry S. Truman signed the bill creating the National Science Foundation. Opponents of the bill included Vannevar Bush and Alexander Smith. 140 notes. J. D. Neville

569. Maddox, Robert J. BANDITS OVER CLARK FIELD. *Am. Hist. Illus. 1974 9(3): 20-27.* In the Japanese attack on Clark Field, Philippines, immediately after the attack on Pearl Harbor in December 1941, the loss of US men and materiel in the attack revealed basic unpreparedness for war.

570. Maddox, Robert J. HARRY S. TRUMAN'S EARLY MONTHS IN THE WHITE HOUSE. *Am. Hist. Illus. 1972 7(4): 12-22.* A brief history of Harry S. Truman and the issues behind the Potsdam Conference. S

571. Maddox, Robert James. ATOMIC DIPLOMACY: A STUDY IN CREATIVE WRITING. *J. of Am. Hist. 1973 59(4): 925-934.* Gar Alperovitz's *Atomic Diplomacy: Hiroshima and Potsdam: The Use of the Atomic Bomb and the American Confrontation with Soviet Power* (New York: Simon and Schuster, 1965) has become a staple of New Left historiography, but Alperovitz' use of his sources distorts and misrepresents the evidence. Arguments cited in support of his thesis in fact refer to other subjects, time sequences are altered, key words are deleted which would invalidate the arguments, certain words are given a sinister weight they do not deserve, and some statements are contradicted by their very sources. The uncritical reception of this lamentable scholarship points to shortcomings in the critical mechanisms of the profession. 43 notes. K. B. West

572. Maddux, Thomas R. WATCHING STALIN MANEUVER BETWEEN HITLER AND THE WEST: AMERICAN DIPLOMATS AND SOVIET DIPLOMACY, 1934-1939. *Diplomatic Hist. 1977 1(2): 140-154.* Most American diplomats residing in the USSR during the late 1930's agreed that Soviet Russia was an unacceptable ally, despite a general difference in assessment of Soviet policy between Soviet specialists, such as George F. Kennan, and other American officers, such as William C. Bullitt. Consequently, they opposed President Franklin D. Roosevelt's efforts to promote Soviet-American cooperation. Furthermore, their evaluations of the 1930's tended to mold their interpretation of Soviet actions after 1945. Unfortunately, these diplomats underestimated the importance of Stalin's overtures to the West and thus failed to fully exploit the possibility of undermining Soviet cooperation with Nazi Germany. Based on primary and secondary sources; 43 notes. G. H. Curtis

573. Maeda, Laura. LIFE AT MINIDOKA: A PERSONAL HISTORY OF THE JAPANESE-AMERICAN RELOCATION. *Pacific Hist. 1976 20(4): 379-387.* During World War II Japanese American Tomeji Mukaida and his

family were sent to a relocation camp at Minidoka, Idaho organized by military procedure. Hardships were numerous, and some stigma have remained to the present. 2 illus., biblio. G. L. Olson

574. Maginnis, John J. MY SERVICE WITH COLONEL DAVID MARCUS. *Am. Jewish Hist. 1980 69(3): 301-324.* There is growing interest in the career of Colonel David Marcus (1902-48), the American organizer of Israeli guerrilla forces in 1948, who became Israel's first general. Marcus's World War II service in Europe, however, has been inaccurately depicted in films. John J. Maginnis, now a retired major general, was on duty with the Berlin District Headquarters when Marcus first arrived as an observer in 1944, and later returned as Secretary of the US Control Council for Germany, 1945-46. This memoir is based on his experiences with Marcus during this time. Based on the author's recollections. J. D. Sarna

575. Makabe, Tomoko. CANADIAN EVACUATION AND NISEI IDENTITY. *Phylon 1980 41(2): 116-125.* The experience of Japanese Canadians was much harsher and more unjust than that of thier counterparts in the United States. However, the Nisei in Canada go to painstaking lengths to avoid consideration of the forced evacuation experience during World War II. The evacuation provided the Nisei with a strong subconscious determination to become fully integrated and assimilated into the Anglo-Canadian society. 14 notes.
N. G. Sapper

576. Mal'kov, V. L. GARRI GOPKINS: STRANITSY POLITICHESKOI BIOGRAFII [Harry Hopkins: pages from a political biography]. *Novaia i Noveishaia Istoriia [USSR] 1979 (3): 108-126, (4): 129-144.* Continued from a previous article (see abstract 17A:7096). Part II. In 1938 Franklin D. Roosevelt's foreign policy was fluctuating, and he shifted priorities away from social welfare toward a buildup of armaments and maintenance of America's international standing. Hopkins believed that admonitions to Hitler were useless and dangerous. He was an influence behind Roosevelt's decision to run for the presidency a third time. In March 1941 he became an official advisor to Roosevelt and attended cabinet meetings. Hopkins was relieved when war on the Eastern Front broke out, as this took pressure off England. Nevertheless, he always had words of praise for the Soviet Union's courage. 78 notes. Part III. A treaty of mutual agreement was signed on 11 June 1942 between the USSR and the United States but the second front did not appear immediately. In the autumn and winter of 1942 Hopkins was already beginning to dwell on postwar Soviet-American relations and sought to make the world more stable for American ambitions. This tendency was apparent in the Teheran declaration of 1943 when the United States, Britain, and the Soviet Union agreed to continue to work together in a peaceful world. Hopkins's influence on American political strategy declined sharply from the end of 1944. During his career he was attacked by conservatives, but he always defended a conservative position. He died on 29 January 1946. 69 notes. L. J. Seymour

577. Manchester, William. THE MAN WHO COULD SPEAK JAPANESE. *Am. Heritage 1975 27(1): 36-39, 91-95.* The story of Harold Dumas, a con-artist who convinced the Marines he could speak Japanese. Serving in the 29th Marine battalion in the Pacific, Dumas was exposed when he tried his line on a graduate of one of the military's Japanese language schools. 2 illus. J. F. Paul

578. Manchester, William. A SECOND LANDING FINALLY ENDS THE WAR. *Marine Corps Gazette 1980 64(4): 53-60.* Personal account of the author's return to Okinawa in 1978 to recall his experiences as a Marine there in 1945 during World War II.

579. Mandelbaum, Michael. THE POLITICAL LESSONS OF TWO WORLD WAR II NOVELS: A REVIEW ESSAY. *Pol. Sci. Q. 1979 94(3): 515-522.* Reviews Herman Wouk's *The Winds of War* (Boston: Little, Brown, 1971) and *War and Remembrance* (Boston: Little, Brown, 1978) and points out that although Wouk's works have been disparaged by most literary critics and totally ignored by historians, the fictional approach to the momentous historical events of the last 40 years is an effective means of depicting deeply felt human reactions to the horrors of war and its aftermath. 11 notes.   S

580. Maness, Lonnie E. A WEST TENNESSEE TOWN AND WORLD WAR II. *West Tennessee Hist. Soc. Papers 1978 (32): 110-119.* Chronicles the response of the people, newspapers, and the University of Tennessee Junior College of Martin, Tennessee, to World War II, beginning with the Lend-lease program. Briefly sketches some Martin men. The community whole-heartedly embraced the war effort. Based on local newspaper accounts and oral interviews; 5 photos, 32 notes.   H. M. Parker, Jr.

581. Manley, J. H. ASSEMBLING THE WARTIME LABS. *Bull. of the Atomic Scientists 1974 30(5): 42-47.* Reminisces about wartime nuclear physics, work in the Massachusetts Institute of Technology Radiation Laboratory, and the Manhattan Project.

582. Mann, Arthur J. PUBLIC EXPENDITURE PATTERNS IN THE DOMINICAN REPUBLIC AND PUERTO RICO 1930-1970. *Social and Econ. Studies [Jamaica] 1975 24(1): 47-82.* Provides data on the growth of public expenditures in the Dominican Republic and Puerto Rico and attempts to identify the reasons for the growth of the public sector. The surplus earned during World War II and increased public acceptance are important reasons for the growth. Finds many similarities in the public spending of the two countries. 6 tables, 24 notes, 29 refs., 3 data appendixes.   E. S. Johnson

583. Mann, Peggy. THE DENTIST AND THE BISHOP: "I KNEW THE MAN WAS A SATAN...." *Present Tense 1974 1(4): 29-35.* Charles H. Kremer has tried to expose Rumanian (now US-based) Bishop Valerian Trifa's role in the murder of Jews during World War II.

584. Markovits, Györgyi. A KANADAI MAGYAR MUNKÁS 1944-BEN [The *Canadian Hungarian Worker* in 1944]. *Magyar Könyvszemle [Hungary] 1979 95(2): 194-197.* The Communist-oriented weekly *Canadian Hungarian Worker* was founded in 1929 by István Szőke. In 1944, it called for the Hungarians to join the fight against Nazism and supported the cause of the USSR. Plate.
R. Hetzron

585. Markowitz, Samuel H. AUTOBIOGRAPHY. *Am. Jewish Arch. 1972 24(2): 128-159.* Reminiscences of a life beginning in Pottstown, Pennsylvania, and culminating in Philadelphia. The author was educated at Bucknell University, where he converted to Christianity and briefly was a Baptist preacher. He

repented soon after, enrolled in the Hebrew Union College in Cincinnati, and became a Reform rabbi. He held pulpits in Lafayette, Indiana, Fort Wayne, Indiana, and Elmira, New York, and was a chaplain during World War II. After the war he became rabbi at the Beth David Reform Congregation in Philadelphia. His primary goal was the re-Judaization of the homes of the members of his various congregations. 2 photos. E. S. Shapiro

586. Marshall, S. L. A. COMBAT BEHAVIOR OF INFANTRY TROOPS. Karsten, Peter, ed. *The Military in America: From the Colonial Era to the Present* (New York: Free Pr., 1980): 333-343. Presents excerpts from the author's book, *Men Against Fire* (1961), which was the result of a study of G.I. combat behavior during World War II.

587. Marshall, S. L. A. GENESIS TO REVELATION. *Military Rev. 1972 52(2): 17-24.* Author discusses his military experiences, 1919-69, including anecdotes concerning both World Wars.

588. Martin, Tony. MARCH ON WASHINGTON MOVEMENT. *J. of African-Afro-American Affairs 1979 3(1): 63-69.* Originally organized in 1941 by A. Philip Randolph and Milton Webster, the March on Washington Movement (which threatened a massive march on Washington, DC, of 10,000 blacks) succeeded in obtaining Executive Order 8802 which proscribed discrimination in defense-related industries and indirectly influenced the establishment of the Fair Employment Practices Committee and then began efforts to end segregation in the armed forces before it lost momentum in 1944.

589. Mashberg, Michael. DOCUMENTS CONCERNING THE AMERICAN STATE DEPARTMENT AND THE STATELESS EUROPEAN JEWS, 1942-1944. *Jewish Social Studies 1977 39(1-2): 163-182.* A collection of documents from the papers of Franklin D. Roosevelt's wartime Secretary of the Treasury, Henry M. Morgenthau, Jr., indicates the efforts of the Treasury Department to investigate and bring to the attention of the President the role of State Department officials in preventing any tangible efforts to rescue European Jewry from extermination at the hands of the Nazis. Treasury Department investigators, especially general counsel Randolph E. Paul, believed that the State Department prevented Jewish rescue through procrastination and failure to act, that it refused to work with private rescue agencies, that it prevented public disclosure of news about the exterminations, and that it covered up its role in regard to the Jewish situation. The actions of Morgenthau and his staff finally resulted in the creation of the War Refugee Board and efforts to retrieve refugees from the hands of the Nazis. Based on documents in the Franklin D. Roosevelt Library.
 N. Lederer

590. Mashberg, Michael. PREJUDICE THAT MEANT DEATH: THE WEST AND THE HOLOCAUST. *Patterns of Prejudice [Great Britain] 1978 12(3): 19-32.* Examines social and scientific attitudes toward Jews, 1880's-1900's, and their effects on US immigration quotas in the 20th century and later, during World War II, on the lethargy displayed by the US government and other Allied governments as well as other Allied nations in organizing the rescue of European Jews.

591. Massicotte, Guy. LES ÉDITORIALISTES CANADIENS-FRANÇAIS ET LES ORIGINES DE LA SECONDE GUERRE MONDIALE [French Canadian editorialists and the origins of World War II]. *Recherches Sociographiques [Canada] 1976 17(2): 139-165.* Juxtaposes the opinions of eight contemporary historians concerning the origins of World War II with the perceptions of French Canadian editorialists writing in five newspapers during 1938-39. The editorialists perceived the movement of international politics in the same light as the contemporary historians. 91 notes. A. E. LeBlanc

592. Matheny, Robert L. LUMBERING IN THE WHITE MOUNTAINS OF ARIZONA, 1919-1942. *Arizona and the West 1976 18(3): 237-256.* Promotion to establish large-scale commercial lumbering in eastern Arizona's White Mountains began as early as 1910. Encouraged by several federal agencies and war needs, companies went into operation in 1919. The efforts proved frustrating and unprofitable in the postwar recession. New investors took over but met financial ruin during the Great Depression. Recapitalized in 1935, the operations limped along until World War II made the White Mountain lumber industry profitable. 7 illus., map, 46 notes. D. L. Smith

593. Mathews, Edward J. WHAT SHIP IS THAT? *US Naval Inst. Pro. 1978 104(7): 61-73.* Shortly after the Japanese attack on Pearl Harbor on 7 December 1941, the US Navy's Director of Naval Intelligence created The Identification and Characteristics Section, Division of Naval Intelligence. Its mission entailed the dissemination of data on the appearance of both friendly and enemy vessels. Eventually, this section also took on the preparation and distribution of ship information for the Allied nations as well. The information was drawn from various sources, and the work of this office was recognized for its importance throughout the war. 17 photos. A. N. Garland

594. Mathews-Klein, Yvonne. HOW THEY SAW US: IMAGES OF WOMEN IN NATIONAL FILM BOARD FILMS OF THE 1940'S AND 1950'S. *Atlantis [Canada] 1979 4(2): 20-33.* Discusses films by the National Film Board of Canada during 1940's-50's depicting conflicting sex roles evident in film titles such as *Women at War, Wings on Her Shoulders, Careers and Cradles,* and *Is It a Woman's World?*

595. Matray, James I. AN END TO INDIFFERENCE: AMERICA'S KOREAN POLICY DURING WORLD WAR II. *Diplomatic Hist. 1978 2(2): 181-196.* After Pearl Harbor, it became evident to US policymakers that future peace in Asia would depend upon postwar stability in Korea. Thanks to 40 years of Japanese domination of the country, an independent government of inexperienced and unprepared Koreans would probably have been unable to maintain that stability in the face of British imperialism, Chinese expansionism, and Soviet Communism. President Franklin D. Roosevelt advocated an international trusteeship for postwar Korea, believing that such an arrangement would bring stability without encouraging imperialism, while preparing Koreans for eventual independence. 67 notes. T. L. Powers

596. Matzozky, Eliyho. AN EPISODE: ROOSEVELT AND THE MASS KILLING. *Midstream 1980 26(7): 17-19.* Examines the attitudes of Franklin D. Roosevelt's administration toward the known destruction of European Jews and Jewish pressure for an active rescue policy.

597. Maurer, D. W. LANGUAGE AND THE SEX REVOLUTION: WORLD WAR I THROUGH WORLD WAR II. *Am. Speech 1976 51(1-2): 5-24.* The dramatic change toward a freer attitude in respect to sexual mores from those of the Victorian Era coalesced in the United States at the end of World War I. The Jazz Age of the 1920's brought about looser attitudes reflected in even politely accepted language. The Great Depression broke down some of the final resistance in society between separate moral codes for males and females further advanced by wartime conditions.　　　　　　　　　　　　　D. A. Yanchisin

598. Mazunan, George T. and Walker, Nancy. RESTRICTED AREAS: GERMAN PRISONER-OF-WAR CAMPS IN WESTERN NEW YORK, 1944-1946. *New York Hist. 1978 59(1): 55-72.* Discusses the organization and administration of prisoner-of-war camps in western New York, from Naples to Fredonia, where 4,500 Germans were encamped during 1944-46. Because of the shortage of civilian labor during World War II, German prisoners were employed in the region's agricultural and food processing industries. Describes the conditions of such prison labor. 7 illus., 37 notes.　　　　　　　　　　　　　R. N. Lokken

599. Mazuzan, George T. THE NATIONAL WAR SERVICE CONTROVERSY, 1942-1945. *Mid-America 1975 57(4): 246-258.* Mobilization needs after US entry into World War II prompted some, including Grenville Clark's Citizens' Committee, to lobby for a national service law. Paul W. McNutt's War Manpower Commission study subcommittee, influenced by anticompulsion capital and labor and a divided cabinet, wished postponement of legislative activity. Clark turned to Congress, wherein Congressman Wadsworth and Senator Austin, though fearing centralization, introduced such legislation followed by lengthy hearings, postponement, Roosevelt's vacillation, and vociferous labor opposition. The controversy did not die down until the substitute May-Bailey and Austin-Wadsworth Bills were defeated and the war ended. Based on Dorr, Clark, Wadsworth, and other papers, National Archives and Library of Congress; Roosevelt, Hopkins, Rosenman papers, Roosevelt Library and secondary sources; 49 notes.
T. H. Wendel

600. McArdle, Kenneth. CHURCHILL TALKS TO AMERICA. *Am. Heritage 1973 25(1): 56-61, 77.* Discusses Winston Churchill's comments about and advice to the American people in the course of his career, particularly his exhortations to the United States during World War II.　　　　　　　　　　　S

601. McBride, Robert M. DON'T BOUNCE OFF THE TREES. *Am. Heritage 1975 26(5): 72-76.* Relates the author's experiences as a lighter-than-air pilot for the US Navy during World War II. 8 illus.　　　　　　　　　　　　J. F. Paul

602. McCain, William D. SOME REMINISCENCES OF THE UNITED STATES ARCHIVIST IN ITALY, 1944-45—DIRECTOR WILLIAM D. MC CAIN ON MILITARY LEAVE FROM MISSISSIPPI DEPARTMENT OF ARCHIVES AND HISTORY. *J. of Mississippi Hist. 1972 34(1): 1-28.* The author records his activities as an American archivist in Italy from June 1944 through August 1945 in "locating and protecting the records of ministries and offices moved north from Rome." Working with British and Italian archivists as a member of the Subcommission for Fine Arts, Monuments, and Archives, he helped to inspect various archival depositories and restore archival service in

northern Italy. Based largely on primary sources, chiefly a journal and the papers of the author; 55 notes. J. W. Hillje

603. McCandless, Bruce. INCIDENT IN THE NANPO SHOTO. *US Naval Inst. Pro. 1973 99(7): 67-77.* In February, 1945, the US Navy destroyer *Gregory* rescued three American airmen floating in the sea near the Japanese occupied island of Chichi Jima. Based on the reminiscences of the author, who was serving as commanding officer of the *Gregory*; 3 illus., map. J. K. Ohl

604. McCorkle, Charles M. THE NUMBER ONE FIGHTER OF WORLD WAR II? SPITFIRE VS MUSTANG. *Aerospace Hist. 1973 20(4): 170-177.* A comparison of the attributes of the P-51 Mustang and the Supermarine Spitfire.

605. McDaniel, Boyce. A PHYSICIST AT LOS ALAMOS. *Bull. of the Atomic Scientists 1974 30(10): 39-43.* Describes graduate studies at Cornell University in physics and the construction of the first plutonium bomb, at Los Alamos, New Mexico, 1940-45.

606. McElroy, John W. REACTION REPORT. *Am. Neptune 1979 39(4): 256-270.* Memoirs of service aboard the attack transport *Marathon* during the assault on Okinawa in April 1945. J. C. Bradford

607. McEvoy, Fred. CANADIAN-IRISH RELATIONS DURING THE SECOND WORLD WAR. *J. of Imperial and Commonwealth Hist. [Great Britain] 1977 5(2): 206-226.* Despite Ireland's choice to remain neutral during World War II, Canada, alone among the British Commonwealth, retained open and friendly relations with Ireland and often arbitrated when other Commonwealth countries attempted to harry Ireland from the group.

608. McGivern, Charles F. BUSH NAVIGATION IN THE SOLOMON ISLANDS. *US Naval Inst. Pro. 1974 100(2): 68-72.* In 1943, US submarines operating in the Solomon Islands discovered that for many of the clandestine missions on which they were dispatched their charts were almost useless. Describes one such mission by the US submarine *Gato* in April 1943 to Tropasino Plantat on the northeast coast of Bougainville, and the crew's successful solutions to the navigational problems encountered. Map, 2 photos. A. N. Garland

609. McGovern, James R. PENSACOLA, FLORIDA: A MILITARY CITY IN THE NEW SOUTH. *Florida Hist. Q. 1980 59(1): 24-41.* Pensacola underwent urbanization as the result of its Naval Air Station, not of industrialization. Immigrants from nearby rural areas diluted the military presence. The city's evolution suggests a model for other southern cities influenced by the presence of military bases. Covers 1900-45. Based on reports in the *Pensacola Journal,* census returns, and city and county statistical records; 75 notes.
N. A. Kuntz

610. McGuire, Phillip. JUDGE HASTIE, WORLD WAR II, AND ARMY RACISM. *J. of Negro Hist. 1977 62(4): 351-362.* William Hastie, the first Afro-American appointed to the federal bench as US District Court Judge for the Virgin Islands (1937-39), left the deanship of the Howard University Law School to serve as a civilian aide to the Secretary of War (1940-43). Although Secretary Henry L. Stimson asked Hastie to be responsible for all black military personnel, most of Hastie's activities related to the US Army. The aide resigned in 1943 in

protest against the racism of the military establishment. The integration of the armed forces by executive order in 1948 was the legacy of Hastie's efforts. Based on primary materials in the Library of Congress, National Archives, the Yale University Library, and secondary sources; 34 notes. N. G. Sapper

611. McGuire, Phillip. JUDGE WILLIAM H. HASTIE AND ARMY RECRUITMENT, 1940-1942. *Military Affairs 1978 42(2): 75-79.* Discusses the work of Judge William H. Hastie, Civilian Aide to the Secretary of War, to persuade the War Department to include the black press in its military recruitment program during 1940-42. Hastie was charged with helping form and implement policies to effectively utilize blacks in the Army. Hastie considered the black press the best medium to aid him in his recruitment campaign. He did increase the number of blacks in the Army, although with great difficulty. Based on the papers of the Civilian Aide and NAACP; 27 notes. A. M. Osur

612. McGuire, Phillip. JUDGE WILLIAM H. HASTIE CIVILIAN AIDE TO THE SECRETARY OF WAR, 1940-1943. *Negro Hist. Bull. 1977 40(3): 712-713.* Evaluates William H. Hastie's fight against racism in the armed forces during World War II. Although unable to convince the War Department to integrate the Army, he helped bring about military reform: the admission of Blacks to officer candidate schools, acceptance of Blacks as blood donors, integration of some recreational facilities, the commissioning of black doctors in the Army Medical Reserve, the training of black pilots as heavy bombardment fliers, the participation of black schools in the Air Force enlistment program, and the beginning of experiments with integrated units. Based on the author's unpublished dissertation; photo, note, biblio. R. E. Noble

613. McIlvenna, Don E. THE HUGHES SUPERPLANE AND THE SECOND FRONT CLAMOR DURING WORLD WAR II. *Southern California Q. 1975 57(4): 371-382.* Appraises the construction of the Hughes HK-1, the largest aircraft ever built, in the light of the climate of thinking about a second front in 1942. Editorials and public opinion polls indicated a large segment of the American people favored an immediate second front against Germany in support of Russia's fight. One alternative to the commitment of large numbers of ground troops was massive movement of supplies, not by sea but by air. Merchant ships invited attack by German submarines, but aircraft could supply men and materiel with relative ease and at little cost. Such views were promoted by Alexander de Seversky, author of *Victory Through Air Power*, and shipbuilder Henry J. Kaiser. In September 1942 the government let out contracts for the construction of plywood superplanes, of which the HK-1 was the only one to be completed, and not until after the war had ended. The beginnings of the project can thus be seen in the fears of the American people that the war could be lost, and the hope that a superplane would make a difference in winning. Based on primary sources, newspapers, published records, and secondary works; 25 notes. A. Hoffman

614. McKenney, Janice. MORE BANG FOR THE BUCK IN THE INTERWAR ARMY: THE 105-MM. HOWITZER. *Military Affairs 1978 42(2): 80-86.* Surveys US Army artillery developments during 1930's-41 and the attitude of artillerymen toward the 75 mm. gun and the 105 mm. howitzer. "It was not until after the fall of France in June 1940 that the War Department made a concerted effort to replace the obsolete 75-mm. gun with the 105-mm. howitzer,

the weapon that was to become the backbone of the divisional artillery in World War II." Primary and secondary sources; 30 notes. A. M. Osur

615. McKenzie, Robert H. CLIO'S PARTNERS: THE SIGNIFICANCE OF ALABAMA HISTORY AND THE CONTRIBUTIONS OF ITS CONTEMPORARY HISTORIANS. *Alabama R. 1975 28(4): 243-259.* Overview of historical studies produced by both professional and amateur historians that have appeared in the *Alabama Review*, relating major local, state, regional, and national themes and topics. Contributions for the Civil War, Reconstruction, the Populist-Progressive eras, and the black experience predominate, while comparatively few deal with the Depression, World War II, and recent events. Secondary sources; 23 notes, biblio. J. F. Vivian

616. McLaren, David R. THE NORTH AMERICAN AVIATION P-51H MUSTANG (PART I). *Am. Aviation Hist. Soc. J. 1980 25(2): 124-139.* Describes the P-51H Mustang produced in 1944 after North American Aviation Corporation engineers had spent one year improving other Mustangs, and traces the development and testing of that airplane until 1952. Article to be continued.

617. McMillan, George. RETURN TO SOPAC. *Marine Corps Gazette 1971 55(11): 48-54.* Describes changes in the environment of south Pacific islands since they were invaded by US Marines during World War II.

618. McNeal, Patricia. CATHOLIC CONSCIENTIOUS OBJECTION DURING WORLD WAR II. *Catholic Hist. 1975 6(2): 222-242.* Focuses on Catholic conscientious objection in World War II. During the war there were 135 Catholics among 11,887 individuals who registered their dissent within the law and were granted conscientious objector (CO) status. These men were placed in Civilian Public Service (CPS) camps. The CPS was created by the Historic Peace Churches as a means of alternative service. The only Catholic group to support CO's was the Catholic Worker. A special group which emerged from the Catholic Worker for this purpose was the Association of Catholic Conscientious Objectors (ACCO). During the war, the ACCO operated two CPS camps for Catholic CO's, published a newspaper, and also worked with 61 Catholics who were imprisoned because they refused to register their dissent within the law. There is no way to show the precise relationship of the Catholic faith to the personal decisions of these men. It is most significant, however, that 73 per cent contended that their faith had a bearing on their decision.

619. Meerse, David E. TO REASSURE A NATION: HOLLYWOOD PRESENTS WORLD WAR II. *Film and Hist. 1976 6(4): 79-91.* Most of the films which Hollywood produced during World War II served as propaganda to keep Americans at home assured that involvement was correct and that America was triumphing in its war effort.

620. Melosi, Martin V. NATIONAL SECURITY MISUSED: THE AFTERMATH OF PEARL HARBOR. *Prologue 1977 9(2): 75-89.* Throughout World War II, the Roosevelt Administration sought to retain absolute secrecy over the circumstances resulting in the Japanese bombing of Pearl Harbor, in order to preserve vital aspects of national security, especially in regard to intelligence operations. The administration attempted to end growing public interest in the matter by casting all blame upon the military commanders on the scene, Admiral

Husband E. Kimmel and Major General Walter C. Short, blaming them for failing to take proper precautions to meet the surprise attack. Roosevelt's obfuscation of this issue had the result of generating more public suspicions of the manner in which the war was being conducted and of providing the Republican opposition with a readymade political issue which they were not slow to exploit. Largely based on Congressional hearings and materials in the National Archives.

N. Lederer

621. Melosi, Martin V. POLITICAL TREMORS FROM A MILITARY DISASTER: 'PEARL HARBOR' AND THE ELECTION OF 1944. *Diplomatic Hist. 1977 1(1): 79-95.* Discusses the debate between Republicans and the Roosevelt administration over personal responsibility for the Pearl Harbor disaster. Republicans failed, however, to make this a vital issue in the 1944 presidential campaign. Criticism of Franklin D. Roosevelt's policies was difficult to achieve while the nation was still at war. Republican presidential nominee Thomas E. Dewey was "reluctant to make a stand on an issue that smacked of disloyalty," and he could not "exploit one spectacular issue—the breaking of the Japanese code—which might give the Republican criticisms legitimacy." Furthermore, the Roosevelt administration effectively denied the release of information which might aid the Republicans. Primary and secondary sources; 49 notes.

G. H. Curtis

622. Mendelsohn, John. TRIAL BY DOCUMENT: THE PROBLEM OF DUE PROCESS FOR WAR CRIMINALS AT NUERNBERG. *Prologue 1975 7(4): 227-234.* The Nuremberg trials pioneered the massive use of documents as court evidence against large groups of defendants. To convict officials who gave orders but did not execute them personally, the prosecution relied heavily on Nazi records. The defendants were treated fairly, considering the intense hatreds engendered by World War II. The prosecution enjoyed easier access to documents in the early cases, and case procedures were disadvantageous to SS defendants. "Yet considering the crimes charged one wonders if there were many exonerating records at all." Primary and secondary sources; 6 photos, 31 notes.

W. R. Hively

623. Mihelich, Dennis N. WORLD WAR II AND THE TRANSFORMATION OF THE OMAHA URBAN LEAGUE. *Nebraska Hist. 1979 60(3): 401-423.* Examines the activities of the Omaha Urban League which was started in 1928. Indicates that while the league entered the war period as a dispenser of social services, it emerged from it as a mediator for social justice. In the former capacity it enhanced the quality of life for a significant number in the black community; in the latter capacity it helped to initiate the struggle to include blacks in the mainstream of American life. 4 photos, map, 54 notes.

R. Lowitt

624. Mikesh, Robert C. THE EMPEROR'S ENVOYS. *Air Force Mag. 1975 58(8): 62-67.* Two Japanese members of the delegation to General Douglas MacArthur's headquarters in Manila describe their part in the surrender arrangements at at the end of World War II.

625. Millar, T. B. TWO NEW WORLDS: THE UNITED STATES AND AUSTRALIA. *Round Table [Great Britain] 1976 (263): 243-248.* Examines similarities in the historical development of Australia and America, their ties with Great Britain, links with Europe, and the shared concerns which led to the formation of ANZUS. World War II outlined the common American-Australian interests in the Pacific, while fear of Japanese resurgence after the war convinced the Australian government that only American power could provide adequate defense in the area. The two countries no longer demonstrably need each other today, but a wide range of financial, industrial, and personal links have sustained a close relationship.
C. Anstey

626. Miller, James E. CARLO SFORZA E L'EVOLUZIONE DELLA POLITICA AMERICANA VERSO L'ITALIA: 1940-1943 [Carlo Sforza and the evolution of American policy toward Italy: 1940-43]. *Storia Contemporanea [Italy] 1976 7(4): 825-853.* Count Carlo Sforza, in the United States after 1940, galvanized Italian American public opinion against Fascism, and helped make clear to other Americans the distinction between Fascists and the Italian people. He tried to win recognition of a free Italian government-in-exile similar to DeGaulle's Free French, but the effort was unsuccessful, due in part to British opposition. After the fall of Fascism, Sforza soon returned to Italy. He sought to drive a wedge between King Victor Emmanuel and General Pietro Badoglio, and was so successful that only the intervention of Churchill and Eisenhower saved Victor Emmanuel's throne. He also succeeded in blocking an Allied effort to deal with moderate Fascists like Dino Grandi. By their successes and their failures the exiles led by Sforza contributed to the moderate solution of Allied-Italian relations and to the relative postwar stability. 95 notes.
J. C. Billigmeier

627. Miller, James E. A QUESTION OF LOYALTY: AMERICAN LIBERALS, PROPAGANDA, AND THE ITALIAN-AMERICAN COMMUNITY, 1939-1940. *Maryland Hist. 1978 9(1): 49-71.* Examines the extensive effort of the Roosevelt administration to counter Fascist support among the Italian Americans. Despite massive efforts by the Office of War Information, conservative Italians remained in control of media and Italian fraternal organizations. The fear of fifth column activity was baseless. The entire campaign was led by liberals and illustrates the increasing tendency of liberals to turn to the government to achieve their ends. Based on US archives and secondary sources; 3 illus., 59 notes.
G. O. Gagnon

628. Miller, James Edward. LA CONDUITE DE LA GUERRE ECONOMIQUE AUX U.S.A.: ORGANISATION, SOURCES ET BIBLIOGRAPHIE [The conduct of the economic war in the U.S.A.: Organisation, sources, and bibliography]. *Cahiers d'Hist. de la Seconde Guerre Mondiale [Belgium] 1976 4: 203-220.* It is important to study whether the objective of US economic warfare was to strengthen capitalism or just to contain Hitler. A chronology of this policy is followed by a detailed catalogue of American civil and military archives bearing on this subject. As the United States was the only country to emerge from the war stronger than she went in, and her preeminence in the world dates from this period, a study of this activity is integral to any analysis of her postwar superiority. Archival records; table, 23 notes, biblio., 3 appendixes.
M. K. Palat

629. Miller, John R. THE CHIANG-STILWELL CONFLICT, 1942-1944. *Military Affairs 1979 43(2): 59-62.* After Pearl Harbor, China was granted Great Power status because America expected it to tie down much of the Japanese war machine and hoped to use Chinese bases for air and sea attacks against Japan. Lieutenant General Joseph W. Stilwell implemented American strategy in China. General Stilwell and Generalissimo Chiang Kai-shek disagreed, however, over many issues: strategy, supply, use of Chinese troops, air versus ground priorities, prosecution of the war, and use of Chinese Communist forces. "The real difficulty was that Stilwell expected more of Chiang than Chiang could deliver." 27 notes.
A. M. Osur

630. Miller, Marc. WORKING WOMEN AND WORLD WAR II. *New England Q. 1980 53(1): 42-61.* Before World War II most of the working women of Lowell, Massachusetts, were employed in textile factories where they composed 35% of the labor force. This percentage rose to a high of 60% in 1943 after which it declined as women moved to higher paying jobs in the new defense industries. During the war wages rose and overtime was regularly available; mobility increased as women moved about and filled previously male positions. They used their income to support their families, not for "pin money." After the war most women left the plants and it became clear that war only provided a respite from depression and narrowing employment opportunities in the town. The war was not a turning point for Lowell women, many of whom had traditionally worked. Based on interviews, newspapers and secondary sources; 49 notes.
J. C. Bradford

631. Millett, Allan R. THE STUDY OF AMERICAN MILITARY HISTORY IN THE UNITED STATES. *Military Affairs 1977 41(2): 58-61.* Three factors have contributed to the health of military history: World War II and its impact on military history, the expansion of university education since World War II, and a lively library and bookstore market. Other influences are the concept of a new military history, which avoids the more traditional stress on command and battles, and the effort to synthesize the American military experience and relate it to American history in the broadest sense. One can look to the future with optimism. 18 notes.
A. M. Osur

632. Milton, T. R. V-E DAY: MAY 7, 1945. *Air Force Mag. 1975 58(5): 8-9.* A brief account of the US Air Force's role in the European war, 1941-45.

633. Milwee, William I. LET'S SALVAGE THE SALVAGE FORCE. *US Naval Inst. Pro. 1979 105(12): 54-59.* During World War II, the US Navy created a large and efficient salvage force. Although much of that force was done away with in the years immediately following the end of the war, the salvage force was expanded again during the Korean War. It also received a boost during the Vietnam War. But today, largely because of the lack of manpower and money, the Navy's salvage forces are less than adequate for all they are required to do, and they certainly could not support any kind of naval expansion. Too, the commercial salvage establishment is not very active and it cannot be looked to for much help. If the Navy is to continue adequate salvage operations, it must provide the necessary peacetime resources and a proper base for expansion during wartime. 4 photos.
A. N. Garland

634. Minei, Nicolae. DIPLOMATUL NAZIST ŞI PONOASELE SPIONAJULUI "NECONVENABIL" [The Nazi diplomat and the drawbacks of "unsuitable" spying]. *Magazin Istoric [Romania] 1977 11(7): 48-51.* Reproduces an extract from *Les Archives secrètes de Wilhelmstrasse* Vol. 9, Books 1 and 2, (Paris, 1960), preceded by comments on the difficult position of the German chargé d'affaires, Hans Thomsen, in Washington in 1940 because of the agents sent to the United States by Wilhelm Canaris and Heinrich Himmler.

635. Miscamble, Wilson D. ANTHONY EDEN AND THE TRUMAN-MOLOTOV CONVERSATIONS OF APRIL, 1945. *Diplomatic Hist. 1978 2(2): 167-180.* The Truman-Molotov conversation of 23 April 1945 did not indicate a reversal of America's wartime policy of cooperation with the USSR. British Foreign Secretary Sir Anthony Eden considered the intransigence of Soviet Foreign Minister V. M. Molotov the roadblock to an acceptable settlement of the crucial disagreement over Poland. At Eden's instigation, President Harry S. Truman held the unscheduled meeting with Molotov in an effort to convince him of the importance of a quick resolution of this issue. Truman, who had discussed questions of general policy with Molotov in the scheduled meeting the previous day, intended the famous "dressing down" for this limited purpose only. 56 notes.
T. L. Powers

636. Miscamble, Wilson D. THE EVOLUTION OF AN INTERNATIONALIST: HARRY S. TRUMAN AND AMERICAN FOREIGN POLICY. *Australian J. of Pol. and Hist. [Australia] 1977 23(2): 268-283.* Traces President Harry S. Truman's foreign policy ideas back to his experiences in World War I, but especially during his middle political career, 1935-45. He read widely in military history. In 1938 he advocated preparedness. In 1939 he attacked the dictators Hitler, Mussolini, and Stalin. During the war he attacked isolationism and spoke out for collective security and membership in the United Nations. The view he espoused as President had evolved in the previous decade.
W. D. McIntyre

637. Mitchell, Kent. THE FAIRCHILD XNQ-1/T-31 *TRAINER. Am. Aviation Hist. Soc. J. 1977 22(1): 48-55.* Examines the Fairchild T-31, a competitor for use as the official Air Force and Navy trainer airplane, 1941-47; discusses specifics of flight operations, and landing, engine, and maneuvering characteristics.

638. Mitson, Betty E. LOOKING BACK IN ANGUISH: ORAL HISTORY AND JAPANESE-AMERICAN EVACUATION. *Oral Hist. R. 1974: 24-51.* Discusses West Coast oral history projects on the evacuation and incarceration of Japanese Americans during World War II with details from the taped experiences of Togo Tanaka and Karl and Elaine Yoneda. Illus., 53 notes.
D. A. Yanchisin

639. Miyamoto, S. Frank. THE FORCED EVACUATION OF THE JAPANESE MINORITY DURING WORLD WAR II. *J. of Social Issues 1973 29(2): 11-32.* Three general causes of the Japanese American evacuation are examined. *Collective disposition* considers the antagonism toward immigrants special characteristics of California politics, economic competition, segregation and racial stereotypes, and Japanese American international relations as condi

tions which instituted a persistent anti-Japanese attitude on the West Coast. *Situational factors* include the tendency to suspect treachery of all Japanese following Pearl Harbor and the time pressures which curtailed deliberation by government officials on the evacuation question. *Collective interaction* considers the interaction among the main elements which produced the evacuation decision. A short section describes the relocation centers and the evacuees' reaction to detention.
J

640. Miyamoto, S. Frank. THE FORCED EVACUATION OF THE JAPANESE MINORITY DURING WORLD WAR II. *J. of Social Issues 1973 29(2): 11-32.* Three general causes of the Japanese American evacuation are examined. *Collective disposition* considers the antagonism toward immigrants, special characteristics of California politics, economic competition, segregation and racial stereotypes, and Japanese American international relations as conditions which instituted a persistent anti-Japanese attitude on the West Coast. *Situational factors* include the tendency to suspect treachery of all Japanese following Pearl Harbor and the time pressures which curtailed deliberation by government officials on the evacuation question. *Collective interaction* considers the interaction among the main elements which produced the evacuation decision. A short section describes the relocation centers and the evacuees' reaction to detention.
J

641. Moch, Jules. CONVERSATIONS AVEC EINSTEIN, EISENHOWER, KHROUCHTCHEV ET WINSTON CHURCHILL ... [Conversations with Einstein, Eisenhower, Khrushchev, and Winston Churchill ...]. *Nouvelle Rev. des Deux Mondes [France] 1980 (4): 27-34.* The author, a French statesman, recalls his conversations with Albert Einstein in 1932, Dwight D. Eisenhower in 1955, Nikita Khrushchev in 1955, and Winston Churchill in 1942, concerning disarmament.

642. Mohl, Ulrich. HUNDERT JAHRE STERNENBANNER ÜBER ALASKA [100 years of the Stars and Stripes over Alaska]. *Geschichte in Wissenschaft und Unterricht [West Germany] 1969 20(3): 140-150.* Surveys the history and importance of this American outpost and elucidates the decisive economic changes during World War II.
St. Boehnke

643. Mohrmann, G. P. and Scott, F. Eugene. POPULAR MUSIC AND WORLD WAR II: THE RHETORIC OF CONTINUATION. *Q. J. of Speech 1976 62(2): 145-156.* Explores the background and characteristics of popular songs during World War II; the lyrics reflect cultural values and attitudes toward the war.

644. Mondello, Salvatore. THE INTEGRATION OF JAPANESE BAPTISTS IN AMERICAN SOCIETY. *Foundations 1977 20(3): 254-263.* American Baptists began work among the Japanese immigrants in the 1890's. They opposed discrimination against the Japanese in the National Origins Act of 1924. Deals with Baptist involvement with Japanese Americans during and after World War II. Baptists were very successful in their resettlement efforts at this time. 21 notes.
E. E. Eminhizer

645. Moore, Jamie W. ECONOMIC INTERESTS AND AMERICAN-JAPANESE RELATIONS: THE PETROLEUM CONTROVERSY. *Historian 1973 35(4): 551-567.* In March 1934, the Japanese Diet enacted legislation taking the nation's oil industry out of the hands of foreigners. During three years of diplomatic controversy the United States followed a policy which avoided deference to a single corporate interest while defending the right of Americans to trade in the Far East. The incident reveals general aspects of contemporary US State Department policy. The United States believed that the Nationalist government would not be able to continue in power in China, and it was intimated to Japan that American attitudes would have to be taken into account if attempts were made to upset the balance of power in Asia. Based on State Department records in the National Archives, Washington; 66 notes. N. W. Moen

646. Moore, John. THE CONSTANCY OF SEA POWER IN STRATEGIC CONSIDERATIONS. *Int. Perspectives [Canada] 1975 (6): 13-18.* Discusses the role of naval power in the military strategy of Great Britain from 1485-1945, and in the United States, the USSR, and NATO from 1945-70's.

647. Moore, John Hammond. GETTING FRITZ TO TALK. *Virginia Q. Rev. 1978 54(2): 263-280.* During World War II the US Navy operated two interrogation centers, particularly for German and Japanese submarine crews. One was at Fort Hunt, Virginia, and the other at Byron Hot Springs, California. Describes possible breaches of the Geneva Code, the use of stool pigeons, interrogation procedures and the bugging of cells. O. H. Zabel

648. Moore, John Hammond. HITLER'S WEHRMACHT IN VIRGINIA, 1943-1946. *Virginia Mag. of Hist. and Biog. 1977 85(3): 259-273.* During World War II, several thousand prisoners of war, most of them Germans, were held in 27 camps in Virginia. Because the most troublesome Nazis usually were sent to camps in the interior, the Virginia camps were generally free of friction, and the prisoners were an invaluable source of labor. Based on records of the Provost Marshal General's Office in the National Archives and the US Army's Center for Military History, Washington, D.C.; 12 notes. R. F. Oaks

649. Moore, John Hammond. ITALIAN POWS IN AMERICA: WAR IS NOT ALWAYS HELL. *Prologue 1976 8(3): 141-151.* Italy's switch from the ranks of the Axis to that of the Allies in 1943 generated plans to utilize Italian Prisoners of War (POWS) in the United States as a source of labor and reflected an unwillingness to release large numbers of former enemy soldiers while the conflict was still going on. The Italian Service Units were an uneasy compromise to achieve these goals, in which Americans were called upon to view as equals recent POWs. Contacts with the Italian American community helped to make these men feel at home and also led to a considerable number of escapes. The scheme was accompanied by broken promises to the Italians, inefficient work utilization, and a general embarrassment on the part of all concerned. Primarily based on archival materials in the National Archives. N. Lederer

650. Moore, John Hammond. NAZI TROOPERS IN SOUTH CAROLINA, 1944-1946. *South Carolina Hist. Mag. 1980 81(4): 306-315.* Discusses the imprisonment of 8,000 Germans in 20 prisoner-of-war camps in 17 counties of South Carolina; they were used for labor until after the war.

651. Morgan, Chuck. NAVAL AVIATION. *By Valor and Arms 1977 3(2): 55-59.* Describes naval aviation in the first half of the 20th century.

652. Morgan, Lael. AN ARTIST'S WAR IN THE ALEUTIANS. *Alaska J. 1980 10(3): 34-39.* Recounts one year of the Aleutian Campaign of World War II, using the words and paintings of naval artist Lt. William F. Draper. Draper was one of five artists the Navy assigned to record World War II in oil. He painted the scenery, servicemen, and some combat of the Aleutian Islands for about one year (1942-43) until he was transferred to the South Pacific. Based on the recently declassified report that Draper made for the Naval Records Office in 1944; 4 illus.
S

653. Morozov, G. and Krivinski, B. NEKOTORYE UROKI I VYVODY IZ OPYTA BOR'BY NA MORSKIKH KOMMUNIKATSIIAKH VO VTOROI MIROVOI VOINE [Some lessons and conclusions from the experience of combat on maritime lines of communications in World War II]. *Morskoi Sbornik [USSR] 1976 (5): 23-28.* World War II demonstrates an increase in the scale of operations against maritime lanes of supply, that the submarine is a basic weapon against surface vessels, and that submarine warfare must be conducted systematically and scientifically as shown by a comparison between the German and American submarine operations.

654. Moss, Kenneth. GEORGE S. MESSERSMITH: AN AMERICAN DIPLOMAT AND NAZI GERMANY. *Delaware Hist. 1977 17(4): 236-249.* Follows the diplomatic career of George Messersmith, particularly 1933-40, and argues that Messersmith helped to shape American attitudes toward Nazi Germany by convincing American leaders of the dangers of Nazi expansionism and megalomania. Messersmith believed in the principles of balance of power and in an international economy and open trade, and these beliefs informed his approaches to foreign policy. Messersmith was able to convince the American government to apply economic pressure on Nazi Germany in the 1930's to restrain Germany's expansion, but otherwise he was unsuccessful in getting America to adopt aggressive measures against Nazism. Based on the Messersmith Papers and contemporary correspondence; 39 notes. R. M. Miller

655. Mountcastle, John W. FROM BAYOU TO BEACHHEAD: THE MARINES AND MR. HIGGINS. *Military Rev. 1980 60(3): 20-29.* The mid-1930's saw the United States vastly unprepared to launch amphibious operations. No good landing craft existed and there were few plans to build some. Andrew J. Higgins, a civilian boat builder, worked with the Marine Corps (especially Colonel, later General, Holland M. Smith) to plan and build landing craft for both troops and tanks. Often fighting the Navy bureaucracy, Higgins's boats became the landing craft used throughout World War II in every amphibious operation. Based mainly on official histories; 2 photos, 2 tables, 17 notes.
D. H. Cline

656. Mrozek, Donald J. ORGANIZING SMALL BUSINESS DURING WORLD WAR II: THE EXPERIENCE OF THE KANSAS CITY REGION. *Missouri Hist. Rev. 1977 71(2): 174-192.* Kansas City businessmen understood the wisdom of Harold Ickes' remark that the defense emergency of 1941 represented an opportunity to industrialize the Midwest, and an even greater likelihood

that the economic gap between the East and West would widen if the opportunity were lost. Efforts to work through Lou E. Holland's Mid-Central War Resources Board of 1940 and his Mid-Central Associated Defense Industries, Inc. after 1941 and through Senator Harry S. Truman were only modestly successful in redressing the economic imbalance between East and West. MCADI directors failed to get member companies to expand their facilities, or to approach federal agencies to gain support for subcontracting plant expansion for their members, and the members themselves feared expansion when there was danger of postwar depression. This desire to play safe cut midwestern manufacturers from a chance to get the large contracts of the Cold War era. Primary and secondary sources; illus., 32 notes.
W. F. Zornow

657. Mughal, N. A. ANALYSIS OF AMERICAN CONGRESSIONAL AND PUBLIC OPINION ON THE MANCHURIAN CRISIS, 1931-33. *Pakistan Horizon [Pakistan] 1975 28(2): 24-47.* Analyzes American Congressional and public opinion during the Japanese attack on China.

658. Muir, Malcolm, Jr. MISUSE OF THE FAST BATTLESHIP IN WORLD WAR II. *US Naval Inst. Pro. 1979 105(2): 57-62.* The 10 fast battleships that the United States built and deployed during World War II were the most powerful warships ever sent to sea, but they were not used to full advantage in the Pacific. Because of the increasing importance of the aircraft carrier, the fast battleships were split among the various carrier task groups, and, for all practical purposes, the battle line was dissolved. This had a number of unfortunate results, the chief one being that when a battle line could have dealt a devastating blow to the Japanese Navy at Saipan in July 1944 and again in Leyte Gulf four months later, it was not available. Still, the battleships did pose a significant threat to the Japanese Navy throughout the war, and they proved to be a viable weapon in carrying out the Navy's sea control mission. Primary and secondary sources; 4 photos, 23 notes.
A. N. Garland

659. Muir, Malcolm, Jr. UNITED STATES AVIATION UNITS ABOARD FAST BATTLESHIPS IN WORLD WAR II: CHANGING MISSIONS IN MIDSTREAM. *Aerospace Hist. 1980 27(2): 95-100.* A history of the use of aircraft aboard fast battleships in World War II. The original missions—scouting and gun-laying—were made obsolete because of the changing mission of the battleships during the war. Being in a fleet with the carriers, those aircraft assumed the roles of scouting and antisubmarine patrol. The battleship scout planes were so loaded down with armament and equipment that they were not practical for service. Also, the mission of the battleship became a gun platform for shelling shore targets, and the type of projectile used made it difficult for the aircraft to spot the point of impact. The mission at which the floatplanes excelled became that of close-to-shore rescue of downed aviators. Based on official records; 6 photos, 23 notes.
C. W. Ohrvall

660. Mulkin, Barb. LOS ALAMOS—P.O. BOX 1663. *Westways 1977 69(1): 31-34, 72.* History of the town of Los Alamos, New Mexico, centering on its importance as the secret scientific center where the atomic bomb was developed during World War II, 1943-46.

661. Munton, Don and Page, Don. PLANNING IN THE EAST BLOCK: THE POST-HOSTILITIES PROBLEMS COMMITTEES IN CANADA 1943-5. *Int. J. [Canada] 1977 32(4): 687-726.* An account of the creation, successes, and demise of formal foreign policy planning mechanism within the Canadian government. Primary sources; 62 notes. R. V. Kubicek

662. Murphy, Wendy. IN FUROR HORTENSIS. *Am. Heritage 1978 29(5): 94-98.* Garden clubs began during the last quarter of the 19th century, and a Garden Club of America was founded in 1913. Small and exclusive, the clubs worked hard during both World Wars, doing their part. As of 1978, 37 states had 182 clubs, with about 13,800 members. Beautification, conservation, pesticides, and related matters are all part of the clubs' concerns. Illus. J. F. Paul

663. Murphy, William T. JOHN FORD AND THE WARTIME DOCUMENTARY. *Film and Hist. 1976 6(1): 1-8.* John Ford, Hollywood filmmaker, collaborated with the federal government ca. 1941-42 in making two World War II documentary films, *Battle of Midway* and *December 7*, which turned out to be cinematic flops because they were strictly propaganda.

664. Murray, D. R. CANADA'S FIRST DIPLOMATIC MISSIONS IN LATIN AMERICA. *J. of Inter-Am. Studies and World Affairs 1974 16(2): 131-152.* In 1939 Canada declared war on the Axis powers and became the only Western Hemisphere state directly involved in the war. Canada had few diplomatic missions in Latin America and was not a member of the Pan-American Union. The first legations were established in Brazil, Argentina, and Chile. In 1941, the United States blocked Canadian membership in the PAU, and Canadian interest in the inter-American system has remained low. Based on Canadian government documents, private papers, and secondary sources; biblio.
J. R. Thomas

665. Murray, David. GARRISONING THE CARIBBEAN: A CHAPTER IN CANADIAN MILITARY HISTORY. *Rev. Interamericana [Puerto Rico] 1977 7(1): 73-86.* During both World Wars, Canada's soldiers have provided garrison duty for Great Britain in the Caribbean, freeing English troops to serve in Europe. 56 notes. J. A. Lewis

666. Murray, G. E. Patrick. "UNDER URGENT CONSIDERATION": AMERICAN PLANES FOR GREECE, 1940-1941. *Aerospace Hist. 1977 24(2): 61-69.* German advances in Europe, and especially the fall of France in June 1940, threatened Greece. Athens assumed an Italian attack and needed enough air power to counter 500 Italian planes. In June 1940, the Greek government turned to the United States as a source of planes, but delivery did not begin until April 1941, too late to help the Greeks. The failure to assist Greece illuminates the problems of the Roosevelt administration in establishing an "arsenal for democracy." Says "that if delivery had not taken so long, the planes might have become something more than a symbolic gesture." Based on State Department Records; 35 notes. A. M. Osur

667. Murray, G. Patrick. COURTNEY HODGES: MODEST STAR OF WORLD WAR II. *Am. Hist. Illus. 1973 7(9): 12-25.* Tank corps commander Courtney Hodges led the battle for Remagen Bridge during World War II.

S

668. Murray, G. Patrick. THE LOUISIANA MANEUVERS: PRACTICE FOR WAR. *Louisiana Hist. 1972 13(2): 117-138.* During 15-28 September 1941, 19 divisions took part in the United States' "first major army versus army war games," conducted between Lieutenant General Ben Lear's Second Army and Lieutenant General Walter Krueger's Third Army. Describes the planning, execution, and logistics of these maneuvers, held in western Louisiana. Among the officers who played important roles in the maneuvers were Major General George Smith Patton, Jr., Colonel Dwight David Eisenhower, and Lieutenant Colonel LeRoy Lutes. Krueger's Third Army won the manuevers, but both armies received severe criticisms from observing officers. Several high-ranking officers lost their jobs and others were demoted, but some promotions also resulted, notably Eisenhower's promotion to brigadier general. The maneuvers served political and psychological purposes as well as military in preparing the American republic for war. Based on published materials and records in the Eisenhower Library, Abilene, Kansas; 13 photos, 38 notes. R. L. Woodward

669. Muth, Steve. 23RD FIGHTER GROUP. *Aero Album 1972 5(3): 2-11.* The 23rd Fighter Group was the Air Force successor to the American Volunteer Group, the "Flying Tigers." Activated on 4 July 1942 at Kunming, China, the 23rd was the fighter contingent of General Claire Lee Chennault's newly created China Air Task Force, a part of the 10th Air Force. Colonel Robert L. Scott, later the author of *God Is My Copilot,* was its first commander. Other famous aviators in the group included Major (later General) Bruce Keener Holloway and Major David "Tex" Hill. Recounts the combat history of the group. Details of operations in 1945 are scarce due to lack of documentation. Based mainly on unofficial unit histories; illus., 18 photos, charts. C. W. Ohrvall

670. Myrick, David F. A CHAPTER IN THE LIFE OF RASO: A RAILROAD GHOST TOWN. *J. of Arizona Hist. 1976 17(4): 363-374.* Raso, known as Railroad Pass until 1905 and then Glade until 1911, was a Southern Pacific Railroad station a few miles northeast of Willcox, Arizona. Its principal function was to serve as a train-order station where a telegrapher handled communications from the Tucson dispatcher concerning train movements, weather instructions, and other messages for train crews. Raso was especially important during the high traffic period of World War II. Today Raso is only a sidetrack with switches operated by remote control from Tucson. 5 illus., map. D. L. Smith

671. Naida, S. F. and Chuzavkov, L. M. ISTORIOGRAFIIA PROBLEMY POSTAVOK S.SH.A. I VELIKOBRITANII SOVETSKOMU SOIUZU V PERIOD VELIKOI OTECHESTVENNOI VOINY [The historiography of US and British military aid to the USSR during World War II]. *Vestnik Moskovskogo U., Seriia 9: Istoriia [USSR] 1975 30(3): 17-31.* Sees a growing literature about alleged Soviet military self-sufficiency during World War II, and denies Western historical claims that the USSR was unprepared for war and dependent on Allied aid. Divides discussion into the periods 1941-47, 1947-60, and 1960-75. Claims that Western scholarship has changed over these periods depending on the political climate, but that Soviet researchers and military memoirists such as G. K. Zhukov have maintained throughout that the Allies deliberately delayed providing supplies to the USSR. 70 notes. M. R. Colenso

672. Nálevka, Vladimír. SPOJENÉ STÁTY A ARGENTINA V LETECH DRUHÉ SVĚTOVÉ VÁLKY [The United States and Argentina in the years of World War II]. *Československý Časopis historický [Czechoslovakia] 1972 20(2): 173-206.* The traditional United States-Argentine struggle over the leadership of the South American continent entered a new phase during World War II, as the nationalist rivalry evolved against the background of the world conflict as part of the U.S. attempt to convert the prewar world system to an American hegemony according to President Roosevelt's strategic plans. The strong US political position in Latin America achieved during the war was opposed by other South American countries, where the war economy gave birth to a stronger working class and a more nationalist-oriented bourgeoisie. American victory in the war contained the germ of future crises in Latin America. Secondary sources; 155 notes.
G. E. Pergl

673. Napier, Peggy. CHARLES E. YEAGER: SUPERSONIC FLIGHT PIONEER. *West Virginia Hist. 1979 40(3): 293-303.* Charles Yeager (b. 1923) of West Virginia served in the Army Air Corps in World War II and was the first man to fly faster than sound on 14 October 1947 in the SX-1 aircraft. Thereafter he made several dozen more supersonic flights, served in various capacities, and retired in 1975 as a brigadier general. Primary sources; 65 notes.
J. H. Broussard

674. Napoli, Donald S. THE MOBILIZATION OF AMERICAN PSYCHOLOGISTS, 1938-1941. *Military Affairs 1978 42(1): 32-36.* Examines the role of psychologists in the US military, 1938-41. Psychologists operated out of patriotism and concern for their profession. After a slow start in 1938, considerable progress was made, especially with the General Classification Test. By Pearl Harbor, a large part of military psychology had been established. The success during the war was based on the place psychologists had made for themselves during the 1938-41 rearmament program. Primary and secondary sources; 30 notes.
A. M. Osur

675. Nash, Al. A UNIONIST REMEMBERS: MILITANT UNIONISM AND POLITICAL FACTIONS. *Dissent 1977 24(2): 181-189.* Author reminisces about his militancy during World War II in the United Automobile Workers of America and working at the Brewster Aeronautical Corporation which was building Brewster Buffalos and Corsairs in Long Island City, New York, for the Army and Navy.

676. Nelson, William T. THE OLD NAVY: 1,500 MILES IN A FLOATING DRY DOCK. *US Naval Inst. Pro. 1980 106(3): 86-89.* During World War II, the Manitowoc Shipbuilding Company of Wisconsin contracted with the US Navy to build 47 submarines. The company completed 28 before the war ended, and the contract was then terminated. The problem that faced the company was to get the submarines from its yards in Wisconsin to the open sea. The St. Lawrence River route could not be used, so the company turned to the Chicago River-Chicago Sanitary Canal-Illinois River-Mississippi River route. To successfully accomplish the transit, the submarines had to be transported in a floating dry dock towed by Mississippi River tugs. The USS *Peto* (SS-265) was the first submarine to make the trip—between 25 December 1942 and 7 January 1943. On 16 January 1943, the *Peto* moved down the river from New Orleans, Louisiana

(where it had completed its fitting out), and headed for Panama and eventually the western Pacific. 2 photos. A. N. Garland

677. Neu, Charles E. AMERICAN FOREIGN POLICY BETWEEN THE WARS. *Reviews in Am. Hist. 1975 3(3): 376-379.* Review article prompted by Arnold A. Offner's *The Origins of the Second World War: American Foreign Policy and World Politics, 1917-1941* (New York: Praeger, 1975). Sees weaknesses in the book's multinational approach, assesses the book's analysis of the US foreign policymaking process in the 1920's and 1930's, and suggests that the book is not so much an examination of the origins of World War II as it is a study of US foreign policy and world politics, especially in Europe and Japan, 1917-41.

678. Neumann, William L. ROOSEVELT'S FOREIGN POLICY DECISIONS, 1940-1945. *Modern Age 1975 19(3): 272-284.* On difficult questions which required a strong and courageous stand, Franklin D. Roosevelt evaded action and stalled by lying to all parties in order to preserve surface tranquility. Based on primary documents and secondary sources; 40 notes. M. L. Lifka

679. Noelte, Earl. L'ÉBLOUISSEMENT PROVOQUÉ L'IMAGE DE LA RUSSIE: OU LE REFLET DE L'OPINION PUBLIQUE DANS LA POLITIQUE ÉTRANGÈRE DE FRANKLIN D. ROOSEVELT À L'ÉGARD DE L'UNION SOVIÉTIQUE DE 1941 À 1945 [The fascination with the image of Russia: the influence of public opinion on Franklin D. Roosevelt's policy toward the Soviet Union, 1941-45]. *Relations Int. [France] 1975 (4): 137-154.* After Hitler's armies attacked the USSR on 22 June 1941, the US government and media saw in the USSR a potential ally in the struggle against the Axis, and went to work rehabilitating the image of the USSR and its dictator, Joseph Stalin. President Roosevelt repeatedly stressed his view that Communist Russia was less of a threat to democracy, religion, and Western civilization than was Nazi Germany. As Soviet armies came closer to Central Europe, and the USSR's hegemonic intentions towards Eastern Europe became clearer, Roosevelt did little. Still bedazzled by his image of a basically friendly, beneficent Russia, he failed to alert the American people to the true nature of Soviet imperialism and its plans. 63 notes. J. C. Billigmeier

680. Nofi, Albert A. MECHANIZED WARFARE: EXPERIMENT AND EXPERIENCE, 1935-40. *Strategy and Tactics 1973 (41): 5-14.* Discusses armored vehicles and tank warfare 1935-40 in Western Europe and the United States.

681. Norquist, Ernest O. THREE YEARS IN PARADISE: A GI'S PRISONER-OF-WAR DIARY, 1942-1945. *Wisconsin Mag. of Hist. 1979 63(1): 2-35.* After the US Army surrendered during the siege of Bataan in the Philippines, the author was taken prisoner by the Japanese. His diary, partly reprinted here from his manuscripts at the State Historical Society of Wisconsin, reflects the prison life he led as a medic, on various work details, and in a foundry, first at Cabanatuan and then in Japan. 16 illus., 3 notes. N. C. Burckel

682. Norton, Douglas M. THE OPEN SECRET: THE U.S. NAVY IN THE BATTLE OF THE ATLANTIC, APRIL-DECEMBER 1941. *Naval War Coll. Rev. 1974 26(4): 63-83.* The issues of Executive secrecy and the role of the Commander in Chief versus the congressional right to declare war are not unique

to the years of the Indochina war. The preservation of England in 1941 demanded U.S. involvement in the naval battle for the Atlantic long before the declaration of war with Germany. Due almost entirely to Presidential action, often undertaken in secret without approval of either the Congress or the public, the operations were a possible infringement on the warmaking powers of Congress. At the same time they were important to saving England. J

683. Nossal, Kim Richard. BUSINESS AS USUAL: CANADIAN RELATIONS WITH CHINA IN THE 1940'S. *Hist. Papers [Canada] 1978: 134-147.* Traces the evolution of Canadian policy toward the Nationalist government in the years before 1949 when the Nationalist government evacuated the capital of Nanking. Ottawa's intentions had little to do with ideological considerations, but military aid to the Kuomintang was shaped by economic considerations and bureaucratic policies. In 1949, Major General Victor Wentworth Odlum, whose knowledge of the Pacific theater was attractive to William Lyon Mackenzie King, flew into Chunking to establish the first Canadian diplomatic presence in China. "The reason for the creation of goodwill was the lure of increased trade with China after the war." The question of postwar reconstruction aid from Canada was raised in November 1944. "It was a desire to increase trade with China rather than a desire to maintain Chiang in power that motivated the Cabinet." Decisions were made with an eye toward contributions to a depleted Canadian treasury. 72 notes. E. P. Stickney

684. Nuechterlein, James A. THE POLITICS OF CIVIL RIGHTS: THE FEPC, 1941-46. *Prologue 1978 10(3): 171-191.* Despite his lack of a strong political commitment to civil rights, Roosevelt bent to black pressures in 1941 to establish the Fair Employment Practices Committee through Executive Order 8802. The FEPC had no direct enforcement powers to curb job discrimination in war industries and was therefore forced to rely on other governmental agencies to cancel the war contracts of offenders. The principal weapon of the committee was publicity generated through media exposure of their hearings. Placing the FEPC under the supervision and control of hostile Paul V. McNutt, director of the War Production Board, in 1942 brought tensions between the committee and other government agencies to a head. An explosion resulted from McNutt's cancellation of committee hearings into railroad employment discrimination. Roosevelt was forced to step in, reconstituting the FEPC with a larger budget but still without enforcement powers. Between 1943 and the committee's demise in 1946, the body was under continual Congressional attack from conservative Southern Democrats who ended the FEPC in 1946. Based on research in the National Archives. N. Lederer

685. Nyberg, Janet. SWEDISH LANGUAGE NEWSPAPERS IN MINNESOTA. Hasselmo, Nils, ed. *Perspectives on Swedish Immigration* (Chicago: Swedish Pioneer Hist. Soc. and Duluth: U. of Minnesota, 1978): 244-255. Examines the publishing history of Swedish-language newspapers in the United States and particularly in Minnesota from 1851 to 1976. Most of the newspapers were of rather small circulation and expressed the conservative spiritual and social ethos of the Lutheran Church, although later newspapers began to advocate more radical solutions to society's problems following World War I. Swedish newspapers tended to be isolationist and somewhat pro-German on the eves of both World Wars, but once war was declared, editorials urged complete loyalty to the

United States. Today, with circulation dropping and the Swedish-reading population falling sharply, there is little optimism for continued publication of Swedish newspapers in America. None survives in Minnesota. 2 photos, 23 notes.　S

686. Nyström, Sune. OM KRIGETS NYA ANSIKTE [The new face of war]. *Kungliga Krigsvetenskaps Akademiens Handlingar och Tidskrift [Sweden] 1968 172(5): 167-174.* Examines how attitudes to warfare changed concurrently with technical and economic developments between World War I and the Vietnam War, and assesses the impact of nuclear arms on military strategies since 1945.　U. G. Jeyes

687. O'Brien, Michael. YOUNG JOE MCCARTHY, 1908-1944. *Wisconsin Mag. of Hist. 1980 63(3): 178-232.* Examines Joseph R. McCarthy's early life in rural Wisconsin, including his activities in Grand Chute, Manawa, Milwaukee, Waupaca, and Shawano. Details early influences on McCarthy; the failure of his chicken business; his graduation from high school in a single year; his five years at Marquette University as an engineering major, boxing coach, fraternity brother, and law graduate; his law partnership with Michael Eberlein; his unsuccessful bid for district attorney; his campaign for judge of the 10th Judicial Circuit Court; his most controversial case—the Quaker Dairy case—resulting in a reversal by the State Supreme Court; his political friendship with Urban Van Susteren and journalists John Wyngaard and Rex Karney; his voluntary service as an intelligence officer in the Marines during World War II; and his challenge of Alexander Wiley in the 1944 primary for US Senator. 19 illus., 161 notes.
N. C. Burckel

688. O'Connor, Raymond G. THE U. S. MARINES IN THE 20TH CENTURY: AMPHIBIOUS WARFARE AND DOCTRINAL DEBATE. *Military Affairs 1974 38(3): 97-103.* Beginnings of development of amphibious doctrine coincide with the formation of the General Board of the Navy in 1900. The Board's concern about the establishment of advance bases for naval operations in the Orient and the Caribbean provided impetus for the development of equipment designed for amphibious operations. The World War II Marine Corps operations in the Pacific proved the wisdom of the Board. Based upon archival and published sources, notably those of the Divison of Naval History, Navy Department.　K. J. Bauer

689. Oehling, Richard A. [GERMANS IN HOLLYWOOD FILMS].
GERMANS IN HOLLYWOOD FILMS: THE CHANGING IMAGE, 1914-1939. *Film & Hist. 1973 3(2): 1-10, 26.*
GERMANS IN HOLLYWOOD FILMS: THE CHANGING IMAGE, THE EARLY WAR YEARS, 1939-1942. *Film & Hist. 1974 4(2): 8-10.*
GERMANS IN HOLLYWOOD FILMS. *Film & Hist. 1974 4(3): 6-10.*

690. Offner, Arnold A. APPEASEMENT REVISITED: THE UNITED STATES, GREAT BRITAIN, AND GERMANY, 1933-1940. *J. of Am. Hist. 1977 64(2): 373-393.* American historians have followed Cordell Hull's belief that the economic similarities between the United States and Great Britain made them natural allies, and natural antagonists with Germany. Yet during 1936-40, German and American trade increased, as did American investments in Germany. Hull's statement also belies consistent attempts by the United States to appease

Germany's economic and political ambitions. Franklin Roosevelt and his foreign policy advisor, Sumner Welles, were willing to grant Germany a sphere of influence in Central and Eastern Europe in return for disarmament talks and nonaggression pacts. American attempts at appeasing Axis appetites continued until March 1940. Primary and secondary sources; 79 notes.   J. W. Leedom

691. Ohlinger, John F.   HURRICANE CONVOY.   *Aerospace Hist. 1979 26(3): 148-153.* The author, an American pilot, helped ferry British Hurricane fighter planes across Africa in 1942 in support of the North African campaign. 7 photos.   C. W. Ohrvall

692. Ohlinger, John F.   INCIDENT AT FOUL BAY.   *Aerospace Hist. 1976 23(2): 71-74.* Memoir of a World War II experience piloting a C-47 on a mapping mission along the ferry route from Africa to China. All went well to Foul Bay, a Red Sea inlet in Egypt. A salt flat that looked like a suitable landing site from the air turned out to be pock-marked with underground voids, into one of which the plane fell while taxiing. The aircraft was slightly damaged, but they were able to radio for help, and an RAF transport arrived the next day with equipment to get the C-47 back into the air. 2 photos.   C. W. Ohrvall

693. Okihiro, Gary Y.   JAPANESE RESISTANCE IN AMERICA'S CONCENTRATION CAMPS: A REEVALUATION.   *Amerasia J. 1973 1(2): 20-34.* Proposes that the assumptions of the revisionist histories of slave and colonized groups provide a more realistic basis for an analysis of Japanese reaction to concentration camp authority than do the older notions of Japanese loyalty and helplessness.   S

694. Okihiro, Gary Y.   TULE LAKE UNDER MARTIAL LAW: A STUDY IN JAPANESE RESISTANCE.   *J. of Ethnic Studies 1977 5(3): 71-85.* Examines the "orthodox interpretation" of the wartime internment of American Japanese, and the simplistic categorizations of Issei, Kibei, and Nisei found at the base of most treatments of the topic. Also attacks the "myth of the model minority" relative to Japanese Americans, especially as seen in *The Spoilage* by Thomas and Nishimoto. Analyzes the period of military rule by the Army at the Tule Lake Camp for "segregees" or "disloyals" during November 1943-January 1944, with the arrest and detention of the democratically elected representative body for the internees, the *Daihyo Sha Kai,* and the substitution of Army-named "block managers" for maintaining order. The authorities manipulated the famous "Status Quo" ballot of 11 January 1944, but the basic unity of purpose among factions of the internees did not waver; various groupings among the prisoners simply held different approaches to the same goal, that of gaining respect for their basic human rights and bringing reforms into camp administration. Primary sources; 44 notes.   G. J. Bobango

695. O'Leary, Jeremiah.   PARRIS ISLAND REVISITED.   *Marine Corps Gazette 1972 56(9): 38-42.* A veteran of the Marines' World War II boot camp at Parris Island, South Carolina, in 1942 compared his experiences with those of Marine Vietnam War recruits in 1972.

696. Olsen, C. E.   FULL HOUSE AT YALTA.   *Am. Heritage 1972 23(4): 20-25, 100-103.* A firsthand account of the preparations for the Yalta Conference.   S

697. O'Neill, James E. THE ACCESSIBILITY OF SOURCES FOR THE HISTORY OF THE SECOND WORLD WAR: THE ARCHIVIST'S VIEWPOINT. *Prologue 1972 4(1): 21-25.* Surveys the dilemma of the historian working with restricted materials in government agencies. While the historian and the archivist are both concerned with accessibility to the bulk of materials, the archivist also serves a master other than scholarship—the agency to whom he is responsible. Three types of restricted materials (agency-restricted, classified, and donor-restricted) are classified and declassified by some 46 different federal departments and agencies, each with differing policies. In the spirit of Executive Order 10501, a possible solution would be to inaugurate automatic declassification procedures rather than currently followed selective declassification; individual documents could be reclassified for brief periods. Such a policy could bring about "a better balance between the government's need for secrecy and the public's right to know." 5 notes. D. G. Davis, Jr.

698. Orange, Vincent. PEARL HARBOR, 7 DECEMBER 1941. *Hist. News [New Zealand] 1980 (40): 1-8.* Discusses the Japanese attack on the American Pacific fleet in December 1941, emphasizing the Japanese planning of the operation and the reasons why the American command was taken by surprise.

699. Orser, Edward. INVOLUNTARY COMMUNITY: CONSCIENTIOUS OBJECTORS AT PATAPSCO STATE PARK DURING WORLD WAR II. *Maryland Hist. Mag. 1977 72(1): 132-146.* The Patapsco Civilian Public Service System Camp 3 was the first for conscientious objectors in American history. Examines the members' World War II experiences during May 1941-August 1942 as a case study in involuntary community. Considers the establishment of the program, the values the men set for camp life, background factors relevant to achievement of their goals, their sense of distinctiveness or mission, camp structure, and work assignments. Campers were predominantly Friends and mainstream Protestants, from large urban areas, and professionally oriented. Despite efforts to build group cohesion, the community ideal seemed badly tarnished by the end of the first year because members opted for a service ideal instead, especially after Pearl Harbor. The pacifists tried to find expression for their ideals in a constructive way while not fully condoning the compulsion which brought and kept them at Patapsco. This attempt led many to conclude that such a middle way was not possible. This was the ambiguity at the heart of an involuntary community. Primary and secondary sources; 65 notes.
G. J. Bobango

700. Orser, Edward W. WORLD WAR II AND THE PACIFIST CONTROVERSY IN THE MAJOR PROTESTANT CHURCHES. *Am. Studies 1973 14(2): 5-24.* World War II produced serious social tensions in the United States, and the wartime experience of pacifists has been neglected. Pacifism dominated the consciousness of the Protestant churches after the late 1930's, although none endorsed the absolutist position. By 1941, this sentiment had eroded considerably and pacifists had trouble defining their role during the war. Surveys the spectrum of pacifist sentiment and divisions 1941-45. Based on primary and secondary sources; 79 notes. J. Andrew

701. Orser, W. Edward. RACIAL ATTITUDES IN WARTIME: THE PROTESTANT CHURCHES DURING THE SECOND WORLD WAR. *Church Hist. 1972 41(3): 337-353.* World War II proved to be a crucial period for Protestant church involvement in the question of race in America. Prior to the war, little concern was expressed over the status of American blacks, except for general statements of goodwill. The Northern Baptist Convention in 1939 broke new ground by officially condemning segregation, but gave no positive suggestions. Southern churches suggested peaceful racial cooperation but did not challenge segregation. By the end of the war, churches came to recognize the problem of racial injustice plaguing the entire nation. The American Protestant churches' de facto acceptance of segregation and lack of positive racial programs lessened the prestige of these churches among blacks in the civil rights movement of the 1950's and 1960's. Based on contemporary religious publications; 69 notes.
S. C. Pearson, Jr.

702. Orzell, Laurence J. A "PAINFUL PROBLEM": POLAND IN ALLIED DIPLOMACY, FEBRUARY-JULY, 1945. *Mid-America 1977 59(3): 147-170.* The future of Poland seriously affected Allied diplomacy in the winter and spring of 1945; differences among the United States, Great Britain, and the USSR eventually were to lead to the Cold War. In 1945, two different Polish governments existed, each supported by various Allies. Territorial questions also created problems, because the Allies could not agree on Poland's new boundaries. The frictions which evolved from the reconstruction of Poland led to mutual distrust in postwar Soviet-Western relations. Based on published and archival sources; 83 notes.
J. M. Lee

703. Palmer, Howard. PATTERNS OF RACISM: ATTITUDES TOWARDS CHINESE AND JAPANESE IN ALBERTA 1920-1950. *Social Hist. [Canada] 1980 13(25): 137-160.* For much of the 20th century Alberta has had more Japanese and Chinese residents than any Canadian province except British Columbia. While the Chinese faced strident opposition before 1920, anti-Japanese sentiment was less intense. In the 1920's anti-Asian sentiment abated, in part because the Asian population remained small and Asians did not compete with whites. In the 1930's their urban concentration and increasing unemployment made the Chinese more obvious. World War II caused a reversal of attitudes as the war effort allowed the Chinese to prove their loyalty, and confronted Albertans with relocated Japanese. When the war ended, prodeportation sentiment declined. Although discrimination persisted, Albertans realized the value of the Japanese contribution to the economy. 77 notes.
D. F. Chard

704. Papachristou, Judith. AN EXERCISE IN ANTI-IMPERIALISM: THE THIRTIES. *Am. Studies 1974 15(1): 61-77.* Critics of Franklin D. Roosevelt's foreign policy in the 1930's were not really isolationists or pacifists, but anti-imperialists. They criticized American motives, methods, and goals, but were not opposed to internationalism per se. These men saw economic motives guiding foreign policy, especially toward the Pacific, and did not think investments worth the risk of war with Japan. Based on primary and secondary sources; 62 notes.
J. Andrew

705. Pappas, George S. HISTORY IN STAINED GLASS: THE CLASS OF 1944 WINDOWS AT WEST POINT. *Military Collector & Hist. 1976 28(3): 114-120.* Describes and pictures a set of stained glass windows (given to the US Military Academy by the graduating class of 1944) which depict various scenes from military history, 1800-1944.

706. Paraschos, Janet Nyberg. SARATOGA SPRINGS. *Am. Preservation 1978 2(1): 59-72.* Saratoga Springs, New York, was late 19th-century America's prime resort relying on natural mineral springs, horseracing, gambling, and luxury hotels to attract wealthy summer vacationers. The financial fortunes of the town fluctuated with the legal status of gambling and alcohol. World War II financially ruined the elegant but declining hotels and the decaying racetrack failed to draw visitors. However, in the past 10 years the city has experienced a revival. Renovation of the racetrack, a 28-day exclusive racing season, new highways, a winter sports boom, and an influx of young residents have all contributed to the economic and cultural renaissance. Today more than 350 Victorian homes, many previously owned by Skidmore College, have been restored and placed on the National Register of Historic Places. 15 photos. S. C. Strom

707. Parks, Robert J. THE DEVELOPMENT OF SEGREGATION IN U.S. ARMY HOSPITALS, 1940-1942. *Military Affairs 1973 37(4): 145-150.* Before 1940 the Army had few Negro physicians and treated its Negro soldiers in integrated hospitals. Negro doctors served as regimental surgeons, but the Medical Department did not establish an all-Negro-staffed hospital until 1942. Based on Army records; 29 notes. K. J. Bauer

708. Parrish, N. F. HAP ARNOLD AND THE HISTORIANS. *Aerospace Historian 1973 20(3): 113-115.* General H. H. "Hap" Arnold sought the aid of a committee of historians to help him with strategic decisions during World War II. S

709. Partin, John W. THE DILEMMA OF "A GOOD, VERY GOOD MAN": CAPPER AND NONINTERVENTIONISM, 1936-1941. *Kansas Hist. 1979 2(2): 86-95.* Arthur Capper was a Republican senator from Kansas during 1919-49. Always a pacifist, he became a prominent noninterventionist. He made speeches advocating nationalization of the arms industry, reduction of armed forces, strict neutrality legislation, and a constitutional amendment for a popular referendum on war. When war came in 1941, however, Capper gave it his full support. Based on newspapers and manuscripts in the Library of Congress and Kansas State Historical Society; illus., 33 notes. W. F. Zornow

710. Parzen, Herbert. THE ROOSEVELT PALESTINE POLICY, 1943-1945. *Am. Jewish Arch. 1974 26(1): 31-65.* It is astonishing to what degree the President's private views ... reflected the opinions of the State Department officials in charge of Middle Eastern affairs and even of the political leaders of the Arab states as pictured in the current consular dispatches to Washington.
J

711. Paszek, Lawrence J. SEPARATE, BUT EQUAL? THE STORY OF THE 99TH FIGHTER SQUADRON. *Aerospace Hist. 1977 24(3): 135-145.* The Army Air Corps during World War II organized and trained black aviators in segregated units, conforming to the *Plessy* v. *Ferguson* (1896) Supreme Court

ruling. Segregation was proved inefficient and costly however, in terms of military results. Tuskegee Army Air Field, the 99th Fighter Squadron, and the 332nd Fighter Group did well considering the adversity they faced. President Harry S. Truman's Executive Order No.9981 officially ended segregation in 1948 and the Air Force eliminated it the next year. Primary and secondary sources.

A. M. Osur

712. Paterson, Thomas F. POTSDAM, THE ATOMIC BOMB, AND THE COLD WAR: A DISCUSSION WITH JAMES P. BYRNES. *Pacific Hist. R. 1972 41(2): 225-230.* Presents and comments on a memorandum by Senator Warren Robinson Austin concerning a conversation with Secretary of State James Francis Byrnes on 20 August 1945. The document sheds light on Soviet-American diplomacy at the Potsdam conference and includes information about the relationship between the dropping of the atomic bomb and Russian participation in the war against Japan. Based on a memorandum from the Austin Papers, Guy W. Bailey Library, University of Vermont; 8 notes. E. C. Hyslop

713. Paterson, Thomas G. A PROPOSAL FOR PEACE, 1945. *New England Q. 1972 45(1): 105-109.* Reprints the text of a 1945 utopian peace proposal written by an unnamed woman from Lebanon, New Hampshire and read in a radio broadcast by NBC news commentator Robert St. John.

714. Patrick, Stephen B. THE ARDENNES OFFENSIVE, THE BATTLE OF THE BULGE, DECEMBER 1944. *Strategy & Tactics 1973 (37): 4-21.* Discusses the World War II Battle of the Bulge in Western Europe between Germany and the Allies in 1944.

715. Patrick, Stephen B. BATTLE FOR GERMANY: THE DESTRUCTION OF THE REICH, DECEMBER 1944-MAY 1945. *Strategy and Tactics 1975 (50): 5-20.* Discusses the final Allied assaults on Nazi Germany, German countermeasures, and the weapons and strategies of the participants. S

716. Patrick, Stephen B. THE BATTLE FOR GUADALCANAL, 7 AUGUST 1942-7 FEBRUARY 1943. *Strategy & Tactics 1973 (39): 23-38.* Discusses the struggle waged by the United States and Japan for Guadalcanal.

717. Patrick, Stephen B. PARATROOP: A HISTORY OF AIRBORNE OPERATIONS. *Strategy and Tactics 1979 (77): 4-13.* Sketches the evolution of airborne troops and provides a detailed description of Allied and Axis paratroop action during World War II.

718. Patterson, James R. BILL DUNN: OUR FIRST ACE OF WORLD WAR II. *Air Force Mag. 1973 56(4): 78-80.* Bill Dunn's record as the first American ace was confirmed only in 1967, because his early victories were scored while flying for the British Royal Air Force.

719. Pearson, Alden B., Jr. A CHRISTIAN MORALIST RESPONDS TO WAR: CHARLES C. MORRISON, *THE CHRISTIAN CENTURY* AND THE MANCHURIAN CRISIS, 1931-33. *World Affairs 1977 139(4): 296-307.* Discusses *The Christian Century,* the most prominent and outspoken Christian periodical on the Japanese threat to peace during the crisis in Manchuria, and its editor, Charles C. Morrison, who had a significant role in determining American foreign policy.

720. Peatross, Oscar F. THE MAKIN RAID. *Marine Corps Gazette 1979 63(11): 96-103.* The author describes his participation with the 2d Raiders, US Marines, in their raid on the Japanese-held Makin Islands (in the Gilbert Islands), 17-18 August 1942; describes the reactions of the Japanese defenders, their eventual beheading of nine Marine prisoners, and the postwar execution and prison sentences visited upon their officers for that crime.

721. Pechatnov, Vladimir O. ZA KULISAMI VYRABOTKI "NOVOGO KURSA" (F. FRANKFURTER-U. LIPPMAN) [Behind the scenes of the New Deal (F. Frankfurter-W. Lippmann)]. *Voprosy Istorii [USSR] 1979 (7): 112-123.* Analyzes the debates and discussions among Franklin D. Roosevelt, Felix Frankfurter (1882-1965), Walter Lippmann (1889-1974), and others on the eve of the New Deal (1932). The writings of Frankfurter released in 1945 show clearly that the New Deal temporarily quieted the economic crisis of the 1930's; the United States would remain a capitalist society. At the same time one cannot hide the fact that the outcome of the experiment continued to remain uncertain. Finally the economic success of the New Deal could not be proved because World War II completely changed the nature of the economic crisis of the 1930's. Based on correspondence between FDR and Frankfurter, the Walter Lippmann letters, and the Perkins Collection; 62 notes. J. L. Evans

722. Peck, Jeff. THE HEROIC SOVIET ON THE AMERICAN SCREEN. *Film and Hist. 1979 9(3): 54-63.* Traces the history of the portrayal of Russians in American films from 1910 with the release of *Russia, the Land of Oppression,* until 1945 when American patriotism during World War II led to the making of several films portraying Soviet Russians as heroes.

723. Peck, Sarah E. THE CAMPAIGN FOR AN AMERICAN RESPONSE TO THE NAZI HOLOCAUST, 1943-1945. *J. of Contemporary Hist. [Great Britain] 1980 15(2): 367-400.* In 1943, Peter Bergson and a group of Palestinian Jews living in the United States formed the Emergency Committee to Save the Jewish People of Europe to pressure the US government into some sort of rescue operation. Zionist leaders were incensed and tried to thwart the activities of the Bergson group. The result is that "organized American Jews—disunited, in retrospect unduly cautious, and preoccupied with long-range political goals—must also share the blame for the deaths of their six million brethren." Primary sources; 79 notes. M. P. Trauth

724. Peltier, Michel. LES CARNETS SECRETS DE PATTON [The secret notebooks of Patton]. *Écrits de Paris [France] 1976 (360—bis): 66-77.* The recently published notebooks of General George S. Patton confirm the traditional view of Patton as abrupt, contentious, autocratic, and deeply suspicious of the USSR at the close of World War II.

725. Pelz, Stephen E. BIG OIL AND PEARL HARBOR. *Rev. in Am. Hist. 1976 4(1): 115-119.* Review article prompted by Irvine H. Anderson, Jr.'s *The Standard-Vacuum Oil Company and United States East Asian Policy, 1933-1941* (Princeton, New Jersey: Princeton U. Pr., 1975) which examines the interrelationship of American foreign investment in oil production in the Dutch East Indies and foreign policy toward East Asia.

726. Penkower, Monty Noam. JEWISH ORGANIZATIONS AND THE CREATION OF THE U.S. WAR REFUGEE BOARD. *Ann. of the Am. Acad. of Pol. and Social Sci. 1980 (450): 122-139.* Confronted by the Holocaust, the Anglo-American Alliance moved slowly to meet this unique tragedy during World War II. Refusing the initial appeal of Jewish organizations in the free world that food and medical packages be dispatched to the ghettos of Europe, London and Washington argued that supplies would be diverted for the Germans' personal use or would be granted the Jews just to free the Third Reich from its "responsibility" to feed them. A license granted in December 1942 for such shipments had minimal effect. The World Jewish Congress' subsequent plan to rescue Jews through the use of blocked accounts in Switzerland received the US Treasury Department's approval in mid-1943, but the State Department and the British Foreign Office procrastinated further. Jewish groups failed at times to measure up to the catastrophe but the fundamental obligation lay with the Allied councils of war, which discriminated in their unwillingness to save a powerless European Jewry. The persistence of Treasury Secretary Henry Morgenthau, Jr., and his staff in bypassing State and ultimately confronting Franklin D. Roosevelt in January 1944, along with increasing calls from Congress and the public for a presidential rescue commission, resulted in the executive creation of the US War Refugee Board. The lateness of the hour and Hitler's ruthless determination to complete the murder of all the Jews of Europe made the odds for the new board's success more than questionable. J

727. Peragallo, James L. CHENNAULT: GUERRILLA OF THE AIR. *Aerospace Historian 1973 20(1): 1-6.* Claire Lee Chennault and his band of American fliers fought the Japanese in China, 1937-45.

728. Perechnev, Iu. DESANTNYE DEISTVIIA VOORUZHENNYKH SIL SSHA NA TIKHOM OKEANE VO VTOROI MIROVOI VOINE [Landing activities by the armed forces of the USA in the Pacific Ocean in the Second World War]. *Morskoi Sbornik [USSR] 1979 (I): 8-13.* During the war against Japan in the Pacific Ocean, the United States undertook two strategic, 25 operative, and 100 tactical landings. Their characteristic features were long and careful preparations and superiority over the enemy in terms of men and equipment. The drawback of the US approach was the often inadequate reconnaissance and lack of central control over all units concerned in an operation. Details several landing attacks to illustrate these points. 6 notes. V. Sobeslavsky

729. Perkins, Bradford. ALLIES OF THE USUAL KIND. *Rev. in Am. Hist. 1978 6(4): 537-543.* Review article prompted by William Roger Louis's *Imperialism at Bay: The United States and the Decolonization of the British Empire, 1941-1945* (New York: Oxford U. Pr., 1978) and Christopher Thorne's *Allies of a Kind: The United States, Britain, and the War against Japan, 1941-1945* (New York: Oxford U. Pr., 1978).

730. Perkins, John H. RESHAPING TECHNOLOGY IN WARTIME: THE EFFECT OF MILITARY GOALS ON ENTOMOLOGICAL RESEARCH AND INSECT-CONTROL PRACTICES. *Technology and Culture 1978 19(2): 169-186.* Developed before World War II, DDT probably would have changed the world's approach to pest control for economic reasons alone. The war greatly accelerated the process because of the military need for a low mam-

malian toxicity pesticide. After the war, all efforts were given to the development of other synthetic organic pesticides, with the result that "biological control technologies were disrupted," as were "control practices based on habitat sanitation and cultural practices." 60 notes. C. O. Smith

731. Perry, Darby. REHEARSAL FOR WORLD WAR II. *Am. Heritage 1967 18(3): 40-45, 76-81.* Japanese air attack on the USS *Panay* in 1937 on the Yangtze River, China. S

732. Petersen, William. CHINESE AMERICANS AND JAPANESE AMERICANS. Sowell, Thomas, ed. *Essays and Data on American Ethnic Groups* (Washington, D.C.: Urban Inst. Pr., 1978): 65-100. The Chinese were the first immigrant group to be specifically excluded in American immigration policy and established the precedent that immigrants would be judged mainly by their place of origin. This discrimination against the Chinese and Japanese ordinarily would have resulted in ghettoization and low incomes, poor education, unstable family life, and a high crime rate, yet descendents of these immigrants have passed levels of native whites. Includes a history of preimmigration US contact with China and Japan in the 19th century, discussing movement from Hawaiian plantations and labor gangs, their social organization, internment of Japanese Americans during World War II, and their history of social mobility after 1945. Primary and secondary sources; 6 tables, 79 notes. K. A. Talley

733. Petillo, Carol M. DOUGLAS MACARTHUR AND MANUEL QUEZON: A NOTE ON AN IMPERIAL BOND. *Pacific Hist. Rev. 1979 48(1): 107-117.* Executive Order No. 1, issued at Fort Mills, Corregidor, on 3 January 1942 by Manuel Quezon, President of the Commonwealth of the Philippines, and found in the recently opened papers of Richard K. Sutherland in the National Archives, Washington, D.C., discloses rewards totalling $640,000 to General Douglas MacArthur, Major General Sutherland, Brigadier General Richard J. Marshall, Jr., and Lieutenant Colonel Sidney L. Huff. The author explores the reasons for such large gifts from Quezon to US Army officers and raises a question of ethics in the acceptance of such gifts. The full text of Executive Order No. 1 is included. 29 notes. R. N. Lokken

734. Petrov, V. ZHIVAIA SVIAZ' VREMEN [The living link between times]. *Mirovaia Ekonomika i Mezhdunarodnye Otnosheniia [USSR] 1976 (11): 122-125.* Discusses the history and prospects of world cooperation for peace in light of wartime correspondence among the leaders of the USSR, the United States, and Great Britain, 1941-45.

735. Pickett, George B., Jr. LEAD, TRAIN, AND ADMINISTER. *Military Rev. 1972 52(6): 47-53.* Recounts the mobilization of the military establishment in the Philippine Insurrection, World War II, and the Vietnam War; the Army can maintain its current level of professionalism by teaching leadership and administrative skills to its officer cadre.

736. Pickler, Gordon K. UNDERSTANDING THE SHIFTING CHINA SCENE. *Air U. R. 1974 25(5): 59-66.* Reviews John Paton Davies, Jr., *Dragon by the Tail: American, British, Japanese, and Russian Encounters with China and One Another* (New York: W. W. Norton, 1972), which emphasizes the years 1937-49 and US-Soviet policies. J. W. Thacker, Jr.

737. Pienkos, Donald E. THE POLISH AMERICAN CONGRESS: AN APPRAISAL. *Polish Am. Studies 1979 36(2): 5-43.* This interest group (the PAC), created in 1944, has served as the chief advocate for Polish American interests. During this period, its two presidents, Charles Rozmarek and Aloysius Mazewski, derived most influence not from the PAC per se but from their simultaneous service as president of the Polish National Alliance, a fraternal insurance lodge with assets of more than $150 million. Originally the PAC had been launched to put pressure on Franklin Roosevelt to rescue Poland from Communism after World War II. Its mission, however, has shifted to the promotion of Polish American interests. Even that mission is fading, because the budget has fallen from $305,385 in 1948 to $21,229 in 1978. The president of the PAC, however, is still recognized as the "Number One Polish American." English and Polish sources; 30 notes. S. R. Pliska

738. Pierson, Ruth. WOMEN'S EMANCIPATION AND THE RECRUITMENT OF WOMEN INTO THE CANADIAN LABOUR FORCE IN WORLD WAR II. *Can. Hist. Assoc. Hist. Papers [Canada] 1976: 141-173.* The federal and provincial bureaucrats of Canada regarded women as temporary replacements for men in the operation of a war economy. The extent of women's employability was categorized according to their positions in the family system. Because they were required to work in wartime, their needs as working women were handled in the context of the war effort. After World War II they were expected to return to the home or to traditional women's occupations. Based on Public Archives of Canada, Series RG 27 and 35, Orders-in-Council, secondary sources; 176 notes. G. E. Panting

739. Pierson, Ruth Roach. "JILL CANUCK": CWAC OF ALL TRADES, BUT NO "PISTOL PACKING MOMMA." *Hist. Papers [Canada] 1978: 106-133.* Many official women's paramilitry corps had sprung up across Canada by August 1940; the British Columbia Women's Service Corps was to replace medically fit men in support jobs in order to relieve them for duty with forward units. The heaviest demands were for stenographers, typists, cooks, and clerks for stores and equipment. "Exclusion from combat duty and the official bearing of arms remained the most salient feature of Women's Army service in World War II, whether in the CWAC (Canadian Women's Army Corps) or the Royal Canadian Army Medical Corps, the only army corps which women were eligible to join. Members of the CWAC were exempted from use as cannon fodder. Concludes the "women's admittance to the army in World War II had not brought about a change in the distribution of power between the sexes in Canada." E. P. Stickney

740. Pierson, Ruth Roach. LADIES OR LOOSE WOMEN: THE CANADIAN WOMEN'S ARMY CORPS IN WORLD WAR II. *Atlantis [Canada] 1979 4 (2, part 2): 245-266.* Discusses the ambivalence surrounding the admission of women to Canada's Army, Navy, and Air Force, 1941-46, due to the Canadian services' need for women in uniform when military service had been considered a man's duty, and the fear that a woman serving in the military would lose her sexual respectability.

741. Pinney, Charles A.   A MILITARY BUSH PILOT ON THE FORGOTTEN FRONT.   *Aerospace Hist. 1975 22(1): 1-5.* An Air Force pilot in Alaska 1942-43 reminisces. Charles A. Pinney graduated from flying school in May 1942 after a shortened training course, was retrained, then assigned to a B-18 to take supplies, personnel, and luxury items from Anchorage to Adak. The author recalls some of his experiences flying these missions. 4 photos, illus.
C. W. Ohrvall

742.   Plaza, Felicia.   FOOTPRINTS ON THE SANDS OF TIME: JUDGE IGNACIO V. BENAVENTE.   *Guam Recorder 1976 6(1): 14-18.* Discusses the judgeship of Ignacio V. Benavente on the island of Yap, 1942-46, where he came into contact with four different regimes, Spanish, German, Japanese, and finally American.

743.   Pluth, Edward J.   PRISONER OF WAR EMPLOYMENT IN MINNESOTA DURING WORLD WAR II.   *Minnesota Hist. 1975 44(8): 290-303.* The employment of prisoners of war, mainly Germans, in Minnesota agriculture, logging, and factory operations during 1943-45 was of considerable economic importance to the state. The prisoners made a valuable contribution in crop harvesting and canning, less so in logging and factory work. Community resistance to housing prisoners of war in or near populated areas was less than expected. The opposition of labor unions to the use of prisoner labor, especially in the lumbering industry, did not prevent the employment of such labor. Based on primary research and oral interviews.
N. Lederer

744.   Pogue, Forrest C.   LA CONDUITE DE LA GUERRE AUX ETATS UNIS (1942-1945): SES PROBLEMES ET SA PRATIQUE   [The conduct of the war in the United States (1942-45): Problems and practices]. *Rev. d'Hist. de la Deuxième Guerre Mondiale [France] 1975 (100): 67-94.* During World War II the United States had to improvise a world strategy and the structures to pursue it. Under pressure from General George C. Marshall the War Department was reorganized as was the Marine Corps. The Joint Chiefs of Staff was formed and Franklin D. Roosevelt worked out his own mode of supervision. Although he avoided detailed operational direction, he was explicit in opposing support for Charles de Gaulle's claims to leadership. Roosevelt's principal adviser, Harry Hopkins, was a crucial link between the president and the military. Surveys other aspects of US government conduct including the lack of planning for maintenance of troops abroad after the war. 11 notes.
G. H. Davis

745.   Polenberg, Richard.   LES LIBERTÉS CIVILES AUX ÉTATS-UNIS [Civil liberties in the United States]. *Rev. d'Hist. de la Deuxième Guerre Mondiale [France] 1972 22(88): 19-44.* Describes civil liberty restrictions in the United States during World War II. Studies American attitudes towards communism, tolerance of German, Italian, and Japanese immigrants, and fear of espionage and sabotage. Civil rights were guaranteed for all except Japanese and conscientious objectors. Outlines legislative controls, media activities, and the position of the Wilson and Roosevelt Administrations. Primary and secondary sources; 45 notes.
S. Sevilla

746. Poole, Walter S. FROM CONCILIATION TO CONTAINMENT: THE JOINT CHIEFS OF STAFF AND THE COMING OF THE COLD WAR, 1945-1946. *Military Affairs 1978 42(1): 12-16.* Between 1944 and 1946, the Joint Chiefs of Staff's (JCS) view of Soviet-American relations changed completely. At first the JCS saw the United States as simply mediating Anglo-Soviet quarrels, but gradually the wheel turned full circle and they saw the US role as the prime mover in stopping Soviet aggression; by late 1945 they viewed the USSR as an expansionist power. Discusses Cold War historiography, saying that JCS's recommendations were defensive reactions and not offensive threats. Based on JCS papers; 25 notes. A. M. Osur

747. Potter, E. B. ADMIRAL NIMITZ AND THE BATTLE OF MIDWAY. *US Naval Inst. Pro. 1976 102(7): 60-68.* An adaptation from the author's book, *Nimitz*, a biography of Admiral Chester W. Nimitz which will be published shortly by the Naval Institute Press. The author tells how the events of the battle of Midway appeared to Nimitz and his staff in Nimitz's headquarters at Pearl Harbor, of the messages received and sent, and of the difficulty Nimitz encountered in getting correct, up-to-date information from his combat commanders. 6 photos. A. N. Garland

748. Pound, Ezra. LETTERS FROM EZRA POUND TO BENITO MUSSOLINI. *Encounter [Great Britain] 1976 46(5): 35-41.* Reprints the text of several letters (1932-43); focuses on the political issues of the correspondence and on Pound's personal admiration for Mussolini.

749. Pozdeeva, L. V. KANADA V GODY VTOROI MIROVOI VOINY [Canada during World War II]. *Novaia i Noveishaia Istoriia [USSR] 1979 (2): 155-168.* During World War II Canada underwent profound structural changes. Its industry and agriculture rapidly developed to ensure war supplies and the economy experienced war conjuncture. At the same time the country was drawn deeper into the US imperialist system and the growing working class and Communist Party opposed such tendencies. Reviews the contemporary "bourgeois" historiography concerned with this important period. 105 notes.
V. Sobeslavsky

750. Pozzetta, George E. and Kersey, Harry A., Jr. YAMATO COLONY: A JAPANESE PRESENCE IN SOUTH FLORIDA. *Tequesta 1976 36: 66-77.* In 1904 an effort was made to establish a Japanese colony in South Florida, just north of present-day Boca Raton. Failure at pineapple production and anti-Japanese sentiment caused the demise of the colony. During World War II all remaining physical evidence of the Yamato colony was removed when the US government purchased the site. However, those few Japanese remaining were not relocated as in the West Coast; they were restricted, however, to the county they were in. Based on primary and secondary sources; 31 notes. H. S. Marks

751. Prados, John. COBRA: PATTON'S 1944 SUMMER OFFENSIVE IN FRANCE. *Strategy and Tactics 1977 65: 4-8.* Describes the execution of Operation Cobra and the subsequent Falaise battle in mid-July of 1944, in which the Allied forces headed by General George S. Patton extricated themselves from the Normandy lodgement.

752. Prados, John. THE WAR AGAINST JAPAN 1941-45. *Strategy and Tactics 1977 65: 27-32.* US industrial productivity, qualitatively superior aircraft, and naval advantages in radar and damage control decisively affected the Battle of the Pacific.

753. Prasad, Yuvaraj Deva. AMERICAN REACTION TO GANDHI'S ARREST IN 1942: THE CONFLICT OF IDEOLOGY AND NECESSITY. *J. of Indian Hist. [India] 1972 50(149): 611-618.* In August 1942, when the Indian National Congress demanded that the British immediately "quit India," Gandhi and other Indian leaders were arrested. Although the US government had pledged itself in the Atlantic Charter and elsewhere to assist the peoples of the world to achieve democratic self-determination, the exigencies of preserving British-American cooperation in the war against Germany and Japan forestalled any official US support for Indian independence. Presents reactions from the American press, State Department papers, orders of the War Department, and statements of private American citizens. American ideology clearly favored independence for India, but the necessity for cooperation with Britain prevailed. Based on American periodicals and secondary sources; 31 notes.
S. H. Frank

754. Preda, Eugen. SECRETELE "TUBULUI ALLOYS" [The "tube alloys" secret]. *Magazin Istoric [Rumania] 1975 9(8): 35-37.* Presents the diplomatic history of atomic bomb development, 1942-45. 3 notes.
J. M. McCarthy

755. Presley, James. THE BIRTH OF JESSE B. SEMPLE. *Southwest R. 1973 58(3): 219-224.* Discusses the origin and development of Langston Hughes' newspaper-column character Jesse B. Semple, later the "Simple" of humorous stories and books. Semple originated in a conversation Hughes had with a friend in a Harlem bar in 1942 and first appeared in the *Chicago Defender* on 13 February 1943. Gives examples of Semple's subjects of discussion such as racism and the inequities experienced by Negroes in World War
J. Coberly

756. Price, Joseph L. ATTITUDES OF KENTUCKY BAPTISTS TOWARD WORLD WAR II. *Foundations 1978 21(2): 123-138.* Southern Baptists' attitudes toward war are examined in George Kelsey's, *Social Ethics Among Southern Baptists 1917-1969* (Metuchen, N.J.: Scarecrow Pr., Inc., 1973). Argues that the book is not accurate, or is to some degree misleading. Examines indepth expressions on World War II in the reports of the Social Service Commission, Kentucky General Association minutes, the Long Run Association, the *Western Recorder,* and First Baptist Church of Paducah. Finds that little attempt was made by these groups to justify the war on biblical grounds, as was suggested by Kelsey. 59 notes.
E. E. Eminhizer

757. Pritchett, Merrill R. and Shea, William L. THE AFRIKA KORPS IN ARKANSAS, 1943-1946. *Arkansas Hist. Q. 1978 37(1): 3-22.* Approximately 23,000 German prisoners of war, most from Erwin Rommel's Afrika Korps, were quartered in Camp Chaffee, Camp Robinson, and Camp Dermott in Arkansas. Discusses facilities, treatment of prisoners, spare time activities such as sports, music, drama and education, escape attempts, and especially the prisoners' value as agricultural laborers. Primary sources; 2 illus., map, diagram, 32 notes.
G. R. Schroeder

758. Pritchett, Merrill R. and Shea, William L. AXIS PRISONER-OF-WAR CAMPS IN ARKANSAS. *J. of the West 1979 18(2): 30-34.* Thousands of captured German and Italian soldiers and airmen were interned during World War II at isolated camps in the southern and southwestern United States. Troops held in Arkansas had a significant impact on the economy of that state as contract laborers for farmers, businessmen, and local governments. Their work was particulary essential in labor-intensive agriculture because of the wartime shortage of other laborers. Based on US Army records in the National Archives, and on contemporary news articles; 3 photos, 18 notes. B. S. Porter

759. Pritchett, Merrill R. and Shea, William L. THE ENEMY IN MISSISSIPPI (1943-1946). *J. of Mississippi Hist. 1979 41(4): 351-371.* In 1943, after mass surrender of Hitler's Afrika Korps and its Italian counterpart in North Africa, the Americans had to make provision for suitable detention facilities in the United States. Four prisoner-of-war camps were established in Mississippi: Camp McCain, Camp Clinton, Camp Como, and Camp Shelby. The authors discuss each of these large facilities by outlining their structure and organization, detailing the recreational and educational activities available in the various camps, and describing contract work by prisoners in Mississippi agriculture, industry, and forestry. Inspection visits by US and international agencies to the camps also are described. M. S. Legan

760. Queuille, Pierre. LA DIPLOMATIE ANGLO-AMÉRICAINE EN VUE D'UN DÉBARQUEMENT ALLIÉ EN AFRIQUE [Anglo-American diplomacy with a view to the landing of the Allies in Africa]. *Bull. de la Soc. d'Hist. Moderne [France] 1980 79(5): 7-12.* Discusses Anglo-American diplomacy and behind-the-scenes machinations in Algiers with the French in an effort to rally the French army in Africa to the Allied cause before the German Afrika Korps arrived.

761. Quick, Paddy. ROSIE THE RIVETER: MYTHS AND REALITIES. *Radical Am. 1975 9(4-5): 115-132.* Tells of the participation of women in World War II war work. S

762. Rabinowitz, Howard N. GROWTH TRENDS IN THE ALBUQUERQUE STANDARD METROPOLITAN STATISTICAL AREA, 1940-1978. *J. of the West 1979 18(3): 62-74.* World War II and the Cold War brought the development of special weapons and atomic research that became the major economic resource of Albuquerque, New Mexico. The city practiced an aggressive policy of annexation to absorb its suburbs and the fleeing middle class. The result has been a conflict between county residents, who want autonomy as well as urban benefits, and the city government, which wants consolidation and control of urban growth. Based on US Census reports, newspapers, and Albuquerque City Commission Minutes; 16 photos, 9 tables, 32 notes. B. S. Porter

763. Rader, Frank J. THE WORKS PROGRESS ADMINISTRATION AND HAWAIIAN PREPAREDNESS, 1935-1940. *Military Affairs 1979 43(1): 12-17.* Early preparedness activities of the Works Progress Administration (WPA) in Hawaii and other territories proved to be an indication of a changing US foreign policy. President Franklin D. Roosevelt took several surreptitious steps to strengthen the nation's outer defense network; one such move was the

transfer of the Hawaiian WPA to War Department control in 1938. Thus, military projects would receive top priority in the allocation of relief funds and labor. Based on WPA records and secondary sources; 35 notes. A. M. Osur

764. Rae, John B. WARTIME TECHNOLOGY AND COMMERCIAL AVIATION. *Aerospace Historian 1973 20(3): 131-136.* World War II military aeronautical developments are directly related to the aviation industry. S

765. Ramirez, Roland J. AIRBORNE HISTORY AND DEVELOPMENT. *Conflict 1972 (3): 17-23.* Outlines the organization and wartime operations, 1935-45, of airborne units developed by Germany, Great Britain, and the United States.

766. Ramsett, David E. and Heck, Tom R. WAGE AND PRICE CONTROLS: A HISTORICAL SURVEY. *North Dakota Q. 1977 45(4): 5-22.* Compares wage-price controls during World War I, World War II, the Korean War, and 1971; assesses success, impact, decisionmaking, and administration.

767. Randall, Stephen James. COLOMBIA, THE UNITED STATES AND INTERAMERICAN AVIATION RIVALRY, 1927-1940. *J. of Inter-Am. Studies and World Affairs 1972 14(3): 297-324.* Following World War I, the U.S. State Department tried to win inter-American aviation rights for U.S. airlines and eliminate European competition, especially German. The State Department was guided in its policy partly by considerations of defense for the Panama Canal. Later, in World War II, this became a greater consideration and defense of the Venezuelan oil fields also led U.S. diplomats to seek concessions for U.S. commercial airlines. The United States withheld landing rights in the Canal Zone from airlines thought to be dominated by Germans. Ultimately, Pan American Airways became a dominant commercial airline in Colombia and other Latin American nations. Based on Colombian, British, and U.S. Government documents, and on secondary sources; 16 notes, biblio. J. R. Thomas

768. Rausch, David A. OUR HOPE: AN AMERICAN FUNDAMENTALIST JOURNAL AND THE HOLOCAUST, 1937-1945. *Fides et Hist. 1980 12(2): 89-103.* Under the leadership of Arno C. Gaebelin, the fundamentalist journal *Our Hope* (1894-1957) was almost unique among American Protestant periodicals, both liberal and conservative, in accurately chronicling the Nazi abuse of European Jewry. Gaebelin began predicting the Jews' problems shortly after Hitler's accession to power. During the late thirties and World War II, his journal described the persecutions and denounced Nazism both in theory and practice, while it advocated a homeland for the Jews in Palestine. 47 notes.
J. A. Kicklighter

769. Ray, Deborah Wing. THE TAKORADI ROUTE: ROOSEVELT'S PREWAR VENTURE BEYOND THE WESTERN HEMISPHERE. *J. of Am. Hist. 1975 62(2): 340-358.* Describes the tactics used by Franklin D. Roosevelt, Hopkins, advisors, and Pan American Airways to circumvent Lend-Lease and neutrality restrictions to set in operation the Takoradi air route across the South Atlantic Ocean to West Africa and on to Cairo in 1941. The Takoradi route was crucial to the British war effort in the Middle East, and, after Pearl Harbor, to the allied war effort world-wide. The episode was a clear example of Roosevelt's tactics before American entry into the war. Based on memoirs, documents

in the National Archives and the Roosevelt library, records of the State Department, strategic studies, and secondary works; 82 notes.   J. B. Street

770. Reagon, Bernice. WORLD WAR II REFLECTED IN BLACK MUSIC: "UNCLE SAM CALLED ME." *Southern Exposure 1974 1(3/4): 169-184.* Black music serves a communication function in black society and is sometimes a source of precise historical data. During World War II, lyrics of popular black songs portrayed the events important in the black community: the draft, heroics, wives working in defense plants, patriotism, and sadness over the death of President Franklin D. Roosevelt. Based on songs, news accounts, and other publications; 4 illus.   G. A. Bolton

771. Reed, Merl E. THE FEPC, THE BLACK WORKER, AND THE SOUTHERN SHIPYARDS. *South Atlantic Q. 1975 74(4): 446-467.* The outbreak of World War II led to a great upsurge of work activity in the southern shipyards. Labor was scarce, but Negroes were employed only in manual positions. President Franklin D. Roosevelt succumbed to pressure and created the Fair Employment Practices Commission. The FEPC acted to give black workers equal job opportunities. A riot in Mobile, Alabama forced the army to move in and some changes were made. The FEPC, its power weakened, was less active in other southern shipyards, and thus has left a mixed record. 31 notes.
V. L. Human

772. Reed, Randal Penn. FOREIGN POLICY AND THE INITIATION OF WAR: THE CONGRESS AND THE PRESIDENCY IN THE DISPUTE OVER WAR POWERS. *Potomac Rev. 1973 6(1): 1-29.* Covers 1787-1972.

773. Reeve, Robert C. I SHOULD HAVE STAYED IN BED. *Aerospace Historian 1975 22(2): 77-79.* The author was flying a Boeing 80A tri-motor on wartime contract for the US Army in 1943 when he lost an engine and had to land in the wilds. He was able to fly in another engine and install it in five days. Next he was to fly to Amchitka with parts for a radar installation. He arrived over Cold Bay with one hour of gas, and the field was socked in. He finally landed the aircraft in the Bering surf. The aircraft was not flyable but he did salvage the engines. When he returned to Anchorage he found that an officer had had his engines destroyed because he thought they were Japanese engines.
C. W. Ohrvall

774. Reeves, Thomas C. TAIL GUNNER JOE: JOSEPH R. MCCARTHY AND THE MARINE CORPS. *Wisconsin Mag. of Hist. 1979 62(4): 300-313.* Joseph R. McCarthy "served the corps and his country ably and with distinction. He risked his life on several occasions, and not entirely for the later political dividend." Corrects some inaccuracies about the future Wisconsin Senator's military career in World War II (Pacific Theater). McCarthy did not enter the Marines as a buck private, but as a first lieutenant, and did not sustain any wounds in actual combat. His citation from Admiral Chester Nimitz was based on an earlier, apparently forged, document, and he had 11 combat flights to his credit, not 32 as he later claimed. 11 illus., 41 notes.   N. C. Burckel

775. Regnery, Henry. HISTORICAL REVISIONISM AND WORLD WAR II. *Modern Age 1976 20(3): 254-265, (4): 402-411.* Part I. Describes revisionist books by George Morgenstern, Charles A. Beard, William Henry Chamberlain,

and Charles C. Tansill, the circumstances of their publication, and their reception by reviewers. When World War II ended, the great question of American involvement again became a burning issue. Primary and secondary sources; 13 notes. Part II. Reviews books by Admiral Husband E. Kimmel, George N. Crocker, and Harry Elmer Barnes and asks, "Was the fight for what we thought was historical truth worthwhile?" Finds it difficult to believe that telling the true story, for example of Pearl Harbor, will prevent such occurrences in the future, but argues that if we believe in anything, we must believe that the truth is worthwhile for its own sake. Primary and secondary sources; 22 notes. M. L. Lifka

776. Reichardt, Otto H. INDUSTRIAL CONCENTRATION IN WORLD WAR II: THE CASE OF THE AIRCRAFT INDUSTRY. *Aerospace Hist. 1975 22(3): 129-134.* Presents part of a larger study dealing with the economic impact of government procurement policies during World War II. Scholars are divided over the effects of government allocation and contracting policies on business concentration during the war. This study attempts to assess the problem through a multidimensional statistical survey of the aircraft industry. After conducting this survey, the author concludes that more research is needed before the data on the aircraft industry can be fully explained. Based on secondary sources; 5 tables, 31 notes. C. W. Ohrvall

777. Reichardt, Otto H. INDUSTRIAL CONCENTRATION AND WORLD WAR II: A NOTE ON THE AIRCRAFT INDUSTRY. *Business Hist. Rev. 1975 49(4): 498-503.* A statistical case study of the aircraft industry in World War II. Concludes that a trend toward less rather than more concentration took place, thus revising some previous scholarly interpretations. Based on government data and published sources; 2 charts, table, 10 notes.
C. J. Pusateri

778. Relyea, Harold C. NATIONAL EMERGENCY POWERS: A BRIEF OVERVIEW OF PRESIDENTIAL SUSPENSIONS OF THE HABEAS CORPUS PRIVILEGE AND INVOCATION OF MARTIAL LAW. *Presidential Studies Q. 1977 7(4): 238-243.* Chronicles outstanding examples of executive power to suspend habeas corpus and invoke martial law. The issue of his right to suspend habeas corpus is based on precedent, not being clearly outlined in the Constitution. Martial law has often merely meant placing soldiers at the disposal of civil authorities. Hawaii was placed under both martial law and suspension of habeas corpus by its governor at the outbreak of hostilities with Japan, a condition lasting until late 1944. An open question is whether a congressional declaration or presidential proclamation would be mandatory for suspension or martial law in case of wars or national emergencies. 19 notes. J. Tull

779. Remley, David A. CROOKED ROAD: ORAL HISTORY OF THE ALASKAN HIGHWAY. *Alaska J. 1974 4(2):113-121.* Prints 13 short essays about the Alaskan Highway and discusses the difficulties incurred while it was being constructed as a corridor for military supplies through Alaska and the Yukon Territory in 1942-43.

780. Resis, Albert. THE CHURCHILL-STALIN SECRET "PERCENTAGES" AGREEMENT ON THE BALKANS, MOSCOW, OCTOBER 1944. *Am. Hist. Rev. 1978 83(2): 368-387.* British archival evidence now available

shows that the famous "percentages" agreement Churchill claims he concluded with Stalin in Moscow was in fact a bi-lateral spheres-of-influence agreement of unlimited duration, despite Churchill's published denial and Soviet denials since 1958 that Stalin ever agreed to it. Moreover, the agreement was reached without US approval or even full knowledge, notwithstanding Churchill's assurances that he would keep Roosevelt fully apprised. Roosevelt's letter to Stalin of October 4, 1944 asserted that no problem in the war could be solved without US participation. The United States then sought a voice equal to that of the USSR in postwar control of the Bulgarian and Hungarian armistices—the first US direct challenge to Soviet dominance of its sphere. Thus, October 4, 1944 marks the beginning of the Cold War in Southeast Europe. Churchill and Stalin honored their agreement while British power faltered and the United States, which had never recognized the "percentages" agreement, replaced Great Britain in the Balkans. A

781. Reynolds, Clark G. ADMIRAL ERNEST J. KING AND THE STRATEGY FOR VICTORY IN THE PACIFIC. *Naval War Coll. R. 1976 28(3): 57-64.* Even though he was often described as being ruthless and abrasive to both subordinates and contemporaries, Fleet Admiral Ernest J. King was eminently successful as both Chief of Naval Operations and Commander in Chief, U.S. Fleet, during World War II. His skill, forcefulness, and self-confidence were essential elements to his success. In his effort to insure victory in the Pacific, he encountered several obstacles, some of which resulted more from conflicting personalities than from differences in strategic concepts. Clark G. Reynolds examines some of those obstacles and describes how they were overcome. J

782. Reynolds, David. COMPETITIVE CO-OPERATION: ANGLO-AMERICAN RELATIONS IN WORLD WAR TWO. *Hist. J. [Great Britain] 1980 23(1): 233-245.* Studies six books dealing with the special relationship between the United States and Great Britain, 1939-45, initiated by Sir Winston Churchill and Franklin D. Roosevelt, which consisted of cooperation between the countries as they bargained for supremacy.

783. Rhodes, Benjamin D. THE BRITISH ROYAL VISIT OF 1939 AND THE "PSYCHOLOGICAL APPROACH" TO THE UNITED STATES. *Diplomatic Hist. 1978 2(2): 197-211.* The first visit of a British king and queen to the United States in 1939 was not intended as a political move or a public relations ploy, but it turned out to be "of considerable political and psychological importance." The popular reception given the royal couple strengthened President Franklin D. Roosevelt's hand in his struggle against isolationism, enhanced Anglo-American friendship at a critical time, and served as a prelude to wartime collaboration. 57 notes. T. L. Powers

784. Rhodes, Richard. "I AM BECOME DEATH . . .": THE AGONY OF J. ROBERT OPPENHEIMER. *Am. Heritage 1977 28(6): 70-83.* J. Robert Oppenheimer (1904-67) is portrayed as a brilliant but lonely man. After a sheltered childhood (during which he reveled in books and science), he went to Harvard and to Göttingen. In 1929 he went to Berkeley where he helped establish the reputation of the University of California's school of theoretical physics. In 1942, he was selected to direct the Manhattan Project. Success led him to support the use of the bomb in order that mankind would know of its horrible consequences. By the 1950's, he was convinced that a nuclear stalemate had been

reached, and he began to question continued arms development. As a result, he lost his security clearance in 1954. He lived out the remainder of his life in isolation. 8 illus. J. F. Paul

785. Ribuffo, Leo. FASCISTS, NAZIS AND AMERICAN MINDS: PERCEPTIONS AND PRECONCEPTIONS. *Am. Q. 1974 26(4): 417-432.* Review essay of several monographs on the American reaction during the New Deal era to Italian Fascism, German Nazism and the German-American Bund, Father Charles Coughlin's home-grown brand of extremism, and the United States and countersubversives on the eve of World War II: John P. Diggins, *Mussolini and Fascism: The View from America* (Princeton: Princeton U. Press, 1972); Sander A. Diamond, *The Nazi Movement in the United States 1924-1941* (Ithaca, N.Y.: Cornell U. Press, 1973); Leland V. Bell, *In Hitler's Shadow: The Anatomy of American Nazism* (Port Washington: N.Y.: Kennikat Press, 1973); Sheldon Marcus, *Father Coughlin: The Tumultuous Life of the Priest of the Little Flower* (Boston: Little, Brown, 1973); Geoffrey S. Smith, *To Save a Nation: American Countersubversives, the New Deal, and the Coming of World War II* (New York: Basic Books, 1972). 12 notes. C. W. Olson

786. Richardson, James L. COLD-WAR REVISIONISM: A CRITIQUE. *World Pol. 1972 24(4): 579-612.* A review article of Gabriel Kolko's *The Politics of War: Allied Diplomacy and the World Crisis of 1943-45* (London: Weidenfeld and Nicolson, 1968), Gar Alperovitz' *Atomic Diplomacy: Hiroshima and Potsdam* (London: Secker and Warburg, 1966) and *Cold War Essays* (Garden City, N. Y.: Doubleday Anchor Books, 1970), and David Horowitz' *From Yalta to Vietnam: American Foreign Policy in the Cold War* (Harmondsworth, Penguin Books, 1967) [published under the title *The Free World Colossus,* (New York: Hill and Wang, 1965)]. Examines issues which exemplify "general, pervasive weaknesses in the handling of evidence and the testing of hypotheses." These issues are 1) the role of Eastern Europe in the Cold War, 2) the breakdown of East-West economic cooperation, 3) atomic weapons and the issue of international control, 4) Soviet aims in Western Europe, 5) the final division of Europe in 1947, and 6) the founding of NATO and Western rearmament. Revisionist assumptions imply that disturbances in European politics were due solely to American initiatives. The revisionists lack a conception of international order. Moreover, they neglect the actors' perspectives and fail to test their hypotheses against a rounded view of the main actors. They are committed to the counterrevolutionary character of American policy. 44 notes. E. P. Stickney

787. Rila, Carter. A MODERN MYSTERY: CUTLASS OR KLEWANG? THE ELUSIVE U.S. NAVY CUTLASS VARIANT OF WORLD WAR II. *Military Collector and Hist. 1975 27(4): 153-158.* Examines the origins of the US Army and Navy's use of the Naval Cutlass during World War I in 1917 and World War II in 1941-42; discusses historical confusion between the origins of the cutlass and the Dutch klewang as described in Harold L. Peterson's *Swords for Sea Services*.

788. Riste, Olav. AN IDEA AND A MYTH: ROOSEVELT'S FREE PORTS SCHEME FOR NORTH NORWAY. *Americana Norvegica IV: Norwegian Contributions to Am. Studies (Oslo: Universitets forlaget, 1973), pp. 379-397.* Denies that at a White House meeting between President Franklin

Delano Roosevelt and Norwegian Foreign Minister Trygve Lie on 12 March 1943, Roosevelt acted as an intermediary for Soviet demands for ports in North Norway. "Our contention that Lie must have misunderstood the President, and that in fact the Soviet Union had not expressed any 'desires or demands' involving Norwegian territory, is further confirmed by a study of the debate on Soviet war aims that took place among the Allies from the autumn of 1941 onwards. The available evidence suggests that North Norway became the first target for Roosevelt's speculations on the topic of free ports. One piece of evidence also indicates that he may have conceived the idea early in 1942—precisely at the time when the President was casting about for ways to satisfy Soviet desires for expansion short of annexation." 34 notes. — D. D. Cameron

789. Robinson, Arthur H. GEOGRAPHY AND CARTOGRAPHY THEN AND NOW. *Ann. of the Assoc. of Am. Geographers 1979 69(1): 97-102.* Examines the profound effects of World War II on the development of American cartography, 1938-79; from a special issue celebrating the 75th anniversary of the Association of American Geographers.

790. Rockaway, Robert A. THE ROOSEVELT ADMINISTRATION, THE HOLOCAUST, AND THE JEWISH REFUGEES. *Rev. in Am. Hist. 1975 3(1): 113-118.* Review article prompted by Saul S. Friedman's *No Haven for the Oppressed: United States Policy toward Jewish Refugees, 1938-1945* (Detroit, Mich.: Wayne State U. Pr., 1973).

791. Rockoff, Hugh. INDIRECT PRICE INCREASES AND REAL WAGES DURING WORLD WAR II. *Explorations in Econ. Hist. 1978 15(4): 407-420.* If adjustments are made to reflect such factors as shortages of goods, deterioration of quality, and reclassification of workers into higher wage categories even though no additional work or responsibility was involved, real wages may not have been higher in June 1946 than in August 1948. Based on published documents and reports and secondary accounts; 4 tables, fig., 6 notes, 30 ref. — P. J. Coleman

792. Rollins, Peter C. *VICTORY AT SEA*: COLD WAR EPIC. *J. of Popular Culture 1972 6(3): 463-482.* The television series *Victory at Sea*, first shown in 1952, reflects the Cold War mentality of the post-World War II era. Its organizing theme is America's role in the preservation of freedom against the evil designs of totalitarian dictators. Ideology and morality are emphasized while power politics considerations are ignored. 15 notes. — E. S. Shapiro

793. Ropp, Theodore. THE STRATEGIC DIMENSIONS OF GLOBAL WAR. *Air U. Rev. 1980 31(5): 58-64.* Reviews the military strategy, diplomacy, and difficulties of the Allies and their commands during World War II.

794. Rosenberg, David Alan. OFFICER DEVELOPMENT IN THE INTERWAR NAVY: ARLEIGH BURKE—THE MAKING OF A NAVAL PROFESSIONAL, 1919-1940. *Pacific Hist. R. 1975 44(4): 503-526.* Arleigh Burke's (b. 1901) experience as an interwar naval officer exemplified the new tendency for junior officers to become professionalized through technological programs and billets rather than through assignments protecting American commerce and showing the flag. Burke's training and experience prepared him well for wartime service. He attended Annapolis (1919-23) at a time when the

Academy emphasized the molding of midshipmen dedicated to the service above all other considerations. More utilitarian and technical training was gained at sea as a junior officer, and in specialized postgraduate course work. The thorough technical background inculcated an ability in interwar officers to respond creatively to new technology under command situations during World War II, thereby overcoming the traditionalism of senior officers. Based on documents at the Naval History Division Operational Archives (Washington, D.C.), the US Naval Academy Archives, interviews, and published Navy records; 42 notes.

W. K. Hobson

795. Rosenberg, Joseph L. IRISH CONSCRIPTION: 1941. *Éire-Ireland 1979 14(1): 16-25.* In 1939 Neville Chamberlain's proposed levying of military conscription in Northern Ireland, prompted by the Stormont government, was foiled "by a common front of the government in Dublin, northern nationalists, and the [Catholic] bishops—as well as by the apathy of the Unionist rank-and-file." By 1941, "to reinforce ties with Westminster, to ease unemployment, and to conceal the low level of loyalist enlistments" the Stormont government again requested conscription. With extreme reluctance, Winston Churchill rejected the drafting of Irishmen, due to adamant opposition from Dublin and US objections. Discusses the roles of John G. Winant, US ambassador in London, and David Gray, US ambassador in Dublin. Based on secondary sources and especially on the papers of the principals and State Department and military intelligence files; 60 notes.

D. J. Engler

796. Rosengarten, Adolph G., Jr. WITH ULTRA FROM OMAHA BEACH TO WEIMAR, GERMANY: A PERSONAL VIEW. *Military Affairs 1978 42(3): 127-132.* The author discusses his involvement with Ultra, the interception and deciphering of the Germans' secret code, and its use from Omaha Beach to Weimar. The author was the representative of the Special Branch of the Military Intelligence Division of the War Department in the Intelligence, or G-2, section of the US 1st Army. Ultra penetrated the "fog of war" and made an invaluable contribution to Allied intelligence during that critical phase of World War II. Yet, it was not perfect and its weaknesses as well as strengths had to be recognized. Based on personal recollections and secondary sources; 17 notes.

A. M. Osur

797. Roshchin, A. A. POSTWAR SETTLEMENT IN EUROPE. *Int. Affairs [USSR] 1978 (1): 112-121, (3): 102-114.* Part I. A former adviser to the European Consultative Commission recalls efforts from 1942 to 1945 by the United States, the USSR, Great Britain and eventually France to come to some agreement on postwar policies, particularly with respect to the partitioning of Germany. Part II. Reviews in detail the negotiations among the United States, Great Britain, France and the USSR from 1944 to 1945 which resulted in the final partition of Germany and discusses the motivations for the differences in the various countries' recommendations for the numerous partition plans.

798. Rositzke, Harry. AMERICA'S SECRET OPERATIONS: A PERSPECTIVE. *Foreign Affairs 1975 53(2): 334-351.* Traces the history of American secret intelligence operations and raises questions concerning their objectives today. Founded by William J. Donovan in the Second World War as the OSS (Office of Strategic Services), this service was later put under the umbrella of the

Central Intelligence Agency. Long-term national objectives should make for "clean-cut" missions for the AIS, not limited to war and politics. 2 notes.

C. W. Olson

799. Roskin, Michael. FROM PEARL HARBOR TO VIETNAM: SHIFTING GENERATIONAL PARADIGMS AND FOREIGN POLICY. *Pol. Sci. Q.* *1974 89(3): 563-588.* Argues that overall American foreign policy can profitably be understood as being based on a succession of generational paradigms about whether the country's defenses should begin at the near or far side of the oceans. Roskin contends that each generation's foreign policy elite comes to favor such an isolationist or interventionist paradigm by living through the catastrophe brought on by the application *ad absurdum* of the opposite paradigm by the previous elite generation. J

800. Ross, Graham. ALLIED DIPLOMACY IN THE SECOND WORLD WAR. *British J. of Int. Studies [Great Britain] 1975 1(3): 283-292.* Review article prompted by several works and articles on diplomacy during World War II, 1939-44; further study is needed.

801. Rothbard, Murray N. THE FOREIGN POLICY OF THE OLD RIGHT. *J. of Libertarian Studies 1978 2(1): 85-96.* Championing individualism, *laissez-faire* economics, and isolationism in foreign policy, the "Old Right" (a group of conservatives originally united by dissatisfaction over New Deal domestic and foreign policy) steadfastly opposed intervention in World War II and Korea, 1930's-1952.

802. Rothwell, David R. UNITED CHURCH PACIFISM OCTOBER 1939. *Bull. of the United Church of Can. 1973 (22): 36-55.* Examines the reasons for the issuance of "A Witness Against War," a manifesto signed by 68 United Church of Canada ministers in October 1939 proclaiming opposition to Canadian participation in World War II. The central figure was Reverend R. Edis Fairbairn, who hoped to force the church to recognize the moral dilemma posed by the war and to advertise his conscientious commitment. The manifesto called for no action but sought merely "to bring into fellowship ... all the Christian pacifists in the United Church." The church moderator suggested that "it is a very serious thing for a minister to split his congregation through controversy," but counselled "tolerance and acceptance of the conscientious rights of others." Concludes that "the pure form of idealism that underlay both the effort to Christianize the social order and to reform international affairs by pacific means was largely a victim of the Second World War." Based on newspapers, interviews and secondary sources; 90 notes. B. D. Tennyson

803. Rothwell, Richard B. SHANGHAI EMERGENCY. *Marine Corps Gazette 1972 56(11): 45-53.* Describes the experiences of US Marines during the battle between Japan and China for control of Shanghai, China, in 1937.

804. Roucek, Joseph S. GENERAL PATTON'S STOPPED INVASION OF CZECHOSLOVAKIA AND THE ROLE OF VLASOV. *Ukrainian Q. 1957 13(2): 144-149.* When US troops stopped short of invading Czechoslovakia in May 1945, residents of Prague had little hope of repelling invading Germans until a Russian general, Andrei A. Vlasov, who had previously fought with the Germans, decided to side with the Czechs and defend Prague.

805. Roy, Patricia E. BRITISH COLUMBIA'S FEAR OF ASIANS, 1900-1950. *Social Hist. [Canada] 1980 13(25): 161-172.* British Columbia's racial intolerance was rooted in fear of Asian superiority, the province's isolation from the rest of Canada, and the newness of its society. Asian academic accomplishments, and whites' beliefs in Asian moral depravity suggested initially that children and women needed special protection. Before World War I labor organizations spearheaded anti-Asian agitation. By the 1920's and 1930's farmers and retail merchants often led the fight. By the late 1930's the Japanese faced increasing resentment as Japanese military power increased. After World War II racial hostility subsided with postwar prosperity and the dispersal of the Japanese. 74 notes. D. F. Chard

806. Roy, Patricia E. THE SOLDIERS CANADA DIDN'T WANT: HER CHINESE AND JAPANESE CITIZENS. *Can. Hist. Rev. [Canada] 1978 59(3): 341-358.* Draws on the records of many federal government departments and politicians as well as British Columbia sources. Argues that the Mackenzie King government was reluctant to enlist Chinese and Japanese Canadians in the armed forces during World War II partly for considerations of military morale but especially because of its sympathies with British Columbia's fears that military service would give Asian Canadians a strong claim to the franchise. Only late in the war, and under special circumstances, were Chinese and Japanese recruited. A

807. Roy, R. H. MAJOR-GENERAL G. R. PEARKES AND THE CONSCRIPTION CRISIS IN BRITISH COLUMBIA, 1944. *BC Studies [Canada] 1975/76 (28): 53-72.* Shows the background of the conscription crisis of 1944 in British Columbia. Pearkes, instead of dragging his feet (as some historians write), really worked to implement the government's policies. Based on primary and secondary sources; 34 notes. W. L. Marr

808. Roy, Reginald H. THE DEFENCE OF PRINCE RUPERT: AN EYE-WITNESS ACCOUNT. *BC Studies [Canada] 1976 (31): 60-77.* Lieutenant R. Thistle was the Area Intelligence Officer for the Prince Rupert Defences when the Japanese attacked Pearl Harbor in 1941. His diary, from which several entries and excerpts from December 1941 to June 1942 are included here, gives a valuable eye-witness account of developments in the northern British Columbia Pacific coastal area. The last entry, 21 June 1942, tells of the first and only enemy shells which fell on British Columbia. 32 notes. D. L. Smith

809. Rubin, Barry. ANGLO-AMERICAN RELATIONS IN SAUDI ARABIA, 1941-45. *J. of Contemporary Hist. [Great Britain] 1979 14(2): 253-267.* From 1941 to 1945, Saudi Arabia repeatedly played off the Americans against the British in order to get financial aid from both Great Britain and the United States. Great Britain was accused of trying to undermine American interests. The US State Department's Near East Affairs Division, animated by national self-righteousness and anti-imperialism, while being prodded by the US oil companies, misread British intentions and involved the United States in a five-year plan "on the assumption that America would have to undertake entire responsibility for aid." Based on British Foreign Office and US State Department Archives; 44 notes. M. P. Trauth

810. Rubin, Norman N. FROM THE SEA WITH WINGS: MARYLAND AND THE FLYING BOAT. *Maryland Hist. Mag. 1977 72(2): 277-287.* Records the 40-year era, 1929-69, of the unique form of vessel called the flying boat, built at Hagerstown, Dundalk, and Middle River, Maryland, primarily by the Martin and Fokker companies. Some of the craft, such as the Model 162, Navy Mariner PBM, went through many versions and thousands of flights during and after World War II. They were used especially by the Coast Guard for rescue work, operating in 10-foot seas where operations previously were prohibited. Discusses the structures, technical capabilities, and varieties of military and civilian use of these flexible clippers. 11 illus., 2 tables. G. J. Bobango

811. Ruetten, Richard T. BURTON K. WHEELER AND THE MONTANA CONNECTION. *Montana 1977 27(3): 2-19.* Burton K. Wheeler (1882-1975) arrived in Butte, Montana, in 1905. His political views were a product of his Montana environment. He had a liberal bent and personally identified with the working man in opposition to the state's corporate influences, primarily the Anaconda Copper Company. Elected to the US Senate in 1922, Wheeler reflected his Montana experience. He opposed concentrated power, both public and private; worked to protect civil liberties; aided farmers and workers; and tried to help Indians. In 1930 Wheeler became an early supporter of Franklin D. Roosevelt for the Presidency, but he broke with Roosevelt over the Supreme Court issue in 1937, fearing concentrated power in the hands of the executive. Wheeler took a noninterventionist stance during 1939-41 and became more identified with conservatism. Always his own man, he did not represent his liberal constituents as much as he reflected them, their fears, and their aspirations. US involvement in World War II contributed to Wheeler's decline as a national political figure. He lost the Democratic primary in 1946 to liberal Leif Erickson and thus ironically preserved Montana's Democratic Party as a vehicle of the liberalism which he himself had constructed early in his career. Adapted from a 1976 lecture at Montana State University, Bozeman; 22 illus. R. C. Myers

812. Rulon, Philip Reed. THE CAMPUS CADETS: A HISTORY OF COLLEGIATE MILITARY TRAINING, 1891-1951. *Chronicles of Oklahoma 1979 57(1): 67-90.* Oklahoma State University opened its doors in 1891 and during its first year the school created a corps of male and female cadets. Early university presidents stressed the value of discipline and exercise for the student cadets, as well as the potential value for military preparedness. During the First and Second World Wars, Oklahoma State University resembled a military installation as the Reserve Officers' Training Corps (ROTC) and Women Appointed for Volunteer Emergency Service (WAVES) expanded their activities on campus. Following World War II, the university organized a very effective program for returning war veterans who used their financial aid from the GI Bill of Rights to return to school. Primary and secondary sources; 4 photos, 43 notes.
M. L. Tate

813. Rundell, Walter, Jr. TROOP LIFE: THE FINANCE DEPARTMENT IN WORLD WAR II. *Historian 1978 41(1): 94-106.* Historians assessing the quality of soldier life in World War II have emphasized the combat soldier at the expense of the men who served in the technical and administrative services. A recognition of these differences is important for an accurate assessment of the impact of the war on the American soldier. Analysis of the type of men assigned

to Army finance, their attitudes toward work, their racial attitudes, and the conditions that affected their morale reveals that 1) Soldiers assigned to finance had higher intellectual abilities and a better grasp of the military situation, 2) Finance units were close-knit, supportive, and self-confident, and the troops showed great enthusiasm and aptitude for their work, and 3) The morale of the finance units, although affected by recreation, promotion, assignment, and social opportunities, was eased by an understanding that these soldiers enjoyed protection from much of the unpleasantness of war. M. S. Legan

814. Rupp, Leila J. WOMAN'S PLACE IS IN THE WAR: PROPAGANDA AND PUBLIC OPINION IN THE UNITED STATES AND GERMANY, 1939-1945. Berkin, Carol Ruth and Norton, Mary Beth. *Women of America: a History* (Boston: Houghton Mifflin Co., 1979): 342-359. Compares US and German exhortations for women to join in the war effort. Though both societies encouraged women to participate, neither altered traditional concepts of women's roles. The American female labor force increased by 32% during the war, the German only 1%, although many women were mobilized before the war. Both countries took a patriotic approach, particularily seen in the American Office of War Information campaigns. Primary sources; 12 notes. K. Talley

815. Rutledge, Philip J. FEDERAL-LOCAL RELATIONS AND THE MISSION OF THE CITY. *Ann. of the Am. Acad. of Pol. and Social Sci. 1974 416: 77-90.* ' The administration's emphasis on New Federalism requires those concerned with governing to reexamine the complex intergovernmental system, and particularly the role of the city in that system. Traditionally, municipal government has been the level of government closest to the people and responsible for answering their needs. With the advent of World War II, however, the traditional roles reversed themselves to the point where, in 1944, federal government accounted for 89 percent of total government expenditures, whereas local governments expended only 6.4 percent of that total. The modern inclination to create 'paragovernments' for special purposes has compounded the imbalance of the intergovernmental system. The current dilemma is to find a suitable split for governmental services, supported by a more equitable financial split. In resolving this dilemma, cities must be accepted as an integral part of the federal system. Local governments should have a clear voice in decisions in such policy areas as growth management, taxation, transfer payments and quality of life enhancement. The resources of cities should be conserved and fully utilized, and the mission of the city to create 'a visible regional and civic structure, designed to make man feel at home with his deeper self and his larger world,' should be implemented. J

816. Ryon, Ted. HISTORY OF BUILDING D. *Aerospace Hist. 1979 26(1): 25-29.* Building "D" was the aircraft assembly built in 1941 at Fort Crook, now Offutt AFB, Nebraska. It was built at the direction of the War Department by the Glenn L. Martin Company as part of a nine-building aircraft assembly plant. The first aircraft assembled there were B-26 bombers. In 1944 production shifted to B-29 bombers. Building "D" still is used by the Air Force as a recreational activities building. 7 photos. C. W. Ohrvall

817. Rystad, Göran; Mjeldheim, Leiv; and Lundestad, Geir. USA OG ØST-EUROPA 1943-1947 [The United States and Eastern Europe, 1943-47]. *Hist. Tidsskrift [Norway] 1977 56(2): 173-202.* A doctoral disputation between Rystad and Mjeldheim on Lundestad's *The American Non-Policy Towards Eastern Europe 1943-1947* (1975), covering the background of the Cold War. Discussion centers on the sources, methods, and conclusions. The work examines what regimes the United States would have supported and whether American foreign policy was defensive (orthodox interpretation) or interventionist—expansionist (revisionist). Rystad and Mjeldheim are critical of the organization of the book. In defense, Lundestad argues for the complexity of the materials and the interpretive conflicts among the historians and claims these forced him to group concepts and views in a way that may obscure certain aspects. R. E. Lindgren

818. Rzheshevskii, O. NESOSTOIATEL'NOST' BURZHUAZNOI "TEORII RESHAIUSHCHIKH BITV" [Unsoundness of the bourgeois "theory of decisive battles"]. *Voenno-Istoricheskii Zhurnal [USSR] 1978 (2): 111-118.* Disputes the Western evaluation of World War II battles which applies the term "decisive" primarily to American and British operations. Except for Stalingrad, none were ranked with El Alamein, Tunis, Midway, and Guadalcanal; this conveniently forgets that 70% of the German troops fought against the USSR and that more than 600 German and Axis divisions were defeated or captured in the East. Only recently were bourgeois historians forced to acknowledge the impact of the crucial battles for Moscow and Kursk; e.g., Hanson Baldwin's *The Crucial Years: 1939-1941* (New York: Harper & Row, 1976) and Martin Caidin's *The Tigers Are Burning* (New York: Hawthorn Books, 1974). However, even they falsify data to belittle Soviet military acumen. As for Midway and Guadalcanal, they were hard blows to Japan but did not break its military superiority in the Pacific. 35 notes. N. Frenkley

819. Sadler, Charles. THE AMERICANS, EAST PRUSSIA, AND THE ODER-NEISSE LINE. *Mid-America 1979 61(3): 159-177.* Describes the activities of the State Department's Advisory Committee on Post-War Foreign Policy, and its influence on US negotiators at Potsdam. The Subcommittee on Territorial Problems, chaired by Dr. Isaiah Bowman, identified Polish boundaries as the most important problem. Largely prewar boundaries were at first recommended, but Under-Secretary Sumner Welles forced further studies. US willingness, as early as 1942, to see East Prussia transferred to Poland from Germany prepared the way for acquiescence in the more radical Oder-Niesse boundary change at war's end. During 1944-45, the Committee lost influence due to Welles's resignation. The present boundaries were established due to the realities of Soviet occupation. Based on State Department records and secondary sources; 60 notes.
J. M. Lee

820. Sadler, Charles. "POLITICAL DYNAMITE": THE CHICAGO POLONIA AND PRESIDENT ROOSEVELT IN 1944. *J. of the Illinois State Hist. Soc. 1978 71(2): 119-132.* Considers the creation and operation of the Polish-American Congress, founded by moderate groups in Buffalo, New York, to rally support for an independent Poland. National in membership and headquartered in Chicago, the Congress was treated deferentially by Franklin D. Roosevelt and some ethnic-minded officials in industrial states, but failed in the end to influence foreign policy. Based on Congress documents, State Department files, and Polish-American newspapers; 3 illus., map, 63 notes. J

821. Sadler, Charles. 'PRO-SOVIET POLISH-AMERICANS': OSKAR LANGE AND RUSSIA'S FRIENDS IN THE POLONIA, 1941-1945. *Polish Rev. 1977 22(4): 25-39.* Describes Oscar Lange's (1904-65) role in furthering the American public's acceptance of Soviet occupation of eastern Poland. Lange emerged from the pro-Soviet faction of American Poles to become an articulate statesman of its beliefs. He conferred with US, Soviet, and Polish exile government leaders. Later, after Stalin's suggestion, he renounced the US citizenship he had received in 1943, and became the first ambassador to the United States from the postwar Polish government. Mentions the roles of President Franklin D. Roosevelt and others in ceding eastern Poland. 65 notes. J. Tull

822. Sainsbury, Keith. "SECOND FRONT IN 1942": ANGLO-AMERICAN DIFFERENCES OVER STRATEGY. *British J. of Int. Studies [Great Britain] 1978 4(1): 47-58.* Assesses disagreements between British and American strategists pertaining to proposed assault Operations Sledgehammer and Round-Up, 1942-44, which pitted both American and British troops against Germans on the European continent.

823. Salaff, Stephen. THE DIARY AND THE CENOTAPH: RACIAL AND ATOMIC FEVER. *Can. Dimension [Canada] 1978 13(3): 8-11.* Discusses excerpts from the diary of former Canadian Prime Minister William Lyon MacKenzie King dealing with Canada's participation in the atomic bomb enterprise of the 1940's, and the racist (specifically, anti-Japanese) policies carried out during his 1921-48 administration.

824. Samouce, Warren A. POLITICAL WARNING AND MILITARY PLANNING. *Military R. 1973 53(4): 17-24.* Although political warning is a basic concept underlying American force structure planning, the events preceding American entry into World War II show that it is an unreliable basis for military planning. Too often political warning is difficult to perceive correctly, and even if properly perceived, unpredictable factors such as public opinion can prevent decisionmakers from acting in response to the warning indicators. Based on primary and secondary sources; 3 illus., 6 notes. J. K. Ohl

825. Samponaro, Frank N. THE COMMITTEE FOR POLITICAL DEFENSE AND HEMISPHERIC SECURITY. *Social Sci. J. 1979 16(1): 29-41.* The Committee for Political Defense was created out of the Third Meeting of the Ministers of Foreign Affairs of the American Republics in 1942, and played a unique role in hemispheric affairs during World War II.

826. Sandeen, Eric J. ANTI-NAZI SENTIMENT IN FILM: *CONFESSIONS OF A NAZI SPY* AND THE GERMAN-AMERICAN BUND. *Am. Studies (Lawrence, KS) 1979 20(2): 69-81.* The film, *Confessions of a Nazi Spy,* released in 1938, abandoned the US position of neutrality and advocated preparedness for war. It also magnified the importance of the German-American Bund, which it attacked. Traces the relationship between the Bund, the Nazi government, and domestic espionage. By 1940, when it was rereleased, the film failed because it seemed too close to reality. 5 illus., 41 notes. J. A. Andrew

827. Sanders, H. KING OF THE OCEANS. *US Naval Inst. Pro. 1974 100(8): 52-59.* Discusses the career of Ernest J. King in World War II, disclaiming his reputation as a martinet. "His very presence was so commanding and the

force of his character and intellect so great that discipline in his commands, as he expected, came naturally." The author served on Admiral King's personal staff in 1941 when the latter was the Commander-in-Chief of the Atlantic Fleet. 5 photos. — A. N. Garland

828. Santoni, Alberto. COME SI GIUNSE A HIROSHIMA [How one arrived at Hiroshima—The critical analysis of an historical decision]. *R. Marittima [Italy] 1976 109(2): 77-88.* The public interest which the atomic explosion at Hiroshima has always provoked, both as an historical and moral/political event, has however never been able to prevent analysis of it being distorted by prejudice or by insufficient objectivity. The author therefore, intends to re-examine the determining factors which led the United States to use nuclear weapons against Japan, basing his analysis on the most reliable documentation, and stressing the Japanese economic and military situation at the time, which up to now has been so wrongly interpreted. — J

829. Santoni, Alberto. LA BATTAGLIA AERONAVALE DI LEYTE [The naval-air battle at Leyte]. *Riv. Marittima [Italy] 1973 106(11): 51-68.* Discusses the battle of Leyte Gulf in October 1944, in Philippine waters, noting the significance of the suicide missions by Japanese pilots and the virtual disappearance as an effective fighting force of the Japanese fleet once the Americans had won the battle.

830. Santoni, A. LA CAMPAGNA DI GUADALCANAL: DALL'ARRIVO DELL'AMMIRAGLIO HALSEY ALLA CONQUISTA DELL'ISOLA [The Guadalcanal Campaign: Part II: From the arrival of Admiral Halsey to the conquest of the island]. *Riv. Marittima [Italy] 1972 105(10): 41-58.* Describes the conquest of Guadalcanal in late 1942, maintaining that this US victory was the turning point in the Pacific.

831. Sargent, Shirley. WHEN WAR CAME TO YOSEMITE. *Am. West 1975 12(2): 40-47.* During World War II, the US Navy utilized a hotel in Yosemite National Park as a convalescent hospital, while personnel from other branches of the armed services used the park for rest and recreation. 6 illus., bibliographic note. Adapted from a forthcoming book. — D. L. Smith

832. Savin, A. RAZGROM IAPONII V OSVESHCHENII BURZHUAZNOI ISTORIOGRAFII [The defeat of Japan in bourgeois historiography]. *Voenno-Istoricheskii Zhurnal [USSR] 1975 (9): 55-59.* Criticizes Western historians for their attempts to prove that Japan was defeated in World War II exclusively by the US armed forces; emphasizes the Soviet contribution to victory.

833. Sawyer, John Edward. OBITUARY: JAMES PHINNEY BAXTER, 3RD. *Pro. of the Am. Antiquarian Soc. 1975 85(2): 357-360.* James Phinney Baxter, 3d. (1893-1975) was born in Portland, Maine, and educated at Williams College and at Harvard University (where he joined the faculty after graduation). He was always interested in national defense; he served in several civilian military capacities during World War II. A fine historian, he was a charter member of the American Antiquarian Society. Among his publications were *Scientists Against Time,* which chronicled the efforts of scientists and technologists in the war effort and won the Pulitzer Prize in 1947. His presence, fine mind, and unfailing good humor will be sorely missed. — V. L. Human

834. Saxton, Alexander. WORLD WAR II: OPENING THE HOME FRONT. *Rev. in Am. Hist. 1980 8(3): 393-397.* Review essay of Alan Clive's *State of War: Michigan in World War II* (Ann Arbor: U. of Michigan Pr., 1979); 1939-45.

835. Scargle, Russ. MUSIC AND MEN'S MINDS: A WORLD WAR II VIGNETTE. *Pacific Historian 1972 16(1): 28-35.* A group of Bay Area women entertained hospitalized soldiers with music, 1943-45.

836. Schäfer, Peter. KOLLEKTIVE SICHERHEIT ODER APPEASEMENTPOLITIK. ZUR AUSSENPOLITIK DER ROOSEVELT-REGIERUNG BIS ZUR MITTE DER DREISSIGER JAHRE [Collective security or appeasement policy: on the foreign policy of the Roosevelt administration until the mid-thirties]. *Wissenschaftliche Zeitschrift der Humboldt-Universität zu Berlin. Gesellschafts- und Sprachwissenschaftliche Reihe [East Germany] 1973 22(1-2): 81-94.* In 1933 the Roosevelt administration adopted a policy of appeasement toward Nazi Germany. This line did not change until 1936, when the US government realized the aggressive strategy of Nazism. Published documents and secondary literature; 70 notes. R. Wagnleitner

837. Schaffer, Ronald. AMERICAN MILITARY ETHICS IN WORLD WAR II: THE BOMBING OF GERMAN CIVILIANS. *J. of Am. Hist. 1980 67(2): 318-334.* Despite an articulated US Air Force policy against the indiscriminate bombing of civilian targets in Germany, broad intepretations and frequent violations of that policy made it almost meaningless. Any restraints among Air Force generals against indiscriminate bombing arose not because of ethical objections, but because of concern for the service's image and the known inefficiency of such operations. Based on the personal papers of US Air Force generals; 46 notes. T. P. Linkfield

838. Schaffer, Ronald. GENERAL STANLEY D. EMBICK: MILITARY DISSENTER. *Military Affairs 1973 37(3): 98-95.* General Stanley D. Embick (1877-1957) was the leading spokesman for a defensive, isolationist policy among the Army planners. In particular he opposed defending the Philippines, a position gaining strong support throughout the Army following the 1934 promise of Philippine independence. After a visit to Germany in 1937 he grew increasingly concerned about the threat of war and joined in several campaigns of the National Council for the Prevention of War. Despite his strong anti-British and isolationist views he served as head of the American delegation to the secret January-March 1941 conferences with British planners which developed a joint plan for a possible Anglo-American war against the Axis. He strongly opposed active support of Britain in the spring and summer of 1941 and favored reaching an agreement with Japan over the Far East. Nevertheless he remained on duty past retirement age in important semidiplomatic and advisory roles throughout World War II. Based on official records and monographic studies; 28 notes. K. J. Bauer

839. Schaich, Warren. A RELATIONSHIP BETWEEN COLLECTIVE RACIAL VIOLENCE AND WAR. *J. of Black Studies 1975 5(4): 374-394.* A survey of collective racial violence 1910-67 reveals 210 outbreaks. Periods of war (with the exception of the Korean War) saw the highest incidences. There seems to be a correlation between war and internal collective violence. Biblio. K. Butcher

840. Schaller, Michael. AMERICAN AIR STRATEGY IN CHINA, 1939-1941: THE ORIGINS OF CLANDESTINE AIR WARFARE. *Am. Q. 1976 28(1): 3-19.* During 1940-41 influential American officials worked closely with individuals and special interest groups associated with the Chinese Nationalist regime to develop at least two plans for clandestine military attacks on Japan. These schemes, using ostensibly private American aircraft and pilots, were developed outside of the State and War Departments. They had the effect of escalating the Japanese-American military confrontation and set precedents for the use of clandestine military means as an active element of American foreign policy.
N. Lederer

841. Schaller, Michael. THE COMMAND CRISIS IN CHINA, 1944: A ROAD NOT TAKEN. *Diplomatic Hist. 1980 4(3): 327-331.* Contains the text of General George C. Marshall's draft of a proposed reply to Chinese Generalissimo Jiang Jieshi's (Chiang Kai-shek's) demand that General Joseph W. Stillwell be recalled from China. Marshall, who had selected Stillwell for the assignment, proposed that President Franklin D. Roosevelt rebut each point of Jiang's complaint and decline to remove Stillwell. Marshall's draft was rejected in favor of a more conciliatory response, and Stillwell was recalled as demanded. 4 notes.
T. L. Powers

842. Schaller, Michael. SACO! THE UNITED STATES NAVY'S SECRET WAR IN CHINA. *Pacific Hist. Rev. 1975 44(4): 527-553.* The history of Naval Group China (later, Sino-American Cooperation Association [SACO]) explains many of the apparent failures and contradictions of the US World War II China policy. From 1942 to 1945 SACO was the only American unit under effective Chinese control, supplying military aid, training, and political support to the Kuomintang. SACO bolstered the most reactionary and anti-Communist faction in the Kuomintang, under the leadership of General Tai Li, in contrast to the tactical moderation of US official policy, which was based on a fear of civil war and a desire to create a coalition in China that would subsume the Communists in an army and government dominated by Chiang Kai-shek. SACO owed its success in preventing American rapprochement with the Communists to the ultimate American strategic commitment to Chiang and to the shared conservative nationalism of American leaders outside the OSS. The significance of SACO lies both in its active role in stimulating the civil war in China and its commitment to the full logic of America's commitment to Chiang. Based on government documents at Federal Records Center (Suitland, Maryland), Navy Operational Archives, the National Archives, and personal papers in six depositories; 81 notes.
W. K. Hobson

843. Schiesl, Martin J. CITY PLANNING AND THE FEDERAL GOVERNMENT IN WORLD WAR II: THE LOS ANGELES EXPERIENCE. *California Hist. 1980 59(2): 126-143.* Describes how federal and city planning agencies attempted to deal with the problems created by greatly accelerated urban growth in Los Angeles during World War II. Problems included a blighted inner city, inadequate housing, strains on city services, and the need to provide employment for war industry workers in the postwar period. Many challenges were met, but planners and business leaders differed over such issues as directing federal funds into revitalizing commercial districts rather than supporting low-income housing. Neither group invited citizen participation in discussing redevelopment.

Despite the best efforts of wartime redevelopment planners, postwar Los Angeles development has been characterized by commercial considerations rather than social responsibility. Photos, maps, 68 notes. A. Hoffman

844. Schiff, Martin. THE UNITED STATES AND SWEDEN: A TROUBLED RELATIONSHIP. *Am. Scandinavian R. 1973 61(4): 367-372.* Friendship between the United States and Sweden dates from the American revolutionary era. During World War II the first rupture occurred because of Swedish trade with Germany. The Cold War period provided further occasion for cool relationships. The most serious strain occurred during the Vietnam conflict, with mounting criticism in Sweden of US policy. 21 notes.
J. G. Smoot

845. Schleh, Eugene P. BOOKS ABOUT FILM AND WAR. *Film and Hist. 1978 8(1): 16-19.* A number of recently written books discuss the intersection of the film industry and making war films, 1940's-70's.

846. Schleh, Eugene P. A. MODERN WAR AND ITS IMAGES. *Film and Hist. 1973 3(3): 12-16.* Lists and discusses films used in teaching a history course covering World Wars I and II, at the University of Maine, Portland, Gorham.

847. Schlenker, Gerald. THE INTERNMENT OF THE JAPANESE OF SAN DIEGO COUNTY DURING THE SECOND WORLD WAR. *J. of San Diego Hist. 1972 18(1): 1-9.* Pearl Harbor provided anti-Japanese forces in California with an opportunity to exclude Japanese Americans from the West Coast under the flag of national security. The *San Diego Union*, California's Governor Olson, Attorney General Earl Warren, and San Diego Councilman Simpson were among those who spearheaded the movement. General John L. DeWitt, West Coast military commander, recommended evacuation on 14 February 1942 and his request was in part granted by a presidential order five days later. Two days later the Tolan Committee of the US House of Representatives began hearings to determine the need for resettlement. Civilian Exclusion Order No. 4 was issued 1 April 1942, giving the Japanese six days to liquidate or store their possessions and be moved. Many lost their personal property to neighbors who promised to purchase their possessions, and much farm equipment disappeared. Hysteria, economic factors, and politics were the chief causes for the internment. The Native Sons of the Golden West, the American Legion, and prominent California politicians were at least as responsible as Colonel Karl R. Bendetsen, who at one time claimed to have planned the evacuation of 125,000 Japanese Americans for the internment policy. Based on City Council minutes, US Government reports, newspapers, and miscellaneous sources; 8 illus., 36 notes. S. S. Sprague

848. Schlesinger, Arthur M., Jr. CONGRESS AND THE MAKING OF AMERICAN FOREIGN POLICY. *Foreign Affairs 1972 51(1): 78-113.* Traces the constitutional and historical aspects of foreign policy control by Congress and the Executive branch. The Constitution is rather ambiguous on this matter, assigning "joint possession" of war and treaty powers to the two branches of government, thereby causing a source of contention. Joint resolutions and executive agreements enhance presidential treaty powers by evading the Senate's veto. Presidential powers increased further under Franklin D. Roosevelt, during World War II, and ultimately were carried to extreme lengths by Presidents Johnson and

Nixon in Indochina. Historically neither branch has remained dominant. Congress must reassert itself, and the two branches of government must become increasingly sensitive to the joint possession of power.   J. A. Kicklighter

849. Schmidt, William T. THE IMPACT OF CAMP SHELBY IN WORLD WAR II ON HATTIESBURG, MISSISSIPPI. *J. of Mississippi Hist. 1977 39(1): 41-50.* Describes the impact of World War II on "one typical community, the Hattiesburg-Camp Shelby mobilization complex." Discusses population, housing, police, churches, schools, race, and the economy. Primary sources; 10 notes.   J. W. Hillje

850. Schulzinger, Robert D. *YALTA* BY DIANE SHAVER CLEMENS AND *THE YALTA MYTHS: AN ISSUE IN U.S. POLITICS, 1945-1955* BY ATHAN G. THEOHARIS. *Hist. and Theory 1973 12(1): 146-162.* A review essay prompted by Diane Shaver Clemens's *Yalta* (Oxford U. Press, 1970) and Athan G. Theoharis's *The Yalta Myths: An Issue In U.S. Politics, 1945-1955* (U. of Missouri Press, 1970). Clemens unravels diplomatic events of the Yalta conference but fails to understand guiding foreign policy. Theoharis studies the conservative attacks on Roosevelt's diplomacy and the Democratic defense. Neither author views the intellectual and political implications of the conference as a part of the wider battle between defenders of the old diplomacy and advocates of the new. 44 notes.   L. F. Johnson

851. Schwabe, Klaus. AMERIKANISCHE WELTPOLITIK IN "REVISIONISTISCHER" SICHT [The "revisionist" view of American world policy]. *Hist. Zeitschrift [West Germany] 1975 221(1): 96-104.* The German edition of William A. Williams's *Tragedy of American Diplomacy* makes available one of the "neorevisionist" arguments concerning United States foreign policy. Williams's view that preservation of the free market distorted the prodemocracy policy defines one of the consistent American policy trends. Whether it is the chief factor remains questionable. Joyce and Gabriel Kolko in *The Politics of War* (New York, 1968) try to show aggressive Cold War tendencies in American foreign policy growing out of domestic policy during the last two years of World War II. The weakness of this work lies in the lack of attention to secondary sources and excessive adherence to a leftist viewpoint.   G. H. Davis

852. Sears, Betty M. IRA C. EAKER: THE MILITARY CAREER OF OKLAHOMA'S GREATEST AVIATOR. *Red River Valley Hist. Rev. 1978 3(3): 66-77.* General Ira C. Eaker served the Army Air Corps from 1917 to 1947, testing aircraft, making record-breaking flights, formulating military strategy, preparing for World War II, and leading the US 8th Bomber Command's B-17's over Europe.

853. Segal, David R.; Lynch, Barbara Ann; and Blair, John D. THE CHANGING AMERICAN SOLDIER: WORK-RELATED ATTITUDES OF U.S. ARMY PERSONNEL IN WORLD WAR II AND THE 1970'S. *Am. J. of Sociol. 1979 85(1): 95-108.*

854. Semmes, Raphael. A SEAPLANE BUILT FOR TWO. *Aerospace Hist. 1979 26(2): 102-107.* Describes the SOC (Scout-Observation, Curtis) seaplane which the author flew during World War II. Based on personal experience; 5 photos.   C. W. Ohrvall

855. Senarclens, Pierre de. LA POLITIQUE AMÉRICAINE DANS LES BALKANS, 1944-1947: LE CAS DE LA BULGARIE [American policy in the Balkans, 1944-47: The case of Bulgaria]. *Relations Int. [France] 1977 (9): 43-68.* Bulgaria was "the first and most constant source of tensions between the western allies and the USSR in southeast Europe." During World War II both the United States and Great Britain seemed content to assign it to the Soviet sphere. Alarm arose in 1944 and 1945 with revelation of Soviet intention to impose a Communist dictatorship and exclude Western influence, even restricting movement of Western diplomats in Sofia. Growing apprehension did not lead to any policy of attempting to challenge Soviet domination; nevertheless the Bulgarian experience prepared the way for the Truman Doctrine. Based largely on documents in *Foreign Relations of the United States.* R. Stromberg

856. Şerban, Constantin. DEBARCAREA ANGLO-AMERICANĂ ÎN NORMANDIA (6 JUNIE 1944) [The Anglo-American landing in Normandy]. *Rev. de Istorie [Rumania] 1974 27(6): 857-870.* Synthetic presentation of one of the greatest amphibious operations of all times: preliminaries, finalization of the Anglo-American plan, defense measures by Germany's headquarters, the landing itself. The study is based on vast documentary material gathered on the spot.
RSA (11:1776)

857. Service, John S. ONLY IN REJECTION COULD THERE BE VINDICATION... EXCERPTS FROM "LOST CHANCE IN CHINA." *Foreign Service J. 1974 51(3): 14-16.* The World War II dispatches of John S. Service reveal that the United States should have listened to the Foreign Service officer's advice regarding foreign policy toward Communist China in 1945.

858. Shafir, Shlomo. GEORGE S. MESSERSMITH: AN ANTI-NAZI DIPLOMAT'S VIEW OF THE GERMAN-JEWISH CRISIS. *Jewish Social Studies 1973 35(1): 32-41.* George Strausser Messersmith (1883-1960) was an American diplomat in Germany 1928-34 and Austria 1934-37 before becoming an assistant Secretary of State, 1937-39. He was an early, resolute opponent of Nazism and its anti-Semitic policies, but never suggested any proposals for the rescue of Jews because he regarded the humanitarian issue as a minor one in comparison to the national interest. Instead, he called for the direct confrontation of the United States against the Nazis and their allies. His attitude was typical of members of the American Department of State who were neither philo- nor anti-Semitic. Based on primary and secondary sources, especially the Messersmith Papers at the University of Delaware at Newark; 37 notes.
P. E. Schoenberg

859. Shapiro, Edward S. THE MILITARY OPTIONS TO HIROSHIMA: A CRITICAL EXAMINATION OF GAR ALPEROVITZ'S *ATOMIC DIPLOMACY.* *Amerikastudien/Am. Studies [West Germany] 1978 23(1): 60-72.* Gar Alperovitz's *Atomic Diplomacy* (1965) is a polemical revisionist tract. At no time was President Harry S. Truman advised by his military chiefs that Japan was on the verge of surrender or that Japanese capitulation would occur without use of the atomic bomb. Of little value in understanding the circumstances surrounding the dropping of the atomic bomb in 1945, *Atomic Diplomacy* reveals much about the outlook and methodology of one representative revisionist diplomatic historian. J/S

860. Shepardson, D. E. THE DEVIL OR BEELZEBUB: DIPLOMACY AND MORALITY. *Midwest Q. 1976 18(1): 36-52.* Traditionally it is claimed that diplomacy should be pursued according to moral and ideological principles, but often *realpolitik* or national interest predominates. In World War II the West ideally did not want to form an alliance with Stalin in order to contain Hitler and considered both to be equally evil. In reality, the alliance was necessary and created new dilemmas during the Cold War when the United States was forced to cooperate with Fascist governments. In the United States there is a tendency to confuse the ideal with the real which results in the conviction that anything is attainable if the cause is just. This belief led the country into the Vietnam War. The failure of this endeavor caused disillusionment. Successful diplomacy requires a balance between goals and tactics. Biblio. S. J. Quinlan

861. Sherwin, Martin Jay. THE ATOMIC BOMB AND THE ORIGINS OF THE COLD WAR: U.S. ATOMIC ENERGY POLICY AND DIPLOMACY, 1941-'45. *Am. Hist. R. 1973 78(4): 945-968.* An examination of recently opened atomic energy files indicates that President Franklin Delano Roosevelt left no definitive statement on the postwar role of the atomic bomb. Nevertheless, the policies he chose from among the alternatives of international control, advocated by his science advisors, and an Anglo-American postwar monopoly, urged by Churchill, indicates that the potential postwar diplomatic value of the bomb began to shape his atomic energy policies as early as 1943. The assumption that the bomb could be used to secure postwar diplomatic aims was carried over to the Truman administration. Suggests that historians have exaggerated Roosevelt's confidence in (and perhaps his commitment to) amicable postwar relations with the Soviet Union. In light of this study, the widely held assumption that Truman's attitude toward the atomic bomb was substantially different from Roosevelt's must also be revised. A

862. Shiriaev, B. A. VTORAIA MIROVAIA VOINA I PERSPEKTIVY SOVETSKO-AMERIKANSKOGO SOTRUDNICHESTVA [World War II and the perspectives of Soviet-American cooperation]. *Vestnik Leningradskogo U.: Istoriia, Iazyk, Literatura [USSR] 1975 14(3): 39-43.* After 1943 American public opinion was that the two most powerful postwar powers would be the United States and the USSR. The conduct of the Allies during the war held forth the possibilities of a positive relationship after the war's conclusion. So strong was US sympathy for the Soviet Union during the war that traditional anticommunist elements were overwhelmed. At the end of the war, powerful business circles favored a continuation of the relationship. Unfortunately by 1948 the opponents of closer Soviet-American relations became stronger, and cooperation between the two powers was replaced by hostility. 20 notes. G. F. Jewsbury

863. Shisler, Michael F. GEN. OLIVER P. SMITH'S LIFE WAS A COMMITMENT TO EXCELLENCE. *Marine Corps Gazette 1978 62(11): 42-48.* A brief history of Oliver P. Smith's military career, 1917-51; he served in both the Marine Corps and the Army in World Wars I and II and in the Korean War.

864. Shulimson, Jack. MAURICE EVANS, SHAKESPEARE AND THE U.S. ARMY. *J. of Popular Culture 1976 10(2): 255-266.* Explores the resistance to and the eventual triumphs of actor Maurice Evans's efforts to present Shakespeare to the troops in the Pacific Theater of Operations during World War II. Primary and secondary sources; 80 notes. D. G. Nielson

865. Sigal, Leon V. BUREAUCRATIC POLITICS AND TACTICAL USE OF COMMITTEES: THE INTERIM COMMITTEE AND THE DECISION TO DROP THE ATOMIC BOMB. *Polity 1978 10(3): 326-364.* With the publication of Graham Allison's *Essence of Decision* the "bureaucratic politics" model added a new dimension to the decision-making theory of foreign policy. Working within the "bureaucratic politics" framework Leon Sigal calls attention to the largely neglected role of committees in the decision-making process. In his analysis of the events leading to the decision to drop the atomic bomb on Japan, he shows how various types of committees can be used tactically to forge interagency agreement on and secure compliance by governmental agencies with policy decisions. The result is a valuable contribution not only to the "bureaucratic politics" model but also to our understanding of the decision to drop the atomic bomb. J

866. Sih, Paul K. T. A DEPLORABLE PAGE IN CHINESE-AMERICAN RELATIONS. *Issues and Studies [Taiwan] 1972 8(12): 57-62.* Discusses the influence of General Joseph W. Stilwell on foreign relations between China and the United States during and following World War II, 1942-70's.

867. Sims, Robert C. "A FEARLESS, PATRIOTIC, CLEAN-CUT STAND": IDAHO'S GOVERNOR CLARK AND JAPANESE-AMERICAN RELOCATION IN WORLD WAR II. *Pacific Northwest Q. 1979 70(2): 75-81.* Idaho's governor Chase Clark was one of the first political figures to advocate that all Japanese Americans be placed in relocation camps following the Pearl Harbor attack. He opposed the initial plan for allowing voluntary relocation and called instead for barbed-wire stockades, guarded by machine guns. Governor Clark drew upon the west coast's long-standing anti-Japanese sentiment and his policies received overwhelming public support. Based on newspapers and archival sources; 5 photos, 30 notes. M. L. Tate

868. Sims, Robert C. THE JAPANESE AMERICAN EXPERIENCE IN IDAHO. *Idaho Yesterdays 1978 22(1): 2-10.* About 1900 the Japanese came into Idaho to work on the railroads. They stayed to work in agriculture, despite state and federal discriminatory laws. A new dimension of Japanese American settlement occurred when a World War II relocation camp was set up near Hunt, Idaho. Few people stayed in the area after the war. Their experiences had been too unpleasant. Primary sources; 2 illus., 57 notes. B. J. Paul

869. Sirevåg, Torbjørn. THE NEW DEAL OF WAR. *Am. Studies in Scandinavia [Norway] 1975 7(2): 81-99.* The political opponents of Franklin D. Roosevelt perceived that American involvement in World War II would allow him to create a "Super-New Deal" domestically. Conceivably, wartime controls would (and did) become permanent features of New Deal programs. The Japanese attack rallied Roosevelt's political opponents by strengthening their suspicions of his motivations. A portion of the text is to become part of a monograph on the eclipse of the New Deal, 1940-45. P. D. Travis

870. Sisk, John P. AT WAR WITH GENERAL FORREST. *Virginia Q. Rev. 1977 53(2): 288-310.* Describes the author's service in World War II where he served under the "last" General Nathan Bedford Forrest (1905-44), the great-grandson of the better known "first" General Forrest. Makes Civil War comparisons. O. H. Zabel

871. Sivachev, N. V. DISKRIMINITSIIA V TRUDOVYKH OTNO-SHENIIAKH V SSHA PERIODA VTOROI MIROVOI VOINY [Discrimination in labor relations in the United States during the second World War]. *Vestnik Moskovskogo U., Seriia 9: Istoriia [USSR] 1972 27(2): 17-35.* Racial discrimination is the class ideology and policy of the monopolistic bourgeoisie in the United States. During the war it mainly affected Negroes. The Communist Party and trade unions fought against racism. The Congress of Industrial Organizations opposed racial discrimination more directly than the American Federation of Labor. Under trade union pressure, President Franklin D. Roosevelt created the Fair Employment Practices Committee, which had limited success in opening employment to minorities, but President Harry S. Truman refused to make the committee permanent. 121 notes. G. E. Munro

872. Sivachev, N. V. NEGRITIANSKII VOPROS V SSHA V GODY VTOROI MIROVOI VOINY [The negro question in the United States during the Second World War]. *Novaia i Noveishaia Istoriia [USSR] 1976 (6): 50-65.* Recent US historiography on the position of Negroes in the New Deal era, unlike the earlier adulation of Roosevelt, attacks the Democrats' racial policies of 1933-45. Soviet works have not discussed the negroes' position in detail. Investigates the negroes' attitudes toward World War II, their position in the armed forces and at home, and the struggle against discrimination and segregation. Drawing on many sources the analysis gives statistics on blacks in the forces, and their unequal treatment, especially regarding promotion. Instances of racial fights in war zones are stressed, as is the fact that no negroes received high decorations for valour. Figures also show discrimination in civilian occupations. However, the participation of the USSR in the war, the rise of national-liberation movements among colored peoples, prepared the ground for a future struggle to end segregation and racial discrimination in America. Based on many American newspapers, papers of H. S. Truman (Truman Library), US National Archives RG-228, and published studies; 89 notes. D. N. Collins

873. Sivachev, N. V. RABOCHAIA POLITIKA PRAVITEL'STVA SSHA V NACHALE VTOROI MIROVOI VOINY (SENTIABR' 1939 G.-DEKABR' 1941 G.) [The labor policy of the US government at the beginning of World War II, September 1939-December 1941]. *Vestnik Moskovskogo U., Seriia 9: Istoriia [USSR] 1971 26(6): 18-37.* During this 27-month period the liberal-progressive labor policy of the 1930's (Wagner Act, etc.) began a reactionary shift led by Congressman Smith of Virginia. The large corporations sought strict limitations on the rights of labor unions, all in the interest of national defense. The National Labor Relations Board was instituted to handle disputes. When strikes continued to occur, President Franklin D. Roosevelt called out military forces on two occasions to work in defense-related industries in the absence of striking workers. In 1940 the National Defense Advisory Commission (NDAC) and in 1941 the Office of Production Management (a branch of the NDAC) were created. By 7 December 1941, the reactionary forces had won. 106 notes. G. E. Munro

874. Skates, John R., Jr. WORLD WAR II AS A WATERSHED IN MISSISSIPPI HISTORY. *J. of Miss. Hist. 1975 37(2): 131-142.* Concludes World War II "was a watershed for Mississippi, . . . after which nothing ever again was quite the same." During the war prosperity developed, population and agriculture changed, racial issues surfaced, and strains appeared in the Democratic Party. Secondary sources; 14 notes. J. W. Hillje

875. Skold, Karen Beck. THE JOB HE LEFT BEHIND: AMERICAN WOMEN IN THE SHIPYARDS DURING WORLD WAR II. Berkin, Carol Ruth and Lovett, Clara M., ed. *Women, War & Revolution* (New York: Holmes & Meier, 1980): 55-75. Discusses the boom in shipbuilding during World War II and women's participation in the industry, focusing on Portland, Oregon. Women made up one-fourth of the industry's workers in Portland and, thus, had opportunities for learning skilled trades and earning high wages from which they had been previously excluded. Focuses on how and why women entered the industry, compares the work done by men and women, and what women did after the war ended and the shipyards closed. G. L. Smith

876. Sköld, Nils. STYRKERELATIONERNAS BETYDELSE I MARKSTRIDEN: ETT BIDRAG TILL FRÅGAN OM MAKTBALANSENS PROBLEM [The importance of the relations of strength in land warfare: a contribution to the question of the problem of balance of power]. *Kungliga Krigsvetenskaps Akademiens Handlingar och Tidskrift [Sweden] 1963 167(3): 31-52.* Investigates the use of conventional weapons in land warfare with a view to defining how great an impact the balance of power between two parties has on the outcome of a battle. The author illustrates his theory that the balance of power is the determining factor in strife with examples from World War II and the Korean War, and maintains that technical developments favor land defense. Secondary sources; 8 tables, 22 notes. U. G. Jeyes

877. Sledge, Eugene B. PELELIEU: A NEGLECTED BATTLE. *Marine Corps Gazette 1979 63(11): 88-95, (12): 28-41; 1980 64(1): 32-42.* Part I. DEFENSE IN DEPTH. Although the battle of Pelelieu Island (in the Palau Islands) in September-November 1944 largely is overlooked by historians and the public, it was probably the toughest battle of World War II. Notes that Admiral William (Bull) Halsey argued that the entire Palau Islands operation, intended to shore up General Douglas MacArthur's right flank for his invasion of the Philippines, was not even necessary. The author describes the horror of his combat on Pelelieu during 15 September-15 October with Company K, 3d Battalion, 5th Marines, 1st Marine Division, most of them not yet 21 years old, against the *bushido* inspired defense in depth practiced by Colonel Kunio Nakagawa, his 14th Infantry Division, and other Japanese units. Part II. ASSAULT INTO HELL. The author describes the landing on Pelelieu, the move inland, Japanese counterattacks, and more US attacks, including that on adjacent Ngesebus Island, 28 September. Part III. VICTORY AT HIGH COST. The author describes the close quarters and hand-to-hand combat, battle fatigue, the Marines' esprit de corps, their relief by the 81st Infantry on 15 October, the killing of the last Japanese by 27 November, casualty totals, and the effectiveness of Marine Corps training.
D. J. Engler

878. Sluch, S. Z. "FAKTOR SSHA" V OTSENKE KOMANDOVANIIA VERMAKHTA NAKANUNE VTOROI MIROVOI VOINY [The assessment of the USA factor by the Wehrmacht command on the eve of World War II]. *Vestnik Moskovskogo U. Seriia 9: Istoriia [USSR] 1973 28(2): 51-68.* American policy of neutrality and isolationism, its economic crisis of the 1930's, and a comparatively small military budget misled the German High Command and Nazi party leadership to underrate the American factor in an eventual European war. Discusses Nazi speculation about US willingness to join the Allies and

assessment of the American military potential in case of US entry into the war. Primary and secondary sources; 105 notes. N. Frenkley

879. Small, Melvin. BUFFOONS AND BRAVE HEARTS: HOLLYWOOD PORTRAYS THE RUSSIANS, 1939-1944. *California Hist. Q. 1973 52(4): 326-337.* During World War II the U.S. motion picture industry made a number of films dealing with Russian themes. Before the German invasion of the USSR in 1941 the films caricatured the Russians as boors or buffoons (as in *Ninotchka*), but after the USSR joined the fight against the Nazis and U.S. entry, Hollywood portrayed the Russian people as defending freedom against tyranny (*Mission to Moscow* and *North Star*). After the war Hollywood's positive view of the Soviet Union (as in *Song of Russia*) was scrutinized by the House Committee on Un-American Activities. Louis B. Mayer and others assured the committee that the films stressed the USSR's positive side because the two countries had been fighting a common enemy. Despite the lack of subtlety in the films, no conspiracy of Communist directors or writers existed. The films undoubtedly affected the American public, because many Americans were optimistic that postwar relations would reflect the amicability projected in the films. After the war Hollywood moved with the prevailing political winds and produced a number of strongly anti-Communist films. Based on unpublished documents, secondary studies, and newspapers; photos, 39 notes. A. Hoffman

880. Small, Melvin. HOW WE LEARNED TO LOVE THE RUSSIANS: AMERICAN MEDIA AND THE SOVIET UNION DURING WORLD WAR II. *Historian 1974 36(3): 455-478.* An examination of public opinion polls reveals that people changed their minds about the USSR during the course of World War II. A statistical study of the proportion of favorable and unfavorable media presentations regarding Russia during the same period indicates a decided favorable shift. The rapidity with which America again became anticommunist suggests some reservation as to the media's permanent effectiveness on foreign policy. 5 tables; 65 notes. R. V. Ritter

881. Small, Melvin. MOTION PICTURES AND THE STUDY OF ATTITUDES: SOME PROBLEMS FOR HISTORIANS. *Film and Hist. 1972 2(1): 1-5.* The author has been studying American attitudes toward the Soviet Union during World War II and has studied motion pictures as one of the sources which helped shape these attitudes. He considers films to be one of the least developed sources in the writing of history. The historian seeking to use movies in his research must face two questions: How do motion pictures affect images? How can the historian manage such an unusual source? Movies play a role in shaping images of various ethnic and national groups. But while movies may shape public opinion, they may also serve as reflectors of opinion. The problems of studying movies for their effects on popular attitudes are difficult. 20 notes.
B. S. Viault

882. Smiley, Donald V. FEDERAL-PROVINCIAL CONFLICT IN CANADA. *Publius 1974 4(3): 7-24.* World War II saw the establishment of a reasonably strong central government, but the provinces moved to reclaim lost ground during the late 1950's because of the failure of so many national programs. The battle wages warm at present. Judicial review of the constitution, partisan politics, territorial pluralism within the central government, and executive feder-

alism represent forces and forums within which the issues are both fought out and settled. The central government retains control of many critical functions, but lacks the institutional structure to effectively pursue them. 35 notes.
V. L. Human

883. Smith, Alonzo and Taylor, Quintard. RACIAL DISCRIMINATION IN THE WORKPLACE: A STUDY OF TWO WEST COAST CITIES DURING THE 1940S. *J. of Ethnic Studies 1980 8(1): 35-54.* Negroes in the shipyards of Portland (Oregon) and Los Angeles (California) experienced employment discrimination during World War II. The yards were closed shops organized by the International Brotherhood of Boilermakers, Iron Shipbuilders and Helpers. As the number of Negro employees increased, the union established segregated locals, which Negroes had to join or lose their jobs. Promotion to skilled jobs was denied them. Negroes appealed to the Fair Employment Practice Committee, which found in their favor but had no means to enforce its decisions. 55 notes.
S

884. Smith, C. Calvin. DILUTING AN INSTITUTION: THE SOCIAL IMPACT OF WORLD WAR II ON THE ARKANSAS FAMILY. *Arkansas Hist. Q. 1980 39(1): 21-34.* World War II brought serious family problems to Arkansas: working mothers, increased juvenile delinquency, venereal disease, hasty marriages, quick divorces, and abandoned children. Efforts to pass legislation that would control the problems were usually defeated. Based on newspapers; 52 notes.
G. R. Schroeder

885. Smith, Charles. LEND-LEASE AID TO GREAT BRITAIN IN 1941-1945. *Southern Q. 1972 10(2): 195-208.* A review of the U.S.-British lend-lease program during World War II. Data relating to the nature and amount of aid are included, as well as problems, contradictions, and policy conflicts. In the final analysis, questions about the effectiveness and necessity of lend-lease aid must be considered in light of the program's results. Public support in the United States was unflagging, once the policy was initiated, but modifying factors are too varied and numerous to be taken into account individually. The objective of lend-lease assistance was the defeat of the Axis powers. This goal was achieved, thereby stamping the program with the mark of success. Based on secondary sources; 48 notes, appendix.
V. L. Human

886. Smith, David E. PROVINCIAL REPRESENTATION ABROAD: THE OFFICE OF AGENT GENERAL IN LONDON. *Dalhousie Rev. [Canada] 1975 55(2): 315-327.* Recapitulates the growth of the office of agent general through its various titles from the late 18th century through the 1970's. The friction between federal and provincial jurisdictions is noted. The main break in the evolution of the agencies is World War II. Since then the roles of the provincial agents have proliferated and the relationships with the federal high commissioners have been harmonious. 27 notes.
C. Held

887. Smith, E. D. THE RAPIDO FIASCO. *Army Q. and Defence J. [Great Britain] 1972 102(4): 483-495.* Describes the planning and course of the Rapido Battle (1944) and the inquiry which followed. Though planning was careful, some of it was misguided and misdirected; conditions made the attack a catastrophe for the Allied troops. "The verdict of history must be that the Rapido fiasco was

an unnecessary attack, that the conditions made it impossible for 36th Division to succeed, and that the result was not only tragic and inevitable but contributed nothing to Anzio [,Italy,] or the main Fifth Army front." Map.
D. H. Murdoch

888. Smith, Frank F. VPB-106: THE WOLVERATORS. *Aero Album 1972 5(4): 2-7.* A history of US Navy Patrol Bombing Squadron 106 from its formation in July 1944 to the transfer of its first commanding officer, Commander William S. Sampson, in July 1945. The squadron took its PB4B-2 aircraft into combat from Tinian Island in February 1945 and supported Navy and Marine operations as far away as Japan. The squadron moved to the Philippines in May 1945, and flew bombing and reconnaissance missions to Borneo, Malay, Singapore, and Thailand. 10 photos.
C. W. Ohrvall

889. Smith, Jean Edward. SELECTION OF A PROCONSUL FOR GERMANY: THE APPOINTMENT OF GEN. LUCIUS D. CLAY, 1945. *Military Affairs 1976 40(3): 123-129.* Discusses the events leading to the appointment of General Lucius D. Clay (b. 1897) to administer the military occupation of Germany. Civilian, not military, leaders selected him because he was in tune with the goals and aspirations of wartime Washington. In 1945 Clay was no friend of the Germans, yet he organized and conducted an occupation that was a model of propriety. Primary and secondary sources; 57 notes.
A. M. Osur

890. Smith, Julian. REVIEW ESSAY: WHERE HAPPINESS COSTS SO LITTLE: AMERICA AT THE MOVIES IN WORLD WAR TWO. *J. of Popular Film 1974 3(1): 75-78.* Reviews *Hollywood at War: The American Motion Picture and World War II*, edited by Ken D. Jones and Arthur F. McClure (Cranbury, N.J.: A. S. Barnes and Co., 1974) and *The Films of World War II: A Pictorial Treasury of Hollywood's War Years*, edited by Joe Morella, Edward Z. Epstein, and John Griggs (New York: Citadel Press, 1974).
S

891. Smith, Melden E., Jr. THE STRATEGIC BOMBING DEBATE: THE SECOND WORLD WAR AND VIETNAM. *J. of Contemporary Hist. [Great Britain] 1977 12(1): 175-191.* Strategic bombing during World War II was effective in bringing about the defeat of Germany and Japan. It was not so successful in the Vietnam War because the air commanders were hampered by instructions from Washington that violated the principle of immediate and maximal use against highest priority targets first. The bombing of North Vietnam cannot, therefore, be considered a real test of the effectiveness of strategic aerial bombing. 33 notes.
M. P. Trauth

892. Smith, Myron J., Jr. LOG OF THE "WEE VEE": THE U.S. BATTLESHIP *WEST VIRGINIA*. *West Virginia Hist. 1977 38(4): 291-303; 39(1): 3-29.* Part I. The battleship *West Virginia* was authorized by Congress in 1916, postponed by World War I, built in 1920-23, and saved by the Washington Treaty of 1922. The *West Virginia* "took part in every important [US] naval exercise from 1924 to 1941." The *West Virginia* was sunk by two bombs and seven torpedoes at Pearl Harbor, 7 December 1941, losing 103 men and 2 officers, including its Captain, Marvyn Bennion, who received a posthumous Congressional Medal of Honor. 15 notes. Part II. The *West Virginia* was raised, rebuilt, and sent back to the Pacific. It fought at Leyte Gulf, Iwo Jima, and Okinawa,

sustaining minor damage. It was decommissioned in 1947 and sold for scrap in 1959. Based on primary and secondary sources; map, 20 notes.

J. H. Broussard/S

893. Smith, Myron J., Jr. LOG OF THE "WEE VEE": THE US BATTLESHIP *WEST VIRGINIA*. *West Virginia Hist. 1977 38(4): 291-303.* Part I. The USS *West Virginia,* commissioned in 1923, was sunk by Japanese bombs at Pearl Harbor in 1941, with the loss of more than 100 men. Primary and secondary sources; 15 notes.

J. H. Broussard

894. Smith, Myron J., Jr. NOVELS OF THE AIR WAR, 1939-45: AN ANNOTATED LIST. *Aerospace Hist. 1975 22(3): 166-168.* Presents an annotated list of novels in English dealing with the air warfare, 1939-45. Includes books published as late as 1975. Arranged alphabetically by author. 4 photos.

C. W. Ohrvall

895. Smith, Myron J., Jr. [THE USS *INDIANA* STORY]. *Indiana Hist. Bull. 1974 51(1): 3-13, (5): 55-76, (7): 92-99.*
THE THIRD *INDIANA* (BB-58): PART I, FROM CONCEPTION TO THE WARZONE, (1): 3-13.
THE THIRD *INDIANA* (BB-58): PART II [IN THE WARZONE], (5): 55-76.
THE THIRD *INDIANA* (BB-58): PART III, FROM THE WARZONE TO THE SCRAPHEAP, (7): 92-99.
Three-part article on the USS *Indiana* (BB-58), its naval operations in the South Pacific during World War II, and its eventual scrapping in 1962. S

896. Smylie, Robert F. JOHN LEIGHTON STUART: A MISSIONARY IN THE SINO-JAPANESE CONFLICT 1937-1941. *J. of Presbyterian Hist. 1975 53(3): 256-276.* As President of Yenching University in 1937 when the Japanese occupied Peking and north China, John Leighton Stuart's unique outlook on China thrust him into the role of intermediary among the varying forces striving for dominance in China. He was disdainful of Chiang Kai-shek who obstinately refused to meet with Japanese officials and sympathized with liberal Japanese who saw the Sino conflict without purpose or end. In 1937-41, all parties in China had confidence in him, but because he was not a US diplomat, he received little sympathy from Roosevelt. Stuart urged an embargo on Japan, financial assistance to China, and settlement of anachronistic foreign rights in China, such as extraterritoriality. Based largely on documents in State Department Archives and the Franklin D. Roosevelt Library in Hyde Park; biblio., 64 notes.

H. M. Parker, Jr.

897. Smyth, H. D. THE "SMYTH REPORT." *Princeton U. Lib. Chronicle 1976 37(3): 173-189.* Discusses the author's role in preparing a War Department report on the military feasibility of using atomic energy for strategic purposes against Japan during World War II.

898. Sniegoski, Stephen J. UNIFIED DEMOCRACY: AN ASPECT OF AMERICAN WORLD WAR II INTERVENTIONIST THOUGHT, 1939-1941. *Maryland Hist. 1978 9(1): 33-48.* Describes the arguments introduced by interventionists such as Lewis Mumford, Harold Ickes, Max Lerner, and Dorothy Thompson in support of American intervention against fascism. They agreed with fascists that democracies lacked national purpose but argued that war would

counter fascism by creating a national purpose. According to the interventionists, discipline, loyalty, and economic democracy would emerge after the war to enable democracy to continue. Based on interventionists' publications and correspondence; 2 photos, 59 notes.   G. O. Gagnon

899. Socknat, Thomas. AN EXAMPLE OF AN INDEPENDENT ORAL HISTORY PROJECT: THE CANADIAN CONTINGENT TO THE FRIENDS AMBULANCE UNIT, CHINA CONVOY. *Can. Oral Hist. Assoc. J. [Canada] 1978 3(2): 18-22.* Describes an individual's oral history project, the study of the Canadian contingent to the Friends' Ambulance Unit's China Convoy during World War II.

900. Solo, Robert A. THE SAGA OF SYNTHETIC RUBBER. *Bull. of the Atomic Scientists 1980 36(4): 31-36.* Recounts the experience of synthetic rubber production in the United States during World War II as a model for the difficulties inherent in government-mandated production of a politically and economically sensitive commodity such as synthetic fuel.

901. Spector, Ronald. "WHAT THE LOCAL ANNAMITES ARE THINKING": AMERICAN VIEWS OF VIETNAMESE IN CHINA, 1942-1945. *Southeast Asia 1974 3(2): 741-751.* Maintains that little attention has been paid either to the contacts American officials had with the Vietnamese prior to 1945 or to the attitudes that resulted from these contacts. American contacts with the Vietnamese, including Ho Chi Minh, occurred in southern China as early as 1942, when the Vietminh sought American help in securing the release of Ho from a Chinese prison. In 1943 and 1944, American consuls provided Washington with additional assessments of Ho and his followers. American officials consistently underestimated the strength and determination of the Vietnamese independence movement, and at the highest policymaking levels information about Vietnamese nationalism appears to have been ignored. Based largely on US government documents; 48 notes.   R. H. Detrick

902. Speer, R. T. LET PASS SAFELY THE AWA MARU. *US Naval Inst. Pro. 1974 100(4): 69-76.* During the night of 1 April 1945 the US submarine *Queenfish* attacked and sank the Japanese steamship *Awa Maru*, even though the latter had been granted safe passage by the US government to carry relief supplies to prisoner of war camps in the East Indies. The sinking was the result of a series of unfortunate circumstances. The *Queenfish*'s commander was tried by general court-martial and received a light sentence. The US government did express its formal apology to the Japanese government, but the war ended before discussions regarding a replacement ship could be concluded. 7 notes; 3 photos.
A. N. Garland

903. Spidle, Jake W. AXIS INVASION OF THE AMERICAN WEST: POWS IN NEW MEXICO, 1942-1946. *New Mexico Hist. R. 1974 49(2): 93-122.* During World War II a prisoner of war camp was built 14 miles southeast of Roswell, New Mexico. Some of the more than 425,000 enemy captives were placed in this camp. American historians have written very little about the prisoner of war camps because little information is available. Rommel's men predominated in the prisoners held in the New Mexico camp. 147 notes.
J. H. Krenkel

904. Spidle, Jake W., Jr.   AXIS PRISONERS OF WAR IN THE UNITED STATES, 1942-1946: A BIBLIOGRAPHICAL ESSAY.   *Military Affairs 1975 39(2): 61-66.* In 1945 camps scattered across the United States confined over 425,000 prisoners of war. To investigate this subject, researchers can take advantage of a massive German series, the official files of various US government agencies, employers of POW labor, state archives, and local newspapers. Includes a state-by-state listing of the larger base and branch camps; 17 notes.
A. M. Osur

905. Spiller, Robert E.   HIGHER EDUCATION AND THE WAR: COMPRESSION OF COURSES DUE TO WAR MAY BE A CHALLENGE TO ACADEMIC RECONSTRUCTION (JUNE 1942).   *J. of Higher Educ. 1979 50(4): 514-525.* During the defense period, students were clearly justified in putting their education ahead of their military service and in taking a long view of both liberal and vocational training. Discusses the squeezing of the four-year college between the junior college and the graduate school. Another aspect of the adjustment to the war situation is the suddenly increasing emphasis on vocational training, sometimes in the form of night courses. The period of higher liberal education for all students is shortened for the duration. Many students now turn to vocational training. Courses in American literature and American civilization are being introduced, but we still know too little of American culture. Mentions examples of new courses in that field at several eastern institutions. The trend was already established at the outbreak of World War II; US entry has merely reinforced it. 2 notes.
E. P. Stickney

906. Spiller, Roger J.   ASSESSING ULTRA.   *Military Rev. 1979 59(8): 13-23.* The top-secret Ultra project decoded German "enigma codes" in World War II. Considers the impact of this cryptographic breakthrough and its effect on the outcome of World War II. Questions whether current historical treatment of the conflict should be reevaluated given the recently uncovered intelligence role of the operation in World War II. Secondary sources; 34 notes.
J. Moore

907. Spivey, Delmar T. and Durad, Arthur A.   SECRET MISSION TO BERLIN.   *Air Force Mag. 1975 58(9): 115-120.* Recounts the secret mission of two American prisoners of war, who were sent by their German captors to Berlin in a conspiracy to overthrow Adolf Hitler and end the war in the West.

908. Sprague, Claire D.   "TILL YOU COME BACK."   *Pacific Hist. 1980 24(2): 192-195.* Personal account of forced relocation during World War II. The author relates experiences in the assembly centers for Japanese Americans as told to her in letters from her former pupils (French Camp Grammar School) and their families. The evacuees were held in assembly centers before being shipped to relocation centers. 5 photos.
G. L. Lake

909. Stacey, C. P.   POLITIQUE ET OPERATIONS MILITAIRES (1939-1945)   [Canadian politics and military operations, 1939-45]. *Rev. d'Hist. de la Deuxième Guerre Mondiale [France] 1976 26(104): 1-30.* The Canadian Army was very small before revival after 1936 under Prime Minister William Lyon W. L. Mackenzie King. Immediately after Great Britain entered World War II, Canada joined as a loyal member of the Commonwealth. The first task was to train and supply almost 30,000 airmen to support Britain. French Canadians

opposed conscription and many politicians called for "limited engagement." Canada took an active part in the direction and operations of the European but not the Pacific war, although Canadians did defend Hong Kong in 1941. Canadians were involved in the operation at Dieppe in August 1942. Other operations summarized here include the Italian and northwest European campaigns, and aerial and naval activity. One of four articles in a special edition on Canada during World War II. 29 notes. G. H. Davis

910. Stacey, C. P. THE TURNING-POINT: CANADIAN-AMERICAN RELATIONS DURING THE ROOSEVELT-KING ERA. *Can.: An Hist. Mag. 1973 1(1): 1-9.* World War II and the amiability that existed between Franklin D. Roosevelt and William Lyon Mackenzie King led to the formulation of the Ogdensburg Agreement, which established a joint US-Canadian board for studying problems of the defense of North America. S

911. Stackman, R. Robert. THE STRUGGLE OVER TURKISH CHROME DURING WORLD WAR II. *North Dakota Q. 1977 45(1): 19-22.* Remaining neutral through most of World War II, Turkey shipped chrome to both Allied and Axis Powers, 1939-44, until pressure applied by the Allies stopped shipment for the duration of the war.

912. Stathis, Stephen W. MALTA: PRELUDE TO YALTA. *Presidential Studies Q. 1979 9(4): 469-482.* Despite President Franklin D. Roosevelt's fear that an Anglo-American meeting before the Yalta Conference might antagonize the USSR, such a meeting eventually took place. Yielding to British Prime Minister Winston Churchill's wishes, Roosevelt agreed to a meeting of the Joint Chiefs of Staff on Malta at the end of January 1945. Military matters such as Eisenhower's plan for the crossing of the Rhine, the occupation of Germany, and the Polish question received attention. Probably by Roosevelt's design, substantive political issues were not addressed. 69 notes. S

913. Stebbins, Owen T. RIFLE COMPANY VS. FORTRESS. *Marine Corps Gazette 1973 57(4): 36-41.* Examines the role of Company G, 22d Marines, in the May 1945 attack on Sugar Loaf Hill on Okinawa, which started the fiercest and most decisive battle of the last campaign of World War II.

914. Stebbins, Robert A. FORMALIZATION: NOTES ON A THEORY OF THE RISE AND CHANGE OF SOCIAL NORMS. *Int. J. of Contemporary Sociol. 1974 11(2-3): 105-119.* Discusses behavioristic and sociological theory regarding the origin of social norms and values 1940's-70's, emphasizing the example of attitudes toward Japanese Americans during World War II.

915. Steele, Richard W. AMERICAN POPULAR OPINION AND THE WAR AGAINST GERMANY: THE ISSUE OF NEGOTIATED PEACE, 1942. *J. of Am. Hist. 1978 65(3): 704-723.* Outspoken and organized dissent regarding US involvement in World War II was absent, but discontent and even indifference concerning US war aims did exist to a considerable degree, especially in 1942. A substantial "peace bloc," which comprised approximately 20% of the adult population, rejected President Roosevelt's no-compromise position toward Germany. Many Americans believed a negotiated settlement could be secured with Germany by contacting anti-Nazi elements in the German Army. The negotiated peace movement, however, was never able to organize on a national

level, although the threat of such a movement was never totally eliminated. 57 notes.
T. P. Linkfield

916. Steele, Richard W. "THE GREATEST GANGSTER MOVIE EVER FILMED": *PRELUDE TO WAR*. *Prologue 1979 11(4): 220-235.* Sketches the armed forces' struggle for better understanding of the war effort that resulted in the 1942 propaganda film *Prelude to War*. The great American director Frank Capra made the movie and, like many of his films, filled it with patriotic, simple ideas aimed at a mass audience. The film put World War II on a personal level while reducing it to a clash of ideologies rather than of nations. Full of stereotyping, it did not deal with Nazi racial policy, but instead portrayed the Axis as mobsters plotting to grab the world. Yet for all of Capra's artistry, the film had little influence on either military men or civilians. It influenced the least educated the most. Primary sources; 9 photos, 64 notes.
S

917. Steger, Bernd. GENERAL CLAYS STABSKONFERENZEN UND DIE ORGANISATION DER AMERIKANISCHEN MILITÄRREGIERUNG IN DEUTSCHLAND: DIE "CLAY-MINUTES" ALS HISTORISCHE QUELLE [General Clay's staff conferences and the organization of the American military government in Germany: the "Clay Minutes" as a historical source]. *Vierteljahrshefte für Zeitgeschichte [West Germany] 1979 27(1): 113-130.* A brief description of the extant minutes of the staff conferences of the US Group Control Council, Germany (USGCC), 28 July 1944 to 30 September 1945 and its successor, Office of Military Government for Germany (US), (OMGUS), 1 October 1945 to 8 August 1949 under US Military Governor General Lucius D. Clay (1897-1978) in post-World War II Germany. Discovered in 1975 during the German-American OMGUS Papers microfilming project, the minutes are now located in the US National Archives and Institut für Zeitgeschichte in Munich, Germany, the latter copy with a subject and name index. 46 notes.
D. Prowe

918. Steiner, Arthur. BAPTISM OF THE ATOMIC SCIENTISTS. *Bull. of the Atomic Scientists 1975 31(2): 21-28.* Traces the fate of the "Franck Report" to illuminate one aspect of scientists' participation in national policymaking. A seven-member Social and Political Implications Committee, composed of scientists working with the atomic bomb and concerned about its uses, chaired by James Franck, a Nobel laureate in physics, issued a report on 11 June 1945 calling for a "non-lethal demonstration of the soon-to-be-ready atomic bomb." The Franck Report never received "the careful consideration it required" perhaps partly because of a "natural desire to give wider circulation to those views which agree with one's own," and Secretary of War Henry L. Stimson firmly disagreed with the Franck Report's major point. Based on primary and secondary sources; 44 notes.
D. J. Trickey

919. Stern, Nancy. JOHN WILLIAM MAUCHLY: 1907-1980. *Ann. of the Hist. of Computing 1980 2(2): 100-103.* Physicist John William Mauchly, with J. Presper Eckert, Jr., and others invented the first electronic digital computer. As consultant for the Electronic Numerical Integrator and Computer (ENIAC) project during 1943-46, John Mauchly developed the concept of the vacuum tube computer to solve ballistics problems for the military. He also contributed to the development of the first machine with stored-program capability. John Mauchly

believed that computers had commercial as well as military and scientific value, and so developed and marketed the Universal Automic Computer (UNIVAC), which was first utilized by the Census Bureau. 3 notes, biblio.   S

920. Stevens, John D. BLACK CORRESPONDENTS OF WORLD WAR II COVER THE SUPPLY ROUTES. *J. of Negro Hist. 1972 57(4): 395-406.* Discusses 27 black newspaper correspondents who covered World War II for the major black newspapers in the United States. Based on personal interviews and secondary materials; 24 notes.   N. G. Sapper

921. Stevenson, Janet. LOLA MAVERICK LLOYD: "I MUST DO SOMETHING FOR PEACE!" *Chicago Hist. 1980 9(1): 47-57.* Lola Maverick Lloyd's activism in the movement for feminism and pacifism was started by a speech in 1914 by Hungarian Rosika Schwimmer of the International Suffrage Alliance, on how to stop World War I; Lloyd supported the Woman's Peace Party, the International Congress of Women, and the Women's International League for Peace and Freedom, until her death in 1944.

922. Stokesbury, James. BATTLE OF ATTU. *Am. Hist. Illus. 1979 14(1): 30-38.* Chronicles the battle between US and Japanese forces for the island of Attu in the Aleutian Islands, 1942.

923. Stokesbury, James L. 1943 INVASION OF ITALY. *Am. Hist. Illus. 1977 12(8): 26-37.* No one wanted to fight a major campaign in Italy, with the possible exception of Field Marshal Albert Kesselring. Hitler distrusted Italians and thought southern Italy too vulnerable so he ordered Rommel to reorganize a skeleton army in northern Italy. Churchill believed that the Italians would quit and that the Germans would not offer determined resistance south of Rome. The Americans preferred an invasion of France but agreed to invade Italy in return for a British agreement to invade France on 1 May 1944. Montgomery's Eighth Army crossed the Straits of Messina from Sicily and took Reggio di Calabria, the toe of the boot, without major resistance. The Anglo-American invasion at Salerno was met by German troops. The invaders expected Italian troops and had limited air cover and a shortage of landing craft. If Rommel had released his reserves as requested by Kesselring, there might have been another Dunkirk. Hitler accepted Kesselring's position that the Germans should not give the Allies what they were not strong enough to take. Almost a million casualties in Italy resulted. Primary and secondary sources; 13 illus.   D. Dodd

924. Stoler, Mark A. THE "SECOND FRONT" AND AMERICAN FEAR OF SOVIET EXPANSION, 1941-1943. *Military Affairs 1975 39(3): 136-141.* Contrary to accepted belief, American political and military leaders in World War II did consider the danger of Soviet expansionism in planning strategy for victory over Germany. In 1943 Washington acted to insure the presence of American forces in Germany, and three *Rankin* plans were contingencies in the event of Germany's weakening. Americans appreciated the necessity for specific military action to prevent Soviet domination of Europe. Primary and secondary sources; 27 notes.   A. M. Osur

925. Stone, Edward. GROUCHO AND ADOLF: OR, THE SUMMER OF 1941. *J. of Popular Film 1973 2(3): 219-229.* Describes famous film comedians during the 1940's, especially Groucho Marx, who turned the public's eye away from the horror of war.   S

926. Stone, Kirk H. GEOGRAPHY'S WARTIME SERVICE. *Ann. of the Assoc. of Am. Geographers 1979 69(1): 89-96.* Federal bureaus and departments in which geographers served during World War II removed geography from a strictly academic context to a practical one; from a special issue celebrating the 75th anniversary of the Association of American Geographers.

927. Stone, Thomas R. 1630 COMES EARLY ON THE ROER. *Military Rev. 1973 53(10): 3-21.* Examines the role of Lieutenant General William H. Simpson, commander of the American 9th Army, in the preparations for the Allied offensive across the Roer River in Germany in February 1945. Plans called for the 9th Army to cross the river on 10 February. However, faced with a rising water level, Simpson correctly decided to postpone the crossing until conditions were more favorable. Primary and secondary sources; 7 illus., map, 66 notes.
J. K. Ohl

928. Stout, Joseph A., Jr. U.S.S. OKLAHOMA, "MINISTER OF PEACE." *Chronicles of Oklahoma 1974 52(3): 283-289.* Relates the history of the battleship, *U.S.S. Oklahoma*, launched on 23 March 1914, and capsized at Pearl Harbor on 7 December 1941. Based on contemporary magazine and newspaper reports and secondary sources; 3 photos, 17 notes.
N. J. Street

929. Straub, Eleanor F. UNITED STATES GOVERNMENT POLICY TOWARD CIVILIAN WOMEN DURING WORLD WAR II. *Prologue 1973 5(4): 240-254.* Detailed analysis of the actions and inactions of federal programs concerning civilian women during World War II. Total war created mobilization of women workers for war production, but a combination of elements limited their participation in manpower policies and lessened the war's impact on women's status in American society. Primary and secondary sources; 5 illus., 46 notes.
R. W. Tissing, Jr.

930. Strunk, Al and Higham, Robin. THE VULTEE BT-13A. *Aerospace Hist. 1977 24(4): 212-216.* Relates experiences with the Vultee BT-13A during World War II, how to fly it and details of flight training. A. M. Osur

931. Stults, Taylor. HISTORY THROUGH FILM: THE TEACHER. *Film & Hist. 1972 2(2): 23-27.* Describes a course offered at Muskingum College in New Concord, Ohio, 1972, entitled "Films of World War II: Movies as Propaganda"; the course was designed to introduce students to history, film documentation, and the use of propaganda.

932. Sue, Stanley and Kitano, Harry H. L. STEREOTYPES AS A MEASURE OF SUCCESS. *J. of Social Issues 1973 29(2): 83-98.* Chinese and Japanese stereotypes have undergone dramatic changes. Early stereotypes were uniformly negative, reflecting the social, economic, and political climate in America. Labor union members and gold miners were particularly vehement in their denunciation of Asian Americans because of the perceived threat of job competition. With the passage of numerous discriminatory laws and the entrance of other ethnic minorities, the Chinese and Japanese were considered less dangerous and the favorability of stereotypes increased. World War II revived negative stereotypes against the Japanese. Currently, these Asian American groups are viewed as highly successful, model minorities. To what extent are these positive stereotypes and views accurate? Methodological and conceptual problems in the study

of stereotypes have hindered a clear analysis of this question. It is suggested that some stereotypes have kernels of truth. The potential negative consequences of favorable stereotypes are also discussed.   J

933. Sugar, Peter F. THE ROLE OF U.S. MINISTER PLENIPOTENTIARY, ARTHUR B. LANE, IN BELGRADE (JUNE, 1940-APRIL, 1941). *Rev. Roumaine d'Hist. [Rumania] 1977 16(3): 487-505.* Focuses on the role of Arthur B. Lane "as the best example of how American policy worked in East-Central Europe between the fall of France and the German invasion of Yugoslavia." Unlike other American ministers in the region, he did not allow his anti-Axis sentiments to cloud his judgment, nor did he allow British interests to weight his reports. Despite the vagueness of American policy prior to Lend-Lease, Lane desperately tried to keep Yugoslavia from joining the Axis, though he could not prevent the conclusion of the Yugoslav-German agreement nor affect the plans of General Dušan Simović and his friends. "He was respected, a moral force, and a correct representative." Few achieved that much during 1940-41. Primary sources, published documents; 51 notes.   G. J. Bobango

934. Suid, Lawrence. HOLLYWOOD AND THE MARINES. *Marine Corps Gazette 1978 62(4): 36-44.* Discusses the image of bravery and fortitude attached to the Marine Corps in films, 1920's-75.

935. Suid, Lawrence. *THE SANDS OF IWO JIMA,* THE UNITED STATES MARINES, AND THE SCREEN IMAGE OF JOHN WAYNE. *Film and HIst. 1978 8(2): 25-32.* Discusses the making of the film *Sands of Iwo Jima* in 1949 and its image of the Marine Corps after haggling among producer Edmund Grainger, actor John Wayne, and Marine Corps adviser Leonard Fribourg.

936. Sullivan, Robert C. WORLD WAR II ACES IN ARIZONA: THE *EXPERTEN* AND THE FLYING TIGER. *Aerospace Hist. 1976 23(3): 148-153.* Describes Class 57-T—the first class of German aviators to train in the United States (at Luke AFB, AZ). This training was a result of West Germany's entry into NATO in 1955. Tells the World War II flying experiences of Colonel Robert L. Scott, Jr., who was the Base Commander, and three of the German pilot-trainees. Although they were veteran fighter pilots the Germans had not flown for 10 years, so they needed refresher training and jet transition. 6 photos.
                                                                    C. W. Ohrvall

937. Sumrall, Robert F. SHIP CAMOUFLAGE (WWII): DECEPTIVE ART. *US Naval Inst. Pro. 1973 99(2): 67-81.* During World War II the US Navy developed 21 basic ship camouflage measures. Each was designed to satisfy the operational requirements of individual vessels and Fleet units and served to reduce visibility at long distances and/or create optical confusion in close situations. 50 illus., table, note, biblio.   J. K. Ohl

938. Suther, Judith D. RAÏSSA MARITAIN IN AMERICA, 1940-1960. *Research Studies 1977 45(2): 61-72.* Examines the writings (especially poetry) of Raïssa Maritain (1883-1960) during her American tenure, emphasizing her allegiance to Free France during World War II and her continuing dedication to French nationalism, 1940-60.

939. Swanson, Roger Frank. AN ANALYTIC ASSESSMENT OF THE UNITED STATES-CANADIAN DEFENSE ISSUE AREA. *Internat. Organization 1974 28(4): 781-802.* Discusses US-Canadian defense policies and interdependence from World War II to the 1970's in a special issue on foreign relations between the US and Canada.

940. Sweatt, Dennis F. 23RD TACTICAL FIGHTER WING FLYING TIGERS. *Aerospace Hist. 1977 24(2): 107-111.* On 4 July 1977, the 23rd Tactical Fighter Wing, the Flying Tigers, celebrated its 35th anniversary. During World War II it continued the work of General Claire Chennault's American Volunteer Group in the China-Burma-India Theater. During and after World War II the 23rd TFW went through periods of activation and inactivation. Today at England Air Force Base, Louisiana, the Flying Tigers is the only regular USAF group flying the A-7D Corsair. Primary and secondary sources. A. M. Osur

941. Sweeney, J. K. THE FRAMEWORK OF LUSO-AMERICAN DIPLOMATIC RELATIONS DURING THE SECOND WORLD WAR. *Rocky Mountain Social Sci. J. 1973 10(3): 93-100.*

942. Sweeney, J. K. GENESIS OF AN AIRBASE: THE UNITED STATES, PORTUGAL, AND SANTA MARIA. *Aerospace Hist. 1977 24(4): 222-227.* The Azores are important for the United States and NATO today, and the relationship between the islands and American military interests goes back to World War II. Portugal was neutral during the war, and it took long, difficult negotiations before the United States was granted aviation facilities in the Azores in October 1944. R. Henry Norweb handled these negotiations. He was able to use the Japanese control of the Portuguese colony of Timor as his negotiating point, playing Portuguese dictator Antonio de Oliveira Salazar's desire to liberate it. Based on State Department Papers; 56 notes. A. M. Osur

943. Sweeney, J. K. THE PORTUGUESE WOLFRAM EMBARGO: A CASE STUDY IN ECONOMIC WARFARE. *Military Affairs 1974 38(1): 23-26.* For a variety of economic and political reasons Great Britain did not halt Portuguese shipments of wolfram to Germany. American policy, on the other hand, called for a hard line; but it was not until May 1944 that the Portuguese government began to weaken in its opposition to a ban on shipments to Germany. On 6 June 1944 the Portuguese agreed to the ban. Based on U.S. State Department documents; 13 notes. K. J. Bauer

944. Sweeny, J. K. THE LUSO-AMERICAN CONNECTION: THE COURTSHIP 1940-1941. *Iberian Studies [Great Britain] 1977 6(1): 3-8.* Discusses the Portuguese-United States alliance during World War II and contrasts it with the background of mutual suspicion and indifference earlier in the century.

945. Sweet, Morris L. INDUSTRIAL LOCATION POLICY: WESTERN EUROPEAN PRECEDENTS FOR AIDING U.S. IMPACTED REGIONS. *Urbanism Past and Present 1978-79 (7): 1-12.* Americans take municipal zoning for granted, but few consider the utility of central controls over new industrial location as a means of aiding fiscally impaired regions, a practice common in Western Europe. The author discusses locational control systems in Western Europe, especially in Great Britain and its use of Industrial Development Certificates. Covers the history of locational controls in the United States, especially

during World War II, problems with controls as they relate to the US system of government, and current governmental efforts. Map, 4 tables, 38 notes.

B. P. Anderson

946. Szajkowski, Zosa. RELIEF FOR GERMAN JEWRY: PROBLEMS OF AMERICAN INVOLVEMENT. *Am. Jewish Hist. Q. 1972 62(2): 111-145.* Illustrates Jewish disunity (the competition between Zionist and anti-Zionist philosophies) and governmental footdragging, which together made consistent, massive assistance impossible just when additional thousands of Jews might have been saved. Based on archives of various US Jewish organizations and private papers; 89 notes.
S

947. Szasz, Margaret Connell. FEDERAL BOARDING SCHOOLS AND THE INDIAN CHILD: 1920-1960. *South Dakota Hist. 1977 7(4): 371-384.* Various theories have led to variations in the goals and operations of the federal Indian boarding schools. Originally following the ideas of assimilationists, children were taken from their families for white education to prepare them for life in urban American society. Coincidentally they provided the labor for school operation and were directed with military discipline. Crowded conditions, poor food, and hard labor led to problems, including runaway students. Improved conditions and better educational direction resulted after the Meriam Report of 1928. Ironically, some schools were closed, despite the realization that Indians' education needed to be changed to help them return to reservation life. Still, Indian educators were not used. Many Indians served in World War II both in the armed forces and in war-related industries. Training in the postwar years centered on vocational training for veterans. Especially successful was the Navajo Special Program, but it also led to resentment from other tribes. The 1969 Kennedy Report recognized the social and emotional problems of boarding school students. By the 1960's, Indians were asking for, and being given, a greater role in their own education. Primary and secondary sources; 4 photos, 31 notes.

A. J. Larson

948. Szilard, Leo. LEO SZILARD: HIS VERSION OF THE FACTS. *Bull. of the Atomic Scientists 1979 35(2): 37-40, (3): 55-59, (4): 28-32, (5): 34-35.* Part I. THE YOUNG SZILARD. Discusses Szilard's childhood in Budapest, Hungary, and his study of physics in Berlin, 1898-1922. Part II. Chronicles Leo Szilard's years of work in physics in Germany, 1928-33, his escape from Germany in 1933, and his further work in nuclear fission with Albert Einstein, 1933-39. Part III. Discusses the aftermath of a meeting with Washington officials in 1940 explaining the importance of uranium chain reactions and the beginning of nuclear research in the United States, 1940-42. Part IV. Describes Szilard's meeting with James F. Byrnes in 1945 in which Szilard opposed further nuclear testing.

949. Tanaka, June K. FRUIT OF DIASPORA: THE JAPANESE EXPERIENCE IN CANADA. *Japan Interpreter [Japan] 1978 12(1): 110-117.* Anti-Japanese prejudice and discrimination led to early anti-Japanese immigration restrictions in British Columbia, and culminated in the forced relocation of all Japanese from the Province after Pearl Harbor. Relocation proved beneficial for many Japanese Canadians. Stresses the lack of racial prejudice in eastern Canada.

F. W. Iklé

950. Tannehill, Victor C. MEDITERRANEAN MARAUDER MARKINGS. *Am. Aviation Hist. Soc. J. 1979 24(1): 55-67.* The 42nd Bombardment Wing was composed of a number of B-26 Marauder units operating first in the Mediterranean and later in the European Theatre during World War II; describes numbering, insignias, and group identification markings on the airplanes, 1942-44.

951. Taussig, Joseph K., Jr. I REMEMBER PEARL HARBOR. *US Naval Inst. Pro. 1972 98(12/838): 18-24.* The US defeat at Pearl Harbor was basically attributable to the lack of effective anti-aircraft guns, and had the fleet been at sea many more men who survived Pearl Harbor would have drowned as a result of the Japanese attack, because the weapons intended to defend against air attack were not capable of meeting the Japanese threat. Admiral H. E. Kimmel and General Walter C. Short, "were treated in a totally unfair and unethical manner," although "someone had to shoulder the blame for a catastrophic tactical situation —which, in the opinion of many, was merely the inevitable result of the actions of the strategic and political planners in Washington." The real material damage at Pearl Harbor was done by torpedo planes, although it is hard to understand why the Japanese did not attack the Tank Farm at the Naval Supply Depot and the Ammunition Depot at West Lock. Much like the fleet at Pearl Harbor, today's fleet is outdated, improperly designed, or both, and as in 1941 it is the ships, not the men, that are likely to be found wanting. 3 photos, note.
A. N. Garland

952. Taylor, Caroline G. YOKOI'S HIDEAWAY. *Guam Recorder 1975 (1): 49-53.* Shoichi Yokoi, a soldier in the Imperial Japanese Army, hid in the jungles of Guam, 1944-72.

953. Tejchman, Miroslav. ZAHRANIČNÍ POLITIKA USA A JIHOVÝCHODNÍ EVROPA 1939-1941 [US foreign policy and the South-East Europe 1939-1941]. *Slovanský přehled [Czechoslovakia] 1978 64(5): 353-360.* After the fall of Czechoslovakia in March 1939 the US policy developed a stronger interest in European affairs even when the administration faced at home a vigilant isolationism. After events of the spring of 1940 US diplomacy got profoundly involved in Balkan affairs, siding with England in opposition toward German and Italian pressure in this part of Europe. Based on diplomatic papers; 24 notes.
G. E. Pergl

954. Tenney, Craig D. THE 1943 DEBATE ON OPINIONATED BROADCAST NEWS. *Journalism Hist. 1980 7(1): 11-15.* Discusses the Brown-White dispute on opinionated radio broadcast news in 1943 which resulted when CBS news director Paul W. White contended that news analyst Cecil B. Brown editorialized during a news report on President Roosevelt's trip to Quebec to discuss World War II with Winston Churchill, which was against CBS policy and the 1941 Mayflower decision by the FCC which banned broadcast editorials; the issue ended when the FCC passed the Fairness Doctrine in 1946.

955. Terzibaschitsch, Stefan. WAFFENSCHUL- UND ERPROBUNGSSCHIFFE DER U.S. NAVY 1930-76 [Weapons training and test ships of the US Navy, 1930-76]. *Marine Rundschau [West Germany] 1976 73(6): 351-367.* Details the course of naval weapons development through the histories of the four

gunnery training and weapons test ships of the US Navy since 1930. Three were old battleships—*Utah, Wyoming,* and *Mississippi*—and the last a converted seaplane tender, *Norton Sound.* The first two served to train antiaircraft gunners at sea until *Utah* was lost in 1941 and *Wyoming* scrapped in 1947. *Mississippi* replaced them in 1948 and also served as evaluation ship for the new antiaircraft missile system until stricken in 1956. The Navy rebuilt *Norton Sound* as its first true floating weapons laboratory in 1948. She serves with continuing modifications today as a primary test ship for nearly all naval missile systems. 20 photos.

K. W. Estes

956. Thackrah, J. R. ASPECTS OF AMERICAN AND BRITISH POLICY TOWARDS POLAND FROM THE YALTA TO THE POTSDAM CONFERENCES, 1945. *Polish Rev. 1976 21(4): 3-34.* Examines the foreign policy of the United States and Great Britain toward Poland and the attempts by both countries to secure a democratic state for the Polish people in the first six months of 1945.

957. Theoharis, Athan. THE ORIGINS OF THE COLD WAR: A REVISIONIST INTERPRETATION. *Peace and Change 1976 4(1): 3-11.* President Franklin D. Roosevelt's vagueness at the Yalta Conference was a source of the Cold War during the Truman administration, 1945-47.

958. Thomas, James A. COLLAPSE OF THE DEFENSIVE WAR ARGUMENT. *Military R. 1973 53(5): 35-38.* In World War II the United States successfully utilized the defensive war argument, anchored in the American tradition of property rights and fervor for universal moral values, to justify its participation. The Korean War and Vietnam War, however, demonstrated that the defensive war argument is not suitable for an era of protracted political conflict, and "the time to begin thinking of an alternative is now."

J. K. Ohl

959. Thomas, Patricia J. WOMEN IN THE MILITARY: AMERICA AND THE BRITISH COMMONWEALTH: HISTORICAL SIMILARITIES. *Armed Forces and Soc. 1978 4(4): 623-646.* A historical survey of women in the military in the United States, Great Britain, Canada, and Australia in World War I, World War II, and after World War II. In each nation military and political leaders used women volunteers in wartime in narrowly defined categories as nonsoldiers and nonsailors. Only after the World War II era has the military leadership, and only then under the pressure of societal and court rulings, altered attitudes and policies toward women. In general, women in the United States have progressed further toward full integration into the military as soldiers and sailors, although several major questions remain unresolved. Secondary works; 12 notes.

J. P. Harahan

960. Thompson, Dean K. WORLD WAR II, INTERVENTIONISM, AND HENRY PITNEY VAN DUSEN. *J. of Presbyterian Hist. 1977 55(4): 327-345.* Henry Pitney Van Dusen (1897-1975) had immense breadth of experience—teacher of theology, seminary president, international ecumenist. His life reflected religious movements from the 1920's to the 1960's. His statesmanship was a major factor in America's interventionist movement before its involvement in World War II. Discusses his views on America's moral duty toward the international

order in light of the Sino-Japanese conflict and the rise of Nazism, his strong criticism of the pacifistic-isolationist forces of America, his break with the ecumenical weekly, the *Christian Century,* his personal leadership in the war lobby within and beyond ecclesiastical circles, and his role in establishing *Christianity and Crisis.* Based largely on Van Dusen Ecumenical Papers of Union Theological Seminary (New York), the Henry P. Van Dusen Oral History, Union Theological Seminary (Richmond, Virginia), and published materials of Van Dusen; 40 notes. H. M. Parker, Jr.

961. Thorne, Christopher. INDOCHINA AND ANGLO-AMERICAN RELATIONS, 1942-1945. *Pacific Hist. Rev. 1976 45(1): 73-96.* American and British policymakers during World War II failed to agree, or even to communicate effectively, on postwar Indochina policy. Franklin D. Roosevelt at first hoped to see France deprived of Indochina, but changed his view in late 1944 as American policy became less anti-imperialist and more pro-French. However, at no time was Indochina an important policy issue for Roosevelt or other American policymakers. Throughout the war the British Foreign Office believed that Britain urgently needed a strong and friendly France after the war, and that this meant French retention of Indochina. However, Great Britain's policy did not make Indochina a high-priority item. Winston Churchill's main policy consideration was maintaining good relations with Roosevelt. Based on manuscripts in Roosevelt Library, Hoover Institution, National Archives, Library of Congress, Yale University, US Navy Operational Archives, Harvard University, Truman Library, Cambridge University, and the Australian Public Record Office. 110 notes. W. K. Hobson

962. Thorne, Christopher. MACARTHUR, AUSTRALIA AND THE BRITISH, 1942-1943: THE SECRET JOURNAL OF MACARTHUR'S BRITISH LIAISON OFFICER. *Australian Outlook [Australia] 1975 29(1): 53-67, (2): 197-210.* Part I. Colonel Gerald Hugh Williamson, British liaison officer with the American commander in the Philippines, General Douglas MacArthur, made a daily record of his talks with MacArthur and with leading Australian and British officials. At this time relations between Great Britain, Australia, and the United States were in a state of flux. The changing political situation, 1942-43, is described and illustrated with extracts from Williamson's journal. 48 notes. Part II. Examines the political situation in Australia, 1942-43, paying particular attention to the cooperation between Australia, Britain, and the United States. The future relationship between Britain and the Dominions was far from clear; but the United States had clearly established itself as an important factor in Dominion affairs, and MacArthur's presence in Australia was important for these changes. 70 notes. J. M. Sanderson

963. Thyng, Harrison R. THE SERGEANT, HIS PILOT, HIS PLANE. *Air Force Mag. 1975 58(2): 66-68.* The author's memoirs as an American officer in the World War II European campaign.

964. Tilford, Earl H. THE DEVELOPMENT OF SEARCH AND RESCUE: WORLD WAR II TO 1961. *Aerospace Hist. 1977 24(4): 228-239.* Before and during World War II the Germans were pioneers in aircrew rescue and rescue equipment. The British and Americans were slower to develop their efforts but by 1945 had improved considerably. The US Air Rescue Service (ARS) was

established in 1946 and with the helicopter had good success during the Korean War. The ARS gave limited assistance to the French in Indochina, but during the 1950's saw its role expand to include the entire world scene. Important aircraft changes were made after 1954 that would prepare the ARS for its great role in Vietnam. Based on USAF and secondary sources; 91 notes.

A. M. Osur

965. Tillman, Barrett. COACHING THE FIGHTERS. *US Naval Inst. Pro. 1980 106(1): 39-45.* During World War II, the US Navy brought shipboard radars into wide use. As a result, fighter direction came into its own. Actually, the process began some months before the United States entered the war, and much of the information resulted from a prewar exchange program between the United States and Britain. After the United States entered the war in 1941, the Navy's fighter direction program blossomed. By 1943, the original radar plots had evolved into the CIC's, or combat information centers. This kind of electronic warfare heralded the future and introduced a new and important breed of sailor. 4 photos.

A. N. Garland

966. Tillman, Barrett. HELLCATS OVER TRUK. *US Naval Inst. Pro. 1977 103(3): 63-71.* In 1944 Truk Atoll was probably the most important Japanese anchorage outside the home islands, and the US Navy, at least until early that year, had been unable to gather much intelligence about the Japanese establishment at that location. Still, the Navy felt it had to attack Truk to disrupt it. An aerial reconnaissance mission in early February 1944 brought back some helpful photographs. Rear Admiral Marc A. Mitscher's Task Force 58 was ordered to knock out Truk through air power. On 17 February 1944, five US aircraft carriers launched 70 Grumman F6F Hellcat fighters to gain air superiority. The next day was scheduled for attack on ground installations and shipping. Both attacks were spectacular successes. Truk was hit again and again during the ensuing months, but no attack "exceeded the first for prolonged intensity of aerial combat." 10 photos, map, 2 tables.

A. N. Garland

967. Tissing, Robert Warren. STALAG-TEXAS, 1943-1945. *Military Hist. of Texas and the Southwest 1976 13(1): 23-36.* Chronicles the detention and work use of German prisoners of war in Texas, 1943-45.

968. Tolley, Kemp. THE STRANGE MISSION OF THE LANIKAI. *Am. Heritage 1973 24(6): 56-61, 93-95.* President Franklin D. Roosevelt, evidently seeking a *casus belli* with Japan, ordered three lightly armed vessels, including the schooner *Lanikai* (of which the author received command), on a reconnaissance voyage off the coast of Indochina in the first week of December 1941.

S

969. Toshkova, Vitka. BULGARIIA V BALKANSKATA POLITIKA NA SASHT (SEPTEMVTI 1943-IUNI 1944 G.) [Bulgaria in US Balkan politics, September 1943-June 1944]. *Istoricheski Pregled [Bulgaria] 1979 35(1): 27-49.* Describes the secret negotiations between Bulgarian representatives and American and British diplomats concerning Bulgaria's desire to conclude peace with the Allies in World War II. Analyzes American foreign policy toward Bulgaria at this time, particularly with regard to postwar developments. Concludes that American policy strove to maintain the capitalist class in power and prevent the

Communist Party from gaining control of the country. Based chiefly on published and unpublished US State Department documents; 100 notes. F. B. Chary

970. Toshkova, Vitka. SASHT I IZLIZANETO NA BULGARIIA OT TRISTRANNIIA PAKT (IUNI-SEPTEMVRI 1944 G.) [The United States and Bulgaria's withdrawal from the Tripartite Pact (June-September 1944)]. *Istoricheski Pregled [Bulgaria] 1979 35(4-5): 204-217.* Soundings carried out by the US consul-general in Istanbul during June and July 1944 showed that Bulgaria was unlikely to break its alliance with Germany until Soviet forces crossed into Romania. Nonetheless, the State Department opened talks on the terms of Bulgaria's eventual capitulation through N. Balabanov, Bulgaria's minister in Ankara. Further contacts followed in August, but attempts to make progress toward a definitive truce were hampered by disputes over the siting and status of negotiations, and were overtaken by the Soviet declaration of war on Bulgaria on 5 September and by the seizure of power by the Fatherland Front on 9 September. F. A. K. Yasamee

971. Tozer, Warren W. THE FOREIGN CORRESPONDENTS' VISIT TO YENAN IN 1944: A REASSESSMENT. *Pacific Hist. R. 1972 41(2): 207-224.* Discusses the effect of the visit of eight foreign correspondents to Chinese Communist headquarters in 1944 after five years of being banned from that area by Chiang Kai-shek. The reporters were accused of making pro-Communist reports that influenced American public opinion against the Nationalist regime; these charges were not correct. Analyzes the reporters' assessments of the nature and role of Chinese Communists at that time. Their reports were censored, relatively obscure (except for Theodore H. White's article in *Life* 18 December 1944), and overshadowed by other events. Therefore, the reporters were not responsible for declining American support of Chiang, nor did they affect American foreign policy. 61 notes. E. C. Hyslop

972. Tracy, R. J. FOOT GUARDS... ON PARADE. *Can. Forces Sentinel 1972 8(8): 1-7.* In its century of existence the Governor General's Foot Guards experienced only 10 years of war. Like most militia units it spent most of its time at peace, but when called upon performed heroically, earning 22 battle honors on the Canadian Frontier during the Boer War, World War I, and World War II. Today time, budgetary restraints, and changing public opinion have eroded the regiment's importance, both militarily and socially. Nevertheless, it took time out for a parade of old veterans and present members to honor past sacrifices. Walter E. Pittman, Jr.

973. Trey, Joan Ellen. WOMEN IN THE WAR ECONOMY. *Rev. of Radical Pol. Econ. 1972 4(3): 40-57.* Women's experience working in a war economy led to significant change. The war work was popular not only because Hitler was clearly an enemy of women, but also because women were not satisfied at home and wanted work away from it. The same factors work today. Based on contemporary and secondary sources; 49 notes, biblio. C. P. de Young

974. Trimble, William F. PITTSBURGH'S DRAVO CORPORATION AND NAVAL SHIPBUILDING IN WORLD WAR II. *Am. Neptune 1978 38(4): 272-290.* Describes the Dravo Corporation's efforts to construct landing ships (LST's and LSM's), destroyer escorts, and other naval ships during World

War II. Although faced with materials shortages and the federal government's juggling of shipbuilding priorities, the Dravo Corporation, with its two shipbuilding yards, located near Pittsburgh (Pennsylvania) and Wilmington (Delaware) "completed all its contracts on or ahead of schedule." Based primarily on records of the Dravo Corporation and the federal government; 2 tables, 40 notes.

G. H. Curtis

975. Trunk, Isaiah. THE CULTURAL DIMENSION OF THE AMERICAN JEWISH LABOR MOVEMENT. *Yivo Ann. of Jewish Social Sci. 1976 (16): 342-393.* Divides the cultural history of the American Jewish labor movement into three periods. The first period, 1880's-90's, was characterized by socialism, a desire for educational achievement, and a tendency toward assimilation. The second period, 1900-20's, was caused by a new influx of immigrants coming after the Dreyfus trial and the Kishinev pogrom. As a result, they were disillusioned with socialism and tended toward cultural autonomy, radical nationalism, and Zionist socialism. A growth of the Hebrew and Yiddish press and literature characterized the Jewish labor movement during this period. The last period, extending from the 1930's to the end of World War II, saw a rise of national solidarity through such groups as the Workmen's Circle and the Jewish Labor Committee who worked against anti-Semitism. R. J. Wechman

976. Trussell, John B. B., Jr. THE ROLE OF THE PROFESSIONAL MILITARY OFFICER IN THE PRESERVATION OF THE REPUBLIC. *Western Pennsylvania Hist. Mag. 1977 60(1): 1-21.* The professional, career, Army officer has preserved and secured the American republic, from the American Revolution through the Vietnam War.

977. Tsumoda, Jun and Uchida, Kazutomi. THE PEARL HARBOR ATTACK: ADMIRAL YAMAMOTO'S FUNDAMENTAL CONCEPT WITH REFERENCE TO PAUL S. DULL'S *A BATTLE HISTORY OF THE IMPERIAL JAPANESE NAVY (1941-1945)*. *Naval War College Rev. 1978 31(2): 83-88.*

978. Tuchman, Barbara Wertheim. IF MAO HAD COME TO WASHINGTON: AN ESSAY IN ALTERNATIVES. *Foreign Affairs 1972 51(1): 44-64.* History might have been altered had Mao Tse-tung been accorded a requested visit with President Franklin Delano Roosevelt in 1945. U.S. policy was simply too short-sighted. A China without the dominant personality of Chiang Kai-shek could not be imagined at the time. American officials failed to understand conditions in China and to recognize Mao's extensive support among the people. American efforts were initially designed to get the contending factions to cooperate against the Japanese, but this policy soon hardened into a pro-Chiang line. Lesser officials perceived the future clearly enough, but their voices were not heeded. Probably Mao's projected visit would have changed nothing, but records have recently come to light suggesting that Roosevelt might have been receptive. Based on secondary sources; 3 notes. V. L. Human

979. Tudor, William W. KNIGHT SCHOOL: A REPORT ON 25 YEARS OF HELICOPTER TRAINING. *Aerospace Historian 1968 16(3): 9-11, 44-46.* The Army Air Corps first helicopter training school was formed at Freeman Field, Indiana, in 1944. There were no aircraft, students, training manuals, or

trained personnel, because helicopters were so new. A cadre of instructors had to go to Bridgeport, Connecticut, to learn about the machines. The first aircraft was the Sikorsky R-4. Describes the changing contents of the training program and the exploits of Major Gerald O. Young, Vietnam War Medal of Honor winner. Discusses the first helicopter rescue operation, in Burma in March 1944. 7 illus. C. W. Ohrvall

980. Turnbaugh, Roy. THE FBI AND HARRY ELMER BARNES: 1936-1944. *Historian 1980 42(3): 385-398.* The Federal Bureau of Investigation's investigation of historian, reformer, and political commentator Harry Elmer Barnes from 1936 to 1944 reveals much about the motives and priorities of that organization. Initially, Barnes was branded by the FBI as an enemy for his criticism of that agency's failure to pursue organized crime. His opposition to America's entry into World War II before Pearl Harbor and his growing alienation from the Roosevelt administration kept alive the agency's interest in his activities. An ill-considered speech in October 1942 before the Rotary Club in Utica, New York, allowed the FBI to take its revenge by trying to brand him as a seditionist; yet he was not prosecuted in the Sedition Trial of 1944. The entire Barnes affair was more than simply FBI chief J. Edgar Hoover's animosity toward Barnes. In essence, Hoover's attitudes toward hostile criticism had so pervaded the Bureau by 1936 that relatively obscure speeches drew tremendous attention. Primary sources; 44 notes. R. S. Sliwoski

981. Turner, James and McGann, C. Steven. BLACK STUDIES AS AN INTEGRAL TRADITION IN AFRICAN-AMERICAN INTELLECTUAL HISTORY. *J. of Negro Educ. 1980 49(1): 52-59.* Though black studies as an academic discipline is generally thought of as a product of the 1960's, its roots go back much farther. Formally, the idea of the sustained study of black life and history began with W. E. B. Du Bois. The pre-Depression decade saw a good start toward black studies, but the Depression, World War II, and the anticommunist hysteria of the 1950's arrested development until the 1960's. Secondary sources; 5 notes. R. E. Butchart

982. Tuttle, Jim. THE NORTH AMERICAN XB-28. *Am. Aviation Hist. Soc. J. 1979 24(2): 82-89.* Describes the North American Aviation XB-28, a high altitude US Army Air Force bomber plane designed in the 1940's; includes diagrams and photographs.

983. Ugland, Richard M. "EDUCATION FOR VICTORY": THE HIGH SCHOOL VICTORY CORPS AND CURRICULAR ADAPTATION DURING WORLD WAR II. *Hist. of Educ. Q. 1979 19(4): 435-451.* In December 1941, the US Office of Education established a wartime commission to facilitate the adjustment of educational agencies to war needs. In September 1942, the High School Victory Corps under A. L. Threlkeld's direction recommended that American secondary schools follow a three-point program to provide physical fitness, patriotism, and vocational skills. High school students were urged to join in one of five special divisions—land, sea, air, production, and community service. The Victory Corps effort reached its maximum strength in 1943 and declined thereafter. Teacher shortages, especially in mathematics, science, and vocational and physical education, frustrated attempts to adapt the curriculum for technical and military fields. Opposition to the Victory Corps came from the pacifists and

from opponents of federal regimentation. Victory Corps ideas briefly challenged the role of liberal education in American high schools but made little contribution to the war effort. Secondary sources; 57 notes. S. H. Frank

984. Uhlenberg, Peter. NONECONOMIC DETERMINANTS OF NONMIGRATION: SOCIOLOGICAL CONSIDERATIONS FOR MIGRATION THEORY. *Rural Sociol. 1973 38(3): 296-311.* "To further understanding of migration determinants, I examine the experiences of three groupings in the U.S.: Negro movement from the South 1860-1920; Japanese-American migration from internment camps during World War II; and exodus from Southern Appalachia between 1930 and 1960. Each ... illustrates the importance of noneconomic variables in determining migration and the worth to noting nonmigration to understand the migration process. I suggest using a framework which examines motivation for and constraints upon migration for individuals as a starting point in developing migration theory. When migration is viewed within a social structure, dependence upon the local community and potential for assimilation elsewhere appear as critical determinants of whether motivation for migration becomes actual movement.... I encourage future migration research to avoid an overemphasis upon economic factors and to reject the argument that no generalization is possible." A

985. Unsigned. MHS COLLECTIONS: WHEN STARS "FELL" ON MINNESOTA. *Minnesota Hist. 1974 44(3): 108-112.* Two performances by a group of Hollywood stars in Minneapolis during May 1942 raised $65,000 for Army and Navy relief organizations. Primary sources; 15 illus., note. S. S. Sprague

986. Unsigned. TRAINING CAMP FOR THE ATOMIC AGE: WENDOVER FIELD. *Aerospace Historian 1973 20(3): 137-139.* The crew of the *Enola Gay*, the B-29 that dropped the atomic bomb on Hiroshima, Japan, trained at Wendover Field on the Utah-Nevada border, 1944-45. S

987. Urofsky, Melvin I. STEPHEN WISE: THE LAST OF THE SUPERSTARS. *Present Tense 1979 6(4): 21-26.* Recounts the deeds and achievements —especially those devoted to Zionism, ecumenism, charity, and efforts to persuade President Franklin Delano Roosevelt to assist in saving the European Jews during World War II—of the Hungarian-born American rabbi, Stephen Samuel Wise (1874-1949).

988. Utley, Jonathan G. DIPLOMACY IN A DEMOCRACY: THE UNITED STATES AND JAPAN, 1937-1941. *World Affairs 1976 139(2): 130-140.* Discusses conflicts in US foreign policy and diplomacy regarding the issue of trade with Japan, 1937-41.

989. Utley, Jonathan G. UPSTAIRS, DOWNSTAIRS AT FOGGY BOTTOM: OIL EXPORTS AND JAPAN, 1940-41. *Prologue 1976 8(1): 17-28.* Historians have generally failed to investigate the manner in which the cautious foreign policy toward Japan formulated by President Roosevelt and Secretary of State Cordell Hull was implemented at lower levels of the foreign service bureaucracy. Lower echelon administrators such as Assistant Secretary of State Dean Acheson favored a stronger and more aggressive attitude toward Japan than did their superiors and they changed the whole character of their instructions to reflect their personal views. Acheson and independent agencies like the Foreign

Funds Control Committee prevented Japan from obtaining the oil supplies to which it was entitled under the conditions laid down by the president and the secretary of state. Based on secondary and government archival records.

N. Lederer

990. Uyeda, Clifford I. THE PARDONING OF "TOKYO ROSE": A REPORT ON THE RESTORATION OF AMERICAN CITIZENSHIP TO IVA IKUKO TOGURI. *Amerasia J. 1978 5(2): 69-93.* The 1977 presidential pardon of Iva Ikuko Toguri d'Aquino, who, as "Tokyo Rose," had been convicted of treason after World War II, was the result of the work of many people, institutions, and organizations. A committee formed by John Hada and the author coordinated the massive campaign to reeducate the public about the facts of the case, the garnering of support from widespread sources, and the mechanics of filing the petition for pardon. The Japanese American Citizens League had done little or nothing for Toguri prior to the work of the committee and did not order the formation of the committee, but it tried to claim credit for the pardon.

T. L. Powers

991. Valenti, Peter L. THE CULTURAL HERO IN THE WORLD WAR II FANTASY FILM. *J. of Popular Film and Television 1979 7(3): 310-321.* Discusses the fantasy films made in the United States during World War II and the archetypal heroes in them who typically experience suffering while on a quest to lead a group to hope or victory, particularly focusing on two films, *A Guy Named Joe* (1943) and *The Enchanted Cottage* (1945).

992. VanEdgerton, F. THE CARLSON INTELLIGENCE MISSION TO CHINA. *Michigan Academician 1977 9(4): 419-432.* Chronicles an intelligence mission for Franklin D. Roosevelt by Evans Carlson in China during the war with Japan, 1937-38.

993. Varg, Paul G. THE COMING OF THE WAR WITH GERMANY. *Centennial Rev. 1976 20(3): 219-227.* Historians have neglected economic considerations in seeking to explain American intervention in World War II. It is possible to argue that the real threat to America was more economic than military, although the latter was useful in "mobilizing public opinion." The economic threat was obvious to those who looked for it. During the thirties Germany had sought to control portions of Europe's economy and had begun to move into Latin America. This could be understood by the most isolationist congressman. Thus, Hitler's efforts to restrict the free flow of trade set the stage for American intervention. By late 1941 the business community strongly supported Roosevelt's foreign policy including aid to Britain. Free trade became a major war aim of the United States. Note.

A. R. Stoesen

994. Veraksa, E. PLANIROVANIE BOEVYKH DEISTVII STRATEGICHESKIKH VVS SSHA I ANGLII V GODY VTOROI MIROVOI VOINY [Planning of combat operations of US and British strategic air forces during World War II]. *Voenno-Istoricheskii Zhurnal [USSR] 1978 20(9): 87-92.* Discusses the aims and results of British and American bombing of Germany and occupied Western Europe in 1942-44. Directives for operation *Point-Blank* issued by the Combined Chiefs of Staff in June 1943 improved long-range strategic planning and coordination of air raids. However, Great Britain and America

underestimated German recuperative capacity and erred in the choice of key targets. The importance of bombing raids has been overrated in Western historiography. Though they dislocated German communication lines and industry, they were not a decisive factor in the defeat of the Third Reich. Based on published British and American sources; 15 notes. — N. Frenkley

995. Verna, Renato. LA PRIMA GRANDE OPERAZIONE ANFIBIA DEL PACIFICO: LA CONQUISTA DELL'ISOLA DI SAIPAN (GRANDI MARIANNE) E LA BATTAGLIA AERO-NAVALE DEL MAR DELLE FILIPPINE [The first great amphibious operation in the Pacific: the conquest of the Island of Saipan (Mariana) and the aeronaval battle of the Philippine Sea]. *Riv. Militare [Italy] 1969 25(7-8): 870-917.* The successful US conquest of Saipan in June-July 1944 made possible the American attack on Japan itself.

996. Veth, K. L. SHOOTOUT AT PALEMBANG: THE "HELLBIRDS" MINE THE MOESI RIVER. *Am. Aviation Hist. Soc. J. 1980 25(1): 72-74.* Account by the author, then technical adviser for the 462d Bomb Group of the US Navy, known as the "Hellbirds," of the mining of the Moesi River in Palembang, Sumatra, during World War II in 1944.

997. Vieth, Jane Karoline. THE DONKEY AND THE LION: THE AMBASSADORSHIP OF JOSEPH P. KENNEDY AT THE COURT OF ST. JAMES, 1938-1940. *Michigan Academician 1978 10(3): 273-282.* Highlights the hostility between Joseph P. Kennedy and Winston Churchill and outlines the foreign policy of the Roosevelt administration, 1938-40.

998. Villa, Brian L. THE U.S. ARMY, UNCONDITIONAL SURRENDER, AND THE POTSDAM PROCLAMATION. *J. of Am. Hist. 1976 63(1): 66-92.* Examines the critical factors affecting the timing of the Japanese surrender. Clarifies the politico-military position assumed by Roosevelt, the Congress, and the US Army. Conflicts arising from differing goals (Roosevelt desired "the rooting out of evil philosophies"; the Army wanted military supremacy) and semantic interpretations ("surrender" was unknown to the Japanese) delayed peace. 69 notes. — V. P. Rilee

999. Villa, Brian Loring. THE ATOMIC BOMB AND THE NORMANDY INVASION. *Perspectives in Am. Hist. 1977-78 11: 463-502.* Franklin D. Roosevelt skillfully refrained from bringing Great Britain into confidence on the atomic bomb project until Winston Churchill openly committed himself to a cross-channel invasion. Although FDR had acted the country squire, his business methods were ingenious and effective. This conclusion contradicts the school of thought which argues that Roosevelt was inept at diplomacy and weak on goals and objectives. Other Roosevelt diplomatic decisions should be reexamined in light of these findings. — W. A. Wiegand

1000. Villa, Brian Loring. A CONFUSION OF SIGNALS: JAMES FRANCK, THE CHICAGO SCIENTISTS AND EARLY EFFORTS TO STOP THE BOMB. *Bull. of the Atomic Scientists 1975 31(10): 36-42.* Compares James Franck's April 1945 memorandum for Henry A. Wallace with the Franck Committee Report of 11 June 1945, noting that the latter contained contradictory advice. As a result Franck's earlier policy advice on use of the atomic bomb against Japan and the nuclear arms race with the USSR was not superseded at the War Department.

1001. Villa, Brian Loring. MILITARY PREPAREDNESS FOR THE FIRST POSTWAR YEARS, 1943-47. *Rev. in Am. Hist. 1978 6(2): 253-258.* Review article prompted by Michael S. Sherry's *Preparing for the Next War: America Plans for Postwar Defense, 1941-45* (New Haven, Conn.: Yale U. Pr., 1977).

1002. Villa, Brian Loring. A UNIQUE GENERAL: MACARTHUR OF THE PACIFIC. *R. in Am. Hist. 1975 3(4): 494-498.* D. Clayton James' *The Years of MacArthur Volume 2, 1941-1945* (Boston: Houghton Mifflin, 1975) is a biography of Douglas MacArthur, "one of the most political generals in the American army" in World War II (Pacific Theater).

1003. Wadleigh, John R. USS VIXEN (PG 53): THE WAR YEARS OF THE GREEK MOTORSHIP ARGONAUT. *Military Collector and Hist. 1978 30(2): 61-65.* Though originally designed as a yacht in 1929, the *Orion* was commissioned by the US Navy during World War II and saw duty, 1940-46, as the *Vixen*.

1004. Wadley, Janet K. and Lee, Everett S. THE DISAPPEARANCE OF THE BLACK FARMER. *Phylon 1974 35(3): 276-283.* The black farmer in the United States has nearly disappeared. As a result, the remaining black farms are small and concentrated in areas where cotton and tobacco are the chief crops. North Carolina is a critical state for determining the future of blacks in agriculture; many of the small black owners and tenants live in that state. Most farm operators in the South are old, and young farmers continue to leave. World War II and the social and technological changes that it precipitated sounded the knell for the small farmer, and Negroes were the first to be displaced. Based on the census and secondary sources; table, 9 notes. B. A. Glasrud

1005. Wagner, Jonathan F. THE DEUTSCHER BUND CANADA IN SASKATCHEWAN. *Saskatchewan Hist. [Canada] 1978 31(2): 41-50.* The Deutscher Bund Canada, founded in Waterloo, Ontario, during January 1934, was closely linked to the pan-German movement sponsored by Hitler's Germany. Its move into western Canada began in the summer of 1934 with a tour by Karl Gerhard, the first national leader. Explains organizational terms such as *Gau, Gebeit, Bezirke, Ortsgrupper,* and *Stutzpunkt.* The number of members was relatively small, representing less than one percent of Saskatchewan's German population. The attempts to propagandize the Nazi ideology through German cultural programs and the speeches of Bernhard Bott, Horst Jerosch, and Henrich Seelheim were overt, and probably telling, until the summer of 1938. At that time the mood all over Canada began to change toward fear of Hitler's Germany. By late 1939 the movement had notably failed. Photo, map, 55 notes.

C. H. Held

1006. Walker, Samuel. COMMUNISTS AND ISOLATIONISM: THE AMERICAN PEACE MOBILIZATION, 1940-1941. *Maryland Historian 1973 4(1): 1-12.* The short-lived American Peace Mobilization (APM) was dominated by the Communist Party USA. The history of the APM exemplifies the decline of noninterventionism in America and illustrates the problems of the American Communist movement after the signing of the Russo-German nonaggression pact. Based on secondary sources; 50 notes. G. O. Gagnon

1007. Wallace, Michael D. ALLIANCE POLARIZATION, CROSS-CUTTING, AND INTERNATIONAL WAR, 1815-1964: A MEASUREMENT PROCEDURE AND SOME PRELIMINARY EVIDENCE. *J. of Conflict Resolution 1973 17(4): 575-604.* Various authors have posited the relationship between alliance polarization and violent conflict in the global system as positive, negative, and curvilinear. Unfortunately, these hypotheses have not received a thorough test, as previous empirical studies of alliance polarization have tended to neglect the configurational properties of alliance groupings and the nonmilitary dimensions of alignment. Attempts to construct measures of polarization and cross-cutting which take these properties into account. Configurations of alignment patterns are generated by subjecting data on military alliances, diplomatic representation, and intergovernmental organizations to Guttmann-Lingoes Smallest Space Analysis. Several mathematical procedures are developed to measure polarization and cross-cutting within and between these clusters. Using these new indices, the relationships between and among polarization, cross-cutting, and international war are examined. It was found that both independent variables had only a weak linear relationship to war. However, polynomial regression uncovered a strong curvilinear relationship between military alliance polarization and war; periods in which polarization was extremely low or extremely high were far more likely to be followed by increased war, while a moderate level of polarization apparently reduced the likelihood of violent conflict. J

1008. Wankmüller, Armin and Cowen, David L. THE GERMAN APOTHECARY SOCIETIES OF NEW YORK. *Pharmacy in Hist. 1980 22(1): 3-10.* Traces the founding and growth of the German apothecary societies in New York City following the influx of German immigrant pharmacists after 1800. The New-Yorker Pharmazeutischer Leseverein (New York Pharmaceutical Reading Society), started by a small group of German-born pharmacists in September-October 1851, became the Deutscher Pharmazeutischer Verein during 1852-64, and in 1864, the New-Yorker Apotheker-Verein, a society open to interested practicing German American pharmacists. After almost a decade of mutual stimulation and honorable competition to advance the interests of science and pharmacy, the East Side Literary and Scientific Society of the German Apothecaries of the City of New York merged with the New-Yorker Apotheker-Verein to form the Deutscher Apotheker-Verein von New York in 1873. Before the advent of the American Pharmaceutical Association and the state pharmaceutical societies, the new society promoted scientific pharmacy, supported the New York College of Pharmacy, and advanced the nonscientific and business aspects of professional pharmacy. The high point of the New York German Apothecaries Society was in the 35 years before the Depression; its demise occurred during World War II. Based on the records of German American apothecary societies of New York and secondary sources; 3 fig., 29 notes. S. C. Morrison

1009. Ward, W. Peter. BRITISH COLUMBIA AND THE JAPANESE EVACUATION. *Can. Hist. Rev. [Canada] 1976 57(3): 289-309.* Explores fluctuations in popular feeling against Japanese in British Columbia during 1937-42. Particularly examines the outburst of sentiment after the bombing of Pearl Harbor and reveals the great impact which public opinion had on the federal government's decision to evacuate Japanese from the coastal region of the province. This decision was a response to popular and political pressures stimulated by the widespread, irrational westcoast belief that Japanese residents threatened the military security of the region. Based on newspaper reports, published public documents, and unpublished documents in major archival collections, notably the Mackenzie King and Ian Mackenzie papers in the Public Archives of Canada and records of the Canadian departments of External Affairs and National Defence.

A

1010. Warren, Shields. HIROSHIMA AND NAGASAKI THIRTY YEARS AFTER. *Pro. of the Am. Phil. Soc. 1977 121(2): 97-99.* Medical teams from the military and the Manhattan Project began studying the effects of radiation on Japanese civilian survivors five weeks after the atomic bombs fell. In 1946 President Truman ordered the National Academy of Sciences to form the Atomic Bomb Casualty Commission to care for the 100,000 severely affected survivors. The commission also studied death rates, chromosome anomalies, and cancer incidences. In 1975 the joint US-Japanese Radiation Effects Research Foundation took over from the commission. W. L. Olbrich

1011. Watkins, Floyd C. EVEN HIS NAME WILL DIE: THE LAST DAYS OF PAUL NOBUO TATSUGUCHI. *J. of Ethnic Studies 1976 3(4): 37-48.* Paul Nobuo Tatsuguchi, an American-educated physician, was sent back to Japan by the Seventh-Day Adventist Church, drafted into the Japanese army in 1941, and sent to the remote Attu Island in the Aleutians where he was killed in the final suicidal attack against American positions in May 1943. His diary, which he kept during the last two and one half weeks, is a moving picture of a man caught between two cultures, not fully trusted by the Japanese, and forced to fight people he did not consider enemies. Refutes by implication the question of whether he killed his wounded patients to prevent their capture. Details the reactions of his wife, children, and friends to the family tragedy and postwar efforts by Americans to help them. Transciption problems of the diary itself are numerous, but the dramatic picture of the final preparations for death of the remaining 1,000 Japanese on Attu is incomparable. Based on the author's own wartime experience and study of numerous copies of the diary.

G. J. Bobango

1012. Watt, Donald. ROOSEVELT AND NEVILLE CHAMBERLAIN: TWO APPEASERS. *Internat. J. [Canada] 1973 28(2): 185-204.* Although Franklin Delano Roosevelt's sources of information and perspective on Europe were different from Neville Chamberlain's, their assessments of the international order and what to do about it were remarkably similar. 62 notes.

R. V. Kubicek

1013. Watt, Donald C. NUREMBERG RECONSIDERED. *Encounter [Great Britain] 1978 50(5): 81-87.* Examines the origins and course of the Nuremberg war crimes trials, based on a discussion of Werner Maser's *Nurnberg: Tribunal der Sieger* (Dusseldorf: Econ Verlag) and Bradley F. Smith's *Reaching Judgment at Nuremberg: The Untold Story of How the Nazi War Criminals Were Judged* (New York: Basic Books, 1977).

1014. Watt, E. F. B. BOMBS AND BUNDLES. *Can. Forces Sentinel [Canada] 1972 8(3): 14-18.* During World War II naval boarding parties were established at Halifax, point of departure for the Atlantic convoys, to prevent German sabotage. Made up of Canadian reservists, the boarding parties were too few to examine most ships but perhaps deterred some saboteurs. Little sabotage was found but the boarders, mostly seamen themselves, quickly found that low morale was a major problem on the England-bound ships. The low morale was a product of war weariness, danger, German propaganda, and, primarily, the ruthless exploitation of poor living conditions of the seamen. The boarders reported their findings to their naval intelligence superiors and corrective action was soon taken. The naval boarders were viewed by seamen as a way to redress grievances to counter propaganda and defeatism. Collection of military intelligence was another primary mission. They also distributed volunteer gifts of food, magazines, and clothing to the crews. Much of the credit for reversing a declining spirit among merchant crews on the Atlantic convoy run must be attributed to this handful of sympathetic and hard working men. Based upon personal experiences of the author; 8 photos. W. E. Pittman, Jr.

1015. Wattenberg, Albert. THE BUILDING OF THE FIRST CHAIN REACTION PILE. *Bull. of the Atomic Scientists 1974 30(6): 51-57.* Recalls the construction of the first controlled nuclear chain reaction pile at the University of Chicago's Stagg Field in 1942.

1016. Webb, B. H. THE ORIGINS OF THE COLD WAR. *Kleio [South Africa] 1974 6(1): 13-26.* The Western Allies' weakness in delaying the opening of a Second Front was the situation which developed into the Cold War, aggravated for the USSR by the atom bomb and the Marshall Plan, and cooled when it manufactured its own bomb.

1017. Webber, Bert. THE BOMBING OF NORTH AMERICA. *Am. Hist. Illus. 1976 11(8): 30-42.* Discusses the Japanese attempt to bomb North America via air balloons loaded with bombs during World War II.

1018. Webster, Grove. THE CIVILIAN PILOT TRAINING PROGRAM. *Aerospace Hist. 1979 26(1): 34-39.* This article, by the former Director of the Civilian Pilot Training Program, describes the development of the program from its beginning in 1938 as a Private Flying Program to put flying instruction into the colleges and universities so as to "foster and develop" all areas of civil aviation. The war situation in 1940 and the rapid expansion of the Air Corps resulted in a greatly expanded program for the CPTP. The expansion made a pool of partially trained pilots for the Army and Navy and flight instructors for the military. As a result, the CPT program supplied 90 percent of the flight and ground school personnel needed for the Army Primary Flight Training programs as well as for foreign programs in the United States. It was responsible for black youths finally being accepted into cadet training. The program lasted 5 years. 6 photos. C. W. Ohrvall

1019. Weddle, Robert S. TEXAS TO TOKYO BAY: ADMIRAL CHESTER W. NIMITZ. *Am. Hist. Illus. 1975 10(5): 4-9, 39-47.* Sketches the life and naval career of Admiral Chester W. Nimitz with emphasis on his role in the Pacific during World War II.

1020. Wedemeyer, Albert C. RELATIONS WITH WARTIME CHINA: A REMINISCENCE. *Asian Affairs: An Am. Rev. 1977 4(3): 196-201.* Describes the author's experiences as an American emissary to China during and after

World War II. Analyzes his motivations in the light of his military background. Based on the author's remarks at the 18th Annual Conference of the American Association for Chinese Studies held in St. Louis, Missouri. Note.

R. B. Mendel

1021. Wegener, Edward. THEORY OF NAVAL STRATEGY IN THE NUCLEAR AGE. *US Naval Inst. Pro. 1972 98(5): 190-207.* Feels that the "series of technical breakthroughs in the naval sector during and after World War II . . . had a more profound impact than any other previous technical revolution." Among the technological breakthroughs, strategic nuclear weapons have most profoundly changed military theory, and thereby, world politics." Discusses the theories of mastery of the seas, seapower, raider warfare, the strategic offensive at sea, maritime presence, and concludes with an overview of seapower in the nuclear age, stressing that "superior seapower thus becomes an important, even indispensable factor of deterrence for the West . . . it cannot allow Western superiority at sea to be endangered by Eastern naval armament." 6 photos, 6 notes.

A. N. Garland

1022. Weigley, Russell F. TO THE CROSSING OF THE RHINE: AMERICAN STRATEGIC THOUGHT TO WORLD WAR II. *Armed Forces and Soc. 1979 5(2): 302-320.* A study of the history of American military strategy reveals movement from a creative and subtle approach during the Revolution, to a much more direct, confrontational approach that depended for success on massive commitments of arms and men designed to overwhelm the enemy's main forces. This meant commitment to straightforward hard fighting. During World War II this strategy was followed successfully, but it must now be rethought. Primary sources; 45 notes.

R. V. Ritter

1023. Weingartner, Fannia. LOOKING BACKWARD: WORLD WAR II. *Chicago Hist. 1978 7(1): 55-58.* Highlights of a scrapbook which details Chicago's role as a Navy recruitment center during April 1941-January 1943.

1024. Weir, Stan. AMERICAN LABOR ON THE DEFENSIVE: A 1940'S ODYSSEY. *Radical Am. 1975 9(4-5): 163-186.* A personal narrative illustrating the elimination of working-class power in industrial labor unions before, during, and after World War II.

S

1025. Werrell, Kenneth P. MUTINY AT ARMY AIR FORCE STATION 569: BAMBER BRIDGE, ENGLAND, JUNE 1943. *Aerospace Historian 1975 22(4): 202-209.* Places the mutiny at Bamber Bridge in the perspective of black service in the US military after briefly reviewing American racial disorders during World War II. Two white military policemen attempted to arrest black soldiers who were out of uniform. Fearful of the congregated black soldiers and British civilians, they obtained the assistance of two more MP's, after which a general melee ensued. Three black soldiers were shot and two MP's were injured. Rumor, emotion, and excitement caused mutinous action the next day as the Negroes sought to avenge what they considered police brutality. In restoring order, the MP's at times used excessive force on the soldiers. The significance of the incident was threefold: it took place overseas, it was in an Air Force unit, and it led to immediate corrective action. Unfortunately, much of the cause, conduct, and treatment of the affair is sadly familiar and current. Primary and secondary sources; 2 photos, 55 notes.

C. W. Ohrvall

1026. Werrell, Kenneth P. THE USAAF OVER EUROPE AND ITS FOES: A SELECTED, SUBJECTIVE, AND CRITICAL BIBLIOGRAPHY. *Aerospace Hist. 1978 25(4): 231-233, 236-243.* A bibliography of air warfare over Europe in World War II, particularly action of the US 8th Air Force.

1027. Wesbrook, Stephen D. THE RAILEY REPORT AND ARMY MORALE, 1941: ANATOMY OF CRISIS. *Military Rev. 1980 60(6): 11-24.* In 1941, the Army faced a very severe morale crisis. The original draftees' term of service, due to end in October, was extended by six months. This was the catalyst to the morale crisis which was documented in a report by *New York Times* correspondent Hilton H. Railey. He found that the soldiers were underpaid, ill-trained, and left out of the mainstream of American society. The soldiers were given a disproportionate share of the defense of the country while being forced into economic and social inferiority. The Railey report pointed out these problems and helped the War Department revise orientation courses accordingly. Based on the Railey report, contemporary articles, and memoirs; 29 notes.
D. H. Cline

1028. West, J. Thomas. PHYSICAL FITNESS, SPORT, AND THE FEDERAL GOVERNMENT 1909 TO 1954. *Can. J. of Hist. of Sport and Physical Educ. 1973 4(2): 26-42.* The Canadian government has cautiously assisted physical fitness and sport, leaving most problems to the private sector. Federal programs for physical fitness have generally encouraged amateur sport, and cost-sharing arrangements have been worked out with the provinces. Mentions the Strathcona trust fund (1909), the Provincial Recreation Movement Programs of the 1930's, and the National Physical Fitness Act of 1943. Federal interest was strong when military preparedness or international prestige were concerned. Based on primary sources; 60 notes.
R. A. Smith

1029. Whalen, Norman M. PLOESTI: GROUP NAVIGATOR'S EYE VIEW. *Aerospace Hist. 1976 23(1): 1-6.* Provides a firsthand account of the planning and flight of the only World War II bombing mission that was classified as a campaign in itself. The five B-24 Groups selected for the mission were based in the Benghazi-Benina area of Libya. Training in low level formation flying and navigating was conducted over the desert where a simulated Ploesti was marked off in the sand. The author describes the actual flight. His plane destroyed its target and flew to Cyprus with one engine inoperative. Based on the author's memoirs; 2 photos, 2 maps.
C. W. Ohrvall

1030. White, G. Edward. THE UNACKNOWLEDGED LESSON: EARL WARREN AND THE JAPANESE RELOCATION CONTROVERSY. *Virginia Q. Rev. 1979 55(4): 613-629.* While attorney general and governor of California during World War II, Earl Warren strongly approved Japanese "relocation centers." Describes Warren's career and suggests that the Japanese position contrasted with his position on civil rights as chief justice. In stating in his memoirs that "it was wrong to react so impulsively," Warren was "settling accounts with himself" about a matter that "weighed on his conscience." The author was a Warren law clerk who had read drafts of his posthumously-published memoirs.
O. H. Zabel

1031. Whitehill, Walter Muir. MARION VERNON BREWINGTON. *Pro. of the Am. Antiquarian Soc. 1975 85(1): 31-36.* Sketches the life of the late Marion Vernon Brewington (1902-74), who was a maritime historian and a lifelong supporter of the AAS. During World War II Brewington worked in the Navy Department, and after the war he became acting curator of the Naval Historical Foundation. His subsequent work concerned painters of American ship portraits in various ports of the world, as well as a proposed biographical dictionary of marine artists. J. Andrew

1032. Whitfield, Joanne. BYRON HOT SPRINGS. *Pacific Historian 1976 20(2): 143-146.* Provides a brief narrative history of the popular California health resort used as prison camp in World War II, and currently being restored. Based on secondary sources; illus., 10 notes. G. L. Olson

1033. Whitney, Ellen; McElligott, Mary Ellen; and Rannalletta, Kathy. ILLINOIS AND ILLINOISANS, 1876-1976: FROM THE COLLECTIONS OF THE ILLINOIS STATE HISTORICAL LIBRARY. *J. of the Illinois State Hist. Soc. 1976 69(4): 242-329.* The entire issue is based on manuscripts in the Library; sources are given on pages 347-348. Accounts are arranged chronologically. 1876-93 (pp. 243-251): US Centennial Exposition, Women's education, medicine, fashion. 10 illus. 1894-1943 (pp. 252-262): Electricity, Pullman strike, sailor's comments on the Orient, race riots, farming, dentistry, automobiles, Chautauqua. 14 illus. 1914-19 (pp. 266-277): Teacher education, Prohibition, woman suffrage, Red Cross librarian in Paris, Armistice celebration, influenza epidemic. 11 illus. 1920-28 (pp. 278-286): auto tour before hard roads, Ku Klux Klan, 10 illus., map. 1929-40 (pp. 287-299): Prison reform, Czech immigrants, Depression, first woman state senator, Chicago World's Fair, end of Prohibition, marriage parlors, big bands. 14 illus. 1941-46 (pp. 300-310): Preparedness, Italian soldier, yellow fever in the Pacific, WPA, rationing, Hitler's house occupied by GI's. 6 illus. 1947-61 (pp. 311-317): Loyalty oaths, recreation therapy in state mental hospital, polio epidemic, displaced persons, segregation, bingo, Red China. 5 illus. 1962-76 (pp. 318-329): Student Non-violent Coordinating Committee, Fallout shelters, Civil Defense, Japanese trade mission, Viet Nam, progressive education, state lotteries. 11 illus. J

1034. Whittemore, Bert R. A QUIET TRIUMPH: THE MISSION OF JOHN GILBERT WINANT TO LONDON, 1941. *Hist. New Hampshire 1975 30(1): 1-11.* In 1941 John Gilbert Winant replaced Joseph Kennedy as American ambassador to Great Britain. Many contemporaries saw him as shy and inarticulate, but he became "a lasting figure in Anglo-American history," and "a symbol of American steadfastness and good sense." His success derived largely from personal qualities of modesty and sincerity. Winant displayed a "constant and obvious" sympathy for the British people; Anthony Eden said, "He cares much for his work, little for party politics, not at all for himself." Based on primary and secondary sources. 3 illus., 30 notes. D. F. Chard

1035. Wilkins, Wynona H. TWO IF BY SEA: WILLIAM LANGER'S PRIVATE WAR AGAINST WINSTON CHURCHILL. *North Dakota Hist. 1974 41(2): 20-29.* Discusses the anti-British sentiments of US Senator from North Dakota William Langer, 1941-52, emphasizing his diatribes against Winston Churchill.

1036. Williams, J. E. THE JOINT DECLARATION ON THE COLONIES: AN ISSUE IN ANGLO-AMERICAN RELATIONS, 1942-1944. *British J. of Int. Studies [Great Britain] 1976 2(3): 267-292.* Compares British and American attitudes toward colonialism and imperialism in regard to British colonies in Southeast Asia 1942-44; examines the Roosevelt administration's unsuccessful attempt to form a Joint Declaration between the two nations toward the colonies.

1037. Williams, William Appleman. DEMYSTIFYING COLD WAR ORTHODOXY. *Sci. and Soc. 1975 39(3): 346-351.* Based on a review of works by George C. Herring, Jr., and Thomas G. Paterson, it is concluded that the confrontation between the United States and the USSR would have been different under Roosevelt from that which occurred under Truman but that the commitment to the global Open Door was as much a part of Roosevelt's refusals to make firm agreements with Stalin in 1941-42 and 1944, as it was of Truman's call in 1945 for the internationalization of the Danube and the Open Door in Manchuria.

N. Lederer

1038. Williamson, John A. and Lanier, William D. THE TWELVE DAYS OF THE *ENGLAND*. *US Naval Inst. Pro. 1980 106(3): 76-83.* In May 1944, the USS *England* (DE-635) was a recently commissioned destroyer escort operating in the Pacific Ocean. As part of Escort Division 39, the *England,* between 19 May and 30 May 1944, sank six Japanese submarines, one of which, the *I-16,* was one of the largest submarines ever built in Japan. Author Williamson was the *England*'s executive officer during that time. 4 photos, map.

A. N. Garland

1039. Willis, John. VARIATIONS IN STATE CASUALTY RATES IN WORLD WAR II AND THE VIETNAM WAR. *Social Problems 1975 22(4): 558-568.* In World War II the more affluent states had higher casualty rates, but in the Vietnam War the situation was reversed. The affluent states in World War II had a higher percentage of men serving in the military. Education was a factor: the Air Corps suffered 17.9% of all casualties and blacks were often segregated into noncombat service units. Vietnam was an infantryman's war; the infantrymen were drawn disproportionately from lower-class and minority men from less affluent states. Notes, biblio.

A. M. Osur

1040. Willson, John P. CARLTON J. H. HAYES, SPAIN, AND THE REFUGEE CRISIS, 1942-1945. *Am. Jewish Hist. Q. 1972 62(2): 99-110.* Describes the efforts of Hayes, wartime US Ambassador to Spain, to organize and expedite relief efforts for Jewish refugees moving through Spain. Analyzes his conflict with the US War Refugee Board, which advocated a more dynamic policy of rescue rather than mere relief. 42 notes.

S

1041. Wilson, Craig Alan. REHEARSAL FOR A UNITED NATIONS: THE HOT SPRINGS CONFERENCE. *Diplomatic Hist. 1980 4(3): 263-281.* The hitherto-neglected UN Conference on Food and Agriculture, held at Hot Springs, Virginia, in May 1943, merits closer attention from historians. This, the first meeting of all nations at war with the Axis, served as a test of the likelihood of postwar international cooperation. Its success both encouraged and provided guidelines for later Allied meetings at Bretton Woods, Dumbarton Oaks, and San Francisco. Further, it illustrates the links between domestic politics and foreign policy, and reveals a close view of decisionmaking within the administration of President Franklin D. Roosevelt (1933-45). 93 notes.   T. L. Powers

1042. Wilson, E. Raymond. **EVOLUTION OF THE C. O. PROVISIONS IN THE 1940 CONSCRIPTION BILL.** *Quaker Hist. 1975 64(1): 3-15.* At the Burke-Wadsworth bill hearings in the summer of 1940, the author and Paul C. French, representing Friends, combined with Mennonites and Brethren to urge legalizing conscientious objection based on personal conviction, civilian control of drafted C.O.'s, and complete exemption for absolutists (nonregistrants). They failed to achieve most of their objectives, experiencing unfavorable discrimination in the hearings. Selective Service control cost the government millions and did injustice to the C.O., and the peace churches should have refused to operate C.O. camps. 14 notes.   T. D. S. Bassett

1043. Wilson, J. L. **THE CHIEF RETIRES.** *Can. Forces Sentinel 1972 8(8): 26-30.* Chief Petty Officer Bob Hewens retired in May 1972, after 30 years service with the Canadian Navy and Reserves. A gunner during WWII, Hewens served on HMCS *Niagara* where he took part in an historic event, the capture of *U-570* in the North Atlantic. The captured U-boat gave up many secrets to the allies and helped turn the tide against the submarines.   W. E. Pittman, Jr.

1044. Wilson, Robert R. **A RECRUIT FOR LOS ALAMOS.** *Bull. of the Atomic Scientists 1975 31(3): 41-47.* Recounts participation in the construction of a cyclotron at Los Alamos, New Mexico, 1942-43, which preceded the Manhattan Project construction and detonation of the first nuclear bomb.

1045. Wilson, Terry Paul. ***AFRIKA KORPS* IN OKLAHOMA: FORT RENO'S PRISONER OF WAR COMPOUND.** *Chronicles of Oklahoma 1974 52(3): 360-369.* Relates the story of the World War II prisoner of war compound at Fort Reno, Oklahoma. Internees were German captives from the African campaign. They contributed to American effort by filling industrial and agricultural labor force needs. Most prisoners adjusted and cooperated, though some "die-hard" Nazis had to be isolated. There was some adverse public opinion over the "lenient" treatment of the prisoners. The prisoner of war policy, however, was considered successful. Based on US government documents, contemporary newspaper reports, and secondary sources; 2 photos, 34 notes.   N. J. Street

1046. Winkler, Allan M. **THE PHILADELPHIA TRANSIT STRIKE OF 1944.** *J. of Am. Hist. 1972 59(1): 73-89.* On 1 July 1944, the War Manpower Commission ruled that the hiring of all male workers in the United States should be done through the United States Employment Service. This agency followed a policy of nondiscrimination in racial matters, and pressed a reluctant Philadelphia Transportation Company to train eight black applicants for positions as streetcar operators, jobs hitherto regarded as reserved for whites only. By 1 August a massive walkout by protesting white employees paralyzed the city for nearly a week. The costly strike, settled only by military intervention, demonstrated racial tensions in the city, the adamant attitude of the American Federation of Labor (A.F.L.) union (motivated in part by a desire to take political advantage of the Congress of Industrial Organizations (C.I.O.) union which advocated nondiscrimination), and the weakness of the Fair Employment Practice Commission. The NAACP played a role in preserving racial peace, and the strike ended with an agreement to employ black operatives. 74 notes.

K. B. West

1047. Winograd, Leonard. DOUBLE JEOPARDY: WHAT AN AMERICAN ARMY OFFICER, A JEW, REMEMBERS OF PRISON LIFE IN GERMANY. *Am. Jewish Arch. 1976 28(1): 3-17.* The author, who was a prisoner of war held by the Germans 1944-45, emphasizes the treatment of Jewish prisoners of war.

1048. Wittner, Lawrence S. AMERICAN POLICY TOWARD GREECE DURING WORLD WAR II. *Diplomatic Hist. 1979 3(2): 129-149.* Calls inaccurate the traditional views that the United States favored a left-wing victory in Greece and opposed British suppression of leftists during World War II. The US government objected to British tactics, but not to the fundamentals. It rejected the British attempt to restore George II to the throne, because the king was so identified with fascism that his restoration would promote a civil war. The United States did, however, help to establish a regency and did virtually nothing to prevent the destruction of the leftists. Based primarily on documents from the National Archives, Washington, D.C., the Roosevelt Library, Hyde Park, N.Y., and other repositories; 96 notes. S

1049. Wittner, Lawrence S. WHEN CIA HEARTS WERE YOUNG AND GAY: PLANNING THE COLD WAR (SPRING 1945). *Peace and Change 1978 5(2-3): 70-76.* Reprints 2 April and 5 May 1945 memos to Presidents Roosevelt and Truman respectively from the Office of Strategic Services outlining the nature of Soviet-American relations after World War II.

1050. Wojciechowski, Marian. STANY ZJEDNOCZONE AMERYKI POŁNOCNEJ I EUROPA SRODKOWA MIEDZY DWIEMA WOJNAMI (1918-1939/41) [The United States and Central Europe in the interwar period, 1918-41]. *Kwartalnik Hist. [Poland] 1976 83(2): 329-337.* Although the United States was closer to Europe after World War I, it didn't sign the Versailles Treaty or participate in the League of Nations. The United States in fact felt close ties with Germany, especially under the Hoover administration, a pro-German partisanship linked with the fear of communism. The Roosevelt administration arrived as Hitler rose to power. This caused the United States to turn more toward French and British policy. This period was characterized by lack of realistic evaluation of Hitler's aims, due mainly to poor judgment of American diplomats in Europe. Even the German aggression against Czechoslovakia and Poland did not shake that policy—America was ready to approve of German conquests, and only the collapse of France and war in the Pacific brought the United States into the world conflict. 33 notes. H. Heitzman-Wojcicka

1051. Wojciechowski, Marian. THE UNITED STATES AND CENTRAL EUROPE BETWEEN THE TWO WORLD WARS (1918-1939/41). *Polish Western Affairs [Poland] 1975 16(1): 65-73.* Robert Gottwald's and Werner Link's works on US policy of isolationism are valuable. The Hoover administration staked its interests on Germany in its Central European interwar foreign policy because Germany was most likely to succumb to a socialist revolution. A communist victory in Germany could mean victory in the whole of Europe. A radical change of sympathies was brought about in 1933 by Franklin D. Roosevelt and Adolf Hitler. M. A. J. Swiecicka-Ziemianek

1052. Wolk, Herman S. THE B-29, THE A-BOMB, AND THE JAPANESE SURRENDER. *Air Force Mag. 1975 58(2): 55-61.* Discusses the role of air power in the war against Japan, 1941-45, relying on conversations between the author and General Curtis Lemay.

1053. Wolk, Herman S. THE OVERLORD DISPUTE: PRELUDE TO D-DAY: THE BOMBER OFFENSIVE. *Air Force Mag. 1974 57(6): 60-65.* Reconstructs the controversy between the Allied military commanders and Winston Churchill and Franklin D. Roosevelt over the use of airpower in the Normandy invasion, Operation Overlord, 1944, and the compromise which was worked out.

1054. Woll, Allen L. HOLLYWOOD'S GOOD NEIGHBOR POLICY: THE LATIN IMAGE IN AMERICAN FILM, 1939-1946. *J. of Popular Film 1974 3(4): 278-293.*

1055. Wollenberg, Charles. BLACKS VS. NAVY BLUE: THE MARE ISLAND MUTINY COURT MARTIAL. *California Hist. 1979 58(1): 62-75.* Describes the court martial in 1944 of 50 black sailors who refused to load ammunition ships at Port Chicago Naval Magazine on San Francisco Bay, 15 miles east of Mare Island, after two ships exploded with the loss of more than 300 men. Their trial embodied such issues as exclusive use of black sailors in loading ammunition ships, the Navy's segregation policies, and whether the men actually had mutinied. The trial proceedings were marred by admission of hearsay evidence and expressions of prejudice by the prosecution. All 50 men were found guilty. Subsequent appeals reduced the initially harsh sentences, while protests from the black community and the NAACP brought the affair to national attention. Eventually Secretary of the Navy James Forrestal, sensitive to race relations in the Navy, provided amnesties for almost all the men. Forrestal's efforts helped moved the Navy from its segregation policies to one of technical integration before President Truman's 1948 order to integrate the armed forces. Primary and secondary sources; 4 photos, 37 notes. A. Hoffman

1056. Wollenberg, Charles. SCHOOLS BEHIND BARBED WIRE. *California Hist. Q. 1976 55(3): 210-217.* A brief survey of the public school system set up by the War Relocation Authority for the children of Japanese Americans sent to the relocation centers in World War II. Of 110,000 evacuees, 25,000 were school age children. The public schools sought to teach American ideals within the hypocritical framework of prison camps. Supplies, equipment, books, and teachers were characterized as second-rate. Yet school life offered continuity amid the shattering effect of relocation. The traditional emphasis on education continued through the war years. Despite imprisonment because of race and shortcomings in the schools, most Nisei remained committed to the ideals of assimilation and education. Based on contemporary and secondary published works; photos, 24 notes. A. Hoffman

1057. Woodman, Lyman L. THE TRANS-CANADIAN, ALASKA, AND WESTERN RAILWAYS. *Alaska J. 1974 4(4): 194-202.* Discusses 1942-43 plans made by the US War Department to build railways from British Columbia to Alaska in order to provide supplies to the USSR during World War II.

1058. Woods, Randall B. CONFLICT OR COMMUNITY? THE UNITED STATES AND ARGENTINA'S ADMISSION TO THE UNITED NATIONS. *Pacific Hist. Rev. 1977 46(3): 361-386.* Despite appearances, American sponsorship of Argentina's UN membership in 1945 does not support the revisionist interpretation of American foreign policy. Although Argentina had maintained diplomatic ties with the Axis powers, served as a base for German espionage in the Western Hemisphere, and submitted to the rule of two autocratic militaristic governments, American foreign policymakers supported its admission because they were committed to the principles of nonintervention, internationalism, and respect for the sovereignty of all nations. Based on documents in MSS. collections and the National Archives, on published primary sources, and on secondary sources; 77 notes. W. K. Hobson

1059. Woods, Randall B. DECISION-MAKING IN DIPLOMACY: THE RIO CONFERENCE OF 1942. *Social Sci. Q. 1975 55(4): 901-918.* In formulating policy, diplomats respond not only to a concept of national interest, but to the needs of a particular governmental organization, and the demands of a political or bureaucratic career as well. This hypothesis is used to examine the evolution of Argentine-American policy in regard to the Inter-American Conference held in Rio de Janeiro. The article uses the construct to shed new light on this very important meeting called by the United States in the wake of Pearl Harbor to commit the Western Hemisphere to the forthcoming struggle against the Axis. The historical situation is also examined to test the validity of the construct. J

1060. Woods, Randall B. HULL AND ARGENTINA: WILSONIAN DIPLOMACY IN THE AGE OF ROOSEVELT. *J. of Inter-Am. Studies and World Affairs 1974 16(3): 350-371.* In 1943 the United States was anxious to force Argentina to break diplomatic relations with the Axis powers. Washington prodded Argentine President Pedro Ramírez into a diplomatic split with Germany, but then the State Department refused to furnish Ramírez with the proof that some of his military officers were linked to the Nazis. Without this proof the Ramírez government fell to pro-Axis forces. Secretary of State Cordell Hull refused to assist Ramírez because Hull, a product of Wilsonian diplomacy, believed in a clear delineation between right and wrong, saw the Ramírez government as wrong, and thought it deserved to fall. Based on State Department documents, memoirs, newspapers and secondary sources; 11 notes, biblio.
J. Thomas

1061. Wright, Christopher C. et al. THE TALL LADIES: *COLUMBUS, ALBANY, & CHICAGO. Warship Int. 1977 14(2): 104-134.* Discusses (1930-74) three cruisers used during World War II and converted under FRAM (Fleet Rehabilitation and Modernization) to carry Talos guided missiles.

1062. Wright, Howard T. CHANGING INSIGNIAS. *Aerospace Hist. 1980 27(2): 113-115.* The author, at that time a second lieutenant, US Army Air Corps, recounts his flight as a fighter pilot out of Hamilton Field California, around 14 December 1941, when he almost shot down what he thought was a Japanese fighter. The aircraft turned out to be American. The error was made because the national insignia on the side of the aircraft fuselage included a red circle in the middle of the white star. As a result of this confusion he was called to the office of General Ira C. Eaker, the Air Defense Commander. After the author told his story, General Eaker called General Hap Arnold and the decision was made to remove the red circle because it could be confused with the Japanese red circle. Provides a confirming statement from General Eaker. 2 photos.

C. W. Ohrvall

1063. Wyman, David S. WHY AUSCHWITZ WAS NEVER BOMBED. *Commentary 1978 65(5): 37-46.* Chronicles the numerous requests to the War Department to bomb the rail lines evacuating Hungarian Jews to Auschwitz and the camp itself in 1944. The War Department replied that such air strikes required diversion of air support from more strategic targets and were of doubtful efficacy. The Allies controlled the skies of Europe at the time and, on several occasions, the Air Force bombed installations very near Auschwitz with considerable success, so that it could have struck the camp and its gas chambers.

J. Tull

1064. Yavenditti, Michael J. THE AMERICAN PEOPLE AND THE USE OF ATOMIC BOMBS ON JAPAN: THE 1940S. *Historian 1974 36(2): 224-247.* A study of American public opinion in the 1940's on the use of atomic bombs on Japan. The immediate response was largely favorable since it undoubtedly shortened World War II, with little sense of personal responsibility or guilt, especially in view of the secrecy surrounding its development and use. There was adept use of a double standard in evaluation of the conduct of the war, including matters related to the bombs. The controversy which developed was significant but limited in participation. The vocal minority of critics "could not even persuade many members of the intelligentsia to condemn the atomic bombings." 82 notes.

R. V. Ritter

1065. Yavenditti, Michael J. JOHN HERSEY AND THE AMERICAN CONSCIENCE: THE RECEPTION OF "HIROSHIMA." *Pacific Hist. R. 1974 43(1): 24-49.* "Evaluates aspects of the post-World War II American milieu, the circumstances which led to the writing and publication of *Hiroshima* (by John Hersey, New York, 1946), and the techniques which Hersey employed in order to determine the meaning of his study for the Americans who first encountered it." The objective is "to shed some light on the larger implications of the atomic bombings for the American conscience." Hersey's book contributed to activation of the American conscience in regard to the bomb and laid the groundwork for later assessments, especially from the standpoint of its human victims. 86 notes.

R. V. Ritter

1066. Young, Kenneth Ray. THE STILWELL CONTROVERSY: A BIBLIOGRAPHICAL REVIEW. *Military Affairs 1975 39(2): 66-68.* Reviews General Joseph W. Stilwell's career in Asia and examines the controversy over Stilwell's effectiveness as the China-India-Burma Theater commander (1942-44). Summarizes the different viewpoints and concludes that Stilwell's mission to China was doomed from the start. 23 notes.

A. M. Osur

1067. Young, Michael. FACING A TEST OF FAITH: JEWISH PACIFISTS DURING THE SECOND WORLD WAR. *Peace and Change 1975 3(2/3): 34-40.* Pacifist convictions and the necessity to fight the Nazis created a dilemma for the Jews of the Jewish Peace Fellowship in 1943.

1068. Young, Robert T. LESSONS OF THE LIBERTIES. *Sea Hist. 1978 (11): 20-22.* Discusses the 2,710 Liberty Ships used during and after World War II.

1069. Young, William H. THAT INDOMITABLE REDHEAD: LITTLE ORPHAN ANNIE. *J. of Popular Culture 1974 8(2): 309-319.* Examines Harold Gray's famous comic strip "Little Orphan Annie" and the right-wing philosophy it editorialized throughout the Depression and World War II. Annie generally admires the very rich and helps poor people get financially ahead without resorting to handouts. "Daddy" Warbucks, a wealthy war profiteer, symbolizes the Carnegie brand of capitalism. Most of Annie's friends are industrialists or small shopkeepers and farmers whose poverty stems from personal rather than economic causes. Gray used the strip to rage against Roosevelt and the New Deal, implying that stability and traditions were being undermined by liberal ideas. During World War II Gray became engrossed with spies and internal subversion, and during 1941-44 Annie turned to shooting Nazis and blowing up submarines. Always self-reliant, Annie represents the social conservatism of the middle class. 12 notes. K. McElroy

1070. Young, William R. ACADEMICS AND SOCIAL SCIENTISTS *VERSUS* THE PRESS: THE POLICIES OF THE BUREAU OF PUBLIC INFORMATION AND THE WARTIME INFORMATION BOARD, 1939-1945. *Hist. Papers [Canada] 1978: 217-240.* "During the Second World War, the Canadian federal government gradually accepted the social sciences as tools in its information policy." Studies of specific sources of wartime discontent had a positive effect on public opinion and the social scientists had a large part in rectifying morale problems. The press opposed any government wartime information agency in a democratic state. In time, the government came to accept the newspapers' point of view, and, believing that "the dangers of criticism" would prove even greater in peacetime, in 1945 abolished the Wartime Information Board. Politicians expressed concern about the government's arguing contentious issues before the public. The demise of the Board removed the major focus of debate, while "the problem of state manipulation in a democratic society remained." 85 notes. E. P. Stickney

1071. Yui, Daizaburô. BUKITAIYO SEISAKU TO HAN-FASHIZUMU RENGÔ NO KEISEI [Lend-lease policy and the formation of the Anti-fascist Coalition]. *Rekishigaku Kenkyu [Japan] 1972 387: 13-31.* Evaluates the fundamental character of the anti-fascist policy of Roosevelt's government by examining the process of legislation and enforcement of the lend-lease policy and its social basis. Discusses the synthetic understanding of both anti-fascist and imperialistic side of the lend-lease policy and its relation to liberal ideology since the New Deal. Primary sources; map, 5 tables, 107 notes. S. Itô

1072. Zahn, Gordon C. PEACE WITNESS IN WORLD WAR II. *Worldview 1975 18(2): 48-55.* Personal account of participation in the Civilian Public Service (a corps for conscientious objectors) during World War II and a general overview of the state of pacifism, 1940-45.

1073. Zancardi, Pietro and Merlo, Vittorio. LA BATTAGLIA DI MIDWAY [World War II in the Pacific: the battle of Midway]. *Rev. Marittima [Italy] 1974 107(6): 28-40, (7/8): 63-76.* Part I. Emphasizes the strategical importance of the battle of Midway which was the turning point of the war in the Pacific. Outlines the Japanese and American planning of the complex MI operation; describes the development of operations; and critically examines the various stages, stressing the new aspect of the war in the Pacific based on the employment of aircraft carriers. Part II. Explains the errors of Japanese planning, the rigidity of which, together with the non-massing of their forces on sea, favored the success of Nimitz's operative concept of calculated risk and the attainment of surprise and air control by the American forces. The actions of the most important protagonists of the battle are described in detail. J

1074. Zapponi, Niccolò. EZRA POUND E IL FASCISMO [Ezra Pound and Fascism]. *Storia Contemporanea [Italy] 1973 4(3): 423-479.* Ezra Pound's Fascist sympathies led to his trial for treason in 1946 and to his confinement to a mental institution until 1958, but his actual understanding of Fascist ideology and his usefulness to that cause were minimal. When Pound lived in Italy (1924-45), he grew to admire the leadership of Benito Mussolini, whom he attempted to contact several times in the interests of his plan for monetary reform, adapted from C. H. Douglas and Silvio Gesell. Despite his wartime radio broadcasts in support of Fascism during World War II and his newspaper articles published by the weekly *Il Meridiano Di Roma,* Pound's ideas were not taken seriously by the Italian regime or public. 132 notes. G. Pizzimenti

1075. Zeitzer, Glen. THE FELLOWSHIP OF RECONCILIATION ON THE EVE OF THE SECOND WORLD WAR: A PEACE ORGANIZATION PREPARES. *Peace and Change 1975 3(2/3): 46-51.* The Fellowship of Reconciliation prepared a program of non-violent resistance during 1940-41 and tried to find solutions to end World War II.

1076. Zemskov, I. THE DIPLOMATIC HISTORY OF THE OPENING OF THE SECOND FRONT IN EUROPE (1941-1944). *Int. Affairs [USSR] 1975 (1): 93-102, (4): 84-92.* Concluded from a previous article. Part IX. Discusses Allied negotiations (including the USA) in 1943-44 about delayed second front operations in Western Europe, and about unsuccessful diversionary military operations in the Mediterranean area and elsewhere.

1077. Zerner, Ruth. HOLOCAUST: A PAST THAT IS ALSO PRESENT. *J. of Ecumenical Studies 1979 16(3): 518-524.* Reviews recent literature, conferences, and organizations for study related to the Holocaust, and analyzes this resurgence of interest. Survivors of the Holocaust and their children, particularly Jewish refugees who settled in the United States, are unusually curious about the catastrophes of European history. Since the publication of Elie Wiesel's *Night* (English translation, 1960), books, articles, and conferences on the Holocaust have proliferated. J. A. Overbeck

1078. Ziemke, Earl F. CIVIL AFFAIRS REACHES THIRTY. *Military Affairs 1972 36(4): 130-133.* Although studies were made between World Wars I and II about the Army's role in the administration of occupied territory, not until 1940 was the manual on *Military Government* issued. In 1942 the responsibility for training civil affairs officers was given to the Provost Marshal General and the School of Military Government established at the University of Virginia. Not until November 1943, however, was the responsibility for governing occupied territory formally assigned to the Army. Based on official records and monographs; 7 notes. K. J. Bauer

1079. Zobrist, Benedict K. RESOURCES OF PRESIDENTIAL LIBRARIES FOR THE HISTORY OF THE SECOND WORLD WAR. *Military Affairs 1975 39(2): 82-85.* Numerous papers and records from varied sources are contained in the Presidential Libraries, offering unique opportunities for researchers interested in World War II. Major sources are available at the Hoover, Roosevelt, Truman, Eisenhower, and Kennedy Libraries. 8 notes.
A. M. Osur

1080. Zolov, A. V. AMERIKANSKII IZOLIATSIONISM I PRINIATIE ZAKONA O NEITRALITETE 1935 GODA [American isolationism and the enactment of the Neutrality Act (1935)]. *Vestnik Moskovskogo U., Seriia 8: Istoriia [USSR] 1979 (1): 32-44.* Isolationists were divided into four groups. The liberal democratic group feared that war would end domestic reform. The left radical groups feared that war would impede socialism in America. The conservatives feared that war would bring social reform and wanted the United States to be an arbiter of a Europe weakened by war. Fascists such as Fr. Coughlin, Long, and Hearst constituted a fourth group. President Franklin D. Roosevelt saw that isolationist sentiment was strong and so acted cautiously in dealing with the Neutrality Act. Roosevelt did win a concession from Congress that the embargo on the shipment of military goods would last only six months. Many groups in America were happy at the passage of the bill. 81 notes. D. Balmuth

1081. Zuroff, Efraim. RESCUE PRIORITY AND FUND RAISING AS ISSUES DURING THE HOLOCAUST: A CASE STUDY OF THE RELATIONS BETWEEN THE VA'AD HA-HATZALA AND THE JOINT, 1939-1941. *Am. Jewish Hist. 1979 68(3): 305-326.* The rescue of a group of East European rabbis and students by the Orthodox Jews of America through the Yeshiva Aid Committee (Va'ad Ha-Hatzala) was organized by Rabbi Eliezer Silver of the Union of Orthodox Rabbis. In complex dealings with the Joint Distribution Committee (JDC) the Va'ad, even though it needed the funds contributed by the JDC, maintained its independent stance and engaged in some separate fund raising. By December 1941, approximately 625 rabbis, students, and members of their families had been rescued via Japan and Shanghai. 4 illus., 3 photos, 27 notes. F. Rosenthal

1082. —. [AUSTRALIA AND ARTICLE VII]. *Australian Econ. Hist. Rev. [Australia] 1978 18(1): 75-89.*
Schedvin, C. B. A COMMENT, *pp. 75-77.* Criticizes Roger Bell's recent article on economic relations between Australia and the United States during World War II (see abstract 15A:4537). Bell reiterated many of the misconceptions prevalent in wartime Washington. Furthermore, Bell failed to consult the records of the Australian treasury. Therefore his interpretation of the commitment in Article VII of the Anglo-American Mutual Aid Agreement of 1942 is invalid. Primary sources; 6 notes.
Bell, Roger. A REPLY, *pp. 78-84.* Schedvin's comments are based on flimsy

evidence. The author presents additional evidence to demonstrate Schedvin's distortions and misrepresentations of Bell's articles. Primary sources; 23 notes.

Schedvin, C. B.   A FURTHER COMMENT,   *pp. 85-88.*
Bell, Roger.   A FURTHER REPLY,   *pp. 88-89.*   R. B. Orr

1083. —. THE BATTLE FOR THE FUTURE. *Am. Hist. Illus. 1979 14(4): 38-39, 42-44.* The State Department and the War Department, wanting to insure that business, industry, jobs, farms, and cities grew and prospered, during World War II campaigned to convince Americans and the world that big is better.

1084. —. THE BATTLE OF MANPOWER. *Am. Hist. Illus. 1979 14(4): 14-18.* Describes the utilization of Americans for World War II by means of military conscription in the form of the Burke-Wadsworth Act (US, 1940), and industry and scientific research.

1085. —. THE BATTLE OF PRODUCTION. *Am. Hist. Illus. 1979 14(4): 5-14.* Describes conversion of US industry from civilian to war production during World War II.

1086. —. THE BATTLE OF SOCIAL JUSTICE. *Am. Hist. Illus. 1979 14(4): 20, 22-23.* Discusses US social reform programs generated by the need for civilian participation in the work force during World War II, particularly the entrance of blacks into the job market.

1087. —. [BRAZILIAN-AMERICAN RELATIONS DURING WORLD WAR II]. *Hispanic Am. Hist. Rev. 1979 59(4): 691-701.*
McCann, Frank D.   CRITIQUE OF STANLEY E. HILTON'S "BRAZILIAN DIPLOMACY AND THE WASHINGTON-RIO DE JANEIRO 'AXIS' DURING THE WORLD WAR II ERA,"   *pp. 691-700.* Hilton's article (see abstract 17A:7135) indicated that Frank D. McCann in *The Brazilian-American Alliance, 1937-1945* (Princeton, 1973) concluded that the United States was deceitful in dealing with Brazil during World War II and sought to rule it. This interpretation of the book is incorrect. 37 notes.
Hilton, Stanley E.   STANLEY E. HILTON'S REPLY,   *p. 701.* Defends his article and interpretation, seeing conceptual fuzziness in McCann's work.
B. D. Johnson

1088. —. DIN NOU DESPRE CRUCISĂTORUL "INDIANAPOLIS" [More on the cruiser *Indianapolis*]. *Magazin Istoric [Rumania] 1977 11(6): 55-57.*
Hashimoto, Mochitsura.   TORPILE ... [Torpedoes ...], *pp. 55-57.* The author, captain of the Japanese submarine, in his memoirs, *Sunk* (New York, 1954), attributed the sinking of the US cruiser *Indianapolis* in 1945 to torpedoes.
Beach, Edward L.   ... SAU KAITEN-URI? [... or kaitens?], *p. 57.* Admiral Beach criticizes the Japanese account and attributes the sinking to *kaitens,* or manned torpedoes.

1089. —. THE DIPLOMATIC HISTORY OF THE OPENING OF THE SECOND FRONT IN EUROPE (1941-1944). *Int. Affairs [USSR] 1974 (5): 93-102, (7): 121-126, (10): 107-114.* Continued from *Int. Affairs* 1970 (4,7,12).

Discusses the USSR's diplomatic attempts to involve Great Britain and the United States in the opening of a second front in Europe during World War II in 1942-43, emphasizing aspects of military strategy and the roles of Winston Churchill and Franklin D. Roosevelt.

1090. —. THE FIGHTING "I." *Warship Int. 1979 16(2): 157-161.* The aircraft carrier, U.S.S. *Intrepid,* launched 26 April 1943 at Newport News, Virginia, was seriously damaged during World War II by Japanese kamikazes, and is destined to become a memorial museum by the nonprofit organization, Odysseys In Flight, Inc.

1091. —. FORGOTTEN FIFTH. *Aero Album 1972 5(2): 23-25.* A brief history of the "forgotten Fifth" Air Force which served in the Pacific during World War II, as revealed in the markings of the unit aircraft. 6 photos.
C. W. Ohrvall

1092. —. [FRANKLIN D. ROOSEVELT AND HIS FOREIGN POLICY CRITICS]. *Pol. Sci. Q. 1979 94(1): 15-35.*
Steele, Richard W.   FRANKLIN D. ROOSEVELT AND HIS FOREIGN POLICY CRITICS.   *pp. 15-32.* Reexamines the actions and attitudes of President Franklin D. Roosevelt toward critics of his foreign policy just before and in the early years of American entry in World War II. According to Steele, Roosevelt viewed what was mere dissent as evidence of subversion and disloyalty.
Schlesinger, Arthur M., Jr.   A COMMENT ON "ROOSEVELT AND HIS FOREIGN POLICY CRITICS."   *pp. 33-35.* Takes issue with Steel's analysis, contending that presidential critics fared much better under the Roosevelt administration than under earlier wartime administrations such as Lincoln's and Woodrow Wilson's. J

1093. —. HARD BARGAINING: A UNION IN THE WOODS: 1940-1950. *Sound Heritage [Canada] 1978 7(4): 60-75.* Examines Canadian labor policy during World War II, when there were few strikes and the era was characterized by progressive labor policy. After the war there were many orderly strikes, exemplified by British Columbia's International Woodworkers of America, founded in 1937 in Washington; briefly mentions members of the IWA.

1094. —. "LOOKING BACK, IT'S HARD TO BELIEVE . . ." *Am. Hist. Illus. 1979 14(4): 44-49.* Takes a nostalgic look at the spirit of Americans during World War II.

1095. —. [MACARTHUR AS MARITIME STRATEGIST]. *Naval War Coll. Rev. 1980 33(2): 79-102.*
Reynolds, Clark G.   MACARTHUR AS MARITIME STRATEGIST, *pp. 79-91.* Maritime strategy is broader than naval strategy and embodies the Army, Navy, and Air Forces in seaborne operations. General Douglas MacArthur's "consistent advocacy of a maritime strategy for the United States in the Pacific places him alongside the nation's leading admirals who have similarly advocated such a strategy." 36 notes.
Falk, Stanley L.   COMMENTS ON REYNOLDS: "MACARTHUR AS MARITIME STRATEGIST,"   *pp. 92-99.* "Maritime strategy is grand strategy —and MacArthur's strategic concepts were petty and parochial." 29 notes.

Wheeler, Gerald E. A COMMENTARY ON DR. CLARK REYNOLDS' PAPER: "MACARTHUR AS MARITIME STRATEGIST," *pp. 99-102.*

1096. —. MAC-ITS MIDDLE NAME IS AIRLIFT. *Air Force Mag. 1972 55(5): 75-79.* Follows the Military Airlift Command from May 1941 in its wide range of operations, from providing large-scale logistical support to conducting air rescue missions, and points out its invaluable role for the Air Force and other services in World War II, the Cuban missile crisis, and Vietnam.

1097. —. *OKLAHOMA*: UP FROM THE MUD AT PEARL HARBOR. *US Naval Inst. Pro. 1975 101(12): 46-59.* A pictorial presentation of the battleship *Oklahoma* based on newspaper articles, journal proceedings, books, and news magazine accounts, which traces the *Oklahoma*'s career from her commissioning in 1916, to her sinking at Pearl Harbor in December 1941, to her raising in 1943 and, finally, her accidental sinking while under tow in 1947. Includes a detailed drawing of the ship. 40 photos. A. N. Garland

1098. —. [PEARL HARBOR AND THE *COLORADO*, *NEVADA*, *TANEY*, AND *UTAH*]. *US Naval Inst. Pro. 1976 102(12): 46-54.*

Shrader, Grahame F. USS COLORADO: THE "OTHER" BATTLESHIP, *pp. 46-47.* The *Colorado* (BB45), on 7 December 1941, was at the Puget Sound Navy Yard in Bremerton, Washington; she had arrived there for overhaul on 3 August 1941, and was due to return to Pearl Harbor in late November 1941 to relieve the *West Virginia*. She was delayed because of blower trouble, and was spared the fate of her sister ships at Pearl Harbor. Although the crew of the *Colorado* spent a number of tense days after 7 December, 1941, expecting a Japanese attack on the west coast of the United States, nothing happened. She left Bremerton in February 1942 but did not get into actual combat until November, 1943, at Tarawa. Unfortunately, because she had not gone through the Pearl Harbor experience, "the *Colorado* continued throughout the war with an antiquated secondary battery that was virtually useless against enemy aircraft." 2 photos.

Merdinger, Charles J. UNDER WATER AT PEARL HARBOR, *pp. 48-49.* The author was serving on the battleship *Nevada* on 7 December 1941 when that ship, the only battleship at Pearl Harbor to get underway that day, received one torpedo and five bomb hits and was beached. When the *Nevada* sank later in the day, the author was stationed in the ship's plotting room, which was then actually lower than the surface of the water. He and his men stayed in position until 3:00 p.m., when water began to enter the room. They climbed topside through an adjacent communications tube. This article is based on the author's recollections which have been recorded as part of the Naval Institute's Oral History Program. 2 photos.

Kraft, Carl and Kraft, Nell. USCGC TANEY: STILL IN SERVICE 35 YEARS LATER, *pp. 50-51.* Of the 101 US military vessels in the vicinity of Pearl Harbor on 7 December 1941, only one, the US Coast Guard cutter *Taney* (WHEC-37) is still in active service. Because of certain fortuitous happenings, she was ready for combat that Sunday morning, but most of the action took place beyond the range of her guns. For the next week she patrolled the harbor entrance; she served with distinction throughout the war, suffered no major damage, and survived "to fight in two more wars." She now operates from the Coast Guard station at Portsmouth, Virginia. 4 photos.

Eldredge, Michael S. THE OTHER SIDE OF THE ISLAND: USS UTAH AT PEARL HARBOR, *pp. 52-54.* Not many of the US Navy's ships were older than the USS *Utah* on 7 December 1941. She had been commissioned in 1911 and had "served for 19 years as BB-31." In July 1931 she had been redesignated AG-16 and was "destined to serve out her final years as a target ship." At the time of the Japanese attack she was berthed at Fox-11, on the northwest side of Ford Island, which was usually assigned to an aircraft carrier. Struck by two torpedoes, the *Utah* eventually capsized. Two attempts to salvage her failed and Fox-11 remains her final resting place; 54 of her crew are still entombed in her hull. In 1970 Congress authorized construction of a memorial over the ship, and she is now "one of the two remaining hulks that remind us of the tragedy of Pearl Harbor." 5 photos.
A. N. Garland

1099. —. SHANGHAI, 1937-1938: HOW BITTERSWEET IT WAS. *US Naval Inst. Pro. 1974 100(11): 79-91.* A pictorial essay, "the results of efforts by Professor Robert M. Leventhal." Many of the photographs were taken by the late Sergeant Major Albert C. Marts, US Marine Corps, who served with the Fourth Marine Regiment in China during the 1920's and 1930's. For 10 years prior to the summer of 1937, with a brief interlude of fighting between the Chinese and Japanese in 1932, "reality ... was guard duty and liberty" for the Fourth Marines in Shanghai, and after "the daily drudgery of duty" they "entered a kind of oriental Valhalla." War came again to Shanghai in July 1937, and life for the Marines began to change seven months later when the Japanese occupied the city. From that time on, "it was the Japanese whose word was law in China's largest city." 28 photos.
A. N. Garland

1100. —. THE UNITED STATES AIR FORCE IN FACTS AND FIGURES. *Air Force Mag. 1974 (5): 132-146.* Reproduces statistics about the US Air Force, 1907-74, including its personnel, founding, wartime activities, equipment, and heroes.

1101. —. USN IN WWII: A PICTORIAL OF SELECTED VIEWS FROM THE COLLECTION OF ARTHUR DAVIDSON BAKER III. *Warship Int. 1978 15(4): 330-339.* A photographic history of the US Navy in World War II from the collection of Arthur Davidson Baker III.

1102. —. THE U.S.S. TULSA, 1919-1945. *Chronicles of Oklahoma 1977 55(3): 259-265.* For five years after its launching in 1922, the *USS Tulsa* served off Central America and in the military occupation of Nicaragua. During 1929-45 it was assigned to the Far East and served in Pacific escort duty throughout World War II. 4 photos.
M. L. Tate

1103. —. [WARTIME STRIKES IN THE AUTOMOBILE INDUSTRY]. *Radical Am. 1975 9(4-5): 77-114.*
Jennings, Ed. WILDCAT! THE WARTIME STRIKE WAVE IN AUTO, *pp. 77-105.*
Glaberman, Martin. EPILOGUE, *pp. 106-114.* Considers the causes for the worker-initiated wildcat strikes that ignored the official no-strike union policy.
S

1104. —. [WOMEN IN THE CANADIAN MILITARY]. *Atlantis [Canada] 1979 4 (2, part 2): 267-286.*
Simpson, Suzanne; Toole, Doris; and Player, Cindy. WOMEN IN THE CANADIAN FORCES: PAST, PRESENT AND FUTURE, *pp. 267-283.* Traces Canadian women's military service since the late 19th century, particularly during World War II; discusses the current status of women in the Canadian services, and the possibilities for the future.
Jacobsen, Carl G. WOMEN IN THE CANADIAN FORCES: PAST, PRESENT AND FUTURE: A CRITIQUE, *pp. 284-286.* Cites examples of women's participation in the military around the world, rebutting the argument that women's participation is limited.

1105. —. WORKING WOMEN AND THE WAR: FOUR NARRATIVES. *Radical Am. 1975 9(4-5): 133-162.*
Unsigned. INTRODUCTION, *pp. 133-134.*
Clawson, Augusta. SHIPYARD DIARY OF A WOMAN WELDER, *pp. 134-138.*
Archibald, Katherine. WOMEN IN THE SHIPYARD, *pp. 139-144.*
Sonnenberg, Mary. TWO EPISODES, *pp. 145-155.*
Stein, Anne. POST-WAR CONSUMER BOYCOTTS, *pp. 156-162.* Personal narratives include examples of sex discrimination, betrayals by labor unions, and the 1946 meat boycott in Washington, D.C.   S

1106. —. [WORLD WAR II AND FEMALE LABOR FORCE PARTICIPATION RATES]. *J. of Econ. Hist. 1980 40(1): 89-97.*
Schweitzer, Mary M. WORLD WAR II AND FEMALE LABOR FORCE PARTICIPATION RATES, *pp. 89-95.* Between the years 1940 and 1947 the demand for female labor in the United States shifted rapidly. Wages for women rose swiftly during the war, then fell suddenly when industries converted to peacetime production. This paper makes use of household production theory to explore the behavior of different segments of the female labor force as they responded to the radical changes in demand brought by World War II. The analysis suggests that a crucial turning point in the efforts to hire women was reached in the second half of 1943.
Nickless, Pamela J. DISCUSSION, *pp. 96-97.*   J

1107. —. [WORLD WAR II: 30 YEARS AFTER]. *Survey [Great Britain] 1975 21(1/2): 1-42.*
Dallek, Robert. ALLIED LEADERSHIP IN THE SECOND WORLD WAR: ROOSEVELT, *pp. 1-10.* Franklin D. Roosevelt's personal views did not determine US policy. Quite the contrary, Roosevelt himself mirrored American public opinion. He followed the US public from pacifism to neutralism, although he himself was never an isolationist. His call for unconditional surrender grew out of official and unofficial thinking, and while his skepticism about postwar cooperation with the USSR was growing, he never let on to the public. Roosevelt also followed American fantasies about China's role, and when the American public wanted a new Wilsonian League after the war instead of Roosevelt's world policed by the Great Powers, he also went along. Based on secondary sources; 18 notes.
Dallin, Alexander. ALLIED LEADERSHIP IN THE SECOND WORLD WAR: STALIN, *pp. 11-19.* Joseph Stalin did not win the victory nor was

the victory won despite him, but as a symbol of wartime leadership he would have had to have been invented had he not existed. There is no record of any great military ability, but he did mobilize the Russian people. As the head of the Party and the government his behavior exhibited his personal needs more than those of the system. He excelled in using people and in making concessions and then taking them back. The same tactics also applied to the Allies, but Stalin never lost sight of the fact that a clash with them was inevitable. Based on secondary sources; 23 notes.

Dilks, David. ALLIED LEADERSHIP IN THE SECOND WORLD WAR: CHURCHILL, *pp. 19-29.* Winston Churchill was a man with a profound sense of history, and "he was incapable of looking at an issue except in its historical setting." The memory of the slaughter of World War I led him to distrust the military, and he would have looked at German terms had they been offered in 1940. Churchill preferred indirection and one of his greatest contributions may have been getting the invasion of France postponed until 1944, and even then it succeeded only by a narrow margin. Although Stalin fooled him over Poland, his view of Russia was not one of implacable hostility. Based on archival material, memoirs and secondary sources; 12 notes.

Kennan, George F. COMMENT, *pp. 29-36.* Roosevelt's policy by 1940 was to force Japan and Germany into moving against the US; thereby making a war inevitable. For all his charm and political skill, his ability to lead during the war, when it came to foreign policy Roosevelt was a superficial, ignorant dilettante, a man with a severely limited intellectual horizon. Churchill probably had the most straightforward task; he was fighting for Britain's survival. Stalin, until 1943, was also fighting for survival—his, and in his acts he did not so much deceive the Western leaders as they deceived themselves.

Seton-Watson, Hugh. REFLECTIONS, *pp. 37-42.* A comparison of 1815 and 1945, while directly opposite in result is also strikingly similar in many respects. Yet whatever may be fashionable in the West, Cold War, peaceful coexistence, detente, the reality of the Soviet Empire remains the same.

R. B. Valliant

SUBJECT INDEX

Subject Profile Index (ABC-SPIndex) carries both generic and specific index terms. Begin a search at the general term but also look under more specific or related terms.

Each string of index descriptors is intended to present a profile of a given article; however, no particular relationship between any two terms in the profile is implied. Terms within the profile are listed alphabetically after the leading term. The variety of punctuation and capitalization reflects production methods and has no intrinsic meaning; e.g., there is no difference in meaning between "History, study of " and "History (study of)."

Cities, towns, and counties are listed following their respective states or provinces; e.g., "Ohio (Columbus)." Terms beginning with an arabic numeral are listed after the letter Z. The chronology of the bibliographic entry follows the subject index descriptors. In the chronology, "c" stands for "century"; e.g., "19c" means "19th century."

Note that "United States" is not used as a leading index term; if no country is mentioned, the index entry refers to the United States alone. When an entry refers to both Canada and the United States, both "Canada" and "USA" appear in the string of index descriptors, but "USA" is not a leading term.

The last number in the index string, in italics, refers to the bibliographic entry number.

A

Actors and Actresses. Benefit performances. Employment. Minnesota (Minneapolis). 1942. *985*
Adachi, Ken (review article). Immigration. Japanese Canadians. Racism. 1877-1976. *521*
Adoption. Baker, Josephine. Civil rights. Entertainers. Negroes. 1940-75. *434*
Adventist Medical Cadet Corps. Armies. Dick, Everett N. (account). Korean War. 1934-53. *223*
Adventists. Chaplains. Military. 1944-55. *224*
Adventure serials. Americanism. National Characteristics. Radio. 1940-45. *287*
Advisory Commission to the Council of National Defense. Industry. Mobilization. 1940. *102*
Aeronautics, Military. Africa, North. Great Britain. Hurricane (aircraft). Ohlinger, John F. (account). 1942. *691*
—. Arizona. Flying Tigers. Germany, West. Scott, Robert L., Jr. 1941-45. 1955-57. *936*
—. Army Air Corps. Eaker, Ira C. World War I. 8th Bomber Command, US. 1917-47. *852*
—. Battleships, fast. Naval Air Forces. 1941-45. *659*
—. Bombing. Bradshaw, Russell (account). Ukraine. 1944. *119*
—. BT-13A (aircraft). Flight training. Strunk, Al (account). 1941-45. *930*
—. Burma. China. Flying Tigers. 1941-77. *940*
—. B-17 (aircraft). B-24 (aircraft). Eighth Air Force, US. Europe, Western. 1935-45. *255*
—. Circumnavigations. Diplomacy. Harriman, W. Averell. Lend-Lease. USSR. 1941. *323*
—. Civilian Pilot Training Program. 1938-41. *1018*
—. Europe. Hudson, James J. (account). P-39 Airacobra (aircraft). 1941-45. *435*
—. Military Intelligence. O-47 (aircraft). O-52 (aircraft). Puerto Rico. ca 1917-43. *320*
—. Philippines. Wagner, Boyd D. 1941-42. *104*
—. P-47 (aircraft). 1941-45. *253*
—. Sociology (aircraft). 1941-45. *854*
Africa (landing). Diplomacy. French. Great Britain. 1941-42. *760*

Africa, North. Aeronautics, Military. Great Britain. Hurricane (aircraft). Ohlinger, John F. (account). 1942. *691*
—. Air Forces. Military Ground Forces. Patton, George S., Jr. Tactics. 1943. *502*
—. Air Warfare. P-38 (aircraft). 1942-45. *276*
—. Diplomacy. Economic Policy. France, Vichy. USA. 1941-43. *97*
Africa (north, west). France. International Trade. Lend-Lease. USA. 1941-46. *242*
Afro-American Studies. 1913-76. *981*
Agent general, office of. Canada. Great Britain (London). Intergovernmental Relations. 18c-20c. *886*
Agricultural coops. Agriculture and Government. 1900-50. *370*
Agricultural Production. Cotton. Economic Conditions. South or Southern States. Soybeans. 1920's-75. *294*
—. Farmers. Michigan. 1939-45. *179*
Agriculture. Europe. Industrialization. Market economy. North America. Peasant movements (colloquium). ca 1875-1975. *52*
—. Florida (Boca Raton). Japanese Americans. Yamato colony. 1904-75. *750*
—. Idaho. Internment. Japanese Americans. Railroads. 1900-45. *868*
Agriculture and Government. Agricultural coops. 1900-50. *370*
Agriculture Department. California. Emergency Rubber Project. Guayule (plant). Nishimura, Shimpe. Rubber industry! 1942-76. *36*
Air Bases. Alabama (Montgomery). Army Air Corps. Maxwell Field. Military training. Mutiny. 1943. *222*
—. Diplomacy. Norweb, R. Henry. Portugal (Azores). 1941-44. *942*
Air Bases (construction of). Civil-Military Relations. Hammon, Stratton Owen (account). Kentucky (Louisville). Standiford Airfield. 1942-43. *377*
Air Force. Alaska (Anchorage, Adak). Bush pilot. Pinney, Charles A. 1942-43. *741*
Air Forces. Africa, North. Military Ground Forces. Patton, George S., Jr. Tactics. 1943. *502*
—. Bombing, daylight. 1941-44. *241*

213

Air Forces

—. Bombing, indiscriminate. Civilian targets. Ethics. Germany. Military General Staff. 1941-45. *837*
—. Bombing, strategic. Japan (Kyoto). Stimson, Henry L. USA. 1940-45. *160*
—. Dunn, William R. Pilots. 1941-45. 1967. *718*
—. Dunn, William R. (account). Eagle Squadron, No. 71. Great Britain. Spitfire (aircraft). 1941. *252*
—. Europe. Thyng, Harrison R. (reminiscences). 1941-45. *963*
—. Gliders. Riddle, Jack (interview). 1942-45. *175*
—. Insignia. Pacific Area. 5th Air Force, US. 1941-45. *1091*
—. Japan. Military Capability. Philippines. 1941. *385*
—. Leyte Gulf (battle). Navies. Philippines. 1944. *829*
—. Maritime missions. Navies. 1941-78. *150*
—. Military Airlift Command. 1941-72. *1096*
—. Military Strategy. Vietnam War. Weather. 1941-72. *311*
—. Statistics. 1907-74. *1100*
Air Power (television series). Films. History. Wolff, Perry. 1939-56. *8*
Air raids. Air Warfare. Germany. Jablonski, Edward (review article). Regensburg-Schweinfurt. USA. 1943. *380*
Air Rescue Service. Rescue work. 1945-61. *964*
Air support, close. Army Air Corps Tactical School. Europe, Western. Tactics. 1930-45. *454*
Air Warfare. Africa, North. P-38 (aircraft). 1942-45. *276*
—. Air raids. Germany. Jablonski, Edward (review article). Regensburg-Schweinfurt. USA. 1943. *380*
—. Aleutian campaign. Canada. USA. 1938-45. *394*
—. American Volunteer Group. China. Flying Tigers motifs. Shoulder patches. 23d Fighter Group. 1930's-45. *191*
—. Andrews, John A. C. (account). P-40 (aircraft). P-47 (aircraft). Spitfire (aircraft). 1943-45. *26*
—. Army Air Corps. Beeson, Duane. Europe, Western. Idaho (Boise). 1941-45. *309*
—. Army Air Force. Arnold, Henry H. (Hap). 1942. *501*
—. Army Air Forces. China. Flying Tigers. Holloway, Bruce K. (account). P-40 (aircraft). 1942-43. *424*
—. Arnold, H. H. "Hap". Historians. Military Strategy. 1943-44. *708*
—. Atomic bomb. *Enola Gay* (aircraft). Military training. Wendover Field. 1944-45. *986*
—. Atomic Warfare. Baldwin, Paul H. (account). Fighter squadrons, night. Philippines. 1942-45. *44*
—. Auschwitz. Concentration Camps. Jews. Military Strategy. 1944-45. *1063*
—. Balloons. Bombing. Japan. North America. 1940-45. *1017*
—. Bibliographies. Eighth Air Force. Europe. 1941-45. *1026*
—. Bibliographies. Novels. 1939-45. *894*
—. Bombing. 1943-45. *386*
—. Bombing. Bowman, Marvin S. (reminiscences). Great Britain. USSR (Mirgorod, Poltava). 1944. *114*
—. Bombing. B-17 (aircraft). Germany. Poltava (battle). USSR. 1944. *445*
—. Bombing. Churchill, Winston. Military General Staff. Operation Overlord. Roosevelt, Franklin D. 1944. *1053*
—. Bombing. Dresden (attack on). Germany. Great Britain. Total war. 1914-45. *181*

—. Bombing. Germany. Great Britain. Military Strategy. 1942-44. *994*
—. Bombing (inadvertent). Diplomacy. Switzerland. USA. 1943-45. *401*
—. Bombing (strategic). Ships. 1939-80. *468*
—. Bombing, strategic. Vietnam War. 1943-45. 1965-73. *891*
—. Brooks, Jim (reminiscences). Oil fields. Romania. 31st Fighter Group, US. 1944. *127*
—. B-17 (aircraft). Kelly, Colin P., Jr. Philippines. 1941. *144*
—. B-26 (aircraft; markings). 42nd Bombardment Wing. 1942-44. *950*
—. Chennault, Claire Lee. China. Flying Tigers. Japan. 1941-45. *408*
—. Chennault, Claire Lee. China. Japan. USA. 1927-45. *727*
—. China. 23d Fighter Group. 1942-45. *669*
—. Churchill, Winston. Eaker, Ira C. (reminiscences). Great Britain. 1942-47. *256*
—. Civilians, bombing of. Public opinion, changes in. 1937-45. *318*
—. Dunn, William R. (account). Great Britain. Royal Air Force. 1941. *251*
—. Egypt (Foul Bay). Ohlinger, John F. (account). 1943. *692*
—. Europe. 1941-45. *632*
—. F4U (aircraft). Marines. Pacific Area. Zero (aircraft). 1943-45. *419*
—. Japan. Kenney, George. New Britain. Rabaul (battle). 1943. *92*
—. Japan. Marianas (battle). 1944. *293*
—. Japan. Naval Strategy. Pearl Harbor, attack on. 1940-41. *698*
—. Marines. McCarthy, Joseph R. Pacific Area. Politics. Wisconsin. 1942-52. *774*
—. McGuire, Thomas. Philippines. 1945. *16*
—. Ploesti (raid). Rumania. USA. Whalen, Norman M. (reminiscences). 1943. *1029*
—. *P-51* (airplane). 1943-45. *117*
—. P-51 (airplane). 1943-45. *139*
Air warfare, clandestine. China. Japan. USA. 1940-41. *840*
Air Warfare (personal accounts). Germany. USA. 1942. *111*
Airborne operations. Netherlands (Arnhem). Operation Market-Garden. Ryan, Cornelius (review article). 1944. *559*
Airborne troops. 1887-1945. *717*
—. Armies. Gavin, James M. (memoirs). Invasions. Sicily. 1943. *313*
Airborne units. Germany. Great Britain. 1935-45. *765*
Aircraft Carriers. *Intrepid* (vessel). Odysseys In Flight, Inc. Preservation. 1943-79. *1090*
—. *Lexington* (vessel). Navies. *Saratoga* (vessel). 1922-45. *23*
—. Midway (battle). 1942. *369*
—. *Midway* class. Naval Vessels. 1941-75. *24*
Aircraft carriers, small. 1941-45. *278*
Aircraft equipment (long-term storage). B-24 (aircraft). Libyan Desert. 1943-59. *422*
Aircraft industry. Contracting policies. Industrial concentration. 1938-46. *776*
—. Joint Aircraft Committee. National Defense Advisory Commission. Office of Production Management. Technological change. 1940-45. *423*
Aircraft markings. F-105 (aircraft). National Guard. Virginia. 192d Tactical Fighter Group. 1917-79. *544*
Airlines. Latin America. National security. State Department. 1927-40. *767*
Airplane Industry and Trade. Industrial concentration. 1938-47. *777*

—. Labor Unions and Organizations (militancy). Nash, Al (reminiscences). New York (Long Island City). Political factions. 1940-44. *675*
—. Military. Technology. 1937-50. *764*
Airplanes. Alaska (Amchitka). Boeing 80A (aircraft). Personal narratives. 1943. *773*
—. Buller, H. L. "Duffy" (personal account). C-46 (aircraft). C-47 (aircraft). 1940-45. *137*
—. China (Kunming). Ghana (Accra). Laughlin, C. H. (reminiscences). 1942. *520*
Airplanes, Military. Armies. Hoyt, Ross G. (account). P-26 (aircraft). 1937-41. *433*
—. Army Air Corps. California. Eaker, Ira C. Hamilton Field. Military Decorations, Flags, and Symbols. Wright, Howard T. (account). 1941. *1062*
—. B-25 transports. North American Aviation. 1942-49. *37*
—. F6F Hellcats (aircraft). Japan. Truk Islands. USA. 1944. *966*
—. Greece. Military Aid. Roosevelt, Franklin D. (administration). 1940-41. *666*
—. Hughes HK-1 (aircraft). Second front clamor. 1942-47. *613*
—. Industrial productivity. Japan. Navies. 1941-45. *752*
—. P-51 (airplane). Spitfire, Supermarine (airplane). 1939-45. *604*
Airplanes, Military (assembly). Nebraska. Offutt Air Force Base (Building D). Recreation. 1940-77. *816*
Airplanes, Military (fighters). 1940-45. *60*
—. 1933-45. *432*
Airplanes, Military (trainers). T-31 (aircraft). 1941-47. *637*
Alabama. Education, progressive. 1930-51. *519*
Alabama (Mobile). Fair Employment Practices Commission. Negroes. Shipyards. South. 1938-45. *771*
Alabama (Montgomery). Air Bases. Army Air Corps. Maxwell Field. Military training. Mutiny. 1943. *222*
Alabama Review (periodical). Bibliographies. Historians. 1840's-1975. *615*
Alaska. Aleutian Campaign. Artists. Draper, William F. 1942-43. *652*
—. Attu Island (battle). Japan. Tatsuguchi, Paul Nobuo (diary). USA. 1941-43. *1011*
—. Canada. Railways. USSR. 1942-43. *1057*
—. Economic Conditions. 1867-1967. *642*
Alaska (Aleutian Islands). *Arthur Middleton* (vessel). Coast Guard. Japan. Laidlaw, Lansing. 1942-43. *508*
—. Attu (battle). Japan. 1942. *922*
Alaska (Amchitka). Airplanes. Boeing 80A (aircraft). Personal narratives. 1943. *773*
Alaska (Anchorage, Adak). Air Force. Bush pilot. Pinney, Charles A. 1942-43. *741*
Alaskan Highway. Highway Engineering. Logistics. Yukon Territory. 1942-43. *779*
Alberta. Chinese Canadians. Japanese Canadians. Racism. 1920-50. *703*
Alberta, southern. British Columbia. Japanese Canadians (relocation). 1941-45. *450*
Aleutian campaign. Air Warfare. Canada. USA. 1938-45. *394*
—. Alaska. Artists. Draper, William F. 1942-43. *652*
Alliance polarization. Diplomatic representation. Guttmann-Lingoes Smallest Space Analysis. Methodology. War. 1815-1973. *1007*
Alliances. Decisionmaking. Domestic Policy. Foreign policy. Roosevelt, Franklin D. (administration). UN Conference on Food and Agriculture. Virginia (Hot Springs). 1943. *1041*
—. Foreign Relations. Portugal. 1940-41. *944*

Alliances (review article). British Empire. Japan. Louis, William Roger. Thorne, Christopher. 1941-45. *729*
Allies. Axis Powers. Chrome. International Trade. Turkey. 1939-44. *911*
—. Berlin (capture). Germany. Military Strategy. 1941-45. *466*
—. Bibliographies. Diplomacy. 1939-44. *800*
—. Chile. Diplomacy. 1941-45. *298*
—. Cold War (origins). Diplomacy. Poland. 1945. *702*
—. Diplomacy. Military strategy. 1942. *793*
—. Germany. Military occupation. Partition. 1943-48. *475*
—. Germany. Military Strategy. Weapons. 1944-45. *715*
—. Historiography. Lend-Lease. USSR. 1941-45. *250*
—. Nazism. USSR. 1939-45. *499*
—. Peace. Roosevelt, Franklin D. Unconditional surrender (concept). ca 1944-45. *45*
Allison, Graham (*Essence of Decision*). Atomic Warfare. Committees. Decisionmaking. Foreign policy. 1944-45. *865*
Alperovitz, Gar. Atomic Warfare. Foreign Relations. World War II (review article). 1945. *378*
—. Atomic Weapons. Cold War (review article). Europe, Eastern. Foreign Policy. Horowitz, David. Kolko, Gabriel. 1943-50. *786*
—. Diplomacy. Historiography. Nuclear Arms. 1943-46. 1965-73. *571*
Alperovitz, Gar (review article). Atomic Warfare. Decisionmaking. Historiography. Japan (Hiroshima). 1945-65. *859*
Ambulance services. American Field Service. Andrew, Piatt. France. World War I (medical and sanitary affairs). 1914-45. *337*
American Antiquarian Society. Baxter, James Phinney, 3d (obituary). History. 1893-1975. *833*
American Field Service. Ambulance services. Andrew, Piatt. France. World War I (medical and sanitary affairs). 1914-45. *337*
American Jewish Joint Distribution Committee. Diplomacy. Jews. Mayer, Saly. 1944-45. *59*
American Peace Mobilization. Communist Party USA. Isolationism. World War II (antecedents). 1939-41. *1006*
American Revolution. deGaulle, Charles. Europe, Western. Foreign Relations. France. Versailles, Treaty of. 1773-1979. *498*
—. Military strategy. ca 1775-1945. *1022*
American Volunteer Group. Air Warfare. China. Flying Tigers motifs. Shoulder patches. 23d Fighter Group. 1930's-45. *191*
Americanism. Adventure serials. National Characteristics. Radio. 1940-45. *287*
Americas (North and South). Defense policy. Monroe Doctrine. Roosevelt, Franklin D. (administration). 1930's-40. *363*
Amphetamines. Drug Abuse. Popular culture. 1932-75. *451*
Amphibious operations. Hewitt, H. Kent. Navies. 1887-1949. *174*
—. Higgins, Andrew J. Landing craft. Shipbuilding. 1933-45. *655*
—. Japan. Pacific Area. USA. 1942-45. *449*
—. Japan. Philippine Sea (battle). Saipan (battle). 1944. *995*
—. *Marathon* (vessel). McElroy, John W. (account). Okinawa (battle). 1945. *606*
—. Marines. Military Strategy. 20c. *542*
—. Normandy (landing). 1944. *856*
—. Pacific Area. 1942-45. *728*

Amphibious warfare. Armored Vehicles and Tank Warfare. Christie, J. Walter. Landing vehicles, tracked. 1918-45. *418*
—. General Board of the Navy. Marines. Naval Strategy. 1900-74. *688*
Anabaptists. Germany. Mennonites. Switzerland. Taxation. War. 16c-1973. *489*
Anderson, Herbert L. (reminiscences). Chicago, University of. Columbia University. Fermi, Enrico. Nuclear Science and Technology. Szilard, Leo. 1933-45. *20*
—. Chicago, University of. Illinois. Nuclear chain reaction. 1942. *19*
Anderson, Irvine H., Jr. (review article). Asia, East. Foreign Investments. Foreign policy. Oil Industry and Trade. Standard-Vacuum Oil Company. 1933-41. 1975. *725*
Andrew, Piatt. Ambulance services. American Field Service. France. World War I (medical and sanitary affairs). 1914-45. *337*
Andrews, John A. C. (account). Air Warfare. P-40 (aircraft). P-47 (aircraft). Spitfire (aircraft). 1943-45. *26*
Angers, François-Albert. Canada. Catholic Church. French Canadians. Pacifism. Values. 1940-79. *349*
Anglophile sentiments. Catholic Church (hierarchy). Wilberforce, Robert. World War II (antecedents). 1940. *356*
Annexation. Baltic Area. Nonrecognition. USA. USSR. 1940-70's. *467*
—. Intergovernmental Relations. New Mexico (Albuquerque). Nuclear Science and Technology. Weapons. 1940-78. *762*
Antiaircraft gunnery. Great Britain. Inventions. Proximity fuse. 1939-45. *73*
Antiaircraft guns. Destroyers. Navies. Photographs. 1945. *42*
Anti-British sentiments. Churchill, Winston. Langer, William. North Dakota. Senate. 1941-52. *1035*
Anticolonialism. Asia. Roosevelt, Franklin D. USA. 1941-45. *353*
Anti-Communism. Armies. Attitudes. Patton, George S., Jr. (notebooks). 1942-45. *724*
Anti-Communists. China. Navies. Sino-American Cooperation Association. USA. 1942-45. *842*
Antifascism. Lend-Lease. New Deal. Roosevelt, Franklin D. (administration). 1941-45. *1071*
Anti-Fascist Movements. Foreign Relations. Italy. Sforza, Carlo. 1940-43. *626*
Anti-Imperialism. Foreign Policy (critics). Pacific Area. Roosevelt, Franklin D. World War II (antecedents). 1930's. *704*
Anti-Nazi Movements. Boycotts. Fram, Leon (reminiscences). Jews. League for Human Rights. Michigan (Detroit). 1930's-40's. *296*
—. *Confessions of a Nazi Spy* (film). Espionage. Films. German-American Bund. 1938-40. *826*
—. Diplomacy. Messersmith, George Strausser. State Department. 1928-39. *858*
Anti-Semitism. Christians. Holocaust. Toynbee, Arnold. ca 1940-1975. *545*
Anti-Soviet consensus. Interventionism. Isolationism. Vandenberg, Arthur Hendrick, Sr. 1941-46. *413*
Antisubmarine warfare. *Batfish* (vessel). Naval Battles. 1942-45. *128*
—. "Four Stackers". Great Britain. Navies. USA. 1940-45. *120*
Antitank warfare. Tactics. 1941-45. *465*
Antiwar sentiment. Aviation. Lindbergh, Anne Morrow (reminiscences). Lindbergh, Charles A. Values. 1902-79. *543*
—. Cartoons. Hasek, Jaroslav (*The Good Soldier Schweik*). Military life. ca 1920-70. *30*
—. Fellowship of Reconciliation. 1940-41. *1075*
—. Keep America Out of War Congress. Socialist Party. Thomas, Norman. Villard, Oswald Garrison. World War II (antecedents). 1938-41. *236*
Antiwar sentiments. Colleges and Universities. Leftism. Political Protest. 1920-36. *124*
Appalachia. Japanese Americans. Migration, Internal (noneconomic variables). Negroes. 1860-1973. *984*
Appeasement. Chamberlain, Arthur Neville. Foreign Policy. Great Britain. Roosevelt, Franklin Delano. USA. 1937-39. *1012*
—. Foreign policy. Germany. 1933-36. *836*
—. Foreign policy. Germany. Great Britain. International Trade. 1933-40. *690*
Appeasement (proposal). Diplomacy. Great Britain. Japan. 1941. *328*
Apple industry. Exports. Great Britain. Imports. Nova Scotia (Annapolis Valley). 1880-1957. *186*
Arab-Israeli Conflict. Conflict and Conflict Resolution. Decisionmaking. Foreign Policy. Japan. 1941-45. 1967-73. *76*
Archives. Capitalism. Defense Policy. Economic Policy. 1939-45. *628*
—. Diplomacy. France. 1939-45. 1979. *217*
—. Italy, northern. McCain, William D. Personal narratives. 1944-45. *602*
Archives, National. Documents. Europe. Resistance. 1939-45. *218*
Arctic. Discovery and Exploration. Finnie, Richard Sterling (account). North America. Office of the Coordinator of Information. Stefansson, Vilhjalmur. 1931-62. *290*
—. *Georgi Sedov* (vessel). Newfoundland. USSR. World War I. 1908-67. *51*
Argentina. Decisionmaking. Diplomacy. Rio Conference of 1942. USA. 1942. *1059*
—. Foreign Policy. Hull, Cordell. Ramírez, Pedro. USA. 1943. *1060*
—. Foreign policy. UN membership. USA. 1942-45. *1058*
—. Foreign Relations. USA. 1940's. *672*
Arizona. Aeronautics, Military. Flying Tigers. Germany, West. Scott, Robert L., Jr. 1941-45. 1955-57. *936*
—. Bridges, floating. Military. Yuma Proving Ground. 1943-50. *431*
—. Concentration camps. Gila River Relocation Center. Japanese Americans. Public Opinion. Race Relations. 1942-45. *159*
Arizona (Raso). Ghost towns. Railroad stations. Southern Pacific Railroad. 1911-76. *670*
Arizona (White Mountains). Economic Conditions. Lumber and Lumbering. 1919-42. *592*
Arkansas. Family. Legislation. Social Problems. 1941-45. *884*
—. Germans. Italians. Labor, contract. Prisoners of War. 1943-46. *758*
—. Germany. Prisoners of war. 1943-46. *757*
Armaments. Embargoes. Isolationism. Neutrality Act (US, 1935). 1935. *1080*
—. Industry. Production. 1941-45. *1085*
—. Navy. *Tiny Tim* (rocket). 1944. *317*
Armed Forces Radio Service. Barnouw, Erik. Education. Radio. 1942-45. *199*
Armies. Adventist Medical Cadet Corps. Dick, Everett N. (account). Korean War. 1934-53. *223*
—. Airborne troops. Gavin, James M. (memoirs). Invasions. Sicily. 1943. *313*
—. Airplanes, Military. Hoyt, Ross G. (account). P-26 (aircraft). 1937-41. *433*
—. Anti-Communism. Attitudes. Patton, George S., Jr. (notebooks). 1942-45. *724*
—. Artillery. Howitzer, 105 mm. War Department. 1930's-41. *614*

—. Attitudes. Labor. Social Change. 1940's-70's. *853*
—. Behavior. Combat. Marshall, S. L. A. (account). 1941-45. *586*
—. Canol Project. National Security. Northwest Territories. Pipelines. USA. 1942-45. *226*
—. Cawthon, Charles (reminiscences). France (Normandy). 1944. *161*
—. Discrimination. Government. Great Britain. Negroes. 1942-45. *358*
—. Discrimination. Great Britain. White, Walter F. 1943-44. *354*
—. Documentaries. Films. Heisler, Stuart. *Negro Soldier* (film). Propaganda. Race Relations. 1944. *195*
—. Europe, Western. Military organization. 1944-45. *288*
—. Evans, Maurice. Pacific Area. Shakespeare, William. Theater Production and Direction. 1942-45. *864*
—. Flight training. Helicopters. 1944-68. *979*
—. Hastie, William H. Military recruitment. Negroes. Press, black. 1940-42. *611*
—. Imprisonment. Italy (Pisa). Pound, Ezra. Steele, John L. (interview). 1945. *485*
—. Japan. Marines. Peleliu (battle). Sledge, Eugene B. (account). 1944. *877*
—. Military force structuring. Reorganization Objective Army Divisions. 1861-1977. *91*
—. Military Government. 1847-1971. *1078*
—. Morale. *New York Times.* Railey, Hilton H. Reporters and Reporting. 1941. *1027*
—. Philippine Insurrection. Professionalism. Vietnam War. 1901-71. *735*
Armies (Finance Department). Military Finance. 1941-45. *813*
Armies (officers). 1919-41. *182*
Armies (review article). Bureaucracies. Gabriel, Richard A. Military (officers). Savage, Paul L. 1914-80. *64*
Armistice question. Government. Great Britain. Italy. Military Occupation. 1944. *29*
Armored Vehicles and Tank Warfare. Amphibious warfare. Christie, J. Walter. Landing vehicles, tracked. 1918-45. *418*
—. Europe, Western. USA. 1935-40. *680*
—. Hodges, Courtney. Remagen Bridge (battle of). 1944. *667*
Armstrong, David M. (personal account). Hawaii. Japan. Pearl Harbor, attack on. 1942. *32*
Armstrong, David M. (reminiscence). Guadalcanal (battle of). Sealark Channel (battle of). 1942. *31*
Army. Camp Beauregard. Cawthon, John Ardis. Conscription, Military. Louisiana. Personal narratives. 1940-42. *163*
Army Air Corps. Aeronautics, Military. Eaker, Ira C. World War I. 8th Bomber Command, US. 1917-47. *852*
—. Air Bases. Alabama (Montgomery). Maxwell Field. Military training. Mutiny. 1943. *222*
—. Air Warfare. Beeson, Duane. Europe, Western. Idaho (Boise). 1941-45. *309*
—. Airplanes, Military. California. Eaker, Ira C. Hamilton Field. Military Decorations, Flags, and Symbols. Wright, Howard T. (account). 1941. *1062*
—. Flight testing. Supersonic planes. SX-1 aircraft. Yeager, Charles. 1944-75. *673*
—. Segregation. Tuskegee Army Air Field. 332d Fighter Group. 99th Fighter Squadron. 1941-49. *711*
Army Air Corps Tactical School. Air support, close. Europe, Western. Tactics. 1930-45. *454*
Army Air Force. Air Warfare. Arnold, Henry H. (Hap). 1942. *501*
Army Air Force Station 569. Great Britain (Bamber Bridge). Mutiny. Negroes. USA. 1943. *1025*

Army Air Forces. Air Warfare. China. Flying Tigers. Holloway, Bruce K. (account). P-40 (aircraft). 1942-43. *424*
—. Arnold, H. H. (Hap). Military Organization. Planning. 1942. *503*
—. Bernhard, George K., Jr. (account). Flight training. PT-17 (aircraft). 1942-43. *81*
—. Bombing. XB-28 (aircraft). 1940's. *982*
—. B-29 (aircraft). China. Ground crews. Johnston, Francis J. (account). Mariana Islands (Tinian). 1944-45. *462*
—. Flight training. 1942-45. *261*
Army Chief of Staff. Artillery (Field and Coast). War Department. 1907-54. *4*
Army hospitals. Hospitals. Negroes (physicians, soldiers). Segregation, development of. 1940-42. *707*
Arnold, H. H. "Hap". Air Warfare. Historians. Military Strategy. 1943-44. *708*
—. Army Air Forces. Military Organization. Planning. 1942. *503*
Arnold, Henry H. (Hap). Air Warfare. Army Air Force. 1942. *501*
Arthur Middleton (vessel). Alaska (Aleutian Islands). Coast Guard. Japan. Laidlaw, Lansing. 1942-43. *508*
Artillery. Armies. Howitzer, 105 mm. War Department. 1930's-41. *614*
—. British Columbia. Coast defenses. 1862-1941. *437*
Artillery (Field and Coast). Army Chief of Staff. War Department. 1907-54. *4*
Artists. Alaska. Aleutian Campaign. Draper, William F. 1942-43. *652*
Asia. Anticolonialism. Roosevelt, Franklin D. USA. 1941-45. *353*
—. Callahan, Raymond. Foreign Relations. Great Britain. Louis, William Roger. Lowe, Peter. World War II (review article). 1939-45. *12*
—. Gibbon, Elwyn H. (memoirs). Pilots. 1937-42. *524*
—. Historiography. Immigration. ca 1849-1974. *206*
Asia, East. Anderson, Irvine H., Jr. (review article). Foreign Investments. Foreign policy. Oil Industry and Trade. Standard-Vacuum Oil Company. 1933-41. 1975. *725*
—. Japan. Military strategy. 1944-45. *173*
Asia, Southeast. Colonialism. Great Britain. Joint declaration (proposed). Roosevelt, Franklin D. (administration). USA. 1942-44. *1036*
Asia, Southeast (coast). India. *Lanikai* (vessel). Navies. Roosevelt, Franklin D. Tolley, Kemp (personal account). World War II (antecedents). 1941. *968*
Asian Americans. Race Relations. Stereotypes, positive. 1850-1973. *932*
Asian Canadians. British Columbia. Racism. 1900-50. *805*
Assimilation. Canada. Evacuation, forced. Japanese Canadians (Nisei). 1941-75. *575*
—. Education. Jews. Labor movement. Socialism. 1880's-1945. *975*
Atlantic, battle of the. Great Britain. Navies. Roosevelt, Franklin D. Secrecy. Warmaking powers. 1941. *682*
Atlantic Fleet. King, Ernest J. Military General Staff. Naval Biography. 1940's. *827*
Atlantic Ocean. Canada. Great Britain. Navies. USA. 1941-43. *557*
Atlantic Ocean (North). Canada. Hewens, Bob. Navies. *Niagara* (vessel). *U-570* (vessel). 1934-72. *1043*
Atlantic Ocean, South. Great Britain. Neutrality (circumvention). Roosevelt, Franklin D. Takoradi air route. World War II (antecedents). 1941-42. *769*

218 Atomic bomb

Atomic bomb. Air Warfare. *Enola Gay* (aircraft). Military training. Wendover Field. 1944-45. *986*
—. Franck, James. Nuclear arms race. Political Attitudes. Truman, Harry S. (administration). 1944-45. *1000*
—. Franck, James. Policymaking. Scientists. Stimson, Henry L. 1945. *918*
—. New Mexico (Los Alamos). 1943-46. *660*
Atomic Bomb Casualty Commission. Civilian survivors. Japan (Hiroshima, Nagasaki). Medical Research. Radiation Effects Research Foundation. 1945-75. *1010*
Atomic bomb development. Diplomacy. Nuclear Science and Technology. 1942-45. *754*
Atomic bombs. Japan. Public opinion. USA. 1945-49. *1064*
Atomic energy. Japan. Military Strategy. Smyth Report, 1945. USA. 1940-45. *897*
Atomic Warfare. Air Warfare. Baldwin, Paul H. (account). Fighter squadrons, night. Philippines. 1942-45. *44*
—. Allison, Graham *(Essence of Decision)*. Committees. Decisionmaking. Foreign policy. 1944-45. *865*
—. Alperovitz, Gar. Foreign Relations. World War II (review article). 1945. *378*
—. Alperovitz, Gar (review article). Decisionmaking. Historiography. Japan (Hiroshima). 1945-65. *859*
—. B-29 (aircraft). Japan. Lemay, Curtis. Surrender. 1945. *1052*
—. Canada. Diaries. King, William Lyon MacKenzie. Racism. 1921-48. *823*
—. Decisionmaking. Hiroshima (attack on). Japan. 1944-45. *828*
—. Decisionmaking. Japan (Hiroshima, Nagasaki). Military Strategy. 1944-45. *304*
—. Foreign Policy. Gowing, Margaret. Great Britain. Nuclear Science and Technology (review article). Sherwin, Martin J. 1938-52. *529*
—. Frisch, Otto R. (account). Nuclear Physics. 1945. *307*
—. Groves, Leslie R. Hirohito, Emperor. Japan (Nagasaki). Potsdam Conference. Truman, Harry S. 1944-45. *546*
—. Hersey, John (*Hiroshima*). Literature. Morality. 1945-74. *1065*
—. History Teaching. Japan. Simulation and Games. 1945. 1978. *265*
—. Japan. Military strategy. USA. 1945. *429*
—. Japan. Politics. Surrender offer. Truman, Harry S. (administration). 1945. *84*
—. Japan (Hiroshima; Nagasaki). Military Strategy. 1945. *267*
—. Japan (Hiroshima, Nagasaki). Military Strategy. USA. 1945. *83*
—. Japan (Hiroshima, Nagasaki). USA. USSR. 1942-47. *86*
Atomic Weapons. Alperovitz, Gar. Cold War (review article). Europe, Eastern. Foreign Policy. Horowitz, David. Kolko, Gabriel. 1943-50. *786*
—. Austin, Warren Robinson. Byrnes, James F. Cold War. Documents. Potsdam Conference. USSR. 1945. *712*
Attitudes. Anti-Communism. Armies. Patton, George S., Jr. (notebooks). 1942-45. *724*
—. Armies. Labor. Social Change. 1940's-70's. *853*
—. Balkans. Diplomacy (foreign service officers). USSR. 1944-46. *221*
—. Business. International trade. Japan. 1931-41. *417*
—. Civil rights. Conscientious objectors. Japanese Americans. 1940-45. *745*
—. Economic development. Military Strategy. Nuclear arms. Technology. War. 1914-68. *686*
—. Executive Behavior. Foreign policy. Political Protest. Roosevelt, Franklin D. 1940-72. *1092*
—. Genocide. Immigration. Jews. 1880's-1940's. *590*
—. Kelsey, George (review article). Kentucky. Southern Baptists. 1941-45. 1973. *756*
—. Morality. Sex. 1918-55. *597*
—. Music, popular. Rhetoric. 1940-45. *643*
Attu (battle). Alaska (Aleutian Islands). Japan. 1942. *922*
Attu Island (battle). Alaska. Japan. Tatsuguchi, Paul Nobuo (diary). USA. 1941-43. *1011*
Audiovisual materials, cataloging. Radio newscasts. Washington, University of (Milo Ryan Phonoarchives). 1956-73. *321*
Auschwitz. Air Warfare. Concentration Camps. Jews. Military Strategy. 1944-45. *1063*
Austin, Warren Robinson. Atomic Weapons. Byrnes, James F. Cold War. Documents. Potsdam Conference. USSR. 1945. *712*
Australia. Bell, Roger. Economic Aid. Foreign Relations. 1941-46. *1082*
—. Curtin, John. Hasluck, Paul. MacArthur, Douglas. Military Recruitment. 1942-43. *551*
—. Diaries. Great Britain. MacArthur, Douglas. Philippines. Williamson, Gerald Hugh. 1942-43. *962*
—. Economic Aid (reciprocal). USA. 1941-46. *68*
—. Foreign Relations. 20c. *625*
—. Foreign Relations. Japan. Pacific Area. Peace settlement. USA. 1942-46. *70*
—. Foreign Relations. Military Bases. National Security. 1944-46. *69*
—. Foreign Relations. USA. 1939-42. *48*
—. Great Britain. Menzies, Robert Gordon. Military Aid. 1940. *263*
Automobile industry. Employment. Labor Unions and Organizations. Strikes, wildcat. 1941-45. *1103*
Automobile Industry and Trade. Labor (militancy). Michigan (Detroit). Production standards. United Automobile Workers of America. Working Conditions. 1937-55. *540*
Autonomy. Congress. Politics. Puerto Rico. Roosevelt, Franklin D. (administration). 1940-45. *89*
Avery, Sewell. Economic Conditions. Illinois (Chicago). Labor Disputes (arbitration). Montgomery Ward (federal seizure of). War Labor Board. 1941. *490*
Aviation. Antiwar sentiment. Lindbergh, Anne Morrow (reminiscences). Lindbergh, Charles A. Values. 1902-79. *543*
Awa Maru (vessel). Japan. *Queenfish* (vessel). Submarines. USA. 1945. *902*
Axis Powers. Allies. Chrome. International Trade. Turkey. 1939-44. *911*
—. Chile. Economic Conditions. Foreign Investments. 1939-45. *11*
—. Diplomatic relations (rupture). Latin America. Rio Conference (1942). USA. 1941-42. *297*
—. Foreign Policy. Latin America. Office of the Coordinator of Inter-American Affairs. Rockefeller, Nelson A. Roosevelt, Franklin D. (administration). 1933-42. *364*

B

Bache, William B. Germany (Ludwigshafen). McAuliffe, Anthony. Personal narratives. 1945. *38*

Bainbridge, Kenneth T. (reminiscences). Manhattan Project. New Mexico (Los Alamos). Nuclear Arms. 1945. *40*
Baker, Arthur Davidson, III (collection). Navies. Photography. 1941-45. *1101*
Baker, Josephine. Adoption. Civil rights. Entertainers. Negroes. 1940-75. *434*
Balance of power. Korean War. Military Strategy. Technology. Weapons. 1918-53. *876*
Baldwin, Paul H. (account). Air Warfare. Atomic Warfare. Fighter squadrons, night. Philippines. 1942-45. *44*
Balkans. Attitudes. Diplomacy (foreign service officers). USSR. 1944-46. *221*
—. Foreign policy. 1939-41. *953*
Balloons. Air Warfare. Bombing. Japan. North America. 1940-45. *1017*
—. Dirigibles. McBride, Robert M. Navy. Personal narratives. 1941-44. *601*
Balloons, armed. Japan. Project FUGO. South Dakota. 1944-45. *517*
Baltic Area. Annexation. Nonrecognition. USA. USSR. 1940-70's. *467*
Bankhead Bill (1943). Federal government. Newspapers. Subsidies. War Bond advertising. 1943. *112*
Baptists. Discrimination. Japanese Americans. Resettlement. 1890-1970. *644*
Barham, Wayne (reminiscences). Guam. Invasion. USA. 1944. *50*
Barnes, Harry Elmer. Crime and Criminals (organized). Federal Bureau of Investigation. Hoover, J. Edgar. 1936-44. *980*
—. Intellectual establishment. 1940-68. *230*
Barnouw, Erik. Armed Forces Radio Service. Education. Radio. 1942-45. *199*
Barrett, Allen M. (account). Iwo Jima (battle). Marines. 1945. *53*
Batfish (vessel). Antisubmarine warfare. Naval Battles. 1942-45. *128*
Battillo, Anthony (reminiscences). Italy. Po Valley campaign. 1945. *58*
Battle cruisers. Naval Strategy. World War I. 1900-47. *25*
Battles. Historiography. USSR. USSR. 1939-78. *818*
—. Historiography. World War I. 1914-45. *473*
Battleship. *Oklahoma* (vessel). Pearl Harbor (attack). 1912-47. *928*
Battleship era. Dreadnought. Naval warfare. 1905-71. *448*
Battleships. Naval Strategy. Pacific Area. 1942-45. *658*
—. Pearl Harbor, attack on. 1941. *427*
—. *West Virginia* (vessel). 1916-59. *892*
Battleships, fast. Aeronautics, Military. Naval Air Forces. 1941-45. *659*
Baxter, James Phinney, 3d (obituary). American Antiquarian Society. History. 1893-1975. *833*
Beach, Edward L. (account). Hashimoto, Mochitsura (account). *Indianapolis* (vessel; sinking). Navies. 1945. *1088*
Beaverbrook, 1st Baron. Diplomacy. Harriman, W. Averell. Military Aid. USSR. 1941. *510*
Beeson, Duane. Air Warfare. Army Air Corps. Europe, Western. Idaho (Boise). 1941-45. *309*
Behavior. Armies. Combat. Marshall, S. L. A. (account). 1941-45. *586*
Bell, Roger. Australia. Economic Aid. Foreign Relations. 1941-46. *1082*
Benavente, Ignacio V. Caroline Islands (Yap). Judges. 1942-46. *742*
Benefit performances. Actors and Actresses. Employment. Minnesota (Minneapolis). 1942. *985*

Bergson, Peter. Emergency Committee to Save the Jewish People of Europe. Genocide. Rescues. Zionism. 1943-45. *723*
Berlin (capture). Allies. Germany. Military Strategy. 1941-45. *466*
Berlin, Isaiah. Congress. Foreign policy. Great Britain. USA. 1943. *355*
Bernhard, George K., Jr. (account). Army Air Forces. Flight training. PT-17 (aircraft). 1942-43. *81*
Bibliographies. Air warfare. Eighth Air Force. Europe. 1941-45. *1026*
—. Air warfare. Novels. 1939-45. *894*
—. *Alabama Review* (periodical). Historians. 1840's-1975. *615*
—. Allies. Diplomacy. 1939-44. *800*
—. Dissertations. Military. 1977-78. *169*
—. Dissertations. Military History. 5c BC-1980. *171*
—. Documents. Italy. 1939-45. *271*
—. Labor Unions and Organizations. Working class. 1940's. *342*
—. Prisoners of War (Axis). USA. 1945. 1975. *904*
Blair, Frederick Charles. Canada. Federal Policy. Jews. Refugees. 1930's. *2*
Blockades. Chamberlain, Neville. China. Great Britain. Japan. Roosevelt, Franklin D. World War II (antecedents). 1937-38. *362*
Bloom, Lynn Z. Crouter, Natalie Stark. Diaries. Philippines. Prisoners of War. 1941-45. 1970's. *101*
Blum, John Morton (review article). Federal government. Politics. Propaganda. 1940-45. *525*
Boarding schools. Children. Federal Government. Indians. 1920-60's. *947*
Boehler, Hurley. Interstate Aircraft and Engineering Corporation. Navies. TDR-1 (aircraft). 1943-77. *554*
Boeing 80A (aircraft). Airplanes. Alaska (Amchitka). Personal narratives. 1943. *773*
Boilermakers, Iron Shipbuilders and Helpers, International Brotherhood of. California (Los Angeles). Discrimination, employment. Labor Unions and Organizations. Negroes. Oregon (Portland). Shipbuilding. 1941-46. *883*
Bolivia. Foreign Relations. Germany. Nazism. USA. 1941-46. *99*
Bombing. Aeronautics, Military. Bradshaw, Russell (account). Ukraine. 1944. *119*
—. Air Warfare. 1943-45. *386*
—. Air Warfare. Balloons. Japan. North America. 1940-45. *1017*
—. Air Warfare. Bowman, Marvin S. (reminiscences). Great Britain. USSR (Mirgorod, Poltava). 1944. *114*
—. Air Warfare. B-17 (aircraft). Germany. Poltava (battle). USSR. 1944. *445*
—. Air Warfare. Churchill, Winston. Military General Staff. Operation Overlord. Roosevelt, Franklin D. 1944. *1053*
—. Air Warfare. Dresden (attack on). Germany. Great Britain. Total war. 1914-45. *181*
—. Air Warfare. Germany. Great Britain. Military Strategy. 1942-44. *994*
—. Army Air Forces. XB-28 (aircraft). 1940's. *982*
—. B-24 (aircraft). 1942-45. *421*
—. France. Military Strategy. Operation Overlord. Zuckerman, Solly (review article). 1944. *484*
Bombing, daylight. Air Forces. 1941-44. *241*
Bombing (inadvertent). Air Warfare. Diplomacy. Switzerland. USA. 1943-45. *401*
Bombing, indiscriminate. Air Forces. Civilian targets. Ethics. Germany. Military General Staff. 1941-45. *837*

220 Bombing ranges

Bombing ranges. Hawaii National Park. Military. 1938-50. *452*
Bombing, strategic. Air Forces. Japan (Kyoto). Stimson, Henry L. USA. 1940-45. *160*
—. Air Warfare. Ships. 1939-80. *468*
—. Air Warfare. Vietnam War. 1943-45. 1965-73. *891*
Bombs, balloon-carried. Japan. Pacific Northwest. 1945. *461*
Books. Films. War. 1940's-70's. *845*
Bookselling. Higher Education. Military history. 1945-70's. *631*
Borg thesis. Foreign Policy. Georgia. Press. Quarantine speech. Roosevelt, Franklin D. 1937. *132*
Borinquen Field ("battle"). Goldsworthy, Harry E. (personal account). Puerto Rico. 1941. *322*
Bowman, Isaiah. East Prussia. Oder-Neisse Line. Poland. State Department (Advisory Committee on Post-War Foreign Policy). Welles, Sumner. 1942-45. *819*
Bowman, Marvin S. (reminiscences). Air Warfare. Bombing. Great Britain. USSR (Mirgorod, Poltava). 1944. *114*
Boycott activities. Economic Conditions. Jews. Joint Boycott Council. Non-Sectarian Anti-Nazi League to Champion Human Rights. 1939-41. *326*
Boycotts. Anti-Nazi Movements. Fram, Leon (reminiscences). Jews. League for Human Rights. Michigan (Detroit). 1930's-40's. *296*
Boycotts, consumer. District of Columbia. Employment. Sex discrimination. Women. 1941-46. *1105*
Bradley, Omar Nelson (*A Soldier's Story*). 1944-45. *118*
Bradshaw, Russell (account). Aeronautics, Military. Bombing. Ukraine. 1944. *119*
Brazil. Diplomacy. 1935-45. *416*
—. Foreign Relations. McCann, Frank D. 1937-45. *1087*
Brewington, Marion Vernon (obituary). Maritime historians. Ship portraits. 1930's-74. *1031*
Bridges. Burma (Kwae Mae Khlong River). B-24 (aircraft). Davis, W. L. (personal account). Prisoners of War. 1942-45. *212*
—. Germany. Remagen (battle). 1945. *165*
—. Kwai, River. Thailand. USA. 1942-45. *403*
Bridges, floating. Arizona. Military. Yuma Proving Ground. 1943-50. *431*
British Columbia. Alberta, southern. Japanese Canadians (relocation). 1941-45. *450*
—. Artillery. Coast defenses. 1862-1941. *437*
—. Asian Canadians. Racism. 1900-50. *805*
—. Canada. Chinese Canadians. Japanese Canadians. Military Service (denied). 1939-45. *806*
—. Canada. Discrimination. India. Suffrage. 1939-45. *414*
—. Chinese. Immigration. Japanese. Suffrage. 1935-49. *523*
—. Conscription, Military (crisis). Pearkes, G. R. 1943-44. *807*
—. Evacuation, forced. Federal government. Japanese. Public opinion. 1937-42. *1009*
—. Films. Naval Vessels. Submarines. World War I. 1914-45. *156*
—. Industrial Relations. International Woodworkers of America. Lumber and Lumbering. 1940-50. *1093*
—. Japanese communities. Minorities. Public schools, challenge to. 1900-72. *203*
British Columbia (Prince Rupert). Coastal defense. Diaries. Thistle, R. 1941-42. *808*
British Columbia, University of. Japanese Canadians. Race relations. 1939-42. *80*
British Commonwealth. Canada. Foreign Relations. Ireland. Neutrality. 1939-45. *607*

—. Integration. Military. USA. Women. World War I. 1900-78. *959*
British Empire. Alliances (review article). Japan. Louis, William Roger. Thorne, Christopher. 1941-45. *729*
Brooks, Jim (reminiscences). Air Warfare. Oil fields. Romania. 31st Fighter Group, US. 1944. *127*
Brown, Anthony Cave. Germany. Great Britain. Kahn, David. Military Intelligence (review article). 1939-45. *518*
Brown, Cecil B. Columbia Broadcasting System. Editorials. News. Radio. White, Paul W. 1943. *954*
Brown, William Eustis (interview). Oral history. Public health. 1942-45. *379*
Brussels Conference (1937). China. Expansionism. Japan. World War II (antecedents). 1937. *107*
BT-13A (aircraft). Aeronautics, Military. Flight training. Strunk, Al (account). 1941-45. *930*
Bulgaria. Communist Party. Foreign policy. 1943-44. *969*
—. Diplomacy. Surrender. 1944. *970*
—. Foreign Policy. 1944. *116*
—. Foreign Policy. Intervention. USSR. 1944-47. *855*
Bulge (battle). China. Cuban Missile Crisis. Korean War. Military intelligence. 1944-80. *34*
—. Germany. Military Strategy. 1944. *714*
Buller, H. L. "Duffy" (personal account). Airplanes. C-46 (aircraft). C-47 (aircraft). 1940-45. *137*
Bureau of Public Information. Canada. Federal government. Press. Public opinion. Social scientists. Wartime Information Board. 1939-45. *1070*
Bureaucracies. Armies (review article). Gabriel, Richard A. Military (officers). Savage, Paul L. 1914-80. *64*
Burke, Arleigh. Military Service, Professional. Naval Education. US Naval Academy. 1919-40. *794*
Burma. Aeronautics, Military. China. Flying Tigers. 1941-77. *940*
Burma (Kwae Mae Khlong River). Bridges. B-24 (aircraft). Davis, W. L. (personal account). Prisoners of War. 1942-45. *212*
Bush pilot. Air Force. Alaska (Anchorage, Adak). Pinney, Charles A. 1942-43. *741*
Business. Attitudes. International trade. Japan. 1931-41. *417*
—. California (Los Angeles). City planning. Federal government. Social Problems. 1941-59. *843*
—. Canada. Federal Government. Labor Unions and Organizations. Social control. Unemployment Insurance Act (1941). Wages. 1910-41. *202*
—. Labor Unions and Organizations. New Deal. Taft-Hartley Act (US, 1947). Wagner Act (US, 1935). 1935-47. *108*
Byrnes, James F. Atomic Weapons. Austin, Warren Robinson. Cold War. Documents. Potsdam Conference. USSR. 1945. *712*
—. Federal Government. Germany. Memoirs. Nuclear Science and Technology. Szilard, Leo. 1898-1945. *948*
B-17 (aircraft). Aeronautics, Military. B-24 (aircraft). Eighth Air Force, US. Europe, Western. 1935-45. *255*
—. Air Warfare. Bombing. Germany. Poltava (battle). USSR. 1944. *445*
—. Air Warfare. Kelly, Colin P., Jr. Philippines. 1941. *144*
—. Eighth Air Force (1st, 3d Air Divisions). 1942-45. *27*

B-24 (aircraft). Aeronautics, Military. B-17 (aircraft). Eighth Air Force, US. Europe, Western. 1935-45. *255*
—. Aircraft equipment (long-term storage). Libyan Desert. 1943-59. *422*
—. Bombing. 1942-45. *421*
—. Bridges. Burma (Kwae Mae Khlong River). Davis, W. L. (personal account). Prisoners of War. 1942-45. *212*
B-25 transports. Airplanes, Military. North American Aviation. 1942-49. *37*
B-26 (aircraft; markings). Air Warfare. 42nd Bombardment Wing. 1942-44. *950*
B-29 (aircraft). Army Air Forces. China. Ground crews. Johnston, Francis J. (account). Mariana Islands (Tinian). 1944-45. *462*
—. Atomic Warfare. Japan. Lemay, Curtis. Surrender. 1945. *1052*

C

California. Agriculture Department. Emergency Rubber Project. Guayule (plant). Nishimura, Shimpe. Rubber industry. 1942-76. *36*
—. Airplanes, Military. Army Air Corps. Eaker, Ira C. Hamilton Field. Military Decorations, Flags, and Symbols. Wright, Howard T. (account). 1941. *1062*
—. Concentration Camps. Japanese Americans. Manzanar War Relocation Center. Riots. Ueno, Harry (arrest). 1942. *381*
—. Concentration Camps. Japanese Americans. Race Relations. 1941-42. *639*
—. Detention. Japanese Americans. Racism. 1941-45. *640*
—. Interrogation centers. Navies. Prisoners of War. Virginia. 1941-45. *647*
—. Japanese Americans. Relocation camps. Warren, Earl. 1941-45. *1030*
California (Byron Hot Springs). Prison camp. Resorts. 1868-1976. *1032*
California (Long Beach). Great Britain. *Queen Mary* (vessel). Ships. ca 1930-74. *566*
California (Los Angeles). Boilermakers, Iron Shipbuilders and Helpers, International Brotherhood of. Discrimination, employment. Labor Unions and Organizations. Negroes. Oregon (Portland). Shipbuilding. 1941-46. *883*
—. Business. City planning. Federal government. Social Problems. 1941-59. *843*
California (Los Angeles, San Diego, San Francisco). City Planning. Navy-yards and Naval Stations. Ports. 1919-41. *548*
California (San Diego). Photographs. 1943. *106*
California (San Diego County). Internment. Japanese Americans. 1941-42. *847*
California (San Francisco Bay). Courts Martial and Courts of Inquiry. Mare Island Mutiny. Navies. Negroes. Port Chicago Naval Magazine. Race relations. 1944-48. *1055*
California (San Francisco Bay area). Military Medicine. Music. Voluntary Associations. 1943-45. *835*
California (San Rafael). Hamilton Air Force Base. Pacific Area. 1931-50. *382*
Callahan, Raymond. Asia. Foreign Relations. Great Britain. Louis, William Roger. Lowe, Peter. World War II (review article). 1939-45. *12*
Camouflage. Naval Vessels. 1940-45. *937*
Camp Beauregard. Army. Cawthon, John Ardis. Conscription, Military. Louisiana. Personal narratives. 1940-42. *163*
Camp Blanding. Florida. Germans. Prisoners of war. 1942-46. *90*

Camp Lejeune. Lamb Studios. Marines. New Jersey (Tenafly). North Carolina. Stained glass. Windows. 1775-1943. *480*
Camp Shelby. Daily Life. Mississippi (Hattiesburg). Mobilization effects. 1940-45. *849*
Canada. Agent general, office of. Great Britain (London). Intergovernmental Relations. 18c-20c. *886*
—. Air Warfare. Aleutian campaign. USA. 1938-45. *394*
—. Alaska. Railways. USSR. 1942-43. *1057*
—. Angers, François-Albert. Catholic Church. French Canadians. Pacifism. Values. 1940-79. *349*
—. Assimilation. Evacuation, forced. Japanese Canadians (Nisei). 1941-75. *575*
—. Atlantic Ocean. Great Britain. Navies. USA. 1941-43. *557*
—. Atlantic Ocean (North). Hewens, Bob. Navies. *Niagara* (vessel). *U-570* (vessel). 1934-72. *1043*
—. Atomic Warfare. Diaries. King, William Lyon MacKenzie. Racism. 1921-48. *823*
—. Blair, Frederick Charles. Federal Policy. Jews. Refugees. 1930's. *2*
—. British Columbia. Chinese Canadians. Japanese Canadians. Military Service (denied). 1939-45. *806*
—. British Columbia. Discrimination. India. Suffrage. 1939-45. *414*
—. British Commonwealth. Foreign Relations. Ireland. Neutrality. 1939-45. *607*
—. Bureau of Public Information. Federal government. Press. Public opinion. Social scientists. Wartime Information Board. 1939-45. *1070*
—. Business. Federal Government. Labor Unions and Organizations. Social control. Unemployment Insurance Act (1941). Wages. 1910-41. *202*
—. Canol project. Dickins, C. H. "Punch". Letters. Mackenzie Air Route. Pipelines. USA. 1942. *56*
—. Canol (project). Foster, W. W. Oil Industry and Trade. USA. War Department. 1942-45. *54*
—. Caribbean. Garrison duty. Great Britain. Military. 1914-45. *665*
—. China. Foreign Policy. International Trade. Odlum, Victor Wentworth. ca 1944-49. *683*
—. China. Hurford, Grace Gibberd (reminiscences). Missions and Missionaries. Teaching. 1928-45. *439*
—. China Convoy. Friends' Ambulance Unit. Oral history. 1939-45. *899*
—. Defense policies. Interdependence. USA. 1940's-70's. *939*
—. deGaulle, Charles. France. Propaganda. Quebec. Vichy Regime. 1940-42. *193*
—. Dieppe (air battle). Great Britain. Leigh-Mallory, Trafford. Royal Canadian Air Force. 1942. *151*
—. Diplomacy. Europe. Peace negotiations. USA. 1943-47. *415*
—. Diplomacy. Foreign Relations. Latin America. Pan-American Union. USA. 1939-44. *664*
—. Drew, George. Duff, Lyman. Hong Kong Inquiry. King, William Lyon Mackenzie. 1941. *140*
—. Economic Structure. 1939-45. *749*
—. Europe. Military operations. Politics. 1939-45. *909*
—. Fairbairn, R. Edis. Pacifism. Protestantism. United Church of Canada. 1939. *802*
—. Federal Government. Physical Education and Training. Sport. 1909-54. *1028*
—. Federal government. Physical fitness programmes. 1850-1972. *314*

Canada

—. Federal Government. Provincial Government. 1940-74. *882*
—. Films. National Film Board of Canada. Sex roles. Women. 1940's-50's. *594*
—. Foreign policy. Great Britain. USA. 1939-45. *332*
—. Foreign policy. Planning. 1943-45. *661*
—. Foreign Relations. King, William Lyon Mackenzie. USA. 1939-45. *330*
—. French Canadians. Military Service. 1939-45. *336*
—. Governor General's Foot Guards. Military History. Militia. 1872-1972. *972*
—. Great Britain. Hyde Park Declaration (1941). Military finance. USA. 1939-41. *331*
—. Great Britain. International Trade. USA. 1943-47. *109*
—. Great Britain. Military Finance. 1943-45. *334*
—. Great Britain. Prisoners of war, German. 1940-47. *477*
—. Highlanders, 48th. Hunter, William A. (reminiscences). Leftism. Liberalism. Military Service. 1939-45. *438*
—. Historiography. 1939-45. *243*
—. Historiography. 1939-78. *343*
—. Historiography. 1939-45. *344*
—. Historiography. Press. World War II (antecedents). 1938-39. *591*
—. Japanese Canadians. Race Relations. Relocation, forced. 1890's-1940's. *949*
—. King, William Lyon Mackenzie. Ogdensburg Agreement. Roosevelt, Franklin D. 1933-45. *910*
—. Labor. Women. 1942-46. *738*
—. Military service. Women. 20c. *1104*
—. Murray, Leonard W. Navies. World War I. 1913-45. *308*
Canadian Hungarian Worker (newspaper). Hungarians. Szőke, István. USSR. 1929-44. *584*
Canadian Labour Congress. Cooperative Commonwealth Federation. Federal Government. Industrial relations. Trades and Labour Congress. 1939-46. *565*
Canadian Women's Army Corps. Military service. Morality. Sex roles. Women. 1941-46. *740*
—. Royal Canadian Army Medical Corps. 1940-43. *739*
Cane, Cyril H. Diplomatic reports. Great Britain. Michigan (Detroit). Riots. 1943. *359*
Canol Project. Armies. National Security. Northwest Territories. Pipelines. USA. 1942-45. *226*
—. Canada. Dickins, C. H. "Punch". Letters. Mackenzie Air Route. Pipelines. USA. 1942. *56*
—. Canada. Foster, W. W. Oil Industry and Trade. USA. War Department. 1942-45. *54*
—. Northwest Territories. Oil and Petroleum Products. Pipelines. Yukon Territory. 1942-45. *470*
—. Northwest Territories (Mackenzie Valley). Oil Industry and Trade. Pipelines. Planning. 1942-45. *55*
Capitalism. Archives. Defense Policy. Economic Policy. 1939-45. *628*
Capper, Arthur. Legislation. Neutrality. Political Speeches. 1936-41. *709*
Capra, Frank. Films. *Prelude to War* (film). Propaganda. 1939-42. *916*
Caribbean. Canada. Garrison duty. Great Britain. Military. 1914-45. *665*
Carlson, Evans. China. Intelligence mission. Japan. Roosevelt, Franklin D. USA. 1937-38. *992*
Caroline Islands (Yap). Benavente, Ignacio V. Judges. 1942-46. *742*
Cartoonists. Depressions. Gray, Harold. "Little Orphan Annie", comic strip. Social conservatism. 1930's-40's. *1069*
Cartoons. Antiwar Sentiment. Hasek, Jaroslav (*The Good Soldier Schweik*). Military life. ca 1920-70. *30*
Casualty rates. Social Status. Vietnam War. 1941-45. 1961-73. *1039*
Catholic Church. Angers, François-Albert. Canada. French Canadians. Pacifism. Values. 1940-79. *349*
—. National Catholic Welfare Conference. National Council of Catholic Women. Peace Movements. Women. 1919-46. *561*
Catholic Church (hierarchy). Anglophile sentiments. Wilberforce, Robert. World War II (antecedents). 1940. *356*
Catholic influence. Isolationism. Nicoll, John R. A. Roosevelt, Franklin D. (administration). 1943. *357*
Catholics. Conscientious Objectors. 1941-45. *618*
Cavalry. Luzon (battle). MacArthur, Douglas. Philippine Scouts. 1941. *244*
—. McClellan, George Brinton. Saddles. 1857-1943. *303*
Cawthon, Charles (reminiscences). Armies. France (Normandy). 1944. *161*
Cawthon, John Ardis. Army. Camp Beauregard. Conscription, Military. Louisiana. Personal narratives. 1940-42. *163*
Cedar Rapids Gazette (newspaper). Iowa. Marshall, Verne. No Foreign War Committee. World War II (antecedents). 1940-41. *238*
Censorship. *Chicago Tribune*. Grand Juries. Japan. Midway Island (attack on). Navies. 1942. *300*
Central America. Military occupation. Pacific Area. *Tulsa* (vessel). 1919-45. *1102*
Central Intelligence Agency (secret operations). Donovan, William J. Intelligence Service. National Security. 1940's-74. *798*
Chamberlain, Arthur Neville. Appeasement. Foreign Policy. Great Britain. Roosevelt, Franklin Delano. USA. 1937-39. *1012*
Chamberlain, Neville. Blockades. China. Great Britain. Japan. Roosevelt, Franklin D. World War II (antecedents). 1937-38. *362*
Chaplains. Adventists. Military. 1944-55. *224*
Chennault, Claire Lee. Air warfare. China. Flying Tigers. Japan. 1941-45. *408*
—. Air Warfare. China. Japan. USA. 1927-45. *727*
Chiang Kai-shek. China. Military strategy. Stilwell, Joseph W. 1942-44. *629*
—. Diplomacy. Mao Tse-tung. Political leadership. 1945. *978*
Chicago Tribune. Censorship. Grand Juries. Japan. Midway Island (attack on). Navies. 1942. *300*
Chicago, University of. Anderson, Herbert L. (reminiscences). Columbia University. Fermi, Enrico. Nuclear Science and Technology. Szilard, Leo. 1933-45. *20*
—. Anderson, Herbert L. (reminiscences). Illinois. Nuclear chain reaction. 1942. *19*
—. Illinois. Nuclear chain reaction. Wattenberg, Albert (reminiscences). 1942. *1015*
Children. Boarding schools. Federal Government. Indians. 1920-60's. *947*
Chile. Allies. Diplomacy. 1941-45. *298*
—. Axis powers. Economic Conditions. Foreign Investments. 1939-45. *11*
China. Aeronautics, Military. Burma. Flying Tigers. 1941-77. *940*
—. Air Warfare. American Volunteer Group. Flying Tigers motifs. Shoulder patches. 23d Fighter Group. 1930's-45. *191*

Cities   223

—. Air Warfare. Army Air Forces. Flying Tigers. Holloway, Bruce K. (account). P-40 (aircraft). 1942-43. *424*
—. Air warfare. Chennault, Claire Lee. Flying Tigers. Japan. 1941-45. *408*
—. Air Warfare. Chennault, Claire Lee. Japan. USA. 1927-45. *727*
—. Air Warfare. 23d Fighter Group. 1942-45. *669*
—. Air warfare, clandestine. Japan. USA. 1940-41. *840*
—. Anti-Communists. Navies. Sino-American Cooperation Association. USA. 1942-45. *842*
—. Army Air Forces. B-29 (aircraft). Ground crews. Johnston, Francis J. (account). Mariana Islands (Tinian). 1944-45. *462*
—. Blockades. Chamberlain, Neville. Great Britain. Japan. Roosevelt, Franklin D. World War II (antecedents). 1937-38. *362*
—. Brussels Conference (1937). Expansionism. Japan. World War II (antecedents). 1937. *107*
—. Bulge (battle). Cuban Missile Crisis. Korean War. Military intelligence. 1944-80. *34*
—. Canada. Foreign Policy. International Trade. Odlum, Victor Wentworth. ca 1944-49. *683*
—. Canada. Hurford, Grace Gibberd (reminiscences). Missions and Missionaries. Teaching. 1928-45. *439*
—. Carlson, Evans. Intelligence mission. Japan. Roosevelt, Franklin D. USA. 1937-38. *992*
—. Chiang Kai-shek. Military strategy. Stilwell, Joseph W. 1942-44. *629*
—. China. Historiography. Stilwell, Joseph W. 1942-44. *1066*
—. China. Historiography. Stilwell, Joseph W. 1942-44. *1066*
—. Churchill, Winston. de Gaulle, Charles. Foreign Policy. French colonies. Indochina. Roosevelt, Franklin D. 1942-45. *507*
—. Cohen, Warren I. (review article). Foreign policy. Japan. Leadership. Public opinion. ca 1900-50. 1978. *205*
—. Communism. Ho Chi Minh. Independence movement. USA. Vietnamese. 1942-45. *901*
—. Diplomacy. Japan. Stuart, John Leighton. USA. 1937-41. *896*
—. Extraterritoriality. Great Britain. Treaties. 1929-43. *164*
—. Foreign policy. Service, John Stewart (*Lost Chance in China*, excerpts). State Department (Foreign Service). USA. 1945-50's. *857*
—. Foreign relations. Stilwell, Joseph W. 1942-70's. *866*
—. Foreign Relations. USA. Wedemeyer, Albert C. (reminiscences). 1920-48. *1020*
—. Great Britain. International Relations (discipline). Japan. USA. USSR. 1937-49. *736*
—. Japan. Marines. Shanghai (battle). 1937. *803*
—. Jiang Jieshi. Marshall, George C. Military General Staff. Stillwell, Joseph W. 1944. *841*
—. *Keys of the Kingdom* (film). Office of War Information. Propaganda. Stereotypes. USA. 1940-45. *94*
China Convoy. Canada. Friends' Ambulance Unit. Oral history. 1939-45. *899*
China (Kunming). Airplanes. Ghana (Accra). Laughlin, C. H. (reminiscences). 1942. *520*
China, north. Civil wars. Marines. Military Occupation. 1945-47. *228*
China (Shanghai). Japan. Marines. Photographs. USA. 1920's-30's. *1099*
China (Yangtze River). Japan. Panay (vessel). World War II (antecedents). 1937. *731*

China (Yenan). Communist Party. Reporters and reporting. 1944. *971*
China-Burma-India Theater. Emmerson, John K. (reminiscences). State Department (Foreign Service). 1941-44. *272*
Chinese. British Columbia. Immigration. Japanese. Suffrage. 1935-49. *523*
Chinese Americans. Discrimination. Economic Conditions. Japanese Americans. Social Status. 1840's-1978. *732*
Chinese Canadians. Alberta. Japanese Canadians. Racism. 1920-50. *703*
—. British Columbia. Canada. Japanese Canadians. Military Service (denied). 1939-45. *806*
Christian Century (periodical). Foreign policy. Japan. Manchurian crisis. Morrison, Charles C. USA. 1931-33. *719*
Christians. Anti-Semitism. Holocaust. Toynbee, Arnold. ca 1940-1975. *545*
—. Genocide. Jews. Theology. 1945-74. *259*
Christie, J. Walter. Amphibious warfare. Armored Vehicles and Tank Warfare. Landing vehicles, tracked. 1918-45. *418*
Chrome. Allies. Axis Powers. International Trade. Turkey. 1939-44. *911*
Churchill, Winston. Air Warfare. Bombing. Military General Staff. Operation Overlord. Roosevelt, Franklin D. 1944. *1053*
—. Air Warfare. Eaker, Ira C. (reminiscences). Great Britain. 1942-47. *256*
—. Anti-British sentiments. Langer, William. North Dakota. Senate. 1941-52. *1035*
—. China. de Gaulle, Charles. Foreign Policy. French colonies. Indochina. Roosevelt, Franklin D. 1942-45. *507*
—. Correspondence. Great Britain. Neutrality. Roosevelt, Franklin D. 1939-40. *531*
—. Diplomacy. Great Britain. Kennedy, Joseph P. Roosevelt, Franklin D. (administration). 1938-40. *997*
—. Diplomacy. Great Britain. Military Strategy. Roosevelt, Franklin D. 1942-44. *999*
—. Diplomacy. Roosevelt, Franklin D. Stalin, J. V. Yalta Conference (preparations). 1945. *696*
—. Disarmament. Einstein, Albert. Eisenhower, Dwight D. Europe. Khrushchev, Nikita. Memoirs. Moch, Jules. 1932-55. *641*
—. Foreign policy. Great Britain. Military preparedness. USA. World War II (antecedents). 1933-39. 1976. *560*
—. Foreign policy. Political Leadership. Roosevelt, Franklin D. Stalin, Joseph. 1939-45. *1107*
—. Foreign Relations. Great Britain. Lash, Joseph P. (review article). Roosevelt, Franklin D. 1939-41. 1976. *227*
—. Foreign Relations. Great Britain. Roosevelt, Franklin D. 1939-45. *782*
—. Germany (partition). Potsdam Conference. Roosevelt, Franklin D. Stettinius, Edward Reilley. Yalta Conference. 1945. *329*
—. Great Britain. Joint Chiefs of Staff. Malta Conference. Military Strategy. Roosevelt, Franklin D. 1945. *912*
—. Great Britain. USA. White House Map Room. 1944. *491*
—. Speeches, Addresses, etc. (to Americans). 1901-46. *600*
Churchill, Winston (correspondence). Great Britain. Roosevelt, Franklin D. (correspondence). USA. 1938-45. *481*
Circumnavigations. Aeronautics, Military. Diplomacy. Harriman, W. Averell. Lend-Lease. USSR. 1941. *323*
Cities (functions). Federal-local relations. Intergovernmental system. Public Finance. 1930's-74. *815*

224 Citizenship

Citizenship. Ford, Gerald R. Hada, John. Japanese American Citizens League. Pardon. Tokyo Rose (Iva Toguri d'Aquino). Uyeda, Clifford I. (account). 1973-77. *990*
City boosters. Nevada (Las Vegas). Public relations. Tourism. 1905-74. *471*
City of Flint (vessel; capture). Contraband. Foreign relations. Germany. Ships. USSR. 1939. *177*
City planning. Business. California (Los Angeles). Federal government. Social Problems. 1941-59. *843*
—. California (Los Angeles, San Diego, San Francisco). Navy-yards and Naval Stations. Ports. 1919-41. *548*
Civic Unity Committee. Defense industries. Japanese Americans. Negroes. Race relations. Washington (Seattle). 1940-45. *248*
Civil rights. Adoption. Baker, Josephine. Entertainers. Negroes. 1940-75. *434*
—. Attitudes. Conscientious objectors. Japanese Americans. 1940-45. *745*
—. Congress. Discrimination, employment. Fair Employment Practices Committee. Roosevelt, Franklin D. (administration). 1941-46. *684*
—. Counterintelligence. Internment. Japanese Americans. Munson, Curtis B. Peiper, N. J. L. 1931-42. *500*
—. Nebraska (Omaha). Negroes. Quality of life. Social services. Urban League. 1928-50. *623*
Civil rights movement. NAACP. Negroes. South Dakota. 1804-1970. *82*
Civil War. Collectivization. History Teaching. Textbooks. USSR. 1917-79. *207*
—. Forrest, Nathan Bedford. Forrest, Nathan Bedford (1905-44). Military Service. Sisk, John P. (personal account). 1861-1945. *870*
Civil wars. China, north. Marines. Military Occupation. 1945-47. *228*
Civilian Pilot Training Program. Aeronautics, Military. 1938-41. *1018*
Civilian Public Service. Conscientious objectors. Protestantism. Wives. 1941-45. *301*
—. Pacifism. Zahn, Gordon C. (account). 1940-45. *1072*
Civilian service. Conscription, military. Mennonites. 1930's-45. *476*
Civilian survivors. Atomic Bomb Casualty Commission. Japan (Hiroshima, Nagasaki). Medical Research. Radiation Effects Research Foundation. 1945-75. *1010*
Civilian targets. Air Forces. Bombing, indiscriminate. Ethics. Germany. Military General Staff. 1941-45. *837*
Civilians, bombing of. Air Warfare. Public opinion, changes in. 1937-45. *318*
Civil-Military Relations. Air Bases (construction of). Hammon, Stratton Owen (account). Kentucky (Louisville). Standiford Airfield. 1942-45. *377*
—. Nelson, Donald M. War Production Board. 1942-45. *172*
Clark, Chase. Far Western States. Internment. Japanese Americans. Politics. 1941-45. *867*
Clark Field, attack on. Japan. Philippines. 1941-42. *569*
Clark, Grenville. Mobilization needs. National service law (proposed). Roosevelt, Franklin D. (administration). 1942-45. *599*
—. New York. Plattsburg Movement. Selective Service, origins of the. 1940-41. *176*
Clay, Lucius D. Documents. Germany. Military General Staff (meetings). Military government. Office of Military Government for Germany (US). US Group Control Council, Germany. 1944-49. *917*
Clay, Lucius D. (appointment). Germany. Military occupation. USA. 1945. *889*

Clayton, Will. Surplus Property Act of 1944. ca 1942-48. *229*
Clive, Alan (review article). Michigan. 1939-45. *834*
Coast defenses. Artillery. British Columbia. 1862-1941. *437*
Coast Guard. Alaska (Aleutian Islands). *Arthur Middleton* (vessel). Japan. Laidlaw, Lansing. 1942-43. *508*
—. Maryland. Seaplanes. 1929-69. *810*
Coastal defense. British Columbia (Prince Rupert). Diaries. Thistle, R. 1941-42. *808*
Coates, Eugene Butler. Merchant Marine. Nova Scotia. 20c. *258*
Codes, secret. Cryptography. Foreign policy. 1789-1942. *410*
Coffee, John M. Congress. Embargo (sought). Japan. Schellenbach, Lewis B. Washington. 1930's-40. *536*
Cohen, Warren I. (review article). China. Foreign policy. Japan. Leadership. Public opinion. ca 1900-50. 1978. *205*
Cold War. Atomic Weapons. Austin, Warren Robinson. Byrnes, James F. Documents. Potsdam Conference. USSR. 1945. *712*
—. Diplomacy. Europe, Eastern. Historiography. USA. 1942-74. *376*
—. Diplomacy. Morality. Vietnam War. 1945-70's. *860*
—. Diplomacy. Nuclear Arms. Roosevelt, Franklin Delano. 1941-45. *861*
—. Diplomacy, atomic. Foreign policy. Nuclear Arms. USA. USSR. 1942-46. *85*
—. Economic Conditions. International Trade. 1943-46. *260*
—. Europe, Eastern. Great Britain. "Percentages" agreement. Roosevelt, Franklin D. USSR. 1944. *780*
—. Europe, Eastern. Lundestad, Geir (views). 1943-47. *817*
—. Historiography. Nazism. Revisionism. ca 1930-50. *515*
—. Isolationism. 1944-54. *231*
—. Joint Chiefs of Staff. USSR. 1944-46. *746*
—. Michigan. Poland. Vandenberg, Arthur Hendrick, Sr. Yalta Conference. 1944-48. *149*
—. Office of Strategic Services (memos). USSR. 1945. *1049*
—. Open Door, global. Roosevelt, Franklin D. Truman, Harry S. USA. USSR. 1941-50. *1037*
Cold War mentality. Propaganda. Television. *Victory at Sea* series. 1952-72. *792*
Cold War (origins). Allies. Diplomacy. Poland. 1945. *702*
—. Diplomacy. Europe. Harriman, W. Averell. USSR. 1943-45. *98*
—. Diplomacy (review article). Great Britain. USSR. 1941-48. *57*
—. Historiography. 1946-75. *14*
—. Historiography (revisionist). 1941-48. *312*
—. Italy. Kolko, Gabriel. Military Strategy. Negotiations. Operation Crossword. 1945. *166*
—. Marshall Plan. Nuclear Arms. Second Front. USSR. 1940's. *1016*
—. Public opinion. USSR. 1941-45. *133*
—. Roosevelt, Franklin D. Truman, Harry S. (administration). Yalta Conference. 1945-47. *957*
Cold War (origins; review article). Economic Policy. Politics. 1941-71. 1973-74. *338*
Cold War (review article). Alperovitz, Gar. Atomic Weapons. Europe, Eastern. Foreign Policy. Horowitz, David. Kolko, Gabriel. 1943-50. *786*

Constitutionalism 225

—. Determinists. Historiography. Left-revisionists. 1945-70. *482*
Collectivism. Dennis, Lawrence. Germany. Political Commentary. Public Opinion. 1941-45. *233*
Collectivization. Civil War. History Teaching. Textbooks. USSR. USSR. 1917-79. *207*
Colleges and Universities. Antiwar sentiments. Leftism. Political Protest. 1920-36. *124*
—. Manhattan Project. Nuclear Arms. Oppenheimer, J. Robert. 1904-67. *784*
Colleges and Universities (presidents). Dalhousie University. Mackenzie, A. Stanley. New Brunswick. Stanley, Carleton. 1911-45. *395*
Colonialism. Asia, Southeast. Great Britain. Joint declaration (proposed). Roosevelt, Franklin D. (administration). USA. 1942-44. *1036*
Columbia Broadcasting System. Brown, Cecil B. Editorials. News. Radio. White, Paul W. 1943. *954*
Columbia University. Anderson, Herbert L. (reminiscences). Chicago, University of. Fermi, Enrico. Nuclear Science and Technology. Szilard, Leo. 1933-45. *20*
Combat. Armies. Behavior. Marshall, S. L. A. (account). 1941-45. *586*
Comedians. Film. Marx, Groucho. 1940's. *925*
Commando operations. Entebbe (raid). Vietnam War. 1940-77. *406*
Commission for the Protection and Salvage of Artistic and Historic Monuments. Europe. Historical Sites and Parks. USA. 1941-45. *365*
Committee for Political Defense. Foreign Policy. Latin America. State Department. 1942-45. *825*
Committees. Allison, Graham *(Essence of Decision)*. Atomic Warfare. Decisionmaking. Foreign policy. 1944-45. *865*
Communications. Germany. Submarine Warfare. USA. 1939-45. *653*
Communism. China. Ho Chi Minh. Independence movement. USA. Vietnamese. 1942-45. *901*
—. United Automobile Workers of America. 1941-46. *474*
Communist Party. Bulgaria. Foreign policy. 1943-44. *969*
—. China (Yenan). Reporters and reporting. 1944. *971*
—. National Maritime Union. Negroes. Racism. United Electrical Radio and Machine Workers. 1941-45. *196*
Communist Party USA. American Peace Mobilization. Isolationism. World War II (antecedents). 1939-41. *1006*
Community, involuntary. Conscientious objectors. Maryland. Patapsco Civilian Public Service System (Camp 3). Values. 1941-42. *699*
Computers. Mauchly, John William (obituary). 1932-78. *919*
Concentration Camps. Air Warfare. Auschwitz. Jews. Military Strategy. 1944-45. *1063*
—. Arizona. Gila River Relocation Center. Japanese Americans. Public Opinion. Race Relations. 1942-45. *159*
—. California. Japanese Americans. Manzanar War Relocation Center. Riots. Ueno, Harry (arrest). 1942. *381*
—. California. Japanese Americans. Race Relations. 1941-42. *639*
—. Genocide. Germany. Jews. Press. 1939-42. *348*
—. Japanese Americans. 1942-46. *693*
—. Japanese Americans. Public schools. 1942-45. *1056*
—. Japanese Americans. Racism. 1940-45. *444*

Conference on Security and Cooperation in Europe (1969). Europe, Eastern. Foreign Policy. Treaties. USA. USSR. 1945-75. *148*
Confessions of a Nazi Spy (film). Anti-Nazi Movements. Espionage. Films. German-American Bund. 1938-40. *826*
Conflict and Conflict Resolution. Arab-Israeli Conflict. Decisionmaking. Foreign Policy. Japan. 1941-45. 1967-73. *76*
Congress. Autonomy. Politics. Puerto Rico. Roosevelt, Franklin D. (administration). 1940-45. *89*
—. Berlin, Isaiah. Foreign policy. Great Britain. USA. 1943. *355*
—. Civil rights. Discrimination, employment. Fair Employment Practices Committee. Roosevelt, Franklin D. (administration). 1941-46. *684*
—. Coffee, John M. Embargo (sought). Japan. Schellenbach, Lewis B. Washington. 1930's-40. *536*
—. Conscription, Military. Isolationism. Kansas. Selective Training and Service Act (US, 1940). State Politics. 1940. *335*
—. Executive Power. Foreign policy. 1789-1972. *848*
—. Foreign policy. Presidency. War powers. 1787-1972. *772*
—. Japan. Manchurian crisis. Public opinion. 1931-33. *657*
—. Japan. World War II (antecedents). 1940-41. *535*
Congress of Industrial Organizations. Employment. Strikes and Lockouts. 1941-45. *541*
—. Isolationism. Leftism. Pacific Northwest. USSR. 1937-41. *552*
—. Oil Industry and Trade. Texas. 1942-43. *459*
Conscientious objectors. Attitudes. Civil rights. Japanese Americans. 1940-45. *745*
—. Catholics. 1941-45. *618*
—. Civilian Public Service. Protestantism. Wives. 1941-45. *301*
—. Community, involuntary. Maryland. Patapsco Civilian Public Service System (Camp 3). Values. 1941-42. *699*
—. Conscription, Military (hearings). French, Paul C. Friends, Society of. Wilson, E. Raymond (personal account). 1940. *1042*
—. Courts. Flag salute. Jehovah's Witnesses. 1930's-40's. *387*
Conscription, Military. Army. Camp Beauregard. Cawthon, John Ardis. Louisiana. Personal narratives. 1940-42. *163*
—. Civilian service. Mennonites. 1930's-45. *476*
—. Congress. Isolationism. Kansas. Selective Training and Service Act (US, 1940). State Politics. 1940. *335*
—. Elections. King, William Lyon Mackenzie. Ligue pour la Défense du Canada. Quebec. 1942-44. *333*
—. Foreign Relations. Great Britain. Ireland. Northern Ireland. 1941. *795*
—. Industry. Scientific Experiments and Research. 1940-44. *1084*
Conscription, Military (crisis). British Columbia. Pearkes, G. R. 1943-44. *807*
Conscription, Military (hearings). Conscientious Objectors. French, Paul C. Friends, Society of. Wilson, E. Raymond (personal account). 1940. *1042*
Conservatism. Foreign policy. Isolationism. 1930's-52. *801*
Conspiracies. Germany (Berlin). Hitler, Adolf. Prisoners of War. 1945. *907*
Constitutionalism. Law. Political theory. ca 1936-70. *72*

Consular dispatches. Eden, Anthony. Foreign relations. Great Britain. Lindsay, Ronald. 1937. *360*
Contraband. *City of Flint* (vessel; capture). Foreign relations. Germany. Ships. USSR. 1939. *177*
Contracting policies. Aircraft industry. Industrial concentration. 1938-46. *776*
Cooperative Commonwealth Federation. Canadian Labour Congress. Federal Government. Industrial relations. Trades and Labour Congress. 1939-46. *565*
Corregidor (battles). Philippines (Manila Bay). 1795-1945. *39*
Correspondence. Churchill, Winston. Great Britain. Neutrality. Roosevelt, Franklin D. 1939-40. *531*
Cotton. Agricultural Production. Economic Conditions. South or Southern States. Soybeans. 1920's-75. *294*
Coughlin, Charles. Countersubversives. Fascism (review article). German-American Bund. Nazism, American (review article). 1924-41. *785*
Counterintelligence. Civil rights. Internment. Japanese Americans. Munson, Curtis B. Peiper, N. J. L. 1931-42. *500*
Countersubversives. Coughlin, Charles. Fascism (review article). German-American Bund. Nazism, American (review article). 1924-41. *785*
Court evidence. Documents, use of. Due process. Nuremberg Trials. War criminals. 1945-48. *622*
Courts. Conscientious Objectors. Flag salute. Jehovah's Witnesses. 1930's-40's. *387*
—. Discrimination, Employment. Labor law. Women. 1876-1979. *412*
Courts Martial and Courts of Inquiry. California (San Francisco Bay). Mare Island Mutiny. Navies. Negroes. Port Chicago Naval Magazine. Race relations. 1944-48. *1055*
Crawford, David L. Hawaii, University of. Japan. Peace pact (proposed). USA. 1940-41. *428*
Crime and Criminals (organized). Barnes, Harry Elmer. Federal Bureau of Investigation. Hoover, J. Edgar. 1936-44. *980*
Crouter, Natalie. Diaries. Philippines. Prisoners of War. 1941-44. *197*
Crouter, Natalie Stark. Bloom, Lynn Z. Diaries. Philippines. Prisoners of War. 1941-45. 1970's. *101*
Cruisers. Navies. 1930-74. *1061*
Crumb, Charles V. (account). Leadership. Marines. 1936-67. 1979. *198*
Cryptography. Codes, secret. Foreign policy. 1789-1942. *410*
Cuban Missile Crisis. Bulge (battle). China. Korean War. Military intelligence. 1944-80. *34*
Culbertson, William S. Economic policy. Foreign Relations. Great Britain. Middle East. USA. 1944-45. *219*
Curricula. High School Victory Corps. Patriotism. Physical Education and Training. Vocational Education. 1941-45. *983*
Curtin, John. Australia. Hasluck, Paul. MacArthur, Douglas. Military Recruitment. 1942-43. *551*
Curtiss-Wright Corp. Foreign Policy. France. Great Britain. P-40 (H-81; aircraft). 1938-40. *389*
Cutlass, Naval. Klewang, Dutch. Peterson, Harold L. World War I. 1917. 1941-42. *787*
Cyclotrons. Manhattan Project. New Mexico (Los Alamos). Nuclear Science and Technology. Wilson, Robert R. (reminiscences). 1942-43. *1044*
Czechoslovakia. Czechs. Slovaks. 1940-45. *325*
—. Diplomatic recognition. Germany. Government-in-exile. USA. 1939-45. *533*
Czechoslovakia (Prague). Germany. Invasions. Patton, George S., Jr. USSR. Vlasov, Andrei. 1945. *804*
Czechs. Czechoslovakia. Slovaks. 1940-45. *325*
C-46 (aircraft). Airplanes. Buller, H. L. "Duffy" (personal account). C-47 (aircraft). 1940-45. *137*
C-47 (aircraft). Airplanes. Buller, H. L. "Duffy" (personal account). C-46 (aircraft). 1940-45. *137*

D

Daily Life. Camp Shelby. Mississippi (Hattiesburg). Mobilization effects. 1940-45. *849*
Dalhousie University. Colleges and Universities (presidents). Mackenzie, A. Stanley. New Brunswick. Stanley, Carleton. 1911-45. *395*
Dallek, Robert (review article). Foreign Policy. Roosevelt, Franklin D. 1932-45. 1979. *446*
Darilek, Richard E. Foreign Policy (review article). Leigh, Michael. Levering, Ralph B. Public opinion. 1936-47. 1976. *315*
Davies, Joseph Edward. Diplomacy. USSR. 1941-43. *567*
Davis, Elmer. Films. Hollywood. Office of War Information, Bureau of Intelligence. Propaganda. 1942-43. *96*
—. Interventionist, making of an. News broadcasts. Radio. World War II (antecedents). 1939-42. *463*
Davis, W. L. (personal account). Bridges. Burma (Kwae Mae Khlong River). B-24 (aircraft). Prisoners of War. 1942-45. *212*
Decisionmaking. Alliances. Domestic Policy. Foreign policy. Roosevelt, Franklin D. (administration). UN Conference on Food and Agriculture. Virginia (Hot Springs). 1943. *1041*
—. Allison, Graham *(Essence of Decision).* Atomic Warfare. Committees. Foreign policy. 1944-45. *865*
—. Alperovitz, Gar (review article). Atomic Warfare. Historiography. Japan (Hiroshima). 1945-65. *859*
—. Arab-Israeli Conflict. Conflict and Conflict Resolution. Foreign Policy. Japan. 1941-45. 1967-73. *76*
—. Argentina. Diplomacy. Rio Conference of 1942. USA. 1942. *1059*
—. Atomic Warfare. Hiroshima (attack on). Japan. 1944-45. *828*
—. Atomic Warfare. Japan (Hiroshima, Nagasaki). Military Strategy. 1944-45. *304*
—. Europe, Western. History Teaching. Simulation and Games. USA. War games. 1939-45. 1970's. *153*
—. Military planning. Political warning. 1941. *824*
—. Military Strategy. Pacific Area. 1941-45. *75*
—. Organizations. System analysis. 20c. *3*
Declassification. Documents. Europe. Resistance. USA. 1939-45. 1972-75. *270*
Defense industries. Civic Unity Committee. Japanese Americans. Negroes. Race relations. Washington (Seattle). 1940-45. *248*
—. Discrimination. Executive Order 8802. March on Washington Movement. Military. Randolph, A. Philip. Webster, Milton. 1941-44. *588*
—. Employment. Massachusetts (Lowell). Textile Industry. Women. 1940-45. *630*
—. Industrialization. Missouri (Kansas City). Small Business. 1940-45. *656*

Defense policies. Canada. Interdependence. USA. 1940's-70's. *939*
Defense policy. Americas (North and South). Monroe Doctrine. Roosevelt, Franklin D. (administration). 1930's-40. *363*
—. Archives. Capitalism. Economic Policy. 1939-45. *628*
—. Federal Policy. Industry. Labor Unions and Organizations. 1939-41. *873*
—. Foreign policy. Generations. 1941-74. *799*
—. Latin America. 1940-45. *487*
Defensive war argument. Foreign Policy. Ideology. War. 1941-73. *958*
deGaulle, Charles. American Revolution. Europe, Western. Foreign Relations. France. Versailles, Treaty of. 1773-1979. *498*
—. Canada. France. Propaganda. Quebec. Vichy Regime. 1940-42. *193*
—. China. Churchill, Winston. Foreign Policy. French colonies. Indochina. Roosevelt, Franklin D. 1942-45. *507*
—. Diplomacy. France. Great Britain. Indochina. 1940-45. *246*
Delaware (Wilmington). Dravo Corp. Navies. Pennsylvania (Pittsburgh). Shipbuilding. 1940-47. *974*
Demobilization. Discrimination, Employment. Literature. Social Status. Women. 1944-46. *392*
Democracies. Developing Nations. Dictatorships. Foreign policy. Nixon, Richard M. USA. 1790-1975. *138*
Democracy. Fascism. Intervention. World War II (antecedents). 1939-41. *898*
Democratic Party. Economic Development. Mississippi. Racial issues. 1941-45. *874*
—. German Americans. Isolationism. Kentucky (Kenton County). 1930-40. *247*
Denmark. Great Britain. Iceland. Independence Movements. USA. 1940-44. *457*
Dennis, Lawrence. Collectivism. Germany. Political Commentary. Public Opinion. 1941-45. *233*
Depressions. Cartoonists. Gray, Harold. "Little Orphan Annie", comic strip. Social conservatism. 1930's-40's. *1069*
Destroyer escorts. *England* (vessel). Japan. Pacific Area. Submarine Warfare. Williamson, John A. (account). 1944. *1038*
Destroyers. Antiaircraft guns. Navies. Photographs. 1945. *42*
—. Military Aid. Navies. Spain. 1942-60. *35*
Detention. California. Japanese Americans. Racism. 1941-45. *640*
Determinists. Cold War (review article). Historiography. Left-revisionists. 1945-70. *482*
Deutscher Bund Canada. German Canadians. Nazism. Saskatchewan. 1934-39. *1005*
Developing Nations. Democracies. Dictatorships. Foreign policy. Nixon, Richard M. USA. 1790-1975. *138*
Dewey, Thomas E. Elections (presidential). Pearl Harbor, attack on (issue). Roosevelt, Franklin D. (administration). 1944. *621*
Diamond, Sander A. (review article). German Americans. Nazism. USA. 1924-41. 1974. *284*
Diaries. Atomic Warfare. Canada. King, William Lyon MacKenzie. Racism. 1921-48. *823*
—. Australia. Great Britain. MacArthur, Douglas. Philippines. Williamson, Gerald Hugh. 1942-43. *962*
—. Bloom, Lynn Z. Crouter, Natalie Stark. Philippines. Prisoners of War. 1941-45. 1970's. *101*
—. British Columbia (Prince Rupert). Coastal defense. Thistle, R. 1941-42. *808*

—. Crouter, Natalie. Philippines. Prisoners of War. 1941-44. *197*
—. Foreign Policy (review article). Roosevelt, Franklin D. (administration). Stettinius, Edward Reilley. 1943-46. 1975. *483*
—. Internment. Japanese Americans. Oregon. Portland Assembly Center. Tomita, Saku. 1942. *492*
—. Japan. Norquist, Ernest O. Philippines. Prisoners of War. 1942-45. *681*
Dick, Everett N. (account). Adventist Medical Cadet Corps. Armies. Korean War. 1934-53. *223*
Dickins, C. H. "Punch". Canada. Canol project. Letters. Mackenzie Air Route. Pipelines. USA. 1942. *56*
Dictatorships. Democracies. Developing Nations. Foreign policy. Nixon, Richard M. USA. 1790-1975. *138*
Dieppe (air battle). Canada. Great Britain. Leigh-Mallory, Trafford. Royal Canadian Air Force. 1942. *151*
Diplomacy. 1939-45. *527*
—. Aeronautics, Military. Circumnavigations. Harriman, W. Averell. Lend-Lease. USSR. 1941. *323*
—. Africa (landing). French. Great Britain. 1941-42. *760*
—. Africa, North. Economic Policy. France, Vichy. USA. 1941-43. *97*
—. Air Bases. Norweb, R. Henry. Portugal (Azores). 1941-44. *942*
—. Air Warfare. Bombing (inadvertent). Switzerland. USA. 1943-45. *401*
—. Allies. Bibliographies. 1939-44. *800*
—. Allies. Chile. 1941-45. *298*
—. Allies. Cold War (origins). Poland. 1945. *702*
—. Allies. Military strategy. 1942. *793*
—. Alperovitz, Gar. Historiography. Nuclear Arms. 1943-46. 1965-73. *571*
—. American Jewish Joint Distribution Committee. Jews. Mayer, Saly. 1944-45. *59*
—. Anti-Nazi Movements. Messersmith, George Strausser. State Department. 1928-39. *858*
—. Appeasement (proposal). Great Britain. Japan. 1941. *328*
—. Archives. France. 1939-45. 1979. *217*
—. Argentina. Decisionmaking. Rio Conference of 1942. USA. 1942. *1059*
—. Atomic bomb development. Nuclear Science and Technology. 1942-45. *754*
—. Beaverbrook, 1st Baron. Harriman, W. Averell. Military Aid. USSR. 1941. *510*
—. Brazil. 1935-45. *416*
—. Bulgaria. Surrender. 1944. *970*
—. Canada. Europe. Peace negotiations. USA. 1943-47. *415*
—. Canada. Foreign Relations. Latin America. Pan-American Union. USA. 1939-44. *664*
—. Chiang Kai-shek. Mao Tse-tung. Political leadership. 1945. *978*
—. China. Japan. Stuart, John Leighton. USA. 1937-41. *896*
—. Churchill, Winston. Great Britain. Kennedy, Joseph P. Roosevelt, Franklin D. (administration). 1938-40. *997*
—. Churchill, Winston. Great Britain. Military Strategy. Roosevelt, Franklin D. 1942-44. *999*
—. Churchill, Winston. Roosevelt, Franklin D. Stalin, J. V. Yalta Conference (preparations). 1945. *696*
—. Cold War. Europe, Eastern. Historiography. USA. 1942-74. *376*
—. Cold War. Morality. Vietnam War. 1945-70's. *860*
—. Cold War. Nuclear Arms. Roosevelt, Franklin Delano. 1941-45. *861*

228 Diplomacy

—. Cold War (origins). Europe. Harriman, W. Averell. USSR. 1943-45. *98*
—. Davies, Joseph Edward. USSR. 1941-43. *567*
—. deGaulle, Charles. France. Great Britain. Indochina. 1940-45. *246*
—. Drought, James M. Japan. John Doe Associates. Konoye, Fumimaro. Roosevelt, Franklin. Summit conferences. 1941. *143*
—. Embick, Stanley D., Gen. Military (policy). National Council for the Prevention of War. 1937-45. *838*
—. Emmerson, John K. (memoirs). Japan (Tokyo). State Department. World War II (antecedents). 1941. *275*
—. Emmerson, John K. (reminiscences). Internment. Japanese Peruvians. Peru. USA. 1942-43. *273*
—. Espionage. Germany. Nazis. Thomsen, Hans. 1940. *634*
—. Europe. Murphy, Robert (tribute). 1941-45. *204*
—. Europe. Repatriation, forced. USA. USSR. 1944-47. *268*
—. Europe. Roosevelt, Franklin D. (death). 1945. *78*
—. Faymonville, Philip R. Military Service, Professional. USA. USSR. 1917-52. *511*
—. Foreign policy. International Trade. Japan. World War II (antecedents). 1937-41. *988*
—. *Foreign Relations* (documents series). 1943-46. *528*
—. Free ports. Norway. Roosevelt, Franklin Delano. USA. USSR. 1941-43. *788*
—. Germany. Lane, Arthur B. Yugoslavia. 1940-41. *933*
—. Germany. Roosevelt, Franklin D. USSR. 1934-39. *572*
—. Great Britain. Historiography. Langer, William L. (account). Vichy Regime. 1941-54. *512*
—. Great Britain. Second front. USA. USSR. 1942-43. *1089*
—. Great Britain. USA. Winant, John Gilbert. 1941-46. *1034*
—. Hayes, Carlton J. H. Historians. Spain. 1942-45. *372*
—. Hornbeck, Stanley K. Japan. USA. World War II (antecedents). 1937-41. *526*
—. Hull, Cordell. Indochina. Japan. Philippines. World War II (antecedents). 1941. *131*
—. Ibn-Saud, King. *Murphy* (vessel). Roosevelt, Franklin D. Saudi Arabia. USA. 1945. *472*
—. Indochina. International trusteeships. Roosevelt, Franklin D. 1941-45. *407*
—. Japan. Konoe Fumimaro. 1934-41. *430*
—. Japan. MacArthur, Douglas. Philippines (Manila). Surrender. 1945. *624*
—. Japan (Tokyo). USA. World War II (antecedents). 1941. *274*
—. National Telephone Company (Spain). Spain. USA. Weddell, Alexander Wilbourne. *367*
—. Pius XII, Pope. Taylor, Myron C. USA. Vatican. 1940-50. *188*
—. Roosevelt, Franklin D. Yalta Conference (review essay). 1945-55. *850*
—. Vatican. 1937-45. *15*
Diplomacy, atomic. Cold War. Foreign policy. Nuclear Arms. USA. USSR. 1942-46. *85*
Diplomacy (foreign service officers). Attitudes. Balkans. USSR. 1944-46. *221*
Diplomacy, mistakes in. Europe. Japan. USA. World War II (review article). 1930's-41. *405*
Diplomacy (review article). Cold War (origins). Great Britain. USSR. 1945. *57*
Diplomatic recognition. Czechoslovakia. Germany. Government-in-exile. USA. 1939-45. *533*

Diplomatic relations (rupture). Axis powers. Latin America. Rio Conference (1942). USA. 1941-42. *297*
Diplomatic reports. Cane, Cyril H. Great Britain. Michigan (Detroit). Riots. 1943. *359*
Diplomatic representation. Alliance polarization. Guttmann-Lingoes Smallest Space Analysis. Methodology. War. 1815-1973. *1007*
Dirigibles. Balloons. McBride, Robert M. Navy. Personal narratives. 1941-44. *601*
Disarmament. Churchill, Winston. Einstein, Albert. Eisenhower, Dwight D. Europe. Khrushchev, Nikita. Memoirs. Moch, Jules. 1932-55. *641*
Discovery and Exploration. Arctic. Finnie, Richard Sterling (account). North America. Office of the Coordinator of Information. Stefansson, Vilhjalmur. 1931-62. *290*
Discrimination. Armies. Government. Great Britain. Negroes. 1942-45. *358*
—. Armies. Great Britain. White, Walter F. 1943-44. *354*
—. Baptists. Japanese Americans. Resettlement. 1890-1970. *644*
—. British Columbia. Canada. India. Suffrage. 1939-45. *414*
—. Chinese Americans. Economic Conditions. Japanese Americans. Social Status. 1840's-1978. *732*
—. Defense industries. Executive Order 8802. March on Washington Movement. Military. Randolph, A. Philip. Webster, Milton. 1941-44. *588*
—. Fair Employment Practices Committee. Negroes. Railroads. Southeastern Carriers Conference. 1941-45. *402*
Discrimination, employment. Boilermakers, Iron Shipbuilders and Helpers, International Brotherhood of. California (Los Angeles). Labor Unions and Organizations. Negroes. Oregon (Portland). Shipbuilding. 1941-46. *883*
—. Civil rights. Congress. Fair Employment Practices Committee. Roosevelt, Franklin D. (administration). 1941-46. *684*
—. Courts. Labor law. Women. 1876-1979. *412*
—. Demobilization. Literature. Social Status. Women. 1944-46. *392*
—. Fair Employment Practices Committee. Negroes. Roosevelt, Franklin D. (administration). 1940-45. *871*
—. Military Service (enlistees). Navies. Negroes. Race Relations. Segregation. 1798-1970's. *388*
Dissertations. Bibliographies. Military. 1977-78. *169*
—. Bibliographies. Military History. 5c BC-1980. *171*
District of Columbia. Boycotts, consumer. Employment. Sex discrimination. Women. 1941-46. *1105*
Documentaries. Armies. Films. Heisler, Stuart. *Negro Soldier* (film). Propaganda. Race Relations. 1944. *195*
Documentation. Evacuation, forced. Internment. Japanese Americans. Photographs. War Relocation Authority. 1941-43. *208*
Documents. Archives, National. Europe. Resistance. 1939-45. *218*
—. Atomic Weapons. Austin, Warren Robinson. Byrnes, James F. Cold War. Potsdam Conference. USSR. 1945. *712*
—. Bibliographies. Italy. 1939-45. *271*

Economic Structure   229

—. Clay, Lucius D. Germany. Military General Staff (meetings). Military government. Office of Military Government for Germany (US). US Group Control Council, Germany. 1944-49. *917*

—. Declassification. Europe. Resistance. USA. 1939-45. 1972-75. *270*

—. Foreign Relations. Taylor, Myron. USA. Vatican. 1940-42. *6*

—. Harry S. Truman Library. Public Policy. Truman, Harry S. Western States. 1940-66. *460*

Documents (accessibility of). Federal Government. 1972. *697*

Documents, use of. Court evidence. Due process. Nuremberg Trials. War criminals. 1945-48. *622*

Domestic Policy. Alliances. Decisionmaking. Foreign policy. Roosevelt, Franklin D. (administration). UN Conference on Food and Agriculture. Virginia (Hot Springs). 1943. *1041*

Dominican Republic. Public expenditures. Puerto Rico. 1930-70. *582*

Donovan, William J. Central Intelligence Agency (secret operations). Intelligence Service. National Security. 1940's-74. *798*

Draper, William F. Alaska. Aleutian Campaign. Artists. 1942-43. *652*

Dravo Corp. Delaware (Wilmington). Navies. Pennsylvania (Pittsburgh). Shipbuilding. 1940-47. *974*

Dreadnought. Battleship era. Naval warfare. 1905-71. *448*

Dresden (attack on). Air Warfare. Bombing. Germany. Great Britain. Total war. 1914-45. *181*

Drew, George. Canada. Duff, Lyman. Hong Kong Inquiry. King, William Lyon Mackenzie. 1941. *140*

Drones. Fahrney, Delmar S. (account). Missiles. Navy Bureau of Aeronautics. N2C-2 (aircraft). Radio. Research and development. TG-2 (aircraft). 1936-45. *279*

Drought, James M. Diplomacy. Japan. John Doe Associates. Konoye, Fumimaro. Roosevelt, Franklin. Summit conferences. 1941. *143*

Drug Abuse. Amphetamines. Popular culture. 1932-75. *451*

Dry dock, floating. Louisiana (New Orleans). Manitowoc Shipbuilding Co. Mississippi River. Navigation, Inland. *Peto* (vessel). Submarines. 1942-45. *676*

Due process. Court evidence. Documents, use of. Nuremberg Trials. War criminals. 1945-48. *622*

Duff, Lyman. Canada. Drew, George. Hong Kong Inquiry. King, William Lyon Mackenzie. 1941. *140*

Dull, Paul S. (review article). Japan. Naval Strategy. Pearl Harbor, attack on. Yamamoto, Isoroku. 1941-45. *977*

Dumas, Harold. Japanese language. Marines. 1944-45. *577*

Dunn, William R. Air Forces. Pilots. 1941-45. 1967. *718*

Dunn, William R. (account). Air Forces. Eagle Squadron, No. 71. Great Britain. Spitfire (aircraft). 1941. *252*

—. Air Warfare. Great Britain. Royal Air Force. 1941. *251*

Dwight D. Eisenhower Library. Kansas (Abilene). Military records. Research. 1916-52. 1977. *361*

E

Eagle Squadron, No. 71. Air Forces. Dunn, William R. (account). Great Britain. Spitfire (aircraft). 1941. *252*

Eaker, Ira C. Aeronautics, Military. Army Air Corps. World War I. 8th Bomber Command, US. 1917-47. *852*

—. Airplanes, Military. Army Air Corps. California. Hamilton Field. Military Decorations, Flags, and Symbols. Wright, Howard T. (account). 1941. *1062*

Eaker, Ira C. (reminiscences). Air Warfare. Churchill, Winston. Great Britain. 1942-47. *256*

East Prussia. Bowman, Isaiah. Oder-Neisse Line. Poland. State Department (Advisory Committee on Post-War Foreign Policy). Welles, Sumner. 1942-45. *819*

Economic agreements. Foreign Relations. Neutrality. Switzerland. World War I. 1919. 1944-45. *292*

Economic Aid. Australia. Bell, Roger. Foreign Relations. 1941-46. *1082*

—. Foreign Relations. Great Britain. Saudi Arabia. State Department (Near East Affairs Division). 1941-45. *809*

Economic Aid (reciprocal). Australia. USA. 1941-46. *68*

Economic Conditions. Agricultural Production. Cotton. South or Southern States. Soybeans. 1920's-75. *294*

—. Alaska. 1867-1967. *642*

—. Arizona (White Mountains). Lumber and Lumbering. 1919-42. *592*

—. Avery, Sewell. Illinois (Chicago). Labor Disputes (arbitration). Montgomery Ward (federal seizure of). War Labor Board. 1941. *490*

—. Axis powers. Chile. Foreign Investments. 1939-45. *11*

—. Boycott activities. Jews. Joint Boycott Council. Non-Sectarian Anti-Nazi League to Champion Human Rights. 1939-41. *326*

—. Chinese Americans. Discrimination. Japanese Americans. Social Status. 1840's-1978. *732*

—. Cold War. International Trade. 1943-46. *260*

—. Manufacturers, small. Roosevelt, Franklin D. 1939-43. *398*

—. Prisoners of war. World War I. 1914-45. *211*

—. Wages. 1939-50. *791*

Economic development. Attitudes. Military Strategy. Nuclear arms. Technology. War. 1914-68. *686*

—. Democratic Party. Mississippi. Racial issues. 1941-45. *874*

—. Liberia. Military Strategy. State Department. 1938-45. *66*

Economic Growth. Industry. Population. South. Western States. 1940-79. *1*

—. Propaganda. State Department. War Department. 1939-45. *1083*

Economic Policy. Africa, North. Diplomacy. France, Vichy. USA. 1941-43. *97*

—. Archives. Capitalism. Defense Policy. 1939-45. *628*

—. Cold War (origins; review article). Politics. 1941-71. 1973-74. *338*

—. Culbertson, William S. Foreign Relations. Great Britain. Middle East. USA. 1944-45. *219*

Economic Regulations. Europe, Western. Industrial location. 1930's-70's. *945*

Economic Structure. Canada. 1939-45. *749*

230   Economic threat

Economic threat. Free trade. World War II (antecedents). 1930's-41. *993*
Ecuador (Galapagos Islands). Europe. Expansionism. 1830-1946. *324*
Ecumenism. Europe. Protestant Churches. 1900-45. *555*
Eden, Anthony. Consular dispatches. Foreign relations. Great Britain. Lindsay, Ronald. 1937. *360*
—. Foreign Policy. Molotov, V. M. Poland. Truman, Harry S. USSR. 1945. *635*
Editorials. Brown, Cecil B. Columbia Broadcasting System. News. Radio. White, Paul W. 1943. *954*
—. Freedom of the Press. Newspapers. 1920. 1940. *113*
Education. Armed Forces Radio Service. Barnouw, Erik. Radio. 1942-45. *199*
—. Assimilation. Jews. Labor movement. Socialism. 1880's-1945. *975*
—. Lawyers. Marines. McCarthy, Joseph R. State Politics. Wisconsin. 1908-44. *687*
Education, progressive. Alabama. 1930-51. *519*
Egypt. Great Britain. State Department. Suez Canal. 1930's-45. *47*
Egypt (Foul Bay). Air Warfare. Ohlinger, John F. (account). 1943. *692*
Eicher, Edward Clayton. Sedition. Trials. 1944. *319*
Eighth Air Force. Air warfare. Bibliographies. Europe. 1941-45. *1026*
Eighth Air Force, US. Aeronautics, Military. B-17 (aircraft). B-24 (aircraft). Europe, Western. 1935-45. *255*
Eighth Air Force (1st, 3d Air Divisions). B-17 (aircraft). 1942-45. *27*
Einstein, Albert. Churchill, Winston. Disarmament. Eisenhower, Dwight D. Europe. Khrushchev, Nikita. Memoirs. Moch, Jules. 1932-55. *641*
—. Hungarian Americans. Nuclear Arms (program). Szilárd, Leo. USA. 1941-74. *366*
Eisenhower, Dwight D. Churchill, Winston. Disarmament. Einstein, Albert. Europe. Khrushchev, Nikita. Memoirs. Moch, Jules. 1932-55. *641*
—. Germany (Berlin). Great Britain. Military Strategy. USSR. 1945. *495*
—. Marshall, George C. Military General Staff. Operation Overlord. Roosevelt, Franklin D. 1942-44. *295*
Elections. Conscription, Military. King, William Lyon Mackenzie. Ligue pour la Défense du Canada. Quebec. 1942-44. *333*
Elections (presidential). Dewey, Thomas E. Pearl Harbor, attack on (issue). Roosevelt, Franklin D. (administration). 1944. *621*
—. Poland (issue). Polish Americans. Roosevelt, Franklin D. 1942-44. *374*
Electric Boat Company. McKee, Andrew Irwin. Military Engineering. Navies. Submarines. 1930's-61. *10*
Embargo, Allied. Portugal (shipping to Germany). Wolfram. 1939-44. *943*
Embargo, de facto. Foreign Policy. Japan. Oil. Roosevelt, Franklin D. 1941. *22*
Embargo (sought). Coffee, John M. Congress. Japan. Schellenbach, Lewis B. Washington. 1930's-40. *536*
Embargoes. Armaments. Isolationism. Neutrality Act (US, 1935). 1935. *1080*
Embick, Stanley D., Gen. Diplomacy. Military (policy). National Council for the Prevention of War. 1937-45. *838*
Emergencies, national. Executive power. Habeas corpus. Martial law. War. 1861-1944. *778*

Emergency Committee to Save the Jewish People of Europe. Bergson, Peter. Genocide. Rescues. Zionism. 1943-45. *723*
Emergency Rubber Project. Agriculture Department. California. Guayule (plant). Nishimura, Shimpe. Rubber industry. 1942-76. *36*
Emmerson, John K. (memoirs). Diplomacy. Japan (Tokyo). State Department. World War II (antecedents). 1941. *275*
Emmerson, John K. (reminiscences). China-Burma-India Theater. State Department (Foreign Service). 1941-44. *272*
—. Diplomacy. Internment. Japanese Peruvians. Peru. USA. 1942-43. *541*
Employment. Actors and Actresses. Benefit performances. Minnesota (Minneapolis). 1942. *985*
—. Automobile industry. Labor Unions and Organizations. Strikes, wildcat. 1941-45. *1103*
—. Boycotts, consumer. District of Columbia. Sex discrimination. Women. 1941-46. *1105*
—. Congress of Industrial Organizations. Strikes and Lockouts. 1941-45. *541*
—. Defense industries. Massachusetts (Lowell). Textile Industry. Women. 1940-45. *630*
—. Employment. Women. 1941-45. *761*
—. Employment. Women. 1941-45. *761*
—. Federal programs. Women (status of). 1941-45. *929*
—. Germans. Minnesota. Prisoners of war. 1942-46. *743*
—. Holland, Lou E. Nelson, Donald M. War Production Board, Smaller Plants Division and Corporation. 1940-44. *399*
—. Industry. Negroes. Social justice. 1942-43. *1086*
—. Labor. Women. 1940-47. *1106*
—. Labor unions. Negroes. Women. Working-class militancy. 1940's. *341*
—. Labor unions, industrial. Working class power (elimination of). 1930-47. *1024*
—. Oklahoma (Oklahoma City). Tinker Air Force Base. 1941-45. *257*
—. Women. 1941-45. *973*
—. Women's liberation movement. 1920's-70's. *79*
England (vessel). Destroyer escorts. Japan. Pacific Area. Submarine Warfare. Williamson, John A. (account). 1944. *1038*
Enola Gay (aircraft). Air Warfare. Atomic bomb. Military training. Wendover Field. 1944-45. *986*
Entebbe (raid). Commando operations. Vietnam War. 1940-77. *406*
Enterprise (vessels). Navies. 1799-1978. *458*
Entertainers. Adoption. Baker, Josephine. Civil rights. Negroes. 1940-75. *434*
Environment. Marines. Pacific Area. Pacific Dependencies (US). 1943-71. *617*
Espionage. Anti-Nazi Movements. *Confessions of a Nazi Spy* (film). Films. German-American Bund. 1938-40. *826*
—. Diplomacy. Germany. Nazis. Thomsen, Hans. 1940. *634*
Ethics. Air Forces. Bombing, indiscriminate. Civilian targets. Germany. Military General Staff. 1941-45. *837*
Europe. Aeronautics, Military. Hudson, James J. (account). P-39 Airacobra (aircraft). 1941-45. *435*
—. Agriculture. Industrialization. Market economy. North America. Peasant movements (colloquium). ca 1875-1975. *52*
—. Air Forces. Thyng, Harrison R. (reminiscences). 1941-45. *963*
—. Air Warfare. 1941-45. *632*
—. Air warfare. Bibliographies. Eighth Air Force. 1941-45. *1026*

Farmers 231

—. Archives, National. Documents. Resistance. 1939-45. *218*
—. Canada. Diplomacy. Peace negotiations. USA. 1943-47. *415*
—. Canada. Military operations. Politics. 1939-45. *909*
—. Churchill, Winston. Disarmament. Einstein, Albert. Eisenhower, Dwight D. Khrushchev, Nikita. Memoirs. Moch, Jules. 1932-55. *641*
—. Cold War (origins). Diplomacy. Harriman, W. Averell. USSR. 1943-45. *98*
—. Commission for the Protection and Salvage of Artistic and Historic Monuments. Historical Sites and Parks. USA. 1941-45. *365*
—. Declassification. Documents. Resistance. USA. 1939-45. 1972-75. *270*
—. Diplomacy. Murphy, Robert (tribute). 1941-45. *204*
—. Diplomacy. Repatriation, forced. USA. USSR. 1944-47. *268*
—. Diplomacy. Roosevelt, Franklin D. (death). 1945. *78*
—. Diplomacy, mistakes in. Japan. USA. World War II (review article). 1930's-41. *405*
—. Ecuador (Galapagos Islands). Expansionism. 1830-1946. *324*
—. Ecumenism. Protestant Churches. 1900-45. *555*
—. Federal Government (response). Jews. USA. War crimes. 1938-45. *5*
—. Foreign policy (review article). Japan. Offner, Arnold A. USA. 1917-41. *677*
—. Genocide. Jews. Public Policy. Roosevelt, Franklin D. (administration). 1942-44. *596*
—. Great Britain. Invasions (proposed). Military Strategy. 1942-44. *822*
—. Historiography. 1939-75. *411*
—. Jews. McDonald, James G. (paper). Refugees. Resettlement. 1938-43. *285*
Europe, Central. Foreign policy. Germany. Isolationism. USA. 1918-41. *1051*
—. Foreign Policy. USA. World War II (antecedents). 1918-41. *1050*
Europe, East. Foreign policy. Isolationism. Neutrality Laws. Roosevelt, Franklin D. World War II (antecedents). 1920's-30's. *249*
Europe, Eastern. Alperovitz, Gar. Atomic Weapons. Cold War (review article). Foreign Policy. Horowitz, David. Kolko, Gabriel. 1943-50. *786*
—. Cold War. Diplomacy. Historiography. USA. 1942-74. *376*
—. Cold War. Great Britain. "Percentages" agreement. Roosevelt, Franklin D. USSR. 1944. *780*
—. Cold War. Lundestad, Geir (views). 1943-47. *817*
—. Conference on Security and Cooperation in Europe (1969). Foreign Policy. Treaties. USA. USSR. 1945-75. *148*
Europe, Western. Aeronautics, Military. B-17 (aircraft). B-24 (aircraft). Eighth Air Force, US. 1935-45. *255*
—. Air support, close. Army Air Corps Tactical School. Tactics. 1930-45. *454*
—. Air Warfare. Army Air Corps. Beeson, Duane. Idaho (Boise). 1941-45. *309*
—. American Revolution. deGaulle, Charles. Foreign Relations. France. Versailles, Treaty of. 1773-1979. *498*
—. Armies. Military organization. 1944-45. *288*
—. Armored vehicles and tank warfare. USA. 1935-40. *680*
—. Decisionmaking. History Teaching. Simulation and Games. USA. War games. 1939-45. 1970's. *153*

—. Economic Regulations. Industrial location. 1930's-70's. *945*
—. Huertgen Forest (battle). 28th Infantry Division, US. 1944. *563*
Evacuation, forced. Assimilation. Canada. Japanese Canadians (Nisei). 1941-75. *575*
—. British Columbia. Federal government. Japanese. Public opinion. 1937-42. *1009*
—. Documentation. Internment. Japanese Americans. Photographs. War Relocation Authority. 1941-43. *208*
Evans, Maurice. Armies. Pacific Area. Shakespeare, William. Theater Production and Direction. 1942-45. *864*
Exchange programs. Great Britain. Medical research. USSR. ca 1941-45. *62*
Executive Behavior. Attitudes. Foreign policy. Political Protest. Roosevelt, Franklin D. 1940-72. *1092*
Executive Order No. 1. Gifts. MacArthur, Douglas. Military General Staff. Philippines. Quezon, Manuel. Sutherland, Richard K. (papers). 1942. *733*
Executive Order 8802. Defense industries. Discrimination. March on Washington Movement. Military. Randolph, A. Philip. Webster, Milton. 1941-44. *588*
Executive Power. Congress. Foreign policy. 1789-1972. *848*
—. Emergencies, national. Habeas corpus. Martial law. War. 1861-1944. *778*
Expansionism. Brussels Conference (1937). China. Japan. World War II (antecedents). 1937. *107*
—. Ecuador (Galapagos Islands). Europe. 1830-1946. *324*
—. Military Strategy. *Rankin* plans. USA. USSR. 1943. *924*
Exports. Apple industry. Great Britain. Imports. Nova Scotia (Annapolis Valley). 1880-1957. *186*
Extraterritoriality. China. Great Britain. Treaties. 1929-43. *164*

F

Fahrney, Delmar S. (account). Drones. Missiles. Navy Bureau of Aeronautics. N2C-2 (aircraft). Radio. Research and development. TG-2 (aircraft). 1936-45. *279*
Fair Employment Practices Commission. Alabama (Mobile). Negroes. Shipyards. South. 1938-45. *771*
Fair Employment Practices Committee. Civil rights. Congress. Discrimination, employment. Roosevelt, Franklin D. (administration). 1941-46. *684*
—. Discrimination. Negroes. Railroads. Southeastern Carriers Conference. 1941-45. *402*
—. Discrimination, Employment. Negroes. Roosevelt, Franklin D. (administration). 1940-45. *871*
Fairbairn, R. Edis. Canada. Pacifism. Protestantism. United Church of Canada. 1939. *802*
Falaise (battle). France. France (Normandy). Military Strategy. Operation Cobra. Patton, George S., Jr. USA. 1944. *751*
Family. Arkansas. Legislation. Social Problems. 1941-45. *884*
Fantasy. Films. Heroes. 1943-45. *991*
Far Western States. Clark, Chase. Internment. Japanese Americans. Politics. 1941-45. *867*
Farmers. Agricultural production. Michigan. 1939-45. *179*

Farmers, black. Negroes. North Carolina. Social Change. South. 1950-70. *1004*
Fascism. Democracy. Intervention. World War II (antecedents). 1939-41. *898*
—. Italy. Pound, Ezra. USA. 1924-58. *1074*
Fascism (alleged). Italian Americans. Liberalism. Loyalty. Office of War Information. Propaganda. 1939-40. *627*
Fascism (review article). Coughlin, Charles. Countersubversives. German-American Bund. Nazism, American (review article). 1924-41. *785*
Faymonville, Philip R. Diplomacy. Military Service, Professional. USA. USSR. 1917-52. *511*
Federal Bureau of Investigation. Barnes, Harry Elmer. Crime and Criminals (organized). Hoover, J. Edgar. 1936-44. *980*
Federal government. Bankhead Bill (1943). Newspapers. Subsidies. War Bond advertising. 1943. *112*
—. Blum, John Morton (review article). Politics. Propaganda. 1940-45. *525*
—. Boarding schools. Children. Indians. 1920-60's. *947*
—. British Columbia. Evacuation, forced. Japanese. Public opinion. 1937-42. *1009*
—. Bureau of Public Information. Canada. Press. Public opinion. Social scientists. Wartime Information Board. 1939-45. *1070*
—. Business. California (Los Angeles). City planning. Social Problems. 1941-59. *843*
—. Business. Canada. Labor Unions and Organizations. Social control. Unemployment Insurance Act (1941). Wages. 1910-41. *202*
—. Byrnes, James F. Germany. Memoirs. Nuclear Science and Technology. Szilard, Leo. 1898-1945. *948*
—. Canada. Physical Education and Training. Sport. 1909-54. *1028*
—. Canada. Physical fitness programmes. 1850-1972. *314*
—. Canada. Provincial Government. 1940-74. *882*
—. Canadian Labour Congress. Cooperative Commonwealth Federation. Industrial relations. Trades and Labour Congress. 1939-46. *565*
—. Documents (accessibility of). 1972. *697*
—. Geography. 1941-45. *926*
—. Great Britain. Jews. Morgenthau, Henry, Jr. Relief organizations. War Refugee Board. 1940-44. *726*
—. Intelligence service. 1941-77. *123*
—. Propaganda. Radio. *Treasury Star Parade* (program). 1942-43. *564*
Federal Government (response). Europe. Jews. USA. War crimes. 1938-45. *5*
Federal Policy. Blair, Frederick Charles. Canada. Jews. Refugees. 1930's. *2*
—. Defense Policy. Industry. Labor Unions and Organizations. 1939-41. *873*
Federal programs. Employment. Women (status of). 1941-45. *929*
Federal-local relations. Cities (functions). Intergovernmental system. Public Finance. 1930's-74. *815*
Fellowship of Reconciliation. Antiwar Sentiment. 1940-41. *1075*
Feminism. Lloyd, Lola Maverick. Peace Movements. 1914-44. *921*
Fermi, Enrico. Anderson, Herbert L. (reminiscences). Chicago, University of. Columbia University. Nuclear Science and Technology. Szilard, Leo. 1933-45. *20*
Field Artillery Battalion, 920th. France (Metz). 3d Army, US. 1944. *18*
Fighter squadrons, night. Air Warfare. Atomic Warfare. Baldwin, Paul H. (account). Philippines. 1942-45. *44*

Film. Comedians. Marx, Groucho. 1940's. *925*
—. Hollywood. Latin Americans (image). 1939-46. *1054*
Films. 1941-45. *890*
—. *Air Power* (television series). History. Wolff, Perry. 1939-56. *8*
—. Anti-Nazi Movements. *Confessions of a Nazi Spy* (film). Espionage. German-American Bund. 1938-40. *826*
—. Armies. Documentaries. Heisler, Stuart. *Negro Soldier* (film). Propaganda. Race Relations. 1944. *195*
—. Books. War. 1940's-70's. *845*
—. British Columbia. Naval Vessels. Submarines. World War I. 1914-45. *156*
—. Canada. National Film Board of Canada. Sex roles. Women. 1940's-50's. *594*
—. Capra, Frank. *Prelude to War* (film). Propaganda. 1939-42. *916*
—. Davis, Elmer. Hollywood. Office of War Information, Bureau of Intelligence. Propaganda. 1942-43. *96*
—. Fantasy. Heroes. 1943-45. *991*
—. Foreign Relations. Hollywood. USA. USSR. 1939-44. *879*
—. Germans (image of). Stereotypes. 1914-45. *689*
—. Heroes. USSR. 1910-45. *722*
—. History Teaching. Maine, University of. World War I. 20c. *846*
—. History Teaching. Muskingum College. Ohio (New Concord). 1971-72. *931*
—. Hollywood. Liberalism. National Self-image. Office of War Information. 1942-45. *494*
—. Hollywood. Propaganda. 1940-45. *619*
—. Marines. 1920's-75. *934*
—. Propaganda. 1942-45. *436*
—. Propaganda. Public opinion. *Why We Fight* series. 1941-45. *562*
—. Public Opinion (American). USSR. 1939-47. *881*
Films (accuracy). Historical license. *Meeting at Potsdam* (film). Potsdam Conference. Truman, Harry S. 1945. 1970's. *310*
Films (analysis of). Hollywood. Office of War Information. Propaganda. 1942-43. *95*
Films, documentary. Ford, John. Propaganda. 1941-42. *663*
Finnie, Richard Sterling (account). Arctic. Discovery and Exploration. North America. Office of the Coordinator of Information. Stefansson, Vilhjalmur. 1931-62. *290*
Fire Department. Hawaii (Honolulu). Hickam Field. Pearl Harbor, attack on. 1941. *110*
Fishbein, Morris (obituary). Historians. Medicine. 1977. *215*
Flag, American. Iwo Jima (battle). Photograph, famous. 1945. *299*
Flag salute. Conscientious Objectors. Courts. Jehovah's Witnesses. 1930's-40's. *387*
Flight testing. Army Air Corps. Supersonic planes. SX-1 aircraft. Yeager, Charles. 1944-75. *673*
Flight training. Aeronautics, Military. BT-13A (aircraft). Strunk, Al (account). 1941-45. *930*
—. Armies. Helicopters. 1944-68. *979*
—. Army Air Forces. 1942-45. *261*
—. Army Air Forces. Bernhard, George K., Jr. (account). PT-17 (aircraft). 1942-45. *81*
—. Hutchinson Naval Air Station. Kansas. Naval Air Forces. Olathe Naval Air Station. 1942-69. *441*
—. Military General Staff. Negroes. Parrish, Noel F. (interview). Tuskegee Army Air Field. 1941-45. *393*
Florida. Camp Blanding. Germans. Prisoners of war. 1942-46. *90*

Foreign policy 233

Florida (Boca Raton). Agriculture. Japanese Americans. Yamato colony. 1904-75. *750*
Florida (Pensacola). Naval Air Forces. Urbanization. 1900-45. *609*
Flying Tigers. Aeronautics, Military. Arizona. Germany, West. Scott, Robert L., Jr. 1941-45. 1955-57. *936*
—. Aeronautics, Military. Burma. China. 1941-77. *940*
—. Air Warfare. Army Air Forces. China. Holloway, Bruce K. (account). P-40 (aircraft). 1942-43. *424*
—. Air warfare. Chennault, Claire Lee. China. Japan. 1941-45. *408*
Flying Tigers motifs. Air Warfare. American Volunteer Group. China. Shoulder patches. 23d Fighter Group. 1930's-45. *191*
Folktales. Vietnam War. 1941-71. *7*
Food shortages. Puerto Rico. Unemployment, rural. 1940-45. *280*
Ford, Gerald R. Citizenship. Hada, John. Japanese American Citizens League. Pardon. Tokyo Rose (Iva Toguri d'Aquino). Uyeda, Clifford I. (account). 1973-77. *990*
Ford, John. Films, documentary. Propaganda. 1941-42. *663*
Foreign Broadcast Information Service. Intelligence Service. State Department (Foreign Service). World War II (antecedents). 1939-41. *178*
Foreign Investments. Anderson, Irvine H., Jr. (review article). Asia, East. Foreign policy. Oil Industry and Trade. Standard-Vacuum Oil Company. 1933-41. 1975. *725*
—. Axis powers. Chile. Economic Conditions. 1939-45. *11*
Foreign policy. Alliances. Decisionmaking. Domestic Policy. Roosevelt, Franklin D. (administration). UN Conference on Food and Agriculture. Virginia (Hot Springs). 1943. *1041*
—. Allison, Graham (*Essence of Decision*). Atomic Warfare. Committees. Decisionmaking. 1944-75. *865*
—. Alperovitz, Gar. Atomic Weapons. Cold War (review article). Europe, Eastern. Horowitz, David. Kolko, Gabriel. 1943-50. *779*
—. Anderson, Irvine H., Jr. (review article). Asia, East. Foreign Investments. Oil Industry and Trade. Standard-Vacuum Oil Company. 1933-41. 1975. *725*
—. Appeasement. Chamberlain, Arthur Neville. Great Britain. Roosevelt, Franklin Delano. USA. 1937-39. *1012*
—. Appeasement. Germany. 1933-36. *836*
—. Appeasement. Germany. Great Britain. International Trade. 1933-40. *690*
—. Arab-Israeli Conflict. Conflict and Conflict Resolution. Decisionmaking. Japan. 1941-45. 1967-73. *76*
—. Argentina. Hull, Cordell. Ramírez, Pedro. USA. 1943. *1060*
—. Argentina. UN membership. USA. 1942-45. *1058*
—. Atomic Warfare. Gowing, Margaret. Great Britain. Nuclear Science and Technology (review article). Sherwin, Martin J. 1938-52. *529*
—. Attitudes. Executive Behavior. Political Protest. Roosevelt, Franklin D. 1940-72. *1092*
—. Axis Powers. Latin America. Office of the Coordinator of Inter-American Affairs. Rockefeller, Nelson A. Roosevelt, Franklin D. (administration). 1933-42. *364*
—. Balkans. 1939-41. *953*
—. Berlin, Isaiah. Congress. Great Britain. USA. 1943. *355*
—. Borg thesis. Georgia. Press. Quarantine speech. Roosevelt, Franklin D. 1937. *132*
—. Bulgaria. 1944. *116*
—. Bulgaria. Communist Party. 1943-44. *969*
—. Bulgaria. Intervention. USSR. 1944-47. *855*
—. Canada. China. International Trade. Odlum, Victor Wentworth. ca 1944-49. *683*
—. Canada. Great Britain. USA. 1939-45. *332*
—. Canada. Planning. 1943-45. *661*
—. China. Churchill, Winston. de Gaulle, Charles. French colonies. Indochina. Roosevelt, Franklin D. 1942-45. *507*
—. China. Cohen, Warren I. (review article). Japan. Leadership. Public opinion. ca 1900-50. 1978. *205*
—. China. Service, John Stewart (*Lost Chance in China*, excerpts). State Department (Foreign Service). USA. 1945-50's. *857*
—. *Christian Century* (periodical). Japan. Manchurian crisis. Morrison, Charles C. USA. 1931-33. *719*
—. Churchill, Winston. Great Britain. Military preparedness. USA. World War II (antecedents). 1933-39. 1976. *560*
—. Churchill, Winston. Political Leadership. Roosevelt, Franklin D. Stalin, Joseph. 1939-45. *1107*
—. Codes, secret. Cryptography. 1789-1942. *410*
—. Cold War. Diplomacy, atomic. Nuclear Arms. USA. USSR. 1942-46. *85*
—. Committee for Political Defense. Latin America. State Department. 1942-45. *825*
—. Conference on Security and Cooperation in Europe (1969). Europe, Eastern. Treaties. USA. USSR. 1945-75. *148*
—. Congress. Executive Power. 1789-1972. *848*
—. Congress. Presidency. War powers. 1787-1972. *772*
—. Conservatism. Isolationism. 1930's-52. *801*
—. Curtiss-Wright Corp. France. Great Britain. P-40 (H-81; aircraft). 1938-40. *389*
—. Dallek, Robert (review article). Roosevelt, Franklin D. 1932-45. 1979. *446*
—. Defense Policy. Generations. 1941-74. *799*
—. Defensive war argument. Ideology. War. 1941-73. *958*
—. Democracies. Developing Nations. Dictatorships. Nixon, Richard M. USA. 1790-1975. *138*
—. Diplomacy. International Trade. Japan. World War II (antecedents). 1937-41. *988*
—. Eden, Anthony. Molotov, V. M. Poland. Truman, Harry S. USSR. 1945. *635*
—. Embargo, de facto. Japan. Oil. Roosevelt, Franklin D. 1941. *22*
—. Europe, Central. Germany. Isolationism. USA. 1918-41. *1051*
—. Europe, Central. USA. World War II (antecedents). 1918-41. *1050*
—. Europe, East. Isolationism. Neutrality Laws. Roosevelt, Franklin D. World War II (antecedents). 1920's-30's. *249*
—. France. Great Britain. Indochina. USA. 1942-45. *961*
—. France. Preparedness. Surrender. 1940-44. *549*
—. Genocide. Jews. 1939-45. *286*
—. Germany. Messersmith, George. Nazism. 1933-45. *654*
—. Gleason, Sarell Everett (obituary). Historians. 1905-74. *530*
—. Great Britain. Greece. 1941-45. *1048*
—. Great Britain. Independence Movements. India. 1900-47. *220*
—. Great Britain. Neutrality. Spain. 1939-45. *266*
—. Great Britain. Palestine. USA. 1941-45. *183*
—. Great Britain. Poland. USA. 1945. *956*

234 Foreign policy

—. Great Britain. USA. USSR. Warsaw uprising. 1944. *556*
—. Harriman, W. Averell. Poland. USA. USSR. Warsaw Ghetto Uprising. 1943-44. *167*
—. Hawaii. Preparedness. Roosevelt, Franklin D. Works Progress Administration. 1935-40. *763*
—. Hearst, William Randolph. Isolationism. Newspapers. 1936-41. *157*
—. Historiography (neorevisionist; review article). Kolko, Gabriel. Kolko, Joyce. Williams, William Appleman. 1975. *851*
—. Hopkins, Harry. Roosevelt, Franklin D. USSR. 1938-46. *576*
—. Illinois (Chicago). Poland. Polish-American Congress. Roosevelt, Franklin D. 1944. *820*
—. Internationalism. Norris, George W. 1939-41. *351*
—. Internationalism. Truman, Harry S. 1935-45. *636*
—. Japan. Netherlands East Indies. 1941-46. *426*
—. Japan. Oil exports, restricted. State Department. USA. 1940-41. *989*
—. Japan. Oil industry. USA. 1934-37. *645*
—. Korea. 1941-45. *595*
—. Latin America. Military Strategy. USA. 1850-1976. *168*
—. MacArthur, Douglas. Military. Philippines. 1945-46. *262*
—. Mass Media. Public opinion. USA. USSR. ca 1939-49. *880*
—. Middle East. 1941-45. *383*
—. Middle East. Palestine. Roosevelt, Franklin D. USA. 1943-45. *710*
—. Nationalism. UN. USA. 1944-45. *152*
—. NATO. UN. 1941-55. *71*
—. Poland. Roosevelt, Franklin D. Truman, Harry S. USA. USSR. 1943-46. *558*
—. Potsdam Conference. Presidents. Truman, Harry S. 1945. *570*
—. Public opinion. Roosevelt, Franklin D. USSR. 1941-45. *679*
—. Roosevelt, Franklin D. USA. USSR. 1933-45. *443*
—. Roosevelt, Franklin D. USSR. 1933-45. *442*
Foreign Policy (balance of power, multipolar). USA. World War II (antecedents). 1930's. 1970's. *122*
Foreign Policy (critics). Anti-Imperialism. Pacific Area. Roosevelt, Franklin D. World War II (antecedents). 1930's. *704*
Foreign policy decisions. Roosevelt, Franklin D. 1940-45. *678*
Foreign Policy (Pacific area). Military preparedness. Military Strategy. USA. 1940-41. *505*
Foreign Policy (preconceptions). Japan. USA. World War II (antecedents). 1976. *74*
Foreign Policy (review article). Darilek, Richard E. Leigh, Michael. Levering, Ralph B. Public opinion. 1936-47. 1976. *315*
—. Diaries. Roosevelt, Franklin D. (administration). Stettinius, Edward Reilley. 1943-46. 1975. *483*
—. Europe. Japan. Offner, Arnold A. USA. 1917-41. *677*
Foreign Relations. Alliances. Portugal. 1940-41. *944*
—. Alperovitz, Gar. Atomic Warfare. World War II (review article). 1945. *378*
—. American Revolution. deGaulle, Charles. Europe, Western. France. Versailles, Treaty of. 1773-1979. *498*
—. Anti-Fascist Movements. Italy. Sforza, Carlo. 1940-43. *626*
—. Argentina. USA. 1940's. *672*

—. Asia. Callahan, Raymond. Great Britain. Louis, William Roger. Lowe, Peter. World War II (review article). 1939-45. *12*
—. Australia. 20c. *625*
—. Australia. Bell, Roger. Economic Aid. 1941-46. *1082*
—. Australia. Japan. Pacific Area. Peace settlement. USA. 1942-46. *70*
—. Australia. Military Bases. National Security. 1944-46. *69*
—. Australia. USA. 1939-42. *48*
—. Bolivia. Germany. Nazism. USA. 1941-46. *99*
—. Brazil. McCann, Frank D. 1937-45. *1087*
—. British Commonwealth. Canada. Ireland. Neutrality. 1939-45. *607*
—. Canada. Diplomacy. Latin America. Pan-American Union. USA. 1939-44. *664*
—. Canada. King, William Lyon Mackenzie. USA. 1939-45. *330*
—. China. Stilwell, Joseph W. 1942-70's. *866*
—. China. USA. Wedemeyer, Albert C. (reminiscences). 1920-48. *1020*
—. Churchill, Winston. Great Britain. Lash, Joseph P. (review article). Roosevelt, Franklin D. 1939-41. 1976. *227*
—. Churchill, Winston. Great Britain. Roosevelt, Franklin D. 1939-45. *782*
—. *City of Flint* (vessel; capture). Contraband. Germany. Ships. USSR. 1939. *177*
—. Conscription, military. Great Britain. Ireland. Northern Ireland. 1941. *795*
—. Consular dispatches. Eden, Anthony. Great Britain. Lindsay, Ronald. 1937. *360*
—. Culbertson, William S. Economic policy. Great Britain. Middle East. USA. 1944-45. *219*
—. Documents. Taylor, Myron. USA. Vatican. 1940-42. *6*
—. Economic agreements. Neutrality. Switzerland. World War I. 1919. 1944-45. *292*
—. Economic Aid. Great Britain. Saudi Arabia. State Department (Near East Affairs Division). 1941-45. *809*
—. Films. Hollywood. USA. USSR. 1939-44. *879*
—. France. Lafayette myth. National Characteristics. 1763-1976. *254*
—. Gandhi, Mahatma (arrest). Great Britain. India. Public Opinion. USA. 1942. *753*
—. George VI (visit). Great Britain. World War II (antecedents). 1939. *783*
—. Great Britain. Navies. Technology. USA. 1938-46. *532*
—. Great Britain. Nuclear Arms. Roosevelt, Franklin D. USA. 1940-45. *87*
—. International Security. Political Leadership. 1941-45. 1976. *734*
—. Japan. King, William. Thomas, Elbert. USA. Utah. ca 1922-40. *538*
—. Japan. Pittman, Key. USA. 1920-40. *537*
—. Latin America. Military Aid. Military Assistance Program. 1932-72. *41*
—. Portugal. Salazar, Antonio. 1939-45. *941*
—. Prisoners and prisons. Repatriation. USA. USSR. 1945. *136*
—. Soviet-American cooperation. USA. 1941-48. *862*
—. Sweden. USA. 1776-1970's. *844*
—. USA. USSR. 1917-76. *479*
Foreign Relations (documents series). Diplomacy. 1943-46. *528*
Foreign Relations of the United States (series). Research. 1940-50. 1978. *350*
Forestry. France. Great Britain. Military Intelligence. USA. 1943-47. *65*

Forrest, Nathan Bedford. Civil War. Forrest, Nathan Bedford (1905-44). Military Service. Sisk, John P. (personal account). 1861-1945. *870*
Forrest, Nathan Bedford (1905-44). Civil War. Forrest, Nathan Bedford. Military Service. Sisk, John P. (personal account). 1861-1945. *870*
Fort Reno. Oklahoma. Prisoners of War. 1943-46. *1045*
Fort Wallace. Hunting grounds, deprivation of. Indian-White Relations. Kansas. Settlers, protection for. 1865-82. *440*
Foster, W. W. Canada. Canol (project). Oil Industry and Trade. USA. War Department. 1942-45. *54*
"Four Stackers". Antisubmarine warfare. Great Britain. Navies. USA. 1940-45. *120*
Fram, Leon (reminiscences). Anti-Nazi Movements. Boycotts. Jews. League for Human Rights. Michigan (Detroit). 1930's-40's. *296*
France. Africa (north, west). International Trade. Lend-Lease. USA. 1941-46. *242*
—. Ambulance services. American Field Service. Andrew, Piatt. World War I (medical and sanitary affairs). 1914-45. *337*
—. American Revolution. deGaulle, Charles. Europe, Western. Foreign Relations. Versailles, Treaty of. 1773-1979. *498*
—. Archives. Diplomacy. 1939-45. 1979. *217*
—. Bombing. Military Strategy. Operation Overlord. Zuckerman, Solly (review article). 1944. *484*
—. Canada. deGaulle, Charles. Propaganda. Quebec. Vichy Regime. 1940-42. *193*
—. Curtiss-Wright Corp. Foreign Policy. Great Britain. P-40 (H-81; aircraft). 1938-40. *389*
—. deGaulle, Charles. Diplomacy. Great Britain. Indochina. 1940-45. *246*
—. Falaise (battle). France (Normandy). Military Strategy. Operation Cobra. Patton, George S., Jr. USA. 1944. *751*
—. Foreign Policy. Great Britain. Indochina. USA. 1942-45. *961*
—. Foreign Policy. Preparedness. Surrender. 1940-44. *549*
—. Foreign Relations. Lafayette myth. National Characteristics. 1763-1976. *254*
—. Forestry. Great Britain. Military Intelligence. USA. 1943-47. *65*
—. Germany. Great Britain. Partition. Roshchin, A. A. (memoirs). USSR. 1942-45. *797*
—. Great Britain. Nuclear arms testing. Secrecy. 1939-45. *327*
—. Haygood, William Converse. Letters. Luxembourg. USA. 1945. *396*
—. Intellectuals. Maritain, Raïssa. Nationalism. Poetry. USA. 1940-60. *938*
—. Lorraine campaign. Metz (battle). Patton, George S., Jr. Third Army. 1944. *46*
—. Normandy invasion. St. Lô (battle). USA. 1944. *162*
—. Roosevelt, Franklin D. 1938-45. *281*
—. USA. World War II (antecedents). 1939-40. *240*
France (Metz). Field Artillery Battalion, 920th. 3d Army, US. 1944. *18*
France (Normandy). Armies. Cawthon, Charles (reminiscences). 1944. *161*
—. Falaise (battle). France. Military Strategy. Operation Cobra. Patton, George S., Jr. USA. 1944. *751*
France, Vichy. Africa, North. Diplomacy. Economic Policy. USA. 1941-43. *97*
Franck, James. Atomic bomb. Nuclear arms race. Political Attitudes. Truman, Harry S. (administration). 1944-45. *1000*

—. Atomic bomb. Policymaking. Scientists. Stimson, Henry L. 1945. *918*
Frankfurter, Felix. Lippmann, Walter. New Deal. Roosevelt, Franklin D. 1932-45. *721*
Free ports. Diplomacy. Norway. Roosevelt, Franklin Delano. USA. USSR. 1941-43. *788*
Free trade. Economic threat. World War II (antecedents). 1930's-41. *993*
Freedom of the Press. Editorials. Newspapers. 1920. 1940. *113*
French. Africa (landing). Diplomacy. Great Britain. 1941-42. *760*
French Canadians. Angers, François-Albert. Canada. Catholic Church. Pacifism. Values. 1940-79. *349*
—. Canada. Military Service. 1939-45. *336*
French colonies. China. Churchill, Winston. de Gaulle, Charles. Foreign Policy. Indochina. Roosevelt, Franklin D. 1942-45. *507*
French, Paul C. Conscientious Objectors. Conscription, Military (hearings). Friends, Society of. Wilson, E. Raymond (personal account). 1940. *1042*
Fribourg, Leonard. Grainger, Edmund. Hollywood. Marines (image). *Sands of Iwo Jima* (film). Wayne, John. 1949. *935*
Friedman, Saul S. (review article). Genocide. Jews. Public Policy. Refugees. Roosevelt, Franklin D. (administration). 1938-45. 1973. *790*
Friends' Ambulance Unit. Canada. China Convoy. Oral history. 1939-45. *899*
Friends, Society of. Conscientious Objectors. Conscription, Military (hearings). French, Paul C. Wilson, E. Raymond (personal account). 1940. *1042*
Friendship. Literature. Morality. Politics. Pound, Ezra. Treason. 1909-72. *192*
Frisch, Otto R. (account). Atomic Warfare. Nuclear Physics. 1945. *307*
Fund raising. Genocide. Joint Distribution Committee. Judaism (Orthodox). Rescue work. Yeshiva Aid Committee. 1939-41. *1081*
Fundamentalism. Gaebelin, Arno C. Genocide. Germany. Jews. *Our Hope* (periodical). 1937-45. *768*
F-105 (aircraft). Aircraft markings. National Guard. Virginia. 192d Tactical Fighter Group. 1917-79. *544*
F4U (aircraft). Air warfare. Marines. Pacific Area. Zero (aircraft). 1943-45. *419*
F6F (aircraft). Harp, A. Norman (account). Naval Air Forces. 1945. *384*
F6F Hellcats (aircraft). Airplanes, Military. Japan. Truk Islands. USA. 1944. *966*

G

Gabriel, Richard A. Armies (review article). Bureaucracies. Military (officers). Savage, Paul L. 1914-80. *64*
Gaebelin, Arno C. Fundamentalism. Genocide. Germany. Jews. *Our Hope* (periodical). 1937-45. *768*
Gandhi, Mahatma (arrest). Foreign Relations. Great Britain. India. Public Opinion. USA. 1942. *753*
Garden clubs. ca 1875-1978. *662*
Garrison duty. Canada. Caribbean. Great Britain. Military. 1914-45. *665*
Gato (vessel). Navigation, bush. Solomon Islands. Submarine Warfare. 1943. *608*
Gavin, James M. (memoirs). Airborne troops. Armies. Invasions. Sicily. 1943. *313*
General Board of the Navy. Amphibious warfare. Marines. Naval Strategy. 1900-74. *688*

236 Generations

Generations. Defense Policy. Foreign policy. 1941-74. *799*
Geneva Convention. Prisoners of War (Germans). USA. 1941-45. *496*
Genocide. Attitudes. Immigration. Jews. 1880's-1940's. *590*
—. Bergson, Peter. Emergency Committee to Save the Jewish People of Europe. Rescues. Zionism. 1943-45. *723*
—. Christians. Jews. Theology. 1945-74. *259*
—. Concentration camps. Germany. Jews. Press. 1939-42. *348*
—. Europe. Jews. Public Policy. Roosevelt, Franklin D. (administration). 1942-44. *596*
—. Foreign Policy. Jews. 1939-45. *286*
—. Friedman, Saul S. (review article). Jews. Public Policy. Refugees. Roosevelt, Franklin D. (administration). 1938-45. 1973. *790*
—. Fund raising. Joint Distribution Committee. Judaism (Orthodox). Rescue work. Yeshiva Aid Committee. 1939-41. *1081*
—. Fundamentalism. Gaebelin, Arno C. Germany. Jews. *Our Hope* (periodical). 1937-45. *768*
—. Germany. Great Britain. Jews. Rescues. 1939-44. *283*
—. Germany. Historiography. Jews. Psychology. 1940's. *514*
Genocide (review article). Historiography. Jews. Refugees. Wiesel, Elie. 1939-45. 1960-79. *1077*
Genocide, toleration of. Germany. Immigration laws. Jews. Refugees. Roosevelt, Franklin D. (administration). 1933-45. *282*
Geography. Federal Government. 1941-45. *926*
—. Map Drawing. 1938-79. *789*
George VI (visit). Foreign Relations. Great Britain. World War II (antecedents). 1939. *783*
Georgi Sedov (vessel). Arctic. Newfoundland. USSR. World War I. 1908-67. *51*
Georgia. Borg thesis. Foreign Policy. Press. Quarantine speech. Roosevelt, Franklin D. 1937. *132*
German Americans. Democratic Party. Isolationism. Kentucky (Kenton County). 1930-40. *247*
—. Diamond, Sander A. (review article). Nazism. USA. 1924-41. 1974. *284*
—. New York City. Pharmacy. Societies, apothecary. 19c-1940's. *1008*
German Canadians. Deutscher Bund Canada. Nazism. Saskatchewan. 1934-39. *1005*
German-American Bund. Anti-Nazi Movements. *Confessions of a Nazi Spy* (film). Espionage. Films. 1938-40. *826*
—. Coughlin, Charles. Countersubversives. Fascism (review article). Nazism, American (review article). 1924-41. *785*
Germans. Arkansas. Italians. Labor, contract. Prisoners of War. 1943-46. *758*
—. Camp Blanding. Florida. Prisoners of war. 1942-46. *90*
—. Employment. Minnesota. Prisoners of war. 1942-46. *743*
—. Labor, prison. New York, western. Prisoners of War (camps). 1944-46. *598*
—. Prisoners of war. Texas. 1943-46. *497*
—. Prisoners of war. Texas. 1943-46. *967*
—. Prisoners of war. Virginia. 1943-46. *648*
—. Prisoners of War (camps). South Carolina. 1944-46. *650*
Germans (image of). Films. Stereotypes. 1914-45. *689*
Germany. Air Forces. Bombing, indiscriminate. Civilian targets. Ethics. Military General Staff. 1941-45. *837*
—. Air raids. Air Warfare. Jablonski, Edward (review article). Regensburg-Schweinfurt. USA. 1943. *380*

—. Air Warfare. Bombing. B-17 (aircraft). Poltava (battle). USSR. 1944. *445*
—. Air Warfare. Bombing. Dresden (attack on). Great Britain. Total war. 1914-45. *181*
—. Air Warfare. Bombing. Great Britain. Military Strategy. 1942-44. *994*
—. Air Warfare (personal accounts). USA. 1942. *111*
—. Airborne units. Great Britain. 1935-45. *765*
—. Allies. Berlin (capture). Military Strategy. 1941-45. *466*
—. Allies. Military occupation. Partition. 1943-48. *475*
—. Allies. Military Strategy. Weapons. 1944-45. *715*
—. Anabaptists. Mennonites. Switzerland. Taxation. War. 16c-1973. *489*
—. Appeasement. Foreign policy. 1933-36. *836*
—. Appeasement. Foreign policy. Great Britain. International Trade. 1933-40. *690*
—. Arkansas. Prisoners of war. 1943-46. *757*
—. Bolivia. Foreign Relations. Nazism. USA. 1941-46. *99*
—. Bridges. Remagen (battle). 1945. *165*
—. Brown, Anthony Cave. Great Britain. Kahn, David. Military Intelligence (review article). 1939-45. *518*
—. Bulge (battle). Military Strategy. 1944. *714*
—. Byrnes, James F. Federal Government. Memoirs. Nuclear Science and Technology. Szilard, Leo. 1898-1945. *948*
—. *City of Flint* (vessel; capture). Contraband. Foreign relations. Ships. USSR. 1939. *177*
—. Clay, Lucius D. Documents. Military General Staff (meetings). Military government. Office of Military Government for Germany (US). US Group Control Council, Germany. 1944-49. *917*
—. Clay, Lucius D. (appointment). Military occupation. USA. 1945. *889*
—. Collectivism. Dennis, Lawrence. Political Commentary. Public Opinion. 1941-45. *233*
—. Communications. Submarine Warfare. USA. 1939-45. *653*
—. Concentration camps. Genocide. Jews. Press. 1939-42. *348*
—. Czechoslovakia. Diplomatic recognition. Government-in-exile. USA. 1939-45. *533*
—. Czechoslovakia (Prague). Invasions. Patton, George S., Jr. USSR. Vlasov, Andrei. 1945. *804*
—. Diplomacy. Espionage. Nazis. Thomsen, Hans. 1940. *634*
—. Diplomacy. Lane, Arthur B. Yugoslavia. 1940-41. *933*
—. Diplomacy. Roosevelt, Franklin D. USSR. 1934-39. *572*
—. Europe, Central. Foreign policy. Isolationism. USA. 1918-41. *1051*
—. Foreign policy. Messersmith, George. Nazism. 1933-45. *654*
—. France. Great Britain. Partition. Roshchin, A. A. (memoirs). USSR. 1942-45. *797*
—. Fundamentalism. Gaebelin, Arno C. Genocide. Jews. *Our Hope* (periodical). 1937-45. *768*
—. Genocide. Great Britain. Jews. Rescues. 1939-44. *283*
—. Genocide. Historiography. Jews. Psychology. 1940's. *514*
—. Genocide, toleration of. Immigration laws. Jews. Refugees. Roosevelt, Franklin D. (administration). 1933-45. *282*
—. Halle, Louis J. (reminiscences). Koichwitz, Otto ("O.K."). Propaganda. Teachers. USA. 1920's-40's. *371*
—. Intelligence service. USA. 1933-41. *277*
—. Jews. Prisoners of war. USA. Winograd, Leonard (reminiscences). 1944-45. *1047*

Great Britain   237

—. Jews. Refugees. Relief organizations. USA. 1933-45. *316*
—. Jews (stateless). Morgenthau, Henry, Jr. State Department. Treasury Department. USA. 1942-44. *589*
—. Labor. Propaganda. Public opinion. Sex roles. Women. 1939-45. *814*
—. Military History. Ultra project. 1940-45. *906*
—. Military Strategy. 1933-39. *878*
—. National Reich Church (suggested). Propaganda campaign. Roosevelt, Franklin D. USA. World War II (antecedents). 1941. *187*
—. Peace Movements. Public Opinion. 1942. *915*
—. Propaganda (review article). Rupp, Leila J. Winkler, Allan M. Women. 1939-45. *373*
Germany (Berlin). Conspiracies. Hitler, Adolf. Prisoners of War. 1945. *907*
—. Eisenhower, Dwight D. Great Britain. Military Strategy. USSR. 1945. *495*
Germany (Ludwigshafen). Bache, William B. McAuliffe, Anthony. Personal narratives. 1945. *38*
Germany (partition). Churchill, Winston. Potsdam Conference. Roosevelt, Franklin D. Stettinius, Edward Reilley. Yalta Conference. 1945. *329*
Germany (Roer River). Simpson, William H. 9th Army, US. 1945. *927*
Germany, West. Aeronautics, Military. Arizona. Flying Tigers. Scott, Robert L., Jr. 1941-45. 1955-57. *936*
Ghana (Accra). Airplanes. China (Kunming). Laughlin, C. H. (reminiscences). 1942. *520*
Ghost towns. Arizona (Raso). Railroad stations. Southern Pacific Railroad. 1911-76. *670*
Gibbon, Elwyn B. (memoirs). Asia. Pilots. 1937-42. *524*
Gifts. Executive Order No. 1. MacArthur, Douglas. Military General Staff. Philippines. Quezon, Manuel. Sutherland, Richard K. (papers). 1942. *733*
Gila River Relocation Center. Arizona. Concentration camps. Japanese Americans. Public Opinion. Race Relations. 1942-45. *159*
Gilbert Islands. Haley, J. Frederick (account). Marines. Reconnaissance. Tarawa (battle). 1943. *368*
—. Japan. Makin Islands (raid). Marines (2d Raiders). Peatross, Oscar F. (account). Prisoners of War. 1942-47. *720*
—. Marines. Tarawa (battle). 1943. *130*
Gleason, Sarell Everett (obituary). Foreign Policy. Historians. 1905-74. *530*
Gliders. Air Forces. Riddle, Jack (interview). 1942-45. *175*
Gold Star (vessel). Guam. Navies. USA. 1941-42. *506*
Goldsworthy, Harry E. (personal account). Borinquen Field ("battle"). Puerto Rico. 1941. *322*
Government. Armies. Discrimination. Great Britain. Negroes. 1942-45. *358*
—. Armistice question. Great Britain. Italy. Military Occupation. 1944. *29*
—. Rubber. Synthetic products. 1939-45. *900*
Government-in-exile. Czechoslovakia. Diplomatic recognition. Germany. USA. 1939-45. *533*
Governor General's Foot Guards. Canada. Military History. Militia. 1872-1972. *972*
Gowing, Margaret. Atomic Warfare. Foreign Policy. Great Britain. Nuclear Science and Technology (review article). Sherwin, Martin J. 1938-52. *529*

Grainger, Edmund. Fribourg, Leonard. Hollywood. Marines (image). *Sands of Iwo Jima* (film). Wayne, John. 1949. *935*
Grand Juries. Censorship. *Chicago Tribune*. Japan. Midway Island (attack on). Navies. 1942. *300*
Gray, Harold. Cartoonists. Depressions. "Little Orphan Annie", comic strip. Social conservatism. 1930's-40's. *1069*
Great Britain. Aeronautics, Military. Africa, North. Hurricane (aircraft). Ohlinger, John F. (account). 1942. *691*
—. Africa (landing). Diplomacy. French. 1941-42. *760*
—. Air Forces. Dunn, William R. (account). Eagle Squadron, No. 71. Spitfire (aircraft). 1941. *252*
—. Air Warfare. Bombing. Bowman, Marvin S. (reminiscences). USSR (Mirgorod, Poltava). 1944. *114*
—. Air Warfare. Bombing. Dresden (attack on). Germany. Total war. 1914-45. *181*
—. Air Warfare. Bombing. Germany. Military Strategy. 1942-44. *994*
—. Air Warfare. Churchill, Winston. Eaker, Ira C. (reminiscences). 1942-47. *256*
—. Air Warfare. Dunn, William R. (account). Royal Air Force. 1941. *251*
—. Airborne units. Germany. 1935-45. *765*
—. Antiaircraft gunnery. Inventions. Proximity fuse. 1939-45. *73*
—. Antisubmarine warfare. "Four Stackers". Navies. USA. 1940-45. *120*
—. Appeasement. Chamberlain, Arthur Neville. Foreign Policy. Roosevelt, Franklin Delano. USA. 1937-39. *1012*
—. Appeasement. Foreign policy. Germany. International Trade. 1933-40. *690*
—. Appeasement (proposal). Diplomacy. Japan. 1941. *328*
—. Apple industry. Exports. Imports. Nova Scotia (Annapolis Valley). 1880-1957. *186*
—. Armies. Discrimination. Government. Negroes. 1942-45. *358*
—. Armies. Discrimination. White, Walter F. 1943-44. *354*
—. Armistice question. Government. Italy. Military Occupation. 1944. *29*
—. Asia. Callahan, Raymond. Foreign Relations. Louis, William Roger. Lowe, Peter. World War II (review article). 1939-45. *12*
—. Asia, Southeast. Colonialism. Joint declaration (proposed). Roosevelt, Franklin D. (administration). USA. 1942-44. *1036*
—. Atlantic, battle of the. Navies. Roosevelt, Franklin D. Secrecy. Warmaking powers. 1941. *682*
—. Atlantic Ocean. Canada. Navies. USA. 1941-43. *557*
—. Atlantic Ocean, South. Neutrality (circumvention). Roosevelt, Franklin D. Takoradi air route. World War II (antecedents). 1941-42. *769*
—. Atomic Warfare. Foreign Policy. Gowing, Margaret. Nuclear Science and Technology (review article). Sherwin, Martin J. 1938-52. *529*
—. Australia. Diaries. MacArthur, Douglas. Philippines. Williamson, Gerald Hugh. 1942-43. *962*
—. Australia. Menzies, Robert Gordon. Military Aid. 1940. *263*
—. Berlin, Isaiah. Congress. Foreign policy. USA. 1943. *355*
—. Blockades. Chamberlain, Neville. China. Japan. Roosevelt, Franklin D. World War II (antecedents). 1937-38. *362*

Great Britain

—. Brown, Anthony Cave. Germany. Kahn, David. Military Intelligence (review article). 1939-45. *518*
—. California (Long Beach). *Queen Mary* (vessel). Ships. ca 1930-74. *566*
—. Canada. Caribbean. Garrison duty. Military. 1914-45. *665*
—. Canada. Dieppe (air battle). Leigh-Mallory, Trafford. Royal Canadian Air Force. 1942. *151*
—. Canada. Foreign policy. USA. 1939-45. *332*
—. Canada. Hyde Park Declaration (1941). Military finance. USA. 1939-41. *331*
—. Canada. International Trade. USA. 1943-47. *109*
—. Canada. Military Finance. 1943-45. *334*
—. Canada. Prisoners of war, German. 1940-47. *477*
—. Cane, Cyril H. Diplomatic reports. Michigan (Detroit). Riots. 1943. *359*
—. China. Extraterritoriality. Treaties. 1929-43. *164*
—. China. International Relations (discipline). Japan. USA. USSR. 1937-49. *736*
—. Churchill, Winston. Correspondence. Neutrality. Roosevelt, Franklin D. 1939-40. *531*
—. Churchill, Winston. Diplomacy. Kennedy, Joseph P. Roosevelt, Franklin D. (administration). 1938-40. *997*
—. Churchill, Winston. Diplomacy. Military Strategy. Roosevelt, Franklin D. 1942-44. *999*
—. Churchill, Winston. Foreign policy. Military preparedness. USA. World War II (antecedents). 1933-39. 1976. *560*
—. Churchill, Winston. Foreign Relations. Lash, Joseph P. (review article). Roosevelt, Franklin D. 1939-41. 1976. *227*
—. Churchill, Winston. Foreign Relations. Roosevelt, Franklin D. 1939-45. *782*
—. Churchill, Winston. Joint Chiefs of Staff. Malta Conference. Military Strategy. Roosevelt, Franklin D. 1945. *912*
—. Churchill, Winston. USA. White House Map Room. 1944. *491*
—. Churchill, Winston (correspondence). Roosevelt, Franklin D. (correspondence). USA. 1938-45. *481*
—. Cold War. Europe, Eastern. "Percentages" agreement. Roosevelt, Franklin D. USSR. 1944. *780*
—. Cold War (origins). Diplomacy (review article). USSR. 1941-48. *57*
—. Conscription, military. Foreign Relations. Ireland. Northern Ireland. 1941. *795*
—. Consular dispatches. Eden, Anthony. Foreign relations. Lindsay, Ronald. 1937. *360*
—. Culbertson, William S. Economic policy. Foreign Relations. Middle East. USA. 1944-45. *219*
—. Curtiss-Wright Corp. Foreign Policy. France. P-40 (H-81; aircraft). 1938-40. *389*
—. deGaulle, Charles. Diplomacy. France. Indochina. 1940-45. *246*
—. Denmark. Iceland. Independence Movements. USA. 1940-44. *457*
—. Diplomacy. Historiography. Langer, William L. (account). Vichy Regime. 1941-54. *512*
—. Diplomacy. Second front. USA. USSR. 1942-43. *1089*
—. Diplomacy. USA. Winant, John Gilbert. 1941-46. *1034*
—. Economic Aid. Foreign Relations. Saudi Arabia. State Department (Near East Affairs Division). 1941-45. *809*

—. Egypt. State Department. Suez Canal. 1930's-45. *47*
—. Eisenhower, Dwight D. Germany (Berlin). Military Strategy. USSR. 1945. *495*
—. Europe. Invasions (proposed). Military Strategy. 1942-44. *822*
—. Exchange programs. Medical research. USSR. ca 1941-45. *62*
—. Federal Government. Jews. Morgenthau, Henry, Jr. Relief organizations. War Refugee Board. 1940-44. *726*
—. Foreign Policy. France. Indochina. USA. 1942-45. *961*
—. Foreign Policy. Greece. 1941-45. *1048*
—. Foreign Policy. Independence Movements. India. 1900-47. *220*
—. Foreign Policy. Neutrality. Spain. 1939-45. *266*
—. Foreign Policy. Palestine. USA. 1941-45. *183*
—. Foreign policy. Poland. USA. 1945. *956*
—. Foreign Policy. USA. USSR. Warsaw uprising. 1944. *556*
—. Foreign Relations. Gandhi, Mahatma (arrest). India. Public Opinion. USA. 1942. *753*
—. Foreign Relations. George VI (visit). World War II (antecedents). 1939. *783*
—. Foreign Relations. Navies. Technology. USA. 1938-46. *532*
—. Foreign Relations. Nuclear Arms. Roosevelt, Franklin D. USA. 1940-45. *87*
—. Forestry. France. Military Intelligence. USA. 1943-47. *65*
—. France. Germany. Partition. Roshchin, A. A. (memoirs). USSR. 1942-45. *797*
—. France. Nuclear arms testing. Secrecy. 1939-45. *327*
—. Genocide. Germany. Jews. Rescues. 1939-44. *283*
—. Historiography. Military aid. Military Capability. USSR. 1941-75. *671*
—. Howard, Michael (review article). Mediterranean Sea and Area. Military Strategy. USA. 1942-43. *453*
—. Information exchange. Science. USSR. 1940-45. *63*
—. Japan. Navies (communications, tactics). USA. 1943-45. *225*
—. Lend-Lease. 1941-45. *885*
—. Lend-Lease. Naval Vessels (destroyer-escorts). 1943-45. *269*
—. Military Aid. Murrow, Edward R. Radio. 1939-41. *200*
—. Military Campaigns. 1942-45. *486*
—. Military Strategy. Singapore, defense of. USA. 1939-41. *49*
—. NATO. Naval Strategy. USA. USSR. 1945-70's. *646*
—. Navies. Pacific Area. Winton, John (review article). 1941-45. *170*
—. Ocean travel. *Queen Mary* (vessel). ca 1930-67. *103*
—. Okinawa (battle). Parker, Willard. Rescues. *Undine* (vessel). 1945. *409*
—. Physicians. USA. 1940. *61*
—. Second front. USSR. 1943-44. *1076*
Great Britain (Bamber Bridge). Army Air Force Station 569. Mutiny. Negroes. USA. 1943. *1025*
Great Britain (London). Agent general, office of. Canada. Intergovernmental Relations. 18c-20c. *886*
Greece. Airplanes, Military. Military Aid. Roosevelt, Franklin D. (administration). 1940-41. *666*
—. Foreign Policy. Great Britain. 1941-45. *1048*

Gregory (vessel). Japan (Bonin Islands). McCandless, Bruce (reminiscences). Navy. 1945. *603*

Griffith, Samuel B., Jr. (reminiscences). Guadalcanal (battle). Marines. Tulagi (battle). 1942-43. *346*

Ground crews. Army Air Forces. B-29 (aircraft). China. Johnston, Francis J. (account). Mariana Islands (Tinian). 1944-45. *462*

Groves, Leslie R. Atomic Warfare. Hirohito, Emperor. Japan (Nagasaki). Potsdam Conference. Truman, Harry S. 1944-45. *546*

Guadalcanal (battle). 1942. *830*
—. Griffith, Samuel B., Jr. (reminiscences). Marines. Tulagi (battle). 1942-43. *346*
—. Japan. USA. 1942-43. *716*
—. King, Ernest J. Marshall, George C. Navies. 1942-43. *135*

Guadalcanal (battle of). Armstrong, David M. (reminiscence). Sealark Channel (battle of). 1942. *31*

Guam. Barham, Wayne (reminiscences). Invasion. USA. 1944. *50*
—. *Gold Star* (vessel). Navies. 1941-42. *506*
—. Japan. Yokoi, Shoichi. 1944-72. *952*

Guam (liberation). Japan. USA. 1944. *155*

Guayule (plant). Agriculture Department. California. Emergency Rubber Project. Nishimura, Shimpe. Rubber industry. 1942-76. *36*

Guttmann-Lingoes Smallest Space Analysis. Alliance polarization. Diplomatic representation. Methodology. War. 1815-1973. *1007*

H

Habeas corpus. Emergencies, national. Executive power. Martial law. War. 1861-1944. *778*

Hada, John. Citizenship. Ford, Gerald R. Japanese American Citizens League. Pardon. Tokyo Rose (Iva Toguri d'Aquino). Uyeda, Clifford I. (account). 1973-77. *990*

Haley, J. Frederick (account). Gilbert Islands. Marines. Reconnaissance. Tarawa (battle). 1943. *368*

Halle, Louis J. (reminiscences). Germany. Koichwitz, Otto ("O.K."). Propaganda. Teachers. USA. 1920's-40's. *371*

Hamilton Air Force Base. California (San Rafael). Pacific Area. 1931-50. *382*

Hamilton Field. Airplanes, Military. Army Air Corps. California. Eaker, Ira C. Military Decorations, Flags, and Symbols. Wright, Howard T. (account). 1941. *1062*

Hammon, Stratton Owen (account). Air Bases (construction of). Civil-Military Relations. Kentucky (Louisville). Standiford Airfield. 1942-43. *377*

Harp, A. Norman (account). F6F (aircraft). Naval Air Forces. 1945. *384*

Harriman, W. Averell. Aeronautics, Military. Circumnavigations. Diplomacy. Lend-Lease. USSR. 1941. *323*
—. Beaverbrook, 1st Baron. Diplomacy. Military Aid. USSR. 1941. *510*
—. Cold War (origins). Diplomacy. Europe. USSR. 1943-45. *98*
—. Foreign policy. Poland. USA. USSR. Warsaw Ghetto Uprising. 1943-44. *167*

Harry S. Truman Library. Documents. Public Policy. Truman, Harry S. Western States. 1940-66. *460*

Hasek, Jaroslav (*The Good Soldier Schweik*). Antiwar Sentiment. Cartoons. Military life. ca 1920-70. *30*

Hashimoto, Mochitsura (account). Beach, Edward L. (account). *Indianapolis* (vessel; sinking). Navies. 1945. *1088*

Hasluck, Paul. Australia. Curtin, John. MacArthur, Douglas. Military Recruitment. 1942-43. *551*

Hastie, William. Military. Negroes. Racism. Stimson, Henry L. 1940-43. *610*

Hastie, William H. Armies. Military recruitment. Negroes. Press, black. 1940-42. *611*
—. Military reform. Racism. 1940-43. *612*

Hawaii. Armstrong, David M. (personal account). Japan. Pearl Harbor, attack on. 1942. *32*
—. Foreign policy. Preparedness. Roosevelt, Franklin D. Works Progress Administration. 1935-40. *763*
—. Hechler, Ted, Jr. (account). Navies. Pearl Harbor, attack on. *Phoenix* (vessel). 1941. *400*
—. Holmes, Wilfrid J. (account). Military Intelligence. Navies. Nimitz, Chester W. Pearl Harbor. 1941. *425*
—. Japan. Naval Vessels. Pearl Harbor (attack on). 1941. *1098*
—. *Oklahoma* (vessel). Pearl Harbor. 1916-47. *1097*

Hawaii (Honolulu). Fire Department. Hickam Field. Pearl Harbor, attack on. 1941. *110*

Hawaii National Park. Bombing ranges. Military. 1938-50. *452*

Hawaii, University of. Crawford, David L. Japan. Peace pact (proposed). USA. 1940-41. *428*

Hayes, Carlton J. H. Diplomacy. Historians. Spain. 1942-45. *372*
—. Jews. Refugees (rescue, relief). Spain. 1942-45. *1040*

Haygood, William Converse. France. Letters. Luxembourg. USA. 1945. *396*

Hearst, William Randolph. Foreign policy. Isolationism. Newspapers. 1936-41. *157*

Hechler, Ted, Jr. (account). Hawaii. Navies. Pearl Harbor, attack on. *Phoenix* (vessel). 1941. *400*

Heisler, Stuart. Armies. Documentaries. Films. *Negro Soldier* (film). Propaganda. Race Relations. 1944. *195*

Helicopters. Armies. Flight training. 1944-68. *979*

Heroes. Fantasy. Films. 1943-45. *991*
—. Films. USSR. 1910-45. *722*

Hersey, John (*Hiroshima*). Atomic Warfare. Literature. Morality. 1945-74. *1065*

Hewens, Bob. Atlantic Ocean (North). Canada. Navies. *Niagara* (vessel). *U-570* (vessel). 1934-72. *1043*

Hewitt, H. Kent. Amphibious operations. Navies. 1887-1949. *174*

Hickam Field. Fire Department. Hawaii (Honolulu). Pearl Harbor, attack on. 1941. *110*

Higgins, Andrew J. Amphibious operations. Landing craft. Shipbuilding. 1933-45. *655*

High School Victory Corps. Curricula. Patriotism. Physical Education and Training. Vocational Education. 1941-45. *983*

Higher education. 1941-42. *905*
—. Bookselling. Military history. 1945-70's. *631*

Highlanders, 48th. Canada. Hunter, William A. (reminiscences). Leftism. Liberalism. Military Service. 1939-45. *438*

Highway Engineering. Alaskan Highway. Logistics. Yukon Territory. 1942-43. *779*

Hirohito, Emperor. Atomic Warfare. Groves, Leslie R. Japan (Nagasaki). Potsdam Conference. Truman, Harry S. 1944-45. *546*

Hiroshima (attack on). Atomic Warfare. Decisionmaking. Japan. 1944-45. *828*

240 Historians

Historians. Air Warfare. Arnold, H. H. "Hap". Military Strategy. 1943-44. *708*
—. *Alabama Review* (periodical). Bibliographies. 1840's-1975. *615*
—. Diplomacy. Hayes, Carlton J. H. Spain. 1942-45. *372*
—. Fishbein, Morris (obituary). Medicine. 1977. *215*
—. Foreign Policy. Gleason, Sarell Everett (obituary). 1905-74. *530*
Historians, Western. Japan. Military defeat. Pacific Area. USSR. 1942-45. *832*
Historical license. Films (accuracy). *Meeting at Potsdam* (film). Potsdam Conference. Truman, Harry S. 1945. 1970's. *310*
Historical Sites and Parks. Commission for the Protection and Salvage of Artistic and Historic Monuments. Europe. USA. 1941-45. *365*
Historiography. Allies. Lend-Lease. USSR. 1941-45. *250*
—. Alperovitz, Gar. Diplomacy. Nuclear Arms. 1943-46. 1965-73. *571*
—. Alperovitz, Gar (review article). Atomic Warfare. Decisionmaking. Japan (Hiroshima). 1945-65. *859*
—. Asia. Immigration. ca 1849-1974. *206*
—. Battles. USSR. USSR. 1939-78. *818*
—. Battles. World War I. 1914-45. *473*
—. Canada. 1939-45. *243*
—. Canada. 1939-78. *343*
—. Canada. 1939-45. *344*
—. Canada. Press. World War II (antecedents). 1938-39. *591*
—. China. China. Stilwell, Joseph W. 1942-44. *1066*
—. Cold War. Diplomacy. Europe, Eastern. USA. 1942-74. *376*
—. Cold War. Nazism. Revisionism. ca 1930-50. *515*
—. Cold War (origins). 1946-75. *14*
—. Cold War (review article). Determinists. Left-revisionists. 1945-70. *482*
—. Diplomacy. Great Britain. Langer, William L. (account). Vichy Regime. 1941-54. *512*
—. Europe. 1939-75. *411*
—. Genocide. Germany. Jews. Psychology. 1940's. *514*
—. Genocide (review article). Jews. Refugees. Wiesel, Elie. 1939-45. 1960-79. *1077*
—. Great Britain. Military aid. Military Capability. USSR. 1941-75. *671*
—. Industry. Labor Unions and Organizations. 1941-45. *305*
—. Isolationism. 1930's-40's. *235*
—. Military Intelligence. 1941-45. *469*
—. Negroes. Roosevelt, Franklin D. (administration). USSR. 1939-45. *872*
—. Novels. Wouk, Herman (review article). 1940-80. *579*
Historiography (neorevisionist; review article). Foreign policy. Kolko, Gabriel. Kolko, Joyce. Williams, William Appleman. 1975. *851*
Historiography (revisionist). 1930's-79. *232*
—. Cold War (origins). 1941-48. *312*
—. Publishers and Publishing. Regnery, Henry (account). Truth, historical. 20c. *775*
History. *Air Power* (television series). Films. Wolff, Perry. 1939-56. *8*
—. American Antiquarian Society. Baxter, James Phinney, 3d (obituary). 1893-1975. *833*
History Teaching. Atomic Warfare. Japan. Simulation and Games. 1945. 1978. *265*
—. Civil War. Collectivization. Textbooks. USSR. USSR. 1917-79. *207*
—. Decisionmaking. Europe, Western. Simulation and Games. USA. War games. 1939-45. 1970's. *153*

—. Films. Maine, University of. World War I. 20c. *846*
—. Films. Muskingum College. Ohio (New Concord). 1971-72. *931*
Hitler, Adolf. Conspiracies. Germany (Berlin). Prisoners of War. 1945. *907*
Ho Chi Minh. China. Communism. Independence movement. USA. Vietnamese. 1942-45. *901*
Hodges, Courtney. Armored Vehicles and Tank Warfare. Remagen Bridge (battle of). 1944. *667*
Holland, Lou E. Employment. Nelson, Donald M. War Production Board, Smaller Plants Division and Corporation. 1940-44. *399*
Holloway, Bruce K. (account). Air Warfare. Army Air Forces. China. Flying Tigers. P-40 (aircraft). 1942-43. *424*
Hollywood. Davis, Elmer. Films. Office of War Information, Bureau of Intelligence. Propaganda. 1942-43. *96*
—. Film. Latin Americans (image). 1939-46. *1054*
—. Films. Foreign Relations. USA. USSR. 1939-44. *879*
—. Films. Liberalism. National Self-image. Office of War Information. 1942-45. *494*
—. Films. Propaganda. 1940-45. *619*
—. Films (analysis of). Office of War Information. Propaganda. 1942-43. *95*
—. Fribourg, Leonard. Grainger, Edmund. Marines (image). *Sands of Iwo Jima* (film). Wayne, John. 1949. *935*
Holmes, Wilfrid J. (account). Hawaii. Military Intelligence. Navies. Nimitz, Chester W. Pearl Harbor. 1941. *425*
Holocaust. Anti-Semitism. Christians. Toynbee, Arnold. ca 1940-1975. *545*
—. Kremer, Charles H. Rumania. Trifa, Valerian. USA. War crimes. 1941-74. *583*
Hong Kong Inquiry. Canada. Drew, George. Duff, Lyman. King, William Lyon Mackenzie. 1941. *140*
Hoover, Herbert C. Intervention (opposed). Peace. Totalitarianism. USSR. 1939-45. *88*
Hoover, J. Edgar. Barnes, Harry Elmer. Crime and Criminals (organized). Federal Bureau of Investigation. 1936-44. *980*
Hopkins, Harry. Foreign policy. Roosevelt, Franklin D. USSR. 1938-46. *576*
—. Marshall, George C. Military reorganization. Roosevelt, Franklin D. 1942-45. *744*
Hornbeck, Stanley K. Diplomacy. Japan. USA. World War II (antecedents). 1937-41. *526*
Horowitz, David. Alperovitz, Gar. Atomic Weapons. Cold War (review article). Europe, Eastern. Foreign Policy. Kolko, Gabriel. 1943-50. *786*
Hospital. Navy. Yosemite National Park. 1943-45. *831*
Hospitals. Army hospitals. Negroes (physicians, soldiers). Segregation, development of. 1940-42. *707*
Howard, Michael (review article). Great Britain. Mediterranean Sea and Area. Military Strategy. USA. 1942-43. *453*
Howitzer, 105 mm. Armies. Artillery. War Department. 1930's-41. *614*
Hoyt, Ross G. (account). Airplanes, Military. Armies. P-26 (aircraft). 1937-41. *433*
Hudson, James J. (account). Aeronautics, Military. Europe. P-39 Airacobra (aircraft). 1941-45. *435*
Huertgen Forest (battle). Europe, Western. 28th Infantry Division, US. 1944. *563*
Hughes HK-1 (aircraft). Airplanes, Military. Second front clamor. 1942-47. *613*

Hughes, Langston. Negro Literature. Popular culture. Semple, Jesse B. (fictitious character). 1942-43. *755*
Hull, Cordell. Argentina. Foreign Policy. Ramírez, Pedro. USA. 1943. *1060*
—. Diplomacy. Indochina. Japan. Philippines. World War II (antecedents). 1941. *131*
Hungarian Americans. Einstein, Albert. Nuclear Arms (program). Szilárd, Leo. USA. 1941-74. *366*
—. Jews. Wise, Stephen Samuel. 1890's-1949. *987*
Hungarians. *Canadian Hungarian Worker* (newspaper). Szőke, István. USSR. 1929-44. *584*
Hunter, William A. (reminiscences). Canada. Highlanders, 48th. Leftism. Liberalism. Military Service. 1939-45. *438*
Hunting grounds, deprivation of. Fort Wallace. Indian-White Relations. Kansas. Settlers, protection for. 1865-82. *440*
Hurford, Grace Gibberd (reminiscences). Canada. China. Missions and Missionaries. Teaching. 1928-45. *439*
Hurricane (aircraft). Aeronautics, Military. Africa, North. Great Britain. Ohlinger, John F. (account). 1942. *691*
Hutchinson Naval Air Station. Flight training. Kansas. Naval Air Forces. Olathe Naval Air Station. 1942-69. *441*
Hyde Park Declaration (1941). Canada. Great Britain. Military finance. USA. 1939-41. *331*

I

Ibn-Saud, King. Diplomacy. *Murphy* (vessel). Roosevelt, Franklin D. Saudi Arabia. USA. 1945. *472*
Iceland. Denmark. Great Britain. Independence Movements. USA. 1940-44. *457*
—. Marines. Military Decorations, Flags, and Symbols (shoulder patches). Polar bear motif. 1941-42. *93*
Idaho. Agriculture. Internment. Japanese Americans. Railroads. 1900-45. *868*
Idaho (Boise). Air Warfare. Army Air Corps. Beeson, Duane. Europe, Western. 1941-45. *309*
Idaho (Minidoka). Japanese Americans. Mukaida, Tomeji (reminiscences). Relocation camps. 1940's. *573*
Ideology. Defensive war argument. Foreign Policy. War. 1941-73. *958*
Illinois. Anderson, Herbert L. (reminiscences). Chicago, University of. Nuclear chain reaction. 1942. *19*
—. Chicago, University of. Nuclear chain reaction. Wattenberg, Albert (reminiscences). 1942. *1015*
Illinois (Chicago). Avery, Sewell. Economic Conditions. Labor Disputes (arbitration). Montgomery Ward (federal seizure of). War Labor Board. 1941. *490*
—. Foreign policy. Poland. Polish-American Congress. Roosevelt, Franklin D. 1944. *820*
—. Military Recruitment. Navies. 1941-43. *1023*
Illinois State Historical Library (collections). 1876-1976. *1033*
Immigration. Adachi, Ken (review article). Japanese Canadians. Racism. 1877-1976. *521*
—. Asia. Historiography. ca 1849-1974. *206*
—. Attitudes. Genocide. Jews. 1880's-1940's. *590*
—. British Columbia. Chinese. Japanese. Suffrage. 1935-49. *523*

Immigration laws. Genocide, toleration of. Germany. Jews. Refugees. Roosevelt, Franklin D. (administration). 1933-45. *282*
Imperialism. Japan. Navigation. Pacific Area. Pearl Harbor, attack on. World War II (antecedents). Prehistory-1941. *216*
Imports. Apple industry. Exports. Great Britain. Nova Scotia (Annapolis Valley). 1880-1957. *186*
Imprisonment. Armies. Italy (Pisa). Pound, Ezra. Steele, John L. (interview). 1945. *485*
Independence movement. China. Communism. Ho Chi Minh. USA. Vietnamese. 1942-45. *901*
Independence Movements. Denmark. Great Britain. Iceland. USA. 1940-44. *457*
—. Foreign Policy. Great Britain. India. 1900-47. *220*
India. Asia, Southeast (coast). *Lanikai* (vessel). Navies. Roosevelt, Franklin D. Tolley, Kemp (personal account). World War II (antecedents). 1941. *968*
—. British Columbia. Canada. Discrimination. Suffrage. 1939-45. *414*
—. Foreign Policy. Great Britain. Independence Movements. 1900-47. *220*
—. Foreign Relations. Gandhi, Mahatma (arrest). Great Britain. Public Opinion. USA. 1942. *753*
Indiana (BB-58, vessel). Navies. Pacific Area (South). 1922-62. *895*
Indiana (Calumet region). Local history. *Steel Shavings* (periodical). 1933-45. 1975-80. *509*
Indianapolis (vessel). *I-58* (vessel). Japan. Pacific Area. Submarine Warfare. USA. 1945. *115*
Indianapolis (vessel; sinking). Beach, Edward L. (account). Hashimoto, Mochitsura (account). Navies. 1945. *1088*
Indians. Boarding schools. Children. Federal Government. 1920-60's. *947*
Indian-White Relations. Fort Wallace. Hunting grounds, deprivation of. Kansas. Settlers, protection for. 1865-82. *440*
Indochina. China. Churchill, Winston. de Gaulle, Charles. Foreign Policy. French colonies. Roosevelt, Franklin D. 1942-45. *507*
—. deGaulle, Charles. Diplomacy. France. Great Britain. 1940-45. *246*
—. Diplomacy. Hull, Cordell. Japan. Philippines. World War II (antecedents). 1941. *131*
—. Diplomacy. International trusteeships. Roosevelt, Franklin D. 1941-45. *407*
—. Foreign Policy. France. Great Britain. USA. 1942-45. *961*
Indonesia (Sumatra; Palembang; Moesi River). Mines, military. Naval Air Forces. 462d Bomb Group. 1944. *996*
Industrial concentration. Aircraft industry. Contracting policies. 1938-46. *776*
—. Airplane Industry and Trade. 1938-47. *777*
Industrial location. Economic Regulations. Europe, Western. 1930's-70's. *945*
Industrial productivity. Airplanes, Military. Japan. Navies. 1941-45. *752*
Industrial Relations. British Columbia. International Woodworkers of America. Lumber and Lumbering. 1940-50. *1093*
—. Canadian Labour Congress. Cooperative Commonwealth Federation. Federal Government. Trades and Labour Congress. 1939-46. *565*
Industrialization. Agriculture. Europe. Market economy. North America. Peasant movements (colloquium). ca 1875-1975. *52*
—. Defense Industries. Missouri (Kansas City). Small Business. 1940-45. *656*
Industry. Advisory Commission to the Council of National Defense. Mobilization. 1940. *102*

242 Industry

—. Armaments. Production. 1941-45. *1085*
—. Conscription, Military. Scientific Experiments and Research. 1940-44. *1084*
—. Defense Policy. Federal Policy. Labor Unions and Organizations. 1939-41. *873*
—. Economic Growth. Population. South. Western States. 1940-79. *1*
—. Employment. Negroes. Social justice. 1942-43. *1086*
—. Historiography. Labor Unions and Organizations. 1941-45. *305*
—. Labor Unions and Organizations. Roosevelt, Franklin D. (administration). War Manpower Commission. War Production Board. 1939-45. *493*
Information exchange. Great Britain. Science. USSR. 1940-45. *63*
Insignia. Air Forces. Pacific Area. 5th Air Force, US. 1941-45. *1091*
Integration. British Commonwealth. Military. USA. Women. World War I. 1900-78. *959*
Intellectual establishment. Barnes, Harry Elmer. 1940-68. *230*
Intellectuals. France. Maritain, Raïssa. Nationalism. Poetry. USA. 1940-60. *938*
Intelligence mission. Carlson, Evans. China. Japan. Roosevelt, Franklin D. USA. 1937-38. *992*
Intelligence Service. Central Intelligence Agency (secret operations). Donovan, William J. National Security. 1940's-74. *798*
—. Federal Government. 1941-77. *123*
—. Foreign Broadcast Information Service. State Department (Foreign Service). World War II (antecedents). 1939-41. *178*
—. Germany. USA. 1933-41. *277*
Interdependence. Canada. Defense policies. USA. 1940's-70's. *939*
Intergovernmental Relations. Agent general, office of. Canada. Great Britain (London). 18c-20c. *886*
—. Annexation. New Mexico (Albuquerque). Nuclear Science and Technology. Weapons. 1940-78. *762*
Intergovernmental system. Cities (functions). Federal-local relations. Public Finance. 1930's-74. *815*
International Organizations. USA. 1776-1976. *455*
International Relations (discipline). China. Great Britain. Japan. USA. USSR. 1937-49. *736*
International Security. Foreign Relations. Political Leadership. 1941-45. 1976. *734*
International Trade. Africa (north, west). France. Lend-Lease. USA. 1941-46. *242*
—. Allies. Axis Powers. Chrome. Turkey. 1939-44. *911*
—. Appeasement. Foreign policy. Germany. Great Britain. 1933-40. *690*
—. Attitudes. Business. Japan. 1931-41. *417*
—. Canada. China. Foreign Policy. Odlum, Victor Wentworth. ca 1944-49. *683*
—. Canada. Great Britain. USA. 1943-47. *109*
—. Cold War. Economic Conditions. 1943-46. *260*
—. Diplomacy. Foreign policy. Japan. World War II (antecedents). 1937-41. *988*
International trusteeships. Diplomacy. Indochina. Roosevelt, Franklin D. 1941-45. *407*
International Woodworkers of America. British Columbia. Industrial Relations. Lumber and Lumbering. 1940-50. *1093*
Internationalism. Foreign Policy. Norris, George W. 1939-41. *351*
—. Foreign policy. Truman, Harry S. 1935-45. *636*
Internment. Agriculture. Idaho. Japanese Americans. Railroads. 1900-45. *868*
—. California (San Diego County). Japanese Americans. 1941-42. *847*
—. Civil rights. Counterintelligence. Japanese Americans. Munson, Curtis B. Peiper, N. J. L. 1931-42. *500*
—. Clark, Chase. Far Western States. Japanese Americans. Politics. 1941-45. *867*
—. Diaries. Japanese Americans. Oregon. Portland Assembly Center. Tomita, Saku. 1942. *492*
—. Diplomacy. Emmerson, John K. (reminiscences). Japanese Peruvians. Peru. USA. 1942-43. *273*
—. Documentation. Evacuation, forced. Japanese Americans. Photographs. War Relocation Authority. 1941-43. *208*
—. Japanese Americans. Letters. 1942. *908*
—. Japanese Americans. Martial law. Tule Lake Camp. 1941-44. *694*
Interrogation centers. California. Navies. Prisoners of War. Virginia. 1941-45. *647*
Interstate Aircraft and Engineering Corporation. Boehler, Hurley. Navies. TDR-1 (aircraft). 1943-77. *554*
Intervention. Bulgaria. Foreign Policy. USSR. 1944-47. *855*
—. Democracy. Fascism. World War II (antecedents). 1939-41. *898*
Intervention (opposed). Hoover, Herbert C. Peace. Totalitarianism. USSR. 1939-41. *88*
Interventionism. Anti-Soviet consensus. Isolationism. Vandenberg, Arthur Hendrick, Sr. 1941-46. *413*
—. Presbyterian Church. VanDusen, Henry Pitney. World War II (antecedents). 1920-45. *960*
Interventionist, making of an. Davis, Elmer. News broadcasts. Radio. World War II (antecedents). 1939-42. *463*
Intrepid (vessel). Aircraft Carriers. Odysseys In Flight, Inc. Preservation. 1943-79. *1090*
Invasion. Barham, Wayne (reminiscences). Guam. USA. 1944. *50*
Invasions. Airborne troops. Armies. Gavin, James M. (memoirs). Sicily. 1943. *313*
—. Czechoslovakia (Prague). Germany. Patton, George S., Jr. USSR. Vlasov, Andrei. 1945. *804*
Invasions (proposed). Europe. Great Britain. Military Strategy. 1942-44. *822*
Inventions. Antiaircraft gunnery. Great Britain. Proximity fuse. 1939-45. *73*
Iowa. *Cedar Rapids Gazette* (newspaper). Marshall, Verne. No Foreign War Committee. World War II (antecedents). 1940-41. *238*
Ireland. British Commonwealth. Canada. Foreign Relations. Neutrality. 1939-45. *607*
—. Conscription, military. Foreign Relations. Great Britain. Northern Ireland. 1941. *795*
—. Neutrality. 1939-41. *158*
Isolationism. American Peace Mobilization. Communist Party USA. World War II (antecedents). 1939-41. *1006*
—. Anti-Soviet consensus. Interventionism. Vandenberg, Arthur Hendrick, Sr. 1941-46. *413*
—. Armaments. Embargoes. Neutrality Act (US, 1935). 1935. *1080*
—. Catholic influence. Nicoll, John R. A. Roosevelt, Franklin D. (administration). 1943. *357*
—. Cold War. 1944-54. *231*
—. Congress. Conscription, Military. Kansas. Selective Training and Service Act (US, 1940). State Politics. 1940. *335*
—. Congress of Industrial Organizations. Leftism. Pacific Northwest. USSR. 1937-41. *552*
—. Conservatism. Foreign policy. 1930's-52. *801*

—. Democratic Party. German Americans. Kentucky (Kenton County). 1930-40. *247*
—. Europe, Central. Foreign policy. Germany. USA. 1918-41. *1051*
—. Europe, East. Foreign policy. Neutrality Laws. Roosevelt, Franklin D. World War II (antecedents). 1920's-30's. *249*
—. Foreign policy. Hearst, William Randolph. Newspapers. 1936-41. *157*
—. Historiography. 1930's-40's. *235*
—. Nye, Gerald P. Political Speeches. Roosevelt, Franklin D. 1941. *516*
Isolationism (review article). Politics. 1935-52. *234*
Italian Americans. Fascism (alleged). Liberalism. Loyalty. Office of War Information. Propaganda. 1939-40. *627*
—. Italy. 1922-41. *154*
—. Labor. Prisoners of War, Italian. USA. 1943-45. *649*
Italians. Arkansas. Germans. Labor, contract. Prisoners of War. 1943-46. *758*
Italy. Anti-Fascist Movements. Foreign Relations. Sforza, Carlo. 1940-43. *626*
—. Armistice question. Government. Great Britain. Military Occupation. 1944. *29*
—. Battillo, Anthony (reminiscences). Po Valley campaign. 1945. *58*
—. Bibliographies. Documents. 1939-45. *271*
—. Cold War (origins). Kolko, Gabriel. Military Strategy. Negotiations. Operation Crossword. 1945. *166*
—. Fascism. Pound, Ezra. USA. 1924-58. *1074*
—. Italian Americans. 1922-41. *154*
—. Italy, invasion of. Kesselring, Albert. Military Strategy. 1943. *923*
—. Mussolini, Benito. Political issues. Pound, Ezra (letters). USA. 1932-43. *748*
Italy (Anzio front). Rapido (battle). 5th Army, US (36th Division). 1944. *887*
Italy, invasion of. Italy. Kesselring, Albert. Military Strategy. 1943. *923*
Italy, northern. Archives. McCain, William D. Personal narratives. 1944-45. *602*
Italy (Pisa). Armies. Imprisonment. Pound, Ezra. Steele, John L. (interview). 1945. *485*
Iwo Jima (battle). 1945. *146*
—. Barrett, Allen M. (account). Marines. 1945. *53*
—. Flag, American. Photograph, famous. 1945. *299*
I-58 (vessel). *Indianapolis* (vessel). Japan. Pacific Area. Submarine Warfare. USA. 1945. *115*

J

Jablonski, Edward (review article). Air raids. Air Warfare. Germany. Regensburg-Schweinfurt. USA. 1943. *380*
James, D. Clayton (review article). MacArthur, Douglas. Pacific Area. Politics and the Military. 1941-45. *1002*
Japan. Air Forces. Military Capability. Philippines. 1941. *385*
—. Air Warfare. Balloons. Bombing. North America. 1940-45. *1017*
—. Air Warfare. Chennault, Claire Lee. China. Flying Tigers. 1941-45. *408*
—. Air Warfare. Chennault, Claire Lee. China. USA. 1927-45. *727*
—. Air Warfare. Kenney, George. New Britain. Rabaul (battle). 1943. *92*
—. Air Warfare. Marianas (battle). 1944. *293*
—. Air Warfare. Naval Strategy. Pearl Harbor, attack on. 1940-41. *698*
—. Air warfare, clandestine. China. USA. 1940-41. *840*

—. Airplanes, Military. F6F Hellcats (aircraft). Truk Islands. USA. 1944. *966*
—. Airplanes, Military. Industrial productivity. Navies. 1941-45. *752*
—. Alaska. Attu Island (battle). Tatsuguchi, Paul Nobuo (diary). USA. 1941-43. *1011*
—. Alaska (Aleutian Islands). *Arthur Middleton* (vessel). Coast Guard. Laidlaw, Lansing. 1942-43. *508*
—. Alaska (Aleutian Islands). Attu (battle). 1942. *922*
—. Alliances (review article). British Empire. Louis, William Roger. Thorne, Christopher. 1941-45. *729*
—. Amphibious operations. Pacific Area. USA. 1942-45. *449*
—. Amphibious operations. Philippine Sea (battle). Saipan (battle). 1944. *995*
—. Appeasement (proposal). Diplomacy. Great Britain. 1941. *328*
—. Arab-Israeli Conflict. Conflict and Conflict Resolution. Decisionmaking. Foreign Policy. 1941-45. 1967-73. *76*
—. Armies. Marines. Peleliu (battle). Sledge, Eugene B. (account). 1944. *877*
—. Armstrong, David M. (personal account). Hawaii. Pearl Harbor, attack on. 1942. *32*
—. Asia, East. Military strategy. 1944-45. *173*
—. Atomic bombs. Public opinion. USA. 1945-49. *1064*
—. Atomic energy. Military Strategy. Smyth Report, 1945. USA. 1940-45. *897*
—. Atomic Warfare. B-29 (aircraft). Lemay, Curtis. Surrender. 1945. *1052*
—. Atomic Warfare. Decisionmaking. Hiroshima (attack on). 1944-45. *828*
—. Atomic Warfare. History Teaching. Simulation and Games. 1945. 1978. *265*
—. Atomic Warfare. Military strategy. USA. 1945. *429*
—. Atomic Warfare. Politics. Surrender offer. Truman, Harry S. (administration). 1945. *84*
—. Attitudes. Business. International trade. 1931-41. *417*
—. Australia. Foreign Relations. Pacific Area. Peace settlement. USA. 1942-46. *70*
—. *Awa Maru* (vessel). *Queenfish* (vessel). Submarines. USA. 1945. *902*
—. Balloons, armed. Project FUGO. South Dakota. 1944-45. *517*
—. Blockades. Chamberlain, Neville. China. Great Britain. Roosevelt, Franklin D. World War II (antecedents). 1937-38. *362*
—. Bombs, balloon-carried. Pacific Northwest. 1945. *461*
—. Brussels Conference (1937). China. Expansionism. World War II (antecedents). 1937. *107*
—. Carlson, Evans. China. Intelligence mission. Roosevelt, Franklin D. USA. 1937-39. *992*
—. Censorship. *Chicago Tribune*. Grand Juries. Midway Island (attack on). Navies. 1942. *300*
—. China. Cohen, Warren I. (review article). Foreign policy. Leadership. Public opinion. ca 1900-50. 1978. *205*
—. China. Diplomacy. Stuart, John Leighton. USA. 1937-41. *896*
—. China. Great Britain. International Relations (discipline). USA. USSR. 1937-49. *736*
—. China. Marines. Shanghai (battle). 1937. *803*
—. China (Shanghai). Marines. Photographs. USA. 1920's-30's. *1099*
—. China (Yangtze River). *Panay* (vessel). World War II (antecedents). 1937. *731*

244 Japan

—. *Christian Century* (periodical). Foreign policy. Manchurian crisis. Morrison, Charles C. USA. 1931-33. *719*
—. Clark Field, attack on. Philippines. 1941-42. *569*
—. Coffee, John M. Congress. Embargo (sought). Schellenbach, Lewis B. Washington. 1930's-40. *536*
—. Congress. Manchurian crisis. Public opinion. 1931-33. *657*
—. Congress. World War II (antecedents). 1940-41. *535*
—. Crawford, David L. Hawaii, University of. Peace pact (proposed). USA. 1940-41. *428*
—. Destroyer escorts. *England* (vessel). Pacific Area. Submarine Warfare. Williamson, John A. (account). 1944. *1038*
—. Diaries. Norquist, Ernest O. Philippines. Prisoners of War. 1942-45. *681*
—. Diplomacy. Drought, James M. John Doe Associates. Konoye, Fumimaro. Roosevelt, Franklin. Summit conferences. 1941. *143*
—. Diplomacy. Foreign policy. International Trade. World War II (antecedents). 1937-41. *988*
—. Diplomacy. Hornbeck, Stanley K. USA. World War II (antecedents). 1937-41. *526*
—. Diplomacy. Hull, Cordell. Indochina. Philippines. World War II (antecedents). 1941. *131*
—. Diplomacy. Konoe Fumimaro. 1934-41. *430*
—. Diplomacy. MacArthur, Douglas. Philippines (Manila). Surrender. 1945. *624*
—. Diplomacy, mistakes in. Europe. USA. World War II (review article). 1930's-41. *405*
—. Dull, Paul S. (review article). Naval Strategy. Pearl Harbor, attack on. Yamamoto, Isoroku. 1941-45. *977*
—. Embargo, de facto. Foreign Policy. Oil. Roosevelt, Franklin D. 1941. *22*
—. Europe. Foreign policy (review article). Offner, Arnold A. USA. 1917-41. *677*
—. Foreign Policy. Netherlands East Indies. 1941-46. *426*
—. Foreign policy. Oil exports, restricted. State Department. USA. 1940-41. *989*
—. Foreign Policy. Oil industry. USA. 1934-37. *645*
—. Foreign Policy (preconceptions). USA. World War II (antecedents). 1940-41. *74*
—. Foreign Relations. King, William. Thomas, Elbert. USA. Utah. ca 1922-40. *538*
—. Foreign Relations. Pittman, Key. USA. 1920-40. *537*
—. Gilbert Islands. Makin Islands (raid). Marines (2d Raiders). Peatross, Oscar F. (account). Prisoners of War. 1942-47. *720*
—. Great Britain. Navies (communications, tactics). USA. 1943-45. *225*
—. Guadalcanal (battle). USA. 1942-43. *716*
—. Guam. Yokoi, Shoichi. 1944-72. *952*
—. Guam (liberation). USA. 1944. *155*
—. Hawaii. Naval Vessels. Pearl Harbor (attack on). 1941. *1098*
—. Historians, Western. Military defeat. Pacific Area. USSR. 1942-45. *832*
—. Imperialism. Navigation. Pacific Area. Pearl Harbor, attack on. World War II (antecedents). Prehistory-1941. *216*
—. *Indianapolis* (vessel). *I-58* (vessel). Pacific Area. Submarine Warfare. USA. 1945. *115*
—. Leyte Gulf (battle). Navies. Philippines. USA. 1944. *352*
—. Midway (battle). Military Strategy. USA. 1942. *1073*
—. Midway (battle). Navies. USA. 1942. *147*
—. Missions and Missionaries. Mormons. USA. 1901-24. *125*
—. Naval Tactics. Pacific Area. USA. 1920's-43. *447*
—. Navies. Pacific Area. Savo Island (battle). USA. 1942. *67*
—. Navies. Philippine Sea (battle). USA. 1944. *145*
—. Navies. Solomon Islands (Vella Lavella). USA. 1943. *547*
—. Peace (delayed). Potsdam Conference. Surrender, unconditional. USA. 1945. *998*
Japan (Bonin Islands). *Gregory* (vessel). McCandless, Bruce (reminiscences). Navy. 1945. *603*
Japan (Bonin Islands; Chichi Jima). 1675-1968. *397*
Japan (Hiroshima). Alperovitz, Gar (review article). Atomic Warfare. Decisionmaking. Historiography. 1945-65. *859*
Japan (Hiroshima, Nagasaki). Atomic Bomb Casualty Commission. Civilian survivors. Medical Research. Radiation Effects Research Foundation. 1945-75. *1010*
—. Atomic Warfare. Decisionmaking. Military Strategy. 1944-45. *304*
—. Atomic Warfare. Military Strategy. 1945. *267*
—. Atomic warfare. Military Strategy. USA. 1945. *83*
—. Atomic Warfare. USA. USSR. 1942-47. *86*
Japan, invasion of. Military Strategy. Operation Olympic (planned). 1945. *210*
Japan (Kyoto). Air Forces. Bombing, strategic. Stimson, Henry L. USA. 1940-45. *160*
Japan (Nagasaki). Atomic Warfare. Groves, Leslie R. Hirohito, Emperor. Potsdam Conference. Truman, Harry S. 1944-45. *546*
Japan (Tokyo). Diplomacy. Emmerson, John K. (memoirs). State Department. World War II (antecedents). 1941. *275*
—. Diplomacy. USA. World War II (antecedents). 1941. *274*
Japanese. British Columbia. Chinese. Immigration. Suffrage. 1935-49. *523*
—. British Columbia. Evacuation, forced. Federal government. Public opinion. 1937-42. *1009*
Japanese American Citizens League. Citizenship. Ford, Gerald R. Hada, John. Pardon. Tokyo Rose (Iva Toguri d'Aquino). Uyeda, Clifford I. (account). 1973-77. *990*
Japanese Americans. Agriculture. Florida (Boca Raton). Yamato colony. 1904-75. *750*
—. Agriculture. Idaho. Internment. Railroads. 1900-45. *868*
—. Appalachia. Migration, Internal (noneconomic variables). Negroes. 1860-1973. *984*
—. Arizona. Concentration camps. Gila River Relocation Center. Public Opinion. Race Relations. 1942-45. *159*
—. Attitudes. Civil rights. Conscientious objectors. 1940-45. *745*
—. Baptists. Discrimination. Resettlement. 1890-1970. *644*
—. California. Concentration Camps. Manzanar War Relocation Center. Riots. Ueno, Harry (arrest). 1942. *381*
—. California. Concentration Camps. Race Relations. 1941-42. *639*
—. California. Detention. Racism. 1941-45. *640*
—. California. Relocation camps. Warren, Earl. 1941-45. *1030*
—. California (San Diego County). Internment. 1941-42. *847*
—. Chinese Americans. Discrimination. Economic Conditions. Social Status. 1840's-1978. *732*

Joint Chiefs   245

—. Civic Unity Committee. Defense industries. Negroes. Race relations. Washington (Seattle). 1940-45. *248*
—. Civil rights. Counterintelligence. Internment. Munson, Curtis B. Peiper, N. J. L. 1931-42. *500*
—. Clark, Chase. Far Western States. Internment. Politics. 1941-45. *867*
—. Concentration Camps. 1942-46. *693*
—. Concentration Camps. Public schools. 1942-45. *1056*
—. Concentration camps. Racism. 1940-45. *444*
—. Diaries. Internment. Oregon. Portland Assembly Center. Tomita, Saku. 1942. *492*
—. Documentation. Evacuation, forced. Internment. Photographs. War Relocation Authority. 1941-43. *208*
—. Idaho (Minidoka). Mukaida, Tomeji (reminiscences). Relocation camps. 1940's. *573*
—. Internment. Letters. 1942. *908*
—. Internment. Martial law. Tule Lake Camp. 1941-44. *694*
Japanese Americans (attitudes toward). Sociological theory. Values. 1940's-70's. *914*
Japanese Americans, incarceration of. Oral history. Tanaka, Togo. Yoneda, Elaine. Yoneda, Karl. 1941-45. *638*
Japanese Americans (Nisei). Language School. Military Intelligence Service. Minnesota. Rasmussen, Kai E. 1941-46. *28*
Japanese Canadians. Adachi, Ken (review article). Immigration. Racism. 1877-1976. *521*
—. Alberta. Chinese Canadians. Racism. 1920-50. *703*
—. British Columbia. Canada. Chinese Canadians. Military Service (denied). 1939-45. *806*
—. British Columbia, University of. Race relations. 1939-42. *80*
—. Canada. Race Relations. Relocation, forced. 1890's-1940's. *949*
Japanese Canadians (Nisei). Assimilation. Canada. Evacuation, forced. 1941-75. *575*
Japanese Canadians (relocation). Alberta, southern. British Columbia. 1941-45. *450*
Japanese communities. British Columbia. Minorities. Public schools, challenge to. 1900-72. *203*
Japanese language. Dumas, Harold. Marines. 1944-45. *577*
Japanese Peruvians. Diplomacy. Emmerson, John K. (reminiscences). Internment. Peru. USA. 1942-43. *273*
Jehovah's Witnesses. Conscientious Objectors. Courts. Flag salute. 1930's-40's. *387*
Jeremiah O'Brien (vessel). Liberty Ships. Maritime Preservation Office. Patterson, Thomas J. Preservation. 1940-80. *184*
Jesuits. McCormick, Vincent A. (diary). Vatican. 1942-45. *404*
Jewish Peace Fellowship. Peace Movements. 1943. *1067*
Jews. Air Warfare. Auschwitz. Concentration Camps. Military Strategy. 1944-45. *1063*
—. American Jewish Joint Distribution Committee. Diplomacy. Mayer, Saly. 1944-45. *59*
—. Anti-Nazi Movements. Boycotts. Fram, Leon (reminiscences). League for Human Rights. Michigan (Detroit). 1930's-40's. *296*
—. Assimilation. Education. Labor movement. Socialism. 1880's-1945. *975*
—. Attitudes. Genocide. Immigration. 1880's-1940's. *590*
—. Blair, Frederick Charles. Canada. Federal Policy. Refugees. 1930's. *2*
—. Boycott activities. Economic Conditions. Joint Boycott Council. Non-Sectarian Anti-Nazi League to Champion Human Rights. 1939-41. *326*
—. Christians. Genocide. Theology. 1945-74. *259*
—. Concentration camps. Genocide. Germany. Press. 1939-42. *348*
—. Europe. Federal Government (response). USA. War crimes. 1938-45. *5*
—. Europe. Genocide. Public Policy. Roosevelt, Franklin D. (administration). 1942-44. *596*
—. Europe. McDonald, James G. (paper). Refugees. Resettlement. 1938-43. *285*
—. Federal Government. Great Britain. Morgenthau, Henry, Jr. Relief organizations. War Refugee Board. 1940-44. *726*
—. Foreign Policy. Genocide. 1939-45. *286*
—. Friedman, Saul S. (review article). Genocide. Public Policy. Refugees. Roosevelt, Franklin D. (administration). 1938-45. 1973. *790*
—. Fundamentalism. Gaebelin, Arno C. Genocide. Germany. *Our Hope* (periodical). 1937-45. *768*
—. Genocide. Germany. Great Britain. Rescues. 1939-44. *283*
—. Genocide. Germany. Historiography. Psychology. 1940's. *514*
—. Genocide (review article). Historiography. Refugees. Wiesel, Elie. 1939-45. 1960-79. *1077*
—. Genocide, toleration of. Germany. Immigration laws. Refugees. Roosevelt, Franklin D. (administration). 1933-45. *282*
—. Germany. Prisoners of war. USA. Winograd, Leonard (reminiscences). 1944-45. *1047*
—. Germany. Refugees. Relief organizations. USA. 1933-45. *316*
—. Hayes, Carlton J. H. Refugees (rescue, relief). Spain. 1942-45. *1040*
—. Hungarian Americans. Wise, Stephen Samuel. 1890's-1949. *987*
—. Pell, Herbert Claiborne. State Department. UN War Crimes Commission. War crimes. 1943-45. *100*
—. Poland. Press, Jewish. USA. Warsaw ghetto uprising. 1942-43. *347*
—. Refugees. Zionist/Anti-Zionist disunity. 1932-45. *946*
Jews (stateless). Germany. Morgenthau, Henry, Jr. State Department. Treasury Department. USA. 1942-44. *589*
Jiang Jieshi. China. Marshall, George C. Military General Staff. Stillwell, Joseph W. 1944. *841*
John Doe Associates. Diplomacy. Drought, James M. Japan. Konoye, Fumimaro. Roosevelt, Franklin. Summit conferences. 1941. *143*
Johnston, Francis J. (account). Army Air Forces. B-29 (aircraft). China. Ground crews. Mariana Islands (Tinian). 1944-45. *462*
Joint Aircraft Committee. Aircraft industry. National Defense Advisory Commission. Office of Production Management. Technological change. 1940-45. *423*
Joint Boycott Council. Boycott activities. Economic Conditions. Jews. Non-Sectarian Anti-Nazi League to Champion Human Rights. 1939-41. *326*
Joint Chiefs of Staff. Churchill, Winston. Great Britain. Malta Conference. Military Strategy. Roosevelt, Franklin D. 1945. *912*
—. Cold War. USSR. 1944-46. *746*
—. MacArthur, Douglas. Nimitz, Chester W. Pacific Area. Roosevelt, Franklin D. 1941-42. *189*

246 Joint declaration

Joint declaration (proposed). Asia, Southeast. Colonialism. Great Britain. Roosevelt, Franklin D. (administration). USA. 1942-44. *1036*

Joint Distribution Committee. Fund raising. Genocide. Judaism (Orthodox). Rescue work. Yeshiva Aid Committee. 1939-41. *1081*

Judaism. Markowitz, Samuel H. (autobiography). Pennsylvania. 1920-65. *585*

Judaism (Orthodox). Fund raising. Genocide. Joint Distribution Committee. Rescue work. Yeshiva Aid Committee. 1939-41. *1081*

Judges. Benavente, Ignacio V. Caroline Islands (Yap). 1942-46. *742*

K

Kahn, David. Brown, Anthony Cave. Germany. Great Britain. Military Intelligence (review article). 1939-45. *518*

Kansas. Congress. Conscription, Military. Isolationism. Selective Training and Service Act (US, 1940). State Politics. 1940. *335*

—. Flight training. Hutchinson Naval Air Station. Naval Air Forces. Olathe Naval Air Station. 1942-69. *441*

—. Fort Wallace. Hunting grounds, deprivation of. Indian-White Relations. Settlers, protection for. 1865-82. *440*

Kansas (Abilene). Dwight D. Eisenhower Library. Military records. Research. 1916-52. 1977. *361*

Keep America Out of War Congress. Antiwar Sentiment. Socialist Party. Thomas, Norman. Villard, Oswald Garrison. World War II (antecedents). 1938-41. *236*

Kelly, Colin P., Jr. Air Warfare. B-17 (aircraft). Philippines. 1941. *144*

Kelsey, George (review article). Attitudes. Kentucky. Southern Baptists. 1941-45. 1973. *756*

Kennedy, Joseph P. Churchill, Winston. Diplomacy. Great Britain. Roosevelt, Franklin D. (administration). 1938-40. *997*

Kenney, George. Air Warfare. Japan. New Britain. Rabaul (battle). 1943. *92*

Kentucky. Attitudes. Kelsey, George (review article). Southern Baptists. 1941-45. 1973. *756*

Kentucky (Kenton County). Democratic Party. German Americans. Isolationism. 1930-40. *247*

Kentucky (Louisville). Air Bases (construction of). Civil-Military Relations. Hammon, Stratton Owen (account). Standiford Airfield. 1942-43. *377*

Kesselring, Albert. Italy. Italy, invasion of. Military Strategy. 1943. *923*

Keys of the Kingdom (film). China. Office of War Information. Propaganda. Stereotypes. USA. 1940-45. *94*

Khrushchev, Nikita. Churchill, Winston. Disarmament. Einstein, Albert. Eisenhower, Dwight D. Europe. Memoirs. Moch, Jules. 1932-55. *641*

Kilgore, Harley M. Legislation. National Science Foundation. Science and Government. Senate. 1942-50. *568*

Kimmel, Husband E. Pearl Harbor, attack on. Personal narratives. Short, Walter C. Weapons (ineffectiveness). 1941. *951*

King, Ernest J. Atlantic Fleet. Military General Staff. Naval Biography. 1940's. *827*

—. Guadalcanal (battle). Marshall, George C. Navies. 1942-45. *135*

—. Naval Strategy. Pacific Area. 1926-44. *781*

—. Navies. Press. Public relations. 1939-43. *339*

King, William. Foreign Relations. Japan. Thomas, Elbert. USA. Utah. ca 1922-40. *538*

King, William Lyon MacKenzie. Atomic Warfare. Canada. Diaries. Racism. 1921-48. *823*

—. Canada. Drew, George. Duff, Lyman. Hong Kong Inquiry. 1941. *140*

—. Canada. Foreign Relations. USA. 1939-45. *330*

—. Canada. Ogdensburg Agreement. Roosevelt, Franklin D. 1933-45. *910*

—. Conscription, Military. Elections. Ligue pour la Défense du Canada. Quebec. 1942-44. *333*

Klewang, Dutch. Cutlass, Naval. Peterson, Harold L. World War I. 1917. 1941-42. *787*

Koichwitz, Otto ("O.K."). Germany. Halle, Louis J. (reminiscences). Propaganda. Teachers. USA. 1920's-40's. *371*

Kolko, Gabriel. Alperovitz, Gar. Atomic Weapons. Cold War (review article). Europe, Eastern. Foreign Policy. Horowitz, David. 1943-50. *786*

—. Cold War (origins). Italy. Military Strategy. Negotiations. Operation Crossword. 1945. *166*

—. Foreign policy. Historiography (neorevisionist; review article). Kolko, Joyce. Williams, William Appleman. 1975. *851*

Kolko, Joyce. Foreign policy. Historiography (neorevisionist; review article). Kolko, Gabriel. Williams, William Appleman. 1975. *851*

Konoe Fumimaro. Diplomacy. Japan. 1934-41. *430*

Konoye, Fumimaro. Diplomacy. Drought, James M. Japan. John Doe Associates. Roosevelt, Franklin. Summit conferences. 1941. *143*

Korea. Foreign Policy. 1941-45. *595*

Korean War. Adventist Medical Cadet Corps. Armies. Dick, Everett N. (account). 1934-53. *223*

—. Balance of power. Military Strategy. Technology. Weapons. 1918-53. *876*

—. Bulge (battle). China. Cuban Missile Crisis. Military intelligence. 1944-80. *34*

—. Military rescue concepts. Vietnam War. 1941-74. *141*

Kremer, Charles H. Holocaust. Rumania. Trifa, Valerian. USA. War crimes. 1941-74. *583*

Kwai, River. Bridges. Thailand. USA. 1942-45. *403*

L

Labor. Armies. Attitudes. Social Change. 1940's-70's. *853*

—. Canada. Women. 1942-46. *738*

—. Employment. Women. 1940-47. *1106*

—. Germany. Propaganda. Public opinion. Sex roles. Women. 1939-45. *814*

—. Italian Americans. Prisoners of War, Italian. USA. 1943-45. *649*

—. Michigan. Sex roles. Women. 1941-45. *180*

Labor, contract. Arkansas. Germans. Italians. Prisoners of War. 1943-46. *758*

Labor Disputes (arbitration). Avery, Sewell. Economic Conditions. Illinois (Chicago). Montgomery Ward (federal seizure of). War Labor Board. 1941. *490*

Labor, forced. Louisiana (Lafourche Parish). Prisoners of war, German. Sugar cane fields. 1943-44. *142*

Labor law. Courts. Discrimination, Employment. Women. 1876-1979. *412*

Labor (militancy). Automobile Industry and Trade. Michigan (Detroit). Production standards. United Automobile Workers of America. Working Conditions. 1937-55. *540*

Labor movement. Assimilation. Education. Jews. Socialism. 1880's-1945. *975*
Labor, prison. Germans. New York, western. Prisoners of War (camps). 1944-46. *598*
Labor unions. Employment. Negroes. Women. Working-class militancy. 1940's. *341*
Labor Unions and Organizations. 1941-45. *539*
—. Automobile industry. Employment. Strikes, wildcat. 1941-45. *1103*
—. Bibliographies. Working class. 1940's. *342*
—. Boilermakers, Iron Shipbuilders and Helpers, International Brotherhood of. California (Los Angeles). Discrimination, employment. Negroes. Oregon (Portland). Shipbuilding. 1941-46. *883*
—. Business. Canada. Federal Government. Social control. Unemployment Insurance Act (1941). Wages. 1910-41. *202*
—. Business. New Deal. Taft-Hartley Act (US, 1947). Wagner Act (US, 1935). 1935-47. *108*
—. Defense Policy. Federal Policy. Industry. 1939-41. *873*
—. Historiography. Industry. 1941-45. *305*
—. Industry. Roosevelt, Franklin D. (administration). War Manpower Commission. War Production Board. 1939-45. *493*
Labor Unions and Organizations (militancy). Airplane Industry and Trade. Nash, Al (reminiscences). New York (Long Island City). Political factions. 1940-44. *675*
Labor unions, industrial. Employment. Working class power (elimination of). 1930-47. *1024*
Lafayette myth. Foreign Relations. France. National Characteristics. 1763-1976. *254*
Laidlaw, Lansing. Alaska (Aleutian Islands). *Arthur Middleton* (vessel). Coast Guard. Japan. 1942-43. *508*
Lake Michigan. Navies. 1941-45. *126*
Lamb Studios. Camp Lejeune. Marines. New Jersey (Tenafly). North Carolina. Stained glass. Windows. 1775-1943. *480*
Landing craft. Amphibious operations. Higgins, Andrew J. Shipbuilding. 1933-45. *655*
Landing vehicles, tracked. Amphibious warfare. Armored Vehicles and Tank Warfare. Christie, J. Walter. 1918-45. *418*
Lane, Arthur B. Diplomacy. Germany. Yugoslavia. 1940-41. *933*
Lange, Oscar. Poland, eastern. Pro-Communism. Roosevelt, Franklin D. USSR. 1941-45. *821*
Langer, William. Anti-British sentiments. Churchill, Winston. North Dakota. Senate. 1941-52. *1035*
Langer, William L. (account). Diplomacy. Great Britain. Historiography. Vichy Regime. 1941-54. *512*
Language School. Japanese Americans (Nisei). Military Intelligence Service. Minnesota. Rasmussen, Kai E. 1941-46. *28*
Lanikai (vessel). Asia, Southeast (coast). India. Navies. Roosevelt, Franklin D. Tolley, Kemp (personal account). World War II (antecedents). 1941. *968*
Lash, Joseph P. (review article). Churchill, Winston. Foreign Relations. Great Britain. Roosevelt, Franklin D. 1939-41. 1976. *227*
Latin America. Airlines. National security. State Department. 1927-40. *767*
—. Axis powers. Diplomatic relations (rupture). Rio Conference (1942). USA. 1941-42. *297*
—. Axis Powers. Foreign Policy. Office of the Coordinator of Inter-American Affairs. Rockefeller, Nelson A. Roosevelt, Franklin D. (administration). 1933-42. *364*
—. Canada. Diplomacy. Foreign Relations. Pan-American Union. USA. 1939-44. *664*

—. Committee for Political Defense. Foreign Policy. State Department. 1942-45. *825*
—. Defense policy. 1940-45. *487*
—. Foreign Policy. Military Strategy. USA. 1850-1976. *168*
—. Foreign Relations. Military Aid. Military Assistance Program. 1932-72. *41*
Latin Americans (image). Film. Hollywood. 1939-46. *1054*
Laughlin, C. H. (reminiscences). Airplanes. China (Kunming). Ghana (Accra). 1942. *520*
Law. Constitutionalism. Political theory. ca 1936-70. *72*
Lawyers. Education. Marines. McCarthy, Joseph R. State Politics. Wisconsin. 1908-44. *687*
Leadership. China. Cohen, Warren I. (review article). Foreign policy. Japan. Public opinion. ca 1900-50. 1978. *205*
—. Crumb, Charles V. (account). Marines. 1936-67. 1979. *198*
League for Human Rights. Anti-Nazi Movements. Boycotts. Fram, Leon (reminiscences). Jews. Michigan (Detroit). 1930's-40's. *296*
Leftism. Antiwar sentiments. Colleges and Universities. Political Protest. 1920-36. *124*
—. Canada. Highlanders, 48th. Hunter, William A. (reminiscences). Liberalism. Military Service. 1939-45. *438*
—. Congress of Industrial Organizations. Isolationism. Pacific Northwest. USSR. 1937-41. *552*
Left-revisionists. Cold War (review article). Determinists. Historiography. 1945-70. *482*
Legislation. Arkansas. Family. Social Problems. 1941-45. *884*
—. Capper, Arthur. Neutrality. Political Speeches. 1936-41. *709*
—. Kilgore, Harley M. National Science Foundation. Science and Government. Senate. 1942-50. *568*
Leigh, Michael. Darilek, Richard E. Foreign Policy (review article). Levering, Ralph B. Public opinion. 1936-47. 1976. *315*
Leigh-Mallory, Trafford. Canada. Dieppe (air battle). Great Britain. Royal Canadian Air Force. 1942. *151*
Lemay, Curtis. Atomic Warfare. B-29 (aircraft). Japan. Surrender. 1945. *1052*
Lend-Lease. Aeronautics, Military. Circumnavigations. Diplomacy. Harriman, W. Averell. USSR. 1941. *323*
—. Africa (north, west). Foreign Policy. International Trade. USA. 1941-46. *242*
—. Allies. Historiography. USSR. 1941-45. *250*
—. Antifascism. New Deal. Roosevelt, Franklin D. (administration). 1941-45. *1071*
—. Great Britain. 1941-45. *853*
—. Great Britain. Naval Vessels (destroyer-escorts). 1943-45. *269*
—. Lobbying. Oil Industry and Trade. Saudi Arabia. 1943. *21*
Letters. Canada. Canol project. Dickins, C. H. "Punch". Mackenzie Air Route. Pipelines. USA. 1942. *56*
—. France. Haygood, William Converse. Luxembourg. USA. 1945. *396*
—. Internment. Japanese Americans. 1942. *908*
Levering, Ralph B. Darilek, Richard E. Foreign Policy (review article). Leigh, Michael. Public opinion. 1936-47. 1976. *315*
Lexington (vessel). Aircraft carriers. Navies. *Saratoga* (vessel). 1922-45. *23*
Leyte Gulf (battle). Air Forces. Navies. Philippines. 1944. *829*
—. Japan. Navies. Philippines. USA. 1944. *352*

248 Libby

Libby, Frederick J. Malmédy massacre. National Council for the Prevention of War. Trials. War crimes (standards). 1944-49. *237*
Liberalism. Canada. Highlanders, 48th. Hunter, William A. (reminiscences). Leftism. Military Service. 1939-45. *438*
—. Fascism (alleged). Italian Americans. Loyalty. Office of War Information. Propaganda. 1939-40. *627*
—. Films. Hollywood. National Self-image. Office of War Information. 1942-45. *494*
Liberia. Economic development. Military Strategy. State Department. 1938-45. *66*
Liberty Ships. *Jeremiah O'Brien* (vessel). Maritime Preservation Office. Patterson, Thomas J. Preservation. 1940-80. *184*
—. Merchant Marine. 1941-78. *1068*
Libraries. War information centers. 1941-45. *345*
Libyan Desert. Aircraft equipment (long-term storage). B-24 (aircraft). 1943-59. *422*
Ligue pour la Défense du Canada. Conscription, Military. Elections. King, William Lyon Mackenzie. Quebec. 1942-44. *333*
Lindbergh, Anne Morrow (reminiscences). Antiwar sentiment. Aviation. Lindbergh, Charles A. Values. 1902-79. *543*
Lindbergh, Charles A. Antiwar sentiment. Aviation. Lindbergh, Anne Morrow (reminiscences). Values. 1902-79. *543*
Lindsay, Ronald. Consular dispatches. Eden, Anthony. Foreign relations. Great Britain. 1937. *360*
Lippmann, Walter. Frankfurter, Felix. New Deal. Roosevelt, Franklin D. 1932-45. *721*
Literature. Atomic Warfare. Hersey, John (*Hiroshima*). Morality. 1945-74. *1065*
—. Demobilization. Discrimination, Employment. Social Status. Women. 1944-46. *392*
—. Friendship. Morality. Politics. Pound, Ezra. Treason. 1909-72. *192*
"Little Orphan Annie", comic strip. Cartoonists. Depressions. Gray, Harold. Social conservatism. 1930's-40's. *1069*
Little Theatre Group. Manhattan Project. New Mexico (Los Alamos). Nuclear Arms. Theater Production and Direction. 1943-46. *13*
Lloyd, Lola Maverick. Feminism. Peace Movements. 1914-44. *921*
Lobbying. Lend-Lease. Oil Industry and Trade. Saudi Arabia. 1943. *21*
—. Mazewski, Aloysius. Polish American Congress. Polish National Alliance. Rozmarek, Charles. 1944-79. *737*
Local history. Indiana (Calumet region). *Steel Shavings* (periodical). 1933-45. 1975-80. *509*
Logistics. Alaskan Highway. Highway Engineering. Yukon Territory. 1942-43. *779*
Lorraine campaign. France. Metz (battle). Patton, George S., Jr. Third Army. 1944. *46*
Louis, William Roger. Alliances (review article). British Empire. Japan. Thorne, Christopher. 1941-45. *729*
—. Asia. Callahan, Raymond. Foreign Relations. Great Britain. Lowe, Peter. World War II (review article). 1939-45. *12*
Louisiana. Army. Camp Beauregard. Cawthon, John Ardis. Conscription, Military. Personal narratives. 1940-42. *163*
Louisiana (Lafourche Parish). Labor, forced. Prisoners of war, German. Sugar cane fields. 1943-44. *142*
Louisiana (New Orleans). Dry dock, floating. Manitowoc Shipbuilding Co. Mississippi River. Navigation, Inland. *Peto* (vessel). Submarines. 1942-45. *676*
Louisiana (western). Military General Staff. War Games. 2nd Army, US. 3d Army, US. 1941. *668*
Lowe, Peter. Asia. Callahan, Raymond. Foreign Relations. Great Britain. Louis, William Roger. World War II (review article). 1939-45. *12*
Loyalty. Fascism (alleged). Italian Americans. Liberalism. Office of War Information. Propaganda. 1939-40. *627*
Luke, Frank, Jr. P-38 (aircraft). Rickenbacker, Edward V. 1st Pursuit Group. 1918-76. *534*
Lumber and Lumbering. Arizona (White Mountains). Economic Conditions. 1919-42. *592*
—. British Columbia. Industrial Relations. International Woodworkers of America. 1940-50. *1093*
Lundestad, Geir (views). Cold War. Europe, Eastern. 1943-47. *817*
Luxembourg. France. Haygood, William Converse. Letters. USA. 1945. *396*
Luzon (battle). Cavalry. MacArthur, Douglas. Philippine Scouts. 1941. *244*

M

MacArthur, Douglas. Australia. Curtin, John. Hasluck, Paul. Military Recruitment. 1942-43. *551*
—. Australia. Diaries. Great Britain. Philippines. Williamson, Gerald Hugh. 1942-43. *962*
—. Cavalry. Luzon (battle). Philippine Scouts. 1941. *244*
—. Diplomacy. Japan. Philippines (Manila). Surrender. 1945. *624*
—. Executive Order No. 1. Gifts. Military General Staff. Philippines. Quezon, Manuel. Sutherland, Richard K. (papers). 1942. *733*
—. Foreign Policy. Military. Philippines. 1945-46. *262*
—. James, D. Clayton (review article). Pacific Area. Politics and the Military. 1941-45. *1002*
—. Joint Chiefs of Staff. Nimitz, Chester W. Pacific Area. Roosevelt, Franklin D. 1941-42. *189*
—. Military Strategy. Naval strategy. 1942-51. *1095*
Mackenzie, A. Stanley. Colleges and Universities (presidents). Dalhousie University. New Brunswick. Stanley, Carleton. 1911-45. *395*
Mackenzie Air Route. Canada. Canol project. Dickins, C. H. "Punch". Letters. Pipelines. USA. 1942. *56*
Maginnis, John J. Marcus, David. Memoirs. US Control Council for Germany. 1944-46. *574*
Maine, University of. Films. History Teaching. World War I. 20c. *846*
Makin Islands (raid). Gilbert Islands. Japan. Marines (2d Raiders). Peatross, Oscar F. (account). Prisoners of War. 1942-47. *720*
Malmédy massacre. Libby, Frederick J. National Council for the Prevention of War. Trials. War crimes (standards). 1944-49. *237*
Malta Conference. Churchill, Winston. Great Britain. Joint Chiefs of Staff. Military Strategy. Roosevelt, Franklin D. 1945. *912*
Manchester, William (account). Marines. Okinawa (battle). 1945. 1978. *578*
Manchurian crisis. *Christian Century* (periodical). Foreign policy. Japan. Morrison, Charles C. USA. 1931-33. *719*
—. Congress. Japan. Public opinion. 1931-33. *657*
Manhattan Project. Bainbridge, Kenneth T. (reminiscences). New Mexico (Los Alamos). Nuclear Arms. 1945. *40*

—. Colleges and Universities. Nuclear Arms. Oppenheimer, J. Robert. 1904-67. *784*
—. Cyclotrons. New Mexico (Los Alamos). Nuclear Science and Technology. Wilson, Robert R. (reminiscences). 1942-43. *1044*
—. Little Theatre Group. New Mexico (Los Alamos). Nuclear Arms. Theater Production and Direction. 1943-46. *13*
Manitowoc Shipbuilding Co. Dry dock, floating. Louisiana (New Orleans). Mississippi River. Navigation, Inland. *Peto* (vessel). Submarines. 1942-45. *676*
Manley, John H. (reminiscences). New Mexico (Los Alamos). Nuclear Science and Technology. 1942-45. *581*
Manufacturers, small. Economic Conditions. Roosevelt, Franklin D. 1939-43. *398*
Manzanar War Relocation Center. California. Concentration Camps. Japanese Americans. Riots. Ueno, Harry (arrest). 1942. *381*
Mao Tse-tung. Chiang Kai-shek. Diplomacy. Political leadership. 1945. *978*
Map Drawing. Geography. 1938-79. *789*
Marathon (vessel). Amphibious operations. McElroy, John W. (account). Okinawa (battle). 1945. *606*
March on Washington Movement. Defense industries. Discrimination. Executive Order 8802. Military. Randolph, A. Philip. Webster, Milton. 1941-44. *588*
Marcus, David. Maginnis, John J. Memoirs. US Control Council for Germany. 1944-46. *574*
Mare Island Mutiny. California (San Francisco Bay). Courts Martial and Courts of Inquiry. Navies. Negroes. Port Chicago Naval Magazine. Race relations. 1944-48. *1055*
Mariana Islands (Tinian). Army Air Forces. B-29 (aircraft). China. Ground crews. Johnston, Francis J. (account). 1944-45. *462*
Marianas (battle). Air Warfare. Japan. 1944. *293*
Marines. Air warfare. F4U (aircraft). Pacific Area. Zero (aircraft). 1943-45. *419*
—. Air Warfare. McCarthy, Joseph R. Pacific Area. Politics. Wisconsin. 1942-52. *774*
—. Amphibious operations. Military Strategy. 20c. *542*
—. Amphibious warfare. General Board of the Navy. Naval Strategy. 1900-74. *688*
—. Armies. Japan. Peleliu (battle). Sledge, Eugene B. (account). 1944. *877*
—. Barrett, Allen M. (account). Iwo Jima (battle). 1945. *53*
—. Camp Lejeune. Lamb Studios. New Jersey (Tenafly). North Carolina. Stained glass. Windows. 1775-1943. *480*
—. China. Japan. Shanghai (battle). 1937. *803*
—. China, north. Civil wars. Military Occupation. 1945-47. *228*
—. China (Shanghai). Japan. Photographs. USA. 1920's-30's. *1099*
—. Crumb, Charles V. (account). Leadership. 1936-67. 1979. *198*
—. Dumas, Harold. Japanese language. 1944-45. *577*
—. Education. Lawyers. McCarthy, Joseph R. State Politics. Wisconsin. 1908-44. *687*
—. Environment. Pacific Area. Pacific Dependencies (US). 1943-71. *617*
—. Films. 1920's-75. *934*
—. Gilbert Islands. Haley, J. Frederick (account). Reconnaissance. Tarawa (battle). 1943. *368*
—. Gilbert Islands. Tarawa (battle). 1943. *130*
—. Griffith, Samuel B., Jr. (reminiscences). Guadalcanal (battle). Tulagi (battle). 1942-43. *346*
—. Iceland. Military Decorations, Flags, and Symbols (shoulder patches). Polar bear motif. 1941-42. *93*
—. Manchester, William (account). Okinawa (battle). 1945. 1978. *578*
—. Military Service. Women. 1918-22. 1943-73. *456*
—. Military training. Parris Island (camp). Vietnam War. 1942-72. *695*
—. Okinawa (battle; Sugar Loaf Hill). 1945. *913*
Marines (image). Fribourg, Leonard. Grainger, Edmund. Hollywood. *Sands of Iwo Jima* (film). Wayne, John. 1949. *935*
Marines (2d Raiders). Gilbert Islands. Japan. Makin Islands (raid). Peatross, Oscar F. (account). Prisoners of War. 1942-47. *720*
Maritain, Raïssa. France. Intellectuals. Nationalism. Poetry. USA. 1940-60. *938*
Maritime historians. Brewington, Marion Vernon (obituary). Ship portraits. 1930's-74. *1031*
Maritime missions. Air Forces. Navies. 1941-78. *150*
Maritime Preservation Office. *Jeremiah O'Brien* (vessel). Liberty Ships. Patterson, Thomas J. Preservation. 1940-80. *184*
Market economy. Agriculture. Europe. Industrialization. North America. Peasant movements (colloquium). ca 1875-1975. *52*
Markowitz, Samuel H. (autobiography). Judaism. Pennsylvania. 1920-65. *585*
Marshall, George C. China. Jiang Jieshi. Military General Staff. Stillwell, Joseph W. 1944. *841*
—. Eisenhower, Dwight D. Military General Staff. Operation Overlord. Roosevelt, Franklin D. 1942-44. *295*
—. Guadalcanal (battle). King, Ernest J. Navies. 1942-43. *135*
—. Hopkins, Harry. Military reorganization. Roosevelt, Franklin D. 1942-45. *744*
Marshall, George C. (strategic thought). Strategy. USSR. 1939-50. *121*
Marshall Plan. Cold War (origins). Nuclear Arms. Second Front. USSR. 1940's. *1016*
Marshall, S. L. A. (account). Armies. Behavior. Combat. 1941-45. *586*
Marshall, S. L. A. (reminiscences). Military. World War I. 1919-69. *587*
Marshall, Verne. *Cedar Rapids Gazette* (newspaper). Iowa. No Foreign War Committee. World War II (antecedents). 1940-41. *238*
Martial law. Emergencies, national. Executive power. Habeas corpus. War. 1861-1944. *778*
—. Internment. Japanese Americans. Tule Lake Camp. 1941-45. *694*
Marx, Groucho. Comedians. Film. 1940's. *925*
Maryland. Coast Guard. Seaplanes. 1929-69. *810*
—. Community, involuntary. Conscientious objectors. Patapsco Civilian Public Service System (Camp 3). Values. 1941-42. *699*
Maryland (Annapolis). Photography, Military. Streichen, Edward J. US Naval Academy (Edward J. Streichen Collection). 1930's-75. *194*
Maser, Werner. Nuremberg trials (review article). Smith, Bradley F. War crimes. 1945-46. 1970's. *1013*
Mass Media. Foreign policy. Public opinion. USA. USSR. ca 1939-49. *880*
Massachusetts (Lowell). Defense industries. Employment. Textile Industry. Women. 1940-45. *630*
Mauchly, John William (obituary). Computers. 1932-78. *919*

Maxwell Field. Air Bases. Alabama (Montgomery). Army Air Corps. Military training. Mutiny. 1943. *222*

Mayer, Saly. American Jewish Joint Distribution Committee. Diplomacy. Jews. 1944-45. *59*

Mazewski, Aloysius. Lobbying. Polish American Congress. Polish National Alliance. Rozmarek, Charles. 1944-79. *737*

McAuliffe, Anthony. Bache, William B. Germany (Ludwigshafen). Personal narratives. 1945. *38*

McBride, Robert M. Balloons. Dirigibles. Navy. Personal narratives. 1941-44. *601*

McCain, William D. Archives. Italy, northern. Personal narratives. 1944-45. *602*

McCandless, Bruce (reminiscences). *Gregory* (vessel). Japan (Bonin Islands). Navy. 1945. *603*

McCann, Frank D. Brazil. Foreign Relations. 1937-45. *1087*

McCarthy, Joseph R. Air Warfare. Marines. Pacific Area. Politics. Wisconsin. 1942-52. *774*

—. Education. Lawyers. Marines. State Politics. Wisconsin. 1908-44. *687*

McClellan, George Brinton. Cavalry. Saddles. 1857-1943. *303*

McCormick, Vincent A. (diary). Jesuits. Vatican. 1942-45. *404*

McDaniel, Boyce (reminiscences). New Mexico (Los Alamos). Nuclear Arms. Plutonium. 1940-45. *605*

McDonald, James G. (paper). Europe. Jews. Refugees. Resettlement. 1938-43. *285*

McElroy, John W. (account). Amphibious operations. *Marathon* (vessel). Okinawa (battle). 1945. *606*

McGuire, Thomas. Air Warfare. Philippines. 1945. *16*

McKee, Andrew Irwin. Electric Boat Company. Military Engineering. Navies. Submarines. 1930's-61. *10*

Medical Research. Atomic Bomb Casualty Commission. Civilian survivors. Japan (Hiroshima, Nagasaki). Radiation Effects Research Foundation. 1945-75. *1010*

—. Exchange programs. Great Britain. USSR. ca 1941-45. *62*

Medicine. Fishbein, Morris (obituary). Historians. 1977. *215*

Mediterranean Sea and Area. Great Britain. Howard, Michael (review article). Military Strategy. USA. 1942-43. *453*

Meeting at Potsdam (film). Films (accuracy). Historical license. Potsdam Conference. Truman, Harry S. 1945. 1970's. *310*

Memoirs. Byrnes, James F. Federal Government. Germany. Nuclear Science and Technology. Szilard, Leo. 1898-1945. *948*

—. Churchill, Winston. Disarmament. Einstein, Albert. Eisenhower, Dwight D. Europe. Khrushchev, Nikita. Moch, Jules. 1932-55. *641*

—. Maginnis, John J. Marcus, David. US Control Council for Germany. 1944-46. *574*

Mennonites. Anabaptists. Germany. Switzerland. Taxation. War. 16c-1973. *489*

—. Civilian service. Conscription, military. 1930's-45. *476*

Menzies, Robert Gordon. Australia. Great Britain. Military Aid. 1940. *263*

Merchant Marine. Coates, Eugene Butler. Nova Scotia. 20c. *258*

—. Liberty Ships. 1941-78. *1068*

—. Military intelligence. Morale. Nova Scotia (Halifax). 1940-45. *1014*

—. Military Sealift Command. National Defense Reserve Fleet. Victory ships. Vietnam War. 1944-77. *201*

Messersmith, George. Foreign policy. Germany. Nazism. 1933-45. *654*

Messersmith, George Strausser. Anti-Nazi Movements. Diplomacy. State Department. 1928-39. *858*

Methodology. Alliance polarization. Diplomatic representation. Guttmann-Lingoes Smallest Space Analysis. War. 1815-1973. *1007*

Metz (battle). France. Lorraine campaign. Patton, George S., Jr. Third Army. 1944. *46*

Michigan. Agricultural production. Farmers. 1939-45. *179*

—. Clive, Alan (review article). 1939-45. *834*

—. Cold War. Poland. Vandenberg, Arthur Hendrick, Sr. Yalta Conference. 1944-48. *149*

—. Labor. Sex roles. Women. 1941-45. *180*

Michigan (Detroit). Anti-Nazi Movements. Boycotts. Fram, Leon (reminiscences). Jews. League for Human Rights. 1930's-40's. *296*

—. Automobile Industry and Trade. Labor (militancy). Production standards. United Automobile Workers of America. Working Conditions. 1937-55. *540*

—. Cane, Cyril H. Diplomatic reports. Great Britain. Riots. 1943. *359*

Middle East. Culbertson, William S. Economic policy. Foreign Relations. Great Britain. USA. 1944-45. *219*

—. Foreign Policy. 1941-45. *383*

—. Foreign Policy. Palestine. Roosevelt, Franklin D. USA. 1943-45. *710*

Midway (battle). Aircraft carriers. 1942. *369*

—. Japan. Military Strategy. USA. 1942. *1073*

—. Japan. Navies. USA. 1942. *147*

Midway, battle of. Naval Biography. Nimitz, Chester W. 1942. *747*

Midway class. Aircraft carriers. Naval Vessels. 1941-75. *24*

Midway Island (attack on). Censorship. *Chicago Tribune*. Grand Juries. Japan. Navies. 1942. *300*

Migration, Internal (noneconomic variables). Appalachia. Japanese Americans. Negroes. 1860-1973. *984*

Military. Adventists. Chaplains. 1944-55. *224*

—. Airplane Industry and Trade. Technology. 1937-50. *764*

—. Arizona. Bridges, floating. Yuma Proving Ground. 1943-50. *431*

—. Bibliographies. Dissertations. 1977-78. *169*

—. Bombing ranges. Hawaii National Park. 1938-50. *452*

—. British Commonwealth. Integration. USA. Women. World War I. 1900-78. *959*

—. Canada. Caribbean. Garrison duty. Great Britain. 1914-45. *665*

—. Defense industries. Discrimination. Executive Order 8802. March on Washington Movement. Randolph, A. Philip. Webster, Milton. 1941-44. *588*

—. Foreign Policy. MacArthur, Douglas. Philippines. 1945-46. *262*

—. Hastie, William. Negroes. Racism. Stimson, Henry L. 1940-43. *610*

—. Marshall, S. L. A. (reminiscences). World War I. 1919-69. *587*

—. Pesticides. 1939-50. *730*

—. Professionalism. Social Change. 1941-76. *129*

—. System analysis. 1940-71. *105*

Military Aid. Airplanes, Military. Greece. Roosevelt, Franklin D. (administration). 1940-41. *666*

—. Australia. Great Britain. Menzies, Robert Gordon. 1940. *263*
—. Beaverbrook, 1st Baron. Diplomacy. Harriman, W. Averell. USSR. 1941. *510*
—. Destroyers. Navies. Spain. 1942-60. *35*
—. Foreign Relations. Latin America. Military Assistance Program. 1932-72. *41*
—. Great Britain. Historiography. Military Capability. USSR. 1941-75. *671*
—. Great Britain. Murrow, Edward R. Radio. 1939-41. *200*
Military Airlift Command. Air Forces. 1941-72. *1096*
Military Assistance Program. Foreign Relations. Latin America. Military Aid. 1932-72. *41*
Military Bases. Australia. Foreign Relations. National Security. 1944-46. *69*
Military Campaigns. Great Britain. 1942-45. *486*
Military Capability. Air Forces. Japan. Philippines. 1941. *385*
—. Great Britain. Historiography. Military aid. USSR. 1941-75. *671*
Military Decorations, Flags, and Symbols. Airplanes, Military. Army Air Corps. California. Eaker, Ira C. Hamilton Field. Wright, Howard T. (account). 1941. *1062*
Military Decorations, Flags, and Symbols (shoulder patches). Iceland. Marines. Polar bear motif. 1941-42. *93*
Military defeat. Historians, Western. Japan. Pacific Area. Military. 1942-45. *832*
Military Engineering. Electric Boat Company. McKee, Andrew Irwin. Navies. Submarines. 1930's-61. *10*
Military Finance. Armies (Finance Department). 1941-45. *813*
—. Canada. Great Britain. 1943-45. *334*
—. Canada. Great Britain. Hyde Park Declaration (1941). USA. 1939-41. *331*
Military force structuring. Armies. Reorganization Objective Army Divisions. 1861-1977. *91*
Military General Staff. Air Forces. Bombing, indiscriminate. Civilian targets. Ethics. Germany. 1941-45. *837*
—. Air Warfare. Bombing. Churchill, Winston. Operation Overlord. Roosevelt, Franklin D. 1944. *1053*
—. Atlantic Fleet. King, Ernest J. Naval Biography. 1940's. *827*
—. China. Jiang Jieshi. Marshall, George C. Stillwell, Joseph W. 1944. *841*
—. Eisenhower, Dwight D. Marshall, George C. Operation Overlord. Roosevelt, Franklin D. 1942-44. *295*
—. Executive Order No. 1. Gifts. MacArthur, Douglas. Philippines. Quezon, Manuel. Sutherland, Richard K. (papers). 1942. *733*
—. Flight training. Negroes. Parrish, Noel F. (interview). Tuskegee Army Air Field. 1941-45. *393*
—. Louisiana (western). War Games. 2nd Army, US. 3d Army, US. 1941. *668*
Military General Staff (meetings). Clay, Lucius D. Documents. Germany. Military government. Office of Military Government for Germany (US). US Group Control Council, Germany. 1944-49. *917*
Military Government. Armies. 1847-1971. *1078*
—. Clay, Lucius D. Documents. Germany. Military General Staff (meetings). Office of Military Government for Germany (US). US Group Control Council, Germany. 1944-49. *917*
Military Ground Forces. Africa, North. Air Forces. Patton, George S., Jr. Tactics. 1943. *502*
Military History. Bibliographies. Dissertations. 5c BC-1980. *171*

—. Bookselling. Higher Education. 1945-70's. *631*
—. Canada. Governor General's Foot Guards. Militia. 1872-1972. *972*
—. Germany. Ultra project. 1940-45. *906*
—. Stained glass windows. US Military Academy. 1800-1944. *705*
—. Surprise attacks. 1940's-70's. *77*
Military Intelligence. Aeronautics, Military. O-47 (aircraft). O-52 (aircraft). Puerto Rico. ca 1917-43. *320*
—. Bulge (battle). China. Cuban Missile Crisis. Korean War. 1944-80. *34*
—. Forestry. France. Great Britain. USA. 1943-47. *65*
—. Hawaii. Holmes, Wilfrid J. (account). Navies. Nimitz, Chester W. Pearl Harbor. 1941. *425*
—. Historiography. 1941-45. *469*
—. Merchant Marine. Morale. Nova Scotia (Halifax). 1940-45. *1014*
—. Normandy Landing. Rosengarten, Adolph G., Jr. (reminiscences). Ultra project. War Department (Military Intelligence Division; Special Branch). 1st Army, US. 1944-45. *796*
Military Intelligence (review article). Brown, Anthony Cave. Germany. Great Britain. Kahn, David. 1939-45. *518*
Military Intelligence Service. Japanese Americans (Nisei). Language School. Minnesota. Rasmussen, Kai E. 1941-46. *28*
Military life. Antiwar Sentiment. Cartoons. Hasek, Jaroslav (*The Good Soldier Schweik*). ca 1920-70. *30*
Military Medicine. California (San Francisco Bay area). Music. Voluntary Associations. 1943-45. *835*
—. Mobilization. Psychologists. World War II (antecedents). 1938-41. *674*
Military occupation. Allies. Germany. Partition. 1943-48. *475*
—. Armistice question. Government. Great Britain. Italy. 1944. *29*
—. Central America. Pacific Area. *Tulsa* (vessel). 1919-45. *1102*
—. China, north. Civil wars. Marines. 1945-47. *228*
—. Clay, Lucius D. (appointment). Germany. USA. 1945. *889*
Military (officers). Armies (review article). Bureaucracies. Gabriel, Richard A. Savage, Paul L. 1914-80. *64*
Military operations. Canada. Europe. Politics. 1939-45. *909*
Military organization. Armies. Europe, Western. 1944-45. *288*
—. Army Air Forces. Arnold, H. H. (Hap). Planning. 1942. *503*
Military planning. Decisionmaking. Political warning. 1941. *824*
Military (policy). Diplomacy. Embick, Stanley D., Gen. National Council for the Prevention of War. 1937-45. *838*
Military preparedness. Churchill, Winston. Foreign policy. Great Britain. USA. World War II (antecedents). 1933-39. 1976. *560*
—. Foreign Policy (Pacific area). Military Strategy. USA. 1940-41. *505*
Military records. Dwight D. Eisenhower Library. Kansas (Abilene). Research. 1916-52. 1977. *361*
Military recruitment. Armies. Hastie, William H. Negroes. Press, black. 1940-42. *611*
—. Australia. Curtin, John. Hasluck, Paul. MacArthur, Douglas. 1942-43. *551*
—. Illinois (Chicago). Navies. 1941-43. *1023*
Military reform. Hastie, William H. Racism. 1940-43. *612*

252 Military reorganization

Military reorganization. Hopkins, Harry. Marshall, George C. Roosevelt, Franklin D. 1942-45. *744*
Military rescue concepts. Korean War. Vietnam War. 1941-74. *141*
Military Sealift Command. Merchant Marine. National Defense Reserve Fleet. Victory ships. Vietnam War. 1944-77. *201*
Military Service. Canada. French Canadians. 1939-45. *336*
—. Canada. Highlanders, 48th. Hunter, William A. (reminiscences). Leftism. Liberalism. 1939-45. *438*
—. Canada. Women. 20c. *1104*
—. Canadian Women's Army Corps. Morality. Sex roles. Women. 1941-46. *740*
—. Civil War. Forrest, Nathan Bedford. Forrest, Nathan Bedford (1905-44). Sisk, John P. (personal account). 1861-1945. *870*
—. Marines. Women. 1918-22. 1943-73. *456*
Military Service (denied). British Columbia. Canada. Chinese Canadians. Japanese Canadians. 1939-45. *806*
Military Service (enlistees). Discrimination, Employment. Navies. Negroes. Race Relations. Segregation. 1798-1970's. *388*
Military Service, Professional. Burke, Arleigh. Naval Education. US Naval Academy. 1919-40. *794*
—. Diplomacy. Faymonville, Philip R. USA. USSR. 1917-52. *511*
—. Ridgway, Matthew B. War. 1917-60. *9*
—. Smith, Oliver P. 1917-51. *863*
Military Service, Professional (officers). National Security. War. 1783-1973. *976*
Military Strategy. Air Forces. Vietnam War. Weather. 1941-72. *311*
—. Air Warfare. Arnold, H. H. "Hap". Historians. 1943-44. *708*
—. Air Warfare. Auschwitz. Concentration Camps. Jews. 1944-45. *1063*
—. Air Warfare. Bombing. Germany. Great Britain. 1942-44. *994*
—. Allies. Berlin (capture). Germany. 1941-45. *466*
—. Allies. Diplomacy. 1942. *793*
—. Allies. Germany. Weapons. 1944-45. *715*
—. American Revolution. ca 1775-1945. *1022*
—. Amphibious operations. Marines. 20c. *542*
—. Asia, East. Japan. 1944-45. *173*
—. Atomic energy. Japan. Smyth Report, 1945. USA. 1940-45. *897*
—. Atomic Warfare. Decisionmaking. Japan (Hiroshima, Nagasaki). 1944-45. *304*
—. Atomic Warfare. Japan. USA. 1945. *429*
—. Atomic Warfare. Japan (Hiroshima; Nagasaki). 1945. *267*
—. Atomic warfare. Japan (Hiroshima, Nagasaki). USA. 1945. *83*
—. Attitudes. Economic development. Nuclear arms. Technology. War. 1914-68. *686*
—. Balance of power. Korean War. Technology. Weapons. 1918-53. *876*
—. Bombing. France. Operation Overlord. Zuckerman, Solly (review article). 1944. *484*
—. Bulge (battle). Germany. 1944. *714*
—. Chiang Kai-shek. China. Stilwell, Joseph W. 1942-44. *629*
—. Churchill, Winston. Diplomacy. Great Britain. Roosevelt, Franklin D. 1942-44. *999*
—. Churchill, Winston. Great Britain. Joint Chiefs of Staff. Malta Conference. Roosevelt, Franklin D. 1945. *912*
—. Cold War (origins). Italy. Kolko, Gabriel. Negotiations. Operation Crossword. 1945. *166*
—. Decisionmaking. Pacific Area. 1941-45. *75*

—. Economic development. Liberia. State Department. 1938-45. *66*
—. Eisenhower, Dwight D. Germany (Berlin). Great Britain. USSR. 1945. *495*
—. Europe. Great Britain. Invasions (proposed). 1942-44. *822*
—. Expansionism. *Rankin* plans. USA. USSR. 1943. *924*
—. Falaise (battle). France. France (Normandy). Operation Cobra. Patton, George S., Jr. USA. 1944. *751*
—. Foreign Policy. Latin America. USA. 1850-1976. *168*
—. Foreign Policy (Pacific area). Military preparedness. USA. 1940-41. *505*
—. Germany. 1933-39. *878*
—. Great Britain. Howard, Michael (review article). Mediterranean Sea and Area. USA. 1942-43. *453*
—. Great Britain. Singapore, defense of. USA. 1939-41. *49*
—. Italy. Italy, invasion of. Kesselring, Albert. 1943. *923*
—. Japan. Midway (battle). USA. 1942. *1073*
—. Japan, invasion of. Operation Olympic (planned). 1945. *210*
—. MacArthur, Douglas. Naval strategy. 1942-51. *1095*
—. Philippines. Rainbow-5 (plan). 1941-42. *190*
Military training. Air Bases. Alabama (Montgomery). Army Air Corps. Maxwell Field. Mutiny. 1943. *222*
—. Air Warfare. Atomic bomb. *Enola Gay* (aircraft). Wendover Field. 1944-45. *986*
—. Marines. Parris Island (camp). Vietnam War. 1942-72. *695*
—. Oklahoma State University. Preparedness. Reserve Officers' Training Corps. Veterans. Women Appointed for Volunteer Emergency Service. 1891-1951. *812*
Militia. Canada. Governor General's Foot Guards. Military History. 1872-1972. *972*
Mines, military. Indonesia (Sumatra; Palembang; Moesi River). Naval Air Forces. 462d Bomb Group. 1944. *996*
Minnesota. Employment. Germans. Prisoners of war. 1942-46. *743*
—. Japanese Americans (Nisei). Language School. Military Intelligence Service. Rasmussen, Kai E. 1941-46. *28*
—. Newspapers. Swedish language. 1851-1976. *685*
Minnesota (Minneapolis). Actors and Actresses. Benefit performances. Employment. 1942. *985*
Minorities. British Columbia. Japanese communities. Public schools, challenge to. 1900-72. *203*
—. Violence, racial. War. 1910-67. *839*
Missiles. Drones. Fahrney, Delmar S. (account). Navy Bureau of Aeronautics. N2C-2 (aircraft). Radio. Research and development. TG-2 (aircraft). 1936-45. *279*
Missions and Missionaries. Canada. China. Hurford, Grace Gibberd (reminiscences). Teaching. 1928-45. *439*
—. Japan. Mormons. USA. 1901-24. *125*
Mississippi. Democratic Party. Economic Development. Racial issues. 1941-45. *874*
—. Prisoners of War. 1943-46. *759*
Mississippi (Hattiesburg). Camp Shelby. Daily Life. Mobilization effects. 1940-45. *849*
Mississippi River. Dry dock, floating. Louisiana (New Orleans). Manitowoc Shipbuilding Co. Navigation, Inland. *Peto* (vessel). Submarines. 1942-45. *676*

Missouri (Kansas City). Defense Industries. Industrialization. Small Business. 1940-45. *656*
Mobilization. Advisory Commission to the Council of National Defense. Industry. 1940. *102*
—. Military Medicine. Psychologists. World War II (antecedents). 1938-41. *674*
Mobilization effects. Camp Shelby. Daily Life. Mississippi (Hattiesburg). 1940-45. *849*
Mobilization needs. Clark, Grenville. National service law (proposed). Roosevelt, Franklin D. (administration). 1942-45. *599*
Moch, Jules. Churchill, Winston. Disarmament. Einstein, Albert. Eisenhower, Dwight D. Europe. Khrushchev, Nikita. Memoirs. 1932-55. *641*
Molotov, V. M. Eden, Anthony. Foreign Policy. Poland. Truman, Harry S. USSR. 1945. *635*
Monroe Doctrine. Americas (North and South). Defense policy. Roosevelt, Franklin D. (administration). 1930's-40. *363*
Montana. Political Attitudes. Roosevelt, Franklin D. Senate. Wheeler, Burton K. 1904-46. *811*
Montgomery Ward (federal seizure of). Avery, Sewell. Economic Conditions. Illinois (Chicago). Labor Disputes (arbitration). War Labor Board. 1941. *490*
Morale. Armies. *New York Times.* Railey, Hilton H. Reporters and Reporting. 1941. *1027*
—. Merchant Marine. Military intelligence. Nova Scotia (Halifax). 1940-45. *1014*
Morality. Atomic Warfare. Hersey, John (*Hiroshima*). Literature. 1945-74. *1065*
—. Attitudes. Sex. 1918-55. *597*
—. Canadian Women's Army Corps. Military service. Sex roles. Women. 1941-46. *740*
—. Cold War. Diplomacy. Vietnam War. 1945-70's. *860*
—. Friendship. Literature. Politics. Pound, Ezra. Treason. 1909-72. *192*
—. War (justification of). 1940-74. *391*
Morgenthau, Henry, Jr. Federal Government. Great Britain. Jews. Relief organizations. War Refugee Board. 1940-44. *726*
—. Germany. Jews (stateless). State Department. Treasury Department. USA. 1942-44. *589*
Mormons. Japan. Missions and Missionaries. USA. 1901-24. *125*
Morrison, Charles C. *Christian Century* (periodical). Foreign policy. Japan. Manchurian crisis. USA. 1931-33. *719*
Mukaida, Tomeji (reminiscences). Idaho (Minidoka). Japanese Americans. Relocation camps. 1940's. *573*
Munson, Curtis B. Civil rights. Counterintelligence. Internment. Japanese Americans. Peiper, N. J. L. 1931-42. *500*
Murphy, Robert (tribute). Diplomacy. Europe. 1941-45. *204*
Murphy (vessel). Diplomacy. Ibn-Saud, King. Roosevelt, Franklin D. Saudi Arabia. USA. 1945. *472*
Murray, Leonard W. Canada. Navies. World War I. 1913-45. *308*
Murrow, Edward R. Great Britain. Military Aid. Radio. 1939-41. *200*
Music. California (San Francisco Bay area). Military Medicine. Voluntary Associations. 1943-45. *835*
—. Negroes. 1941-45. *770*
Music, popular. Attitudes. Rhetoric. 1940-45. *643*
Muskingum College. Films. History Teaching. Ohio (New Concord). 1971-72. *931*
Mussolini, Benito. Italy. Political issues. Pound, Ezra (letters). USA. 1932-43. *748*

Mutiny. Air Bases. Alabama (Montgomery). Army Air Corps. Maxwell Field. Military training. 1943. *222*
—. Army Air Force Station 569. Great Britain (Bamber Bridge). Negroes. USA. 1943. *1025*

N

NAACP. Civil rights movement. Negroes. South Dakota. 1804-1970. *82*
Nash, Al (reminiscences). Airplane Industry and Trade. Labor Unions and Organizations (militancy). New York (Long Island City). Political factions. 1940-44. *675*
National Catholic Welfare Conference. Catholic Church. National Council of Catholic Women. Peace Movements. Women. 1919-46. *561*
National Characteristics. Adventure serials. Americanism. Radio. 1940-45. *287*
—. Foreign Relations. France. Lafayette myth. 1763-1976. *254*
—. Patriotism. 1941-45. *1094*
National Council for the Prevention of War. Diplomacy. Embick, Stanley D., Gen. Military (policy). 1937-45. *838*
—. Libby, Frederick J. Malmédy massacre. Trials. War crimes (standards). 1944-49. *237*
National Council of Catholic Women. Catholic Church. National Catholic Welfare Conference. Peace Movements. Women. 1919-46. *561*
National Defense Advisory Commission. Aircraft industry. Joint Aircraft Committee. Office of Production Management. Technological change. 1940-45. *423*
National Defense Reserve Fleet. Merchant Marine. Military Sealift Command. Victory ships. Vietnam War. 1944-77. *201*
National Film Board of Canada. Canada. Films. Sex roles. Women. 1940's-50's. *594*
National Guard. Aircraft markings. F-105 (aircraft). Virginia. 192d Tactical Fighter Group. 1917-79. *544*
National Maritime Union. Communist Party. Negroes. Racism. United Electrical Radio and Machine Workers. 1941-45. *196*
National Reich Church (suggested). Germany. Propaganda campaign. Roosevelt, Franklin D. USA. World War II (antecedents). 1941. *187*
National Science Foundation. Kilgore, Harley M. Legislation. Science and Government. Senate. 1942-50. *568*
National security. Airlines. Latin America. State Department. 1927-40. *767*
—. Armies. Canol Project. Northwest Territories. Pipelines. USA. 1942-45. *226*
—. Australia. Foreign Relations. Military Bases. 1944-46. *69*
—. Central Intelligence Agency (secret operations). Donovan, William J. Intelligence Service. 1940's-74. *798*
—. Military Service, Professional (officers). War. 1783-1973. *976*
—. Peace Movements. Preparedness. 1941-71. *214*
—. Pearl Harbor question. Roosevelt, Franklin D. (administration). 1941-46. *620*
National Self-image. Films. Hollywood. Liberalism. Office of War Information. 1942-45. *494*
National service law (proposed). Clark, Grenville. Mobilization needs. Roosevelt, Franklin D. (administration). 1942-45. *599*
National Telephone Company (Spain). Diplomacy. Spain. USA. Weddell, Alexander Wilbourne. *367*
Nationalism. Foreign Policy. UN. USA. 1944-45. *152*

254 Nationalism

—. France. Intellectuals. Maritain, Raïssa. Poetry. USA. 1940-60. *938*
NATO. Foreign Policy. UN. 1941-55. *71*
—. Great Britain. Naval Strategy. USA. USSR. 1945-70's. *646*
Naval Air Forces. 1911-78. *33*
—. 1910's-50. *651*
—. Aeronautics, Military. Battleships, fast. 1941-45. *659*
—. Flight training. Hutchinson Naval Air Station. Kansas. Olathe Naval Air Station. 1942-69. *441*
—. Florida (Pensacola). Urbanization. 1900-45. *609*
—. F6F (aircraft). Harp, A. Norman (account). 1945. *384*
—. Indonesia (Sumatra; Palembang; Moesi River). Mines, military. 462d Bomb Group. 1944. *996*
—. Radar. 1940-44. *965*
Naval Battles. Antisubmarine warfare. *Batfish* (vessel). 1942-45. *128*
—. *Platte* (vessel). Shipbuilding. 1939-71. *213*
Naval Biography. Atlantic Fleet. King, Ernest J. Military General Staff. 1940's. *827*
—. Midway, battle of. Nimitz, Chester W. 1942. *747*
Naval Education. Burke, Arleigh. Military Service, Professional. US Naval Academy. 1919-40. *794*
Naval History. Nimitz, Chester W. Pacific Area. 1885-1966. *1019*
Naval Intelligence (The Identification and Characteristics Section). 1941-45. *593*
Naval Strategy. Air Warfare. Japan. Pearl Harbor, attack on. 1940-41. *698*
—. Amphibious warfare. General Board of the Navy. Marines. 1900-74. *688*
—. Battle cruisers. World War I. 1900-47. *25*
—. Battleships. Pacific Area. 1942-45. *658*
—. Dull, Paul S. (review article). Japan. Pearl Harbor, attack on. Yamamoto, Isoroku. 1941-45. *977*
—. Great Britain. NATO. USA. USSR. 1945-70's. *646*
—. King, Ernest J. Pacific Area. 1926-44. *781*
—. MacArthur, Douglas. Military Strategy. 1942-51. *1095*
—. Nuclear Arms. Technology. 1945-72. *1021*
—. Pacific Area. 1934-42. *420*
—. Pacific Area. Surrender. Wake Island. 1941. *340*
—. USSR. 1943-45. *504*
—. War Plan ORANGE. World War II (antecedents). 1933-40. *245*
Naval Tactics. Japan. Pacific Area. USA. 1920's-43. *447*
—. Philippine Sea, battle. Spruance, Raymond A. 1943. *134*
Naval Vessels. Aircraft carriers. *Midway* class. 1941-75. *24*
—. British Columbia. Films. Submarines. World War I. 1914-45. *156*
—. Camouflage. 1940-45. *937*
—. Hawaii. Japan. Pearl Harbor (attack on). 1941. *1098*
—. *New England* (vessel). 1937-44. *264*
—. Scrap metal industry. 1941-79. *302*
—. Weapons. 1930-76. *955*
Naval Vessels (destroyer-escorts). Great Britain. Lend-Lease. 1943-45. *269*
Naval warfare. Battleship era. Dreadnought. 1905-71. *448*
Navies. Air Forces. Leyte Gulf (battle). Philippines. 1944. *829*
—. Air Forces. Maritime missions. 1941-78. *150*

—. Aircraft carriers. *Lexington* (vessel). *Saratoga* (vessel). 1922-45. *23*
—. Airplanes, Military. Industrial productivity. Japan. 1941-45. *752*
—. Amphibious operations. Hewitt, H. Kent. 1887-1949. *174*
—. Antiaircraft guns. Destroyers. Photographs. 1945. *42*
—. Anti-Communists. China. Sino-American Cooperation Association. USA. 1942-45. *842*
—. Antisubmarine warfare. "Four Stackers". Great Britain. USA. 1940-45. *120*
—. Asia, Southeast (coast). India. *Lanikai* (vessel). Roosevelt, Franklin D. Tolley, Kemp (personal account). World War II (antecedents). 1941. *968*
—. Atlantic, battle of the. Great Britain. Roosevelt, Franklin D. Secrecy. Warmaking powers. 1941. *682*
—. Atlantic Ocean. Canada. Great Britain. USA. 1941-43. *557*
—. Atlantic Ocean (North). Canada. Hewens, Bob. *Niagara* (vessel). *U-570* (vessel). 1934-72. *1043*
—. Baker, Arthur Davidson, III (collection). Photography. 1941-45. *1101*
—. Beach, Edward L. (account). Hashimoto, Mochitsura (account). *Indianapolis* (vessel; sinking). 1945. *1088*
—. Boehler, Hurley. Interstate Aircraft and Engineering Corporation. TDR-1 (aircraft). 1943-77. *554*
—. California. Interrogation centers. Prisoners of War. Virginia. 1941-45. *647*
—. California (San Francisco Bay). Courts Martial and Courts of Inquiry. Mare Island Mutiny. Negroes. Port Chicago Naval Magazine. Race relations. 1944-48. *1055*
—. Canada. Murray, Leonard W. World War I. 1913-45. *308*
—. Censorship. *Chicago Tribune.* Grand Juries. Japan. Midway Island (attack on). 1942. *300*
—. Cruisers. 1930-74. *1061*
—. Delaware (Wilmington). Dravo Corp. Pennsylvania (Pittsburgh). Shipbuilding. 1940-47. *974*
—. Destroyers. Military Aid. Spain. 1942-60. *35*
—. Discrimination, Employment. Military Service (enlistees). Negroes. Race Relations. Segregation. 1798-1970's. *388*
—. Electric Boat Company. McKee, Andrew Irwin. Military Engineering. Submarines. 1930's-61. *10*
—. *Enterprise* (vessels). 1799-1978. *458*
—. Foreign Relations. Great Britain. Technology. USA. 1938-46. *532*
—. *Gold Star* (vessel). Guam. 1941-42. *506*
—. Great Britain. Pacific Area. Winton, John (review article). 1941-45. *170*
—. Guadalcanal (battle). King, Ernest J. Marshall, George C. 1942-43. *135*
—. Hawaii. Hechler, Ted, Jr. (account). Pearl Harbor, attack on. *Phoenix* (vessel). 1941. *400*
—. Hawaii. Holmes, Wilfrid J. (account). Military Intelligence. Nimitz, Chester W. Pearl Harbor. 1941. *425*
—. Illinois (Chicago). Military Recruitment. 1941-43. *1023*
—. *Indiana* (BB-58, vessel). Pacific Area (South). 1922-62. *895*
—. Japan. Leyte Gulf (battle). Philippines. USA. 1944. *352*
—. Japan. Midway (battle). USA. 1942. *147*

—. Japan. Pacific Area. Savo Island (battle). USA. 1942. *67*
—. Japan. Philippine Sea (battle). USA. 1944. *145*
—. Japan. Solomon Islands (Vella Lavella). USA. 1943. *547*
—. King, Ernest J. Press. Public relations. 1939-43. *339*
—. Lake Michigan. 1941-45. *126*
—. Salvage. 1943-79. *633*
—. Submarines. 17c-1943. *522*
—. *Vixen* (vessel). 1940-46. *1003*
Navies (communications, tactics). Great Britain. Japan. USA. 1943-45. *225*
Navigation. Imperialism. Japan. Pacific Area. Pearl Harbor, attack on. World War II (antecedents). Prehistory-1941. *216*
Navigation, bush. *Gato* (vessel). Solomon Islands. Submarine Warfare. 1943. *608*
Navigation, Inland. Dry dock, floating. Louisiana (New Orleans). Manitowoc Shipbuilding Co. Mississippi River. *Peto* (vessel). Submarines. 1942-45. *676*
Navy. Armaments. *Tiny Tim* (rocket). 1944. *317*
—. Balloons. Dirigibles. McBride, Robert M. Personal narratives. 1941-44. *601*
—. *Gregory* (vessel). Japan (Bonin Islands). McCandless, Bruce (reminiscences). 1945. *603*
—. Hospital. Yosemite National Park. 1943-45. *831*
Navy Bureau of Aeronautics. Drones. Fahrney, Delmar S. (account). Missiles. N2C-2 (aircraft). Radio. Research and development. TG-2 (aircraft). 1936-45. *279*
Navy Patrol Bombing Squadron 106. PB4B-2 (aircraft). Regimental histories. 1944-45. *888*
Navy-yards and Naval Stations. California (Los Angeles, San Diego, San Francisco). City Planning. Ports. 1919-41. *548*
Nazis. Diplomacy. Espionage. Germany. Thomsen, Hans. 1940. *634*
Nazism. Allies. USSR. 1939-45. *499*
—. Bolivia. Foreign Relations. Germany. USA. 1941-46. *99*
—. Cold War. Historiography. Revisionism. ca 1930-50. *515*
—. Deutscher Bund Canada. German Canadians. Saskatchewan. 1934-39. *1005*
—. Diamond, Sander A. (review article). German Americans. USA. 1924-41. 1974. *284*
—. Foreign policy. Germany. Messersmith, George. 1933-45. *654*
Nazism, American (review article). Coughlin, Charles. Countersubversives. Fascism (review article). German-American Bund. 1924-41. *785*
Nebraska. Airplanes, Military (assembly). Offutt Air Force Base (Building D). Recreation. 1940-77. *816*
Nebraska (Omaha). Civil Rights. Negroes. Quality of life. Social services. Urban League. 1928-50. *623*
Negotiations. Cold War (origins). Italy. Kolko, Gabriel. Military Strategy. Operation Crossword. 1945. *166*
Negro Literature. Hughes, Langston. Popular culture. Semple, Jesse B. (fictitious character). 1942-43. *755*
Negro Soldier (film). Armies. Documentaries. Films. Heisler, Stuart. Propaganda. Race Relations. 1944. *195*
Negroes. Adoption. Baker, Josephine. Civil rights. Entertainers. 1940-75. *434*
—. Alabama (Mobile). Fair Employment Practices Commission. Shipyards. South. 1938-45. *771*

—. Appalachia. Japanese Americans. Migration, Internal (noneconomic variables). 1860-1973. *984*
—. Armies. Discrimination. Government. Great Britain. 1942-45. *358*
—. Armies. Hastie, William H. Military recruitment. Press, black. 1940-42. *611*
—. Army Air Force Station 569. Great Britain (Bamber Bridge). Mutiny. USA. 1943. *1025*
—. Boilermakers, Iron Shipbuilders and Helpers, International Brotherhood of. California (Los Angeles). Discrimination, employment. Labor Unions and Organizations. Oregon (Portland). Shipbuilding. 1941-46. *883*
—. California (San Francisco Bay). Courts Martial and Courts of Inquiry. Mare Island Mutiny. Navies. Port Chicago Naval Magazine. Race relations. 1944-48. *1055*
—. Civic Unity Committee. Defense industries. Japanese Americans. Race relations. Washington (Seattle). 1940-45. *248*
—. Civil Rights. Nebraska (Omaha). Quality of life. Social services. Urban League. 1928-50. *623*
—. Civil rights movement. NAACP. South Dakota. 1804-1970. *82*
—. Communist Party. National Maritime Union. Racism. United Electrical Radio and Machine Workers. 1941-45. *196*
—. Discrimination. Fair Employment Practices Committee. Railroads. Southeastern Carriers Conference. 1941-45. *402*
—. Discrimination, Employment. Fair Employment Practices Committee. Roosevelt, Franklin D. (administration). 1940-45. *871*
—. Discrimination, Employment. Military Service (enlistees). Navies. Race Relations. Segregation. 1798-1970's. *388*
—. Employment. Industry. Social justice. 1942-43. *1086*
—. Employment. Labor unions. Women. Working-class militancy. 194)'s. *341*
—. Farmers, black. North Caroli\a. Social Change. South. 1950-70. *1004*
—. Flight training. Military General Staff. Parrish, Noel F. (interview). Tuskegee Army Air Field. 1941-45. *393*
—. Hastie, William. Military. Racism. Stimson, Henry L. 1940-43. *610*
—. Historiography. Roosevelt, Franklin D. (administration). USSR. 1939-45. *872*
—. Music. 1941-45. *770*
—. Newspapers. 1941-45. *920*
—. Newspapers. Political Protest. Race relations. 1941-45. *289*
—. Pennsylvania (Philadelphia). Public transportation. Racism. Strikes. US Employment Service. War Manpower Commission. 1944. *1046*
Negroes (physicians, soldiers). Army hospitals. Hospitals. Segregation, development of. 1940-42. *707*
Nelson, Donald M. Civil-military relations. War Production Board. 1942-45. *172*
—. Employment. Holland, Lou E. War Production Board, Smaller Plants Division and Corporation. 1940-44. *399*
Netherlands (Arnhem). Airborne operations. Operation Market-Garden. Ryan, Cornelius (review article). 1944. *559*
Netherlands East Indies. Foreign Policy. Japan. 1941-46. *426*
Neutrality. British Commonwealth. Canada. Foreign Relations. Ireland. 1939-45. *607*
—. Capper, Arthur. Legislation. Political Speeches. 1936-41. *709*

256   Neutrality

—. Churchill, Winston. Correspondence. Great Britain. Roosevelt, Franklin D. 1939-40. *531*
—. Economic agreements. Foreign Relations. Switzerland. World War I. 1919. 1944-45. *292*
—. Foreign Policy. Great Britain. Spain. 1939-45. *266*
—. Ireland. 1939-41. *158*
Neutrality Act (US, 1935). Armaments. Embargoes. Isolationism. 1935. *1080*
Neutrality (circumvention). Atlantic Ocean, South. Great Britain. Roosevelt, Franklin D. Takoradi air route. World War II (antecedents). 1941-42. *769*
Neutrality Laws. Europe, East. Foreign policy. Isolationism. Roosevelt, Franklin D. World War II (antecedents). 1920's-30's. *249*
Nevada (Las Vegas). City boosters. Public relations. Tourism. 1905-74. *471*
New Britain. Air Warfare. Japan. Kenney, George. Rabaul (battle). 1943. *92*
New Brunswick. Colleges and Universities (presidents). Dalhousie University. Mackenzie, A. Stanley. Stanley, Carleton. 1911-45. *395*
New Deal. Antifascism. Lend-Lease. Roosevelt, Franklin D. (administration). 1941-45. *1071*
—. Business. Labor Unions and Organizations. Taft-Hartley Act (US, 1947). Wagner Act (US, 1935). 1935-47. *108*
—. Frankfurter, Felix. Lippmann, Walter. Roosevelt, Franklin D. 1932-45. *721*
New Deal programs. Roosevelt, Franklin D. 1940-45. *869*
New England (vessel). Naval Vessels. 1937-44. *264*
New Hampshire (Lebanon). Peace proposal, utopian. Radio. St. John, Robert. 1945. *713*
New Jersey (Tenafly). Camp Lejeune. Lamb Studios. Marines. North Carolina. Stained glass. Windows. 1775-1945. *480*
New Mexico. Prisoners and prisons. 1942-46. *903*
New Mexico (Albuquerque). Annexation. Intergovernmental Relations. Nuclear Science and Technology. Weapons. 1940-78. *762*
New Mexico (Los Alamos). Atomic bomb. 1943-46. *660*
—. Bainbridge, Kenneth T. (reminiscences). Manhattan Project. Nuclear Arms. 1945. *40*
—. Cyclotrons. Manhattan Project. Nuclear Science and Technology. Wilson, Robert R. (reminiscences). 1942-43. *1044*
—. Little Theatre Group. Manhattan Project. Nuclear Arms. Theater Production and Direction. 1943-46. *13*
—. Manley, John H. (reminiscences). Nuclear Science and Technology. 1942-45. *581*
—. McDaniel, Boyce (reminiscences). Nuclear Arms. Plutonium. 1940-45. *605*
—. Nuclear Arms. Trinity test. White Sands military reservation. 1945. *488*
—. Nuclear Arms (first testing). 1945. *291*
New York. Clark, Grenville. Plattsburg Movement. Selective Service, origins of the. 1940-41. *176*
New York City. German Americans. Pharmacy. Societies, apothecary. 19c-1940's. *1008*
New York (Long Island City). Airplane Industry and Trade. Labor Unions and Organizations (militancy). Nash, Al (reminiscences). Political factions. 1940-44. *675*
New York (Saratoga Springs). Resorts. Restorations. 1810-1978. *706*
New York Times. Armies. Morale. Railey, Hilton H. Reporters and Reporting. 1941. *1027*
New York, western. Germans. Labor, prison. Prisoners of War (camps). 1944-46. *598*

Newfoundland. Arctic. *Georgi Sedov* (vessel). USSR. World War I. 1908-67. *51*
News. Brown, Cecil B. Columbia Broadcasting System. Editorials. Radio. White, Paul W. 1943. *954*
News broadcasts. Davis, Elmer. Interventionist, making of an. Radio. World War II (antecedents). 1939-42. *463*
Newspapers. Bankhead Bill (1943). Federal government. Subsidies. War Bond advertising. 1943. *112*
—. Editorials. Freedom of the Press. 1920. 1940. *113*
—. Foreign policy. Hearst, William Randolph. Isolationism. 1936-41. *157*
—. Minnesota. Swedish language. 1851-1976. *685*
—. Negroes. 1941-45. *920*
—. Negroes. Political Protest. Race relations. 1941-45. *289*
Niagara (vessel). Atlantic Ocean (North). Canada. Hewens, Bob. Navies. *U-570* (vessel). 1934-72. *1043*
Nicoll, John R. A. Catholic influence. Isolationism. Roosevelt, Franklin D. (administration). 1943. *357*
Nimitz, Chester W. Hawaii. Holmes, Wilfrid J. (account). Military Intelligence. Navies. Pearl Harbor. 1941. *425*
—. Joint Chiefs of Staff. MacArthur, Douglas. Pacific Area. Roosevelt, Franklin D. 1941-42. *189*
—. Midway, battle of. Naval Biography. 1942. *747*
—. Naval History. Pacific Area. 1885-1966. *1019*
Nishimura, Shimpe. Agriculture Department. California. Emergency Rubber Project. Guayule (plant). Rubber industry. 1942-76. *36*
Nixon, Richard M. Democracies. Developing Nations. Dictatorships. Foreign policy. USA. 1790-1975. *138*
No Foreign War Committee. *Cedar Rapids Gazette* (newspaper). Iowa. Marshall, Verne. World War II (antecedents). 1940-41. *238*
Nonrecognition. Annexation. Baltic Area. USA. USSR. 1940-70's. *467*
Non-Sectarian Anti-Nazi League to Champion Human Rights. Boycott activities. Economic Conditions. Jews. Joint Boycott Council. 1939-41. *326*
Normandy invasion. France. St. Lô (battle). USA. 1944. *162*
Normandy (landing). Amphibious operations. 1944. *856*
—. Military Intelligence. Rosengarten, Adolph G., Jr. (reminiscences). Ultra project. War Department (Military Intelligence Division; Special Branch). 1st Army, US. 1944-45. *796*
Norquist, Ernest O. Diaries. Japan. Philippines. Prisoners of War. 1942-45. *681*
Norris, George W. Foreign Policy. Internationalism. 1939-41. *351*
North America. Agriculture. Europe. Industrialization. Market economy. Peasant movements (colloquium). ca 1875-1975. *52*
—. Air Warfare. Balloons. Bombing. Japan. 1940-45. *1017*
—. Arctic. Discovery and Exploration. Finnie, Richard Sterling (account). Office of the Coordinator of Information. Stefansson, Vilhjalmur. 1931-62. *290*
North American Aviation. Airplanes, Military. B-25 transports. 1942-49. *37*
North American Aviation Corporation. P-51H (aircraft). 1943-52. *616*

Office 257

North Carolina. Camp Lejeune. Lamb Studios. Marines. New Jersey (Tenafly). Stained glass. Windows. 1775-1943. *480*
—. Farmers, black. Negroes. Social Change. South. 1950-70. *1004*
North Dakota. Anti-British sentiments. Churchill, Winston. Langer, William. Senate. 1941-52. *1035*
Northern Ireland. Conscription, military. Foreign Relations. Great Britain. Ireland. 1941. *795*
Northwest Territories. Armies. Canol Project. National Security. Pipelines. USA. 1942-45. *226*
—. Canol Project. Oil and Petroleum Products. Pipelines. Yukon Territory. 1942-45. *470*
Northwest Territories (Mackenzie Valley). Canol Project. Oil Industry and Trade. Pipelines. Planning. 1942-45. *55*
Norway. Diplomacy. Free ports. Roosevelt, Franklin Delano. USA. USSR. 1941-43. *788*
Norweb, R. Henry. Air Bases. Diplomacy. Portugal (Azores). 1941-44. *942*
Nova Scotia. Coates, Eugene Butler. Merchant Marine. 20c. *258*
Nova Scotia (Annapolis Valley). Apple industry. Exports. Great Britain. Imports. 1880-1957. *186*
Nova Scotia (Halifax). Merchant Marine. Military intelligence. Morale. 1940-45. *1014*
Novels. Air warfare. Bibliographies. 1939-45. *894*
—. Historiography. Wouk, Herman (review article). 1940-80. *579*
Nuclear Arms. Alperovitz, Gar. Diplomacy. Historiography. 1943-46. 1965-73. *571*
—. Attitudes. Economic development. Military Strategy. Technology. War. 1914-68. *686*
—. Bainbridge, Kenneth T. (reminiscences). Manhattan Project. New Mexico (Los Alamos). 1945. *40*
—. Cold War. Diplomacy. Roosevelt, Franklin Delano. 1941-45. *861*
—. Cold War. Diplomacy, atomic. Foreign policy. USA. USSR. 1942-46. *85*
—. Cold War (origins). Marshall Plan. Second Front. USSR. 1940's. *1016*
—. Colleges and Universities. Manhattan Project. Oppenheimer, J. Robert. 1904-67. *784*
—. Foreign Relations. Great Britain. Roosevelt, Franklin D. USA. 1940-45. *87*
—. Little Theatre Group. Manhattan Project. New Mexico (Los Alamos). Theater Production and Direction. 1943-46. *13*
—. McDaniel, Boyce (reminiscences). New Mexico (Los Alamos). Plutonium. 1940-45. *605*
—. Naval strategy. Technology. 1945-72. *1021*
—. New Mexico (Los Alamos). Trinity test. White Sands military reservation. 1945. *488*
Nuclear Arms (first testing). New Mexico (Los Alamos). 1945. *291*
Nuclear Arms (program). Einstein, Albert. Hungarian Americans. Szilárd, Leo. USA. 1941-74. *366*
Nuclear arms race. Atomic bomb. Franck, James. Political Attitudes. Truman, Harry S. (administration). 1944-45. *1000*
Nuclear arms testing. France. Great Britain. Secrecy. 1939-45. *327*
Nuclear chain reaction. Anderson, Herbert L. (reminiscences). Chicago, University of. Illinois. 1942. *19*
—. Chicago, University of. Illinois. Wattenberg, Albert (reminiscences). 1942. *1015*
Nuclear Physics. Atomic Warfare. Frisch, Otto R. (account). 1945. *307*

Nuclear Science and Technology. Anderson, Herbert L. (reminiscences). Chicago, University of. Columbia University. Fermi, Enrico. Szilard, Leo. 1933-45. *20*
—. Annexation. Intergovernmental Relations. New Mexico (Albuquerque). Weapons. 1940-78. *762*
—. Atomic bomb development. Diplomacy. 1942-45. *754*
—. Byrnes, James F. Federal Government. Germany. Memoirs. Szilard, Leo. 1898-1945. *948*
—. Cyclotrons. Manhattan Project. New Mexico (Los Alamos). Wilson, Robert R. (reminiscences). 1942-43. *1044*
—. Manley, John H. (reminiscences). New Mexico (Los Alamos). 1942-45. *581*
Nuclear Science and Technology (review article). Atomic Warfare. Foreign Policy. Gowing, Margaret. Great Britain. Sherwin, Martin J. 1938-52. *529*
Nuremberg Trials. Court evidence. Documents, use of. Due process. War criminals. 1945-48. *622*
—. War crimes. Yamashita, Tomoyuki. 1945-46. *390*
Nuremberg trials (review article). Maser, Werner. Smith, Bradley F. War crimes. 1945-46. 1970's. *1013*
Nye, Gerald P. Isolationism. Political Speeches. Roosevelt, Franklin D. 1941. *516*
N2C-2 (aircraft). Drones. Fahrney, Delmar S. (account). Missiles. Navy Bureau of Aeronautics. Radio. Research and development. TG-2 (aircraft). 1936-45. *279*

O

Ocean travel. Great Britain. *Queen Mary* (vessel). ca 1930-67. *103*
Oder-Neisse Line. Bowman, Isaiah. East Prussia. Poland. State Department (Advisory Committee on Post-War Foreign Policy). Welles, Sumner. 1942-45. *819*
Odlum, Victor Wentworth. Canada. China. Foreign Policy. International Trade. ca 1944-49. *683*
Odysseys In Flight, Inc. Aircraft Carriers. *Intrepid* (vessel). Preservation. 1943-79. *1090*
Office of Military Government for Germany (US). Clay, Lucius D. Documents. Germany. Military General Staff (meetings). Military government. US Group Control Council, Germany. 1944-49. *917*
Office of Production Management. Aircraft industry. Joint Aircraft Committee. National Defense Advisory Commission. Technological change. 1940-45. *423*
Office of Strategic Services (memos). Cold War. USSR. 1945. *1049*
Office of the Coordinator of Information. Arctic. Discovery and Exploration. Finnie, Richard Sterling (account). North America. Stefansson, Vilhjalmur. 1931-62. *290*
Office of the Coordinator of Inter-American Affairs. Axis Powers. Foreign Policy. Latin America. Rockefeller, Nelson A. Roosevelt, Franklin D. (administration). 1933-42. *364*
Office of War Information. China. *Keys of the Kingdom* (film). Propaganda. Stereotypes. USA. 1940-45. *94*
—. Fascism (alleged). Italian Americans. Liberalism. Loyalty. Propaganda. 1939-40. *627*
—. Films. Hollywood. Liberalism. National Self-image. 1942-45. *494*

258 Office

—. Films (analysis of). Hollywood. Propaganda. 1942-43. *95*
—. Poland. Propaganda. USA. USSR. 1943-45. *375*
Office of War Information, Bureau of Intelligence. Davis, Elmer. Films. Hollywood. Propaganda. 1942-43. *96*
Offner, Arnold A. Europe. Foreign policy (review article). Japan. USA. 1917-41. *677*
Offutt Air Force Base (Building D). Airplanes, Military (assembly). Nebraska. Recreation. 1940-77. *816*
Ogdensburg Agreement. Canada. King, William Lyon Mackenzie. Roosevelt, Franklin D. 1933-45. *910*
Ohio (Lucas County). Price controls. Rationing. 1942-43. *17*
Ohio (New Concord). Films. History Teaching. Muskingum College. 1971-72. *931*
Ohlinger, John F. (account). Aeronautics, Military. Africa, North. Great Britain. Hurricane (aircraft). 1942. *691*
—. Air Warfare. Egypt (Foul Bay). 1943. *692*
Oil. Embargo, de facto. Foreign Policy. Japan. Roosevelt, Franklin D. 1941. *22*
Oil and Petroleum Products. Canol Project. Northwest Territories. Pipelines. Yukon Territory. 1942-45. *470*
Oil exports, restricted. Foreign policy. Japan. State Department. USA. 1940-41. *989*
Oil fields. Air Warfare. Brooks, Jim (reminiscences). Romania. 31st Fighter Group, US. 1944. *127*
Oil industry. Foreign Policy. Japan. USA. 1934-37. *645*
Oil Industry and Trade. Anderson, Irvine H., Jr. (review article). Asia, East. Foreign Investments. Foreign policy. Standard-Vacuum Oil Company. 1933-41. 1975. *725*
—. Canada. Canol (project). Foster, W. W. USA. War Department. 1942-45. *54*
—. Canol Project. Northwest Territories (Mackenzie Valley). Pipelines. Planning. 1942-45. *55*
—. Congress of Industrial Organizations. Texas. 1942-43. *459*
—. Lend-Lease. Lobbying. Saudi Arabia. 1943. *21*
Okinawa (battle). Amphibious operations. *Marathon* (vessel). McElroy, John W. (account). 1945. *606*
—. Great Britain. Parker, Willard. Rescues. *Undine* (vessel). 1945. *409*
—. Manchester, William (account). Marines. 1945. 1978. *578*
Okinawa (battle; Sugar Loaf Hill). Marines. 1945. *913*
Oklahoma. Fort Reno. Prisoners of War. 1943-46. *1045*
—. War. 1890-1968. *209*
Oklahoma (Oklahoma City). Employment. Tinker Air Force Base. 1941-45. *257*
Oklahoma State University. Military training. Preparedness. Reserve Officers' Training Corps. Veterans. Women Appointed for Volunteer Emergency Service. 1891-1951. *812*
Oklahoma (vessel). Battleship. Pearl Harbor (attack). 1912-47. *928*
—. Hawaii. Pearl Harbor. 1916-47. *1097*
Olathe Naval Air Station. Flight training. Hutchinson Naval Air Station. Kansas. Naval Air Forces. 1942-69. *441*
Open Door, global. Cold War. Roosevelt, Franklin D. Truman, Harry S. USA. USSR. 1941-50. *1037*
Operation Cobra. Falaise (battle). France. France (Normandy). Military Strategy. Patton, George S., Jr. USA. 1944. *751*

Operation Crossword. Cold War (origins). Italy. Kolko, Gabriel. Military Strategy. Negotiations. 1945. *166*
Operation Market-Garden. Airborne operations. Netherlands (Arnhem). Ryan, Cornelius (review article). 1944. *559*
Operation Olympic (planned). Japan, invasion of. Military Strategy. 1945. *210*
Operation Overlord. Air Warfare. Bombing. Churchill, Winston. Military General Staff. Roosevelt, Franklin D. 1944. *1053*
—. Bombing. France. Military Strategy. Zuckerman, Solly (review article). 1944. *484*
—. Eisenhower, Dwight D. Marshall, George C. Military General Staff. Roosevelt, Franklin D. 1942-44. *295*
Oppenheimer, J. Robert. Colleges and Universities. Manhattan Project. Nuclear Arms. 1904-67. *784*
Oral history. Brown, William Eustis (interview). Public health. 1942-45. *379*
—. Canada. China Convoy. Friends' Ambulance Unit. 1939-45. *899*
—. Japanese Americans, incarceration of. Tanaka, Togo. Yoneda, Elaine. Yoneda, Karl. 1941-45. *638*
Ordnance. San Jacinto Ordnance Depot. Texas. 1939-64. *478*
Oregon. Diaries. Internment. Japanese Americans. Portland Assembly Center. Tomita, Saku. 1942. *492*
Oregon (Portland). Boilermakers, Iron Shipbuilders and Helpers, International Brotherhood of. California (Los Angeles). Discrimination, employment. Labor Unions and Organizations. Negroes. Shipbuilding. 1941-46. *883*
—. Shipbuilding. Women. 1941-45. *875*
Organizations. Decisionmaking. System analysis. 20c. *3*
Our Hope (periodical). Fundamentalism. Gaebelin, Arno C. Genocide. Germany. Jews. 1937-45. *768*
O-47 (aircraft). Aeronautics, Military. Military Intelligence. O-52 (aircraft). Puerto Rico. ca 1917-43. *320*
O-52 (aircraft). Aeronautics, Military. Military Intelligence. O-47 (aircraft). Puerto Rico. ca 1917-43. *320*

P

Pacific Area. Air Forces. Insignia. 5th Air Force, US. 1941-45. *1091*
—. Air warfare. F4U (aircraft). Marines. Zero (aircraft). 1943-45. *419*
—. Air Warfare. Marines. McCarthy, Joseph R. Politics. Wisconsin. 1942-52. *774*
—. Amphibious operations. 1942-45. *728*
—. Amphibious operations. Japan. USA. 1942-45. *449*
—. Anti-Imperialism. Foreign Policy (critics). Roosevelt, Franklin D. World War II (antecedents). 1930's. *704*
—. Armies. Evans, Maurice. Shakespeare, William. Theater Production and Direction. 1942-45. *864*
—. Australia. Foreign Relations. Japan. Peace settlement. USA. 1942-46. *70*
—. Battleships. Naval Strategy. 1942-45. *658*
—. California (San Rafael). Hamilton Air Force Base. 1931-50. *382*
—. Central America. Military occupation. *Tulsa* (vessel). 1919-45. *1102*
—. Decisionmaking. Military Strategy. 1941-45. *75*

—. Destroyer escorts. *England* (vessel). Japan. Submarine Warfare. Williamson, John A. (account). 1944. *1038*
—. Environment. Marines. Pacific Dependencies (US). 1943-71. *617*
—. Great Britain. Navies. Winton, John (review article). 1941-45. *170*
—. Historians, Western. Japan. Military defeat. USSR. 1942-45. *832*
—. Imperialism. Japan. Navigation. Pearl Harbor, attack on. World War II (antecedents). Prehistory-1941. *216*
—. *Indianapolis* (vessel). *I-58* (vessel). Japan. Submarine Warfare. USA. 1945. *115*
—. James, D. Clayton (review article). MacArthur, Douglas. Politics and the Military. 1941-45. *1002*
—. Japan. Naval Tactics. USA. 1920's-43. *447*
—. Japan. Navies. Savo Island (battle). USA. 1942. *67*
—. Joint Chiefs of Staff. MacArthur, Douglas. Nimitz, Chester W. Roosevelt, Franklin D. 1941-42. *189*
—. King, Ernest J. Naval Strategy. 1926-44. *781*
—. Naval History. Nimitz, Chester W. 1885-1966. *1019*
—. Naval Strategy. 1934-42. *420*
—. Naval Strategy. Surrender. Wake Island. 1941. *340*
Pacific Area (South). *Indiana* (BB-58, vessel). Navies. 1922-62. *895*
Pacific Dependencies (US). Environment. Marines. Pacific Area. 1943-71. *617*
Pacific Northwest. Bombs, balloon-carried. Japan. 1945. *461*
—. Congress of Industrial Organizations. Isolationism. Leftism. USSR. 1937-41. *552*
Pacifism. Angers, François-Albert. Canada. Catholic Church. French Canadians. Values. 1940-79. *349*
—. Canada. Fairbairn, R. Edis. Protestantism. United Church of Canada. 1939. *802*
—. Civilian Public Service. Zahn, Gordon C. (account). 1940-45. *1072*
—. Protestant churches. Public opinion. 1939-45. *700*
Palestine. Foreign Policy. Great Britain. USA. 1941-45. *183*
—. Foreign Policy. Middle East. Roosevelt, Franklin D. USA. 1943-45. *710*
Pan-American Union. Canada. Diplomacy. Foreign Relations. Latin America. USA. 1939-44. *664*
Panay (vessel). China (Yangtze River). Japan. World War II (antecedents). 1937. *731*
Pardon. Citizenship. Ford, Gerald R. Hada, John. Japanese American Citizens League. Tokyo Rose (Iva Toguri d'Aquino). Uyeda, Clifford I. (account). 1973-77. *990*
Parker, Willard. Great Britain. Okinawa (battle). Rescues. *Undine* (vessel). 1945. *409*
Parris Island (camp). Marines. Military training. Vietnam War. 1942-72. *695*
Parrish, Noel F. (interview). Flight training. Military General Staff. Negroes. Tuskegee Army Air Field. 1941-45. *393*
Partition. Allies. Germany. Military occupation. 1943-48. *475*
—. France. Germany. Great Britain. Roshchin, A. A. (memoirs). USSR. 1942-45. *797*
Patapsco Civilian Public Service System (Camp 3). Community, involuntary. Conscientious objectors. Maryland. Values. 1941-42. *699*
Patriotism. Curricula. High School Victory Corps. Physical Education and Training. Vocational Education. 1941-45. *983*
—. National Characteristics. 1941-45. *1094*

Patterson, Thomas J. *Jeremiah O'Brien* (vessel). Liberty Ships. Maritime Preservation Office. Preservation. 1940-80. *184*
Patton, George S., Jr. Africa, North. Air Forces. Military Ground Forces. Tactics. 1943. *502*
—. Czechoslovakia (Prague). Germany. Invasions. USSR. Vlasov, Andrei. 1945. *804*
—. Falaise (battle). France. France (Normandy). Military Strategy. Operation Cobra. USA. 1944. *751*
—. France. Lorraine campaign. Metz (battle). Third Army. 1944. *46*
Patton, George S., Jr. (notebooks). Anti-Communism. Armies. Attitudes. 1942-45. *724*
PB4B-2 (aircraft). Navy Patrol Bombing Squadron 106. Regimental histories. 1944-45. *888*
Peace. Allies. Roosevelt, Franklin D. Unconditional surrender (concept). ca 1942-45. *45*
—. Hoover, Herbert C. Intervention (opposed). Totalitarianism. USSR. 1939-41. *88*
Peace (delayed). Japan. Potsdam Conference. Surrender, unconditional. USA. 1945. *998*
Peace Movements. Catholic Church. National Catholic Welfare Conference. National Council of Catholic Women. Women. 1919-46. *561*
—. Feminism. Lloyd, Lola Maverick. 1914-44. *921*
—. Germany. Public Opinion. 1942. *915*
—. Jewish Peace Fellowship. 1943. *1067*
—. National security. Preparedness. 1941-71. *214*
Peace negotiations. Canada. Diplomacy. Europe. USA. 1943-47. *415*
Peace pact (proposed). Crawford, David L. Hawaii, University of. Japan. USA. 1940-41. *428*
Peace proposal, utopian. New Hampshire (Lebanon). Radio. St. John, Robert. 1945. *713*
Peace settlement. Australia. Foreign Relations. Japan. Pacific Area. USA. 1942-46. *70*
Pearkes, G. R. British Columbia. Conscription, Military (crisis). 1943-44. *807*
Pearl Harbor. Hawaii. Holmes, Wilfrid J. (account). Military Intelligence. Navies. Nimitz, Chester W. 1941. *425*
—. Hawaii. *Oklahoma* (vessel). 1916-47. *1097*
Pearl Harbor (attack). Battleship. *Oklahoma* (vessel). 1912-47. *928*
Pearl Harbor, attack on. Air Warfare. Japan. Naval Strategy. 1940-41. *698*
—. Armstrong, David M. (personal account). Hawaii. Japan. 1942. *32*
—. Battleships. 1941. *427*
—. Dull, Paul S. (review article). Japan. Naval Strategy. Yamamoto, Isoroku. 1941-45. *977*
—. Fire Department. Hawaii (Honolulu). Hickam Field. 1941. *110*
—. Hawaii. Hechler, Ted, Jr. (account). Navies. *Phoenix* (vessel). 1941. *400*
—. Hawaii. Japan. Naval Vessels. 1941. *1098*
—. Imperialism. Japan. Navigation. Pacific Area. World War II (antecedents). Prehistory-1941. *216*
—. Kimmel, Husband E. Personal narratives. Short, Walter C. Weapons (ineffectiveness). 1941. *951*
—. *West Virginia* (vessel). 1916-41. *893*
Pearl Harbor, attack on (issue). Dewey, Thomas E. Elections (presidential). Roosevelt, Franklin D. (administration). 1944. *621*
Pearl Harbor question. National security. Roosevelt, Franklin D. (administration). 1941-46. *620*
Peasant movements (colloquium). Agriculture. Europe. Industrialization. Market economy. North America. ca 1875-1975. *52*

Peatross, Oscar F. (account). Gilbert Islands. Japan. Makin Islands (raid). Marines (2d Raiders). Prisoners of War. 1942-47. *720*
Peiper, N. J. L. Civil rights. Counterintelligence. Internment. Japanese Americans. Munson, Curtis B. 1931-42. *500*
Pelelieu (battle). Armies. Japan. Marines. Sledge, Eugene B. (account). 1944. *877*
Pell, Herbert Claiborne. Jews. State Department. UN War Crimes Commission. War crimes. 1943-45. *100*
Pennsylvania. Judaism. Markowitz, Samuel H. (autobiography). 1920-65. *585*
Pennsylvania (Philadelphia). Negroes. Public transportation. Racism. Strikes. US Employment Service. War Manpower Commission. 1944. *1046*
Pennsylvania (Pittsburgh). Delaware (Wilmington). Dravo Corp. Navies. Shipbuilding. 1940-47. *974*
"Percentages" agreement. Cold War. Europe, Eastern. Great Britain. Roosevelt, Franklin D. USSR. 1944. *780*
Personal narratives. Airplanes. Alaska (Amchitka). Boeing 80A (aircraft). 1943. *773*
—. Archives. Italy, northern. McCain, William D. 1944-45. *602*
—. Army. Camp Beauregard. Cawthon, John Ardis. Conscription, Military. Louisiana. 1940-42. *163*
—. Bache, William B. Germany (Ludwigshafen). McAuliffe, Anthony. 1945. *38*
—. Balloons. Dirigibles. McBride, Robert M. Navy. 1941-44. *601*
—. Kimmel, Husband E. Pearl Harbor, attack on. Short, Walter C. Weapons (ineffectiveness). 1941. *951*
Peru. Diplomacy. Emmerson, John K. (reminiscences). Internment. Japanese Peruvians. USA. 1942-43. *273*
Pesticides. Military. 1939-50. *730*
Peterson, Harold L. Cutlass, Naval. Klewang, Dutch. World War I. 1917. 1941-42. *787*
Peto (vessel). Dry dock, floating. Louisiana (New Orleans). Manitowoc Shipbuilding Co. Mississippi River. Navigation, Inland. Submarines. 1942-45. *676*
Pharmacy. German Americans. New York City. Societies, apothecary. 19c-1940's. *1008*
Philippine Insurrection. Armies. Professionalism. Vietnam War. 1901-71. *735*
Philippine Scouts. Cavalry. Luzon (battle). MacArthur, Douglas. 1941. *244*
Philippine Sea (battle). Amphibious operations. Japan. Saipan (battle). 1944. *995*
—. Japan. Navies. USA. 1944. *145*
—. Naval Tactics. Spruance, Raymond A. 1943. *134*
Philippines. Aeronautics, Military. Wagner, Boyd D. 1941-42. *104*
—. Air Forces. Japan. Military Capability. 1941. *385*
—. Air Forces. Leyte Gulf (battle). Navies. 1944. *829*
—. Air Warfare. Atomic Warfare. Baldwin, Paul H. (account). Fighter squadrons, night. 1942-45. *44*
—. Air Warfare. B-17 (aircraft). Kelly, Colin P., Jr. 1941. *144*
—. Air Warfare. McGuire, Thomas. 1945. *16*
—. Australia. Diaries. Great Britain. MacArthur, Douglas. Williamson, Gerald Hugh. 1942-43. *962*
—. Bloom, Lynn Z. Crouter, Natalie Stark. Diaries. Prisoners of War. 1941-45. 1970's. *101*
—. Clark Field, attack on. Japan. 1941-42. *569*

—. Crouter, Natalie. Diaries. Prisoners of War. 1941-44. *197*
—. Diaries. Japan. Norquist, Ernest O. Prisoners of War. 1942-45. *681*
—. Diplomacy. Hull, Cordell. Indochina. Japan. World War II (antecedents). 1941. *131*
—. Executive Order No. 1. Gifts. MacArthur, Douglas. Military General Staff. Quezon, Manuel. Sutherland, Richard K. (papers). 1942. *733*
—. Foreign Policy. MacArthur, Douglas. Military. 1945-46. *262*
—. Japan. Leyte Gulf (battle). Navies. USA. 1944. *352*
—. Military strategy. Rainbow-5 (plan). 1941-42. *190*
Philippines (Manila). Diplomacy. Japan. MacArthur, Douglas. Surrender. 1945. *624*
Philippines (Manila Bay). Corregidor (battles). 1795-1945. *39*
Phoenix (vessel). Hawaii. Hechler, Ted, Jr. (account). Navies. Pearl Harbor, attack on. 1941. *400*
Photograph, famous. Flag, American. Iwo Jima (battle). 1945. *299*
Photographs. Antiaircraft guns. Destroyers. Navies. 1945. *47*
—. California (San Diego). 1943. *106*
—. China (Shanghai). Japan. Marines. USA. 1920's-30's. *1099*
—. Documentation. Evacuation, forced. Internment. Japanese Americans. War Relocation Authority. 1941-43. *208*
Photography. Baker, Arthur Davidson, III (collection). Navies. 1941-45. *1101*
Photography, Military. Maryland (Annapolis). Streichen, Edward J. US Naval Academy (Edward J. Streichen Collection). 1930's-75. *194*
Physical Education and Training. Canada. Federal Government. Sport. 1909-54. *1028*
—. Curricula. High School Victory Corps. Patriotism. Vocational Education. 1941-45. *983*
Physical fitness programmes. Canada. Federal government. 1850-1972. *314*
Physicians. Great Britain. USA. 1940. *61*
Pilots. Air Forces. Dunn, William R. 1941-45. 1967. *718*
—. Asia. Gibbon, Elwyn H. (memoirs). 1937-42. *524*
Pinney, Charles A. Air Force. Alaska (Anchorage, Adak). Bush pilot. 1942-43. *741*
Pipelines. Armies. Canol Project. National Security. Northwest Territories. USA. 1942-45. *226*
—. Canada. Canol project. Dickins, C. H. "Punch". Letters. Mackenzie Air Route. USA. 1942. *56*
—. Canol Project. Northwest Territories. Oil and Petroleum Products. Yukon Territory. 1942-45. *470*
—. Canol Project. Northwest Territories (Mackenzie Valley). Oil Industry and Trade. Planning. 1942-45. *55*
Pittman, Key. Foreign Relations. Japan. USA. 1920-40. *537*
Pius XII, Pope. Diplomacy. Taylor, Myron C. USA. Vatican. 1940-50. *188*
Planning. Army Air Forces. Arnold, H. H. (Hap). Military Organization. 1942. *503*
—. Canada. Foreign policy. 1943-45. *661*
—. Canol Project. Northwest Territories (Mackenzie Valley). Oil Industry and Trade. Pipelines. 1942-45. *55*
—. Preparedness. Sherry, Michael S. (review article). 1943-47. 1977. *1001*

Platte (vessel). Naval Battles. Shipbuilding. 1939-71. *213*
Plattsburg Movement. Clark, Grenville. New York. Selective Service, origins of the. 1940-41. *176*
Ploesti (raid). Air Warfare. Rumania. USA. Whalen, Norman M. (reminiscences). 1943. *1029*
Plutonium. McDaniel, Boyce (reminiscences). New Mexico (Los Alamos). Nuclear Arms. 1940-45. *605*
Po Valley campaign. Battillo, Anthony (reminiscences). Italy. 1945. *58*
Poetry. France. Intellectuals. Maritain, Raïssa. Nationalism. USA. 1940-60. *938*
Poland. Allies. Cold War (origins). Diplomacy. 1945. *702*
—. Bowman, Isaiah. East Prussia. Oder-Neisse Line. State Department (Advisory Committee on Post-War Foreign Policy). Welles, Sumner. 1942-45. *819*
—. Cold War. Michigan. Vandenberg, Arthur Hendrick, Sr. Yalta Conference. 1944-48. *149*
—. Eden, Anthony. Foreign Policy. Molotov, V. M. Truman, Harry S. USSR. 1945. *635*
—. Foreign policy. Great Britain. USA. 1945. *956*
—. Foreign policy. Harriman, W. Averell. USA. USSR. Warsaw Ghetto Uprising. 1943-44. *167*
—. Foreign policy. Illinois (Chicago). Polish-American Congress. Roosevelt, Franklin D. 1944. *820*
—. Foreign Policy. Roosevelt, Franklin D. Truman, Harry S. USA. USSR. 1943-46. *558*
—. Jews. Press, Jewish. USA. Warsaw ghetto uprising. 1942-43. *347*
—. Office of War Information. Propaganda. USA. USSR. 1943-45. *375*
Poland, eastern. Lange, Oscar. Pro-Communism. Roosevelt, Franklin D. USSR. 1941-45. *821*
Poland (issue). Elections (presidential). Polish Americans. Roosevelt, Franklin D. 1942-44. *374*
Polar bear motif. Iceland. Marines. Military Decorations, Flags, and Symbols (shoulder patches). 1941-42. *93*
Policymaking. Atomic bomb. Franck, James. Scientists. Stimson, Henry L. 1945. *918*
Polish American Congress. Lobbying. Mazewski, Aloysius. Polish National Alliance. Rozmarek, Charles. 1944-79. *737*
Polish Americans. Elections (presidential). Poland (issue). Roosevelt, Franklin D. 1942-44. *374*
Polish National Alliance. Lobbying. Mazewski, Aloysius. Polish American Congress. Rozmarek, Charles. 1944-79. *737*
Polish-American Congress. Foreign policy. Illinois (Chicago). Poland. Roosevelt, Franklin D. 1944. *820*
Political Attitudes. Atomic bomb. Franck, James. Nuclear arms race. Truman, Harry S. (administration). 1944-45. *1000*
—. Montana. Roosevelt, Franklin D. Senate. Wheeler, Burton K. 1904-46. *811*
Political change. Women's Liberation Movement. 19c-1970's. *513*
Political Commentary. Collectivism. Dennis, Lawrence. Germany. Public Opinion. 1941-45. *233*
Political factions. Airplane Industry and Trade. Labor Unions and Organizations (militancy). Nash, Al (reminiscences). New York (Long Island City). 1940-44. *675*
Political issues. Italy. Mussolini, Benito. Pound, Ezra (letters). USA. 1932-43. *748*

Political leadership. Chiang Kai-shek. Diplomacy. Mao Tse-tung. 1945. *978*
—. Churchill, Winston. Foreign policy. Roosevelt, Franklin D. Stalin, Joseph. 1939-45. *1107*
—. Foreign Relations. International Security. 1941-45. 1976. *734*
Political Protest. Antiwar sentiments. Colleges and Universities. Leftism. 1920-36. *124*
—. Attitudes. Executive Behavior. Foreign policy. Roosevelt, Franklin D. 1940-72. *1092*
—. Negroes. Newspapers. Race relations. 1941-45. *289*
Political Speeches. Capper, Arthur. Legislation. Neutrality. 1936-41. *709*
—. Isolationism. Nye, Gerald P. Roosevelt, Franklin D. 1941. *516*
Political theory. Constitutionalism. Law. ca 1936-70. *72*
Political warning. Decisionmaking. Military planning. 1941. *824*
Politics. Air Warfare. Marines. McCarthy, Joseph R. Pacific Area. Wisconsin. 1942-52. *774*
—. Atomic Warfare. Japan. Surrender offer. Truman, Harry S. (administration). 1945. *84*
—. Autonomy. Congress. Puerto Rico. Roosevelt, Franklin D. (administration). 1940-45. *89*
—. Blum, John Morton (review article). Federal government. Propaganda. 1940-45. *525*
—. Canada. Europe. Military operations. 1939-45. *909*
—. Clark, Chase. Far Western States. Internment. Japanese Americans. 1941-45. *867*
—. Cold War (origins; review article). Economic Policy. 1941-71. 1973-74. *338*
—. Friendship. Literature. Morality. Pound, Ezra. Treason. 1909-72. *192*
—. Isolationism (review article). 1935-52. *234*
Politics and the Military. James, D. Clayton (review article). MacArthur, Douglas. Pacific Area. 1941-45. *1002*
Poltava (battle). Air Warfare. Bombing. B-17 (aircraft). Germany. USSR. 1944. *445*
Popular culture. Amphetamines. Drug Abuse. 1932-75. *451*
—. Hughes, Langston. Negro Literature. Semple, Jesse B. (fictitious character). 1942-43. *755*
Population. Economic Growth. Industry. South. Western States. 1940-79. *1*
Port Chicago Naval Magazine. California (San Francisco Bay). Courts Martial and Courts of Inquiry. Mare Island Mutiny. Navies. Negroes. Race relations. 1944-48. *1055*
Portland Assembly Center. Diaries. Internment. Japanese Americans. Oregon. Tomita, Saku. 1942. *492*
Ports. California (Los Angeles, San Diego, San Francisco). City Planning. Navy-yards and Naval Stations. 1919-41. *548*
Portugal. Alliances. Foreign Relations. 1940-41. *944*
—. Foreign Relations. Salazar, Antonio. 1939-45. *941*
Portugal (Azores). Air Bases. Diplomacy. Norweb, R. Henry. 1941-44. *942*
Portugal (shipping to Germany). Embargo, Allied. Wolfram. 1939-44. *943*
Potsdam Conference. Atomic Warfare. Groves, Leslie R. Hirohito, Emperor. Japan (Nagasaki). Truman, Harry S. 1944-45. *546*
—. Atomic Weapons. Austin, Warren Robinson. Byrnes, James F. Cold War. Documents. USSR. 1945. *712*
—. Churchill, Winston. Germany (partition). Roosevelt, Franklin D. Stettinius, Edward Reilley. Yalta Conference. 1945. *329*

—. Films (accuracy). Historical license. *Meeting at Potsdam* (film). Truman, Harry S. 1945. 1970's. *310*
—. Foreign Policy. Presidents. Truman, Harry S. 1945. *570*
—. Japan. Peace (delayed). Surrender, unconditional. USA. 1945. *998*
Pound, Ezra. Armies. Imprisonment. Italy (Pisa). Steele, John L. (interview). 1945. *485*
—. Fascism. Italy. USA. 1924-58. *1074*
—. Friendship. Literature. Morality. Politics. Treason. 1909-72. *192*
Pound, Ezra (letters). Italy. Mussolini, Benito. Political issues. USA. 1932-43. *748*
Prelude to War (film). Capra, Frank. Films. Propaganda. 1939-42. *916*
Preparedness. Foreign Policy. France. Surrender. 1940-44. *549*
—. Foreign policy. Hawaii. Roosevelt, Franklin D. Works Progress Administration. 1935-40. *763*
—. Military training. Oklahoma State University. Reserve Officers' Training Corps. Veterans. Women Appointed for Volunteer Emergency Service. 1891-1951. *812*
—. National security. Peace Movements. 1941-71. *214*
—. Planning. Sherry, Michael S. (review article). 1943-47. 1977. *1001*
Presbyterian Church. Interventionism. VanDusen, Henry Pitney. World War II (antecedents). 1920-45. *960*
Preservation. Aircraft Carriers. *Intrepid* (vessel). Odysseys In Flight, Inc. 1943-79. *1090*
—. *Jeremiah O'Brien* (vessel). Liberty Ships. Maritime Preservation Office. Patterson, Thomas J. 1940-80. *184*
Presidency. Congress. Foreign policy. War powers. 1787-1972. *772*
Presidential libraries. 1940-45. *1079*
Presidents. Foreign Policy. Potsdam Conference. Truman, Harry S. 1945. *570*
Press. Borg thesis. Foreign Policy. Georgia. Quarantine speech. Roosevelt, Franklin D. 1937. *132*
—. Bureau of Public Information. Canada. Federal government. Public opinion. Social scientists. Wartime Information Board. 1939-45. *1070*
—. Canada. Historiography. World War II (antecedents). 1938-39. *591*
—. Concentration camps. Genocide. Germany. Jews. 1939-42. *348*
—. King, Ernest J. Navies. Public relations. 1939-43. *339*
Press, black. Armies. Hastie, William H. Military recruitment. Negroes. 1940-42. *611*
Press, Jewish. Jews. Poland. USA. Warsaw ghetto uprising. 1942-43. *347*
Price controls. Ohio (Lucas County). Rationing. 1942-43. *17*
Prison camp. California (Byron Hot Springs). Resorts. 1868-1976. *1032*
Prisoners and prisons. Foreign Relations. Repatriation. USA. USSR. 1945. *136*
—. New Mexico. 1942-46. *903*
Prisoners of War. Arkansas. Germans. Italians. Labor, contract. 1943-46. *758*
—. Arkansas. Germany. 1943-46. *757*
—. Bloom, Lynn Z. Crouter, Natalie Stark. Diaries. Philippines. 1941-45. 1970's. *101*
—. Bridges. Burma (Kwae Mae Khlong River). B-24 (aircraft). Davis, W. L. (personal account). 1942-45. *212*
—. California. Interrogation centers. Navies. Virginia. 1941-45. *647*
—. Camp Blanding. Florida. Germans. 1942-46. *90*
—. Conspiracies. Germany (Berlin). Hitler, Adolf. 1945. *907*
—. Crouter, Natalie. Diaries. Philippines. 1941-44. *197*
—. Diaries. Japan. Norquist, Ernest O. Philippines. 1942-45. *681*
—. Economic Conditions. World War I. 1914-45. *211*
—. Employment. Germans. Minnesota. 1942-46. *743*
—. Fort Reno. Oklahoma. 1943-46. *1045*
—. Germans. Texas. 1943-46. *497*
—. Germans. Texas. 1943-45. *967*
—. Germans. Virginia. 1943-46. *648*
—. Germany. Jews. USA. Winograd, Leonard (reminiscences). 1944-45. *1047*
—. Gilbert Islands. Japan. Makin Islands (raid). Marines (2d Raiders). Peatross, Oscar F. (account). 1942-47. *720*
—. Mississippi. 1943-46. *759*
Prisoners of War (Axis). Bibliographies. USA. 1945. 1975. *904*
Prisoners of War (camps). Germans. Labor, prison. New York, western. 1944-46. *598*
—. Germans. South Carolina. 1944-46. *650*
Prisoners of war, German. Canada. Great Britain. 1940-47. *477*
—. Labor, forced. Louisiana (Lafourche Parish). Sugar cane fields. 1943-44. *142*
Prisoners of War (Germans). Geneva Convention. USA. 1941-45. *496*
Prisoners of War, Italian. Italian Americans. Labor. USA. 1943-45. *649*
Pro-Communism. Lange, Oscar. Poland, eastern. Roosevelt, Franklin D. USSR. 1941-45. *821*
Production. Armaments. Industry. 1941-45. *1085*
Production standards. Automobile Industry and Trade. Labor (militancy). Michigan (Detroit). United Automobile Workers of America. Working Conditions. 1937-55. *540*
Professionalism. Armies. Philippine Insurrection. Vietnam War. 1901-71. *735*
—. Military. Social Change. 1941-76. *129*
Project FUGO. Balloons, armed. Japan. South Dakota. 1944-45. *517*
Propaganda. Armies. Documentaries. Films. Heisler, Stuart. *Negro Soldier* (film). Race Relations. 1944. *195*
—. Blum, John Morton (review article). Federal government. Politics. 1940-45. *525*
—. Canada. deGaulle, Charles. France. Quebec. Vichy Regime. 1940-42. *193*
—. Capra, Frank. Films. *Prelude to War* (film). 1939-42. *916*
—. China. *Keys of the Kingdom* (film). Office of War Information. Stereotypes. USA. 1940-45. *94*
—. Cold War mentality. Television. *Victory at Sea* series. 1952-72. *792*
—. Davis, Elmer. Films. Hollywood. Office of War Information, Bureau of Intelligence. 1942-43. *96*
—. Economic Growth. State Department. War Department. 1939-45. *1083*
—. Fascism (alleged). Italian Americans. Liberalism. Loyalty. Office of War Information. 1939-40. *627*
—. Federal Government. Radio. *Treasury Star Parade* (program). 1942-43. *564*
—. Films. 1942-45. *436*
—. Films. Hollywood. 1940-45. *619*
—. Films. Public opinion. *Why We Fight* series. 1941-45. *562*
—. Films (analysis of). Hollywood. Office of War Information. 1942-43. *95*
—. Films, documentary. Ford, John. 1941-42. *663*

Quebec 263

—. Germany. Halle, Louis J. (reminiscences). Koichwitz, Otto ("O.K."). Teachers. USA. 1920's-40's. *371*
—. Germany. Labor. Public opinion. Sex roles. Women. 1939-45. *814*
—. Office of War Information. Poland. USA. USSR. 1943-45. *375*
Propaganda campaign. Germany. National Reich Church (suggested). Roosevelt, Franklin D. USA. World War II (antecedents). 1941. *187*
Propaganda (review article). Germany. Rupp, Leila J. Winkler, Allan M. Women. 1939-45. *373*
Protestant Churches. Ecumenism. Europe. 1900-45. *555*
—. Pacifism. Public opinion. 1939-45. *700*
—. Race Relations. Segregation. 1939-45. *701*
Protestantism. Canada. Fairbairn, R. Edis. Pacifism. United Church of Canada. 1939. *802*
—. Civilian Public Service. Conscientious objectors. Wives. 1941-45. *301*
Provincial Government. Canada. Federal Government. 1940-74. *882*
Proximity fuse. Antiaircraft gunnery. Great Britain. Inventions. 1939-45. *73*
Psychologists. Military Medicine. Mobilization. World War II (antecedents). 1938-41. *674*
Psychology. Genocide. Germany. Historiography. Jews. 1940's. *514*
PT-17 (aircraft). Army Air Forces. Bernhard, George K., Jr. (account). Flight training. 1942-43. *81*
Public expenditures. Dominican Republic. Puerto Rico. 1930-70. *582*
Public Finance. Cities (functions). Federal-local relations. Intergovernmental system. 1930's-74. *815*
Public health. Brown, William Eustis (interview). Oral history. 1942-45. *379*
Public Opinion. Arizona. Concentration camps. Gila River Relocation Center. Japanese Americans. Race Relations. 1942-45. *159*
—. Atomic bombs. Japan. USA. 1945-49. *1064*
—. British Columbia. Evacuation, forced. Federal government. Japanese. 1937-42. *1009*
—. Bureau of Public Information. Canada. Federal government. Press. Social scientists. Wartime Information Board. 1939-45. *1070*
—. China. Cohen, Warren I. (review article). Foreign policy. Japan. Leadership. ca 1900-50. 1978. *205*
—. Cold War (origins). USSR. 1941-45. *133*
—. Collectivism. Dennis, Lawrence. Germany. Political Commentary. 1941-45. *233*
—. Congress. Japan. Manchurian crisis. 1931-33. *657*
—. Darilek, Richard E. Foreign Policy (review article). Leigh, Michael. Levering, Ralph B. 1936-47. 1976. *315*
—. Films. Propaganda. *Why We Fight* series. 1941-45. *562*
—. Foreign policy. Mass Media. USA. USSR. ca 1939-49. *880*
—. Foreign Policy. Roosevelt, Franklin D. USSR. 1941-45. *679*
—. Foreign Relations. Gandhi, Mahatma (arrest). Great Britain. India. USA. 1942. *753*
—. Germany. Labor. Propaganda. Sex roles. Women. 1939-45. *814*
—. Germany. Peace Movements. 1942. *915*
—. Pacifism. Protestant churches. 1939-45. *700*
—. Tennessee (Martin). 1940-46. *580*
Public Opinion (American). Films. USSR. 1939-47. *881*
Public opinion, changes in. Air Warfare. Civilians, bombing of. 1937-45. *318*

Public Policy. Documents. Harry S. Truman Library. Truman, Harry S. Western States. 1940-66. *460*
—. Europe. Genocide. Jews. Roosevelt, Franklin D. (administration). 1942-44. *596*
—. Friedman, Saul S. (review article). Genocide. Jews. Refugees. Roosevelt, Franklin D. (administration). 1938-45. 1973. *790*
Public relations. City boosters. Nevada (Las Vegas). Tourism. 1905-74. *471*
—. King, Ernest J. Navies. Press. 1939-43. *339*
Public schools. Concentration Camps. Japanese Americans. 1942-45. *1056*
Public schools, challenge to. British Columbia. Japanese communities. Minorities. 1900-72. *203*
Public transportation. Negroes. Pennsylvania (Philadelphia). Racism. Strikes. US Employment Service. War Manpower Commission. 1944. *1046*
Public welfare. 1932-64. *306*
Publishers and Publishing. Historiography (revisionist). Regnery, Henry (account). Truth, historical. 20c. *775*
Puerto Rico. Aeronautics, Military. Military Intelligence. O-47 (aircraft). O-52 (aircraft). ca 1917-43. *320*
—. Autonomy. Congress. Politics. Roosevelt, Franklin D. (administration). 1940-45. *89*
—. Borinquen Field ("battle"). Goldsworthy, Harry E. (personal account). 1941. *322*
—. Dominican Republic. Public expenditures. 1930-70. *582*
—. Food shortages. Unemployment, rural. 1940-45. *280*
P-26 (aircraft). Airplanes, Military. Armies. Hoyt, Ross G. (account). 1937-41. *433*
P-38 (aircraft). Africa, North. Air Warfare. 1942-45. *276*
—. Luke, Frank, Jr. Rickenbacker, Edward V. 1st Pursuit Group. 1918-76. *534*
P-39 Airacobra (aircraft). Aeronautics, Military. Europe. Hudson, James J. (account). 1941-45. *435*
P-40 (aircraft). Air Warfare. Andrews, John A. C. (account). P-47 (aircraft). Spitfire (aircraft). 1943-45. *26*
—. Air Warfare. Army Air Forces. China. Flying Tigers. Holloway, Bruce K. (account). 1942-43. *424*
P-40 (H-81; aircraft). Curtiss-Wright Corp. Foreign Policy. France. Great Britain. 1938-40. *389*
P-47 (aircraft). Aeronautics, Military. 1941-45. *253*
—. Air Warfare. Andrews, John A. C. (account). P-40 (aircraft). Spitfire (aircraft). 1943-45. *26*
P-51 (airplane). Air Warfare. 1943-45. *117*
—. Air Warfare. 1943-45. *139*
—. Airplanes, Military. Spitfire, Supermarine (airplane). 1939-45. *604*
P-51H (aircraft). North American Aviation Corporation. 1943-52. *616*

Q

Quality of life. Civil Rights. Nebraska (Omaha). Negroes. Social services. Urban League. 1928-50. *623*
Quarantine speech. Borg thesis. Foreign Policy. Georgia. Press. Roosevelt, Franklin D. 1937. *132*
Quebec. Canada. deGaulle, Charles. France. Propaganda. Vichy Regime. 1940-42. *193*

264   Quebec

—. Conscription, Military. Elections. King, William Lyon Mackenzie. Ligue pour la Défense du Canada. 1942-44. *333*
Queen Mary (vessel). California (Long Beach). Great Britain. Ships. ca 1930-74. *566*
—. Great Britain. Ocean travel. ca 1930-67. *103*
Queenfish (vessel). *Awa Maru* (vessel). Japan. Submarines. USA. 1945. *902*
Quezon, Manuel. Executive Order No. 1. Gifts. MacArthur, Douglas. Military General Staff. Philippines. Sutherland, Richard K. (papers). 1942. *733*

R

Rabaul (battle). Air Warfare. Japan. Kenney, George. New Britain. 1943. *92*
Race Relations. Arizona. Concentration camps. Gila River Relocation Center. Japanese Americans. Public Opinion. 1942-45. *159*
—. Armies. Documentaries. Films. Heisler, Stuart. *Negro Soldier* (film). Propaganda. 1944. *195*
—. Asian Americans. Stereotypes, positive. 1850-1973. *932*
—. British Columbia, University of. Japanese Canadians. 1939-42. *80*
—. California. Concentration Camps. Japanese Americans. 1941-42. *639*
—. California (San Francisco Bay). Courts Martial and Courts of Inquiry. Mare Island Mutiny. Navies. Negroes. Port Chicago Naval Magazine. 1944-48. *1055*
—. Canada. Japanese Canadians. Relocation, forced. 1890's-1940's. *949*
—. Civic Unity Committee. Defense industries. Japanese Americans. Negroes. Washington (Seattle). 1940-45. *248*
—. Discrimination, Employment. Military Service (enlistees). Navies. Negroes. Segregation. 1798-1970's. *388*
—. Negroes. Newspapers. Political Protest. 1941-45. *289*
—. Protestant churches. Segregation. 1939-45. *701*
Racial issues. Democratic Party. Economic Development. Mississippi. 1941-45. *874*
Racism. Adachi, Ken (review article). Immigration. Japanese Canadians. 1877-1976. *521*
—. Alberta. Chinese Canadians. Japanese Canadians. 1920-50. *703*
—. Asian Canadians. British Columbia. 1900-50. *805*
—. Atomic Warfare. Canada. Diaries. King, William Lyon MacKenzie. 1921-48. *823*
—. California. Detention. Japanese Americans. 1941-45. *640*
—. Communist Party. National Maritime Union. Negroes. United Electrical Radio and Machine Workers. 1941-45. *196*
—. Concentration camps. Japanese Americans. 1940-45. *444*
—. Hastie, William. Military. Negroes. Stimson, Henry L. 1940-43. *610*
—. Hastie, William H. Military reform. 1940-43. *612*
—. Negroes. Pennsylvania (Philadelphia). Public transportation. Strikes. US Employment Service. War Manpower Commission. 1944. *1046*
Radar. Naval Air Forces. 1940-44. *965*
Radiation Effects Research Foundation. Atomic Bomb Casualty Commission. Civilian survivors. Japan (Hiroshima, Nagasaki). Medical Research. 1945-75. *1010*
Radio. Adventure serials. Americanism. National Characteristics. 1940-45. *287*

—. Armed Forces Radio Service. Barnouw, Erik. Education. 1942-45. *199*
—. Brown, Cecil B. Columbia Broadcasting System. Editorials. News. White, Paul W. 1943. *954*
—. Davis, Elmer. Interventionist, making of an. News broadcasts. World War II (antecedents). 1939-42. *463*
—. Drones. Fahrney, Delmar S. (account). Missiles. Navy Bureau of Aeronautics. N2C-2 (aircraft). Research and development. TG-2 (aircraft). 1936-45. *279*
—. Federal Government. Propaganda. *Treasury Star Parade* (program). 1942-43. *564*
—. Great Britain. Military Aid. Murrow, Edward R. 1939-41. *200*
—. New Hampshire (Lebanon). Peace proposal, utopian. St. John, Robert. 1945. *713*
Radio newscasts. Audiovisual materials, cataloging. Washington, University of (Milo Ryan Phonoarchives). 1956-73. *321*
Railey, Hilton H. Armies. Morale. *New York Times*. Reporters and Reporting. 1941. *1027*
Railroad stations. Arizona (Raso). Ghost towns. Southern Pacific Railroad. 1911-76. *670*
Railroads. Agriculture. Idaho. Internment. Japanese Americans. 1900-45. *868*
—. Discrimination. Fair Employment Practices Committee. Negroes. Southeastern Carriers Conference. 1941-45. *402*
Railways. Alaska. Canada. USSR. 1942-43. *1057*
Rainbow-5 (plan). Military strategy. Philippines. 1941-42. *190*
Ramírez, Pedro. Argentina. Foreign Policy. Hull, Cordell. USA. 1943. *1060*
Randolph, A. Philip. Defense industries. Discrimination. Executive Order 8802. March on Washington Movement. Military. Webster, Milton. 1941-44. *588*
Rankin plans. Expansionism. Military Strategy. USA. USSR. 1943. *924*
Rapido (battle). Italy (Anzio front). 5th Army, US (36th Division). 1944. *887*
Rasmussen, Kai E. Japanese Americans (Nisei). Language School. Military Intelligence Service. Minnesota. 1941-46. *28*
Rationing. Ohio (Lucas County). Price controls. 1942-43. *17*
Reconnaissance. Gilbert Islands. Haley, J. Frederick (account). Marines. Tarawa (battle). 1943. *368*
Recreation. Airplanes, Military (assembly). Nebraska. Offutt Air Force Base (Building D). 1940-77. *816*
Refugees. Blair, Frederick Charles. Canada. Federal Policy. Jews. 1930's. *2*
—. Europe. Jews. McDonald, James G. (paper). Resettlement. 1938-43. *285*
—. Friedman, Saul S. (review article). Genocide. Jews. Public Policy. Roosevelt, Franklin D. (administration). 1938-45. 1973. *790*
—. Genocide (review article). Historiography. Jews. Wiesel, Elie. 1939-45. 1960-79. *1077*
—. Genocide, toleration of. Germany. Immigration laws. Jews. Roosevelt, Franklin D. (administration). 1933-45. *282*
—. Germany. Jews. Relief organizations. USA. 1933-45. *316*
—. Jews. Zionist/Anti-Zionist disunity. 1932-45. *946*
Refugees (rescue, relief). Hayes, Carlton J. H. Jews. Spain. 1942-45. *1040*
Regensburg-Schweinfurt. Air raids. Air Warfare. Germany. Jablonski, Edward (review article). USA. 1943. *380*

Regimental histories. Navy Patrol Bombing Squadron 106. PB4B-2 (aircraft). 1944-45. *888*

Regnery, Henry (account). Historiography (revisionist). Publishers and Publishing. Truth, historical. 20c. *775*

Relief organizations. Federal Government. Great Britain. Jews. Morgenthau, Henry, Jr. War Refugee Board. 1940-44. *726*

—. Germany. Jews. Refugees. USA. 1933-45. *316*

Relocation camps. California. Japanese Americans. Warren, Earl. 1941-45. *1030*

—. Idaho (Minidoka). Japanese Americans. Mukaida, Tomeji (reminiscences). 1940's. *573*

Relocation, forced. Canada. Japanese Canadians. Race Relations. 1890's-1940's. *949*

Remagen (battle). Bridges. Germany. 1945. *165*

Remagen Bridge (battle of). Armored Vehicles and Tank Warfare. Hodges, Courtney. 1944. *667*

Reorganization Objective Army Divisions. Armies. Military force structuring. 1861-1977. *91*

Repatriation. Foreign Relations. Prisoners and prisons. USA. USSR. 1945. *136*

Repatriation, forced. Diplomacy. Europe. USA. USSR. 1944-47. *268*

Reporters and Reporting. Armies. Morale. *New York Times.* Railey, Hilton H. 1941. *1027*

—. China (Yenan). Communist Party. 1944. *971*

Rescue work. Air Rescue Service. 1945-61. *964*

—. Fund raising. Genocide. Joint Distribution Committee. Judaism (Orthodox). Yeshiva Aid Committee. 1939-41. *1081*

Rescues. Bergson, Peter. Emergency Committee to Save the Jewish People of Europe. Genocide. Zionism. 1943-45. *723*

—. Genocide. Germany. Great Britain. Jews. 1939-44. *283*

—. Great Britain. Okinawa (battle). Parker, Willard. *Undine* (vessel). 1945. *409*

Research. Dwight D. Eisenhower Library. Kansas (Abilene). Military records. 1916-52. 1977. *361*

—. *Foreign Relations of the United States* (series). 1940-50. 1978. *350*

—. Science and Government. 1945. *464*

Research and development. Drones. Fahrney, Delmar S. (account). Missiles. Navy Bureau of Aeronautics. N2C-2 (aircraft). Radio. TG-2 (aircraft). 1936-45. *279*

Reserve Officers' Training Corps. Military training. Oklahoma State University. Preparedness. Veterans. Women Appointed for Volunteer Emergency Service. 1891-1951. *812*

Resettlement. Baptists. Discrimination. Japanese Americans. 1890-1970. *644*

—. Europe. Jews. McDonald, James G. (paper). Refugees. 1938-43. *285*

Resistance. Archives, National. Documents. Europe. 1939-45. *218*

—. Declassification. Documents. Europe. USA. 1939-45. 1972-75. *270*

Resorts. California (Byron Hot Springs). Prison camp. 1868-1976. *1032*

—. New York (Saratoga Springs). Restorations. 1810-1978. *706*

Restorations. New York (Saratoga Springs). Resorts. 1810-1978. *706*

Revisionism. Cold War. Historiography. Nazism. ca 1930-50. *515*

Rhetoric. Attitudes. Music, popular. 1940-45. *643*

Rickenbacker, Edward V. Luke, Frank, Jr. P-38 (aircraft). 1st Pursuit Group. 1918-76. *534*

Riddle, Jack (interview). Air Forces. Gliders. 1942-45. *175*

Ridgway, Matthew B. Military Service, Professional. War. 1917-60. *9*

Rio Conference of 1942. Argentina. Decisionmaking. Diplomacy. USA. 1942. *1059*

Rio Conference (1942). Axis powers. Diplomatic relations (rupture). Latin America. USA. 1941-42. *297*

Riots. California. Concentration Camps. Japanese Americans. Manzanar War Relocation Center. Ueno, Harry (arrest). 1942. *381*

—. Cane, Cyril H. Diplomatic reports. Great Britain. Michigan (Detroit). 1943. *359*

Rockefeller, Nelson A. Axis Powers. Foreign Policy. Latin America. Office of the Coordinator of Inter-American Affairs. Roosevelt, Franklin D. (administration). 1933-42. *364*

Romania. Air Warfare. Brooks, Jim (reminiscences). Oil fields. 31st Fighter Group, US. 1944. *127*

Roosevelt, Franklin. Diplomacy. Drought, James M. Japan. John Doe Associates. Konoye, Fumimaro. Summit conferences. 1941. *143*

Roosevelt, Franklin D. Air Warfare. Bombing. Churchill, Winston. Military General Staff. Operation Overlord. 1944. *1053*

—. Allies. Peace. Unconditional surrender (concept). ca 1942-45. *45*

—. Anticolonialism. Asia. USA. 1941-45. *353*

—. Anti-Imperialism. Foreign Policy (critics). Pacific Area. World War II (antecedents). 1930's. *704*

—. Asia, Southeast (coast). India. *Lanikai* (vessel). Navies. Tolley, Kemp (personal account). World War II (antecedents). 1941. *968*

—. Atlantic, battle of the. Great Britain. Navies. Secrecy. Warmaking powers. 1941. *682*

—. Atlantic Ocean, South. Great Britain. Neutrality (circumvention). Takoradi air route. World War II (antecedents). 1941-42. *769*

—. Attitudes. Executive Behavior. Foreign policy. Political Protest. 1940-72. *1092*

—. Blockades. Chamberlain, Neville. China. Great Britain. Japan. World War II (antecedents). 1937-38. *362*

—. Borg thesis. Foreign Policy. Georgia. Press. Quarantine speech. 1937. *132*

—. Canada. King, William Lyon Mackenzie. Ogdensburg Agreement. 1933-45. *910*

—. Carlson, Evans. China. Intelligence mission. Japan. USA. 1937-38. *992*

—. China. Churchill, Winston. de Gaulle, Charles. Foreign Policy. French colonies. Indochina. 1942-45. *507*

—. Churchill, Winston. Correspondence. Great Britain. Neutrality. 1939-40. *531*

—. Churchill, Winston. Diplomacy. Great Britain. Military Strategy. 1942-44. *999*

—. Churchill, Winston. Diplomacy. Stalin, J. V. Yalta Conference (preparations). 1945. *696*

—. Churchill, Winston. Foreign policy. Political Leadership. Stalin, Joseph. 1939-45. *1107*

—. Churchill, Winston. Foreign Relations. Great Britain. 1939-45. *782*

—. Churchill, Winston. Foreign Relations. Great Britain. Lash, Joseph P. (review article). 1939-41. 1976. *227*

—. Churchill, Winston. Germany (partition). Potsdam Conference. Stettinius, Edward Reilley. Yalta Conference. 1945. *329*

—. Churchill, Winston. Great Britain. Joint Chiefs of Staff. Malta Conference. Military Strategy. 1945. *912*

—. Cold War. Europe, Eastern. Great Britain. "Percentages" agreement. USSR. 1944. *780*

—. Cold War. Open Door, global. Truman, Harry S. USA. USSR. 1941-50. *1037*

Roosevelt

—. Cold War (origins). Truman, Harry S. (administration). Yalta Conference. 1945-47. *957*
—. Dallek, Robert (review article). Foreign Policy. 1932-45. 1979. *446*
—. Diplomacy. Germany. USSR. 1934-39. *572*
—. Diplomacy. Ibn-Saud, King. *Murphy* (vessel). Saudi Arabia. USA. 1945. *472*
—. Diplomacy. Indochina. International trusteeships. 1941-45. *407*
—. Diplomacy. Yalta Conference (review essay). 1945-55. *850*
—. Economic Conditions. Manufacturers, small. 1939-43. *398*
—. Eisenhower, Dwight D. Marshall, George C. Military General Staff. Operation Overlord. 1942-44. *295*
—. Elections (presidential). Poland (issue). Polish Americans. 1942-44. *374*
—. Embargo, de facto. Foreign Policy. Japan. Oil. 1941. *22*
—. Europe, East. Foreign policy. Isolationism. Neutrality Laws. World War II (antecedents). 1920's-30's. *249*
—. Foreign policy. Hawaii. Preparedness. Works Progress Administration. 1935-40. *763*
—. Foreign policy. Hopkins, Harry. USSR. 1938-46. *576*
—. Foreign policy. Illinois (Chicago). Poland. Polish-American Congress. 1944. *820*
—. Foreign Policy. Middle East. Palestine. USA. 1943-45. *710*
—. Foreign Policy. Poland. Truman, Harry S. USA. USSR. 1943-46. *558*
—. Foreign Policy. Public opinion. USSR. 1941-45. *679*
—. Foreign Policy. USA. USSR. 1933-45. *443*
—. Foreign Policy. USSR. 1933-45. *442*
—. Foreign policy decisions. 1940-45. *678*
—. Foreign Relations. Great Britain. Nuclear Arms. USA. 1940-45. *87*
—. France. 1938-45. *281*
—. Frankfurter, Felix. Lippmann, Walter. New Deal. 1932-45. *721*
—. Germany. National Reich Church (suggested). Propaganda campaign. USA. World War II (antecedents). 1941. *187*
—. Hopkins, Harry. Marshall, George C. Military reorganization. 1942-45. *744*
—. Isolationism. Nye, Gerald P. Political Speeches. 1941. *516*
—. Joint Chiefs of Staff. MacArthur, Douglas. Nimitz, Chester W. Pacific Area. 1941-42. *189*
—. Lange, Oscar. Poland, eastern. Pro-Communism. USSR. 1941-45. *821*
—. Montana. Political Attitudes. Senate. Wheeler, Burton K. 1904-46. *811*
—. New Deal programs. 1940-45. *869*
Roosevelt, Franklin D. (administration). Airplanes, Military. Greece. Military Aid. 1940-41. *666*
—. Alliances. Decisionmaking. Domestic Policy. Foreign policy. UN Conference on Food and Agriculture. Virginia (Hot Springs). 1943. *1041*
—. Americas (North and South). Defense policy. Monroe Doctrine. 1930's-40. *363*
—. Antifascism. Lend-Lease. New Deal. 1941-45. *1071*
—. Asia, Southeast. Colonialism. Great Britain. Joint declaration (proposed). USA. 1942-44. *1036*
—. Autonomy. Congress. Politics. Puerto Rico. 1940-45. *89*
—. Axis Powers. Foreign Policy. Latin America. Office of the Coordinator of Inter-American Affairs. Rockefeller, Nelson A. 1933-42. *364*

—. Catholic influence. Isolationism. Nicoll, John R. A. 1943. *357*
—. Churchill, Winston. Diplomacy. Great Britain. Kennedy, Joseph P. 1938-40. *997*
—. Civil rights. Congress. Discrimination, employment. Fair Employment Practices Committee. 1941-46. *684*
—. Clark, Grenville. Mobilization needs. National service law (proposed). 1942-45. *599*
—. Dewey, Thomas E. Elections (presidential). Pearl Harbor, attack on (issue). 1944. *621*
—. Diaries. Foreign Policy (review article). Stettinius, Edward Reilley. 1943-46. 1975. *483*
—. Discrimination, Employment. Fair Employment Practices Committee. Negroes. 1940-45. *871*
—. Europe. Genocide. Jews. Public Policy. 1942-44. *596*
—. Friedman, Saul S. (review article). Genocide. Jews. Public Policy. Refugees. 1938-45. 1973. *790*
—. Genocide, toleration of. Germany. Immigration laws. Jews. Refugees. 1933-45. *282*
—. Historiography. Negroes. USSR. 1939-45. *872*
—. Industry. Labor Unions and Organizations. War Manpower Commission. War Production Board. 1939-45. *493*
—. National security. Pearl Harbor question. 1941-46. *620*
Roosevelt, Franklin D. (correspondence). Churchill, Winston (correspondence). Great Britain. USA. 1938-45. *481*
Roosevelt, Franklin D. (death). Diplomacy. Europe. 1945. *78*
Roosevelt, Franklin Delano. Appeasement. Chamberlain, Arthur Neville. Foreign Policy. Great Britain. USA. 1937-39. *1012*
—. Cold War. Diplomacy. Nuclear Arms. 1941-45. *861*
—. Diplomacy. Free ports. Norway. USA. USSR. 1941-43. *788*
Rosengarten, Adolph G., Jr. (reminiscences). Military Intelligence. Normandy Landing. Ultra project. War Department (Military Intelligence Division; Special Branch). 1st Army, US. 1944-45. *796*
Roshchin, A. A. (memoirs). France. Germany. Great Britain. Partition. USSR. 1942-45. *797*
Royal Air Force. Air Warfare. Dunn, William R. (account). Great Britain. 1941. *251*
Royal Canadian Air Force. Canada. Dieppe (air battle). Great Britain. Leigh-Mallory, Trafford. 1942. *151*
Royal Canadian Army Medical Corps. Canadian Women's Army Corps. 1940-43. *739*
Rozmarek, Charles. Lobbying. Mazewski, Aloysius. Polish American Congress. Polish National Alliance. 1944-79. *737*
Rubber. Government. Synthetic products. 1939-45. *900*
Rubber industry. Agriculture Department. California. Emergency Rubber Project. Guayule (plant). Nishimura, Shimpe. 1942-76. *36*
Rumania. Air Warfare. Ploesti (raid). USA. Whalen, Norman M. (reminiscences). 1943. *1029*
—. Holocaust. Kremer, Charles H. Trifa, Valerian. USA. War crimes. 1941-74. *583*
Rupp, Leila J. Germany. Propaganda (review article). Winkler, Allan M. Women. 1939-45. *373*
Russett, Bruce M. USA. World War II (antecedents) (review article). 1939-41. *239*
Ryan, Cornelius (review article). Airborne operations. Netherlands (Arnhem). Operation Market-Garden. 1944. *559*

S

Saddles. Cavalry. McClellan, George Brinton. 1857-1943. *303*
St. John, Robert. New Hampshire (Lebanon). Peace proposal, utopian. Radio. 1945. *713*
St. Lô (battle). France. Normandy invasion. USA. 1944. *162*
Saipan (battle). Amphibious operations. Japan. Philippine Sea (battle). 1944. *995*
Salazar, Antonio. Foreign Relations. Portugal. 1939-45. *941*
Salvage. Navies. 1943-79. *633*
San Jacinto Ordnance Depot. Ordnance. Texas. 1939-64. *478*
Sands of Iwo Jima (film). Fribourg, Leonard. Grainger, Edmund. Hollywood. Marines (image). Wayne, John. 1949. *935*
Saratoga (vessel). Aircraft carriers. *Lexington* (vessel). Navies. 1922-45. *23*
Saskatchewan. Deutscher Bund Canada. German Canadians. Nazism. 1934-39. *1005*
Saudi Arabia. Diplomacy. Ibn-Saud, King. *Murphy* (vessel). Roosevelt, Franklin D. USA. 1945. *472*
—. Economic Aid. Foreign Relations. Great Britain. State Department (Near East Affairs Division). 1941-45. *809*
—. Lend-Lease. Lobbying. Oil Industry and Trade. 1943. *21*
Savage, Paul L. Armies (review article). Bureaucracies. Gabriel, Richard A. Military (officers). 1914-80. *64*
Savo Island (battle). Japan. Navies. Pacific Area. USA. 1942. *67*
Schellenbach, Lewis B. Coffee, John M. Congress. Embargo (sought). Japan. Washington. 1930's-40. *536*
Science. Great Britain. Information exchange. USSR. 1940-45. *63*
Science and Government. Kilgore, Harley M. Legislation. National Science Foundation. Senate. 1942-50. *568*
—. Research. 1945. *464*
Scientific Experiments and Research. Conscription, Military. Industry. 1940-44. *1084*
Scientists. Atomic bomb. Franck, James. Policymaking. Stimson, Henry L. 1945. *918*
Scott, Robert L., Jr. Aeronautics, Military. Arizona. Flying Tigers. Germany, West. 1941-45. 1955-57. *936*
Scrap metal industry. Naval Vessels. 1941-79. *302*
Sealark Channel (battle of). Armstrong, David M. (reminiscence). Guadalcanal (battle of). 1942. *31*
Seaplanes. Coast Guard. Maryland. 1929-69. *810*
Second Front. Cold War (origins). Marshall Plan. Nuclear Arms. USSR. 1940's. *1016*
—. Diplomacy. Great Britain. USA. USSR. 1942-43. *1089*
—. Great Britain. USSR. 1943-44. *1076*
Second front clamor. Airplanes, Military. Hughes HK-1 (aircraft). 1942-47. *613*
Secrecy. Atlantic, battle of the. Great Britain. Navies. Roosevelt, Franklin D. Warmaking powers. 1941. *682*
—. France. Great Britain. Nuclear arms testing. 1939-45. *327*
Sedition. Eicher, Edward Clayton. Trials. 1944. *319*
Segregation. Army Air Corps. Tuskegee Army Air Field. 332d Fighter Group. 99th Fighter Squadron. 1941-49. *711*

—. Discrimination, Employment. Military Service (enlistees). Navies. Negroes. Race Relations. 1798-1970's. *388*
—. Protestant churches. Race Relations. 1939-45. *701*
Segregation, development of. Army hospitals. Hospitals. Negroes (physicians, soldiers). 1940-42. *707*
Selective Service, origins of the. Clark, Grenville. New York. Plattsburg Movement. 1940-41. *176*
Selective Training and Service Act (US, 1940). Congress. Conscription, Military. Isolationism. Kansas. State Politics. 1940. *335*
Semple, Jesse B. (fictitious character). Hughes, Langston. Negro Literature. Popular culture. 1942-43. *755*
Senate. Anti-British sentiments. Churchill, Winston. Langer, William. North Dakota. 1941-52. *1035*
—. Kilgore, Harley M. Legislation. National Science Foundation. Science and Government. 1942-50. *568*
—. Montana. Political Attitudes. Roosevelt, Franklin D. Wheeler, Burton K. 1904-46. *811*
Service, John Stewart (*Lost Chance in China*, excerpts). China. Foreign policy. State Department (Foreign Service). USA. 1945-50's. *857*
Settlers, protection for. Fort Wallace. Hunting grounds, deprivation of. Indian-White Relations. Kansas. 1865-82. *440*
Seversky Aircraft Corporation. YP-43 Lancer (aircraft). 1939-59. *553*
Sex. Attitudes. Morality. 1918-55. *597*
Sex discrimination. Boycotts, consumer. District of Columbia. Employment. Women. 1941-46. *1105*
Sex roles. Canada. Films. National Film Board of Canada. Women. 1940's-50's. *594*
—. Canadian Women's Army Corps. Military service. Morality. Women. 1941-46. *740*
—. Germany. Labor. Propaganda. Public opinion. Women. 1939-45. *814*
—. Labor. Michigan. Women. 1941-45. *180*
Sforza, Carlo. Anti-Fascist Movements. Foreign Relations. Italy. 1940-43. *626*
Shakespeare, William. Armies. Evans, Maurice. Pacific Area. Theater Production and Direction. 1942-45. *864*
Shanghai (battle). China. Japan. Marines. 1937. *803*
Sherry, Michael S. (review article). Planning. Preparedness. 1943-47. 1977. *1001*
Sherwin, Martin J. Atomic Warfare. Foreign Policy. Gowing, Margaret. Great Britain. Nuclear Science and Technology (review article). 1938-52. *529*
Ship portraits. Brewington, Marion Vernon (obituary). Maritime historians. 1930's-74. *1031*
Shipbuilding. Amphibious operations. Higgins, Andrew J. Landing craft. 1933-45. *655*
—. Boilermakers, Iron Shipbuilders and Helpers, International Brotherhood of. California (Los Angeles). Discrimination, employment. Labor Unions and Organizations. Negroes. Oregon (Portland). 1941-46. *883*
—. Delaware (Wilmington). Dravo Corp. Navies. Pennsylvania (Pittsburgh). 1940-47. *974*
—. Naval Battles. *Platte* (vessel). 1939-71. *213*
—. Oregon (Portland). Women. 1941-45. *875*
Ships. Air Warfare. Bombing (strategic). 1939-80. *468*
—. California (Long Beach). Great Britain. *Queen Mary* (vessel). ca 1930-74. *566*

268 Ships

—. *City of Flint* (vessel; capture). Contraband. Foreign relations. Germany. USSR. 1939. *177*

Shipyards. Alabama (Mobile). Fair Employment Practices Commission. Negroes. South. 1938-45. *771*

Short, Walter C. Kimmel, Husband E. Pearl Harbor, attack on. Personal narratives. Weapons (ineffectiveness). 1941. *951*

Shoulder patches. Air Warfare. American Volunteer Group. China. Flying Tigers motifs. 23d Fighter Group. 1930's-45. *191*

Sicily. Airborne troops. Armies. Gavin, James M. (memoirs). Invasions. 1943. *313*

Simpson, William H. Germany (Roer River). 9th Army, US. 1945. *927*

Simulation and Games. Atomic Warfare. History Teaching. Japan. 1945. 1978. *265*

—. Decisionmaking. Europe, Western. History Teaching. USA. War games. 1939-45. 1970's. *153*

Singapore, defense of. Great Britain. Military Strategy. USA. 1939-41. *49*

Sino-American Cooperation Association. Anti-Communists. China. Navies. USA. 1942-45. *842*

Sisk, John P. (personal account). Civil War. Forrest, Nathan Bedford. Forrest, Nathan Bedford (1905-44). Military Service. 1861-1945. *870*

Sledge, Eugene B. (account). Armies. Japan. Marines. Pelelieu (battle). 1944. *877*

Slovaks. Czechoslovakia. Czechs. 1940-45. *325*

Small Business. Defense Industries. Industrialization. Missouri (Kansas City). 1940-45. *656*

Smith, Bradley F. Maser, Werner. Nuremberg trials (review article). War crimes. 1945-46. 1970's. *1013*

Smith, Oliver P. Military Service, Professional. 1917-51. *863*

Smyth Report, 1945. Atomic energy. Japan. Military Strategy. USA. 1940-45. *897*

Social Change. Armies. Attitudes. Labor. 1940's-70's. *853*

—. Farmers, black. Negroes. North Carolina. South. 1950-70. *1004*

—. Military. Professionalism. 1941-76. *129*

Social conservatism. Cartoonists. Depressions. Gray, Harold. "Little Orphan Annie", comic strip. 1930's-40's. *1069*

Social control. Business. Canada. Federal Government. Labor Unions and Organizations. Unemployment Insurance Act (1941). Wages. 1910-41. *202*

Social justice. Employment. Industry. Negroes. 1942-43. *1086*

Social Problems. Arkansas. Family. Legislation. 1941-45. *884*

—. Business. California (Los Angeles). City planning. Federal government. 1941-59. *843*

Social scientists. Bureau of Public Information. Canada. Federal government. Press. Public opinion. Wartime Information Board. 1939-45. *1070*

Social services. Civil Rights. Nebraska (Omaha). Negroes. Quality of life. Urban League. 1928-50. *623*

Social Status. Casualty rates. Vietnam War. 1941-45. 1961-73. *1039*

—. Chinese Americans. Discrimination. Economic Conditions. Japanese Americans. 1840's-1978. *732*

—. Demobilization. Discrimination, Employment. Literature. Women. 1944-46. *392*

Socialism. Assimilation. Education. Jews. Labor movement. 1880's-1945. *975*

Socialist Party. Antiwar Sentiment. Keep America Out of War Congress. Thomas, Norman. Villard, Oswald Garrison. World War II (antecedents). 1938-41. *236*

Societies, apothecary. German Americans. New York City. Pharmacy. 19c-1940's. *1008*

Sociological theory. Japanese Americans (attitudes toward). Values. 1940's-70's. *914*

Sociology (aircraft). Aeronautics, Military. 1941-43. *854*

Solomon Islands. *Gato* (vessel). Navigation, bush. Submarine Warfare. 1943. *608*

Solomon Islands (Vella Lavella). Japan. Navies. USA. 1943. *547*

South. Alabama (Mobile). Fair Employment Practices Commission. Negroes. Shipyards. 1938-45. *771*

—. Economic Growth. Industry. Population. Western States. 1940-79. *1*

—. Farmers, black. Negroes. North Carolina. Social Change. 1950-70. *1004*

South Carolina. Germans. Prisoners of War (camps). 1944-46. *650*

South Dakota. Balloons, armed. Japan. Project FUGO. 1944-45. *517*

—. Civil rights movement. NAACP. Negroes. 1804-1970. *82*

South or Southern States. Agricultural Production. Cotton. Economic Conditions. Soybeans. 1920's-75. *294*

Southeastern Carriers Conference. Discrimination. Fair Employment Practices Committee. Negroes. Railroads. 1941-45. *402*

Southern Baptists. Attitudes. Kelsey, George (review article). Kentucky. 1941-45. 1973. *756*

Southern Pacific Railroad. Arizona (Raso). Ghost towns. Railroad stations. 1911-76. *670*

Soviet-American cooperation. Foreign Relations. USA. 1941-48. *862*

Soybeans. Agricultural Production. Cotton. Economic Conditions. South or Southern States. 1920's-75. *294*

Spain. Destroyers. Military Aid. Navies. 1942-60. *35*

—. Diplomacy. Hayes, Carlton J. H. Historians. 1942-45. *372*

—. Diplomacy. National Telephone Company (Spain). USA. Weddell, Alexander Wilbourne. *367*

—. Foreign Policy. Great Britain. Neutrality. 1939-45. *266*

—. Hayes, Carlton J. H. Jews. Refugees (rescue, relief). 1942-45. *1040*

Speeches, Addresses, etc. (to Americans). Churchill, Winston. 1901-46. *600*

Spitfire (aircraft). Air Forces. Dunn, William R. (account). Eagle Squadron, No. 71. Great Britain. 1941. *252*

—. Air Warfare. Andrews, John A. C. (account). P-40 (aircraft). P-47 (aircraft). 1943-45. *26*

Spitfire, Supermarine (airplane). Airplanes, Military. P-51 (airplane). 1939-45. *604*

Sport. Canada. Federal Government. Physical Education and Training. 1909-54. *1028*

Spruance, Raymond A. Naval Tactics. Philippine Sea, battle. 1943. *134*

Stained glass. Camp Lejeune. Lamb Studios. Marines. New Jersey (Tenafly). North Carolina. Windows. 1775-1943. *480*

Stained glass windows. Military history. US Military Academy. 1800-1944. *705*

Stalin, J. V. Churchill, Winston. Diplomacy. Roosevelt, Franklin D. Yalta Conference (preparations). 1945. *696*

Stalin, Joseph. Churchill, Winston. Foreign policy. Political Leadership. Roosevelt, Franklin D. 1939-45. *1107*

Standard-Vacuum Oil Company. Anderson, Irvine H., Jr. (review article). Asia, East. Foreign Investments. Foreign policy. Oil Industry and Trade. 1933-41. 1975. *725*
Standiford Airfield. Air Bases (construction of). Civil-Military Relations. Hammon, Stratton Owen (account). Kentucky (Louisville). 1942-43. *377*
Stanley, Carleton. Colleges and Universities (presidents). Dalhousie University. Mackenzie, A. Stanley. New Brunswick. 1911-45. *395*
State Department. Airlines. Latin America. National security. 1927-40. *767*
—. Anti-Nazi Movements. Diplomacy. Messersmith, George Strausser. 1928-39. *858*
—. Committee for Political Defense. Foreign Policy. Latin America. 1942-45. *825*
—. Diplomacy. Emmerson, John K. (memoirs). Japan (Tokyo). World War II (antecedents). 1941. *275*
—. Economic development. Liberia. Military Strategy. 1938-45. *66*
—. Economic Growth. Propaganda. War Department. 1939-45. *1083*
—. Egypt. Great Britain. Suez Canal. 1930's-45. *47*
—. Foreign policy. Japan. Oil exports, restricted. USA. 1940-41. *989*
—. Germany. Jews (stateless). Morgenthau, Henry, Jr. Treasury Department. USA. 1942-44. *589*
—. Jews. Pell, Herbert Claiborne. UN War Crimes Commission. War crimes. 1943-45. *100*
State Department (Advisory Committee on Post-War Foreign Policy). Bowman, Isaiah. East Prussia. Oder-Neisse Line. Poland. Welles, Sumner. 1942-45. *819*
State Department (Foreign Service). China. Foreign policy. Service, John Stewart (*Lost Chance in China*, excerpts). USA. 1945-50's. *857*
—. China-Burma-India Theater. Emmerson, John K. (reminiscences). 1941-44. *272*
—. Foreign Broadcast Information Service. Intelligence Service. World War II (antecedents). 1939-41. *178*
State Department (Near East Affairs Division). Economic Aid. Foreign Relations. Great Britain. Saudi Arabia. 1941-45. *809*
State Politics. Congress. Conscription, Military. Isolationism. Kansas. Selective Training and Service Act (US, 1940). 1940. *335*
—. Education. Lawyers. Marines. McCarthy, Joseph R. Wisconsin. 1908-44. *687*
Statistics. Air Forces. 1907-74. *1100*
Steel Shavings (periodical). Indiana (Calumet region). Local history. 1933-45. 1975-80. *509*
Steele, John L. (interview). Armies. Imprisonment. Italy (Pisa). Pound, Ezra. 1945. *485*
Stefansson, Vilhjalmur. Arctic. Discovery and Exploration. Finnie, Richard Sterling (account). North America. Office of the Coordinator of Information. 1931-62. *290*
Stereotypes. China. *Keys of the Kingdom* (film). Office of War Information. Propaganda. USA. 1940-45. *94*
—. Films. Germans (image of). 1914-45. *689*
Stereotypes (combatants). Students. Values (change in). War, perceptions of. 1961-71. *185*
Stereotypes, positive. Asian Americans. Race Relations. 1850-1973. *932*
Stettinius, Edward Reilley. Churchill, Winston. Germany (partition). Potsdam Conference. Roosevelt, Franklin D. Yalta Conference. 1945. *329*
—. Diaries. Foreign Policy (review article). Roosevelt, Franklin D. (administration). 1943-46. 1975. *483*

Stillwell, Joseph W. China. Jiang Jieshi. Marshall, George C. Military General Staff. 1944. *841*
Stilwell, Joseph W. Chiang Kai-shek. China. Military strategy. 1942-44. *629*
—. China. China. Historiography. 1942-44. *1066*
—. China. Foreign relations. 1942-70's. *866*
Stimson, Henry L. Air Forces. Bombing, strategic. Japan (Kyoto). USA. 1940-45. *160*
—. Atomic bomb. Franck, James. Policymaking. Scientists. 1945. *918*
—. Hastie, William. Military. Negroes. Racism. 1940-43. *610*
Strategy. Marshall, George C. (strategic thought). USSR. 1939-50. *121*
Streichen, Edward J. Maryland (Annapolis). Photography, Military. US Naval Academy (Edward J. Streichen Collection). 1930's-75. *194*
Strikes. Negroes. Pennsylvania (Philadelphia). Public transportation. Racism. US Employment Service. War Manpower Commission. 1944. *1046*
Strikes and Lockouts. Congress of Industrial Organizations. Employment. 1941-45. *541*
Strikes, wildcat. Automobile industry. Employment. Labor Unions and Organizations. 1941-45. *1103*
Strunk, Al (account). Aeronautics, Military. BT-13A (aircraft). Flight training. 1941-45. *930*
Stuart, John Leighton. China. Diplomacy. Japan. USA. 1937-41. *896*
Students. Stereotypes (combatants). Values (change in). War, perceptions of. 1961-71. *185*
Submarine Warfare. Communications. Germany. USA. 1939-45. *653*
—. Destroyer escorts. *England* (vessel). Japan. Pacific Area. Williamson, John A. (account). 1944. *1038*
—. *Gato* (vessel). Navigation, bush. Solomon Islands. 1943. *608*
—. *Indianapolis* (vessel). *I-58* (vessel). Japan. Pacific Area. USA. 1945. *115*
Submarines. *Awa Maru* (vessel). Japan. *Queenfish* (vessel). USA. 1945. *902*
—. British Columbia. Films. Naval Vessels. World War I. 1914-45. *156*
—. Dry dock, floating. Louisiana (New Orleans). Manitowoc Shipbuilding Co. Mississippi River. Navigation, Inland. *Peto* (vessel). 1942-45. *676*
—. Electric Boat Company. McKee, Andrew Irwin. Military Engineering. Navies. 1930's-61. *10*
—. Navies. 17c-1943. *522*
Subsidies. Bankhead Bill (1943). Federal government. Newspapers. War Bond advertising. 1943. *112*
Subversive Activities. Xenophobia. 1939-41. *550*
Suez Canal. Egypt. Great Britain. State Department. 1930's-45. *47*
Suffrage. British Columbia. Canada. Discrimination. India. 1939-45. *414*
—. British Columbia. Chinese. Immigration. Japanese. 1935-49. *523*
Sugar cane fields. Labor, forced. Louisiana (Lafourche Parish). Prisoners of war, German. 1943-44. *142*
Summit conferences. Diplomacy. Drought, James M. Japan. John Doe Associates. Konoye, Fumimaro. Roosevelt, Franklin. 1941. *143*
Supersonic planes. Army Air Corps. Flight testing. SX-1 aircraft. Yeager, Charles. 1944-75. *673*
Surplus Property Act of 1944. Clayton, Will. ca 1942-48. *229*
Surprise attacks. Military History. 1940's-70's. *77*

Surrender. Atomic Warfare. B-29 (aircraft). Japan. Lemay, Curtis. 1945. *1052*
—. Bulgaria. Diplomacy. 1944. *970*
—. Diplomacy. Japan. MacArthur, Douglas. Philippines (Manila). 1945. *624*
—. Foreign Policy. France. Preparedness. 1940-44. *549*
—. Naval Strategy. Pacific Area. Wake Island. 1941. *340*
Surrender offer. Atomic Warfare. Japan. Politics. Truman, Harry S. (administration). 1945. *84*
Surrender, unconditional. Japan. Peace (delayed). Potsdam Conference. USA. 1945. *998*
Sutherland, Richard K. (papers). Executive Order No. 1. Gifts. MacArthur, Douglas. Military General Staff. Philippines. Quezon, Manuel. 1942. *733*
Sweden. Foreign Relations. USA. 1776-1970's. *844*
Swedish language. Minnesota. Newspapers. 1851-1976. *685*
Switzerland. Air Warfare. Bombing (inadvertent). Diplomacy. USA. 1943-45. *401*
—. Anabaptists. Germany. Mennonites. Taxation. War. 16c-1973. *489*
—. Economic agreements. Foreign Relations. Neutrality. World War I. 1919. 1944-45. *292*
SX-1 aircraft. Army Air Corps. Flight testing. Supersonic planes. Yeager, Charles. 1944-75. *673*
Synthetic products. Government. Rubber. 1939-45. *900*
System analysis. Decisionmaking. Organizations. 20c. *3*
—. Military. 1940-71. *105*
Szilard, Leo. Anderson, Herbert L. (reminiscences). Chicago, University of. Columbia University. Fermi, Enrico. Nuclear Science and Technology. 1933-45. *20*
—. Byrnes, James F. Federal Government. Germany. Memoirs. Nuclear Science and Technology. 1898-1945. *948*
—. Einstein, Albert. Hungarian Americans. Nuclear Arms (program). USA. 1941-74. *366*
Szőke, István. *Canadian Hungarian Worker* (newspaper). Hungarians. USSR. 1929-44. *584*

T

Tactics. Africa, North. Air Forces. Military Ground Forces. Patton, George S., Jr. 1943. *502*
—. Air support, close. Army Air Corps Tactical School. Europe, Western. 1930-45. *454*
—. Antitank warfare. 1941-45. *465*
Taft-Hartley Act (US, 1947). Business. Labor Unions and Organizations. New Deal. Wagner Act (US, 1935). 1935-47. *108*
Takoradi air route. Atlantic Ocean, South. Great Britain. Neutrality (circumvention). Roosevelt, Franklin D. World War II (antecedents). 1941-42. *769*
Tanaka, Togo. Japanese Americans, incarceration of. Oral history. Yoneda, Elaine. Yoneda, Karl. 1941-45. *638*
Tarawa (battle). Gilbert Islands. Haley, J. Frederick (account). Marines. Reconnaissance. 1943. *368*
—. Gilbert Islands. Marines. 1943. *130*
Tatsuguchi, Paul Nobuo (diary). Alaska. Attu Island (battle). Japan. USA. 1941-43. *1011*
Taxation. Anabaptists. Germany. Mennonites. Switzerland. War. 16c-1973. *489*

Taylor, Myron. Documents. Foreign Relations. USA. Vatican. 1940-42. *6*
Taylor, Myron C. Diplomacy. Pius XII, Pope. USA. Vatican. 1940-50. *188*
TDR-1 (aircraft). Boehler, Hurley. Interstate Aircraft and Engineering Corporation. Navies. 1943-77. *554*
Teachers. Germany. Halle, Louis J. (reminiscences). Koichwitz, Otto ("O.K."). Propaganda. USA. 1920's-40's. *371*
Teaching. Canada. China. Hurford, Grace Gibberd (reminiscences). Missions and Missionaries. 1928-45. *439*
Technological change. Aircraft industry. Joint Aircraft Committee. National Defense Advisory Commission. Office of Production Management. 1940-45. *423*
Technology. Airplane Industry and Trade. Military. 1937-50. *764*
—. Attitudes. Economic development. Military Strategy. Nuclear arms. War. 1914-68. *686*
—. Balance of power. Korean War. Military Strategy. Weapons. 1918-53. *876*
—. Foreign Relations. Great Britain. Navies. USA. 1938-46. *532*
—. Naval strategy. Nuclear Arms. 1945-72. *1021*
Television. Cold War mentality. Propaganda. *Victory at Sea* series. 1952-72. *792*
Tennessee (Martin). Public Opinion. 1940-46. *580*
Texas. Congress of Industrial Organizations. Oil Industry and Trade. 1942-43. *459*
—. Germans. Prisoners of war. 1943-46. *497*
—. Germans. Prisoners of war. 1943-45. *967*
—. Ordnance. San Jacinto Ordnance Depot. 1939-64. *478*
Textbooks. Civil War. Collectivization. History Teaching. USSR. USSR. 1917-79. *207*
Textile Industry. Defense industries. Employment. Massachusetts (Lowell). Women. 1940-45. *630*
TG-2 (aircraft). Drones. Fahrney, Delmar S. (account). Missiles. Navy Bureau of Aeronautics. N2C-2 (aircraft). Radio. Research and development. 1936-85. *279*
Thailand. Bridges. Kwai, River. USA. 1942-45. *403*
Theater Production and Direction. Armies. Evans, Maurice. Pacific Area. Shakespeare, William. 1942-45. *864*
—. Little Theatre Group. Manhattan Project. New Mexico (Los Alamos). Nuclear Arms. 1943-46. *13*
Theology. Christians. Genocide. Jews. 1945-74. *259*
Third Army. France. Lorraine campaign. Metz (battle). Patton, George S., Jr. 1944. *46*
Thistle, R. British Columbia (Prince Rupert). Coastal defense. Diaries. 1941-42. *808*
Thomas, Elbert. Foreign Relations. Japan. King, William. USA. Utah. ca 1922-40. *538*
Thomas, Norman. Antiwar Sentiment. Keep America Out of War Congress. Socialist Party. Villard, Oswald Garrison. World War II (antecedents). 1938-41. *236*
Thomsen, Hans. Diplomacy. Espionage. Germany. Nazis. 1940. *634*
Thorne, Christopher. Alliances (review article). British Empire. Japan. Louis, William Roger. 1941-45. *729*
Thyng, Harrison R. (reminiscences). Air Forces. Europe. 1941-45. *963*
Tinker Air Force Base. Employment. Oklahoma (Oklahoma City). 1941-45. *257*
Tiny Tim (rocket). Armaments. Navy. 1944. *317*

Tokyo Rose (Iva Toguri d'Aquino). Citizenship. Ford, Gerald R. Hada, John. Japanese American Citizens League. Pardon. Uyeda, Clifford I. (account). 1973-77. *990*

Tolley, Kemp (personal account). Asia, Southeast (coast). India. *Lanikai* (vessel). Navies. Roosevelt, Franklin D. World War II (antecedents). 1941. *968*

Tomita, Saku. Diaries. Internment. Japanese Americans. Oregon. Portland Assembly Center. 1942. *492*

Total war. Air Warfare. Bombing. Dresden (attack on). Germany. Great Britain. 1914-45. *181*

Totalitarianism. Hoover, Herbert C. Intervention (opposed). Peace. USSR. 1939-41. *88*

Tourism. City boosters. Nevada (Las Vegas). Public relations. 1905-74. *471*

Toynbee, Arnold. Anti-Semitism. Christians. Holocaust. ca 1940-1975. *545*

Trades and Labour Congress. Canadian Labour Congress. Cooperative Commonwealth Federation. Federal Government. Industrial relations. 1939-46. *565*

Treason. Friendship. Literature. Morality. Politics. Pound, Ezra. 1909-72. *192*

Treasury Department. Germany. Jews (stateless). Morgenthau, Henry, Jr. State Department. USA. 1942-44. *589*

Treasury Star Parade (program). Federal Government. Propaganda. Radio. 1942-43. *564*

Treaties. China. Extraterritoriality. Great Britain. 1929-43. *164*

—. Conference on Security and Cooperation in Europe (1969). Europe, Eastern. Foreign Policy. USA. USSR. 1945-75. *148*

Trials. Eicher, Edward Clayton. Sedition. 1944. *319*

—. Libby, Frederick J. Malmédy massacre. National Council for the Prevention of War. War crimes (standards). 1944-49. *237*

Trifa, Valerian. Holocaust. Kremer, Charles H. Rumania. USA. War crimes. 1941-74. *583*

Trinity test. New Mexico (Los Alamos). Nuclear Arms. White Sands military reservation. 1945. *488*

Truk Islands. Airplanes, Military. F6F Hellcats (aircraft). Japan. USA. 1944. *966*

Truman, Harry S. Atomic Warfare. Groves, Leslie R. Hirohito, Emperor. Japan (Nagasaki). Potsdam Conference. 1944-45. *546*

—. Cold War. Open Door, global. Roosevelt, Franklin D. USA. USSR. 1941-50. *1037*

—. Documents. Harry S. Truman Library. Public Policy. Western States. 1940-66. *460*

—. Eden, Anthony. Foreign Policy. Molotov, V. M. Poland. USSR. 1945. *635*

—. Films (accuracy). Historical license. *Meeting at Potsdam* (film). Potsdam Conference. 1945. 1970's. *310*

—. Foreign policy. Internationalism. 1935-45. *636*

—. Foreign Policy. Poland. Roosevelt, Franklin D. USA. USSR. 1943-46. *558*

—. Foreign Policy. Potsdam Conference. Presidents. 1945. *570*

Truman, Harry S. (administration). Atomic bomb. Franck, James. Nuclear arms race. Political Attitudes. 1944-45. *1000*

—. Atomic Warfare. Japan. Politics. Surrender offer. 1945. *48*

—. Cold War (origins). Roosevelt, Franklin D. Yalta Conference. 1945-47. *957*

Truth, historical. Historiography (revisionism). Publishers and Publishing. Regnery, Henry (account). 20c. *775*

Tulagi (battle). Griffith, Samuel B., Jr. (reminiscences). Guadalcanal (battle). Marines. 1942-43. *346*

Tule Lake Camp. Internment. Japanese Americans. Martial law. 1941-44. *694*

Tulsa (vessel). Central America. Military occupation. Pacific Area. 1919-45. *1102*

Turkey. Allies. Axis Powers. Chrome. International Trade. 1939-44. *911*

Tuskegee Army Air Field. Army Air Corps. Segregation. 332d Fighter Group. 99th Fighter Squadron. 1941-49. *711*

—. Flight training. Military General Staff. Negroes. Parrish, Noel F. (interview). 1941-45. *393*

T-31 (aircraft). Airplanes, Military (trainers). 1941-47. *637*

U

Ueno, Harry (arrest). California. Concentration Camps. Japanese Americans. Manzanar War Relocation Center. Riots. 1942. *381*

Ukraine. Aeronautics, Military. Bombing. Bradshaw, Russell (account). 1944. *119*

Ultra project. Germany. Military History. 1940-45. *906*

—. Military Intelligence. Normandy Landing. Rosengarten, Adolph G., Jr. (reminiscences). War Department (Military Intelligence Division; Special Branch). 1st Army, US. 1944-45. *796*

UN. Foreign Policy. Nationalism. USA. 1944-45. *152*

—. Foreign Policy. NATO. 1941-55. *71*

UN Conference on Food and Agriculture. Alliances. Decisionmaking. Domestic Policy. Foreign policy. Roosevelt, Franklin D. (administration). Virginia (Hot Springs). 1943. *1041*

UN membership. Argentina. Foreign policy. USA. 1942-45. *1058*

UN War Crimes Commission. Jews. Pell, Herbert Claiborne. State Department. War crimes. 1943-45. *100*

Unconditional surrender (concept). Allies. Peace. Roosevelt, Franklin D. ca 1942-45. *45*

Undine (vessel). Great Britain. Okinawa (battle). Parker, Willard. Rescues. 1945. *409*

Unemployment Insurance Act (1941). Business. Canada. Federal Government. Labor Unions and Organizations. Social control. Wages. 1910-41. *202*

Unemployment, rural. Food shortages. Puerto Rico. 1940-45. *280*

United Automobile Workers of America. Automobile Industry and Trade. Labor (militancy). Michigan (Detroit). Production standards. Working Conditions. 1937-55. *540*

—. Communism. 1941-46. *474*

United Church of Canada. Canada. Fairbairn, R. Edis. Pacifism. Protestantism. 1939. *802*

United Electrical Radio and Machine Workers. Communist Party. National Maritime Union. Negroes. Racism. 1941-45. *196*

Urban League. Civil Rights. Nebraska (Omaha). Negroes. Quality of life. Social services. 1928-50. *623*

Urbanization. Florida (Pensacola). Naval Air Forces. 1900-45. *609*

US Control Council for Germany. Maginnis, John J. Marcus, David. Memoirs. 1944-46. *574*

US Employment Service. Negroes. Pennsylvania (Philadelphia). Public transportation. Racism. Strikes. War Manpower Commission. 1944. *1046*

272 US Group

US Group Control Council, Germany. Clay, Lucius D. Documents. Germany. Military General Staff (meetings). Military government. Office of Military Government for Germany (US). 1944-49. *917*
US Military Academy. Military history. Stained glass windows. 1800-1944. *705*
US Naval Academy. Burke, Arleigh. Military Service, Professional. Naval Education. 1919-40. *794*
US Naval Academy (Edward J. Streichen Collection). Maryland (Annapolis). Photography, Military. Streichen, Edward J. 1930's-75. *194*
USSR. Aeronautics, Military. Circumnavigations. Diplomacy. Harriman, W. Averell. Lend-Lease. 1941. *323*
—. Air Warfare. Bombing. B-17 (aircraft). Germany. Poltava (battle). 1944. *445*
—. Alaska. Canada. Railways. 1942-43. *1057*
—. Allies. Historiography. Lend-Lease. 1941-45. *250*
—. Allies. Nazism. 1939-45. *499*
—. Annexation. Baltic Area. Nonrecognition. USA. 1940-70's. *467*
—. Arctic. *Georgi Sedov* (vessel). Newfoundland. World War I. 1908-67. *51*
—. Atomic Warfare. Japan (Hiroshima, Nagasaki). USA. 1942-47. *86*
—. Atomic Weapons. Austin, Warren Robinson. Byrnes, James F. Cold War. Documents. Potsdam Conference. 1945. *712*
—. Attitudes. Balkans. Diplomacy (foreign service officers). 1944-46. *221*
—. Battles. Historiography. USSR. 1939-78. *818*
—. Battles. Historiography. USSR. 1939-78. *818*
—. Beaverbrook, 1st Baron. Diplomacy. Harriman, W. Averell. Military Aid. 1941. *510*
—. Bulgaria. Foreign Policy. Intervention. 1944-47. *855*
—. *Canadian Hungarian Worker* (newspaper). Hungarians. Szőke, István. 1929-44. *584*
—. China. Great Britain. International Relations (discipline). Japan. USA. 1937-49. *736*
—. *City of Flint* (vessel; capture). Contraband. Foreign relations. Germany. Ships. 1939. *177*
—. Civil War. Collectivization. History Teaching. Textbooks. USSR. 1917-79. *207*
—. Civil War. Collectivization. History Teaching. Textbooks. USSR. 1917-79. *207*
—. Cold War. Diplomacy, atomic. Foreign policy. Nuclear Arms. USA. 1942-46. *85*
—. Cold War. Europe, Eastern. Great Britain. "Percentages" agreement. Roosevelt, Franklin D. 1944. *780*
—. Cold War. Joint Chiefs of Staff. 1944-46. *746*
—. Cold War. Office of Strategic Services (memos). 1945. *1049*
—. Cold War. Open Door, global. Roosevelt, Franklin D. Truman, Harry S. USA. 1941-50. *1037*
—. Cold War (origins). Diplomacy. Europe. Harriman, W. Averell. 1943-45. *98*
—. Cold War (origins). Diplomacy (review article). Great Britain. 1941-48. *57*
—. Cold War (origins). Marshall Plan. Nuclear Arms. Second Front. 1940's. *1016*
—. Cold War (origins). Public opinion. 1941-45. *133*
—. Conference on Security and Cooperation in Europe (1969). Europe, Eastern. Foreign Policy. Treaties. USA. 1945-75. *148*
—. Congress of Industrial Organizations. Isolationism. Leftism. Pacific Northwest. 1937-41. *552*

—. Czechoslovakia (Prague). Germany. Invasions. Patton, George S., Jr. Vlasov, Andrei. 1945. *804*
—. Davies, Joseph Edward. Diplomacy. 1941-43. *567*
—. Diplomacy. Europe. Repatriation, forced. USA. 1944-47. *268*
—. Diplomacy. Faymonville, Philip R. Military Service, Professional. USA. 1917-52. *511*
—. Diplomacy. Free ports. Norway. Roosevelt, Franklin Delano. USA. 1941-43. *788*
—. Diplomacy. Germany. Roosevelt, Franklin D. 1934-39. *572*
—. Diplomacy. Great Britain. Second front. USA. 1942-43. *1089*
—. Eden, Anthony. Foreign Policy. Molotov, V. M. Poland. Truman, Harry S. 1945. *635*
—. Eisenhower, Dwight D. Germany (Berlin). Great Britain. Military Strategy. 1945. *495*
—. Exchange programs. Great Britain. Medical research. ca 1941-45. *62*
—. Expansionism. Military Strategy. *Rankin* plans. USA. 1943. *924*
—. Films. Foreign Relations. Hollywood. USA. 1939-44. *879*
—. Films. Heroes. 1910-45. *722*
—. Films. Public Opinion (American). 1939-47. *881*
—. Foreign Policy. Great Britain. USA. Warsaw uprising. 1944. *556*
—. Foreign policy. Harriman, W. Averell. Poland. USA. Warsaw Ghetto Uprising. 1943-44. *167*
—. Foreign policy. Hopkins, Harry. Roosevelt, Franklin D. 1938-46. *576*
—. Foreign policy. Mass Media. Public opinion. USA. ca 1939-49. *880*
—. Foreign Policy. Poland. Roosevelt, Franklin D. Truman, Harry S. USA. 1943-46. *558*
—. Foreign Policy. Public opinion. Roosevelt, Franklin D. 1941-45. *679*
—. Foreign Policy. Roosevelt, Franklin D. 1933-45. *442*
—. Foreign Policy. Roosevelt, Franklin D. USA. 1933-45. *443*
—. Foreign Relations. Prisoners and prisons. Repatriation. USA. 1945. *136*
—. Foreign Relations. USA. 1917-76. *479*
—. France. Germany. Great Britain. Partition. Roshchin, A. A. (memoirs). 1942-45. *797*
—. Great Britain. Historiography. Military aid. Military Capability. 1941-75. *671*
—. Great Britain. Information exchange. Science. 1940-45. *63*
—. Great Britain. NATO. Naval Strategy. USA. 1945-70's. *646*
—. Great Britain. Second front. 1943-44. *1076*
—. Historians, Western. Japan. Military defeat. Pacific Area. 1942-45. *832*
—. Historiography. Negroes. Roosevelt, Franklin D. (administration). 1939-45. *872*
—. Hoover, Herbert C. Intervention (opposed). Peace. Totalitarianism. 1939-41. *88*
—. Lange, Oscar. Poland, eastern. Pro-Communism. Roosevelt, Franklin D. 1941-45. *821*
—. Marshall, George C. (strategic thought). Strategy. 1939-50. *121*
—. Naval Strategy. 1943-45. *504*
—. Office of War Information. Poland. Propaganda. USA. 1943-45. *375*
—. USSR. World War II (review article). 1942. *43*
—. USSR. World War II (review article). 1942. *43*
USSR (Mirgorod, Poltava). Air Warfare. Bombing. Bowman, Marvin S. (reminiscences). Great Britain. 1944. *114*

War crimes 273

Utah. Foreign Relations. Japan. King, William. Thomas, Elbert. USA. ca 1922-40. *538*
Uyeda, Clifford I. (account). Citizenship. Ford, Gerald R. Hada, John. Japanese American Citizens League. Pardon. Tokyo Rose (Iva Toguri d'Aquino). 1973-77. *990*
U-570 (vessel). Atlantic Ocean (North). Canada. Hewens, Bob. Navies. *Niagara* (vessel). 1934-72. *1043*

V

Values. Angers, François-Albert. Canada. Catholic Church. French Canadians. Pacifism. 1940-79. *349*
—. Antiwar sentiment. Aviation. Lindbergh, Anne Morrow (reminiscences). Lindbergh, Charles A. 1902-79. *543*
—. Community, involuntary. Conscientious objectors. Maryland. Patapsco Civilian Public Service System (Camp 3). 1941-42. *699*
—. Japanese Americans (attitudes toward). Sociological theory. 1940's-70's. *914*
Values (change in). Stereotypes (combatants). Students. War, perceptions of. 1961-71. *185*
Vandenberg, Arthur Hendrick, Sr. Anti-Soviet consensus. Interventionism. Isolationism. 1941-46. *413*
—. Cold War. Michigan. Poland. Yalta Conference. 1944-48. *149*
VanDusen, Henry Pitney. Interventionism. Presbyterian Church. World War II (antecedents). 1920-45. *960*
Vatican. Diplomacy. 1937-45. *15*
—. Diplomacy. Pius XII, Pope. Taylor, Myron C. USA. 1940-50. *188*
—. Documents. Foreign Relations. Taylor, Myron. USA. 1940-42. *6*
—. Jesuits. McCormick, Vincent A. (diary). 1942-45. *404*
Versailles, Treaty of. American Revolution. deGaulle, Charles. Europe, Western. Foreign Relations. France. 1773-1979. *498*
Veterans. Military training. Oklahoma State University. Preparedness. Reserve Officers' Training Corps. Women Appointed for Volunteer Emergency Service. 1891-1951. *812*
Vichy Regime. Canada. deGaulle, Charles. France. Propaganda. Quebec. 1940-42. *193*
—. Diplomacy. Great Britain. Historiography. Langer, William L. (account). 1941-54. *512*
Victory at Sea series. Cold War mentality. Propaganda. Television. 1952-72. *792*
Victory ships. Merchant Marine. Military Sealift Command. National Defense Reserve Fleet. Vietnam War. 1944-77. *201*
Vietnam War. Air Forces. Military Strategy. Weather. 1941-72. *311*
—. Air Warfare. Bombing, strategic. 1943-45. 1965-73. *891*
—. Armies. Philippine Insurrection. Professionalism. 1901-71. *735*
—. Casualty rates. Social Status. 1941-45. 1961-73. *1039*
—. Cold War. Diplomacy. Morality. 1945-70's. *860*
—. Commando operations. Entebbe (raid). 1940-77. *406*
—. Folktales. 1941-71. *7*
—. Korean War. Military rescue concepts. 1941-74. *141*
—. Marines. Military training. Parris Island (camp). 1942-72. *695*
—. Merchant Marine. Military Sealift Command. National Defense Reserve Fleet. Victory ships. 1944-77. *201*

Vietnamese. China. Communism. Ho Chi Minh. Independence movement. USA. 1942-45. *901*
Villard, Oswald Garrison. Antiwar Sentiment. Keep America Out of War Congress. Socialist Party. Thomas, Norman. World War II (antecedents). 1938-41. *236*
Violence, racial. Minorities. War. 1910-67. *839*
Virginia. Aircraft markings. F-105 (aircraft). National Guard. 192d Tactical Fighter Group. 1917-79. *544*
—. California. Interrogation centers. Navies. Prisoners of War. 1941-45. *647*
—. Germans. Prisoners of war. 1943-46. *648*
Virginia (Hot Springs). Alliances. Decisionmaking. Domestic Policy. Foreign policy. Roosevelt, Franklin D. (administration). UN Conference on Food and Agriculture. 1943. *1041*
Vixen (vessel). Navies. 1940-46. *1003*
Vlasov, Andrei. Czechoslovakia (Prague). Germany. Invasions. Patton, George S., Jr. USSR. 1945. *804*
Vocational Education. Curricula. High School Victory Corps. Patriotism. Physical Education and Training. 1941-45. *983*
Voluntary Associations. California (San Francisco Bay area). Military Medicine. Music. 1943-45. *835*

W

Wage-price controls. 1914-71. *766*
Wages. Business. Canada. Federal Government. Labor Unions and Organizations. Social control. Unemployment Insurance Act (1941). 1910-41. *202*
—. Economic Conditions. 1939-50. *791*
Wagner Act (US, 1935). Business. Labor Unions and Organizations. New Deal. Taft-Hartley Act (US, 1947). 1935-47. *108*
Wagner, Boyd D. Aeronautics, Military. Philippines. 1941-42. *104*
Wake Island. Naval Strategy. Pacific Area. Surrender. 1941. *340*
War. Alliance polarization. Diplomatic representation. Guttmann-Lingoes Smallest Space Analysis. Methodology. 1815-1973. *1007*
—. Anabaptists. Germany. Mennonites. Switzerland. Taxation. 16c-1973. *489*
—. Attitudes. Economic development. Military Strategy. Nuclear arms. Technology. 1914-68. *686*
—. Books. Films. 1940's-70's. *845*
—. Defensive war argument. Foreign Policy. Ideology. 1941-73. *958*
—. Emergencies, national. Executive power. Habeas corpus. Martial law. 1861-1944. *778*
—. Military Service, Professional. Ridgway, Matthew B. 1917-60. *9*
—. Military Service, Professional (officers). National Security. 1783-1973. *976*
—. Minorities. Violence, racial. 1910-67. *839*
—. Oklahoma. 1890-1968. *209*
War Bond advertising. Bankhead Bill (1943). Federal government. Newspapers. Subsidies. 1943. *112*
War crimes. Europe. Federal Government (response). Jews. USA. 1938-45. *5*
—. Holocaust. Kremer, Charles H. Rumania. Trifa, Valerian. USA. 1941-74. *583*
—. Jews. Pell, Herbert Claiborne. State Department. UN War Crimes Commission. 1943-45. *100*
—. Maser, Werner. Nuremberg trials (review article). Smith, Bradley F. 1945-46. 1970's. *1013*

274 War crimes

—. Nuremberg Trials. Yamashita, Tomoyuki. 1945-46. *390*
War crimes (standards). Libby, Frederick J. Malmédy massacre. National Council for the Prevention of War. Trials. 1944-49. *237*
War criminals. Court evidence. Documents, use of. Due process. Nuremberg Trials. 1945-48. *622*
War Department. Armies. Artillery. Howitzer, 105 mm. 1930's-41. *614*
—. Army Chief of Staff. Artillery (Field and Coast). 1907-54. *4*
—. Canada. Canol (project). Foster, W. W. Oil Industry and Trade. USA. 1942-45. *54*
—. Economic Growth. Propaganda. State Department. 1939-45. *1083*
War Department (Military Intelligence Division; Special Branch). Military Intelligence. Normandy Landing. Rosengarten, Adolph G., Jr. (reminiscences). Ultra project. 1st Army, US. 1944-45. *796*
War games. Decisionmaking. Europe, Western. History Teaching. Simulation and Games. USA. 1939-45. 1970's. *153*
—. Louisiana (western). Military General Staff. 2nd Army, US. 3d Army, US. 1941. *668*
War information centers. Libraries. 1941-45. *345*
War (justification of). Morality. 1940-74. *391*
War Labor Board. Avery, Sewell. Economic Conditions. Illinois (Chicago). Labor Disputes (arbitration). Montgomery Ward (federal seizure of). 1941. *490*
War Manpower Commission. Industry. Labor Unions and Organizations. Roosevelt, Franklin D. (administration). War Production Board. 1939-45. *493*
—. Negroes. Pennsylvania (Philadelphia). Public transportation. Racism. Strikes. US Employment Service. 1944. *1046*
War, perceptions of. Stereotypes (combatants). Students. Values (change in). 1961-71. *185*
War Plan ORANGE. Naval Strategy. World War II (antecedents). 1933-40. *245*
War powers. Congress. Foreign policy. Presidency. 1787-1972. *772*
War Production Board. Civil-military relations. Nelson, Donald M. 1942-45. *172*
—. Industry. Labor Unions and Organizations. Roosevelt, Franklin D. (administration). War Manpower Commission. 1939-45. *493*
War Production Board, Smaller Plants Division and Corporation. Employment. Holland, Lou E. Nelson, Donald M. 1940-44. *399*
War Refugee Board. Federal Government. Great Britain. Jews. Morgenthau, Henry, Jr. Relief organizations. 1940-44. *726*
War Relocation Authority. Documentation. Evacuation, forced. Internment. Japanese Americans. Photographs. 1941-43. *208*
Warmaking powers. Atlantic, battle of the. Great Britain. Navies. Roosevelt, Franklin D. Secrecy. 1941. *682*
Warren, Earl. California. Japanese Americans. Relocation camps. 1941-45. *1030*
Warsaw Ghetto Uprising. Foreign policy. Harriman, W. Averell. Poland. USA. USSR. 1943-44. *167*
—. Jews. Poland. Press, Jewish. USA. 1942-43. *347*
Warsaw uprising. Foreign Policy. Great Britain. USA. USSR. 1944. *556*
Wartime Information Board. Bureau of Public Information. Canada. Federal government. Press. Public opinion. Social scientists. 1939-45. *1070*

Washington. Coffee, John M. Congress. Embargo (sought). Japan. Schellenbach, Lewis B. 1930's-40. *536*
Washington (Seattle). Civic Unity Committee. Defense industries. Japanese Americans. Negroes. Race relations. 1940-45. *248*
Washington, University of (Milo Ryan Phonoarchives). Audiovisual materials, cataloging. Radio newscasts. 1956-73. *321*
Wattenberg, Albert (reminiscences). Chicago, University of. Illinois. Nuclear chain reaction. 1942. *1015*
Wayne, John. Fribourg, Leonard. Grainger, Edmund. Hollywood. Marines (image). *Sands of Iwo Jima* (film). 1949. *935*
Weapons. Allies. Germany. Military Strategy. 1944-45. *715*
—. Annexation. Intergovernmental Relations. New Mexico (Albuquerque). Nuclear Science and Technology. 1940-78. *762*
—. Balance of power. Korean War. Military Strategy. Technology. 1918-53. *876*
—. Naval Vessels. 1930-76. *955*
Weapons (ineffectiveness). Kimmel, Husband E. Pearl Harbor, attack on. Personal narratives. Short, Walter C. 1941. *951*
Weather. Air Forces. Military Strategy. Vietnam War. 1941-72. *311*
Webster, Milton. Defense industries. Discrimination. Executive Order 8802. March on Washington Movement. Military. Randolph, A. Philip. 1941-44. *588*
Weddell, Alexander Wilbourne. Diplomacy. National Telephone Company (Spain). Spain. USA. *367*
Wedemeyer, Albert C. (reminiscences). China. Foreign Relations. USA. 1920-48. *1020*
Welles, Sumner. Bowman, Isaiah. East Prussia. Oder-Neisse Line. Poland. State Department (Advisory Committee on Post-War Foreign Policy). 1942-45. *819*
Wendover Field. Air Warfare. Atomic bomb. *Enola Gay* (aircraft). Military training. 1944-45. *986*
West Virginia (vessel). Battleships. 1916-59. *892*
—. Pearl Harbor (attack on). 1916-41. *893*
Western States. Documents. Harry S. Truman Library. Public Policy. Truman, Harry S. 1940-66. *460*
—. Economic Growth. Industry. Population. South. 1940-79. *1*
Whalen, Norman M. (reminiscences). Air Warfare. Ploesti (raid). Rumania. USA. 1943. *1029*
Wheeler, Burton K. Montana. Political Attitudes. Roosevelt, Franklin D. Senate. 1904-46. *811*
White House Map Room. Churchill, Winston. Great Britain. USA. 1944. *491*
White, Paul W. Brown, Cecil B. Columbia Broadcasting System. Editorials. News. Radio. 1943. *954*
White Sands military reservation. New Mexico (Los Alamos). Nuclear Arms. Trinity test. 1945. *488*
White, Walter F. Armies. Discrimination. Great Britain. 1943-44. *354*
Why We Fight series. Films. Propaganda. Public opinion. 1941-45. *562*
Wiesel, Elie. Genocide (review article). Historiography. Jews. Refugees. 1939-45. 1960-79. *1077*
Wilberforce, Robert. Anglophile sentiments. Catholic Church (hierarchy). World War II (antecedents). 1940. *356*
Williams, William Appleman. Foreign policy. Historiography (neorevisionist; review article). Kolko, Gabriel. Kolko, Joyce. 1975. *851*

Williamson, Gerald Hugh. Australia. Diaries. Great Britain. MacArthur, Douglas. Philippines. 1942-43. *962*

Williamson, John A. (account). Destroyer escorts. *England* (vessel). Japan. Pacific Area. Submarine Warfare. 1944. *1038*

Wilson, E. Raymond (personal account). Conscientious Objectors. Conscription, Military (hearings). French, Paul C. Friends, Society of. 1940. *1042*

Wilson, Robert R. (reminiscences). Cyclotrons. Manhattan Project. New Mexico (Los Alamos). Nuclear Science and Technology. 1942-43. *1044*

Winant, John Gilbert. Diplomacy. Great Britain. USA. 1941-46. *1034*

Windows. Camp Lejeune. Lamb Studios. Marines. New Jersey (Tenafly). North Carolina. Stained glass. 1775-1943. *480*

Winkler, Allan M. Germany. Propaganda (review article). Rupp, Leila J. Women. 1939-45. *373*

Winograd, Leonard (reminiscences). Germany. Jews. Prisoners of war. USA. 1944-45. *1047*

Winton, John (review article). Great Britain. Navies. Pacific Area. 1941-45. *170*

Wisconsin. Air Warfare. Marines. McCarthy, Joseph R. Pacific Area. Politics. 1942-52. *774*

—. Education. Lawyers. Marines. McCarthy, Joseph R. State Politics. 1908-44. *687*

Wise, Stephen Samuel. Hungarian Americans. Jews. 1890's-1949. *987*

Wives. Civilian Public Service. Conscientious objectors. Protestantism. 1941-45. *301*

Wolff, Perry. *Air Power* (television series). Films. History. 1939-56. *8*

Wolfram. Embargo, Allied. Portugal (shipping to Germany). 1939-44. *943*

Women. Boycotts, consumer. District of Columbia. Employment. Sex discrimination. 1941-46. *1105*

—. British Commonwealth. Integration. Military. USA. World War I. 1900-78. *959*

—. Canada. Films. National Film Board of Canada. Sex roles. 1940's-50's. *594*

—. Canada. Labor. 1942-46. *738*

—. Canada. Military service. 20c. *1104*

—. Canadian Women's Army Corps. Military service. Morality. Sex roles. 1941-46. *740*

—. Catholic Church. National Catholic Welfare Conference. National Council of Catholic Women. Peace Movements. 1919-46. *561*

—. Courts. Discrimination, Employment. Labor law. 1876-1979. *412*

—. Defense industries. Employment. Massachusetts (Lowell). Textile Industry. 1940-45. *630*

—. Demobilization. Discrimination, Employment. Literature. Social Status. 1944-46. *392*

—. Employment. 1941-45. *973*

—. Employment. Employment. 1941-45. *761*

—. Employment. Labor. 1940-47. *1106*

—. Employment. Labor unions. Negroes. Working-class militancy. 1940's. *341*

—. Germany. Labor. Propaganda. Public opinion. Sex roles. 1939-45. *814*

—. Germany. Propaganda (review article). Rupp, Leila J. Winkler, Allan M. 1939-45. *373*

—. Labor. Michigan. Sex roles. 1941-45. *180*

—. Marines. Military Service. 1918-22. 1943-73. *456*

—. Oregon (Portland). Shipbuilding. 1941-45. *875*

Women Appointed for Volunteer Emergency Service. Military training. Oklahoma State University. Preparedness. Reserve Officers' Training Corps. Veterans. 1891-1951. *812*

Women (status of). Employment. Federal programs. 1941-45. *929*

Women's liberation movement. Employment. 1920's-70's. *79*

—. Political change. 19c-1970's. *513*

Working class. Bibliographies. Labor Unions and Organizations. 1940's. *342*

Working class power (elimination of). Employment. Labor unions, industrial. 1930-47. *1024*

Working Conditions. Automobile Industry and Trade. Labor (militancy). Michigan (Detroit). Production standards. United Automobile Workers of America. 1937-55. *540*

Working-class militancy. Employment. Labor unions. Negroes. Women. 1940's. *341*

Works Progress Administration. Foreign policy. Hawaii. Preparedness. Roosevelt, Franklin D. 1935-40. *763*

World War I. Aeronautics, Military. Army Air Corps. Eaker, Ira C. 8th Bomber Command, US. 1917-47. *852*

—. Arctic. *Georgi Sedov* (vessel). Newfoundland. USSR. 1908-67. *51*

—. Battle cruisers. Naval Strategy. 1900-47. *25*

—. Battles. Historiography. 1914-45. *473*

—. British Columbia. Films. Naval Vessels. Submarines. 1914-45. *156*

—. British Commonwealth. Integration. Military. USA. Women. 1900-78. *959*

—. Canada. Murray, Leonard W. Navies. 1913-45. *308*

—. Cutlass, Naval. Klewang, Dutch. Peterson, Harold L. 1917. 1941-42. *787*

—. Economic agreements. Foreign Relations. Neutrality. Switzerland. 1919. 1944-45. *292*

—. Economic Conditions. Prisoners of war. 1914-45. *211*

—. Films. History Teaching. Maine, University of. 20c. *846*

—. Marshall, S. L. A. (reminiscences). Military. 1919-69. *587*

World War I (medical and sanitary affairs). Ambulance services. American Field Service. Andrew, Piatt. France. 1914-45. *337*

World War II (antecedents). American Peace Mobilization. Communist Party USA. Isolationism. 1939-41. *1006*

—. Anglophile sentiments. Catholic Church (hierarchy). Wilberforce, Robert. 1940. *356*

—. Anti-Imperialism. Foreign Policy (critics). Pacific Area. Roosevelt, Franklin D. 1930's. *704*

—. Antiwar Sentiment. Keep America Out of War Congress. Socialist Party. Thomas, Norman. Villard, Oswald Garrison. 1938-41. *236*

—. Asia, Southeast (coast). India. *Lanikai* (vessel). Navies. Roosevelt, Franklin D. Tolley, Kemp (personal account). 1941. *968*

—. Atlantic Ocean, South. Great Britain. Neutrality (circumvention). Roosevelt, Franklin D. Takoradi air route. 1941-42. *769*

—. Blockades. Chamberlain, Neville. China. Great Britain. Japan. Roosevelt, Franklin D. 1937-38. *362*

—. Brussels Conference (1937). China. Expansionism. Japan. 1937. *107*

—. Canada. Historiography. Press. 1938-39. *591*

—. *Cedar Rapids Gazette* (newspaper). Iowa. Marshall, Verne. No Foreign War Committee. 1940-41. *238*

—. China (Yangtze River). Japan. Panay (vessel). 1937. *731*

—. Churchill, Winston. Foreign policy. Great Britain. Military preparedness. USA. 1933-39. 1976. *560*

—. Congress. Japan. 1940-41. *535*

World War

—. Davis, Elmer. Interventionist, making of an. News broadcasts. Radio. 1939-42. *463*
—. Democracy. Fascism. Intervention. 1939-41. *898*
—. Diplomacy. Emmerson, John K. (memoirs). Japan (Tokyo). State Department. 1941. *275*
—. Diplomacy. Foreign policy. International Trade. Japan. 1937-41. *988*
—. Diplomacy. Hornbeck, Stanley K. Japan. USA. 1937-41. *526*
—. Diplomacy. Hull, Cordell. Indochina. Japan. Philippines. 1941. *131*
—. Diplomacy. Japan (Tokyo). USA. 1941. *274*
—. Economic threat. Free trade. 1930's-41. *993*
—. Europe, Central. Foreign Policy. USA. 1918-41. *1050*
—. Europe, East. Foreign policy. Isolationism. Neutrality Laws. Roosevelt, Franklin D. 1920's-30's. *249*
—. Foreign Broadcast Information Service. Intelligence Service. State Department (Foreign Service). 1939-41. *178*
—. Foreign Policy (balance of power, multipolar). USA. 1930's. 1970's. *122*
—. Foreign Policy (preconceptions). Japan. USA. 1940-41. *74*
—. Foreign Relations. George VI (visit). Great Britain. 1939. *783*
—. France. USA. 1939-40. *240*
—. Germany. National Reich Church (suggested). Propaganda campaign. Roosevelt, Franklin D. USA. 1941. *187*
—. Imperialism. Japan. Navigation. Pacific Area. Pearl Harbor, attack on. Prehistory-1941. *216*
—. Interventionism. Presbyterian Church. VanDusen, Henry Pitney. 1920-45. *960*
—. Military Medicine. Mobilization. Psychologists. 1938-41. *674*
—. Naval Strategy. War Plan ORANGE. 1933-40. *245*
World War II (antecedents) (review article). Russett, Bruce M. USA. 1939-41. *239*
World War II (review article). Alperovitz, Gar. Atomic Warfare. Foreign Relations. 1945. *378*
—. Asia. Callahan, Raymond. Foreign Relations. Great Britain. Louis, William Roger. Lowe, Peter. 1939-45. *12*
—. Diplomacy, mistakes in. Europe. Japan. USA. 1930's-41. *405*
—. USSR. USSR. 1942. *43*
Wouk, Herman (review article). Historiography. Novels. 1940-80. *579*
Wright, Howard T. (account). Airplanes, Military. Army Air Corps. California. Eaker, Ira C. Hamilton Field. Military Decorations, Flags, and Symbols. 1941. *1062*

X

XB-28 (aircraft). Army Air Forces. Bombing. 1940's. *982*
Xenophobia. Subversive Activities. 1939-41. *550*

Y

Yalta Conference. Churchill, Winston. Germany (partition). Potsdam Conference. Roosevelt, Franklin D. Stettinius, Edward Reilley. 1945. *329*
—. Cold War. Michigan. Poland. Vandenberg, Arthur Hendrick, Sr. 1944-48. *149*
—. Cold War (origins). Roosevelt, Franklin D. Truman, Harry S. (administration). 1945-47. *957*
Yalta Conference (preparations). Churchill, Winston. Diplomacy. Roosevelt, Franklin D. Stalin, J. V. 1945. *696*
Yalta Conference (review essay). Diplomacy. Roosevelt, Franklin D. 1945-55. *850*
Yamamoto, Isoroku. Dull, Paul S. (review article). Japan. Naval Strategy. Pearl Harbor, attack on. 1941-45. *977*
Yamashita, Tomoyuki. Nuremberg Trials. War crimes. 1945-46. *390*
Yamato colony. Agriculture. Florida (Boca Raton). Japanese Americans. 1904-75. *750*
Yeager, Charles. Army Air Corps. Flight testing. Supersonic planes. SX-1 aircraft. 1944-75. *673*
Yeshiva Aid Committee. Fund raising. Genocide. Joint Distribution Committee. Judaism (Orthodox). Rescue work. 1939-41. *1081*
Yokoi, Shoichi. Guam. Japan. 1944-72. *952*
Yoneda, Elaine. Japanese Americans, incarceration of. Oral history. Tanaka, Togo. Yoneda, Karl. 1941-45. *638*
Yoneda, Karl. Japanese Americans, incarceration of. Oral history. Tanaka, Togo. Yoneda, Elaine. 1941-45. *638*
Yosemite National Park. Hospital. Navy. 1943-45. *831*
YP-43 Lancer (aircraft). Seversky Aircraft Corporation. 1939-59. *553*
Yugoslavia. Diplomacy. Germany. Lane, Arthur B. 1940-41. *933*
Yukon Territory. Alaskan Highway. Highway Engineering. Logistics. 1942-43. *779*
—. Canol Project. Northwest Territories. Oil and Petroleum Products. Pipelines. 1942-45. *470*
Yuma Proving Ground. Arizona. Bridges, floating. Military. 1943-50. *431*

Z

Zahn, Gordon C. (account). Civilian Public Service. Pacifism. 1940-45. *1072*
Zero (aircraft). Air warfare. F4U (aircraft). Marines. Pacific Area. 1943-45. *419*
Zionism. Bergson, Peter. Emergency Committee to Save the Jewish People of Europe. Genocide. Rescues. 1943-45. *723*
Zionist/Anti-Zionist disunity. Jews. Refugees. 1932-45. *946*
Zuckerman, Solly (review article). Bombing. France. Military Strategy. Operation Overlord. 1944. *484*

1st Army, US. Military Intelligence. Normandy Landing. Rosengarten, Adolph G., Jr. (reminiscences). Ultra project. War Department (Military Intelligence Division; Special Branch). 1944-45. *796*
1st Pursuit Group. Luke, Frank, Jr. P-38 (aircraft). Rickenbacker, Edward V. 1918-76. *534*
2nd Army, US. Louisiana (western). Military General Staff. War Games. 3d Army, US. 1941. *668*
3d Army, US. Field Artillery Battalion, 920th. France (Metz). 1944. *18*
—. Louisiana (western). Military General Staff. War Games. 2nd Army, US. 1941. *668*

5th Air Force, US. Air Forces. Insignia. Pacific Area. 1941-45. *1091*
5th Army, US (36th Division). Italy (Anzio front). Rapido (battle). 1944. *887*
8th Bomber Command, US. Aeronautics, Military. Army Air Corps. Eaker, Ira C. World War I. 1917-47. *852*
9th Army, US. Germany (Roer River). Simpson, William H. 1945. *927*
23d Fighter Group. Air Warfare. American Volunteer Group. China. Flying Tigers motifs. Shoulder patches. 1930's-45. *191*
—. Air Warfare. China. 1942-45. *669*
28th Infantry Division, US. Europe, Western. Huertgen Forest (battle). 1944. *563*
31st Fighter Group, US. Air Warfare. Brooks, Jim (reminiscences). Oil fields. Romania. 1944. *127*
42nd Bombardment Wing. Air Warfare. B-26 (aircraft; markings). 1942-44. *950*
99th Fighter Squadron. Army Air Corps. Segregation. Tuskegee Army Air Field. 332d Fighter Group. 1941-49. *711*
192d Tactical Fighter Group. Aircraft markings. F-105 (aircraft). National Guard. Virginia. 1917-79. *544*
332d Fighter Group. Army Air Corps. Segregation. Tuskegee Army Air Field. 99th Fighter Squadron. 1941-49. *711*
462d Bomb Group. Indonesia (Sumatra; Palembang; Moesi River). Mines, military. Naval Air Forces. 1944. *996*

Ref Z 6207 .W8 W67 1983

World War II from an
 American perspective